DATE DUE

# PROTEINS AS HUMAN FOOD

*Published Reports of Previous Easter Schools in Agricultural Science*

SOIL ZOOLOGY
Edited by D. K. McE. Kevan
(Butterworths: London, 1955)

THE GROWTH OF LEAVES
Edited by F. L. Milthorpe
(Butterworths: London, 1956)

CONTROL OF THE PLANT ENVIRONMENT
Edited by J. P. Hudson
(Butterworths: London, 1957)

NUTRITION OF THE LEGUMES
Edited by E. G. Hallsworth
(Butterworths: London, 1958)

THE MEASUREMENT OF GRASSLAND PRODUCTIVITY
Edited by J. D. Ivins
(Butterworths: London, 1959)

DIGESTIVE PHYSIOLOGY AND NUTRITION OF
THE RUMINANT
Edited by D. Lewis
(Butterworths: London, 1960)

NUTRITION OF PIGS AND POULTRY
Edited by J. T. Morgan and D. Lewis
(Butterworths: London, 1961)

ANTIBIOTICS IN AGRICULTURE
Edited by M. Woodbine
(Butterworths: London, 1962)

THE GROWTH OF THE POTATO
Edited by J. D. Ivins and F. L. Milthorpe
(Butterworths: London, 1963)

EXPERIMENTAL PEDOLOGY
Edited by E. G. Hallsworth and D. V. Crawford
(Butterworths: London, 1964)

THE GROWTH OF CEREALS AND GRASSES
Edited by F. L. Milthorpe and J. D. Ivins
(Butterworths: London, 1965)

REPRODUCTION IN THE FEMALE MAMMAL
Edited by G. E. Lamming and E. C. Amoroso
(Butterworths: London, 1967)

GROWTH AND DEVELOPMENT OF MAMMALS
Edited by G. A. Lodge and G. E. Lamming
(Butterworths: London, 1968)

ROOT GROWTH
Edited by W. J. Whittington
(Butterworths: London, 1969)

# PROTEINS

## AS

# HUMAN FOOD

*Proceedings of the Sixteenth Easter School in*
*Agricultural Science, University of Nottingham, 1969*

*Edited by*
## R. A. Lawrie

*Professor of Food Science*
*University of Nottingham School of Agriculture*
*Sutton Bonington, Loughborough*

.

*Published in the United States*
*by*
THE AVI PUBLISHING COMPANY, INC.
WESTPORT, CONNECTICUT
1970

FIRST UNITED STATES EDITION
1970
THE AVI PUBLISHING COMPANY, INC.
*Westport, Connecticut*

*Library of Congress Catalog Card Number: 76-123523*

*ISBN-0-87055-091-8*

*Printed in Great Britain*

# CONTENTS

| | PAGE |
|---|---|
| PREFACE | ix |
| ACKNOWLEDGEMENTS | xi |
| INTRODUCTION<br>SIR DAVID CUTHBERTSON, C.B.E., F.R.S.E. | xiii |

## I.  GENERAL ASPECTS OF SUPPLY AND DEMAND

| | |
|---|---|
| DR. M. AUTRET<br>World Protein Supplies and Needs | 3 |
| PROFESSOR R.H. TUCK<br>Economics of Protein Production | 20 |
| MISS D.F. HOLLINGSWORTH, O.B.E. and DR. J.P. GREAVES<br>Nutrition Policy with Regard to Protein | 32 |
| MR. N.W. PIRIE, F.R.S.<br>Complementary Ways of Meeting the World's Protein Needs | 46 |

## II.  GENERAL ASPECTS OF PROTEIN PRESERVATION AND PROCESSING

| | |
|---|---|
| DR. P.S. ELIAS<br>Toxic Agents and Protein Availability | 65 |
| PROFESSOR D. MOSSEL<br>Microbial Spoilage of Proteinaceous Foods | 89 |
| PROFESSOR E.J. ROLFE<br>Characteristics of Preservation Processes as applied to Proteinaceous Foods | 107 |
| DR. M.P. TOMBS<br>Alterations to Proteins during Processing and the Formation of Structures | 126 |

CONTENTS

## III. PROTEINS FROM ANIMAL SOURCES

DR. G.A. LODGE
  Quantitative and Qualitative Control of Proteins in Meat
  Animals    141

PROFESSOR DR. R. HAMM
  Properties of Meat Proteins    167

DR. G.H.O. BURGESS and DR. J.M. SHEWAN
  Intrinsic and Extrinsic Factors Affecting the Quality of Fish    186

DR. J.J. CONNELL
  Properties of Fish Proteins    200

DR. J.A.B. SMITH, C.B.E., F.R.S.E.
  Milk and Milk Products    213

DR. D.H. SHRIMPTON
  Eggs and Poultry    225

## IV. PROTEINS FROM PLANT SOURCES

PROFESSOR DR. W. SCHUPHAN
  Control of Plant Proteins: The Influence of Genetics and
  Ecology of Plant Foods    245

DR. D. ROSENFIELD
  Enrichment of Plant Protein    266

DR. N.L. KENT
  Structural and Nutritional Properties of Cereal Proteins    280

DR. N. CHAMBERLAIN
  Baking: the Significance of Modern Processing Methods    300

## V. UNCONVENTIONAL PROTEIN SOURCES

MR. C.A. SHACKLADY
  Hydrocarbon-Grown Yeasts in Nutrition    317

DR. J.F. GORDON
  Algal Proteins and the Human Diet    328

DR. E.W. MEYER
  Soya Protein Isolates for Food    346

# CONTENTS

PAGE

## VI.  PRESENTATION

MRS. D.A. PARRY
The Organoleptic Qualities of Protein Foods (with Special
Reference to Cooking Procedures)                                365
MISS E. TELFORD
Protein Problems of Large Scale Catering                        388

## VII.  ASSIMILATION

PROFESSOR H.N. MUNRO, F.R.S.E.
Regulatory Mechanisms in Mammalian Protein Metabolism           403
PROFESSOR A.E. HARPER and DR. N.J. BENEVENGA
Effects of Disproportionate Amounts of Amino Acids              417
PROFESSOR D. LEWIS and DR. K.N. BOORMAN
Procedures of Protein Evaluation                                448
DR. NINA CARSON
Abnormalities of Protein Metabolism                             458

CONCLUDING REMARKS
MR. P. BROWN                                                    474

LIST OF REGISTRANTS                                             479

AUTHOR INDEX                                                    487

SUBJECT INDEX                                                   505

# PREFACE

Hitherto the Easter Schools organized by the School of Agriculture of the University of Nottingham have been concerned with various aspects of food crops and food animals up to the point of their despatch from the farm. It seemed appropriate, however, that the 16th Easter School should extend consideration of these products to include the questions which arise when they react with the human consumer for whom they are eventually intended.

There were several reasons for this view. In the first place there are major problems of malnutrition in the world today. For a substantial proportion of human beings the diet lacks the minimum quantities of those amino acids which are commonly accepted as essential for health. Secondly, the rate of increase of population appears to foreshadow a time, in the not too distant future, when the supply of proteins of high biological value may become inadequate not only for those in under-developed areas but for all mankind. Thirdly, there is increasing interest in the health of those who are fortunate enough to enjoy what has hitherto been supposed to be an adequate diet. This interest has arisen both in regard to overt metabolic abnormalities and to the suspicion that such features of universal experience as ageing and life span may be associated with aspects of individual dietary and metabolic needs which have so far failed to be recognized.

There is concomitant awareness that the quality of food commodities can be scientifically assessed and controlled. This outlook is attested by the establishment of Food Science teaching in the Universities of Strathclyde, Leeds, Nottingham and Reading in recent years. The scientific study of food is not confined to commodities at the moment of their presentation to the consumer. The history of food starts on the farm — at conception of the animal or at germination of the seed. It proceeds through a sequence of logical phases — growth and maturity, harvesting or slaughter, preservation, preparation and cooking — to mastication; but while the attributes of eating quality are appreciated at this point, it is only after the subsequent phase of digestion and assimilation that the basic nutrient quality is exerted. At every phase numerous influences affect eating and nutrient quality. These are amenable to scientific investigation on the basis of which their ultimate control for the benefit of man, as a member of a species and as a unique individual, can be envisaged.

ix

The contributions to the 16th Easter School were intended to reflect the above considerations. It was the purpose of the Symposium to bring together those who had been trained in many different disciplines so that, however distinct their individual approaches to the theme might appear in isolation, they would be seen to be interdependent. All are necessary for a full appreciation of proteins as human food.

*R.A.L.*

# ACKNOWLEDGEMENTS

It is a pleasure to publicly acknowledge the efforts of those who contributed papers at the Easter School in ensuring its success.

I am also indebted to Dr. F. S. Dainton, F.R.S., Vice-Chancellor of the University of Nottingham, who opened the School: to Sir David Cuthbertson, C.B.E., F.R.S.E., who delivered the introductory remarks: to Mr. P. Brown, Secretary of the British Nutrition Foundation Ltd., who concluded the Symposium; and to the following gentlemen who kindly acted as session chairmen: Professor F. Aylward, Head of the Department of Food Science, University of Reading: Professor A. G. Ward, O.B.E., Head of the Procter Department of Food and Leather Science, University of Leeds: Professor E. J. Briskey, Muscle Biology Laboratory, University of Wisconsin: Dr. R. B. Duckworth of the Department of Food Science, University of Strathclyde: Dr. A. W. Holmes, Director, British Food Manufacturing Industries Research Association; and Professor A. D. M. Greenfield, Dean of the Medical School, University of Nottingham.

The University of Nottingham wishes to express its gratitude to the following organizations whose generosity made possible the contributions from overseas speakers:

Boots Pure Drug Co. Ltd.
British Nutrition Foundation Ltd.
Brown and Polson Ltd.
Frigoscandia Ltd.
H. J. Heinz Co. Ltd.
Imperial Chemical Industries Ltd.
J. Lyons & Co. Ltd.
Marks and Spencer Ltd.
Metal Box Co. Ltd.
Milk Marketing Board.
Petfoods Ltd.
Ranks, Hovis, McDougall Ltd.
J. Sainsbury Ltd.
Spillers Ltd.
Unilever Research Laboratory.

In conclusion, I should like to thank warmly all the staff of the School of Agriculture for their assistance. The help of Miss. K. Robson, Mrs. D. Burrows, Mrs. S. Treeby, Mr. G. Millwater and Mr. P. Knowles was particularly appreciated.

# INTRODUCTION

## SIR DAVID CUTHBERTSON, C.B.E., F.R.S.E.

*Department of Pathological Biochemistry,*
*University and Royal Infirmary of Glasgow*

Protein is the most abundant organic constituent of our bodies – some 54 per cent of the total organic mass. It covers our bodies and in its varied forms makes up much of the substance and structure of our tissues including the blood. It has to be remembered that omnivorous man grows relatively slowly compared to farm livestock and experimental animals: he ranges very widely in the amount and quality of the protein he ingests (Cuthbertson, 1940). The high levels of animal protein, such as the Eskimos, the Khirghiz and other hunting and pastoral nomads eat, can be consumed without apparent harm, wasteful though this may be in terms of valuable protein but these peoples are frequently relatively short of carbohydrate. Whereas for the developed countries the daily *per caput* protein intake comes to roughly 90 g, for developing countries the figure is some 60 and for some countries, particularly in South East Asia, it is barely 40 g. As regards available supplies of animal proteins the differences are even wider: whereas in the rich countries they are of the order of from 50 g per day, in regions with emerging countries the figure is some 11 g. In the developing countries, proteins of vegetable origin constitute over 80 per cent of overall available proteins, cereals alone providing some 60 per cent and pulses, oilseeds and nuts about 17 per cent.

For most peoples protein constitutes some 10–14 per cent of the total energy of the diet and this tends to remain constant irrespective of age, sex, pregnancy, lactation, work or recovery from illness (Cuthbertson, 1940; Ministry of Health, 1964). The range is narrower when larger groups are considered (10.5–12 per cent). When it falls below about 8 per cent in a mixed diet, working capacity may be affected (Ferreira, 1965). Where the energy input is inadequate protein will be used even more extensively as a source of energy and this is wasteful, likewise if protein occupies a disproportionately large amount of the intake.

So long as man requires milk additional to that produced by the female of his species, so long as he demands a diet of meat, fish or eggs, so long as he needs leather and wool for his protection, so his need for animals will continue, for they are the most efficient or abundant or sole providers of these requirements. As man increases in his numbers and in his economic circumstances, so his demand for these will increase – unless his religious tenets or taboos forbid particular forms of them. In their recent analysis of the present position, and having regard to population trends through to 1985, the Advisory Committee of the United Nations Economic and Social Council (1967) consider that the bulk of human protein supplies will still probably be derived from traditional sources. On that assumption and assuming a higher intake of protein per day than at present and a high population there should be a corresponding increment of 85 per cent in milk and milk products and a 103 per cent rise in all meats. On the other hand, if the assumption be a low protein level but high population the increments by 1985 will need to be of the order of 67 per cent for milk and milk products and 76 per cent for meats.

In 1881 Voit defined a food as a palatable mixture of foodstuffs capable of maintaining the body in an equilibrium of substance, or capable of bringing it to a desired condition of substance, and the ideal food as one in which the foodstuffs are arranged together in such proportion as to burden the organism with the minimum of labour. Man is continually constituting and reconstituting himself by the habitual assimilation of protein-containing materials once living, or currently in a state of dormancy. We do not meet our amino acid requirements by eating mixtures of amino acids *per se,* nor indeed pure proteins, but traditionally we continue to eat proteins as tissues or secretions smoked or raw, cooked, air dried or freeze-dried, or fermented. In these they are associated in varying degree with the fat, carbohydrate, vitamins, salts and the water of these tissues or secretions. Man is dependent on ingested animal food to supply the bulk of his vitamin $B_{12}$ requirements. There is no significant amount in plants unless there has been fermentation. The physico-chemical state of animal proteins on being cooked or otherwise denatured renders them attractive in a wide range of ultimate states. Consider what the housewife can do with an egg. Cooking also stabilizes them for a time against microbial attack.

It is common knowledge that the proteins of plants and their products, which form the major energy sources of the greater part of the world's population, are often lacking in quantity one or more of the amino acids known to be essential. Proteins of actively metabolizing plant tissues on the other hand are better balanced. In general, cereals are deficient in lysine and threonine, but through plant breeding this is being rectified. The supplemental action of legumes and leaf proteins helps to correct this but some staples like cassava and yams, and to a lesser extent maize, seem to require more considerable supplementation; it is frequently simpler to effect this with proteins of animal origin for, additionally, these provide the amino acids in a concentrated form free of indigestible cellulosic and other matter. Further, legume proteins, like groundnut, soya and cotton seed, are frequently associated with antitryptic or toxic materials prior to appropriate processing, and in some circumstances they are subject to become substrates for fungal attack which may result in mycotoxin production. Modern technology is, however, moving fast and vegetable protein 'steaks' and 'milks' have appeared on the market – some based on old practices. Unless such products are known to be used by the upper crust of society it is unlikely they will be accepted by those who really need them, even if relatively cheap. They are considered as a stigma of poverty. Incaparina, Proflo, and other vegetable protein-rich concentrates including yeast and algal proteins have not gained much acceptance. Some products are suspect. On the other hand, initially if a product is too attractive when presented to a developing community the men may scoop the major share.

Even with protein-rich supplements it is difficult to be sure that the regular diet plus the supplement will supply all needed nutrients for weaned infants and pre-school children in developing countries. Formulating a high protein candy or drink may significantly improve acceptance of the protein mixture, but unless the food actually makes good the spectrum of nutrients that are low the expected benefit will not materialize (Dunn et al., 1967). Even when the cure seems nutritionally obvious as in the case of kwashiorkor the remedy, in practice, may be baulked by lack of sanitation and education.

In agricultural crop planning attention should be given not only to the production of total protein in relation to total yield, since an increase in yield very often results in a decrease in protein content per unit of production, but attention should also be given to the quality of the protein in the crops produced.

As Blaxter (1968) has pointed out, while the calorific return is much greater when good land is used to grow bread grains rather than to produce milk, and at least 50 per cent more biologically useful calories can be obtained from such a cereal crop in terms of flour yield than from the milk produced, nevertheless this is the only major respect in which the cereal crop really excels. Although intensive milk production and wheat growing produce similar amounts of protein the quality of these proteins differs markedly in their biological value for humans. The yields per acre of lysine and of threonine from dairy production are, respectively, three times and twice those from cereal production. The alleged absence of a lactase in the digestive tract of some non-Caucasian adults, however, needs further investigation in respect of tolerance to milk. With the exception of nicotinic acid, yields of the vitamin B complex are greater for dairy production than for cereal production and similarly for yields of calcium and phosphorus. In terms of land use, milk production is probably the most efficient type of animal production. Nevertheless, as Widdowson and McCance (1954) have shown, children can grow well on a diet composed almost entirely of wheaten bread and a good mixture of vegetables and with no milk, though if prolonged, vitamin $B_{12}$ deficiency may well ensue. The apparent emphasis is on selection of a mixture to provide all the essential amino acids and in the right proportions, but it would seem more direct to use, when avilable, animal proteins. In general, they are more definitely related to the tissues of the human body,

Table 1

Total protein expressed as percentage total calories
and animal protein as percentage of total protein
(After Autret, 1970)

| | kcal per caput | Protein as percentage of kcal | Percentage of animal protein |
|---|---|---|---|
| Far East (including Mainland China) | 2,050 | 10.7 | 15.7 |
| Near and Middle East | 2,410 | 11.9 | 19.6 |
| Africa | 2,170 | 10.8 | 18.6 |
| Latin America | 2,590 | 10.5 | 35.7 |
| River Plate countries | 3,090 | 11.3 | 57.7 |
| Developing regions | 2,140 | 10.8 | 18.6 |
| Europe (including U.S.S.R.) | 3,050 | 11.1 | 48.5 |
| Eastern | 3,180 | 11.2 | 36.4 |
| Western | 3,020 | 11.2 | 51.6 |
| North America | 3,140 | 11.9 | 69.9 |
| Oceania | 3,230 | 11.8 | 66.9 |
| Developed regions | 3,070 | 11.6 | 31.8 |

particularly when the demand for protein is high, and possibly in the end less wasteful in terms of nitrogen.

The tragedy of it is that multitudes of the livestock of the world which could supply the animal protein so urgently needed by mankind are themselves suffering from malnutrition and disease, or are precluded from the dietary because of religious or cultural prohibitions. The pig, for example, is prohibited to the orthodox of the Islam, Hebrew and Hindu religions. The cow is sacred to the Hindu. Poultry and eggs are avoided in almost as large a world area as are pig and pig meat products. As a matter of tradition, fish is largely ignored as food by populations living near some of the world's richest fishing grounds. The utilization of the wild life resources on critical marginal lands offers a possible solution to stabilize the debilitating advance of unproductive land while at the same time allowing the land to contribute to the world's food supply.

The biologists of the world are alive to the problem of protein supply. The International Biological Programme initiated by the Royal Society is largely related to meeting the challenge of the expanding world population. UNESCO, impressed with it, has decided on a further study of the Biosphere at inter-governmental level (Man and the Biosphere).

It is right and proper that in Nottingham we should meet to discuss this most important nutritional subject.

## REFERENCES

Autret, M. (1970). This volume, p. 3.
Blaxter, K. L. (1968). *Science J.* May, p.53
British Medical Association (1950). *Report of the Committee on Nutrition,* London; British Medical Association
Cuthbertson, D. P. (1940). *Nutr. Abstr. Rev.* 10, 1
Dunn, W. E., Pao, B. R. H. and Jesudion, G. (1967). *J. Nutr. Diet.* 4, 285
Ferreira, G. (1965). Personal communication
Ministry of Health (1964). *Requirements of Man for Protein.* London; H.M.S.O.
United Nations (1967). *Increasing the Production and Use of Edible Protein,* from: Report of the Advisory Committee on the Application of Science and Technology to Development
Voit, C. (1881). In: *Handbuch der Physiologie* Ed. By L. Hermann 6, Pt. 1, Leipzig, pp. 330, 340
Widdowson, E. M. and McCance, R. A. (1954). *Medical Research Council Special Report* No. 275. 'Studies of Undernutrition'. Wuppertal, 1946–9. London; H.M.S.O.

# I. GENERAL ASPECTS OF SUPPLY AND DEMAND

# WORLD PROTEIN SUPPLIES AND NEEDS

## M. AUTRET

*Nutrition Division, FAO, Rome*

## PROTEIN SUPPLIES AND DISTRIBUTION

Two sources of information are drawn upon to assess the current situation as regards proteins: FAO-compiled food balance sheets, covering over 90 per cent of the world's population, and family food consumption surveys.

### Food balance sheets data

Table 1 gives data derived from the food balance sheets, on available supplies of proteins (animal, vegetable and total) in grammes *per caput* per day for all regions and subregions of the world during the period 1963–1965. Table 2 gives the percentage contribution of the main food groups to total protein supplies.

Whereas for the developed countries the daily *per caput* protein intake comes to roughly 90 g, for developing countries the figure is 50–70 g (average 57 g) and for some countries, particularly in South East Asia, it is barely over 40 g. The discrepancies in available supplies of animal proteins are even wider: whereas in the rich countries they range from 40–60 g per day (averaging 48.3 g), in regions with emerging countries the figures range from 6–20 g per day (average 10.7 g). In the developing countries, proteins of vegetable origin constitute 81.4 per cent of overall available proteins, cereals alone providing 57 per cent and pulses, oilseeds and nuts 16.8 per cent. Owing to the low animal protein content of the diet and lack of diversity of supplies, protein quality is unsatisfactory. The expression of protein intake in terms of reference proteins gives the net protein value of the diet on the basis of which absolute comparisons of diets in different countries can be made. Thus local available proteins that range from 76 g (Spain) to 109.4 g (New Zealand), are equivalent to those from 43 to 61.4 g of the reference proteins, while supplies of from 29 g (Congo–Kinshasa) to 52 g (Madagascar), already inadequate from the overall standpoint, are equivalent to only 16.4 g and 30.6 g of the reference proteins.

3

Table 1. Protein Supplies (1963–65) (*per caput* and per day – by regions and subregions)

| Regions and Subregions | Calories | Animal proteins | Vegetable proteins | Total proteins |
|---|---|---|---|---|
| FAR EAST (incl. China Mainland) | | | | |
| South Asia | 2,050 | 8.6 | 46.2 | 54.8 |
| Southern Asia Mainland | 2,020 | 6.4 | 43.0 | 49.4 |
| Eastern Asia | 2,180 | 13.1 | 36.3 | 49.4 |
| South Eastern Asia Major Islands | 2,350 | 20.5 | 54.6 | 75.1 |
| China Mainland | 2,040 | 7.1 | 33.6 | 40.7 |
| | 2,010 | 8.2 | 50.5 | 58.7 |
| NEAR AND MIDDLE EAST | 2,410 | 14.0 | 57.6 | 71.6 |
| AFRICA | | | | |
| North Africa | 2,170 | 10.9 | 47.6 | 58.5 |
| West and Central Africa | 2,100 | 10.9 | 44.1 | 55.0 |
| East and Southern Africa | 2,120 | 7.8 | 46.9 | 54.7 |
| | 2,270 | 15.0 | 49.8 | 64.8 |
| LATIN AMERICA | | | | |
| Brazil | 2,590 | 24.1 | 43.5 | 67.6 |
| Mexico and Central America | 2,780 | 19.4 | 49.4 | 68.8 |
| Northern and Western countries | 2,500 | 21.3 | 45.0 | 66.3 |
| of South America | | | | |
| River Plate Countries | 2,220 | 22.2 | 36.3 | 58.5 |
| | 3,090 | 50.5 | 37.0 | 87.5 |
| DEVELOPING REGIONS | 2,140 | 10.7 | 46.9 | 57.6 |
| EUROPE (incl. U.S.S.R.) | 3,050 | 42.8 | 44.8 | 87.6 |
| Eastern Europe | 3,180 | 32.4 | 56.7 | 89.1 |
| Western Europe | 3,020 | 45.4 | 41.9 | 87.3 |
| NORTH AMERICA | 3,140 | 65.3 | 27.8 | 93.1 |
| OCEANIA | 3,230 | 63.9 | 31.5 | 95.4 |
| DEVELOPED REGIONS | 3,070 | 48.3 | 40.8 | 89.1 |
| WORLD | 2,380 | 21.0 | 45.1 | 66.1 |

Table 2. Percentage contribution of various commodities to percentage supplies (Protein supplies 1963–65)

| | Cereals | Starchy roots and tubers | Pulses nuts and seeds | Vegetables and fruits | Vegetable proteins | Meat | Eggs | Fish | Milk | Animal proteins |
|---|---|---|---|---|---|---|---|---|---|---|
| FAR EAST (incl. China Mainland) | 59.3 | 3.3 | 18.0 | 3.3 | 84.3 | 6.6 | 0.7 | 4.6 | 3.8 | 15.7 |
| South Asia | 64.5 | 1.0 | 19.6 | 1.0 | 87.1 | 1.4 | 0.2 | 1.4 | 9.9 | 12.9 |
| Southern Asia Mainland | 58.8 | 2.0 | 8.3 | 4.0 | 73.5 | 7.1 | 1.4 | 15.4 | 2.6 | 26.5 |
| Eastern Asia | 48.2 | 2.1 | 14.0 | 8.4 | 72.7 | 6.1 | 2.9 | 15.6 | 2.7 | 27.3 |
| South Eastern Asia Major Islands | 64.4 | 6.4 | 7.4 | 3.9 | 82.6 | 7.1 | 1.0 | 8.6 | 0.7 | 17.4 |
| China Mainland | 57.8 | 4.6 | 20.3 | 3.2 | 86.1 | 10.0 | 0.5 | 2.7 | 0.5 | 13.9 |
| NEAR AND MIDDLE EAST | 67.8 | 1.0 | 6.7 | 4.9 | 80.1 | 8.0 | 0.7 | 1.4 | 9.5 | 19.6 |
| AFRICA | 54.7 | 9.1 | 15.7 | 1.9 | 81.4 | 9.2 | 0.5 | 4.1 | 4.8 | 18.6 |
| North Africa | 69.9 | 1.1 | 5.1 | 4.2 | 80.3 | 7.8 | 0.8 | 1.6 | 9.5 | 19.7 |
| West and Central Africa | 51.2 | 14.8 | 18.1 | 1.6 | 85.7 | 6.8 | 0.4 | 5.1 | 2.0 | 14.3 |
| East and Southern Africa | 55.1 | 4.5 | 15.6 | 1.7 | 76.9 | 12.5 | 0.6 | 3.4 | 6.6 | 23.1 |
| LATIN AMERICA | 39.8 | 4.0 | 16.9 | 3.4 | 64.3 | 18.3 | 1.9 | 2.7 | 12.7 | 35.7 |
| Brazil | 37.9 | 3.6 | 26.6 | 3.7 | 71.8 | 13.5 | 2.2 | 2.3 | 10.2 | 28.2 |
| Mexico and Central America | 44.3 | 2.1 | 18.2 | 3.0 | 67.9 | 12.7 | 1.8 | 2.4 | 14.9 | 32.1 |
| Northern and Western countries of South America | 41.0 | 7.5 | 8.5 | 4.3 | 61.8 | 18.8 | 1.2 | 4.8 | 13.2 | 38.2 |
| River Plate Countries | 32.7 | 4.2 | 2.5 | 2.9 | 42.3 | 41.0 | 2.1 | 1.4 | 13.0 | 57.7 |
| DEVELOPING REGIONS | 57.2 | 3.8 | 16.8 | 3.3 | 81.4 | 8.3 | 0.9 | 4.0 | 5.4 | 18.6 |
| EUROPE (incl. U.S.S.R.) | 36.8 | 5.5 | 3.8 | 5.4 | 51.5 | 21.5 | 3.8 | 4.2 | 18.8 | 48.5 |
| Eastern Europe | 50.0 | 6.4 | 3.0 | 4.2 | 63.6 | 16.4 | 2.5 | 1.5 | 15.1 | 36.4 |
| Western Europe | 33.5 | 5.4 | 3.9 | 5.6 | 48.4 | 22.8 | 4.1 | 4.9 | 19.8 | 51.6 |
| NORTH AMERICA | 17.6 | 2.6 | 4.6 | 5.2 | 30.1 | 36.3 | 5.8 | 2.9 | 24.9 | 69.9 |
| OCEANIA | 24.9 | 2.4 | 2.2 | 3.6 | 33.1 | 36.8 | 4.2 | 3.1 | 22.5 | 66.9 |
| DEVELOPED REGIONS | 31.9 | 4.7 | 3.9 | 5.3 | 45.8 | 25.4 | 4.3 | 3.9 | 20.4 | 54.2 |
| WORLD | 47.9 | 4.1 | 12.1 | 3.9 | 68.2 | 14.7 | 2.1 | 3.9 | 10.9 | 31.8 |

*Figure 1* shows local protein resources and requirements in grammes *per caput* per day for 88 countries, for which FAO in 1967 revised its food balance sheets for the purposes of the Indicative World Plan. Sixty per cent of the world's population or 1800 million inhabitants (mainland China being excluded) live in these 88 countries. *Figure 1* groups these countries under seven headings relating to type of diet according to the nature of their protein resources and, within each group, in order of decreasing total protein intake expressed in grammes *per caput* per day. Protein requirements, expressed in grammes of local proteins *per caput* per day, are shown on the graph by dots; the quantities of protein corresponding to the essential amino acids of each type of diet are shown by full lines on the figure, while the quantities corresponding to non-essential amino acids and non-protein nitrogen appear as dotted lines.

Protein supplies decrease greatly as one goes from the industrialized countries with high consumption of animal products to the countries of the equatorial zone where the diet is based on roots and tubers.

Protein requirements *per caput* per day range from 83 to 51 g. Although certain industrialized countries enjoy a wide safety margin, 43 out of the 88 countries under consideration show a level of consumption lower than estimated requirements. These 43 countries have a combined population of 900 million inhabitants, or half that of the total for all 88 countries.

## Data from the food consumption surveys

A study of the national food consumption surveys (or family dietary surveys) which we have available for a certain number of developing countries confirms the picture derived from the national food balance sheets, though it appears that in the latter, available supplies (particularly as regards proteins) are usually overestimated. The protein gap is therefore greater than would be deduced from these estimates. However, the great merit of these surveys – still too few in number to provide sound bases for national agricultural development plans – is to highlight inequalities of distribution. They show that there are wide discrepancies from one region to another, within one and the same country, between urban and rural areas, at different seasons, between families at different income levels and between the individuals of one and the same family, particularly according to age groups. For instance, surveys in Central America, Colombia, Ghana, India, Ivory Coast, Nigeria, Tunisia and many other countries have revealed that even though families as such may have adequate and satisfactory diets, the protein and calorie requirements of the children are covered only to the extent of 70-80 per cent – a matter of lack of parent education. In urban areas, protein

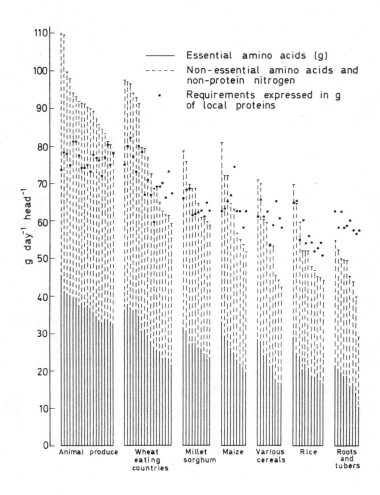

*Figure 1. Protein intake and requirements (g) by country, according to type of diet*

consumption is higher than in rural areas because incomes on the whole are higher.

The Madagascar survey on 5,000 rural households (François, 1968) objectively demonstrated the influence of income on protein quality and level in the diet (Table 3).

Table 3. Madagascar—Rural household survey (5,000 families)

| Annual income per 1000 CFA francs | Families % | Ratio protein cal./ tot. cal. | Net proteins per 100 cal. | Total proteins (g) | Proteins (in % total protein) provided by: | | |
|---|---|---|---|---|---|---|---|
| | | | | | Animal sources | Grain legumes | Rice |
| 1– 10 | 21.4 | 9.3 | 5.3 | 49.8 | 11 | 7 | 55 |
| 10– 20 | 33.3 | 8.5 | 5.0 | 45.9 | 5 | 7 | 64 |
| 20– 30 | 17.3 | 9.4 | 5.5 | 53.9 | 15 | 7 | 58 |
| 30– 40 | 10.4 | 9.6 | 5.6 | 54.5 | 17 | 8 | 56 |
| 40– 60 | 7.3 | 9.3 | 5.5 | 52.7 | 17 | 7 | 61 |
| 60– 80 | 3.6 | 9.9 | 5.8 | 55.5 | 18 | 5 | 58 |
| 80–130 | 3.8 | 10.4 | 6.1 | 61.2 | 25 | 5 | 55 |
| 130–190 | 1.5 | 10.0 | 6.6 | 59.1 | 26 | 3 | 57 |
| 190–390 | 0.8 | 11.0 | 6.0 | 64.6 | 34 | 3 | 54 |
| 390–590 | 0.3 | 10.6 | 6.2 | 65.3 | 36 | 3 | 54 |
| 590 and + | 0.1 | 12.8 | 7.6 | 71.2 | 61 | 0.4 | 30 |

Thus it was found that calories derived from protein foods amounted to less than 10 per cent of total calories (and net protein calories to less than 6 per cent) for 93.3 per cent of the population — that is among all those whose annual income was less than 80,000 CFA francs (US $320). The level of intake of proteins, and especially of animal proteins, rose with income; the quantity of protein derived from rice remained more or less steady, while protein from pulses varied inversely with income. Note that in the well-to-do group (earning 590,000 CFA francs or U.S. $2360 per annum or over) only five families had a European-style diet.

Furthermore, even in rural areas, despite theoretical possibilities of an improved subsistence economy, greater protein intake and better protein quality seem to be linked to higher cash income.

## PRESENT AND FUTURE REQUIREMENTS OF PROTEIN FOODS

Taking present day world protein requirements and supplies, one finds that, generally speaking, the two sets of figures come very close to one another. However, while in countries with food surpluses people consume more than enough to cover their nutritional requirements — so much so that their present diet constitutes a monumental physiological and economic error — quite the contrary is true (as has just been seen) in those countries where supplies barely approximate requirements, where a most privileged social class is also surfeited at the same time that the under-privileged socio-economic groups do not have the means to obtain enough proteins to meet their nutritional needs. Over and above this matter of inequitable distribution, in certain countries included in *Figure 1,* nation-wide supplies do not cover 'practical requirements' or even 'mean requirements'.

Just as it is a vain hope that any important improvement in distribution will be brought about on a world-wide scale, it would be equally naive to expect redistribution according to individual needs on a national scale. The only realisitic solution therefore is to achieve a global increase in production of protein foods under conditions of universal free trade. In such, greater production, combined with higher income, would raise purchasing power to the point where the great majority of the population would be able to satisfy their protein requirements.*

Protein requirements are calculated in accordance with the recommendations of the joint FAO/WHO Expert Group on Protein Requirements (1963), using provisional data on individual body weight and a population breakdown by sex and age. This is how the physiological mean protein requirements (M) of the reference man, woman and child of various ages, for any given country are defined. These protein requirements are stated in terms of grammes of reference protein (NPU = 100), here expressed in grammes of 'local protein', taking into account (operative) net protein utilization (NPUop) in the country in question in accordance with the suggestions of Platt, Miller and Payne (1961) and Miller and Payne (1961a and 1961b).

However, these calculations and field studies show that even when mean requirements (M) are satisfied, half of the population in countries whose total available supplies are marginal do not have their requirements covered. Indeed, in order to cover the requirements of the great majority of the population (97.5 per cent) it is necessary, in principle to have supplies equivalent to 120 per cent of mean requirements (M) available. This figure, representing 'practical requirements' (P), might be considered as a 'recommended allowance' the provision of which it is the prime aim of production to make feasible.

*In the meantime programmes for food distribution, either free of charge or at reduced prices, should be launched to help poorer classes suffering from, or vulnerable to, protein malnutrition.

Finally, protein requirements must be assessed against the background of the diet in respect of which certain principles regarding balance must be applied. In particular, for an adequate diet, at least 10–12 per cent of total calories must be derived from proteins. This criterion is also stated in the form of a calorie/protein balance objective (*O*). These two ways of expressing *per caput* requirements give slightly different figures, depending on the type of diet.

Table 4 gives protein resources (that is, available supplies) and requirements *per caput* per day in local proteins. Protein requirements of the average man are given at three levels:

(1) the average requirement (*M*) at the retail level (based on physiological data), such that if national supplies reached this level, half of the population would have its requirements covered (medium assumption of the report of a joint FAO/WHO Expert Group on Protein Requirements FAO 1963);

(2) practical requirements (*P*) equal to the average plus 20 per cent (translated into practical allowances) considered adequate to cover the requirements of 97.5 per cent of the population;

(3) the target or objective (*O*) ensuring coverage of at least *P* and a type of diet so balanced as to provide a ratio Calories from proteins/Total calories equal or above 10 per cent.

So much for individuals. There remain to be set reasonably close future dates when such requirements might be covered. The Indicative World Plan sets 1985 as the target year with an intermediary stage in 1975.

The next step is to take into account individual requirements and population growth to determine production goals for these two target dates. This has been done country by country, taking into account the changes which are likely to occur by these dates in the socio-economic grounds. Let us consider, for instance, the case of India.

Considering population growth projected into 1975 and 1985 (using the medium variant of the United Nations assumptions), it follows that 50–90 per cent higher protein supplies will be necessary by those dates. Obviously that fraction of the population whose requirements are already covered will grow in number and its comsumption will continue to increase or be of better quality. Assuming for this segment a 2 per cent rise in income per year and an elasticity of protein demand of 0.3 (it is 0.55

*M* –Average requirements, national level (see report on protein requirements)–
This covers only the requirements of 50 per cent of the population.

*P* –Average requirements + 20 per cent (see report on protein requirements)–
This covers the requirements of 97.5 per cent of the population.

*O* –Objectives (qualitative and quantitative)–This ensures a ratio Protein cal./total cal. between 10 and 12 per cent.

Table 4
Available proteins and protein requirements per head and per day
(in local proteins) (Retail level)

| | Supplies | | Requirements | | | |
|---|---|---|---|---|---|---|
| | Calories | Total proteins (g) | Calories | Total Proteins (g) M | P | O |
| FAR EAST (incl. China | | | | | | |
| Mainland) | 2,050 | 54.8 | 2,250 | 49.1 | 59 | 68 |
| South Asia | 2,020 | 49.4 | 2,230 | 49.1 | 59 | 63 |
| Southern Asia Mainland | 2,180 | 49.4 | 2,170 | 41.9 | 50 | 57 |
| Eastern Asia | 2,350 | 75.1 | 2,370 | 52.5 | 75 | 75 |
| South Eastern Asia | | | | | | |
| Major Islands | 2,040 | 40.7 | 2,040 | 41.8 | 50 | 55 |
| China Mainland | 2,010 | 58.7 | 2,300 | 50.7 | 60 | 72 |
| | | | | | | |
| NEAR AND MIDDLE | | | | | | |
| EAST | 2,410 | 71.6 | 2,410 | 56.1 | 72 | 77 |
| | | | | | | |
| AFRICA | 2,170 | 58.5 | 2,250 | 51.6 | 62 | 69 |
| North Africa | 2,100 | 55.0 | 2,350 | 55.2 | 66 | 72 |
| West and Central Africa | 2,120 | 54.7 | 2,220 | 50.3 | 60 | 63 |
| East and Southern | | | | | | |
| Africa | 2,270 | 64.8 | 2,270 | 52.5 | 65 | 73 |
| | | | | | | |
| LATIN AMERICA | 2,590 | 67.6 | 2,360 | 53.3 | 68 | 71 |
| Brazil | 2,780 | 68.8 | 2,350 | 54.9 | 69 | 71 |
| Mexico and Central | | | | | | |
| America | 2,500 | 66.3 | 2,280 | 50.3 | 66 | 69 |
| Northern and Western | | | | | | |
| countries of South | 2,220 | 58.5 | 2,350 | 51.1 | 61 | 72 |
| America | | | | | | |
| River Plate Countries | 3,090 | 87.5 | 2,620 | 61.8 | 88 | 88 |
| | | | | | | |
| DEVELOPING REGIONS | 2,140 | 57.6 | 2,270 | 50.2 | 61 | 69 |
| | | | | | | |
| EUROPE (incl. U.S.S.R.) | 3,050 | 87.6 | 2,690 | 50.2 | 88 | 88 |
| Eastern Europe | 3,180 | 89.1 | 2,690 | 59.7 | 89 | 89 |
| Western Europe | 3,020 | 87.3 | 2,680 | 60.3 | 87 | 87 |
| | | | | | | |
| NORTH AMERICA | 3,140 | 93.1 | 2,520 | 61.0 | 93 | 93 |
| | | | | | | |
| OCEANIA | 3,230 | 95.4 | 2,700 | 56.3 | 95 | 95 |
| | | | | | | |
| DEVELOPED REGIONS | 3,070 | 89.1 | 2,650 | 60.4 | 89 | 89 |
| | | | | | | |
| WORLD | 2,380 | 66.1 | 2,370 | 53.0 | 66 | 74 |

for all of India), the total increase in protein supplies will have to be 60 per cent by 1975 and 95 per cent by 1985.

Table 5 gives indices of protein supplies (i.e. increased production of protein foods) required by 1975 and 1985 to cover practical requirements (*P*) as defined. Higher indices would be obtained for developing countries if the objective (*O*) was to be achieved by those same dates.

Table 5

Increases in protein supplies required by 1975 and 1985 to meet protein targets calculated as 120 per cent of requirements

(1965 = 100)

| Regions and Subregions | 1975 | 1985 |
|---|---|---|
| FAR EAST (incl. China Mainland) | 135 | 167 |
| South Asia | 153 | 193 |
| Southern Asia Mainland | 132 | 166 |
| Eastern Asia | 115 | 133 |
| South Eastern Asia Major Islands | 160 | 214 |
| China Mainland | 126 | 153 |
| NEAR AND MIDDLE EAST | 131 | 172 |
| AFRICA | 135 | 176 |
| North Africa | 160 | 216 |
| West and Central Africa | 142 | 186 |
| East and Southern Africa | 127 | 161 |
| LATIN AMERICA | 134 | 177 |
| Brazil | 133 | 176 |
| Mexico and Central America | 138 | 190 |
| Northern and Western countries of South America | 139 | 187 |
| River Plate Countries | 120 | 138 |
| DEVELOPING REGIONS | 134 | 170 |
| EUROPE (incl. U.S.S.R.) | 109 | 118 |
| Eastern Europe | 114 | 124 |
| Western Europe | 106 | 112 |
| NORTH AMERICA | 115 | 135 |
| OCEANIA | 124 | 153 |
| DEVELOPED REGIONS | 111 | 123 |
| WORLD | 122 | 151 |

## HOW CAN THE PROTEIN GAP BE CLOSED?

We shall not consider here any of the following points:
  (a)  increasing the purchasing power of populations;
  (b)  government and other measures intended to ensure better distribution and more equitable sharing of available monetary and food resources;
  (c)  measures to reduce waste;
  (d)  nutrition education which is indispensable to ensure better use of
available food supplies and household resources.

The only subject being discussed here is the *increasing of available
supplies of protein foods* and the contribution of each of the major food
groups.

The percentage contribution of different food groups as shown in
Table 2 — which could also have been done by countries — indicates
major prospects and priorities.

In fact, planning of production — whether directed, suggested or
induced and whatever the motivations or incentives — will necessarily
follow more or less the type of diet imposed by ecological conditions,
trade, habits and openings for investment in food production,
preservation and distribution. Planning can only provide guidelines,
accelerate efforts in certain sectors, but cannot bring about a dietary
revolution; presumably improvement will come gradually.

*Proteins of vegetable origin*

Foods of vegetable origin constitute from 60 to 87 per cent of the
proteins in countries where proteins are in short supply. Cereals by
themselves constitute the staple food of 95 per cent of the population of
developing countries. Here are percentages of total protein intake derived
from cereals:

| Area | per cent |
|------|----------|
| Brazil | 38 |
| Mexico and Central America | 45 |
| Eastern Europe | 50 |
| Africa | 55 |
| India, Pakistan, Ceylon | 65 |
| Near East | 68 |
| North Africa | 70 |
| Third World | 58 |
| Entire World | 48 |

Hence the main method for increasing production of crude protein is to promote the production of cereals.

However, most cereals, even though their content of calories derived from protein exceeds 10 per cent, have a net protein utilization (*NPU*) of only between 50 and 60 per cent; it is therefore necessary to improve the quality of the diet by simultaneous production of a certain quantity of protein foods for diet supplementation (pulses, animal proteins). For diets based on rice – the protein content of which is low – such supplementation is vital.

Obviously the selection and use of high yielding cereals, such as maize selected in Mexico and rice selected in the Philippines, together with current efforts to obtain high yielding varieties of wheat, millet and sorghum, justify all work of research and distribution of selected seeds. Indeed FAO has decided that this shall be one of the high priority areas of its programme of work, two of the other areas of concentration being the production of protein foods and the war on waste.

It also follows from the preceding discussion that it is equally necessary to select – no matter what the cost – protein-rich varieties. This is a necessity for rice, the common varieties of which have a protein calorie/total calorie ratio of less than 8 per cent.

It is further necessary to pay special attention to the protein quality of selected seeds. At Purdue University, U.S.A., there has been selected a maize variety called 'Opaque 2' with a high lysine and tryptophan content – these usually being limiting amino acids for this cereal. Analogous results can be obtained for rice. The following tables show the effects on the protein content and protein value of the diet of:

(*a*) increasing the protein content by application of nitrogen fertilizer (in the case of wheat) (Table 6)

(*b*) substitution for traditional maize varieties of

(*i*) high yielding hybrid maize

(*ii*) 'Opaque 2' which though it gives slightly lower yields than common varieties, has a higher protein value or protein score. (Table 7)
From the above data it can be deduced that:

(*a*) A higher protein content does not necessarily mean an increase in net utilizable protein in the diet (*see* Iran – national supplies).

(*b*) A major increase (of from 30 to 35 per cent) in net protein level is obtainable without necessarily any increase in yields, merely through the improvement of protein quality (Guatemala, maize variety 'Opaque 2').
*Now to consider pulses, nuts and seeds:* All types of beans, peas, chickpeas, lentils, oilseeds and nuts are grouped together under this heading. Their particular feature is that they contain some 20–25 per cent protein and even up to 38 per cent (in the case of soya beans). Their proteins are

14

Table 6. Influence on the protein value and intake of the replacement of ordinary varieties of cereals by high yield varieties and high protein yield and quality varieties

| IRAN | Total proteins of the diet g/day per head | Proteins calories % | Chemical score | | | | NPU | Ndp cal. % | Net protein g/day per head | Δ% |
|---|---|---|---|---|---|---|---|---|---|---|
| | | | Lysine | S-cont. A.A. | Threon. | Trypt. | | | | |
| NATIONAL FOOD SUPPLY | | | | | | | | | | |
| 1) Common Wheat (Prot. 10.4%) | 55.5 | 10.8 | 72 | 74 | 71 | 72 | 63 | 6.8 | 35.0 | — |
| 2) Wheat obtained with N-fertilizers (Prot. 12.4%) | 61.9 | 12.1 | 65 | 73 | 68 | 72 | 57 | 6.9 | 35.3 | + 0.9 |
| National food supply +10% Wheat obtained with N-fertilizers (Prot. 12.4%) | 65.9 | 12.2 | 64 | 73 | 68 | 72 | 56 | 6.8 | 36.9 | + 2.3 |
| FAMILY CONSUMPTION (Azarbaijan) | | | | | | | | | | |
| 1) Common Wheat (Prot. 10.4%) | 72.4 | 10.6 | 60 | 73 | 66 | 72 | 55 | 5.8 | 39.8 | — |
| 2) Wheat obtained with N-fertilizers (Prot. 12.4%) | 83.5 | 12.3 | 58 | 73 | 65 | 72 | 51 | 6.3 | 42.6 | + 7.0 |
| Family consumption +10% Wheat obtained with N-fertilizers (Prot. 12.4%) | 90.4 | 12.4 | 58 | 73 | 65 | 72 | 51 | 6.3 | 46.1 | +15.8 |

Table 7. Influence on the protein value and intake of the replacement of ordinary varieties of cereals by high yield varieties and high protein yield and quality varieties

| GUATEMALA | Total proteins of the diet g/day per head | Protein calories % | Chemical score | | | | NPU | Ndp Cal. % | Net protein g/day per head | $\Delta\%$ |
|---|---|---|---|---|---|---|---|---|---|---|
| | | | Lysine | S-cont. A.A. | Threon. | Trypt. | | | | |
| NATIONAL FOOD SUPPLY | | | | | | | | | | |
| 1) Common Maize (Prot. 9.5%) | 55.4 | 10.6 | 62 | 61 | 72 | 55 | 51 | 5.4 | 28.3 | — |
| 2) Hybrid Maize (Individuals 521) (Prot.10.0%) | 57.1 | 11.0 | 58 | 57 | 70 | 57 | 49 | 5.5 | 28.0 | − 1.1 |
| 3) High Lysine Maize (Opaque 2–Fleury 2) (Prot. 11.6%) | 62.7 | 12.1 | 79 | 79 | 74 | 80 | 61 | 7.4 | 38.2 | + 35.0 |
| National food supply +10% Maize (Opaque 2–Fleury 2) (Prot.11.6%) | 66.8 | 12.1 | 78 | 80 | 74 | 80 | 61 | 7.4 | 40.7 | + 43.8 |
| FAMILY CONSUMPTION (S. Fernando) | | | | | | | | | | |
| 1) Common Maize (Prot. 9.5%) | 72.0 | 12.6 | 70 | 56 | 74 | 55 | 49 | 6.1 | 35.3 | — |
| 2) Hybrid Maize (Individuals 521) (Prot. 10.0%) | 74.1 | 13.0 | 65 | 52 | 72 | 58 | 46 | 6.0 | 34.1 | − 3.4 |
| 3) High Lysine Maize (Opaque 2–Fleury 2)(Prot. 11.6%) | 78.8 | 13.8 | 85 | 80 | 76 | 79 | 59 | 8.1 | 46.5 | + 31.7 |
| Family Consumption + 10% Maize (Opaque 2–Fleury 2) (Prot. 11.6%) | 83.7 | 13.8 | 84 | 81 | 76 | 79 | 59 | 8.1 | 49.4 | + 39.9 |

excellent sources for supplementation of proteins derived from cereals. Their protein calorie/total calorie ratio is two to three times higher than that of cereals. At the present time they constitute for example 5.1 per cent (North Africa), 15.7 per cent (equatorial Africa), 20.3 per cent (mainland China) and as much as 26.6 per cent (Brazil), of the total protein supply. Their production along with cereals should therefore be promoted by all means possible.

*Proteins of animal origin*

Although theoretically an adult can live on cereals supplemented by a mixture of vegetable proteins, animal proteins do improve the biological value of proteins in the diet. Even well balanced baby foods prepared from plant proteins are improved by the addition of animal proteins. The reason is that animal proteins, aside from their amino acid composition supply other nutrients and improve food flavour. Moreover, the consumer public attaches great significance to the consumption of animal products (for the feeling of satisfaction or as a status symbol, a gain in social prestige). Finally, certain foods of animal origin (milk and eggs) are essential for babies and young children.

Milk, meat, eggs and fish constitute 15, 11, 2 and 4 per cent of world food supplies respectively. The figures vary considerably from one part of the world to another and from one country to another. Thus in North America (where animal proteins constitute 70 per cent of the protein intake) these percentages are, respectively: 36.3, 24.9, 2.9 and 5.8 per cent; whereas in North Africa the figures are: 7.8, 9.5, 1.6 and 0.8 per cent; and in India, Pakistan and Ceylon: 1.4, 9.9, 1.4 and 0.2 per cent (*see* Table 1).

Production planning, country by country, is essential; but whatever the efforts and investments required to increase production of staple protein foods, clearly (in the emerging countries) even if the production indices for 1975 and 1985 were attained, this would mean only a partial improvement — given the low percentage represented by these foods in the total protein intake. Now the limitations upon animal production are well known. Meeting quantitative requirements in those countries which are now suffering from shortages will have to come first through higher crop production and improvement of crop quality.

Another point which should not be overlooked is that the targets or objectives are just that and no more and are rarely attained. Past experience has shown that, in respect of India for instance, even with the most optimistic prospects for a rise in individual income, protein consumption toward 1975 will only have risen by one third; and in 1985 by only two-thirds of the increase envisaged in the practical requirements (*P*) (*see*

Table 5). According to these calculations, an additional 25 years of sustained economic development would be necessary to attain a production level such that the great majority of the population will have an adequate protein intake. The Indicative World Plan for Agricultural Production reaches rather pessimistic conclusions for most parts of the world.

I merely cite one instance taken from the Indicative World Plan for Agricultural Production, Annex on Dietary Levels, Prospects and Food policies in Africa south of the Sahara: according to this (*see* Table 8 below), 11 countries will not have covered their total protein requirements by 1975 while 9 countries, primarily those in the Ghanaian and equatorial zones, will not have covered them even by 1985. There the animal protein gap resulting from insufficient market supplies is expected to amount to around 14,000 tons of proteins in 1975 and 27,000 in 1985.

Table 8
Deficit in protein in certain countries of Africa

| Target year | Economic deficit* (animal protein) | Nutritional deficit† (Total protein) | Number of countries | Population involved | |
|---|---|---|---|---|---|
| | | | | (million) | in % total Africa population |
| 1975 | 14,000 tons | 270,000 tons | 11 | 63 | 27% |
| 1985 | 27,000 tons | 270,000 tons | 9 | 68 | 22% |

*difference between demand and supplies
†difference between requirements and supplies

These are actually small quantities that could easily be covered by imports of some 130,000 tons of fresh fish in 1975 and 250,000 tons in 1985 (equivalent to 4 kg *per caput* per year). What is more serious is the gap in overall protein supplies – a shortfall of some 270,000 tons, equivalent to 1,250,000 tons of pulses (or 18 kg *per caput* per year). This is a widely unreasonable figure whether from the standpoint of production or of acceptability. What then?

The answer is that we must leave the beaten track. We must innovate. All resources of science and technology must be mobilized to create new protein-rich foods or to derive the utmost benefits from hitherto insufficiently utilized resources to feed mankind.

## REFERENCES

François, P. J. (1968). *Budgets et alimentation des ménages ruraux en 1962 Madagascar.* Paris; INSEE

Miller, D. S. and Payne, P. R. (1961a). *Brit. J. Nutr.* **15**, 11

– and – (1961b). *J. Nutr.* **74**, 413

Platt, B. S., Miller, D. S. and Payne, P. R. (1961). In: *Protein Values of Human Food,* from J. F. Brock: *Recent Advances in Human Nutrition,* Ed. Churchill, London

# ECONOMICS OF PROTEIN PRODUCTION

## R.H. TUCK

*Department of Agricultural Economics,
University of Reading*

## INTRODUCTION

If we were to set out to make a list of all the items which human beings (as individuals or groups) buy and sell, or exchange, or use in production or consumption — and I mean the specific items about which the practical decisions to buy and sell etc. are made — then it would have to be an extremely long list.

It would have to include such items as: land, buildings, petrol, cars, milking machines, steel, manual labour, managerial labour, advice, taxi rides, wheat, bread, cows, milk, pigs, pork, opera tickets, and many, many others. It would not include (except in, as yet, very tiny quantities) proteins. These things, in themselves, are not bought or sold. In so far as they are produced, transferred, stored or consumed, it is as constituents of other things. There is no market in proteins. As such they never figure as the precise object of economic calculations or decisions. Therefore, if you wished to be awkward, you might argue that you cannot have an 'economics' of proteins in any exact sense — not, that is, in the sense that you can speak of the economics of steel, or of rice.

In a precisely similar way, one might argue that there is no such thing as, for example, an 'economics of beauty', in any simple sense. Though a straightforward economics of beauty may not exist, no-one can doubt that considerations of beauty affect economic decisions. Thus if I am considering buying a car, I require it to possess certain functional attributes. I also wish it to have certain qualities of line and style, and if it does so I will pay more for it. The manufacturer, knowing this, is influenced to modify the design of his vehicle so that it possesses, to some extent, the desired aesthetic, as well as the desired functional, attributes. Doing this will have repercussions upon the productive resources which have to be bought and used—i.e. upon the costs which have to be incurred—in order to produce the car. Considerations of beauty have thus affected both the conditions of supply and the conditions of demand for this car.

The demand and supply conditions of every other item on the long list of commodities and services which was contemplated above might be similarly affected, in greater or lesser degree. One might consider developing an economics of beauty in terms of the effects considerations of it have upon the demand and supply conditions of all the listed items in which an explicit trade takes place. It is in these terms that we have to develop an 'economics of proteins'.

It will be obvious that the subject thus defined is too vast to be dealt with comprehensively here. Therefore, in the brief survey which follows, I shall concentrate on certain main points.

Broadly speaking it will emerge that in this field, we are either, in certain circumstances, confronted with grave problems of surplus in some sense, or else, in other circumstances, we are confronted with grave problems of deficit, and that these contrasting problems can simultaneously exist in different regions of the world. I shall argue, however, that the reasonable-seeming device of organizing free or concessional transfers of appropriate products from one kind of region to the other cannot offer more, at best, than relatively minor and temporary alleviation to the problems of either. I shall argue further, with reference to 'deficit' regions, that, both in the long and medium term effective solutions to the main problems will not be found solely in terms of production development, but that regard must be had for the other side of the balance, namely, the magnitude of aggregate requirements. Finally, with reference to the production development side, I shall argue that attempts to stimulate the increased production of protein-rich products, will need to be properly related to other aspects of the complex process of economic development if they are to succeed fully.

I must add, straightaway, that in none of this shall I be decrying, or attempting to belittle, the fundamentally important work on proteins with which, in so many different ways, those present are associated. On the contrary, as a humble admirer of this work, I would simply hope, by attempting to place it in a reasonable economic context, to help slightly to make it even more effective in its continuation.

## PROBLEMS OF SURPLUS

Let us examine how considerations of the protein question are likely to bear upon, or be affected by, the conditions of demand and supply for food products, which are the items on our imaginary list most directly relevant in this context. Let us concentrate first of all upon the situation in developed economies, such as those of western Europe and, in particular, this country.

21

It has been characteristic of these economies in recent decades that developments in the techniques and organization of production have been more than adequate to keep pace with population growth. The result has been that both average, and minimal, real incomes per head have risen. This means that, if patterns of production and consumption remain unchanged, each consumer could receive, as time goes on, more of every item he consumes than formerly. For various reasons, however, we would not expect consumers to wish to increase their consumption of agricultural sector products so rapidly as other things (see, National Food Survey Committee 1968). If we neglect the factor of external demand for the time being, this must mean either an unwanted surplus of these products or else a relative decline of the agricultural sector, particularly in respect to the proportion of the total labour force it absorbs; or, more probably, something of both effects, the one moving relative prices and rewards in a direction which stimulates the other. So that the potential surplus is likely to exceed the actual one.

It is true that the extent of this surplus is likely to be somewhat reduced effectively, at least for a time, because of the likely accompanying tendency of consumers in these circumstances to wish to increase the proportions they consume of the higher quality, higher protein, higher cost products of the agricultural sector (see National Food Supply Committee, 1968). So that the discrepancy between their increased demands for agricultural products compared with other products, will be less when the former are measured in terms of the productive task they represent (i.e. in terms of cost) than when they are measured in some other terms, for example, calories or bulk. However, the mitigating effects of this factor will only be felt by certain products, and they will be partially offset by particularly severe problems for others, especially such things as potatoes and bread; moreover, it is unlikely still to be an important factor once incomes generally have risen to a moderately high level.

So it would seem that, in these economies, the prospect for the next few decades is one of potential surplus for the products of the agricultural sector with which we are concerned. The actual surpluses may be expected to be less than the potential ones by an amount which will depend upon the success with which the proportion of productive resources (especially labour) retained within the sector can be reduced. Again, one would expect the position to vary in degree from one developed economy to another because of differences in other factors.

We will now consider how the protein question affects this general prospect. It can be expected to do so both by influencing the demand side, and by influencing the supply side. I will take these in turn.

There are three main ways in which protein considerations could interact with the state of demand for human food products. The first and simplest is via the mere diffusion, among the final consumers themselves, of more knowledge about proteins. Such knowledge might or might not be accurate. Its diffusion might be an aspect of a purely educative process, or it might be something skilfully achieved by an advertising expert contriving to exploit a new gimmick in the interest of his client. Either way there is likely to be an effect upon the consumers' scales of preference for different products, in the sense that, at given prices, they will buy more of some and less of others. On the whole one would expect this effect to be most marked upon those exposed to a real or imagined risk of protein shortage; for example, pregnant and nursing mothers, infants and growing children, and those following some kind of special dietary regime. The impact of this kind of demand change will no doubt be greatest upon food processors, who, over recent decades, have of course greatly modified their methods of preparing certain traditional products, and have introduced certain new ones, in response to it. Examples are not hard to find. It is no doubt a testimonial to somebody's effectiveness that 'Kelloggs Special K' and the 'Cambridge Formula Loaf' come readily to mind. Both are advertised as good sources of protein.

The second main kind of interaction with demand which I had in mind is that which operates via governmental intervention on social and nutritional grounds. There is obviously no need for me to pursue this particular topic far, since Miss Hollingsworth is about to deal with it much more competently than I could hope to. However, there is just one point of principle I should note here. It is that if within its nutrition policy a government wishes to increase the rate of consumption of certain items by certain groups — other than by advice and persuasion to the groups in question — then it will have, in some form or other, to pay part of the price of these items. From the point of view of the producers, it is this total price (including any government subsidy or contribution in some other form) which is the relevant one in any statement of the demand situation of the products in question. Thus governmental action of this kind directly affects demand.

The third aspect of interaction with demand which I should mention is that which is concerned with external demand, that is, demand from other countries. In so far as this demand comes from other developed countries one would expect it to be subject to the same general influences as have just been noted for home demand. It may be a different question, however, where the demand comes from developing countries faced with acute and chronic problems of deficiency. I intend to return to this important factor later in my paper. I therefore leave it on one side for the moment and carry on with my rough assessment of the overall position in developed economies, with this element explicitly left out of the account. We must next turn to a brief consideration of the supply side of the question. Research and thought concerned with nutritional factors and, in particular with proteins, is likely to have far-reaching direct effects upon the techniques and organization of production within the agricultural sector (in the wide sense) in several different ways.

One important way is through the more rapid emergence of new strains and varieties, and of new processing methods, promising enough to be worth commercial trial, which is virtually certain to result from the self-conscious quest for high-yielding protein-rich products. Most of these innovations will prove non-viable commercially. But the fact that the overall flow of new technical possibilities is accelerated will have the effect that the flow of the minority of commercially viable innovations will also be accelerated. There is an analogy here with the process of evolution through natural selection. New technical ideas and discoveries have the role of mutations, and just as most mutations fail to survive, so it is with the new technical possibilities in production. Commercial selection imposes tests no less severe than those undergone by new species in the environment of nature.

A second important way is through the effects of more precise understanding of the parts played in the productive process by items which are not in themselves new. As an example of this one might take the case of animal feeds. More precise understanding of the exact qualities required in a final feed mix, combined with more precise understanding of the contributions made to these by different possible constituents, have led to the development of very sophisticated methods of revising, in changing price situations, the appropriate constituents and quantities to use. Systematic exploitation of these methods brings important gains in efficiency, but is beyond the scope of most farms. There is no doubt that, along these lines, improved nutritional understanding has contributed to what is the most significant of all organizational developments in the agricultural sectors of developed economies. This is the major emergence of non-farming businesses in and around farming which perform in a sophisticated and highly organized way functions which, in an earlier form, had been located on the farms themselves.

We must now try to assess the effect of all these influences, on the demand side and on the supply side, upon the general prospect of surplus which, as I suggested earlier, exists for economies of the kinds we are considering. I do not think there is much doubt that the overall effect is to accentuate the tendency to surplus. For though the influences on the demand side can be expected to sustain *per capita* consumption of protein products to some extent, they will not do so to the extent that the consumption rises in proportion with total income — especially beyond a certain level of income. Moreover, it has to be remembered that there will be converse depressive effects upon consumption of other items of diet, (which must tend to add to the resources available for production of protein products). Meanwhile the direct influences on the supply side, which I have noted, are likely to have a lasting and significant effect upon the effectiveness with which productive resources are used in this field.

The next and obvious question is whether the external demand factor, especially demand from the developing countries, which was discussed briefly above, and which has so far been left out of this assessment, makes, or could make, any great difference to the general conclusion. My general answer to this question is 'no'.

It may well seem at first sight gallingly perverse to deny the possibility that countries with an embarrassing problem of surplus in certain categories of output might find an elegant and humane solution to their problem by transferring these surpluses to other countries which seem to be suffering from the contrary problem in a severe degree. So I must explain my negative answer, by clarifying the sense in which I have been using this very loose term 'surplus'. Slightly more accurately, I am using the word to denote a continuing situation in which a country is so placed that, if it maintains the same proportion as before of its work force in a given line of production, then the resulting output will increasingly exceed what can be disposed of through conventional channels at the level of prices necessary to meet costs.

Where such a situation exists it often happens in practice that the actual relative shift of labour out of the relevant sector lags behind what is called for by the underlying imbalance. In these cases many different devices, (including pathological forms of marketing organization) have been resorted to in the attempt to patch over the immediate difficulties. There then arise surpluses (one thinks of coffee burnt in the 1930s, and of the eggs and dairy products internationally dumped at the present time) which can clearly be transferred at very low extra cost to the donor countries. The point is that, in these instances, the main costs (or wastage of resources) has already been incurred. However, surpluses in this extreme sense are no more than the tip of the iceberg when compared with the continuing implications of the surplus situations of which I am talking.

What I am denying, therefore, is that international transfers to deficiency regions are possible on the scale which could effectively reverse this kind of imbalance. The essential difficulties are connected with the fact that such transfers would have to be paid for. I stress that full payment is unavoidable, whatever it is called, or whoever does it; for the economist it is simply the name given to the act whereby productive resources are released from other activites and sustained in the relevant ones.

Resources for such payment must either derive from the international exchange of other output (e.g. petroleum) originating within the country which wishes to purchase, or else it must derive elsewhere. In cases where the former possibility is open there is no apparent obstacle to the normal development of international trade and one must suppose that such demand is already making its full impact upon the international pattern of demand. No doubt this impact will develop, modified, however, by developments in the home production position in the purchasing countries. Clearly it will be in cases in which the payment must come from elsewhere that we must expect to find any major persistent problems of protein insufficiency — or other material insufficiencies for that matter.

One important source of the means of payment, falling within this second category, is that which involves, in some form, contributions from governments — either as individual governments, or through some kind of international organization. Such government payments imply taxation; and it is important to remember that taxation is subject, not only to political, but also to functional limitations. For beyond a certain level of total taxation, it is hard to levy more without distorting the pattern of price and income differentials upon which all complex high income economies must partially depend for the efficient allocation of resources (*see* Tuck, 1967). This latter point is potentially extremely important; it is a feature of government expenditure which sets a comparatively early limit upon the amounts which can be transferred in this way, through public finance, from person to person or from region to region. I have expressed the point in terms appropriate to a free enterprise economy or a mixed economy of the Western kind, but I believe that similar factors will also operate in economic systems of other kinds once the general level of incomes within them is relatively high.

The fact has to be faced, I believe, that it is not possible to arrange to make available for use elsewhere anything near the whole of the potential surpluses of protein containing products of the agricultural sectors of those developed economies where such surpluses exist and are in continuing prospect. Still less would it be possible to make available the enhanced potential surpluses which would result if the populations of these 'surplus' economies could be persuaded to prefer a less costly form of protein adequate diet, relying less heavily on the expensive animal products they currently choose to consume. It is not even plausible to assume that such 'free' transfers of 'surplus' produce can attain a level which would save many of the economies in question from severe problems of moving resources between sectors, of the kind which underly the intractable issues of 'structural' policy and which currently beset the countries of the E.E.C.

Moreover, since one important limiting factor in these matters is the total availability of government financial contributions out of tax revenue, it is worth considering how far it is wise to use these valuable funds for the transfer of produce (except, of course, in cases of especially severe temporary problems caused by such catastrophes as droughts or wars), rather than for making available or possible other things, such as technical advice, training, education, capital equipment and works, well-chosen research, which, by helping to bring about favourable economic developments in areas of deficiency, might well contribute more to the solution of the world problem

In order to examine this question further, I now turn to the problems of the developing economies.


## PROBLEMS OF DEFICIENCY

When one talks, in a world context, of 'the protein problem' one is usually talking of a problem of shortage. The precise extent of this problem is a matter of definition (as to what constitutes 'shortage') and of some debate (to the extent that many of the relevant facts are not known with precision). M. Autret, in his important paper, has thrown significant further light on these matters. For my part I shall accept that, on the most severe definition (and *a fortiori* for less severe ones), a major world protein problem exists, both currently and in prospect. By this I mean that, in several areas of the world, shortages of protein-containing food products affect mortality rates amongst substantial sections of the population. For this problem to be completely and permanently removed the following would be necessary: first, locality by locality, the current rates of production of protein products (or of other output freely exchangeable against such products) must be on a scale commensurate with the needs of the local population; second, the prospective rates of increase in these rates of production must be at least equal to the potential rates of increase in the needs of the local populations. Of these two conditions, the second is more important than the first.

By 'potential' rate of increase (with reference to populations) I mean the rates of increase which would be in prospect if mortality was in no way affected by shortages (such as protein deficiencies) attributable to low real income levels (*see* Tuck, 1968). In areas where severe shortage affects important sections of the population these potential rates will, by my definition, not be reached. To the extent that this applies, estimates of

27

the prospective future extent of the protein problem made with reference to projections of actual population numbers, are liable to be underestimates. The magnitude of this effect would be hard to estimate exactly even with the fullest and most carefully classified mortality data, because of the devious ways in which, for example, a protein deficiency might influence mortality immediately attributed to other causes; but given the complete absence of mortality data of this order for many of the most relevant areas, this magnitude is in fact unknown. The region by region element is important in this prescription for a solution because of the difficulties which attach to concessional international transfers.

On the basis of this definition of it I think it may now be asserted that the world protein problem will either be over-solved, or not solved. The crucial factors here are, on the one hand, the birth-rate (which is the essential determinant of the potential population growth rate, since, nowadays, one must assume a relatively low death rate if the potential rate of growth is achieved — in other words the mortality of a well-fed, well-sheltered and well-clad population is nowadays likely to be low) and, on the other hand, the possibilities of increase in production capacity. That these should be in exact balance is a coincidence hardly to be expected. An imbalance in one sense will imply rising living standards in the population concerned (including for most of the poorest elements) and ultimately problems of surplus of the kind which have been discussed earlier. An imbalance in the other sense will imply downward-tending standards at least for a substantial section of the poorer elements (overall average standards could be rising) unless, or until, the protein problem and other related problems of low income levels, are sufficiently severe to ensure the discrepancy between 'actual' and 'potential' population growth which is called for by the situation.

I believe that this proposition has applied (i.e. one or other of the two main kinds of imbalance it prescribes has been found) in the various localities of the world in the past, that it applies today, and that it will continue to apply in the future.

That it is inescapable in the very long run (say 100—150 years) seems particularly clear. Unless indeed one can contemplate the ultimate possibility of sustaining indefinitely increasing colonies of human beings in space, able to use materials found in space to extend their life-support environments and to provide the means of subsistence, all in indefinitely increasing amounts. If this is possible — and if it would be desirable above other conceivable objectives (and some of, for example, Dr. Colin Clark's recent writings seem to me almost to suggest that this is in fact his opinion — see *Population Growth and Land Use,* chapters 3 and 4) then perhaps it is arguable that birth-rates should not be allowed to

28

fall – whatever the current and medium term discomforts this implies – for fear lest, without the (questionable) stimulus of population pressure, the necessary technical developments might not be pursued with sufficient determination and persistence.

For my part, after reviewing this, I am left with the conviction that the fundamental element in any lasting solution to the protein problem (or other chronic problems of shortage of necessary output) is the achievement of birth-rates in every region and time which are within the range which are appropriate to the situation. By the word 'situation' here I mean: *(a)* prevailing death-rates (except to the extent that they are attributable to shortages);*(b)* the attainable rate of increase in productive capacity of the region. This latter is limited by several factors (the actual rate of population growth is one). Important among the others are: first, the pace of advance in technical knowledge and of its diffusion among the relevant people; second, the rate at which new additional capital of various kinds (which must all come out of someone's current production) can be found. Except in the ultimate, very long term, quite rapid rates of increase in productive capacity may often be attainable, so that, meanwhile, it is not implied that birth-rates need to be such as to make population numbers stationary; but they will have to be appropriate to the situation if the satisfactory kind of imbalance is to be obtained.

The implication of this latter analysis, which is, perhaps, most directly relevant to the present symposium is the element of flexibility which it reveals as provided in these matters by any possibilities for faster rates of increase in productive capacity. There is, however, a certain danger in separating this production side too completely from the birth rate question. One source of this danger is the fact that, in a given situation, the choice of policy in respect of production development can, for example through sociological side-effects, help, or hinder, desirable developments in respect of birth rates. Another source of danger from too complete a dichotomy is connected with the fact that the resources for any action which may be attempted, either in respect of production development or in respect of birth-rate regulation, all largely derive from the same limited pool of governmental funds. It is important to take thought, as far as possible, to ensure that the amount of action taken on the one side is not pushed beyond the point where it begins to preclude more urgent action on the other.

It is nevertheless clear that effective and well-judged action to enhance the local productive capacity is important and helpful in many under-developed regions. In some cases it may even be an essential preliminary to effective regulation of birth-rates. Moreover, it is also clear that increasing knowledge and experience of the role of the different proteins in human diets, of the widening range of products which can provide them, and of the processes whereby these products can be made available under various conditions, make a crucially important contribution in this context – by permitting the areas of especially urgent need to be more precisely identified, and by suggesting promising activities to include in projects intended to relieve the situation in particular cases.

I have a final cautionary word to offer even here. It is necessary that any such project should be so designed that, when in operation it can be made to pay. That is to say, it must be possible for the resulting output to find buyers able, and (although I do not pursue this avenue) willing, to pay for it. 'Pay' means 'to offer, in effect, acceptable other produce, or services, in exchange'. 'Acceptable' means 'such as will effectively help to meet the running costs of the projects'.

A project must pay if it is to be sustained, for otherwise it will represent a continuing and ultimately unacceptable burden on governmental resources. Moreover (and this may often be even more important) it must pay if it is to be emulated, and so lead to a growing activity. Thus, for example, say an attempt is to be made to introduce improved husbandry methods, including the use of fertilizers and improved seed in a given area. It is essential that this scheme should be accompanied by action, not only to provide the appropriate machinery of distribution and marketing for the resulting produce, but also to provide an effective demand for it (which includes the ability to pay in the foregoing sense). This might be done, perhaps, by arranging in a parallel scheme to set up, in an accessible market area, activities which will manufacture some of the new inputs required by the original productive process – indeed, the choice of this original process might sensibly be influenced by this consideration, i.e. so chosen as to use inputs which might lend themselves to this kind of complementary development. Moreover, the provision of an 'infra-structure' (e.g. roads, credit organizations) needs also to be thought of. It might often be advizable to provide this on a larger scale than would be required just for the initial scheme, so that an environment conducive to expansion is created (see Mosher, 1965).

In other words, I am stressing the need for a sense of proportion, and suggesting that a project to increase the production of protein-rich commodities in an area where these are needed, is more likely to succeed where the project forms part of a larger, well-concerted scheme for more general development in that area, than where it is pursued too single-mindedly on its own, even though on a larger scale.

Rather similar considerations must apply also to schemes to transfer finished products, either free or on concessional terms, from an area where they are in surplus, to an area where they are short. The attempt should be made to incorporate such deliveries within a wider development scheme — say to sustain the expansion of one kind of activity during a period when this is out of phase with the expansion of some complementary activity, and so that, moreover, a term is seen to these deliveries. There is a risk, otherwise, that such deliveries may fail to stimulate local productive capabilities. They may even retard the development of these, (though this, of course, is a complicated question, not adequately to be dealt with in a brief mention (*see* Lewis and Sandford, 1968)) through lowering the local exchange value of the products in question. If either of these eventualities results, then it will not be possible to claim that the longer run problems (i.e. impending future hardships) of the region have been helped, especially if the possibility of an eventual discontinuance of the deliveries must be faced

It was for reasons such as these that I suggested earlier, that where certain governmental funds are available for international co-operative purposes, the merits of any scheme to use part of them to enable the free, or concessional, transfer of finished produce should be weighed rather anxiously against the merits of possible alternative uses of the funds more directly aimed at stimulating general productive capacity in the deficit regions themselves.

## REFERENCES

Anonymous (1968). 'Household Food Consumption and Expenditure': *Rep. natn. Fd. Surv. Comm.*
Clark, C. (1967). *Population Growth and Land Use.* London; Macmillan
Lewis, J. and Sandford, S. (1968). *Food Aid.* University of Cambridge, Overseas Studies Committee Conference 1968. Background paper
Mosher, A. T. (1965). *Getting Agriculture Moving. Essentials for Development and Modernisation.* New York; Praeger
Tuck, R. H. (1967). *J. agric. Econ.* 18, 75
Tuck, R. H. (1968). *Mediterranea* 17, 6

# NUTRITION POLICY WITH REGARD TO PROTEIN

DOROTHY F. HOLLINGSWORTH and J.P. GREAVES

*Food Science Advice Branch,*
*Ministry of Agriculture, Fisheries and Food,*
*London*

## INTRODUCTION

We chose this title for our contribution not only to fit the subject of this symposium, but to acknowledge the recent acceleration of interest in the United Nations and elsewhere in the problems involved in ensuring that sufficient protein is consumed throughout the world. In choosing it, however, we are not suggesting that policy relating to protein can or should be divorced from a general nutritional policy. As protein provides 10–15 per cent of the energy value of most diets it is quantitatively important, and it is often associated in foods with other nutrients, particularly those vitamins of the B complex. Nevertheless, improvement of the nutritional condition of all people, which must be the aim of policy, starts with recognition of the importance of providing an adequate energy intake. It may necessitate ensuring the consumption of sufficient foods rich in vitamins A, C and D or other nutrients which do not necessarily occur in the protein-containing parts of foods. Thus, though it may be desirable to give first place to protein, it would be wrong to give it the only consideration in the development of nutrition policy, which is itself only part of general food policy. It may be mentioned briefly that food and agricultural policy in developing countries will be formulated in the context of the overall planning of economic development; in this regard the 'protein gap' between rich and poor countries, particularly great with respect to animal protein *(see,* for example, *Food and Agriculture Organization 1963,* Table 13), may be held to be a valid indicator of socio-economic status. It seems to be a universal fact that, as circumstances permit, the consumption of protein foods, especially those of animal origin, increases to levels similar to those enjoyed by the developed countries today, and to this extent such levels may be thought of as representing the legitimate aspirations of all people. Thus in global terms the 'protein gap' is not just – or even mainly – a nutritional indicator, but an index of economic and social development.

During the first world war W.M.Bayliss (1917), when Professor of General Physiology at University College, London, expressed his views on man's need for protein, in the context of a Western European type diet, in the phrase: 'Take care of the calories and the protein will take care of itself'. This dictum has stood the tests of time and subsequent research in respect of situations, such as he envisaged, where the food supply is sufficiently rich in protein, for each person in a community to be able to meet his or her needs for protein simply by eating enough food (i.e. by meeting his or her calorie–energy–needs). This condition is met for adults almost everywhere in the world. In other words, almost every mixture of foods liable to be eaten by adults, when eaten in sufficent quantity to meet energy needs, is likely to meet protein needs. The quantity qualification is important. Adults may not get sufficient protein from their local food supply if food is short.

If the basic foods of a country are relatively rich in protein content, of good quality, the above condition may also be met for young children, who require more protein in relation to their size than adults because they are growing – and the more rapid their growth the greater their need for protein. If, however, the staple foods are relatively poor sources of protein, such as maize or rice, or very poor sources such as cassava, sago or plantains, young children will not be able to obtain the quantity and quality of protein they need unless their diets are supplemented by foods rich in protein or improved by fortification with protein isolates or amino acids. In practice, no country without an adequate milk supply has yet wholly solved the problem of assuring the consumption of adequate amounts of good quality protein by young children after they are weaned from the breast, a circumstance almost foretold 50 years ago by the Royal Society Food (War) Committee (1919) which stated that 'The special value of animal proteins, and especially those of milk, for building up the body is one of the reasons why milk is of such supreme value in the feeding of infants and young children, and *no diet for such can be considered satisfactory which does not contain a considerable proportion of milk'.*

## THE DEVELOPMENT OF A NUTRITION POLICY

The problems involved in developing and operating a nutrition policy designed to ensure that everyone gets an adequate protein supply are not simple to solve, because they are not primarily scientific: their solution depends on the behaviour of individual human beings.

The development of an appropriate nutrition policy requires knowledge of the local situation. A balance sheet must be drawn up showing on one side the kinds and quantities of foods available or likely to be available, and on the other the numbers, ages and sex of the people to be fed. The foods must be converted, as precisely as possible, into terms of energy value, protein and a few mineral salts and vitamins; and the nutritional requirements of the people must be calculated in terms of energy value and the same nutrients. Comparison of the two sides of the balance sheet gives an indication, but no more, of what should be done. Additional information, obtained from appropriate surveys, may be needed because of the following considerations.

In any society there are likely to be regional differences in consumption, and perhaps in the composition, of food eaten. In most countries there are likely to be great differences between what is commonly eaten in the towns and in the country, and between the consumption of the rich and the poor. In many countries there are seasonal shortages of particular foods or nutrients. Distribution within the family is rarely, if ever, made according to nutritional needs of individual members of the family. All these factors must be taken into account in the development of a nutrition policy, and the policy when developed must be simple to operate, sensible and understood by the people. Otherwise it will fail.

Enough has been said to make it plain that nutrition is a multi-disciplinary matter, by no means the sole concern or responsibility of nutritional scientists. The first necessity is for a political decision. Someone in some relevant government department must be given, or more probably must take, responsibility for nutrition policy. This person, or persons, must have relevant scientific knowledge and the means of keeping in touch with the international community of nutritional and food scientists and should, preferably, be employed in the Ministry of Food or of Agriculture and Food or its equivalent. Medical support is necessary for any nutritional policy to be accepted because nutrition concerns the health of human beings. Financial support is essential because subsidies may be needed to change or direct agricultural policy or to cause some desired change in the composition of food by manufacturing means. Educational support is needed because it may be necessary to train more agriculturalists, food scientists or nutritionists to operate the policy – and such people are in lamentably short supply in all the developing world – and it will almost certainly be necessary to train the general public sufficiently in nutrition to make the policy recognizably sensible. Such general training should range widely so that school children, housewives, business men, civil servants and politicians all understand that the purpose of the policy is to feed the people adequately and so ensure the full physical growth and mental development of children. This must be seen to be the central point of any programme, for on this depends the progress of any country or community.

To achieve the required support and co-ordination of effort it is probably necessary to institute some kind of council or committee representative of the interests already mentioned. Such a body should be multi-disciplinary and should represent the government departments concerned and the academic world. Provision should be made for the periodic evaluation of the effectiveness of measures introduced.

The first essential is to ensure that sufficient food in terms of energy value is available for the population. Usually this is a matter for home agriculture but in periods of great shortage and in normal times in a country like Great Britain, which in 1966 imported nearly 60 per cent of its energy supplies and nearly 40 per cent of its protein supplies, the food to be imported, and also the means to pay for it, must be available. The second essential is that the people must have the means to buy the available food. Well-organized markets are essential for the prosperity of farmers and for the satisfaction of consumers and both conditions are also necessary for well-fed communitites. As farming and food manufacture become more complicated – and these industries are changing rapidly even in primitive societies – the importance of the marketing aspect increases. The third essential for good nutrition is for families to know that young children need foods richer in protein and certain other nutrients than adults, and to act accordingly. In most parts of the world the realization of this essential demands changes in food practices that are hard to achieve – for almost everywhere the male head of the household, who has relatively smaller needs for protein, mineral salts and vitamins than have his young children, is accorded first choice of the available food supply. And the most prized and palatable foods are usually those richest in proteins and other nutrients. Much experience has accumulated on the problems of teaching and learning better nutrition (Ritchie, 1968).

## BRITISH EXPERIENCE

We shall now consider what lessons for today can be learnt from the British wartime and post-war achievement, for which the Lasker Awards Committee of the American Public Health Association recommended in 1947 'awards for scientific and administrative achievements to the British Ministries of Food and Health and to the four great leaders in this historic enterprise, Lord Woolton, Sir Jack Drummond, Sir Wilson Jameson and

Sir John Orr'. The Committee expressed the opinion that 'this has been one of the greatest demonstrations of public health administration that the world has ever seen'. The steps the Ministries of Food and Health took to promote their policies have already been described (Hollingsworth 1958; Baines, Hollingsworth and Leitch, 1963). Wartime food policy was directed towards improving the nutritional value of the diet for all groups of the population. Hammond (1951) has recorded (page 101) that' . . . experts on nutrition, so far from envisaging any deterioration in the national diet, were urging that the war presented an opportunity to bring about some reform of dietary habits, by pegging the prices of a few of the essential foods, particularly bread, potatoes and milk. The price of milk, they thought, should be specially reduced to encourage its consumption by children and expectant mothers'. Hammond (page 221) considered *A Survey of Wartime Nutrition*, which was prepared by Sir Jack Drummond and appended to the Ministry of Food's import programme for the second year of war, to be 'an important landmark' because it was 'the first example of successful collaboration between food scientists and the statisticians engaged in drawing up forward programmes – the first application of nutritional principles to a piece of economic planning'. He commented that 'the initiative that had begun with the National Milk Scheme was to run through the whole of subsequent food policy'. The development and implementation of food policy in the United Kingdom have recently been discussed (Berry, 1968; Barnell, Coomes and Hollingsworth, 1968).

In this paper we are considering, particularly, nutrition policy in relation to protein. The wartime and post-war nutrition policy was not designed to deal primarily with protein consumption, although the steps that were taken to increase the consumption of milk solids had an important effect on the consumption of protein of good nutritional quality. Those steps have been summarized (Hollingsworth, 1957). They included: increased milk production and increased imports of skimmed dried milk and cheese, measures which were of nutritional benefit to the whole population; the National Milk and Milk Supply Schemes, which ensured supplies of cheap milk for expectant mothers, infants and children up to the age of 5 years; and expansion of the existing Milk-in-Schools Scheme. The National Milk Scheme exists today in the Welfare Foods Scheme. In the judgment of Baines *et al.* (1963), who compared the diets of working-class families with children before and after the Second World War, 'the most important single contribution to improvement of the diet of working-class families during the past generation was the provision of welfare foods, especially welfare and school milk'.

Recently, the Panel on Recommended Allowances of Nutrients, of the Department of Health and Social Security's Committee on Medical Aspects of Food Policy, has recommended intakes of nutrients for the United Kingdom (Department of Health and Social Security, 1969). This report sets out, for different categories of persons, minimum protein requirements. These are derived from nitrogen requirements for maintenance and growth and make allowance for individual variation in need and for the efficiency of utilization of dietary protein (taken as 70 per cent for the mixed proteins of diets eaten in the United Kingdom). It is stated that persons taking such amounts 'are unlikely to suffer from deficiency of protein', but that 'we cannot exclude at the present state of our knowledge the possibility that some tissues may suffer preferentially while the overall nitrogen balance is apparently unaffected. The question of whether the minimum requirements are adequate to maintain health for a lifetime can only be answered by long-term studies, which have not yet been made'. It has been reported (Greaves and Hollingsworth, 1964) that protein provides between 10 and 15 per cent of the energy value of the diets of the majority of people in the United Kingdom, amounts substantially in excess of the minimum requirements proposed by the Panel. The Panel considered that because such a relatively high proportion of protein has been eaten in this country for generations this may play a part 'in making the diets acceptable, and there is no evidence that any harm results from such amounts'. Because diets containing protein at the levels of the minimum requirement would be unlikely to be palatable, and might also be inadequate in riboflavine, nicotinic acid and other B vitamins often found in association with dietary proteins, the Panel recommended that an arbitrary value of 10 per cent of the total energy requirement should be derived from protein – a level at which there were no reservations about adequacy – emphasizing that 'in the construction of diets attention must be paid to palatability as well as to nutrient content'.

If this recommendation is compared with the composition of the average British diet at various times it is found (Berry and Hollingsworth, 1963) that before the war protein supplied 10.3 per cent of the total energy supply; the proportion rose to 12 per cent by 1945, fell again to 10.3 per cent in 1954 and thereafter rose again to 10.9 per cent in 1960; it was 11.1 per cent in 1967 (Ministry of Agriculture, Fisheries and Food, 1968). These are average figures, which apply to the population as a whole. They suggest that before the war and again in the 1950s there may have been families and individuals who obtained less than 10 per cent of their energy requirements in the form of protein, though there can have been few – if any – who obtained less than the minimum requirements of the Panel. (Except for infants up to the age of 3 months and lactating women, for whom the recommended proportions are 9.5 per cent and 8.1 per cent respectively, the minimum proportions are all 7.6 per cent or less). However, the data of Baines *et al.* (1963) shows that no family group studied in 1937–39 obtained less than 11.5 per cent of its energy from protein, though all types of family containing more than 2 children, whether or not the head of the household was in employment, obtained on average less than their estimated requirements of energy; and where the head of the family was unemployed even the families containing one or two children obtained less than their energy requirements.

Thus, although these pre-war diets were apparently adequate in protein, shortage of energy may have resulted in an inefficient utilization of that which was present. In large families in 1966 protein also provided 11.5 per cent or more of the energy intake, but this was itself close to the average energy requirement (Ministry of Agriculture, Fisheries and Food: National Food Survey Committee, 1968), so that the new recommended intakes for protein, and to an even greater extent the minimum requirements, were well exceeded. A pilot survey in 1963 of the nutrition of young children up to 5 years of age (Ministry of Health, 1968) showed that for each age group studied the average protein intake was at or above the new recommended intake, and well in excess of the minimum requirement; while only 2–3 per cent of the individual children were recorded as obtaining less protein than the minimum requirement.

One can conclude from these observations that the present nutritional position in the United Kingdom with regard to protein is satisfactory, but that obtaining before the war may have been less so. The United Kingdom has a basic food supply which contains ample protein – even English wheat with its relatively low protein content contains about 9 per cent of its energy as protein – and special arrangements are made to supply cheap or free milk to expectant mothers, children up to the age of 5 years and primary school children, and to provide school meals containing satisfactory types and amounts of protein (Department of Education and Science, 1965). The greater part of the world does not enjoy such benefits.

## WORLD PROBLEMS: ACTIVITIES IN THE UNITED NATIONS FAMILY

The commonest of the nutritional deficiency diseases in the world today are the protein-calorie deficiency diseases, which result from giving weaned infants diets lacking in sufficient protein of good quality and often not providing enough energy to allow the efficient use of this limited quantity of protein (Food and Agriculture Organization, 1963, page 45). World-wide awareness of this fact is, however, very recent, the first major study on the subject being made for the World Health and the Food and Agriculture Organizations in 1950 (Brock and Autret, 1952). This was followed by widespread activity by the international scientific community to gather and collate evidence on the occurrence of these syndromes among children in developing countries. It was recognized at the outset that the syndrome caused physical stunting, sickness and death, and more recently attention has been directed to the likely detrimental effect of protein-calorie malnutrition on mental development. The types of foods or food mixtures effective in preventing or curing the diseases are known. Recent experiences and thoughts on calorie deficiencies and protein deficiencies were exchanged at a colloquium held in Cambridge, England, in 1967 (McCance and Widdowson, 1968).

In spite of this general awareness of the protein problem, progress towards its solution has not been rapid. As part of the international effort to solve the problem the U.N. Advisory Committee on the Application of Science and Technology to Development, submitted in July 1967 a report (United Nations, 1968a) to the Economic and Social Council of the United Nations. This report proposed a series of fourteen specific measures which would have required increased expenditure by the members of the United Nations family as well as bilateral agencies and governments. International agreement on greatly increased expenditure was not achieved, but the General Assembly at its twenty-second session in December 1967 resolved to call for a report at its next session a year later on activities of governments, and activities within the United Nations family, designed to increase the supply and utilization of protein. As a guide to governments responding to the General Assembly's resolution the Secretary-General sent out to member governments a questionnaire based on the fourteen specific proposals of the Advisory Committee.

The United Nations received replies from a large number of governments and on the basis of these the Secretary-General presented a report on 'The Protein Problem' (United Nations, 1968b) to the twenty-third Session of the General Assembly. The report makes it clear that some governments are aware of, and are beginning to explore, the protein problem in their own countries, but that others are not. There appears to be world-wide recognition that the protein problem is complex and that there are no short cuts to its solution, though many governments appear to understand the urgency of finding a solution. It also appears that some governments are able to draw on and utilize scientific and technical knowledge relevant to various aspects of the problem, while others have great difficulty in doing so. No country gave a comprehensive reply to the last item of the U.N. questionnaire which asked 'What are the present and proposed steps of your Government to review and improve its policies and its legislation and regulations regarding all aspects of food and protein production, processing and marketing so as to remove unnecessary obstacles and encourage appropriate activities?', a result which suggests that the world does not yet understand the importance of good nutrition, particularly to young children, in development — both individual and national.

## THE IMPORTANCE OF CEREALS

However, assuming that the governments of developing countries will increasingly understand the role of nutrition in human development, much scientific and technical information is available for them to apply. Perhaps the single most important event is the increased use of the new high-yielding varieties of grains which require, for the full realization of their potential, modern farm management, including enhanced and efficient use of fertilizers and irrigation. This development is dramatically improving the prospects for expanding food production in the developing countries, particularly Asia. The International Agricultural Development Service of the U.S. Department of Agriculture has given the following estimates of acreages in new high-yielding varieties in Asia (Dalrymple, 1968):

| Year | Acres |
|---|---|
| 1964/65 | 200 |
| 1965/66 | 37,000 |
| 1966/67 | 4,800,000 |
| 1967/68 | 20,000,000 |
| 1968/69(target) | 34,000,000 |

Even if the new varieties are not richer in protein than the old ones, the increased quantities of grains grown will alone increase the gross amount of protein available. If they contain higher concentrations of protein this will, of course, provide extra benefit, and there are signs that effort in plant breeding is beginning to be directed towards improvement of protein content. Reports from many countries show that they are aware of the possibility of improving the protein yields of maize. The recognition of high lysine maize at Purdue University was an important landmark. Maize varieties containing appropriate genes have a protein quality far superior to conventional varieties. Geneticists at the International Rice Research Institute in the Philippines are giving increased attention to the protein content of rice. Of the several hundred varieties so far tested, protein content varies from 7 to 14 per cent. The average for rice varieties now grown in Asia is about 8 per cent. If high-yielding varieties containing more than this could be developed and used this would greatly increase protein intake among Asia's predominantly rice-eating population. In the long run, genetic research to improve the protein content of wheat and sorghum also offers great promise.

Another way to improve the biological quality of proteins, and hence effectively increase the quantity of protein available for utilization, is by fortification with amino acids. There are many proposals to fortify flour from present varieties of wheat, and possibly rice, with lysine, which is the limiting amino acid in cereals. Such proposals should be viewed with caution, and be tested for effectiveness by field experiments before large scale introduction. The protein values of most human diets are not limited by their content of lysine, but by that of sulphur amino acids (Miller and Donoso, 1963), or other amino acids (Autret, Périssé, Sizaret and Cresta, 1968). If lysine is not the limiting amino acid in the total diet of a population, fortification of cereals with this amino acid will not improve the people's nutritional condition. Nevertheless, cereals are a useful vehicle for a fortification programme because they are frequently processed at a relatively few plants where proper control can be maintained; but in situations where most of the people live on grain processed in small village mills the problems of effective fortification may be insuperable.

The choice of agricultural crops and varieties should depend partly on nutritional considerations. If the protein supply for a whole people can be improved by increasing the supply and protein content of cereals this will go far towards meeting the protein needs of that whole population. Other important agricultural steps would be to encourage the production of more pulses, legumes and other greenstuffs, and, if possible, the intensive production of poultry and other livestock.


## THE SPECIAL NEEDS OF CHILDREN

Such measures would help the whole population, including the children. Nevertheless, in addition special measures should be introduced to ensure that suitable foods are available, at prices all can afford, for children at the time of weaning. It is of the utmost importance to find ways of using local raw materials in the preparation of weaning foods suitably rich in protein, and to disseminate information through all existing channels both on the foods available commercially or through clinics, and on recipes for making suitable mixtures in the home. Another way of ensuring that children are given nourishing food is to make generous provision for nutritionally well designed school meals. This is particularly important for children of nursery or young school age.

Many attempts have been made in different countries to formulate foods for infants and young children from mixtures of various kinds of protein concentrates, legumes and cereals, with or without the addition of dried skimmed milk or other sources of animal protein, yeasts, vitamins and mineral salts. Formulated foods made from suitable mixtures of proteins of vegetable origin have proved to be as satisfactory as dried skimmed milk in the prevention of protein-calorie malnutrition. In the past, the main stumbling blocks against the successful production of such products on a large scale in developing countries have been lack of full appreciation of the need to create economically viable industrial operations, with effective marketing arrangements, and lack of understanding that such foods must be palatable if they are to be accepted and used. It cannot be emphasized too strongly that the business of food promotion, involving modern techniques of advertizing and marketing generally, is a highly specialized undertaking which if it is to be effective should be operated only by those with the appropriate expert knowledge and experience. The successful promotion of special foods for children has been found to depend upon the interest shown by Governments and by the food processing industries in developing them for use in government-sponsored feeding schemes or for commercial exploitation. There are signs that several different mixtures are beginning to succeed.

A report on 'the protein paradox' by a group of students at the Harvard Graduate School of Business (Belden *et al.*, 1964) gives case histories of some of the protein-rich foods that have been developed and marketed commercially. The broadest programme to promote the commercial introduction of inexpensive protein-rich foods is the result of pioneering developmental work done by the Institute of Nutrition of Central America and Panama (INCAP). Incaparina, the name given by INCAP to mixtures containing 25 per cent or more of proteins, has proved to be suitable for feeding young children. Different formulations have been developed and are in commercial production in several countries. They are based on concentrates derived from cottonseed or soya beans and contain food yeast, added mineral salts and vitamins and some cheaper cereal such as maize, rice or sorghum whichever is locally available. The resulting enriched flour is used in the home according to traditional food habits. A similar product developed and marketed by a South African food manufacturing firm is called ProNutro. This is based on dried skimmed milk, processed full-fat peanuts and soya beans, fish flour, food yeast, wheat germ, whey powder and bone meal with added iron, iodized salt, B vitamins, vitamins A and C and sugar. Yellow and white maize flours compose about a third of the formula and are used to dilute the product which would otherwise be too concentrated and expensive. This food is apparently having immense success.

Other similar foods developed since the Harvard study include Bal Ahar, made from cereals and oilseed protein concentrate and fortified with vitamins and mineral salts, which is being manufactured under the auspices of the Food Corporation of India and distributed in scarcity areas; and Superamine, based on wheat, chick peas and lentils, recently developed and marketed with promising results in Algeria.

Rather different developments in India are designed to increase the milk supply. There, buffalo milk is being successfully diluted and 'toned' with skimmed dried milk to provide increased quantities of milk without reducing the protein content. Recently, it has been found that toning can be done with a solution of oilseed protein concentrate, the product being of roughly the same protein and fat content as cow's milk. By using this process the milk supply could be doubled at a cost increase of 25 per cent. In Hong Kong a high protein soft drink made from soya beans is being manufactured and there are claims that it has captured 20–25 per cent of the soft drink market in that country. One American firm has developed a high-protein beverage that it plans to produce and market in countries deficient in protein supplies, and another is test marketing a soya based, chocolate flavoured beverage, designed to be the nutritional equivalent of milk.

## CONCLUSION

These developments lead one to hope that eventually the nutritional disadvantage for children of the lack of milk supplies will be overcome. A further ground for hope is that the protein problem is now being debated by politicians and statesmen, and recently by the General Assembly of the United Nations, which in December 1968 considered the report of the Secretary-General (United Nations, 1968b) and passed a resolution (United Nations General Assembly, 1968) on increasing the production and use of edible protein. The resolution aims to hasten action, both national and international, designed to solve the protein problem. It requests the Secretary-General, in consultation with interested organizations within the United Nations system, for periodic progress reports, the first to be submitted in two year's time, and it calls for acceleration of work within the United Nations system 'on objectives and measures designed to narrow the protein gap significantly by the end of the 1970s'. If this is not achieved the outlook for mankind is grave.

REFERENCES

Autret, M., Périssé, J., Sizaret, F. and Cresta, M. (1968). 'Protein Value of Different Types of Diet in the World: Their Appropriate Supplementation.' *Nutr. Newsletter,* Vol. 6, No. 4 FAO, Rome

Baines, A. H. J., Hollingsworth, D. F. and Leitch, I. (1963). *Nutr. Abstr. Rev.,* 33, 653

Bayliss, W. M. (1917). *The Physiology of Food and Economy in Diet.* London; Longmans Green

Barnell, H. R., Coomes, T. J. and Hollingsworth, D. F. (1968). *Proc. Nutr. Soc.,* 27, 8

Belden, G. C., Congleton, W. L., Devoto, W. R., Hurlbut, T. A., Johnston, B., Katz, D. P., Michelson, J. T., Pipkin, A. P., Tibbets, C. D. and Weston, D. R. (1964). 'The Protein Paradox.' *Mgmt. Rep.* Boston, U.S.A.

Berry, W. T. C. (1968). *Proc. Nutr. Soc.* 27, 1

Berry, W. T. C. and Hollingsworth, D. F. (1963). *Proc. Nutr. Soc.* 22, 48

Brock, J. F. and Autret, M. (1952). 'Kwashiorkor in Africa.' *FAO Nutr. Stud.* No. 8, Rome and *W.H.O. Monograph Ser.* No. 8, Geneva

Dalrymple, D. G. (1968). 'Estimated Area of High-Yielding Varieties of Grains in Ten Asian Nations.' *International Agriculture Development Service,* U.S. Department of Agriculture, Washington, D.C.

Department of Education and Science (1965). *The Nutritional Standard of The School Dinner.* London; H.M. Stationery Office

Department of Health and Social Security (1969). 'Recommended Intakes of Nutrients for the United Kingdom.' *Rep. Publ. Hlth. Med. Subj. Lond.* No. 120, London; H.M. Stationery Office

Food and Agriculture Organization of the United Nations (1963). 'Third World Food Survey.' *FFHC. Basic. Study* No. 11, Rome

Greaves, J. P. and Hollingsworth, D. F. (1964). Appendix 5 in 'Requirements of Man for Protein.' *Rep. Publ. Hlth Med. Subj. Lond.,* No. 111. London; H.M. Stationery Office

Hammond, R. J. (1951). *Food.* Vol. 1, 'The Growth of Policy.' London; H.M. Stationery Office and Longmans Green

Hollingsworth, Dorothy (1957). Chapter XXIV. 'The Application of the Newer Knowledge of Nutrition' in *The Englishman's Food* by J. C. Drummond and Anne Wilbraham. London; Jonathan Cape

McCance, R. A. and Widdowson, E. M. (1968). *'Calorie Deficiencies and Protein Deficiencies.'* London; J. & A. Churchill Ltd

Miller, D. S. and Donoso, G. (1963). *J. Sci. Fd Agric.* 14, 345

Ministry of Agriculture, Fisheries and Food (1968). 'Food Consumption Levels in the United Kingdom.' *Board of Trade Journal* 195, 40

NUTRITION POLICY WITH REGARD TO PROTEIN

Ministry of Agriculture, Fisheries and Food: National Food Survey Committee (1968). *Household Food Consumption and Expenditure: 1966.* London; H.M. Stationery Office

Ministry of Health (1968). 'A Pilot Survey of the Nutrition of Young Children in 1963'. *Rep. Publ. Hlth Med. Subj. Lond.* No. 118. London; H.M. Stationery Office

Ritchie, J. A. S. (1968). 'Learning Better Nutrition.' *F.A.O. United Nations,* Rome

Royal Society Food (War) Committee (1919). *Report on the Food Requirements of Man and their Variations according to Age, Sex, Size and Occupation.* London; Harrison and Sons

United Nations (1968a). *Feeding the Expanding World Population:* 'International action to avert the impending protein crisis.' Sales No.:E.68.XIII.2

United Nations (1968b). 'The Protein Problem.' *Rep. Sec. Gen.* E/4592

United Nations General Assembly (1968). A/Res/2416 (XXIII)

# COMPLEMENTARY WAYS OF MEETING

# THE WORLD'S PROTEIN NEEDS

## N.W. PIRIE

*Biochemistry Department*
*Rothamsted Experimental Station, Harpenden, Herts*

## INTRODUCTION

Before considering the various possible protein sources, we must make some sort of estimate of the possible protein need by – say – the end of the century. That estimate controls the amount of effort we should put into work on protein supplies and the degree of novelty that we should envisage. The estimate depends on the number of people to be fed and the amount of protein that each needs. Both quantities are uncertain: the first because it must be guessed, the second because it is hotly disputed. It is therefore obvious that contrary opinions are tenable.

## THE POPULATION TO BE FED

At present our numbers are increasing at a rate that would double the population of the world in about 30 years. This rate is very unlikely to continue indefinitely. The more fecund parts of the world will probably settle down, as the long-industrialized parts have done, and achieve static or slowly increasing populations. No confident prediction can be made about the time when this may happen. With modern methods of contraception, it should, in principle, be easier than in the past to achieve population stability. But it is important to remember that no method of contraception will be used effectively until people understand the basic principles of biology – this understanding will greatly increase the survival rate of those children that are born in spite of contraception. Consequently, the first result of an effective contraception campaign is likely to be an increase in the population. Furthermore, without a degree of coercion that is improbable and that most of us would regard as intolerable, most parents will not accept the two-child family as the norm until experience shows them that both children are likely to survive. Conviction may take a generation; in the meantime "family planning' may mean a plan for 3 or 4 children as an insurance policy. It would be foolish therefore not to envisage the possibility that we may have to feed 7 or 8 G people by the end of the century. It would be even more foolish to rely on wars and epidemics to relieve us of a catering problem.

## PROTEIN REQUIREMENTS

Purely biochemical and physiological considerations should specify how much protein each person needs. Many surveys show that there may be no blatant signs of universal malnutrition in communities in which the average protein consumption is only 40 g per person per day, whereas in other communities the average is 100 without universal plethora. Energy intake varies much less. The question is: would the first communities fare better on more protein, or the second on less? A naive approach to the problem is to measure how much protein an individual needs to be in balance; that is to say, to be in a state in which the protein eaten is equal to or greater than the protein break-down products excreted. Obviously, someone not in balance is getting too little protein and will go on being depleted until an equilibrium is established at which metabolism is depressed so much that it matches intake. It is unwarrantable to assume that as soon as the balance is struck, at about 40 g of protein per person per day, nutrition is adequate. In old-fashioned logical terms, balance is a necessary but not a sufficient factor. Furthermore, if the average protein consumption in a community is 40 g a day, half get less than this. Communities vary in the extent to which food is evenly distributed, but there are few communities in which those most in need of protein — children and pregnant or lactating women — get preferential treatment. Foods rich in protein are usually the most highly esteemed parts of the diet and, through custom and selfishness, men tend to get more than their share of them. Until there has been a revolution in meal-time habits it will be necessary to supply much more than the minimum amount of protein to ensure that everyone gets that minimum.

The ideal is easily stated: a person is not getting enough protein when well-being is increased by eating more protein. That is in accordance with the wise criterion laid down by the World Health Organization. 'Health is a state of complete physical, mental and social well-being and not merely the absence of disease and infirmity'. The ideal is easy to state but less easy to define or measure. With domestic animals we know what we want — rapid growth, a certain bodily conformation, a large milk yield, or abundant eggs. Although children grow much more slowly than

47

domestic animals, their growth-rate is a good index of the amount of protein in the diet, but there is no evidence that rapid growth is desirable. There is indeed evidence from animal experiments that it shortens the ultimate expectation of life. This evidence is not necessarily relevant and Widdowson and Kennedy (1962) remark '... any suggestion that a deliberate restriction of food sufficient to limit growth might prolong the life span of a human population appears to be unsound. Unless the children were also protected from cold and infections there would almost certainly be an increased mortality among them which would far outweigh the advantages of any possible increase in life span among a few of the survivors'. Waterlow (1968), writing of people getting on average 40 g of protein a day, commented 'If they survive infancy, they tend to be small in size'. There is evidence from studies on people (e.g. Graham 1967) and animals (e.g. Dickerson et al., 1967) that nutritional stunting at certain stages of growth is not made good later. There is also contrary evidence. Garrow and Pike (1967), having observed that children who had been treated for acute malnutrition were larger than their siblings when measured several years later, made the very interesting suggestion that the signs of malnutrition become most obvious, and therefore attract treatment, in those with a constitutional tendency to be large. In the well-fed countries we tend to assume that bigger-is-better, but we are not necessarily right.

Similar assumptions are often made about bodily composition. Haemoglobin, plasma protein, and amino acid values found in the blood of the well-fed are taken as the norm even when their bodily fat and blood cholesterol are regarded with dismay. This marks the beginnings of an attempt at physiological standards of good nutrition. The respiratory function of haemoglobin is well understood and there are measurable disadvantages in having too little of it. This is also true of plasma proteins such as the antibodies. There is less certainty about the advantage of maintaining specific concentrations of albumin and amino acids in the blood. These are presumably metabolites on their way to the sites where they will be used; Neale (1968) records the dramatic improvement in a patient given intravenously 25 g of albumin daily. Are there any advantages in maintaining such concentrations that much of the circulating material gets used simply as fuel? This is wasteful according to those who regard nitrogen balance measurements as a sufficient index of the adequacy of protein supplies, but 'waste' may be a concomitant of desirable effects. According to the 'euphoristic theory' of the function of glutathione, its presence, even when not used, is advantageous: some processes may proceed more effectively when circulating protein and amino acids are always plentiful.

The evidence is suggestive rather than positive. Lawes and Gilbert (1852, 1866) disproved Liebig's contention that muscular work involved protein metabolism; Liebig confused the structure of the muscular machine with its fuel. They cautiously added that there could be increased nitrogen metabolism when an animal was overtaxed or '... in the human body, when under excitement or excessive mental exercise'. The effect of stress on nitrogen excretion has had ample recent confirmation. Though work does not increase nitrogen excretion, the impulse to work depends on the amount of protein in the diet. Children become more active when given more than the recommended allowance of protein, primates in the better-managed zoos are livelier now that they get diets containing 25–35 per cent protein, and the performance of trained workers improved when they were given 1.1 rather than 1 g of protein per kg body weight (FAO/WHO 1965).

There is general agreement that malnourishment, particularly protein deficiency, in infancy restricts brain development. It may also lead to impaired intellectual development, though this does not necessarily follow. There is little correlation between brain size and intellectual capacity either within the human species or when species are compared. Large animals, such as elephants and whales, have brains four to five times as big as ours and the brains of some small primates are three to four times as big in proportion to their body weight. Impaired intellectual capacity is not therefore a necessary consequence of early malnutrition but this remains a possibility. The early work on animals, mainly done in the U.S.S.R. by pupils of Pavlov (surveyed by Brozek, 1962), is not easy to interpret because irritability characterizes human cases of kwashiorkor and it could be interpreted as enterprise or inquisitiveness in a laboratory animal. There is however evidence (e.g. Chow and Blackwell, 1968) that the offspring of rats on restricted (in energy as well as protein) diets developed the usual reflexes later than the controls and never learnt to run mazes so efficiently. There are abnormalities in structure and coordination in pups from protein-deficient bitches and these are intensified when the pups are themselves weaned on protein-deficient diets (Steward and Platt, 1968). Because pups grow faster than babies, the diets used in these experiments (7 per cent of the metabolizable calories was in the form of good quality retained protein) might not have had such a disastrous effect on babies. However, as I have already pointed out, to ensure that mothers and infants get the minimum, the average protein intake must be well above that minimum.

The death rate between 1 and 5 years of age is strongly correlated with protein deficiency. Admittedly, protein deficiency is commonest in countries with poor hygiene; infections are the recorded cause of most of these deaths. A suspicion remains that the protein-deficient have less resistance to bacterial infection. Animal experiments supporting this suspicion are reviewed by Dubos (1965). This is one aspect of well-being. Wound-healing is another. Hospital patients suffer less from the 'disuse syndrome' if, by culinary skill, they can be persuaded to eat 150 g of protein a day (Stevenson, 1946). There is evidence that dividing cells in the mucous membrane of the mouth, which is a site of regular mild wounding, are abnormally scarce in protein-deficiency (Squires, 1966). The gut also is subject to abrasion; it would be useful to know whether the great variations in normal structure of the villi in people in different parts of the world (Creamer, 1967) and in different animals (Hofmann, 1968) arise because of diminished regeneration in the protein-deficient. Other possible indices of the adequacy of dietary protein, e.g. regeneration of leucocytes and resistance to inanimate poisons, are discussed by Guggenheim and Szmelcman (1967) and still more were surveyed at a symposium organized jointly by the Biochemical and Nutrition Societies in 1969.

I draw the conclusion that it is premature to decide that enough protein is being eaten as soon as nitrogen balance is struck or a certain growth rate is attained. No one would wish, casually, to increase the difficulties of countries with a food shortage by urging on them inflated nutritional standards; they should not, on the other hand, be encouraged to live in a 'fool's paradise', and much of the money they now spend goes on prestige projects of more debatable value than improved nutrition. When we consider the diets actually eaten by the more productive members of the community, including members of official committees that give niggardly trophological advice to others, it seems reasonable to think that lack of protein makes many members of apparently well-fed communities less healthy and responsive than they could be. It is possible that the average amount of protein eaten in a day should be as great as 100 g a day. This opinion is shared by those who organize the U.S. space programme; astronauts, the most up-to-date elite group, get 120 g.

Infants do not need 100 g of protein a day. However, in regions where poor hygiene causes widespread infection and infestation, adolescents and adults probably need more. To get a measure of the possible need, the round figure may therefore be taken. If 7 G people average 100 g a day, 256 M tons of protein will be eaten in a year. This would mean the production of nearly 300 M tons because there are losses during storage (with some commodities in some countries losses by predation and rotting can be as large as 20 per cent, but losses will presumably be much less by the end of the century) and not all the protein measured at the retail level is, or can be, eaten. The world total of protein, at the retail level, is 90 M tons (FAO, 1964) and the Protein Advisory Group concluded in 1966 that the world deficit was 20 M tons even on its rather ungenerous estimate that individual needs ranged, according to the climate and age distribution in different countries, from 40 to 52 g a day. We seem, therefore, to have a formidable problem now and an even more formidable one is impending.

## CONVENTIONAL SOURCES OF PROTEIN

Table 1 shows the sources of protein in the well-fed (i.e. Europe, North America, Oceania and the River Plate countries) and ill-fed (i.e. Far East, Near East, Africa and South America apart from the River Plate countries) countries. The striking difference is the use of animal products in the well-fed countries. This brings out a point that cannot be too often emphasized: the percentage of protein in a day's food is nearly as important as the amount eaten in a day. Thus, someone doing very heavy work needs 4,000 kcal (17 M joules) a day and so could, in principle, get 100 g of protein by eating the 1,000 g of cereal, containing 9 −11 per cent of protein, that would provide that amount of energy. Sedentary people would get grossly fat if they tried to meet their protein needs in this way; unless some of their food contains 20 per cent or more protein (on the dry matter) they are condemned to a low-protein diet. The recent increases in cereal yields in such countries as India, Mexico and the Philippines are extremely valuable because, in many parts of the world, hunger (i.e. energy shortage) is as great a problem as protein shortage so that much of what protein there is, has to be used by the body merely as fuel. Furthermore, cereals supply, and will probably continue to supply, between half and a third of our protein. Cereals have been found with enhanced protein contents. A tetraploid oat contains 23−30 per cent protein (Murphy *et al.,* 1968) and some sorghums contain 18−26 per cent (Johnson *et al.,* 1968). Even if the promise in these discoveries is substantiated, and protein-rich cereals are bred that can grow in all parts of the world where cereal growing is traditional, other protein concentrates will still be needed. In parts of the wet tropics, cereals do not ripen properly. It is hazardous to become wholly dependent on a single crop for diseases have a disquieting ability to change their virulence. And people want, and are wise to want, variety.

Having suggested the possible scale of the world's need for protein by the end of the century, another set of assumptions must be set out before the complementary ways of meeting this need can be considered. Even if we assume that, by the end of the century, there will be no frank hostility between different countries, it is unreasonable to assume that one group of countries will make itself permanently responsible for supplying protein to another. This means that the most useful contribution a prosperous country, with an efficient research organization, can make is to devise means whereby an ill-fed one can produce its own protein. A few countries may be able to exist, as we do in Great Britain, by importing protein and other foodstuffs, but it is not easy to see what most of the ill-fed parts of the world could export to pay for their imports. Not only should foods rich in protein be produced in the countries where they are needed, they should be produced, in part at least, near the spot where they will be eaten. Ultimately, no doubt, there will be reliable systems of transport throughout all countries; they are not likely to come into existence by the end of the century. Until they exist, protein-rich foods that depend on highly skilled people working in elaborate installations are likely to be mainly consumed in urban areas. Special attention should therefore be given to methods for producing protein from local products for local consumption.

At present, the problem is most acute in densely populated tropical regions with prolonged, or even daily, wet periods. The assumption underlying much agricultural planning is that the ill-fed state of so much of the wet tropics is essentially an accident, which can be corrected by the more widespread adoption of conventional agricultural techniques. I assume, on the other hand, that we have not yet found out how to farm the wet tropics.

The most obvious method for increasing the protein supply is to grow more of those familiar foods that are rich in protein. Table 1 shows the contribution that peas, beans and oilseeds make in the ill-fed parts of the world. These seeds, unlike the traditional cereals, contain 25 per cent or more of protein. Because of the risk that they will rot rather than ripen, they do not thrive in regions where it rains nearly every day, but where the climate is favourable for them, they deserve very much more attention from plant breeders and agronomists than they are getting. Leafy vegetables and immature flowers cannot supply as much protein as the pulses because of the amount of fibre in them, but they could be eaten much more extensively than they are. Many contain 30 per cent of protein (on the dry matter) and some contain even more. Raymond *et al.*, (1941) reported 11 per cent N in cassava leaves that had been boiled for 90 min; they are extensively consumed in tropical Africa (Terra, 1964). Many leaf species, e.g. amaranth, baobab, drumstick and sweet potato, that are unfamiliar in the Temperate Zone are still widely eaten but their popularity is declining as a result of the preconceptions of visiting 'experts'. This is a trend that should be combated: we should increase rather than diminish the number of food plants. In the wet tropics, green vegetables give a greater yield of protein than any other crop that is extensively grown; 400 kg of protein per hectare in 3 months is reported (FAO, 1964). The area devoted to market gardening is increasing (it doubled in Trinidad between 1965 and 1967) and so is the attention that is given in India and elsewhere to school gardens. But much remains to be done People have to be persuaded that green vegetables are more important than crops such as okra and tomato, and work on the school garden must be made part of the normal curriculum and not a punishment.

## LEAF AND SEED PROTEINS

The fibre in leaves limits the amount that can be eaten. Protein can be extracted from many different species (Pirie, 1956, 1966, 1969a) and, when extracted, is easy to make up into acceptable dishes (Byers *et al.,*1965). Like many other food-proteins, it is easily damaged by improper handling, e.g. over heating during drying (Buchanan, 1969). When competently prepared, its nutritional value in chickens and rats (Duckworth and Woodham, 1961; Woodham, 1965), rats (Henry and Ford, 1965), pigs (Duckworth *et al.,* 1961), infants (Waterlow, 1962) and children (Doraiswamy *et al.,* 1969) is greater than that of other vegetable proteins though not so good as exceptional proteins such as milk and egg. Many years ago F.A.O. baselessly asserted that leaf protein would be expensive to manufacture and the statement is repeated from time to time. Actual costs will not be known until large scale production starts; a reasonable estimate makes this protein cheaper than any other (apart from by-products) except for soya when that is grown in favourable climates. The yield at Rothamsted improves yearly and is now 2 tons (dry matter) per hectare (Pirie, 1969b); in India, with no cessation of growth in winter, it is 3 tons. Although these yields of edible protein exceed those attained by any other system of husbandry, there is no reason to think that the limit has been reached. So that systematic agronomic studies can be made in different countries, and with support from the International Biological Programme, we have made laboratory-scale extraction units (Davys and Pirie, 1969; Davys *et al.,* 1969). These are already in use in India and Nigeria and more are being made so that agronomic research can be done in other countries.

Coconuts, like leaves, contain good quality protein (Snyderman *et al.,* 1961; Butterworth and Fox, 1963; Rao *et al.,* 1967) accompanied by so much fibre that people cannot eat much. Rapid progress is being made in perfecting mechanical and enzymic (Ramamurti and Johar, 1963; Chandrasekaran and King, 1967) methods for separating protein from the fibrous mass. Coconuts and leaves have the outstanding advantages as protein sources that they flourish in the wet tropics and that the extraction procedures are simple enough to be feasible as a village industry. These proteins will be important by the end of the century; only lethargy, and the hostility of national and international organizations responsible for agricultural affairs, keeps them from being important now.

The residues from expelling oil from soya, groundnut and cottonseed are the most abundant, unused or inadequately used sources of protein. Estimates of the amount of protein contained in these residues vary somewhat: a conservative one is 10 M tons. That is half the present deficit; and almost all this protein is wasted. Some oil seeds are now being handled with sufficient care to yield residues of edible quality. Soya flour is extensively used in human food, and foodstuffs based on groundnuts and cottonseed are coming into use in India and Central America. At one time the residue was a by-product of little commercial value compared to the oil; now the residue and the oil are of about equal value, and a time can be forseen when the oil will become the by-product with protein as the primary product. The Tropical Products Institute (1967) published a useful set of statistics on these products and surveyed some aspects of their production and use. Bressani *et al.,* (1966a and b) give more information about cottonseed, and Bassir and Loebel (1968) describe the successful use of soya in child nutrition.

Plant-breeding programmes are only slowly becoming attuned to the protein shortage. Varieties of maize, rice and wheat with enhanced protein content, and sometimes with protein of better quality as well, have been produced; there are also strains of cotton from which the harmful constituent, gossypol, has been partly or completely eliminated. If these new varieties yield as much, and are as resistant to diseases, as the old ones, they will contribute greatly to the world's protein resources. Soya, in suitable climates, can yield 2 tons of protein per hectare. Unfortunately the protein is accompanied by carbohydrate that is largely indigestible by people, and by substances that inhibit proteolytic enzymes. Hence the use of elaborate methods of fermentative pretreatment in those countries where the use of soya is traditional. The increased use of soya as a human food would be facilitated if strains could be found containing a useful carbohydrate, such as starch, and less inhibitor. No attention has been paid, so far, to breeding coconuts or leaf-crops in which protein is both abundant and readily extractable. Briefly: a reappraisal of plant-breeding policies is overdue now that protein shortage is known to be the world's most acute nutritional problem.

It is salutary to remember that the strains of maize, that were hailed recently as a 'break through', because of their improved protein quality, had been lying unesteemed on the shelf for 30 years. And it is encouraging to find that the point now rates official attention. In a report to the U.N. Economic and Social Council in 1968 the Protein Advisory Group says: 'In agricultural planning attention should be given to the production of protein as well as total yield, since an increase in yield may often result in a decrease in protein content per unit of production. Attention should also be given to the quality of the protein in the crops produced'.

## ANIMAL CONVERSION

In most parts of the world people use animal products as protein concentrates when they can afford them. So long as animals are not fed on products that people could have eaten, or on products grown on land that could have produced food for people, this is an excellent arrangement; there are many agricultural by-products that would be wasted if not used as fodder and much land that is unsuitable for ploughing but on which cattle can graze. Furthermore, much of the nitrogen that a ruminant needs can be supplied as urea (Briggs, 1967; Preston and Hagelberg, 1967). But the process of animal conversion is too inefficient to be tolerated in any region with a protein shortage, if it uses land to produce fodder rather than food. The issue is confused by lack of precision in terminology. It is now possible to get a pound of chicken from two pounds of feed: but what is measured is dry feed and wet chicken —including guts, neck, feet and other inedible parts. Furthermore, to achieve that conversion rate the chicken has to be fed largely on material that people could have eaten. By the end of the century, the use of animal products is likely to become more uniform than Table 1 shows it now to be. There may also be greater diversity in the species of animal used.

Domestic cattle will probably continue to be more productive than any other species (unless another species is subjected to a comparable amount of skilled selection) when kept on well-managed sward; that usually means on potential arable land. Other species, and especially a mixture of species, may well fare better on the mixed vegetation on unmanaged land – one obvious reason for this is that, by grazing and browsing at different levels, more complete use would be made of the natural mixed vegetation. Different animal species, even when they feed at the same level, select different plant species (Gwynne and Bell, 1968). The whole subject of the merits of wild animals has been comprehensively reviewed recently (e.g. Talbot et al., 1965; Maloiy, 1965; Golley and Buechner, 1968), but properly controlled experiments, comparing the productivity of wild and domestic animals on similar terrain, are long overdue.

55

Table 1

Grammes of protein available per head per day at retail level (From the State of Food and Agriculture, 1964, by courtesy of FAO Rome)

| | Countries | |
| | Well-fed | Ill-fed |
| --- | --- | --- |
| Cereals | 33 | 33 |
| Roots | 5 | 2 |
| Pulses | 4 | 12 |
| Vegetables | 4 | 2 |
| Meat | 20 | 4 |
| Eggs | 3 | 0.4 |
| Fish | 2 | 2 |
| Milk | 18.5 | 3 |
| Total | 89.5 | 58 |

In articles such as this it is traditional to stress the potentialities of fish. Some extravagant claims have been made. FAO cautiously estimates that the catch could not be more than trebled without depleting stocks. The proviso is important for, as the folly of the whalers shows, it is easy to overfish so that the ultimate catch becomes much smaller than a more modest fishing programme would have provided. A great deal of effort is being put into research on the conversion of fish into tasteless powders with a long shelf-life. It is a pity greater effort is not put into improving the marketing, distribution and preservation of fish so that it could be eaten more extensively in a more natural state.

## MICROBIAL CONVERSION

All the foods mentioned so far depend on current photosynthesis. A plant uses sunlight to convert atmospheric carbon dioxide into products that are then used as food, as the raw material for processing into food, or as fodder. An increasing amount of interest is now being taken in the cultivation of yeasts and other micro-organisms on the products, in part, of past photosynthesis. 'In part' because, although the carbon that appears in the microbial mass comes from coal or oil, large amounts of oxygen are also needed and this is the product of current photosynthesis.

The possible scale of production is enormous; the unwanted paraffin fraction of the oil now used would produce 20 M tons of protein per year. Production could become even greater if limestone were used as the carbon source instead of fossil fuels. The supply of oxygen rather than carbon would then limit production, for there are 2 kg of carbon for every square centimetre of Earth's surface but only 200 g of atmospheric oxygen. Ultimately microbial protein may become a very important human food. It does not seem likely to have a great immediate effect on the nutrition of those most in need because the techniques involved in cultivating the micro-organisms, and removing the fuel residues from them, are too sophisticated to be used in their countries. The techniques, and difficulties, of production from oil are discussed by Tannenbaum and Mateles (1968) and by Llewelyn (1968); the potentialities of coal are discussed by Silverman *et al.* (1966). The enterprise that is being shown by the oil companies will direct attention to the potentialities of microbial protein; its most important immediate consequence will probably be that better use will be made of molasses and other existing agricultural by-products on which micro-organisms could be grown.

## ACCEPTANCE OF NOVELTIES

A rough classification of the principal merits and demerits of the more important novel protein sources is attempted in Table 2. That table could have been drawn up 25 years ago. It was obvious then that there was a protein shortage, that it was likely to get worse, and that research would be needed to mitigate it. It is unfortunate that those in control of national and international research policies have shown so much prejudice and unawareness of the possibilities that this research is only now beginning on a serious scale. Although the need for research is now accepted, there is a danger that the various potential sources of protein will be regarded as alternatives rather than as complements. No single novel source of protein is likely to satisfy the impending need, partly because people prefer a mixed diet, and partly because climate and conditions vary. Near the shore of an underexploited sea or lake, fish deserve most attention. In regions with adequate spring rain followed by a hot summer with dry spells, no source of protein is likely to outyield soya and the other oil-seeds. Where there is rain almost every day (about a fifth of the world's population lives in such a climate) coconuts and leaves are the pre-eminent protein sources. In industrialized communities with access to fossil fuels or agricultural wastes, part of the need will be met by centralized production of microbial protein.

Table 2

The ways in which some novel protein sources differ

| Novel protein source | Especial merits | Main limitation |
|---|---|---|
| Fish: fresh, and protein made from mixed marine fauna | Familiarity in principle though the 'fish' used and the end product may be novel | Ultimate probable yield < 5 per cent of total requirement. General consumption depends on efficient transport |
| Leaves: for direct consumption or as sources of extracted protein | Most productive use of arable land in the wet tropics. Little need for transport | The colour is unfamiliar |
| Oil-seed residues | The source material already exists and production could be expanded | None in suitable climates |
| Wild animals | By browsing as well as grazing they make fuller use of land than domestic animals and are more resistant to many diseases | Collection difficult and hygiene uncertain. Ultimate probable yield < 5 per cent of total requirement |
| Yeasts and other micro-organisms | Use made of underused agricultural by-products and fossil fuels | Sophisticated technique needed; this limits the number of centres of production |

Some of the products discussed here, e.g. fish and the flesh of unfamiliar animals, fit easily into accepted culinary patterns and are likely to prove acceptable if propaganda for them is managed skilfully so that they are given prestige and are not presented as substitutes for which there is a brief regretted necessity. The other novelties are less familiar and call for more skill in presentation. Experience in the food industry shows that the success or failure of a new line cannot be predicted; it may depend on accident and chance association as much as on anything else. There is little evidence from animal experiments, but Revusky and Bedarf (1967) found that rats given a dose of X-rays, sufficient to cause mild malaise, when they were eating a novel food, took to the food much less readily than the controls. People probably have an even greater tendency to make logical but unfounded correlations. McConnel (1969) describes a fascinating experiment in which 60 married students were, during several weeks, given beer, all from one batch, but put up in bottles carrying three different labels and with different apparent prices. They quickly built up strong preferences and only one, a woman, is recorded as having maintained throughout that they all tasted the same. A moment's thought about the surprising textures, flavours and antecedents that are relished in different parts of the world, shows that there are few, if any, intrinsically unacceptable potential foods.

## CONCLUSION

I have discussed these issues, and the essential steps to be taken and pitfalls to be avoided in winning acceptance for a novelty, at greater length elsewhere (Pirie, 1969c). Only two more points need be made here. When it is difficult to get a desirable product accepted, it is essential to find out whether there is any factual basis for the reluctance. Factually and emotionally based oppositions are equally real — but different approaches are needed in combating them. A novelty must be produced before it can be assessed, cooked and popularized. By definition, a novelty is novel. One type of official obstruction takes the form 'people will not change their habits'. The changes in food and agriculture in much of the world during the past half century show that this is nonsense. If the thesis is accepted that 20 M tons more protein are needed now and a further 200 M could be needed by the end of the century, change is inevitable. The fact that popularization of novelties may prove difficult is all the more reason for getting started on the job, soon, and the fact that there are many random factors in acceptance is an argument for attempting the job in several different centres. Failure, like success, happens with one group of people, in one set of circumstances, at one

PROTEINS AS HUMAN FOOD

time: it is not a universal. There are conditions in which success is likely, and a few more successes would help enormously in overcoming inertia.

REFERENCES

Bassir, O. and Loebel, W. (1968). *West African J. Biol. Chem.* **11**, 70
Bressani, R., Elias, L. G. and Braham, E. (1966a).*Adv. in Chem. Ser.,* No.57,75
– Elias, L. G., Zaghi, S. de., Mosovich, L. and Viteri, F. (1966b).*J. Agric. Fd. Chem.* **14**, 493
Briggs, M. H. (1967). *Urea as a Protein Supplement,* London; Pergamon Press
Brozek, J. (1962). *Ann. N.Y. Acad. Sci.* **93**, 665
Buchanan, R. A. (1969). *Brit. J. Nutr.* **23**, 533
Butterworth, M. H. and Fox, H. C. (1963). *Brit. J. Nutr.* **17**, 445
Byers, M., Green, S. H. and Pirie, N. W. (1965). *Nutr. (London)* **19**, 63
Chandrasekaran, A. and King, K. W. (1967). *J. agric. Fd.Chem.* **15**, 305
Chow, B. F. and Blackwell, R. Q. (1968). *Borden's Rev. Nutr. Res.* **29**, 25
Creamer, B. (1967). *Br. med. Bull.* **23**, 226
Davys, M. N. G. and Pirie, N. W. (1969). *Biotech. Bioengng.* **11**, 517
Davys, M. N. G., Pirie, N. W. and Street, G. (1969). *Biotech. Bioengng,* **11**, 528
Dickerson, J. W. T., Dobbing, J. and McCance, R. A. (1967).*Proc. R. Soc. (B).,* **166**, 396
Doraiswamy, T. R., Singh, N. and Daniel, V. A. (1969). *Brit. J. Nutr.* **23**, 737
Dubos, R. (1965). *Man Adapting,* p. 527, New Haven and London; Yale University Press
Duckworth, J. and Woodham, A. A. (1961).*J. Sci. Fd. Agric.* **12**, 5
– Hepburn, W. R. and Woodham, A. A. (1961).*J. Sci. Fd. Agric.* **12**, 16
FAO (1964). *The State of Food and Agriculture,* Rome, Table III-4, p. 109
FAO/WHO (1965). *FAO Nutrition Meetings Report Series,* No. 37
Garrow, J. S. and Pike, M. C. (1967). *Lancet.* 1967 **i**, 1
Golley, F. B. and Beuchner, H. K. (1968). *IBP Handbook* No. 7
Graham, G. G, (1967). *Fedn. Proc. Fedn. Am. Socs. exp. Biol.* **26**, 139
Guggenheim, K. and Szmelcman, S. (1967). *Can. J. Biochem.* **45**, 959
Gwynne, M.D. and Bell, R.H.V. (1968). *Nature, Lond.* **220**, 390
Henry, K.M. and Ford, J.E. (1965).*J. Sci. Fd Agric.* **16**, 425
Hofman, R.R. (1968). In *'Comparative Nutrition of Wild Animals'*. Ed. by M.A. Crawford, *Symp. zool. Soc. Lond.*21, 179
Johnson, V.A., Schmidt, J.W. and Mattern, P.J. (1968). *Econ. Bot.* **22**, 16
Lawes, J.B. and Gilbert, J.H. (1852). *Rep. Br. Ass. Advmt. Sci.,* p. 323. Also (1866). *Phil. Mag.* (4th ser.) **32**, 55
Llewelyn, D.A.B. (1968).*Microbology,* Ed. by Hepple, P. Inst. Petroleum, p. 63
Maloiy, G.M.O. (1965). *Nutr. Abstr. Rev.* **35**, 903
McConnell, J.D. (1968). *J. Marketing Res.* **5**, 13
Murphy, H.C. Sadanaga, K., Zillinsky, F.J., Terrell, E.E. and Smith, R.T. (1968). *Science,* **159**, 103
Neale, G. (1968).*Proc. R. Soc. Med.*60, 1069
Pirie, N.W. (1956). *Proc. Nutr. Soc.* **15**, 154
– (1966). *Science, N.Y.* **152**, 1701
– (1969a). *Proc. Nutr. Soc.* **28**, 85
– (1969b). *Ann. Rep. Rothamsted Exp. Sta. for 1968,* p. 112
– (1969c). *Food Resources: Conventional and Novel,* Penguin Books
Preston, T.R. and Hagelberg, G.B. (1967). *New Scientist* **36**, 31
Ramamurti, K. and Johar, D.S. (1963).*Nature, Lond.* **198**, 481

Rao, G.R., Ramanatham, G., Indira, K., Rao, U.S.B., Chandrasekhara, M.R., Carpenter, K.J. and Bhatia, D.S. (1967). *Indian J. exp. Biol.* **5**, 114

Raymond, W.D., Jojo, W. and Nicodemus, Z. (1941). *East African Agric. J.* **6**, 154

Revusky, S. and Bedarf, E. (1967). *Science, N.Y.* **155**, 219

Silverman, M.P., Gordon, J.N. and Wender, I. (1966). In *'World Protein Resources'. Adv. Chem. Series,* No. 57. *Amer. Chem. Soc.* p. 269. Also *Nature, Lond.* **211**, 735

Snyderman, S.E., Boyer, A. and Holt, L.E. (1961). In *'Progress in Meeting Protein Needs of Infants and Preschool Children'. Nat. Acad. Sci. Publ. 843,* and Nat. Res. Council, p. 331

Squires, B.T. (1966). *Cent. Afr. J. Med.,* **12**, 223

Stevenson, J.A.F. (1946). *Proc. Nutr. Soc.* **4**, 212

Stewart, R.J.C. and Platt, B.S. (1968). *Proc. Nutr. Soc.* **27**, 95

Talbot, L.M., Payne, W.J.A., Ledger, H.P., Verdcourt, L.D. and Talbot, M.H. (1965). *'The Meat Production Potential of Wild Animals in Africa'. Tech. Comm.* 19 of Commonwealth Agric. Bureau

Tannenbaum, S. R. and Mateles, R. I. (1968). *Science J.* **4**, (5) 87

Terra, G.J.A. (1964). *Trop. Geogr. Med.* **16**, 97

TPI (1967). *'The Production of Protein Foods and Concentrates from Oilseeds', Publ. G31* of Tropical Products Institute

Waterlow, J.C. (1962). *Brit. J. Nutr.* **16**, 531

– (1968). *Lancet 1968* **ii**, 1091

Widdowson, E.M. and Kennedy, G.C. (1962). *Proc. R. Soc. (B),* **156**, 96

Woodham, A.A. (1965). *Proc. Nutr. Soc.* **24**, 24

# II. GENERAL ASPECTS OF PROTEIN
# PRESERVATION AND PROCESSING

# TOXIC AGENTS AND PROTEIN AVAILABILITY

P.S. ELIAS

*Department of Health and Social Security, London*

## INTRODUCTION

Better supplies of protein for the steadily increasing population of the world may be achieved in a number of ways, but each of these avenues presents ample opportunities for interference by noxious agents, many of which have been designed deliberately for functions inimical to one or other forms of life.

The progress of modern medicine creates its own problems in relation to the availability of proteins. These are less matters of supply but rather, for some, an interference with their use of certain proteins. Examples are the deleterious consequences of drug incompatibility with ingested food such as the interaction between monoamineoxidase inhibitors and foods containing tyramine or tryptophan.

It is not possible in this paper to cover adequately all existing examples of the interrelation between toxic agents and the availability of protein. Discussion will therefore be confined to some illustrative, and I hope, interesting items.

## ANTIBIOTICS

For nearly two decades antibiotics, in addition to their therapeutic application, have been used for non-medical purposes e.g. as feed additives for growth promotion in poultry, pigs and calves, as preservatives for chilled fish or poultry and as antifungal agents applied to cheese rinds or banana skins. Antibiotics are potent substances with known toxicological effects. Some occur naturally in certain foods: a selected few may be added intentionally to food for technological reasons. Residues of antibiotics are found in animals and animal products as a result of non-medical use or after therapeutic treatment.

Generally only traces of antibiotic residues are detected in foods. Further quantitative and qualitative modification results from subsequent treatment of the food material. Residues consist either of unchanged antibiotic or degradation products with or without antibiotic or toxic properties. None of these antibiotic residues is known to have caused any direct toxic effects in consumers of food. The principal indirect toxic effect likely to interfere seriously with subsequent human consumption is an allergic hypersensitivity reaction. Most of these reactions occur in people hypersensitive to penicillin: A more remote indirect effect is, for example, the development of extrachromosomal bacterial resistance, particularly among members of the gram-negative enterobacteriaceae.

In nearly all countries where the penicillins are widely used in medicine, an estimated 1−2 per cent of the population is hypersensitive to them. As little as 0.024 mg of ingested benzyl penicillin may produce an allergic reaction in highly susceptible individuals (Siegel, 1959). Penicillin allergy is of the 'immediate' type and sometimes fatal. The principal determinants of this allergy are probably degradation products of the penicillins but the exact quantitative relationships are not yet fully established (Levine, 1966). Cows' milk is a major source of trouble and is likely to contain significant antibiotic residues. In this country, control is exercised through the Milk Marketing Board's testing and penalty schemes. These aim to exclude from sale milk containing penicillin residues detectable by the inhibition of *Streptococcus thermophilus* BC, an organism very sensitive to penicillin. Milk thus contaminated is therefore lost to consumption. The problem is confined to countries which use antibiotics extensively and consequently have comparatively large numbers of hypersensitive individuals.

## FOOD ADDITIVES

Large urban communities can only be supplied adequately with foodstuffs by the use of depots carrying sufficient stocks, necessitating preservative measures which permit importation, long distance transportation and storage facilities guaranteeing a minimum loss of valuable food. Increased automation has led to a swing towards a diet high in protein and low in fat and to a demand for manufactured convenience foods. As a consequence, the development and use of deliberate food additives has risen sharply to meet the technological demands of modern large-scale food production and of consumer pressure for diversification, improved quality, better appearance and satisfactory texture.

In principle, no chemicals are harmless, there are only harmless ways of using them. It is necessary to balance the benefits against the risks. Most of the population is likely to be exposed continuously to additives in their food, as opposed to drugs, and personal benefits from the presence of these additives are often indirect and not as immediately obvious.

Deliberate food additives are not intrinsically toxic. In single doses, at any rate, enormous quantities would have to be ingested to do any harm, but uncertainty prevails about the consequences of ingesting even tiny quantities throughout life. Obviously such insidious possibilities are not easily checked by direct human observation and epidemiological surveys. Accordingly, in the face of opposition from the antivivisectionists, tests are carried out on animals. Rats and mice, sometimes dogs, and occasionally other species are commonly fed substances under test at levels far in excess of those likely to be put into human food, both for short periods and also throughout their life-span. Any changes are noted in growth, body functions, reproduction and, notably, tumour incidence as a measure of carcinogenic potential. In extrapolating the results to man it is usually accepted that if a substance causes no detectable adverse effects at a level of at least one hundred times the maximum amount likely to be added to food then it is reasonably safe. No absolute assurance of safety of a substance can, of course, be given from this sort of information unless careful study of its ingestion by persons of all ages over long periods has shown conclusively to have had no harmful result or unless its metabolism in man was accurately known. Many other points have to be considered if a more refined evaluation is aimed at and these are set out in Table 1.

Table 1

Main considerations in assessment of potential health hazards of food additives
(After Frazer, 1968)

| | |
|---|---|
| 1. Provision of adequate specifications and methods for identification and assay | |
| 2. Full programmes of toxicity studies on the food additives supplemented by studies on the treated food where necessary | |
| 3, Variability of exposed population | Young, old, sick, healthy |
| 4. Possible daily consumption for life | High or low levels |
| 5. Summation of toxic effects | Separate effects of individual compounds acting at different points along the same metabolic pathway |
| 6. Large amount of negative information | Generally food additives not toxic |
| 7. Changes induced in food by treatment | Nutritional, toxic, carcinogenic risks |
| 8. Synergism with alcohol, drugs, other chemical in food | |

Historically, food has been the obvious and most readily accessible vehicle for the conveyance of deliberate poison and the history of mankind abounds with records of the nefarious effects of toxic 'food additives'. Today it is rare for a chemical rather than a micro-organism to be responsible for food poisoning. When a chemical is to blame, its presence is almost invariably due to accidental contamination – by contact, spillage, misunderstanding etc. Recognition of the inevitability of food additives entails as a corollary the acceptance of the control of food purity. Hence we find food legislation in many countries aiming at the exclusion of all those substances which do not comply with the generally accepted standards of safety evaluation, based either on the opinions of national bodies or on the numerous reports of such international authorities as the Joint FAO/WHO Expert Committee on Food Additives.

Direct toxic effects from the small amounts of approved food additives appearing in foodstuffs are unlikely to affect their availability, but the interaction of a given food additive with certain food constituents may harbour some surprises.

## NITROSAMINES

The ancient observation of the appearance of red patches in cooked meat which had been preserved with rock salt containing impurities of saltpetre led to the deliberate use of nitrates to produce uniform coloration. Later, the microbial reduction of nitrate to nitrite was discovered as the real cause of this colouring effect so that nitrites are now widely used as a valuable preservative for cured meat and some other food products. However, nitrites undergo chemical reactions with secondary and tertiary amines in food which, under certain conditions, lead to the formation of nitrosamines.

Many nitrosamines have been shown to possess remarkable toxic and carcinogenic activities particularly in relation to the liver and kidneys of rats, and other organs in other animal species. Some are teratogenic in rats and several are powerful mutagens (Magee and Barnes, 1967; Druckrey *et al.*, 1967). The unsuspected formation of 30–100 p.p.m. of a carcinogenic nitrosamine, later identified as dimethylnitrosamine, in herring meal preserved with sodium nitrite, was shown to be the cause of severe liver disease in ruminants (Ender *et al.*, 1964). Mink are extremely sensitive and only 2 p.p.m. dimethylnitrosamine in the diet of rats suffice to induce liver tumours (Terracini *et al.*, 1967). If man is sensitive to the carcinogenic action of nitrosamines – and there seems to be no reason to assume that he is not – the implications of the above findings are obvious. Nitrosamines have been claimed to be present, albeit in minute amounts, in cigarette smoke, white flour, meat and fish preserved with nitrites and in other situations; but the estimation and identification of such very minute quantities presents great analytical difficulties. Theroetically, carcinogenic amines could be formed by interaction of nitrites with amines present in food, and hazardous levels might be attained in foods with high amine content. Any possible risk to human health must however be balanced against the outstanding value of nitrites as preservatives of meat and fish proteins, especially against those clostridia which cause fatal botulism (Anonymous, 1968).

Some naturally occurring compounds are either nitroso-carcinogens or break down to biologically active intermediates identical with those that are believed to be concerned in the carcinogenic action of dimethylnitrosamine e.g. the antibiotic streptozotocin, a nitrosamide (Avison and Feudale, 1967) and the carcinogenic glucosides of methyl-azoxymethanol found in cycad plants (Anonymous, 1965). The possibility that some of these compounds may contaminate human food, particularly in the tropics, must not be dismissed.

## AGENE

Nitrogen trichloride or agene had been in use since the early 1920s as an efficient bleach for flour and as a strengthening agent for gluten. Suddenly reports appeared in the U.S.A. and England of a nervous disorder in dogs characterized by running fits, due to a toxic factor present in commercial wheat gluten (Wagner and Elvehjem, 1944). This toxic factor was isolated eventually and identified as methionine sulphoximine (Misani and Reiner, 1950); the precise mechanism of its toxic action has so far remained unknown. Administration of methionine sulphoximine to man in large doses produced (reversibly) hallucinations, disorientation and marked agitation. These reactions could be prevented by administering simultaneously doses of methionine some 20 times greater than those of methionine sulphoximine (Krakoff, 1961; Campbell and Morrison, 1966).

## 3,4–BENZPYRENE

Another instance of contamination as a result of traditional methods of food preservation may be the practice, in some rural areas of Iceland, of preserving fish and mutton by heavy smoking over prolonged periods.

Such treatment appears to have resulted in the deposition of significant amounts of the carcinogen 3,4–benzpyrene. Rats fed this smoked food showed an increased incidence of malignant tumours. Epidemiological observations of those sections of the Icelandic population consuming smoked foods in considerable amounts over many years pointed to a possible increased incidence of gastric carcinoma (Dungal, 1961). Other pertinent investigations revealed the presence of carcinogenic aromatic polycyclic hydrocarbons on charcoal-broiled steaks in concentrations of 8 $\mu$g/kg steak, probably derived from pyrolysis of molten fat (Lijinsky and Shubik, 1964). Luckily for steak lovers, 3,4-benzpyrene is poorly absorbed from the intestine under normal circumstances. It is a widely distributed environmental contaminant in the air of any urban community (Wogan, 1966; Anonymous, 1969).

## NATURALLY OCCURRING TOXIC AGENTS

Increasing awareness of the toxicological importance to human health of factors existing in our natural environment has led to a more searching and critical assessment of the true health of 'natural' foodstuffs. Despite the widespread belief that natural substances are necessarily safer than synthetic chemicals it is gradually being realized that nothing could be further from the truth. Many potent poisons are found in plants, animals or micro-organisms so that certain components of natural foodstuffs may be far from harmless if consumed by man. It is sometimes argued that natural substances must be safe if they have been consumed over centuries without apparent harm to man. This argument is illusory because identification of the cause of relatively minor deleterious effects in human subjects is remarkably difficult nor are these effects likely to be detected by epidemiological studies alone.

On the other hand virtually nothing is known about the mechanisms underlying the wide range of individual susceptibility, and of possible adaptation by man to toxic components of food. Modern studies have revealed the presence of a multiplicity of enzymes in the intestinal mucosa that can act as a first line of defence against ingested deleterious substances. Yet deficiencies in the normal complement of such enzymes might lead to intolerance of normal foodstuffs as exemplified by such pathological conditions as primary lactose intolerance, gluten-sensitive enteropathy or portal-systemic encephalopathy.

Summation of effects at different points along the same biosynthetic metabolic pathway enables collective toxic action by a number of different compounds, each present in food in an amount too small to

## Table 2

Some naturally occurring toxic agents and environmental contaminants
(After Anonymous, 1966a; Mickelsen and Yang, 1966)

| | |
|---|---|
| Cottonseed meal | Gossypol |
| Cycad starch | Cycasin hepatotoxin, possibly neurotoxic, the aglycone methylazoxymethanol has similar activity to nitrosamine metabolite |
| Tonka beans | Coumarins, hepatotoxic and some anticoagulant activity, certain metabolites inhibit hepatic glucose-6-phosphatase |
| Wheat and rye gluten | Toxic metabolite occurs in people with genetic enzyme defect (infantile coeliac disease, adult gluten-induced enteropathy) with resultant mucosal damage |
| Lathyrus seed | $\beta$-Aminopropionitrile causes lathyrism, neurotoxic, collagen disturbance in rats,? $\beta$-cyano-L-alanine causes human lathyrism |
| Sassafras | Safrole, hepatotoxic and carcinogenic, only in certain varieties |
| Senecio, crotalaria, heliotropum sp. | Pyrrolizidine alkaloids hepatotoxic, veno-occlusive disease of liver from West Indian bush-teas |
| *Vicia fava* | Haemolytic anaemia in people with genetic deficiency in glucose-6-phosphate dehydrogenase in red cells |
| Arsenic | Accumulation in shellfish and mineral waters, cancer in vineyard workers |
| Radionuclides | Contaminants and naturally occurring, destroy essential nutrients, haematologic, carcinogenic and mutagenic risks |
| Lactones | Some are carcinogenic e.g. penicillin G, parasorbic acid |
| Nitrosamines | Hepatotoxic, hepatic and neurogenic tumours, occur in some nitrite-preserved material |
| Aflatoxin | Mycotoxin of *Aspergillus flavus* infection of peanuts, hepatotoxic and carcinogenic |
| Ergot | *Claviceps purpurea* of cereals, epidemics in Europe in fifteenth to eighteenth centuries, gangrene of extremities, hallucinogenic, abortifacient, 'St. Anthony's fire' |
| Bacterial toxins | Botulism and staphylococcal toxins |

Table 2—continued

| Mercury | Effluents from Hg-using plants contaminate fish and shellfish, Minimata disease |
| --- | --- |
| Polycyclic hydrocarbons, 3,4-benzpyrene | Charcoal-broiled steaks from pyrolised fat, smoked salmon, smoked Icelandic mutton and fish, ? carcinoma of stomach, overroasted coffee, tobacco |
| Agene (nitrogen trichloride) | Running fits in dogs from methionine sulphoximine |
| Ethylene oxide | Thiamine destruction, epichlorhydrin formation |
| DDT, dieldrin | Vitamin A storage depressed in liver, ? carcinogenic |

cause an effect on its own. Synergism or potentiation of the effects of individual toxic agents might be the result of exposure to alcohol, drugs, industrial solvents or other chemical agents.

Table 2 lists some of the more important naturally occurring toxic and environmental contaminants described in the literature.

For the purposes of this discussion it will suffice to select a few examples which are particularly relevant to dietary protein supply.

## MARINE BIOTOXINS

Marine food products have been part of the human diet for many centuries; some of their potential health hazards relating to acute toxicity have been recognized for a very long time. Concern has arisen recently because greater use will have to be made of marine food products to alleviate world food shortages. Apart from the potential dangers of long-term effects of natural toxins there is evidence, in certain areas, of increasing contamination of sea food by agricultural and industrial chemicals. All these potentially toxic agents may appear in marine protein concentrates.

The oceans produce annually about 400 million tons of animal protein in a variety of species and are therefore a most valuable protein source. Because biotoxins are much more abundant throughout the marine biotope in the warm seas, the recent expansion of fisheries operations from temperate to tropical latitudes will undoubtedly increase opportunities for contact with these poisons. Marine intoxicants involve not only fishes but also many marine invertebrates. Several varieties of ichthyosarcotoxism (toxic fish flesh) are now recognized; other fishes contain various neurotoxins, some estimated to be about 10,000 times more toxic than sodium cyanide. Many of these poisons are heat stable. Geographical distribution and intensity of ichthyosarcotoxism fluctuates considerably and little is known concerning the triggering mechanisms for these outbreaks.

The advent of the marine protein concentrate process introduces new potential health hazards, probably less serious in temperate zones but more dangerous in tropical areas. The process uses biological concentrators which may contain chemical contaminants or natural biotoxins. These proteins will reach eventually human and animal diets. The removal from concentrates of biotoxins or industrial wastes, particularly if they are protein-bound, is unreliable. In spite of these possible health hazards, marine food products including marine protein concentrates can still be useful and safe, provided proper control measures are taken, health educational programmes are established and adequate toxicological testing of the products carried out.

Ciguatera fish poisoning is probably the most important form of ichthyosarcotoxism endemic in the tropical Atlantic, Pacific and Indian oceans. Normally edible valuable food fishes become suddenly poisonous without warning. These outbreaks cannot be forecast. The existing bioassay methods are crude and practised only in large Japanese fish markets. Ciguatera fish constitute, therefore, a significant threat to the utilization of marine food protein resources.

Other types of tropical marine biotoxications are tetrodotoxin poisoning due to puffer fishes in the Far East and scombroid fish poisoning caused by saurine.

Paralytic shellfish poisoning is caused by shellfish which have ingested toxic dinoflagellates and many incidents have been reported from U.S.A., Canada and Europe including the U.K. The causative saxitoxin can be assayed biologically. Routine surveys of districts likely to produce toxic shellfish may help to contain incidents and surveys of dinoflagellate population behaviour are useful for forecasting probable toxicity. These toxic shellfish and many other types of marine organisms affected by biotoxins might be involved in the production of protein concentrates (Halstead, 1965, 1967, 1968).


## CONTAMINANTS OF MARINE ORGANISMS

The extensive agricultural use of the persistent organochlorine pesticides has led to widespread contamination of rivers and the sea. As a result almost all marine vertebrates and invertebrates now contain residues in their tissues at levels ranging from 0.001 to 5 p.p.m. (Robinson *et al.*, 1967).

Industrial waste containing mercury has led to outbreaks of severe neurological disorders in the Minimata and Niigata areas of Japan. These are discussed in greater detail later. In Sweden, fishes caught downstream of industries using mercury have shown high mercury residues particularly in the form of methylmercury and this has led to the banning of commerical fishing in a significant proportion of the coastal and inland fishing areas. This is also discussed more extensively later.

Monitoring of contamination from liquid radioactive waste discharges to the sea has shown that the total exposure of the critical population group is well below the limit considered safe although problems have arisen from contamination with radioactive fallout from nuclear tests or through discharges from nuclear-powered vessels.

The problem of mycotoxin production in food from contaminating fungal organisms should be mentioned here, but is not dealt with in detail.

## BIOLOGICAL AMINES

Many amino-compounds, often possessing considerable physiological activity, exist naturally in food. They include histamine, tyramine, tryptamine and their metabolites, serotonin (5-hydroxytryptamine) and noradrenaline. Although typical constituents of animal tissue, they are found also in plants as shown in Table 3.

The hazards arising from their consumption depend largely on their absorption from the gastro-intestinal tract and subsequent metabolic fate. Primary amines are usually detoxified by enzymatic oxidation (monoamineoxidase) to the corresponding carboxylic acid. Thus the naturally occurring osteolathyrogen, $\beta$-aminopropionitrile, is converted to cyanoacetic acid. Inhibition of monoamineoxidase will cause characteristic symptoms of amine activity at normally ineffective concentrations. Similar potentiation of amine toxicity in man has been described following the eating of matured cheese or pickled herrings by some patients treated simultaneously with monoamineoxidase inhibitors. The typical complications are those due to the hypertensive effect of the accumulating pressor amine serotonin or other catecholamines secondary to blockage of the metabolizing enzyme by drugs. Some fatal cases of brain haemorrhage have been reported (Blackwell, 1963).

The serotonin intake of many African peoples who use plantains as a major article of their diet may reach 100–200 mg per day. It has been suggested, in analogy to carcinoid heart disease which is associated with

Table 3

Some naturally-occurring physiologically-active amino compounds

(After Anonymous, 1966a)

| Food | Amine | Approximate concentration in p.p.m. fresh weight |
|------|-------|--------------------------------------------------|
| Ripe bananas | Serotonin<br>Noradrenaline<br>Dopamine | 30<br>2<br>8 |
| Ripe plantains | Serotonin<br>Noradrenaline | 40 − 100<br>2.5 |
| Ripe pineapples | Serotonin | 20 |
| Pineapple juice | Serotonin | 25 − 35 |
| Ripe tomatoes | Serotonin | 3.4 |
| Cheese | Tyramine<br>Tryptamine<br>Phenylethylamine | 2,000<br>−<br>− |
| Lemons | Octopamine<br>Synephrin | |
| Wine | Histamine | 5 − 20 |

excessive endogenous serotonin production, that this dietary intake may be an aetiological factor in certain heart conditions among Africans (Foy and Parratt, 1962).

## TRACE ELEMENTS

Some trace elements play an essential part in the nutrition of plants, animals and man, while others are of purely toxicological interest. For most of them a wide range exists between the innocuous and the injurious level (Monier-Williams, 1949). They may become concentrated in protein food as a consequence of biological activity as exemplified by the accumulation of Cu, As, Pb, Zn, or Hg in shellfish. Alternatively, they may accumulate as a result of processing of protein concentrates, for instance in certain fish flour preparations where fluorine levels up to 170 p.p.m. and selenium in levels up to 1.8 p.p.m. were found on analysis. Such quantities may have deleterious effects on tooth development and the incidence of dental caries in children whose dietary protein ration is supplemented by such concentrates (Hadjimarkos, 1965).

## ENVIRONMENTAL POLLUTANTS

The role of microchemical pollutants in our environment, particularly their long-term effects on the public health, is becoming more clearly defined. Indeed the food-chain is the major pathway for the transfer of radioactive contaminants and pesticide residues to man. The advances in industrial technology, rapid transportation and comfortable housing, and wastes from communities and from industries contribute to land, river, estuary and sea pollution. Thus pesticide and industrial residues may become absorbed by fresh-water fishes and even marine fishes. American surveys have shown pesticide residue levels of 0.0001–0.005 p.p.m. in major river systems, small concentrations in themselves but injurious to highly sensitive fish species. Some aquatic organisms are capable of concentrating these residues manyfold while the pesticide content of fishes may well suffice to lead to high levels in fish-eating birds and other species. Massive mortality particularly among trout and salmon has occurred due to accidental spraying of land bordering rivers and streams.

Soil contamination from domestic and industrial wastes, as well as from the many agricultural chemicals, has produced new problems. Many of these substances are effectively degraded but others remain as persistent contaminants e.g. lead, mercury, arsenic, some chlorinated hydrocarbons etc.

## NITRATES AND NITRITES

Most plants take up nitrates preferentially whether derived from fertilizers or occurring naturally in the soil, and convert them to amino acids and proteins. Any excess available or unused in photosynthesis accumulates in the plant. The following table indicates typical levels.

Table 4

Typical content of nitrate-nitrogen in vegetables
(From BNF Information Bulletin No. 1 (1968)
by courtesy of The Secretary, BNF)

| Plant | Nitrate-Nitrogen % in dry matter |
|---|---|
| Carrots | 0 –0.30 |
| Beets | 0.09–0.84 |
| Spinach | 0.07–0.82 |

Biologically, the total nitrate of the diet is of significance, arising from contributions by the nitrate content of vegetable crops to that of public water supplies. The nitrates found in drinking water, especially from shallow wells, arise however only in part from nitrates leached out of the soil. Some nitrate appears also to be formed as an end product of nitrogenous metabolism in man, and it and ingested nitrate is rapidly excreted in the urine. Much is known about the behaviour of nitrate in man from its therapeutic use and nitrates have a low toxic potential. The acceptable daily intake for nitrates has been established as 5—10 mg/kg body weight for normal people (FAO/WHO, 1962) but nitrates should be kept as low as possible in baby foods.

In certain circumstances reduction of nitrates to nitrites can take place in the digestive tract by the activity of the intestinal flora or if food is allowed to deteriorate. Ruminants are particularly liable to suffer from nitrite poisoning. Babies less than six months old, especially dyspeptic infants, or other human subjects with little gastric acid secretion and an active flora in the upper regions of the gastro-intestinal tract, may be at risk. Serious poisoning of babies has occurred due to the use of prepared foods containing excessive amounts of nitrite and the preparation of baby feeds with water containing an excess of nitrite. The safe level for babies is thought to be 10 p.p.m.

Inorganic nitrates and nitrites have been used for many years in the bacon and ham industry. Nitrites combine with the myoglobin in the meat to give an acceptable colour and also have a preservative action. Their important toxicological effects are related to the oxidation of haemoglobin and similar compounds to methaemoglobin and to their well known inhibition of plain muscle resulting in vascular dilation, hypotension and circulatory collapse. Methaemoglobin is valueless for oxygen transport in the body and, if excessive amounts are formed, cyanosis will occur. The sub-acute hazard of nitrite rests, therefore, on the ability of the body to reconvert methaemoglobin to haemoglobin. The special susceptibility of babies to nitrites is possibly associated with deficient powers to effect detoxification and with the presence of appreciable amounts of foetal haemoglobin. The acceptable daily intake for nitrites is 0.4—0.8 mg/kg body weight for normal people, about one tenth of that for nitrate. Excessive amounts of nitrite have led to many severe epidemics of poisoning particularly in Germany, where in 1950 alone there were 16 deaths and 327 cases of poisoning recorded from this cause (Marquardt, 1967). Recent Russian experimental work has demonstrated that the feeding of rats on diets containing three times the estimated total dietary intake of nitrates and nitrites resulted in a significant reduction in the absorption of the fat and protein fraction of the animals' diet without showing any effect on the carbohydrate absorption (Popov, 1964).

## PESTICIDES

Of all the potentially toxic agents which might come into contact with food, pesticides occupy the most important position by virtue of their intimate association with the production of food materials. Chemically they can be classified into eight convenient groups as shown in Table 5.

Table 5

Chemical classification of pesticides

| Group | Examples |
| --- | --- |
| Mineral compounds | Carbon disulphide, hydrocyanic acid, zinc phosphide, lead arsenate, mercuric chloride |
| Organo-mercurials | Methoxyethylmercury silicate, phenyl mercuric acetate, methylmercury benzoate, ethylmercury-thiourea |
| Organophosphorus compounds | Dichlorvos, phosphamidon, malathion, diazinon, parathion, fenthion, fenchlorphos, bromophos |
| Organo-halogen compounds | Methyl bromide, trichlorethylene, lindane, DDT, dieldrin, dicofol, fenson, 2,4-D, fluorbenside |
| Nitro derivatives | Dinocap, dinoseb, dinitrophenol, DNOC, sodium dinitro-orthocresylate |
| Carbamates and urea derivatives | Antu, carbaryl, diuron, barban, ziram, di-allate |
| Alkaloids | Nicotine and its salts, strychnine and its salts brucine |
| Miscellaneous | Thiram, fentin hydroxide, metaldehyde, warfarin, pindone, azobenzene, diquat, paraquat |

Pesticides have proved invaluable in economic food production, in combating disease, in making our lives more comfortable and in furthering man's existence. This should be remembered when arguments arise over pesticide residues in food. Table 6 illustrates the magnitude of the wastage involved in certain crops.

On the other side of the balance sheet, however, these compounds are by no means devoid of toxic potentialities.

Much heat has been generated over the physical presence of small

Table 6

Estimated losses in some principal crop-potential production in the U.S.A.
(1965)

| Crop | Source of loss | | | | Loss in tons (Millions) |
|------|---------------|---|---|---|-------------------------|
|      | Disease (%) | Insects (%) | Nematodes (%) | Weeds (%) | |
| Corn | 12 | 12 | 3 | 10 | 37 |
| Wheat | 14 | 6 | – | 12 | 11.5 |
| Rice | 7 | 4 | – | 1 | 0.6 |
| Soy bean | 14 | 3 | 2 | 17 | 3.7 |
| Dry bean | 17 | 20 | – | 15 | 0.5 |
| Snap bean | 20 | 12 | 5 | 9 | 0.3 |
| Potatoes | 19 | 14 | 4 | 3 | 4.7 |
| Tomatoes | 22 | 7 | 8 | 7 | 5.0 |
| Apples | 8 | 13 | – | 3 | 0.7 |
| Oranges | 12 | 6 | 4 | 5 | 1.5 |
| Strawberries | 26 | 25 | – | 25 | 0.2 |
| Alfalfa | 24 | 15 | 3 | – | 30 |
| Pasture and range (as hay equivalent) | 5 | 20 | – | 15 | 100 |
| Sugar beets | 16 | 12 | 4 | 8 | 5.9 |

Modified from:  'The Use of Human Subjects in Safety of Food Chemicals'
*Proceedings of a Conference,* National Academy of Sciences,
Washington D.C., 29-30th November 1966.

residues of comparatively innocuous pesticides in human food while
powerful natural carcinogens like aflatoxin have remained almost acceptable because they are 'natural' and not 'chemical' — a nonsensical distinction to a scientist. Pesticides are widely used to control the vectors of
certain human diseases like malaria so that more people live to demand
food. Once saved from death these people should not go hungry because
their food was found to contain say DDT above some accepted daily
intake level, still much below that absorbed from their sprayed living

quarters (Barnes, 1967). Even if the levels are not acceptable to some highly developed nations, there would be in underdeveloped countries an infinitely greater risk of death and disability from malnutrition than from poisoning by pesticide residues. Exceeding the acceptable daily intakes occasionally, is not unacceptable toxicologically because acceptable daily intakes are designed to achieve safety throughout the whole of the human lifespan. Hence considerable positive and negative variations around this mean value are permissible for brief periods, provided a balance is achieved in the long run.

Hazards to the consumer of pesticide-treated food arise mainly in three ways as acute poisoning only occurs under circumstances of ill-considered or improper use.

(1) *Pesticides leaving insignificant residues:* Examples are pyrethrum, volatile BHC and dichlorvos.

(2) *Pesticides reacting with the treated material:* Examples are methylbromide, ethylene oxide and ethylene dibromide.

Ethylene oxide can be used at different concentrations either as a fumigant or as a sterilant. It reacts with naturally present or added chloride to form 2—chloroethanol or epichlorhydrin, a toxic alcohol. Ethylene oxide-amino acid adducts, as well as other reaction products with carbohydrates, vitamins etc., have also been identified (Lindgren *et al.*, 1968). The amino acid adducts have been reported to be non-toxic (Lehman, 1965). If livestock are fed grain fumigated with ethylene dibromide the residues may affect poultry adversely and reduce egg production thus resulting in a loss of egg protein to the community. Yet the same grain when milled and baked into bread presents no hazard to man (Barnes, 1967). In so far as the action of fumigants on the nutritive value of the food has been examined, the results have been reassuring (FAO/WHO, 1965).

(3) *Pesticides leaving a significant unchanged residue or metabolite in the treated food:* These pesticides are usually stable solids or liquids with low acute toxicity and they largely disappear by the time the final food has been prepared, as a result of various intermediate cleaning and milling processes.

Most of the organophosphorus compounds which are very effective against insects present no problems of chronic or cumulative toxicity. The organochlorine group of pesticides provides an interesting contrast but it should be realized that it is still only one group amongst all the pesticides employed today. Whatever accusations are hurled at organochlorines specifically they must not be employed indiscriminately against all pesticides. The rest, toxicologically, may be better or worse, but at all events they are very different in their properties and behaviour.

DDT has a low toxicity and presents no apparent hazard to men heavily exposed for many months when spraying houses for mosquito control. Unfortunately DDT is metabolized to DDE and DDA and excreted only slowly by mammals, and being fat soluble, a portion accumulates in tissue fat as DDT and DDE. So far, nobody has shown that this contaminant of depot fat causes any adverse physiological effects in man. Its presence was only recognized because of the availability of extremely sensitive methods of analysis. Much anxiety has been generated over these minute residues when much larger quantities were shown to be of no toxicological importance to the whole animal. Epidemiological studies on the health of people exposed for 20 years or more to large doses of DDT have not shown any obvious toxic effect, so that DDT's record as a saviour of many human lives will remain untarnished.

Other members of this group are aldrin, dieldrin, endrine, chlordane, heptachlor, endosulphan, toxaphene and gamma BHC or lindane. They are all very stable, resistant to both chemical and biological degradation, scarcely water-soluble, though readily soluble in lipids. These features, in the main, account for their persistence. They all enter the body by ingestion, inhalation or percutaneous absorption and tend to be deposited in body fat. Aldrin is readily converted to dieldrin, especially in the liver. The accumulation, however, is not indefinite and, given a steady intake, there is a so-called plateau effect of body load. Aldrin and dieldrin, even at very low levels of intake, produce histological changes in mice, rats and dogs, so that a no-effect level has not been established. The interpretation of the observed liver changes is controversial; some pathologists regarding them as neoplastic. Only lindane appears to have a no-effect level. Nevertheless, none of these compounds are as violently poisonous as nicotine or arsenic, and no lasting harm has been demonstrated. Recently some 'market-basket' surveys have been instituted in the U.S.A. and in this country, and have disclosed that residues are reassuringly small (Duggan and Weatherwax, 1967).

It is asserted that these minute residues are sufficient to contribute to enormous build-ups of organochlorine compounds in our bodies. Human fat analyses, carried out in various countries of the world including Great Britain, lend some confirmation to this (Egan *et al.*, 1965; Abbott *et al.*, 1968).

The thought of a load of foreign chemicals in the human body is not, under any circumstances, conducive to tranquillity of mind, the more so as the unavoidable source is food, but are the quantities really so immense — DDT equivalent in 1965 ranging from 0.2 to 8.5 p.p.m., total BHC from a trace to 1.0 p.p.m. and dieldrin from a trace to 0.9 p.p.m.? Also, is there any indication, by any meaningful criteria that one cares to employ, that man is suffering at all from their presence?

Perhaps there may be some adverse effect in time on this account: it is difficult to prophesy; at the moment, anyway, it is scientifically fair to say that there is not one iota of substantiated evidence to the effect that man has suffered any chronic toxic effects at all from organochlorine residues in food. In common with all toxic agents, even carcinogens, a dose-response relationship is assumed in thinking about organochlorine toxicity. Sometimes, however, a claim is made that such idiopathic disorders as disseminated sclerosis, leukaemia, polyneuritis, disseminated lupus erythematosus and so on are due to one or other organochlorine compound with which the unfortunate patient has previously come into contact – not to excess, but in small amounts, even transiently. A hypersensitivity reaction is postulated and such a postulate can neither be sustained nor refuted, but until this hypothesis has been checked with more reliable laboratory tests this sort of allegation may be applied to almost anything in the world.

In Great Britain the mean concentration of the three main pesticides BHC, dieldrin and DDT, in the human body has decreased over the last few years with a concurrent decline in the residue levels of the same pesticides in fatty foods consumed. The parallel drop in dieldrin content in home-produced foodstuffs is undoubtedly the result of the recent restrictions imposed on many of the uses of aldrin and dieldrin.(Egan *et al*., 1965, Abbott *et al*., 1968). During 1968 there appears to have been little change in the levels of organochlorine residues in food except for a further satisfactory decline in the background level of dieldrin in fatty foodstuffs. Those foods with very low levels of residues have shown no rise. Such total diet surveys are therefore very informative and very reassuring.

Although the use of pesticides in agriculture has the essential objective of providing man with more food, and thus more available protein, this aim is not always achieved. Consideration of the situation created by the introduction of organomercurials serves as an illustration.

## ORGANOMERCURIALS

The number of organomercury compounds known to be employed in present-day agriculture as fungicides and seed dressings is large. Table 7 lists some representative examples and Tables 8a and 8b show some residue figures.

The biological significance of these residues of organomercurials must be assessed in relation to man's total environmental exposure to mercury.

---

Minute amounts of mercury enter naturally into foods and beverages and are added to mercury residues from organomercurials. Some years ago the average intake of mercury from the diet was estimated to range from 0.00033–0.00083 mg/kg body weight per day (0.02–0.05 mg for a 60 kg man) with little evidence of accumulation in body tissues (FAO/WHO, 1967a).

Residues in eggs are most likely derived from feeding of mercury-dressed grain. Mercury also accumulates in the feathers of birds and these levels can be used to compare environmental loads and to pinpoint periods of excessive mercury contamination (Berg *et al.*, 1966). Recent work has complicated the issues by producing evidence that inorganic mercury can be transformed in nature by micro-organisms into methyl-

Table 7

Classification of organomercury pesticides

| Alkylmercury compounds<br>A1 - Hg - X | Alkoxyalkylmercury compounds<br>$RO(CH_2)_n$ - Hg - X |
|---|---|
| methylmercury acetate<br>methylmercury pentachlorphenate<br>ethylmercury stearate<br>ethylmercury acetone | methoxyethylmercury dicyandiamide<br>ethoxyethylmercury silicate<br>ethoxyethylmercury hydroxide |
| Arylmercury compounds<br>Ar - Hg - X | Others |
| phenylmercury acetate<br>phenylmercury chloride<br>phenylmercury urea<br>tolylmercury chloride | ethylphenethynyl mercury<br>methoxyacetyl mercury chloride<br>hydroxymercurichlorophenol<br>cresol mercury naphthenate |

Table 8a

Mercury content of commercial foods
(From FAO/WHO, 1967 by courtesy of FAO)

| Product | p.p.m. Hg |
|---|---|
| Cereals grown from dressed seed: | |
| wheat | 0.01 |
| barley | 0.008–0.072 |
| Japanese | 0.4 |
| U.K. imported rice | 0.001 |
| Other articles: | |
| apples | 0.03–0.05 |
| pears | 0.14–0.26 |

Table 8b

Mercury content of Scandinavian food products
(From Löfroth, 1968)

| Product (raw) | p.p.m. Hg | | |
| --- | --- | --- | --- |
| | Swedish | Norwegian | Danish |
| Egg | 0.029 (1965) | 0.019 (1964) | 0.007 (1964)* |
| Pork chops | 0.030 | 0.019 | 0.003 |
| Beef | 0.012 | | 0.003 |
| Bacon | 0.018 | | 0.004 |
| Pig's liver | 0.060 | 0.030 | 0.009 |
| Ox liver | 0.016 | | 0.005 |
| Fish | 0.031–1.30 (mean) 5.0 (individual) | | 0.15† |

\* mean of 6 continental countries
† probable 'normal' mercury level in sea fish (FAO/WHO, 1967)

mercury compounds (IUPAC, 1967). There is also some evidence that, at least with organomercurials, bioconversion, e.g. phenyl to methyl compounds, may occur (Anonymous, 1966).

From the toxicological point of view mercury is not known to serve any essential function in man or other living organisms. It is capable of acting as a cumulative poison and of producing symptoms of acute toxicity, depending upon the level in, and the route of entry into the body, and the chemical form in which the element is ingested, injected or inhaled.

In countries where large sections of the population are poor and food is scarce, the consumption of stolen dressed seed grain has caused many hundreds of cases of illness including blindness and paralysis. There were 331 cases of intoxication (with 36 deaths) which occurred in Iraq between 1956 and 1960 after consumption of grain treated with ethylmercury tolylsulphanilide (Berglund, 1967). Cases of permanent neurological damage have been reported in Sweden following ingestion of methyl-mercury-treated grain (Tejning, 1965).

Contrast these dramatic reports with the absence of any reports of chronic mercury intoxication as evidenced by clinical signs and symptoms during many years of proper handling of organomercurials, particularly the aryl derivatives, in various surveys conducted by the Medical Inspectorate of the Department of Employment and Productivity and by other research workers in Britain (Taylor, 1968; Bidstrup, 1968). Nevertheless, the situation is not as simple as it looks. Evidence has come forward from Sweden that the introduction of liquid seed-dressings containing methylmercury dicyandiamide in the 1940s had led to poisoning of seed-eating birds and their predators. By 1964, Swedish eggs contained four times as much mercury, almost all in the form of methylmercury, as the average found in European eggs. After the use of alkylmercury compounds had been banned in Sweden on 1st February, 1966, the mercury content of Swedish eggs gradually decreased as illustrated in Table 9 (Westöö, 1967).

Table 9

Mercury content of Swedish eggs sampled at different periods
(From Westöö, 1967 by courtesy of The Editor, Vår Föda)

| Sample period | Average Hg p.p.m.* |
|---|---|
| March 1964–April 1966 | 0.029 |
| April 1966–November 1966 | 0.019 |
| April 1967–September 1967 | 0.010 |

* of which about 90 per cent is methylmercury

Mercury-containing industrial waste has been shown to be another potent source of accumulation of toxic forms of mercury in protein foods such as fish. The classical incident which focused attention on this problem occurred in Japan, and is known as Minimata disease. Between 1954 and 1960 some 111 persons contracted methylmercury poisoning having lived predominantly on locally caught fish and shellfish; 41 died, the rest showed more or less permanent neurological disabilities. Nineteen cases occurred among children born from mothers who had eaten contaminated fishes. The active agent was identified as methylmercury which had accumulated from dilute material present in seawater and plankton in fishes and shellfish below the outfall point of a chemical plant. Prolonged intakes of methylmercury at levels as low as 2 mg Hg/day were therefore toxic to man (Irukayama, 1966).

Once attention had been drawn to the health hazards arising from industrial discharges containing mercury, Swedish workers scrutinized the mercury content of freshwater fishes caught in inland lakes and along the nearby Baltic coast. Elevated levels ranging from 0.2 to 1 p.p.m. Hg were found in fishes from 1 per cent of the total Swedish catch. The mercury found in all types of fishes was almost to 100 per cent in the form of methylmercury (Westöö and Norén, 1967).

The implications of these discoveries concern particularly that section of the population which relies on fish as the main supply of their dietary protein or which belongs to the high consumption segment for raw and cooked fish. The existing toxicological information does not permit the setting of meaningful maximum permissible limits to the dietary intake of this element. To prevent possible hazards to health every effort should therefore be made to control and reduce this form of contamination of the environment, and consequently of food (FAO/WHO, 1967a). Calculations would permit the provisional establishment of 0.1 mg Hg/day as an acceptable intake for man using a safety factor of 10 (Löfroth, 1968).

On the basis of pharmacological experience, average amounts of fish and shellfish containing 0.2–0.4 mg Hg/kg wet tissue might be consumed daily without serious hazard or fishes containing 1 mg Hg/kg wet tissue might be eaten safely once per week. Such a policy implies severe restriction for an indefinite time on fishing in certain areas, and on consumption of fishes by the high-consumption segment of the population. (Löfroth, 1968).

## VETERINARY PRODUCTS

Time and space prevent discussion of the large group of toxic agents which are used in the veterinary field either for therapeutic, prophylactic or growth stimulating purposes. Their very nature and intended function decrees that these agents should be inimical to biological organisms and in many cases the same residue problems occur as with plant pesticides. These risks have to be balanced once more against the undoubted benefits they confer in animal husbandry and in ensuring large increases in available animal food, the principal source of first class protein.

Many of these substances leave small but detectable residues in the meat, eggs and milk which reach the consumer. Various control schemes or direct legislative measures ensure that these residues are kept to that toxicologically safe minimum amount which would cause no harm if consumed throughout man's life span. There is a further safety factor in so far as the large variety of substances available ensures a consequently smaller chance of accumulating the same residue; and better control can be exercised over the intake of toxic agents by individual animals than is possible in the large scale treatment of vegetable and fruit crops. The same considerations *qua* the use of animal protein foods containing residues of veterinary substances apply that have been discussed in relation to pesticide residues in plant crops.

## IRRADIATION OF FOOD

Too little is known as yet about the usefulness and risks of irradiation of food for preservation purposes to be able to give an opinion, although this technological development may well become an acceptable alternative to the use of pesticides in the future.

Despite the phenomenal advances in science and technology our world has not yet succeeded in providing adequate, wholesome food for every one of its inhabitants. As methods of food production, preservation and distribution improve so do we find a parallel rise in the contamination of our total environment, and with it of our food, by an ever increasing number of active substances. Constant vigilance will have to be exercised to ensure that toxic agents do not reach levels in our diet at which their biological activities nullify the advantages of the greater provision of foodstuffs and better nutrition of the people, despite the knowledge that our bodies are endowed with tremendous capabilities for coping with most of the deleterious substances to which we are exposed in our food.

## REFERENCES

Abbott, D.C., Goulding, R. and Tatton, J. O'G. (1968). *Br. med. J.* **3**, 146
Anonymous, (1965). *Lancet,* **i**, 593
   –  (1966a). National Academy of Sciences–NRC. *Toxicants occurring naturally in Foods,* Public. 1354
   –  (1966b). Symposium on Mercury. *Royal Comm. Nat. Res. Swed.,* Stockholm, 24.1.1966
   –  (1967). Ministry of Agriculture, Fisheries and Food. *Tech. Rep. FRL* 1
   –  (1968). *Lancet.* 1071
   –  (1969). *Bibra Bull.,* February, in press
Avison, R.N. and Feudale, E.L. (1967). *Nature, London.* **214**, 1254
Barnes, J.M. (1967). *Br. Fd. J.* May/June, 71
Berg, W., Johnels, A., Sjöstrand, B. and Westermark, T. (1966). *Oikos* **17**, 71
Berglund, F. (1967). *Särtr. ur Läkart.* **64**, 3531
Bidstrup, L.P. (1968). Private communication
Blackwell, B. (1963). *Lancet,* **ii**, 849
British Nutrition Foundation (1968). *Inf. Bull.,* No. 1, 24
Campbell, J.A. and Morrison, A.B. (1966). *Fedn. Proc. Fedn. Am. Socs exp. Biol.* **25** (1), 130
Duggan, R.E. and Weatherwax J.R. (1967). *Science,* **157**, 1006
Dungal, N. (1961). *J. Am. med. Ass.* **178**, 789

Druckrey, H., Preussmann, R., Ivankovic, S. and Schmahl, D. (1967). *Z. Krebsforsch.* **69**, 193

Egan, H., Goulding, R., Roburn, J. and Tatton, J. O'G. (1965). *Br. Med. J.* **ii**, 66

Ender, F., Havre, G., Helgebostad, A., Koppang, N., Madsen, R. and Ceh. L. (1964). *Naturwissenschaften*, **51**, 637

FAO/WHO (1962). *Tech. Rep. Ser. Wld Hlth Org.* No. 238

– (1965). *Report No.* PL/1965/10/2

– (1967). *Report No.* WHO/Food Add./68.30

– (1967a). *Tech. Rep. Ser. Wld Hlth Org.* No. 373

Foy, J.M. and Parratt, J.R. (1962). *Lancet*, **i**, 942

Frazer, A.C. (1968). *Brit. Nutr. Found. Inform. Bull.*, No. 2, 21

Hadjimarkos, D.M. (1965). *Lancet* **i**, 605

Halstead, B.W. (1965, 1967, 1968). *Poisonous and Venomous Marine Animals of the World*, U.S. Government Printing Office, Washington

Irukayama, K. (1966). *Third Int. Conf. Water Poll. Res.* **3**, 153

IUPAC (1967). Proc. of the Committee on Pesticide Residue Analysis

Krakoff, I. (1961). *Clin. Pharmacol. and Ther.* **2**, 599

Lehman, A.J. (1965). *Assoc. F. & D.O. of U.S.*, 115

Levine, B.B. (1966). *New Engl. J. Med.*, **275**, 1115

Lindgren, D.L., Sinclair, W.B. and Vincent, L.E. (1968). *Residue Rev.* **21**, 1

Lijinsky, W. and Shubik, P. (1964). *Science, N.Y.* **145**, 53

Löfroth, G. (1968). *Unpub. rep. on methylmercury to WHO,* 10

Magee, P. and Barnes, J.M. (1967). *Adv. Cancer Res.* **10**, 163

Marquardt, P. (1967). *Symp. Gesell, Ernährungs.*, Bonn 9.5.1967

Mickelsen, O. and Yang, M.G. (1966). *Fedn. Proc. Fedn. Am. Socs. exp. Biol.* **25**(1) 104

Misani, F. and Reiner, L. (1950). *Archs. Biochem. Biophys.* **27**, 234

Monier-Williams, G.W. (1949). *Trace Elements in Food,* London; Chapman & Hall

Popov, V.I. (1964). *Gig. Sanit.* **29**, No. 3, 32

Robinson, T., Coulson, J.C., Crabtree, A.N., Potts, G.R. and Richardson, A. (1967). *Nature, Lond.*, **214**, 1307

Siegel, B. B. (1959). *Bull. Wld Hlth Org.* **21**, 703

Stock, A. (1940). *Biochem. Z.* **304**, 73

Taylor, W. (1968). Private communication

Tejning, S. (1965). In: *National Mercury Conference,* 8.9.1965, Sweden, 80

Terracini, B., Magee, P. N. and Barnes, J. M. (1967). *Brit. J. Cancer,* **21**, 559

Wagner, J. R. and Elvehjem, C. A. (1944). *J. Nutr.* **23**, 431

Westöö, G. (1967). *Var Föda* **19**, 121

Westöö, F. and Noren K. (1967). *Var Föda* **19**, 135

Wogan, G.N. (1966). *Fedn. Proc. Fedn. Am. Socs. exp. Biol.* **25**(1), 124

# MICROBIAL SPOILAGE OF PROTEINACEOUS FOODS

## D.A.A. MOSSEL

*Central Institute for Nutrition and
Food Research TNO, Zeist, The Netherlands
and the Catholic University, Louvain, Belgium*

## INTRODUCTION

There are at least two important reasons why the prevention of microbial deterioration of proteinaceous foods merits our full attention. Firstly, the alarming shortage of protein in the world makes any loss of protein by microbial spoilage virtually irreparable. In addition, microbial proliferation in proteinaceous foods or isolated proteins may lead to the formation of harmful products, i.e. commodities containing dangerous levels of enteropathogenic organisms, or clinically active concentrations of orally toxic microbial metabolites. Such foods, as a rule not spoiled, are hence consumed, particularly in regions where malnutrition prevails and where they may do most harm.

In this paper we shall first of all review the underlying mechanisms of both types of deterioration. Based on these fundamental data we shall then outline potentially effective ways of avoiding such losses of food protein.

## SPOILAGE OF PROTEINACEOUS FOODS

It has been well established that the microbial spoilage of foods is a rather specific phenomenon. Different foods show very divergent spoilage microfloras; while fresh meats tend to slime formation, fish spoils by the accumulation of low molecular nitrogenous metabolites, whereas fruit juices tend to fermentation and rolled oats to growing mould. Such specific microfloras are called spoilage associations (Westerdijk, 1949); their genesis has become better understood during the last twenty years (Mossel and Westerdijk, 1949; Mossel and Ingram, 1955; Mossel, 1969). It has become clear that they are determined by three groups of ecological parameters, namely:

*(i)* intrinsic factors, such as nutrient composition of a food, the occurrence of antimicrobial factors, its pH and redox potential and its so-called water activity (Scott, 1957);

*(ii)* extrinsic factors, particularly temperature of storage normally applied to the food and the gaseous atmosphere in which it is conventionally stored or transported, as determined by $pO_2$, $pCO_2$ and relative humidity;

*(iii)* so-called implicit factors, i.e. synergism or antagonism between components of the primary microflora, as resulting from the selective effects of the parameters mentioned under *(i)* and *(ii)*.

Most fresh proteinaceous foods are very moist, i.e. show water activity ($a_w$) values of about 0.97 or more, and are nearly neutral. Because of their susceptibility to microbial spoilage they are usually stored at reduced temperatures. These ecological circumstances lead to the development of a very specific, obviously psychrotrophic microflora, consisting of non-fermentative Gram-negative rod shaped bacteria of the groups, at present taxonomically indicated as the *Pseudomonas/Acinetobacter/Alcaligenes*-group (Shewan, *et al.*, 1960; Thornley, 1960; Thornley, 1967).

*In vitro* it has been demonstrated repeatedly that fresh blood and tissues possess antimicrobial activity against various types of bacteria (Jensen, 1954; Leistner, 1956; Muschel, 1960; Davis and Wedgwood, 1965; Cybulska and Jeljaszewicz, 1966; Joos and Hall, 1968, 1968a). Nevertheless, muscle foods do not appear to contain levels of such natural inhibitors that are of practical significance. The same holds true for most natural sources of vegetable proteins. Only proteinaceous foods of animal secretory origin contain natural antimicrobial factors of any significance. Fresh milk is protected by the lactenins (Auclair, 1964; Randolph and Gould, 1968) and a few other factors (Reiter and Oram, 1967; Ashton and Busta, 1968), while eggs, in addition to mechanical defence mechanisms, possess proteins with antimicrobial properties in the white, particularly Fleming's (1922) lysozyme (Martin, 1963; Roeder and Witzenhausen, 1967), conalbumin (Schade and Caroline, 1944; Williams, 1962) and a few, less well identified factors (Board, 1968). However, the practical importance of these factors should not be overrated. Milk is almost totally pasteurized these days, to protect consumers against overt infectious risks; and the lactenins being rather thermostable, this eliminates virtually all of them from liquid milk as marketed today. Egg white as such is only a commodity of very limited importance; and egg yolk, with which it is mostly mixed, seems to neutralize most of the antimicrobial defence of the white (Board, 1968).

Table 1

*In vitro* destruction of bacteria by fresh hog's blood

(After Jensen, 1954)

| Type of bacterium | Viable count per 1 ml *after exposure to sterile blood at 37°C for* | | | |
|---|---|---|---|---|
| | 0 min | 5 min | 90 min | 240 min |
| E. coli | $0.2 \times 10^6$ | $0.9 \times 10^5$ | $0.3 \times 10^5$ | $0.6 \times 10^3$ |
| Achromobacter | $0.1 \times 10^6$ | $0.2 \times 10^5$ | $<10$ | $<10$ |
| Pseudomonas 1 | $0.1 \times 10^6$ | $0.2 \times 10^5$ | $<10$ | $<10$ |
| Pseudomonas 2 | $0.1 \times 10^6$ | $0.2 \times 10^5$ | $0.4 \times 10^2$ | $<10$ |
| Gram-positive non-sporing rod | $0.2 \times 10^5$ | $0.9 \times 10^3$ | $0.6 \times 10^2$ | $0.8 \times 10^2$ |

Hence, the typical spoilage association of the proteinaceous foods normally develops virtually uninhibited. This does not invariably, or even mostly, lead to proteolysis. In the case of meats, poultry and fish, the typical primary spoilage phenomenon is the formation of a slimy mass of bacterial cells (Haines, 1933; Ingram, 1949; Shewan *et al.*, 1960a; Ayres, 1960a; Ayres, 1960b). Only when microbial growth is allowed to proceed beyond this stage, and/or at slightly higher temperatures, dissimilation of food protein occurs, and this then leads to deamination and desulphydration reactions, resulting in putrefaction (Lerke *et al.*, 1965, 1967).

When proteinaceous foods are not stored as such, but rather to increase their keeping quality after modification, their spoilage microflora changes accordingly. Partial drying, salting (Del Valle and Nickerson, 1968) or curing results in a less $a_w$-sensitive association of *Micrococcaceae,* certain *Lactobacillaceae,* streptococci of Lancefield's group D, moulds and certain yeasts. When the pH of proteinaceous foods is reduced by the addition of vinegar or by fermentation, an association of acid-tolerant organisms such as *Lactobacillaceae,* yeasts and moulds invariably comes to the fore (Pederson, 1960; Holtzapffel and Mossel, 1968).

## LOSS OF WHOLESOMENESS

Historically three types of loss of wholesomeness of proteinaceous foods have to be distinguished. The first and second are rather non-specific: contamination with enteropathogenic organisms and the formation of orally active toxins of microbial origin. The third is very characteristic of proteinaceous foods: diseases contracted by the absorption of more or less toxic microbial metabolites of proteins.

91

*Gastroenteric disorders conveyed by proteinaceous foods*

Swine, calves and poultry, and to a lesser extent cows carry *Salmonellae* in their large intestine, without showing any signs of disease. It is, therefore, logical that freshly slaughtered meats of these animals may harbour these bacteria to an extent dependent on the sanitary conditions prevailing during the holding of such animals before slaughter and in the slaughter houses (Edwards and Galton, 1967). Hence the consumption of fresh as well as processed meats is fraught with the risk of salmonellosis, as the morbidity reports in virtually all countries clearly show. In addition, fish may carry *Salmonellae,* stemming from the fish market or auctions in the case of sea fish and from the animals themselves as far as brackish water fish are concerned (Ruys, 1948; Steiniger, 1951; Floyd and Jones, 1954; Gulasekharam *et al.,* 1956; Jadin *et al.,* 1957). Finally, the aetiological role of shellfish in the spread of enteric diseases is well known (Sherwood and Thomson, 1953; Kelly and Arcisz, 1954; Buttiaux *et al.,* 1955; Baird, 1961; Preston, 1968; Slanetz *et al.,* 1968).

Slaughter animals and fish do not, as a rule, carry *Shigellae.* Yet proteinaceous foods are such excellent media for the proliferation of these bacteria, that, where they become contaminated by a human carrier or from an insanitary environment, they will lead to disease outbreaks. Milk particularly is often involved in shigellosis.

Epidemiologists have long been familiar with food 'poisoning' outbreaks due to at least two types of *Bacillaceae,* the anaerobic type *Clostridium perfringens* and the facultatively anaerobic *B. cereus.* It has been demonstrated recently (Hauschild, 1968; Nikodemuss, 1966) that these diseases are, in fact, infectious enteritis, caused by the absorption with food of large numbers of viable cells — as is also the case in salmonellosis and shigellosis. Enteritis caused by *B. cereus* is mostly transmitted by dairy foods, such as pudding and pastry (Hauge, 1955). *Cl. perfringens* enteritis is, almost invariably, caused by the consumption of severely contaminated cooked meat and poultry (Hobbs and Sutton, 1968; Hauschild, 1968).

Recently it has been established that a mild form of enteritis, observed in the hot season in Japan after the consumption of certain types of fresh fish, is due to the development in the fishes concerned of a halotolerant type of vibrio, called *V. parahaemolyticus* (Sakasaki *et al.,* 1963; Zen-Yoji *et al.,* 1965; Aoki, Hsu and Chun, 1967; Sakazaki *et al.,* 1967). This bacterium has also been detected in seawater and fish in Northern Germany (Nakanishi *et al.,* 1968) and the Americas (Ward, 1968; Baross and Liston, 1968). Fortunately, we have found that the organism is not psychrotrophic so that chilled fish will be no cause of concern. Since these vibrios show no particular thermal resistance, the risk that this type of vibriosis is caused by processed fisheries' products is limited to severe underprocessing or recontamination; but the risks are very much lower here than in salmonellosis, because of the less general spread in the raw materials concerned and the handicap in competition due to the vibrios' requirement for at least *c*. 0.5 per cent of NaCl.

Food-borne viral hepatitis has remained a sort of an epidemiological enigma, because of its long incubation time and lack of methods for the isolation of the aetiological virus. Nevertheless, the role of the consumption of shellfish in this disease seems clear (Roos, 1956; Mason and McLean, 1962; Koff *et al.*, 1967). In addition, foods less rich in protein, such as meat and potato salads may transmit the disease, when exposed to faecal contamination in the course of their preparation. Finally, there is evidence that 'viral dysentery' or winter vomiting disease is indeed spread by a virus probably occurring in food (Reimann, 1963).

The helminthological risks involved in the consumption of uncooked, or undercooked, meats are well known (Morgan, 1968). Where raw fish is consumed on a large scale, another parasitological risk of enteric disease is imminent. Herring frequently contains large numbers of a nematode worm *Anisakis marina*. It has been demonstrated that repeated exposure of the same, relatively limited, area of the human intestinal lining to larvae of this nematode may lead to an allergic reaction, manifesting itself as an eosinophilic ulcer, requiring surgery to relieve the patient (van Thiel *et al.*, 1960; van Thiel, 1966). Consumption of herring that has not been properly cured or frozen (van Mameren *et al.*, 1969) has, therefore, to be discouraged.

### Food intoxications of microbial origin

Botulism remains the most grave example of this type of disease, not because of its incidence, but since it shows an unusually high mortality for food-borne diseases – i.e. of the order of 50 per cent (Lewis and Cassel, 1964; Ingram and Roberts, 1967). At least four types of *Cl. botulinum* are known at present, that biosynthesize the deadly neurotoxins; two of them are psychrotrophic, namely, the non-proteolytic B type (Eklund *et al.*, 1967) and the type E (Dolman *et al.*, 1950; Dolman *et al.*, 1960; Schmidt *et al.*, 1961), which further complicates the picture. Underprocessed canned or otherwise manufactured meat and fish products are the main vectors. Hence, the protein food industry has very valid reasons for a constant alert in this respect.

Paralytic shellfish poisoning is another toxic disease of high mortality transmitted by foods. The disease is caused by the consumption of certain molluscs and other shellfish, that, in turn, have ingested toxic dinoflagellates, mainly of the genus *Gonyaulax*. Paralytic shellfish poisoning has been mainly observed in the Americas (Russell, 1968). However, Europe is not at all free from this risk, as clinical data from Norway (Oftebro, 1965) and Great Britain (McCollum *et al.,* 1968) show, and neither is Australia (Tonge *et al.,* 1967).

Far less serious, but yet quite vexing, is the disease called staphyloenterotoxicosis. It is caused by the absorption of one of at least five different, so-called enterotoxins biosynthesized by strains of *Staph. aureus* (Casman *et al.,* 1967). Since, roughly one third of all strains of *Staph. aureus* examined has been found to be enterotoxinogenic, and some other types of *Staphylococcus* also seem to be capable of forming such toxins (Bergdoll *et al.,* 1967; Hall, 1968), it is clear that the risks in this area are considerable. Foods mostly involved in enterotoxicosis are cream pastry, hams and ice cream—thus, this seems to be another risk area for proteinaceous foods.

Whereas all the toxins just reviewed lead to an acute type of disease, a chronic form of food-borne intoxication has also been recognized since almost a decennium. The factors involved are metabolites of moulds of common occurrence on foods and hence called mycotoxins (Wilson, 1968). Aflatoxin, produced by *Aspergillus flavus* has become the type toxin of this group, although more than 10 years earlier mycotoxins formed by various species of the genus *Fusarium* had been identified as the cause of the dreadful endemic of the syndrome called alimentary toxic aleukia (Joffe, 1963). In Table 2 a summary of the mycotoxins known at present is displayed. Of the majority of factors listed, the

Table 2

Mycotoxinogenic moulds

| Species | Clinical effect | Susceptible species |
|---|---|---|
| Group 1, Producers of well-defined mycotoxins | | |
| *Alternaria tenuis* | ATA | man |
| *A.* sp. | haemorrhages | mouse |
| *Aspergillus amstelodami* | emaciation | poultry |
| *Asp. candidus* | cf. *Pen. citrinum* | |
| *Asp. clavatus* | haemorrhages | poultry |
| *Asp. flavus* | hepatic carcinoma | poultry, man |
| | tremors | mouse |
| | haemorrhages | swine |
| *Asp. fumigatus* | perirenal oedema | swine |
| *Asp. glaucus* | haemorrhages and | |
| | diarrhoea | poultry |
| *Asp. niger* | cf. *Asp. flavus* | |
| *Asp. ochraceus* | hepatic injury | poultry |
| | | rat |

Table 2—*continued*
Mycotoxinogenic moulds

| Species | Clinical effect | Susceptible species |
|---------|-----------------|---------------------|
| Group 1, Producers of well-defined mycotoxins | | |
| *Asp. oryzae* | hepatic necrosis | various |
| *Asp. ostianus* | cf. *Asp. ochraceus* | |
| *Asp. parasiticus* | cf. *Asp. flavus* | |
| *Asp. ruber* | cf. *Asp. flavus* | |
| *Asp. terreus* | cf. *Pen. citrinum* | |
| *Asp. wentii* | emaciation | poultry |
| *Chaetomium globosum* | haemorrhages and paralysis | rat |
| *Cladosporium epiphyllum* | ATA | man |
| *Fusarium culmorum* | anorexia | bovine |
| *Fus. nivale* | emaciation and gangrene | bovine |
| *Fus. roseum (*Syn. *Gibberella saubinetti)* | hepatic necrosis | swine |
| *Fus. sporotrichioides* | ATA | man |
| *Gibberella zeae* | oestromimetic response | swine |
| *Mucor hiemalis* | ATA | man |
| *Penicillium brevicompactum* | ATA | man |
| *Pen. citreoviride* | ascending paralyses | various |
| *Pen. citrinum* | haemorrhages and renal damage | poultry mouse |
| *Pen. cyclopium* | tremors | mouse |
| *Pen. islandicum* | hepatic atrophia cirrhosis | various |
| *Pen. puberulum* | cf. *Asp. flavus* | |
| *Pen. rubrum* | haemorrhages and hepatic injury | swine |
| *Pen. rugulosum* | cf. *Pen. citrinum* | |
| *Pen. tardum* | cf. *Pen. citrinum* | |
| *Pen. variabile* | cf. *Asp. flavus* | |
| *Pen. viridicatum* | renal damage | swine, rat |
| *Pen.* sp. | cf. *Asp. ochraceus* | |
| *Pithomyces chartarum* | angiocholecystitis facial oedema | sheep bovine |
| *Rhizopus* sp. | cf. *Asp. flavus* | |
| *Stachyobotrys atra* | haemorrhages | horse |

Group 2. Producers of less well-defined orally active toxins

*Asp. avenaceus, carneus, chevalieri, nidulans* and *niveus*
*Cladosporium fragi*
*Fusarium moniliforme*
*Paecilomyces varioti* (Syn. *Byssochlamys fulva)*
*Pen. oxalicum, piceum, purpurogenum, urticae*
*Trichoderma lignorum*

pathogenicity for the human consumer is unknown as yet. However, the occurrence of significant levels of not one of these metabolites can be allowed in the human diet, because such a tolerance would, logically, lead to having to accept also those synthetic food additives, that have so far been rigorously banned from the human diet, because of – often only minor – untoward effects noticed in experimental animals. Moulds flourish particularly in the drier types of foods, where competition by bacteria has been eliminated (Mossel, 1969). Hence products such as proteinaceous press cakes are particularly at risk; moulds do not seem to prefer particular precursors for the formation of mycotoxins, since copious formation of, e.g. the N-free aflatoxin has been observed on casein (Lie and Marth, 1968) and fish meal (Love, 1968).

## Nitrogenous bacterial toxins of uncertain oral pathogenicity

In 1830 an Editorial in *The Lancet* (Anonymous, 1830) reported an outbreak of food poisoning that had recently occurred in France, caused by ingestion of a meat pie. The Editor said that those phenomena were frequently observed after the consumption of proteinaceous foods, such as sausage, bacon, ham or cheese. He explained how difficult it often is to differentiate these syndromes – which he attributed to intrinsic toxic properties of such foods – from cases where chemical poisons had been deliberately added to foods with criminal purposes. It is somewhat horrifying to see the Editor remarking subsequently that it was most fortunate for pastry bakers that toxicologists were, at that time, able to disprove claims often made by coroners in such cases with regard to assassination. It was exactly this type of humanitarian motivation that led Selmi somewhat later (1872) to study the properties of the intrinsic poisonous compounds of proteinaceous foods, his reasoning being that the direct detection of such toxins would more readily provide the proof required to prevent the beheading of innocent cooks, etc. These investigations resulted in two monographs (1878 and 1879) on toxic factors which Selmi thought were the reaction products of postmortem autolytic processes and hence named 'ptomaines'. A few years later Brieger (1885a, 1885b and 1886) demonstrated that such compounds are, in fact, formed by the action of proteolytic bacteria on precursors occurring in meat, fish, cheese and bakers' yeast. One of his further achievements was the isolation of cadaverine from proteolysed lysine containing proteins. Again somewhat later Berthelot and Bertrand (1912) identified another ptomaine as histamine, and demonstrated that it was formed by intestinal bacteria from histidine-containing proteins.

The entire concept of ptomaines has always been frowned upon by the majority of British and American pathologists, simply because none of these ptomaines seemed to lead to any untoward effects, when administered orally to man or experimental animals. In addition Dolman (1943) and Dack (1947) have rightly observed that in many of the earlier clinical reports on ptomaine poisoning, the syndromes described were very similar to those of staphyloenterotoxicosis, which was only recognized as a pathological entity after Denys' first observations in 1894, but particularly since those of Barber in 1914. Likewise, observations first made by Jansen and den Dooren de Jong (1930) and later by many others, as reviewed by Taylor and Bettelheim (1966), suggest that some of the alleged ptomaine food poisoning episodes may have been caused by certain serotypes of *E. coli,* while Hobbs *et al.* (1962) have suggested that enteritis due to *Cl. perfringens* might have mimicked some others.

However, there is no doubt among pathologists that a well delineated type of food poisoning, caused by the consumption of foods containing histamine, definitely exists (Legroux and Levaditi, 1947; van Veen and Latuasan, 1950; Boyer *et al.,* 1956; Peeters, 1963; Ramel *et al.,* 1965). Moreover, exactly how histamine exerts its toxic action has also become clear recently. Normally food-borne histamine is deaminated by mono

Table 3

Amino acid decarboxylation potentialities encountered among
bacteria

(After Mossel, 1968)

| Parent amino acid | Enzyme producing organisms |
|---|---|
| Histidine | *Betabact. breve, buchneri, fermenti* |
| | *Brevibact. linens* |
| | *Clost. perfringens* |
| | *Ent. aerogenes* |
| | *Esch. coli* |
| | *Prot. morganii* |
| | *Pseud. reptilivora* |
| | *Ristella* sp. |
| | *Salmonella* sp. |
| | *Shigella* sp. |
| Tyrosine | *Betabact.* sp. |
| | *Brevibact. linens* |
| | *Clost. aerofoetidum, sporogenes* |
| | *Esch. coli* |
| | *Prot. mirabilis* |
| | *Pseud. reptilivora* |
| | *Str. durans, faecalis, faecium* |
| Phenylalanine | *Pseud. reptilivora* |
| | *Str. faecalis* |
| Various other amino acids | *Betabact.* sp. |
| | *Lactob. casei, plantarum* |

amine oxidases occurring in the intestinal system; only when this detoxification mechanism breaks down as a result of therapy by drugs, which as
a side-effect inhibit the action of these enzymes (Blackwell and Mabbitt,
1965), or of slight dysfunctioning of the large intestine (Geiger, 1955;
Weigers and van de Kamer, 1965; Avery *et al.*, 1968) this amine may be
absorbed to such an extent that the corresponding type of pharmaco-
dynamic effect occurs. A similar mechanism has been demonstrated for
tyramine (Asatoor *et al.*, 1963; Blackwell and Mabitt, 1965) and
phenylethylamine (Bachrach *et al.*, 1960). Therefore, bacteria that
decarboxylate amino acids definitely merit the attention of food
bacteriologists; a summary of a few of such organisms is presented in
Table 3 (Mossel, 1968). This newly acquired insight should not, however,
lead to overrating the role of bacteria decarboxylating amino acids in
food-borne disease outbreaks. The amines formed in such reactions when
escaping intraenteric inactivation, lead to a very specific 'pressor amine'
type of disease and not to vomiting, enteric spasms and diarrhoea, with
which they have been so often aetiologically connected.

On the other hand, evidence has recently been obtained (Tansy and
Venturella, 1967) that for example, Lancefield group D streptococci
form, in addition to certain pressor amines, factors that irritate the
intestinal lining. Careful studies of this type might perhaps lead to the
elucidation of the aetiological role of these, and some other bacteria, in
food-borne disease, a subject that has been very much disputed ever since
the end of the last century.

## PRINCIPLES OF THE CONTROL OF MICROBIAL
## DETERIORATION OF FOOD PROTEINS

The prevention of food spoilage and of food-borne disease is generally
regarded as based on the same common action, namely, avoiding
microbial proliferation in foods. However, a few exceptions to this rule
should not be overlooked. Some forms of food-borne bacterial enteritis
such as cholera, typhoid, paratyphoid fever and the Flexner and similar
types of dysentery may be brought about by the absorption of very
few — if not one single — cells of the causal pathogenic organisms. The
same holds true for food-borne hepatitis and helminthic infections. In
addition, paralytic shellfish poisoning results from the absorption of
foods in which no microbial proliferation need have occurred. Although
the listed diseases are only minor causes of food-borne disease as far as
morbidity is concerned, they are yet by far the most severe ones. Hence
this evidence demonstrates that, although prevention of microbial
growth in foods is required for maintaining food wholesomeness, it is

not sufficient. Constant attention should, in addition, always be paid to measures leading to the prevention of contamination of initially wholesome foods, or the use of commodities already contaminated at an earlier stage of harvest or production.

Table 4

Influence of $a_w$-values on the microbial spoilage of foods

| $a_w$-range | Organisms inhibited by the lower value | Examples of foods having this lower $a_w$-value |
| --- | --- | --- |
| 1.00-0.95 | Gram-negative rods; Spores of *Bacillaceae* | Foods containing c. 40 wt.% sucrose or c. 7 wt.% NaCl |
| | | Bread crumb |
| | | Some types of cooked sausage |
| 0.95-0.91 | Most cocci, lactobacilli and vegetative cells of *Bacillaceae* | Foods containing c. 55 wt.% sucrose or c. 12 wt.% NaCl |
| | | Raw ham |
| 0.91-0.88 | Most yeasts | Foods containing c. 65 wt.% sucrose or 15 wt.% NaCl |
| | | Salami |
| | | Fishmeal with c. 10% moisture |
| 0.88-0.80 | Most moulds; *Staph. aureus* | Flour, rice, pulses, etc. with c. 17% moisture |
| | | Fruit cake |
| | | Dry sausage |
| 0.80-0.75 | Most halophilic bacteria | Foods containing c. 26 wt.% NaCl |
| | | Most jams and fondant creams |
| 0.75-0.65 | Xerophilic moulds | Marzipan, marshmallow |
| | | Fishmeal with c. 5% moisture |
| 0.65-0.60 | Osmophilic yeasts | Liquorice, gums |
| | | Medium salted cod with c. 12% moisture |
| < 0.60 | All micro-organisms | Toffees, boiled sweets |
| | | Raisins |

99

The most effective and simple — though not the most frequently used — mode of preservation of proteinaceous foods is reducing their water activity. As is shown in Table 4, drying to a final $a_w$ of approximately 0.60 will guarantee unlimited keeping quality in the microbiological sense of the term. Where foods are 'machine dried', ultimate $a_w$ values attained are much lower and no problems of this sort exist. However, frequently staple foods are either 'sun-dried' or their water activity is reduced by the addition of salt; and these modes of preservation do present microbiological problems. Although proteolytic spoilage is prevented by drying or salting to $a_w = c.$ 0.95, as we have seen before, in this instance other organisms, particularly *Micrococcaceae*, become predominant in the spoilage association, which will eventually lead to souring and or lipolytic rancidity of the fat fraction of the commodity concerned. Sun-drying appears often to lead to a sufficiently low overall $a_w$ value, but may leave moist 'pockets'. These have water activity values that are inhibitory to most bacteria, or at least reduce their development considerably, whereas moulds may still proliferate relatively rapidly. This, clearly is the area of risk for foods becoming contaminated with mycotoxins; and since most mycotoxins are very heat-stable it is difficult to free proteinaceous raw materials, once having become mouldy, from this toxicity.

It may be of interest to emphasize, that dried foods, although mostly quite inhibitory to bacteria, are not at all necessarily free from enteropathogenic organisms, however low their $a_w$-tolerance may be. Practice has shown that dried, protein-rich products of animal origin, such as meat and bone meal and fish meal, but also vegetable meals, e.g. cottonseed presscake meal, sunflower meal, etc. frequently contain *Salmonellae*. It has been demonstrated that this originates from post-drying recontamination of initially pathogen free meals by a severely contaminated environment (Mossel, 1965; Clise and Swecker, 1965; Magwood *et al.*, 1965; Loken *et al.*, 1968). Adequate sanitation of drying plants may, therefore, be expected, and has in practice been demonstrated, to be effective in controlling this type of contamination. Where wholesome food proteins or protein concentrates have to be manufactured, attention has therefore to be paid to sanitary practices in processes such as drying, mixing and packaging. This is particularly urgent in the manufacture of dried weaning foods in developing areas.

Because conventional drying leads to some impairment of the organoleptic properties of foods so treated, while improved methods of dehydration are often too expensive, proteinaceous foods have mostly been preserved by canning. Most meat and fish products are heat-preserved after curing or brining; this eliminates the need for the very intensive degree of heating aiming at 'total' destruction of spores of *Cl. botulinum*, since the water activity of these commodities is such that it will discourage outgrowth of the spores of these bacteria, particularly when already impaired by heat (Roberts and Ingram 1966; Baird-Parker and Freame, 1967; Blanche Koelensmid and van Rhee, 1968; Duncan and Foster, 1968; Perigo and Roberts, 1968; Pivnick and Thatcher, 1968). Heating in pouches made of heat-resistant plastic materials is a possibility that has come to the fore rather recently (Pflug *et al.*, 1963; Heiss and Becker, 1966) and needs careful attention where cost and/or convenience are factors to be taken into account.

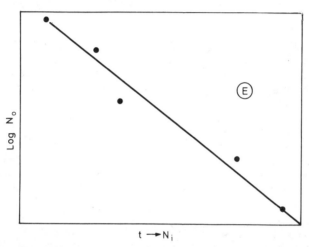

*Figure 1. Time to spoilage* $t \rightarrow N_i$ *as a function of initial contamination with the spoilage association* $(N_0)$ *at given external conditions* (E)

Refrigerated storage of proteinaceous foods is very frequently used. It has its severe shortcomings, as is well known. Even when handled in a rather sanitary way, fish will only keep at *c.* 3°C for some days, and at higher temperatures not much more than one day (Pelroy and Seman, 1968). This is due to predominance in fish market auctions and plants of the psychrotrophic slime forming association dealt with earlier. Poultry is somewhat more stable, because it is easier here to keep the initial counts of the spoilage association low and thereby reduce the time to spoilage; *see Figure 1.* Red meats can be finished with again lower initial counts of spoiling bacteria and can, hence be kept for periods as long as 14 days. When, in addition, the gaseous atmosphere and the relative humidity during storage are carefully controlled, keeping for a month or so becomes a possibility (Ingram, 1949). For developing areas, refrigerated storage has the additional shortcoming that the continuous cold chain, required for successful preservation is difficult or even impossible to maintain; hence our stressing of the importance of drying as a means of preservation of protein in those areas. Turning again to technologically more advanced areas, refrigerated storage is most effective in the preservation of cured products, and particularly of heat-treated commodities such as sausages. If post-process recontamination of such goods is avoided so that they are virtually free from all non-sporing bacteria, including Lancefield Group D streptococci, their microflora consists of spores of *Bacillaceae* only and they will hence keep indefinitely at temperatures below 7 °C (Haines, 1934; Mol, 1957; Wolf and Mahmoud, 1957; Zeller, 1963) provided no psychrotrophic mutants belong to the local biosphere (Larkin and Stokes, 1967 and 1968). Where refrigerated storage is for some reason or another lacking sufficient efficacy, freezing to temperatures of $c.-20$ °C will always confer the required keeping quality. However, this system of preservation has shortcomings similar to refrigeration in developing areas, although the use of liquid nitrogen may have unique possibilities (Holdsworth, 1967).

All other modes of preservation of proteinaceous foods also show severe shortcomings. Fermentation has been tried on a limited scale (van Veen, 1953; Saisithi *et al.,* 1966; Orillo and Pederson, 1968; Burkholder *et al.,* 1968); but, unless the processes are accurately controlled and the products obtained are subsequently packed in hermetically sealed containers and given a pasteurization heat treatment, the resulting commodities have only limited stability due to the development of yeasts, moulds and *Lactobacillaceae* (Pederson, 1960; Gehring, 1965) and to a lesser extent clostridia that dissimilate lactic acid (Bergère *et al.,* 1968). Similar spoilage problems menace vinegar-preserved proteinaceous foods: unless heat-treated after hermetic packaging these may spoil due to the development of micro-organisms that attack acetic acid (Dakin and Stolk, 1968), or at least tolerate it (Erichsen, 1967; Holtzapffel and Mossel, 1968). Preservation by the addition of chemical preservatives and antibiotics has its obvious toxicological and microbiological shortcomings (Mossel and Eijgelaar, 1956). In addition, chemically preserved foods tend to be attacked by associations that are resistant to the factors applied for stabilization, since most of the pharmacologically acceptable antimicrobials have a rather limited spectrum of activity. Finally, irradiation has been evaluated as a tool for preservation of proteinaceous foods. The doses required for straightforward sterilization are such, that, for various reasons, additional processing techniques have to be used, which makes the process intricate, expensive or both (Mehrlich, 1966; Spiher, 1968). Irradiation at low doses, i.e. the order 0.1–0.3 Mrad, may be helpful in prolonging the refrigerated shelf life of fish (Slavin *et al.*, 1966) and meat; but careful temperature control has to be exerted, particularly in the case of fish, to avoid the development of the psychro-trophic *Clostridium botulinum* types, that are presented a unique chance of virtually exclusive development on such commodities (Schmidt *et al.*, 1961, 1962; Ajmal, 1968).

REFERENCES

Ajmal, M. (1968). *J. appl. Bact.* **31**, 124
Anonymous (1830). *Lancet*, **ii**, 838
Aoki, Y., Hsu, S. and Chun, D. (1967). *Endem. Dis. Bull. Nagasaki Univ.* **8**, 191
Asatoor, A. M., Levi, A. J. and Milne, M. D. (1963). *Lancet*, **ii**, 733
Ashton, D. H. and Busta, F. F. (1968). *J. Dairy Sci.* **51**, 842
Auclair, J. (1964). In: *Microbial Inhibitors in Food.* p. 281 (Ed. by N. Molin and A. Erichsen) Stockholm; Almqvist and Wissell
Avery, G. B., Villavicencio, O., Lilly, J. R. and Randolph, J. G. (1968). *Pediatrics, Springfield,* **41**, 712
Ayres, J. C. (1960a). *Fd Res.* **25**, 1
–(1960b). *J. appl. Bact.* **23**, 471
Bachrach, U., Sterk, V. V., Gery, I. and Rozansky, R. (1960). *Am. J. Hyg.* **72**, 1
Baird, T. T. (1961). *Mon. Bull. Minist. Hlth.* **20**, 152
Baird-Parker, A. C. and Freame, B. (1967). *J. appl. Bact.* **30**, 420
Barber, M.A. (1914). *Phillipp. J. Sci. Sect. B.* **9**, 515
Baross, J. and Liston, J. (1968). *Nature, Lond.* **217,** 1263
Bergdoll, M. S., Weiss, K. F. and Muster, M. J. (1967). *Bact. Proc.* 12
Bergère, J. L., Gonet, P., Hermier, J. and Mocquot, G. (1968). *Annls Inst. Pasteur Lille,* **19**, 41
Berthelot, A. and Bertrand, D. M. (1912). *C.r. hebd. Séanc. Acad. Sci., Paris,* **154**, 1643
Blackwell, B. and Mabbitt, L. A. (1965). *Lancet,* **i**, 938
Blanche Koelensmid, W. A. A. and Rhee, R. van (1968). *Antonie van Leeuwenhoek* **34**, 287
Board, R. G. (1968). In: *Egg Quality—A Study of the Hen's Egg.* p.133 (Ed. by T. C. Carter) Edinburgh; Oliver and Boyd
Boyer, J., Depierre, F., Tessier, M. and Jacob, J. (1956). *Presse méd.* **64**, 1003
Brieger, L. (1885a). *Ueber Ptomaine.* p.80. Berlin; Hirschwald
–(1885b). *Weitere Untersuchungen über Ptomaine.* p.83. Berlin; Hirschwald
–(1886). *Untersuchungen über Ptomaine, Dritter Teil.* p. 119. Berlin; Hirschwald
Burkholder, L., Burkholder, P. R., Chu, A., Kostyk, N. and Roels, O. A. (1968). *Fd Technol., Champaign* **22**, 1278
Buttiaux, R., Coin, L., Trochou, P. and Moriamez, J. (1955). *Revue Hyg. Méd. soc.* **3**, 409
Casman, E. P., Bennett, R. W., Dorsey, A. E. and Issa, J. A. (1967). *J. Bact.* **94**, 1875
Clise, J. D. and Swecker, E. E. (1965). *Publ. Hlth Rep. Wash.,* **80**, 899
Cybulska, J. and Jeljaszewicz, J. (1966). *J. Bact.* **91**, 953
Dack, G. M. (1947). *Am. J. publ. Hlth* **37**, 360
Dakin, J. C. and Stolk, A. C. (1968). *J. Fd Technol.* **3**, 49
Davis, S. D. and Wedgwood, R. J. (1965). *J. Immun.* **95**, 75

Del Valle, F. R. and Nickerson, J. T. R. (1968). *Fd Technol.* **22**, 1036, 1135

Denys, J. (1894). *Bull. Acad. R. Méd. Bel.* **8**, 496

Dolman, C. E. (1943). *Can. J. publ. Hlth* **34**, 97, 205

Dolman, C. E., Chang, H., Kerr, D. E. and Shearer, A. R. (1950). *Can. J. publ. Hlth* **41**, 215

Dolman, C. E., Tomsich, M., Campbell, C. C. R. and Laing, W. B. (1960). *J. infect. Dis.* **106**, 5

Duncan, C. L. and Foster, E. M. (1968). *Appl. Microbiol.* **16**, 401

Edwards, P.R. and Galton, M.M. (1967). *Adv. vet. Sci.* **11**, 1

Eklund, M. W., Wieler, D. I. and Poysky, F. T. (1967). *J. Bact.* **93**, 1461

Erichsen, I. (1967). *Antonie van Leeuwenhoek* **33**, 107

Fleming, A. (1922). *Proc. R. Soc.* B, **93**, 306

Floyd, T. M. and Jones, G. B. (1954). *Am. J. trop. Med. Hyg.* **3**, 475

Gehring, F. (1965). *Arch. FischWiss.* **15**, 253

Geiger, E. (1955). *Science, N.Y.* **121**, 865

Gulasekharam, J., Velaudapillai, T. and Niles, G. R. (1956). *J. Hyg. Camb.* **54**, 581

Haines, R. B. (1933). *J. Hyg., Camb.* **33**, 175

–(1934). *J. Hyg., Camb.* **34**, 277

Hall, H. E. (1968). *Bact. Proc.* 77

Hauge, S. (1955). *J. appl. Bact.* **18**, 591

Hauschild, A. H. W. (1968). *Q. Bull. Ass. Fd Drug Off. U.S.* **32**, 135

Heiss, R. and Becker, K. (1966). *Lebensmitteltechnologie und Verpackung, 65.* Bundeswehr-Verwaltung, Sonderh. 6

Hobbs, B. C., Ritchie, J. M. and Ritchie, E. D. (1962). *J. Hyg.* **60**, 259

Hobbs, B. C. and Sutton, R. G. A. (1968). *Annls Inst. Pasteur, Lille,* **19**, 29

Holdsworth, S. D. (1967). *Fd Mf.* **42**, No. 7, 42

Holtzapffel, D. and Mossel, D. A. A. (1968). *J. Fd Technol.* **3**, 223

Ingram, M. (1949). *Jl. R. sanit. Inst.* **69**, 39

Ingram, M. and Roberts, T. A. (1967). *Proc. 5th Int. Symp. Fd Microbiol.* Moscow, July 1966, p. 531

Jadin, J., Resseler, J. and Looy, G. van. (1957). *Bull. Acad. R. Méd. Belg.* **22**, 85

Jansen, J.D. and Dooren de Jong, L.E. den. (1930). *Zentbl. Bakt. Parasitkde,* I Abt. Orig. **117**, 193

Jensen, L.B. (1954). *Microbiology of Meats.* 3rd Ed. p.138 Champaign, Ill. U.S.A: Garrard Press

Joffe, A. Z. (1963). *Pl. Soil* **18**, 31

Joos, R. W. and Hall, W. H. (1968). *Proc. Soc. exp. Biol. Med.* **128**, 49

Joos, R. W. and Hall, W. H. (1968a). *J. Bact.* **96**, 881

Kelly, C. B. and Arcisz, W. (1954). *Publ. Hlth Rep., Wash.* **69**, 1205

Koff, R. S., Grady, G. F., Chalmers, T. C., Mosley, J. W. and Swartz, B. L. (1967). *New Engl. J. Med.* **276**, 703

Larkin, J. M. and Stokes, J. L. (1967). *J. Bact.* **94**, 889

Larkin, J. M. and Stokes, J. L. (1968). *Can. J. Microbiol.* **14**, 97

Legroux, R. and Levaditi, J. (1947). *C.R. Séanc. Soc. Biol.* **141**, 998

Leistner, L. (1956). *Jber. Bundesforschung-Anstalt Fleischwirtschaft,* Kulmbach, 45

Lerke, P., Adams, R. and Farber, L. (1965). *Appl. Microbiol.* **13**, 625

Lerke, P., Farber, L. and Adams, R. (1967). *Appl. Microbiol.* **15**, 770

Lewis, K. H. and Cassel, K. (1964). *Botulism.* U.S. Dept. Hlth Educ. Welfare, Publ. Hlth Service, Publication 999-FP-1, p. 327

Lie, J. L. and Marth, E. H. (1968). *J. Dairy Sci.* **51**, 1743

Loken, K. I., Culbert, K. H., Solee, R. E. and Pomeroy, B. S. (1968). *Appl. Microbiol.* **16**, 1002

Love, T. D. (1968). *Fish. Ind. Res.* **4**, 139

McCollum, J.P.K., Pearson, R.C.M., Ingham, H.R., Wood, P.C. and Dewar, H.A. (1968). *Lancet*, **ii**, 767.

Magwood, S. E., Fung, J. and Byrne, J. L. (1965). *Avian Dis.* **9**, 302

Mameren, J. van (1969). *Proc. Comm. IV,* Inst. Int. Froid, Budapest

Martin, H. H. (1963). *J. theor. Biol.* **5**, 1

Mason, J. O. and McLean, W. R. (1962). *Am. J. Hyg.* **75**, 90

Mehrlich, F.P. (1966). In: *Food Irradiation.* p.673 Vienna: International Atomic Energy Agency

Mol, J. H. H. (1957). *J. appl. Bact.* **20**, 454

Morgan, P.M. (1968). In: *The Safety of Foods.* p.102 Ed. by Ayres, J.C. *et al.,* Westport, Conn. USA; Avi Publishing Cy.

Mossel, D. A. A. (1965). *Bull. Soc. Path. exot.* **58**, 687
— (1968). In: *The Safety of Foods,* p.168 Ed. by Ayres, J. C. *et al,,* Westport, Conn. USA: Avi Publishing Cy.
— (1969). *Alimenta* **8**, 8
— and Westerdijk, J. (1949). *Antonie van Leeuwenhoek* **15**, 190
— and Ingram, M. (1955). *J. appl. Bact.* **18**, 232
— and Eijgelaar, G. (1956). *Conserva* **5**, 7

Muschel, L. H. (1960). *Ann. N.Y. Acad. Sci* **88**, 1265

Nakanishi, H., Leistner, L., Heckelmann, H. and Baumgart, J. (1968). *Archiv. Lebensmittl hyg.* **19**, 49

Nikodemusz, I. (1958). *Z. Hyg. InfektKr.* **145**, 335

Nikodemusz, I. (1966). *Annls Inst. Pasteur Lille,* **17**, 229

Oftebro, T. (1965). *Nordisk VetMed.* **17**, 467

Orillo, C. A. and Pederson, C. S. (1968). *Appl. Microbiol.* **16**, 1669

Pederson, C. S. (1960). *Adv. Fd Res.* **10**, 233

Peeters, E. M. E. (1963). *Archs. belg. Méd. soc.* **21**, 451

Pelroy, G. A. and Seman, J. P. (1968). *J. Milk Fd Technol.* **31**, 231

Perigo, J. A. and Roberts, T. A. (1968). *J. Fd Technol.* **3**, 91

Pflug, I. J., Bock, J. H. and Long, F. E. (1963). *Fd Technol.* **17**, 1167

Pivnick, H. and Thatcher, F. S. (1968). In: *The Safety of Foods.* p.121. Ed. by Ayres, J. C. *et al.,* Westport, Conn. USA; Avi Publishing Cy.

Preston, F. S. (1968). *Aerospace Med.* **39**, 519

Ramel, P., Girard, P., Lanteaume, M. T. and Guezennec, J. (1965). *Rev. Hyg. Méd. soc.* **13**, 73

Randolph, H. E. and Gould, I. A. (1968). *J. Dairy Sci.* **51**, 8

Reimann, H. A. (1963). *Am. J. med. Sci.* **246**, 404

Reiter, B. and Oram, J. D. (1967). *Nature, Lond.* **216**, 328

Roberts, T. A. and Ingram, M. (1966). *J. Fd Technol.* **1**, 147

Roeder, G. and Witzenhausen, R. (1967). *Archiv. Lebensmittl hyg.* **18**, 265

Roos, B. (1956). Svenska Läkartidn **53**, 989

Russell, F. E. (1968). In: *The Safety of Foods.* p.68. Ed. by Ayres, J. C. *et al.,* Westport, Conn. USA: Avi Publishing Cy.

Ruys, A. C. (1948). *Am. J. publ. Hlth* **38**, 1219

Saisithi, P., Kasemsaru, B., Liston, J. and Dollar, A. M. (1966). *J. Fd Sci.* **31**, 105

Sakazaki, R., Iwanami, S. and Fukumi, H. (1963). *Jap. J. med. Sci. Biol.* **16**, 161

Sakazaki, R., Tamura, K. and Saito, M. (1967). *Jap. J. med. Sci. Biol.* **20**, 387

Schade, A. L. and Caroline, L. (1944). *Science N.Y.* **100**, 14

Schmidt, C. F., Lechowich, R. V. and Folinazzo, J. F. (1961). *J. Fd Sci.* **26**, 626

Schmidt, C. F., Lechowich, R. V. and Nank, W. K. (1962). *J. Fd Sci.* **27**, 85
Scott, W. J. (1957). *Adv Food Res.* **7**, 83
Selmi, F. (1872). *Mém. Real. Accad. Sci. Bol.* (III) **2**, 81
Selmi, F. (1878). *Sulle ptomaine od alcaloidi cadaverici, e loro importanza in tossicologia.* p.110. Bologna: Zanichelli
Selmi, F. (1879). *Atti Real. Accad. Lincei* (III) **4**, 75
Sherwood, H. P. and Thomson, S. (1953). *Mon. Bull. Minist. Hlth* **12**, 103
Shewan, J. M., Hobbs, G. and Hodgkiss, W. (1960). *J. appl. Bact.* **23**, 379
Shewan, J. M., Hobbs, G. and Hodgkiss, W. (1960a). *J. appl. Bact.* **23**, 463
Slanetz, L. W., Bartley, C. H. and Stanley, K. W. (1968). *Hlth Lab. Sci.* **5**, 66
Slavin, J. W., Ronsivalli, L. J. and Connors, T. J. (1966). In: *Food Irradiation.* p.509. Vienna: International Atomic Energy Agency
Spiher, A. T. (1968). *FDA Papers* **2**, No. 8, 15
Steiniger, F. (1951). *Z. Hyg. Infekt Kr.* **132**, 228
Tansy, M. F. and Venturella, V. S. (1967). *Lancet*, **ii**, 1314
Taylor, J. and Bettelheim, K. A. (1966). *J. gen. Microbiol.* **42**, 309
Thiel, P. H. van, Kuipers, F. C. and Rosham, R. Th. (1960). *Trop. geogr. Med.* **12**, 97
Thiel, P. H. van (1966). *Trop. geogr. Med.* **18**, 310
Thornley M. J. (1960). *J. appl. Bact.* **23**, 37
Thornley, M. J. (1967). *J. gen. Microbiol.* **49**, 211
Tonge, J. I., Battey, Y., Forbes, J. J. and Grant, E. M. (1967). *Med. J. Aust.* **2**, 1088
Veen, A. G. van and Latuasan, H. E. (1950). *Documenta Neel. indones. Morb. Trop.* **2**, 18
Veen, A. G. van (1953). *Adv Fd Res.* **4**, 209
Ward, B. Q. (1968). *Appl. Microbiol.* **16**, 543
Westerdijk, J. (1949). *Antonie van Leeuwenhoek* **15**, 187
Weijers, H. A. and Kamer, J. H. van de (1965). *Nutr. Abstr. Rev.* **35**, 591
Williams, J. (1962). *Biochem. J.* **83**, 355
Wilson, B.J. (1968). In: *The Safety of Foods.* p.141 Ed. by Ayres, J.C. *et al.* Westport, Conn. USA: Avi Publishing Cy.
Wolf, J. and Mahmoud, S. A. Z. (1957). *J. appl. Bact.* **20**, 124
Zeller, M. (1963). *Arch. Lebensmittl hyg.* **14**, 104
Zen-Yoji, H., Sakai, S., Terayama, T., Kudo, Y., Ito, T., Benoki, M. and Nagasaki, M. (1965). *J. infect. Dis.* **115**, 436

# CHARACTERISTICS OF PRESERVATION PROCESSES AS APPLIED TO PROTEINACEOUS FOODS

E. ROLFE

*National College of Food Technology, Weybridge, Surrey*

## INTRODUCTION

Particular consideration is given here to meat, fish and eggs, all of which have a high moisture content and consequently spoil quickly through attack by micro-organisms if stored at ambient temperatures. The available methods of food preservation seek either to create an environment in and around the food which is inimical to the proliferation of the contaminating micro-organisms, or to destroy them under conditions where re-infection cannot occur. Success in the above respects may not provide the complete solution when long term storage is necessary, as the avoidance of microbial spoilage may make apparent other slower forms of deterioration — for example, those due to enzymic activity or chemical interaction between components of the foodstuff. A common example of chemical deterioration, and one which is particularly difficult to control, is non-enzymic browning (also termed carbonyl-amine browning) due to reactions of the Maillard type between reducing sugars and amino groups of either proteins or amino acids (Maillard, 1912). The reactions give rise to numerous forms of spoilage including discoloration, development of off-flavours, deterioration of texture and loss of nutritive value. Many preservation processes therefore include additional procedures designed to minimize or overcome such spoilage mechanisms.

## CRITICAL MICROBIOLOGICAL FACTORS

Advantage is taken in food preservation methods of the several critical factors which affect microbial activity.

1. *Water* — Micro-organisms can grow only in the presence of adequate water. Its availability is conveniently expressed as water activity $a_w$ (Scott, 1957; Christian, 1962).

107

$$a_w = \frac{P}{P_o}$$

where $P$ = equilibrium vapour pressure of the foodstuff and
$P_o$ = vapour pressure of pure water at the same temperature.

Provided the water remains in the liquid phase, $a_w$ of the food is almost unaffected by temperature within the range permitting microbial growth. The minimum $a_w$ requirements of normal bacteria, yeasts and moulds are 0.91, 0.88 and 0.80 respectively (Mossel and Ingram, 1955).

2. *Temperature* – Micro-organisms can cause food spoilage within the temperature range $-10°C$ to $70°C$. The psychrophiles are able to grow at the lower temperatures and can spoil refrigerated foods. All the so-called psychrophiles are not particularly 'cold-loving' as the name implies; rather they are able to tolerate cold but could be considered mesophiles on the basis of their optimum growth temperature. Eddy (1960) coined the term psychrotrophs to describe bacteria which are able to grow at temperatures below $5°C$ irrespective of their optimum growth temperature. Growth has been observed down to $-10°C$ although months may be required to produce visible colonies (Ingraham and Stokes, 1959); but spoilage may still occur at temperatures below $-10°C$ through the action of microbial enzymes elaborated during previous growth at more favourable temperatures (Michener and Elliott, 1964; Peterson and Gunderson, 1960; Ayres, 1955).

3. *Acidity* – pH has a marked discriminatory effect on microbial flora. The inability of *Clostridium botulinum* to grow in substrates of pH below 4.5 is one factor permitting milder heat treatments in the processing of canned acid foods. Most bacteria grow best in a substrate around neutral pH, yeasts are favoured by slight acidity, and moulds are most tolerant of acidity.

4. *Oxygen* – Availability of oxygen exerts a selective effect on the microbial population. Bacteria are either aerobic, or anaerobic or facultative, whereas moulds and yeasts grow best under aerobic conditions.

5. *Inhibitory substances* – These may be added as preservatives (e.g., benzoic acid). Some foods contain natural protective substances that inhibit the growth of micro-organisms such as lactenin in milk and lysozyme in eggs. Such inhibitors are often specific in their action; lysozyme is particularly active against micrococci.

## PRESERVATION PROCESSES

1. Preservation methods which depend on the provision of an unfavourable environment include:

*(a)* Storage at temperatures near or below the minimum for growth of spoilage organisms — chilling and freezing.

*(b)* Reducing the water activity below that necessary to support the growth of micro-organisms. It can be achieved either by dehydration or by the addition of solutes, e.g., salt, sugar, to reduce $a_w$ by colligative effects.

*(c)* Fermentation to make the food acidic.

*(d)* Addition of chemical preservatives. The nature of the latter varies widely, e.g., antibiotics (nisin), acids (sulphurous acid), and gases (ozone).

2. Preservation methods which rely on the destruction of micro-organisms are:

*(a)* Sterilization: in fact a few micro-organisms may survive the process but remain inactive so that a better term to describe the condition is 'commercial sterility' or 'commercial stability' (Riemann, 1957).

*(b)* Pasteurization is a milder treatment applied to kill the pathogens particularly. The accompanying reduction in the microbial flora improves the shelf life of the food.

Heat is the usual agent in both processes, but $\gamma$-radiation is also effective.

## PRESERVATION BY APPLICATION OF HEAT

*Pasteurization*

The temperatures employed are usually below 100ºC and the heat treatment is carefully controlled to minimize damage to heat labile proteins whilst destroying pathogens.

Because of its unique functional properties large quantities of egg are used in the bakery trade. Raw egg is liable to contain *Salmonellae;* to prevent the possibility of outbreaks of food poisoning legislation was introduced in the U.K. to make pasteurization of liquid egg compulsory as from 1st January 1964. The regulations require liquid egg to be subjected to a temperature not lower than 148ºF for at least 2½ min and immediately thereafter cooled to below 38ºF. The prescribed heat treatment does not adversely affect the baking properties (Heller *et al.,* 1962).

Liquid egg white is more sensitive to heat than is either whole egg or yolk, and changes in physical and functional properties are observed after heating for several minutes at temperatures above 134ºF (57ºC). Reasons for this behaviour are *(a)* the heat lability of conalbumin which in whole egg is converted into the more stable iron-conalbumin complex by iron from the yolk and *(b)* the heating of egg white at pH 9.0 causes a marked increase in viscosity due to the instability of one or more of the proteins.

The heat stability of the major protein ovalbumin varies sharply with pH, and reaches a maximum between pH 6.5 and 7.0 when denaturation is less than 1 per cent after heating for 30 min at 65°C. Both the above factors are remedied by adjusting the pH to about 7 through the addition of lactic acid, and by the addition of certain metal salts, e.g. of aluminium. Pasteurization can then be carried out at 60°–61°C for 3½–4 min whilst retaining the functional properties of the egg white (Cunningham and Lineweaver, 1965).

*Sterilization*

The process is a compromise between supplying enough heat to destroy the contaminating spoilage micro-organisms whilst trying to avoid the adverse effect of excessive heat on texture, flavour and nutritive value of the food. The heat resistance of microbial cells and spores is greatest around neutral pH, so that the low acid foods, which include fish, meat and milk, require the most drastic treatments. A rise in temperature accelerates chemical reactions, including those within the microbial cell (and lead to its death) and those between food components (resulting in loss of quality). The $Q_{10°C}$ for the destruction of bacterial spores is between 6.6 to 15.8, whereas $Q_{10°C}$ for the reactions involved in the cooking of foods is approximately 3.5, and for the destruction of aneurin and riboflavin the values are 2.1 and 2.3 respectively. Thus a high-temperature/short-time process will result in a smaller loss in food quality as compared with a process of equal sterilizing value carried out at a lower temperature (Gillespy, 1962).

The 'no survival' level of *Bacillus botulinum* spores has been interpreted as the reduction of an initial population of approximately $10^{11}$ spores to $10^{-1}$, which is a decrease in numbers of 12 decimal reductions (Esty and Meyer, 1922), and has given rise to the 12D concept in canning. The 12D destruction level is obtained by heating for 2.78 min at 250°F. The latter has subsequently been amended to 3.0 min to allow for the protective effect of food constituents (Townsend *et al.*, 1938). Hence a heat treatment to destroy *Clostridium botulinum* in a non-acid pack has a value $F_o$ = 3.0. The critical resistance index in canning from the aspect of food spoilage is related, however, to the more resistant spores of mesophilic saprophytic types, (particularly putrefactive anaerobes), although occasionally the resistant spores of thermophilic anaerobes constitute the spoilage hazard. A process value $F_o$ = 3.0 provides a 5D to 7D treatment against the latter two spoilage types, but the satisfactory record of canning shows it provides an adequate margin of safety (El-Bisi, 1965).

*Application in the Canning of Fish*

When fish is heated, a considerable amount of water is released from the tissue (e.g., 20–30 per cent of their weight in the case of sardines) because of the reduced water-holding property of the coagulated proteins (Meesemaecker and Sohier, 1959). If the water were allowed to remain in the can, the result would be an unattractive pack, and the shrunken fish would be damaged mechanically by movement within the can during distribution. Fish should therefore be cooked before canning. During heat processing, fish is liable to produce sulphide ions which react with the tinplate of the container to form tin or iron sulphide. Both may impair the appearance of the product, and cans should therefore be treated with a sulphur resistant lacquer (van den Brock, 1965). Fish is also very susceptible to the development of overcooked flavours through non-enzymic browning, and this should be minimized by establishing the optimum time-temperature relationship for the processing of each product (Riemann, 1957), and processing must be followed by immediate and rapid cooling. This reaction between muscle protein and reducing sugars also produces a brown discoloration in many white-fleshed fish, e.g. lemon sole (Tarr, 1952). Ribose appears to be the sugar mainly responsible for browning in fish. It is produced enzymically *post mortem* from ribonucleic acid (Tarr, 1954). A ribose oxidase will remove ribose within 2 days at 0°C when added to fish and no browning occurs subsequently on heating (Tarr and Bissett, 1954).

## PRESERVATION BY USE OF IONIZING RAYS

This method of food preservation is the only new basic method, and is important because it possesses two major advantages. The temperature rise produced in foods is very small, hence they may be preserved in the raw or lightly cooked form. Absorption of the radiation by water raises the temperature by only 2.4°C per Mrad. Also appreciable thicknesses of food can be treated. A particular difficulty hindering its adoption is the induced unpleasant flavours and odours caused by sterilizing doses, and also there is the problem of demonstrating that the irradiation products of the food are non-toxic. The unit of radiation is the 'rad' which is equivalent to an energy absorption of 100 ergs/g foodstuff. 1 Mrad = $10^6$ rad.

Applications of the method may be classified with respect to dose (Ingram and Rhodes, 1962; Rolfe, 1962) and pertinent examples are:
1. Low dose treatments:          0.01–0.1 Mrad
     Destruction of parasites in fresh meat      0.02 Mrad

2. Medium dose treatments         0.1–1.0 Mrad
     Destruction of *Salmonellae*         0.5 Mrad
     'Pasteurization' of meats        0.6–0.8 Mrad
3. High dose treatments         2–5 Mrad
     Such doses provide commercial sterility in foods.

A dose of 4.8 Mrad inactivates the spores of *Clostridium botulinum*, but usually also renders the food inedible (Hannan, 1955; Shea, 1958). The undesirable side reactions are due to the formation and activity of free radicals and activated molecules in the aqueous environment, and their effect may be reduced by irradiation at subzero temperatures or at low oxygen tensions.

Another and more recent classification is (Goresline *et al.*, 1964):

Type I 'Radappertization': an ionizing dose sufficient to produce commercial sterility.

Type II 'Radicidation': a dose sufficient to reduce the number of viable specific non-spore forming pathogenic micro-organisms (e.g. to destroy *Salmonellae*).

Type III 'Radurization': a dose sufficient to enhance keeping quality by causing a substantial reduction in the number of viable specific spoilage organisms.

Because of the problems associated with high dose treatments, efforts currently tend to be directed more to the exploitation of low dose methods (Goldblith, 1964). Two examples are:

*(i)* radurization to destroy most of the non-spore formers that cause food spoilage (e.g., *Pseudomonads*) in meat, followed by storage at chill temperatures,

*(ii)* combination processes where ionizing rays supplement another treatment (e.g., use of both ionizing rays and heat in the canning of hams).

The irradiation odour in raw meat (aptly described as 'wet dog') does not vary in type but increases in intensity in the series pork, chicken, lamb, veal and beef. The contribution which is derived from the protein fraction is mainly sulphur compounds and aromatic hydrocarbons. There is no evidence that irradiation ruptures peptide bonds. The main attack occurs as cleavage of side chains or end groups (Merritt, 1966).

The usually very high radio resistance of tissue enzymes *in situ* may seriously interfere with the success of radurization and radappertization treatments in food. The surviving cathepsins and other proteolytic enzymes may induce the development of nauseating and bitter flavours and mushy texture of irradiated and microbiologically stable fish and meat products (Vas, 1966). A $12D$ value for *Clostridium botulinum* is accepted as giving sufficient microbiological safety, and a $4D$ value for enzyme inactivation should result in a sufficiently low enzyme activity to make the food stable, but whereas the dose for the former is 4.5 Mrad, the latter required 20 Mrad (Hansen, 1966). A physiological combination method has been developed to control proteolytic enzymes in irradiated raw meat (Mouton, 1964a, 1964b, 1965; Radouco-Thomas, 1959; Zender *et al.*, 1958) The animal is injected about 4 h before slaughter with adrenalin. The pH of the tissue of the slaughtered animal is maintained at the original high level which prevents the enzyme activity responsible for autolysis. Microbiological stabilization is then carried out, preferably by applying a surface treatment with electron beams.

Other combination treatments suggested are:

*(a)* Heat addition + irradiation. Cooking or roasting meat to an internal temperature of 74°–80°C (to inactivate enzymes) followed by 4.5 Mrad gave pork and poultry meats which were acceptable after 9–24 months storage at room temperatures (Heiligman, 1965).

*(b)* Heat removal + irradiation. This treatment suppresses not only excessive growth of the micro-organisms which survive medium doses of ionizing rays, but also the activity of undestroyed enzymes. The method is said to be useful for wet fish (Liston *et al.*, 1968). Spoilage of seafoods is caused particularly by *Pseudomonads* (Shewan *et al.*, 1956) which are fortunately highly sensitive to γ-radiation (Thornley, 1963). Pasteurizing doses of radiation (0.1–0.5 Mrad) effectively reduce, to a very low level, the viable count of such organisms naturally present in sea foods (Pelroy *et al.*, 1967) and provide for considerable extension of shelf life of the refrigerated and irradiated product (Masurovsky *et al.*, 1963).


## PRESERVATION BY REFRIGERATION

Storage at low temperatures inhibits spoilage by slowing down the growth of micro-organisms, the activity of enzymes, and chemical reactions involving the food.

Chilling is useful for short term storage or in cases where it is essential to preserve the natural characteristics of the fresh food. Psychrotrophs will increase in number and eventually cause spoilage. Bacteria responsible for food poisoning cannot grow or grow very slowly at temperatures below 10°C, and none have been observed to grow below 4.4°C. Chilled foods should therefore be stored at or below this latter temperature.

The freezing of foodstuffs leads to damage of the tissue and to a consequent effect on texture. The thawed tissue loses its original turgor, and the loss of cell fluid as drip is familiar – for example from frozen meat. Non-cellular material such as cooked egg white behaves similarly. During freezing water separates as ice crystals and after thawing pores

113

filled with water may be formed in the food. In thawed cooked egg white some water is easily pressed out, whilst the gel is made hard from contraction and irreversible loss of water (Davis *et al.*, 1952). The deterioration appears to be due to a combination of effects.

*(a)* Firstly freezing results in the concentration of salts and enzymes in solution within the cells. The enzymes become more active in stronger solution and produce spoilage changes which cannot be reversed when the flesh is thawed (Burgess *et al.*, 1965a). Lovelock (1953) has shown that exposure to concentrated solutions of electrolytes will affect bio-polymers, e.g. structural proteins and lipoproteins of membranes,

*(b)* Water in cells may be considered to exist as polarized multilayers oriented on the surfaces of cell proteins. Its removal by freezing leads to irreversible structural changes in the proteins which become apparent as texture changes and loss of water holding properties.

*(c)* The rate of freezing controls size and location of ice crystals and was first reported by Plank *et al.* (1916). Rapid freezing (measured in minutes) gave intracellular ice crystals in fish muscle. As the rate of freezing is decreased the intracellular ice crystals become larger and with slow freezing intercellular ice in comparatively large masses is formed. To ensure good quality frozen fish the Ministry of Food in the early 1950s defined quick freezing as a rate of freezing at which no part of a fish or packet of fish takes more than 2 h to cool from $0°C$ to $-5°C$. Times in excess of 2 h have an adverse effect both on appearance and on suitability of the fish for subsequent filleting and smoking (Burgess *et al.*, 1965b) The proteins of meat are more resistant to damage by freezing and whole sides of beef can be frozen successfully.

Ice nucleation particles are present in all but highly purified aqueous materials, so that the freezing of foodstuffs will occur by heterogeneous nucleation (Lusena, 1955; Meryman, 1956). Due to the presence of solutes and 'organized' water in tissues, unfrozen water will remain present in apparently hard frozen foods (e.g., at $-10°C$), and will become gradually less as the temperature is lowered (Riedel, 1957).

*Application to the preservation of eggs*

If egg yolk is frozen and stored below $-6°C$, the thawed product possesses a plastic or gel-like character. The rate of viscosity increase is dependent on the storage temperature, being much faster at $-10°C$ than $-14°C$ (Powrie *et al.*, 1963). At $-6°C$, 81 per cent of the water in yolk is converted to ice (Riedel, 1957), and the yolk salts are concentrated in about 19 per cent of the initial water. The fivefold concentration of salts may cause irreversible damage to yolk lipoproteins. It seems probable that lipoproteins in the soluble phase are involved in gelation

114

since it occurs less in crotoxin treated yolk (crotoxin degrades lipoproteins to lysophospholipoproteins) than in untreated yolk (Lightbody and Fevold, 1948).

The first reported chemical protection of frozen yolk was by Moran (1925) who noted the effectiveness of 10 per cent added sucrose. As little as 1 per cent sucrose inhibits gelation in whole egg magma (Thomas and Bailey, 1933). Addition of 10 per cent sodium chloride is widely used to inhibit gelation; but in contrast to sugar, it causes striking physical alterations. The yolk becomes more translucent but its fluid character is retained. The physical changes may be due to solubilization of yolk granules (Burley and Cook, 1961). Proteolytic enzymes are also effective in preventing gelation (e.g., the addition of 0.05 per cent papain to yolk and incubation at $24^{\circ}$ C for 15–20 min; Lopez et al., 1955). Mechanical treatment of yolk by either homogenization or colloid milling prior to freezing can retard gelation (Pearce and Lavers, 1949; Lopez et al., 1954). The rheological properties of yolk are primarily dependent on the uniform dispersion of low density lipoproteins and granules in an aqueous medium. Aggregation of the granules and low density lipoproteins may give rise to a weak three dimensional network and the entrapment of a large amount of free water. Such a yolk system could have viscoplastic properties (Powrie, 1969) and account for the gelation.

## PRESERVATION BY DEHYDRATION

Because of its peculiar advantages, considerable interest is attached to dehydration as a means of food preservation. Thus long storage life is achieved without refrigeration; processing does not require the use of excessive heat as the destruction of bacterial spores is unnecessary; and provided also are logistical advantages of reduction in weight and bulk, the latter being very large if compression of the product is permissible. In order to retain as much as possible of the natural characteristics of the foodstuff, dehydration must entail more than controlled drying by artificial thermal means. The process must include the selection of raw material, and in addition, a knowledge of the biochemistry of the foodstuff and of the chemistry of spoilage reactions will suggest appropriate additional treatments for maximum quality retention (Rolfe, 1965).

The methods for dehydration may be classified as follows.

1. *Drying at atmospheric pressure*
   *(a)* Drying in a current of warm air is widely used and numerous types of equipment have been designed for the purpose. During drying, water

evaporates from the surface of the foodstuff whilst at the same time moisture diffuses from inside the food to the surface. The evaporation of water may be considered to occur in two stages. The first stage takes place whilst the surface remains moist and drying depends only on the condition of the air surrounding the food, particularly its temperature, relative humidity and air speed. Provided these conditions remain constant, the rate of drying does not change and hence this stage is called the constant rate period.

The second stage occurs when all the surface moisture has evaporated, and the rate of loss of moisture is then controlled by the speed with which water can reach the surface from within. In other words, it is independent of the surrounding air provided the latter is not saturated. As the residual water in the food becomes less, the water takes progressively longer to diffuse from the deeper parts to the surface, and drying becomes progressively slower. Hence the second stage is termed the 'falling rate period' of drying.

The utilization of warm air drying for the development of stable palatable products in the form of dehydrated minced cooked meats and fish (particularly white fish, beef and pork) occurred during the Second World War (Anonymous, 1944; Sharp, 1953). To facilitate drying, the meat must be trimmed to a fat content not exceeding 30 per cent on a dry weight basis, and the selection of pork carcasses is necessary to avoid the development of incipient rancidity during the exposure to warm air in the drying process and subsequent instability of the product (Gooding and Rolfe, 1957). Drying becomes very protracted as the size of piece is increased. Thus ½ in cubes of cooked meat require about 22 h of drying to reach 8 per cent moisture content, whereas a cooked mince (passed through a cutter with 3/8 in diameter holes) dries in 4–5 h. Raw meats, even though minced, dry slowly and irregularly. The product is hard, requires many hours to reconstitute, and when cooked, is very tough and of characteristic flavour.

*(b)* Dehydration by means of solvent extraction to remove water and lipids has been applied on a considerable scale for the preparation of fish protein concentrate (FPC). The solvent used should be non-toxic and of low boiling point to permit inexpensive de-solventization. The products are bland-tasting, light-coloured protein powders. Much of the pioneering work was done in U.S.A. where a process was developed of simultaneously dehydrating and defatting whole raw fish with ethylene dichloride, followed by an extraction de-odourization step in which methyl or iso-propyl alcohol is used (VioBin Corporation, 1956; Lewin, 1959). Many other similar processes have also been described (Guttman *et al.*, 1957; Dreosti *et al.*, 1956; Hammerle *et al.*, 1964; Snyder, 1967).

## 2. *Vacuum drying*

Vacuum drying offers three main advantages, namely the ability to dry foods *(a)* as large and recognizable pieces, *(b)* at low temperatures, which becomes important to slow down enzymic deterioration and reduce damage to foods rich in heat-labile materials such as proteins, and *(c)* in almost complete absence of oxygen (which prevents undesirable oxidation of, e.g., fats and lipids).

There are two main techniques for vacuum drying (Rolfe, 1958). One utilizes a moderate vacuum of 5–10 mm Hg absolute pressure. In this case water is evaporated from the liquid phase and the foodstuff shrinks and decreases in size as the water is removed. The second technique is freeze drying. This requires an absolute pressure of about 1 mm Hg. Freeze drying is possible only when the water vapour pressure inside the vacuum drying cabinet is at such low levels; and less than the saturation water vapour pressure of hard frozen food. For rapid drying the heat input must balance the rate of heat loss through sublimation of ice crystals, and one of the most difficult problems associated with the process is to provide an adequate rate of heating. The water is removed by sublimation of ice crystals from the frozen foodstuff, and the product is a porous low-density solid which retains the original size and shape of the foodstuff. The porosity promotes rapid reconstitution. Commercial interest in the freeze drying of foodstuffs was stimulated markedly by the Accelerated Freeze Drying Process (AFD). A description of the basic AFD technique was first reported and described by Rolfe (1956), but the name AFD did not appear in the literature until 1958 when the process was discussed in some detail (Rolfe, 1958).

The vacuuum contact-plate dehydration (VCD) process (Hay, 1955; Gooding and Rolfe, 1955) offers important advantages when applied to minced cooked meats, for example, as compared with warm air drying.

*(i)* The fat content of the mince is not critical, and a mince containing 45 per cent fat (drying weight basis) is dried without difficulty (Rolfe, a).

*(ii)* Absence of air avoids oxidative changes. A batch of pork mince yielded products containing fat of peroxide value 19.8 m-equiv. oxygen/kg and 2 m-equiv. oxygen/kg when dried in warm air and by VCD respectively (Rolfe, b).

*(iii)* The low temperatures employed prevent incipient non-enzymic browning from occurring during drying, and together with avoidance of oxidation a product is obtained with a fresh flavour.

Freeze drying, such as AFD, is the best process for the dehydration of raw meats. The muscle fibres still retain their contractility, and between 40 to 80 per cent of original ATP-ase activity of the raw meat is retained (Hunt and Matheson, 1958), features which indicate little damage to the labile proteins has occurred. But even so, the product after reconstitution and cooking is less tender and juicy than the fresh meat when cooked. Meat of high pH has superior water holding properties, and may be achieved through inhibiting post mortem glycolysis by pre-slaughter injection of adrenalin (Cori and Cori, 1928; Radouco-Thomas *et al.*, 1959). Such 'adrenalin' meat yields a freeze dried product of superior texture (Penny *et al.*, 1963 and 1964). In addition the glucose content of the meat is depleted which confers added stability by limiting deterioration due to non-enzymic browning.

## PRESERVATION WITH PROTEIN MODIFICATION

In the above described procedures the intention is to provide a preserved food with the minimum change in its characteristics. However, processing may also be employed to convert a protein food into a more desirable product, either by simulating a more expensive product or one which is currently unavailable, or by preparing an entirely new product.

Wiking Eiweiss was a fish protein food developed for human consumption in Germany during the Second World War and used as an egg substitute. It was prepared by heating minced fish muscle at 70°–80°C for one hour in 0.5 per cent acetic acid. The water content of the mass was reduced to about 40 per cent by pressing, and after extraction with ethyl alcohol or trichlorethylene, the protein was hydrolysed with alkali. The solution of proteins so obtained was neutralized with either acetic or lactic acid and spray dried to give Wiking Eiweiss as a pure white water-soluble powder.

Fermented fish represents one of the oldest techniques for food preservation the name of which varies with country. It is known as fish sauce in Indonesia and Nagapi in Burma. Fish tissue is broken down by use of either proteolytic micro-organisms, e.g., yeasts, or proteolytic enzymes and the product is characterized by a strong flavour. It is commonly used in the form of pastes and sauces as a condiment in the Far East. Salt in large quantities is added as a preservative rendering the food unsuitable for small children, though a low pH in many of the products enhances stability. Preparation is simple and requires no expensive equipment.

## PROTEIN DETERIORATION ARISING FROM PRESERVATION

The major observed protein spoilage reactions may be divided into two groups i.e. non-enzymic browning and structural changes such as de-naturation and aggregation.

118

*Non-enzymic browning*

The biochemical significance of the non-enzymic browning reaction was first pointed out by the French chemist Maillard (1912) and since then it has been shown that the reaction induces a wide range of defects in processed foods – darkening in colour, development of scorched off-flavours and odours, loss of nutritive value particularly by destruction of lysine, (and in the case of dehydrated foods – toughening of texture and reduction in water absorption). The fundamental reaction involved is a condensation between the aldehyde group of a reducing sugar and a free amino group usually of an amino acid or protein. In proteins the $\epsilon$-amino groups of the lysine residues, together with such terminal $\alpha$-amino groups as remain exposed at the ends of the polypeptide chains, are available to react. Reynolds (1963, 1965) has extensively reviewed the reaction.

The rate of the reaction is very sensitive to three parameters within the system.

*(i) Moisture content.* The rate is at a maximum in the solid state at 65–70 per cent relative humidity. In the dry food (e.g., 2 per cent moisture on a fat free basis) or in aqueous solution the interaction is very slow.

*(ii) pH.* The reaction is inhibited at acidic pH, and increases rapidly with rise in pH above neutrality.

*(iii) Temperature.* The rate of reaction increases rapidly with a rise in temperature (Lea, 1958; Sharp and Rolfe, 1958; Thomson *et al.*, 1962). The temperature coefficient $Q_{10^\circ C}$ lies between 3.2 and 4.3 over the temperature range $15^\circ-50^\circ C$ which explains the marked reduction in shelf-life when, e.g., dehydrated meat is stored under tropical conditions. Dehydrated cooked meat minces and egg may be stabilized by removing the glucose by a yeast fermentation or by use of glucose oxidase (Henrickson *et al.*, 1955; Brooks *et al.*, 1955).

*Protein Denaturation and Aggregation*

Dehydration and freezing of proteinaceous foods may have an adverse effect on texture through structural changes in the protein initiated by environmental changes due to freezing or dehydration of the tissue. The responsible changes could be the increase in concentration of soluble salts, pH effects arising from precipitation of buffering salts, removal of 'bound' water and perhaps also surface activity at ice-solution interfaces.

The conformation of the protein macromolecule is stabilized by non-covalent bonds of three categories: hydrogen bonds, ionic bonds and hydrophobic bonds. Non-polar groups tend to come together in order to reduce the number of water-solute contacts because of the strong solute-solute van der Waals forces. This aggregation of non-polar groups is

119

termed hydrophobic bonding and it is believed to be one of the major contributions to the stability of compact protein conformations. Presumably protein molecules are folded in such a way that the majority of the non-polar groups are on the inside of the molecule while the charged groups are on the surface exposed to water (Nemethy, 1969). These ideas about the folding of the protein molecules have been confirmed generally in those proteins for which the detailed structures have been determined by means of X-ray diffraction, e.g. Perutz (1965) in respect of haemoglobin. The hydrophobic side chains are mostly buried in the protein molecule in the native state: with the unfolding of the molecule in the denatured state they become exposed to the solvent. The ionic side chains are largely solvated in both the native and denatured states.

Although loss of the native conformation, caused by a rise in temperature or by the addition of some denaturing agent, has been shown to be completely reversible for a number of different proteins (Brandts, 1964; 1965), conditions must be carefully controlled before a complete return to the native configuration can be observed. The content of irreversibility for most conformational unfolding reactions increases as the concentration of protein is increased, implying that failure to revert to the native conformation is due to an aggregation reaction subsequent to the unimolecular unfolding reaction, the aggregation step being kinetically irreversible. In the case of ribonuclease, reversibility can be demonstrated only at low protein concentrations; with other proteins e.g., ovalbumin, the aggregation reaction is so favourable that it occurs even at very low concentrations (Brandts, 1967; Holme, 1963). The mode of aggregation can be influenced by the environment. Orosomucoid, a glycoprotein, when heated at pH 4.1 in a solution of low ionic strength, produced a chain polymer whereas similar treatment in high ionic strength produced a spherical polymer. The polymers can be depolymerized in 3M guanidine hydrochloride, showing the bonding is either by hydrogen bonds or by electrostatic attraction between the monomers. The monomer could be repolymerized on heating; but whereas the 'chain monomer' only formed chains (at all ionic strengths), the 'spherical monomer' was indistinguishable from the original monomer in its behaviour. Evidently the formation of the chain is accompanied by irreversible rearrangements in the molecule (Spragg et al., 1969).

The macromolecular structures of biopolymers such as collagen, ribonuclease and DNA are grossly different, yet von Hippel and Wong (1964) point out that the effects of certain simple compounds on the conformation of these macromolecules in aqeous solutions are strikingly similar. They studied the thermal disorganization of ribonuclease and myosin in the presence of a variety of neutral compounds, and observed that the latter substances fell into two separate classes with respect to their influence on the transition temperature. It is lowered by urea, lithium bromide and potassium thiocyanate, and is raised by ammonium sulphate and sugar. Similar studies have been reported on DNA (Hamaguchi *et al.,* 1962) and collagen (Gustavson, 1956) and it is observed that the stabilizing and destabilizing effects of the simple molecules are similar in these cases too. It would appear that the small molecules generate their effects by modifying the structure of the solvent. Such modifications could, in turn, perturb interactions between solvent and macromolecule, and thus indirectly change the conformation and behaviour of the biopolymer (Klotz, 1965).

Around a biopolymer and its side groups there is a quite rigid, first layer of hydration. This remains unchanged on freezing whereas the bulk of the water goes into ordinary α-ice. Apparently therefore, apart from the aggregation of non-polar groups in the native protein molecule, there is a possibility also of an interaction between these non-polar groups and water structure. Water is very versatile in regard to hydrate formation and is capable of forming a large variety of cage-like structures to accommodate itself to non-polar groups. Klotz (1960) has suggested that similar structures could form around non-polar groups projecting from a macromolecule. There is a parallelism between the non-polar side chains of proteins and those small molecules known to form clathrate-like hydrates (e.g., $-CH_3$ of alanine, $-CH(CH_3)_2$ of valine, $-CH_2.CH(CH_3)_2$ of leucine). In the protein the local concentration of side chains is high and there could be a co-operative effect of adjacent non-polar groups to induce a stabilized arrangement of water in a microscopically crystalline array. Klotz attributes non-polar bond stabilization in these macromolecules to the formation of these ordered water regions or 'hydrotactoids'. The effect of temperature on the denaturation of proteins is attributed to the disorganization or melting of hydrotactoids. Likewise the denaturing effect of urea is attributed to its ability to disorganize the hydration lattice and thereby decrease the stabilization of the protein originating from the presence of non-polar groups.

The multilayer concept of water on the surface of proteins is consistent with the behaviour of cell water during freeezing. The cell water of supercooled muscle fibres freezes unidirectionally in thin columns when the cut end of a muscle fibre is seeded by means of ice crystals. Within a single muscle cell there will be numerous spikes whose direction follows that of the muscle fibre (Chambers and Hale, 1932). However, even when freezing is complete, considerable water can still be detected in the protoplasm (Luyet, 1965). This evidence suggests that the water located near the centre of the spaces between the columns of proteins will freeze, whereas the water immediately absorbed on the proteins is not readily freezable because its molecular arrangement is dictated by the unique structure of the protein at that location, and its transformation into another structure (i.e., ice) is energetically unfavourable (Ling, 1965). Such protein-oriented water structure is exemplified by its structure in partially dried collagen as revealed by nuclear magnetic resonance studies of Berendesen (1962).

Some doubts regarding the possibility of any marked increase in concentration of salts arising in a tissue as a result of freezing is expressed by Ling (1965). His work suggests that more than 90 per cent of the intracellular ions are absorbed on cell proteins; dehydration therefore does not necessarily give rise to a very high concentration inside the cell. However, should ice formation damage the cell proteins, release of absorbed ions may be expected.

## REFERENCES

Anonymous (1944). Committee on Dehydration of Meat. *Agric. Res. Adm. Circ.* 706, U.S. Dep. Agriculture

Ayres, J. C. (1955). In *Adv. Fd Res.* 6, Ed. by Mrak, E. M. and Stewart, G. F. New York; Academic Press

Berendsen, H. J. C. (1962). *J. chem. Phys.,* 36, 3297

Brandts, J. F. (1964). *J. Am. chem. Soc.,* 86, 4291

Brandts, J. F. (1965). *J. Am. chem. Soc.,* 87, 2759

Brandts, J. F. (1967). In *Heat Effects on Proteins and Enzymes.* Ed. by Rose, A. H. New York; Academic Press

Brooks, J., Taylor, D. J. (1955). *Spec. Rept. Fd Invest. Bd D.S.I.R. No. 60.* London: H.M. Stationery Office p.85

Burgess. G. H. O., Cutting, C. L., Lovern, J. A. and Waterman, J. J. (1965a). *Fish Handling and Processing.* Edinburgh: H.M. Stationery Office p.14

– Cutting, C. L., Lovern, J. A. and Waterman, J. J. (1965b). *Ibid* p.142

Burley, R. W. and Cook, W. H. (1961). *Can. J. Biochem. Physiol.* 39, 1295

Chambers, R. and Hale, H. P. (1932) *Proc. R. Soc.* 110B, 336

Christian, J. H. B. (1962). In *Rec. Adv. Fd Sci.,* 3, Ed. by Leitch, J. M. and Rhodes, D. London: Butterworths.

Cori, C. F. and Cori, G. T. (1928). *J. biol. Chem.* 79, 309

Cunningham, F. E. and Lineweaver, H. (1965). *Fd Technol. Champaign,* 19, 1442

Davis, J. G., Hanson, H. L. and Lineweaver, H. (1952). *Fd Res.,* 17, 393

Dreosti, G. M. and Van der Merue, R. P. (1956). *Tenth A. Rep. Fishg Inds Res. Inst. S. Afr.* p. 36

Eddy, B. P. (1960). *J. Appl. Bact.* 23, 189

El-Bisi, H. M. (1965). In *Radiat. Preserv. Fd, Publ. 1273,* Natn. Acad. Sci., Wash., D.C., Natn. Res. Counc.

Esty, J. R. and Meyer, K. F. (1922). *J. infect. Dis.,* 31, 650

Gillespy, T. G. (1962). In *Rec. Adv. Fd Sci.,* 2, Ed. by Hawthorn, J. and Leitch, J. M. London: Butterworths. p. 93

Goldblith, S. A. (1964). *Fd Technol. Champaign,* 18, 1384

Gooding, E. G. B. and Rolfe, E. J. (1955). *J. Sci. Fd Agric.*, **6**, 427

Gooding, E. G. B. and Rolfe, E. J. (1957). *Fd Technol. Champaign*, **11**, 302

Goresline, H. E., Ingram, M., Macuch, P., Mocquot, C., Mossel, D. A. A., Niven, C. F. and Thatcher, F. S. (1964). *Nature, Lond.*, **204**, 237

Guttman, A. and Van den Leuval, F. A. (1957). *Prog. Rep. Atlant. Cst Stns, No. 67*, p. 29

Gustavson, K. H. (1956). *The Chemistry and Reactivity of Collagen.* New York: Academic Press

Hamaguchi, K. and Geiduschok, P. (1962). *J. Am. Chem. Soc.*, **84**, 1329

Hammerle, O. A., Knobl, G. M., Pariser, E. R. and Snyder, D. G. (1964). In *Technology of Fish Util.*, pp. 217-222. London: Fishing New (Books) Ltd.

Hannan, R. S. (1955). *Spec. Rep. Fd Invest. Bd D.S.I.R. No. 61.* London: H.M. Stationery Office

Hansen, P. I. E. (1966). *Process Biochemistry*, **1**, 487

Hay, J. M. (1955). *J. Sci. Fd Agric.*, **6**, 433

Heiligman, F. (1965). *Fd Technol. Champaign.* **19**, 114

Heller, C. L., Roberts, B. C., Amos, A. J., Smith, M. E. and Hobbs, B. C. (1962). *J. Hyg., Camb.* **60**, 135

Henrickson, R. L., Brady, D. E., Gehrke, C. W. and Brooks, R. F. (1955). *Agric. Exp. Stn Res. Bull. No. 587*, Univ. Mo. Coll. Agric.

Holme, J. (1963). *J. phys. Chem. Ithaca*, **67**, 788

Hunt, S. M. V. and Matheson, N. A. (1958). *Nature, Lond.*, **181**, 472

Hunt, S. M. V. and Matheson, N. A. (1959). *Fd Res.* **24**, 262

Ingraham, J. L. and Stokes, J. L. (1959). *Bact. Rev.* **23**, 97

Ingram, M. and Rhodes, D. N. (1962). *Fd Mf.* **37**, 318

Klotz, I. M. (1960). *Brookhaven, Symp. Biol.* **13**, 25

Klotz, I. M. (1965). *Fedn Proc. Fedr Am. Socs exp Biol.*,**24**, Suppl. **15**, S-24

Lea, C.H. (1958). In *Fundamental Aspects of the Dehydration of foodstuffs.* London: Soc. chem. Ind.

Lewin, E. (1959). *Fd Technol. Champaign.* **13** (2), 132

Lightbody, H. D., and Fevold, H. L., (1948). In *Adv. Fd Res.*, **1**. Ed. by Mrak, E. M. and Stewart, G. F., New York: Academic Press

Ling, G. N. (1965). *Fedn Proc. Fedn Am. Soc exp. Biol.*, **24**, Suppl. 15, S-111

Liston, J. and Matches, T. R. (1968). *Fd Technol. Champaign.* **22**, 893

Lopez, A., Fellers, C. R. and Powrie, W. D. (1954). *J. Milk Fd Technol.*, **17**, 334

− Fellers, C. R. and Powrie, W. D. (1955). *Ibid*, **18**, 77

Lovelock, J. E. (1953). *Biochim. Biophys. Acta*, **10**, 414

Lusena, C. V. (1955). *Arch. Biochem. Biophys.*, **57**, 277

Luyet, B. J. (1965). *Fedn Proc. Fedn Am. Socs. Exp. Biol.*, **24**, Suppl. 15. S-315

Maillard, L. C. (1912). *C.r. hebd. Séanc. Acad. Sci. Paris.* **154**, 66

Masurovsky, E. B., Goldblith, S. A. and Nickerson, J. T. R. (1963). *Appl. Microbiol.*, **11**, 330

Meesemaecker, R. and Sohier, Y. (1959). *Fd Mf.*, **34**, 193

Merritt, C. (1966). In *Food Irradiation.* Vienna: Int. atom. Energy Ag. p. 197

Meryman, H. T. (1956). *Science, N.Y.* **124**, 515

Michener, H. D. and Elliott, R. P. (1964). In *Adv. Fd. Res.* **13**, Ed. by Chichester. C.O., Mrak E. M. and Stewart, G. F. New York: Academic Press

Moran, T. (1925). *Proc. R. Soc.*, **98B**, 436

Mossel, D. A. A., and Ingram, M. (1955). *J. Appl. Bact.* **18**, 232

Mouton, R. F. (1964a). *Inds atom.*, **8**, 5/6, 53

− (1964b). *Ibid*, **8**, 7/8, 103

− (1965). *Ibid.* **9**, 1/2 65

Nemethy, G. (1969). In *Low Temperature Biology of Foodstuffs,* Ed. by
  Hawthorn, J. and Rolfe, E. Oxford: Pergamon Press. p. 17
Pearce, J. A. and Lavers, C. G. (1949). *Can. J. Res.* 27F. 231
Pelroy, G. A., Seaman, J. P. and Eklund, M. W. (1967). *Appl. Microbiol.,* 15, 92
Penny, I. F., Voyle, C. A. and Lawrie, R. A. (1963). *J. Sci. Fd Agric.,* 14, 535
  — Voyle, C. A. and Lawrie, R. A. (1964). *Ibid,* 15, 559
Perutz, M. F. (1965). *J. molec. Biol.,* 13, 646
Peterson, A. C. and Gunderson, M. F. (1960). *Fd Technol. Champaign.* 14, 413
Plank, R., Ehrenbaum, E. and Reuter, K. (1916). In *Abhandlungen zur
  Volksernahrung,* Vol. 5 Part I Berlin p. 6
Powrie, W. D. (1969). In *Low Temperature Biology of Foodstuffs.* Ed. by
  Hawthorn, J. and Rolfe, E. Oxford: Pergamon Press. p. 328
  —      Little, H. and Lopez, A. (1963). *J. Fd Sci.,* 28, 38
Radouco-Thomas, C. (1959). *Int. J. Appl. Radiat. Isotopes,* 6, 129
Reynolds, T. M. (1963). In *Adv. Fd Res.* 12, Ed. by Chichester, C.O., Mrak, E. M.
  and Stewart, G. F. New York: Academic Press, p. 1
  —          (1965). *Ibid.* 14, 167
Riedel, L. (1957). *Kältetechnik,* 9, 38, 342
Riemann, H. (1957). *Fd Mf.,* 32, 265, 333
Rolfe, E. (1956). *Food,* 25, 199
  —      (1958). In *Fundamental Aspects of the Dehydration of Foodstuffs.*
  London: Soc. Chem. Ind.
  —      (1962). *Trends and Developments in Food Technology in O.E.C.D.
  Countries.* O.E.C.D. Directorate Agric. Fd Div. Tech. Action. AGR/T (62), 29
  —      (1965). *Fd Mf.,* 40(7), 46
  —      (a) unpublished data.
  —      (b) unpublished data.
Scott, W. J. (1957). In *Adv. Fd Res.* 1, Ed. by Mrak, E. M. and Stewart, G. F. New
  York: Academic Press
Sharp, J. G. (1953). *Spec. Rept. Fd Invest. Bd D.S.I.R. No. 57.,* London: H.M.
  Stationery Office
Sharp, J. G. and Rolfe, E. (1958). In *Fundamental Aspects of the Dehydration
  of Foodstuffs.* London: Soc. Chem. Ind.
Shea, K. G. (1958). *Fd Technol. Champaign.* 12(8), 6
Shewan, J. M. and Liston, J. (1956). *Bull. int. Inst. Refrig., Suppl. Annexe
  1956–1,* 137
Spragg, S. P., Halsall, H. B., Flewett, T. H. and Barclay, G. R. (1969). *Biochem. J.*
  111, 345
Snyder, D. G. (1967). *Fd Technol. Champaign,* 21, 1234
Tarr, H. L. A. (1952). *Prog. Rep. Pacif. Cst Stns., No. 92,* p. 23
Tarr, H. L. A. (1954). *Fd Technol. Champaign.* 8, 15
Tarr, H. L. A. and Bissett, H. M. (1954). *Prog. Rep. Pacif. Cst Stns, No. 98,* p. 3
The Liquid Egg (Pasteurization) Regulations (1963). (S.I. 1963 No. 1503). Dated
  28 August 1963
Thomas, A. W. and Bailey, M. (1933). *Ind. Eng Chem. ind. Edn,* 25, 669
Thomson, J. S., Fox, J. B. and Landman, W. A. (1962). *Fd Technol. Champaign,*
  16(9), 131
Thornley, M. J. (1963). *J. appl. Bact.* 26, 334
Townsend, C. T., Esty, T. R. and Basel, F. C. (1938). *Fd Res.* 3, 323
Van den Brock, C. J. H. (1965). In *Fish as Food* Vol. IV, Ed. by Borgstrom, G.
  New York: Academic Press

Vas, K. (1966). In *Food Irradiation,* Vienna: Int. Atom. Energy ag. p. 253

VioBin Corporation (1956). *Fish Flour—a Review of Progress.* VioBin Corporation, Monticello, Ill

Von Hippel, P. H. and Wong, K. Y. (1964). *Science, N.Y.* **145**, 577

Zender, R., Lataste-Dorolle, C., Collet, R. A., Rowinski, P. and Mouton, R. F. (1958). *Proc. 2nd U.N. Int. Conf. PUAE,* **27**, 384

# ALTERATIONS TO PROTEINS DURING PROCESSING AND THE FORMATION OF STRUCTURES

## M.P. TOMBS

*Unilever Research Laboratory, Colworth House, Sharnbrook, Beds.*

## INTRODUCTION

We are interested in the role of proteins as structural elements in food-stuffs, in the belief that an understanding of protein behaviour will lead to some insight into the characteristics of proteinaceous foods. Ultimately we hope that an understanding of the main factors may lead to better control of the structure of foods and in particular of the group of properties generally classified as texture.

We believe that we have to deal mainly with protein–protein inter-actions of various strengths and frequencies, which may be described under the inclusive term of aggregation. All changes, such as precipitation, gelation, or simply the development of turbidity involve such inter-actions.

We have investigated arachin, a groundnut protein (Tombs, 1965; Tombs and Lowe, 1967) and bovine serum albumin as examples of two types of globular proteins to try and identify the main factors in aggregation leading to gelations and precipitations and why one is preferred rather than the other in different conditions.

## ALBUMIN AGGREGATION

We have followed heat aggregation by measuring the molecular weight, and we chose to measure the number average molecular weight by osmometry. This is defined as

$$M_{\bar{n}} = \sum_{m}^{j} \frac{n_m M_m \ldots n_j M_j}{\sum_{m}^{j} n_m \ldots n_j}$$

126

where $n_m$ is the number of molecules of weight, $M_m$ and so on. If we have an initial molecular weight

$$M_{\bar{n}_i} = \frac{n_i M_i}{n_i}$$

But $n_i\, M_i$ is the concentration and similarly, at any degree of aggregation

$$\sum_{m}^{j} \; n_m M_m \ldots n_j M_j$$

is also the concentration. The total weight concentration is not changed by aggregation so that

$$n_i M_i = \sum_{m}^{j} n_m M_m \ldots n_j M_j$$

and

$$\frac{M\bar{n}}{Mn_i} = a \qquad (1)$$

where $a$ is the average degree of aggregation. It is the ratio between the initial number of particles and the final. (It should be noted that weight average measurements will not give this result.) If the initial particle is a single chain, then at least one interchain link is needed to form a dimer, two for a trimer, and so on; $(a-1)/a$ is the average number of interchain links, per chain, so that

$$K = \frac{a-1}{a} \qquad (2)$$

$K$ may be used to estimate progress towards gelation, because when $K = 1$ in principle a continuous network could be formed.

Gelation may of course, occur before all the molecules are linked into a network, and determination of $K$ can lead to some information on this.

The time course of aggregation was first dealt with by Smoluchowski (1918) who derived the expression

127

$$n_t = \frac{n_0}{1 + \beta n_0 t} \tag{3}$$

where $n_t$ is the number of particles after time $t$, $n_0$ the initial number and $\beta$ is a 'constant'. Clearly $n_0/n_t = a$ as defined above, so

$$a = 1 + \beta n_0 t \tag{4}$$

$\beta$ is equal to $4\pi RD\epsilon$ where $R$ and $D$ are the radius and diffusion constant of the interacting particles. These are changing during the aggregation, and so are not exactly constant. The product $RD$ will probably change less than the individual quantities, but $\beta$ may show some variations. $\epsilon$ is the collision frequency efficiency factor and is a measure of the fraction of the number of collisions which leads to interaction.

*Figure 1* shows a plot of $a$ against $t$ for albumin solutions in sodium phosphate buffer pH 6.24 (8 volumes of 9.45 g/l $NaH_2PO_4$ and 2 volumes 10.4 g/l $Na_2HPO_4$), heated at 69°C. The molecular weights were measured with a modified Rowe–Abrahams osmometer (1957). Samples removed at the indicated times were cooled quickly in ice, a series of dilutions made, and $M_n$ determined from $\pi/c$ in the usual way (Tombs and Lowe, 1967). The $\pi/c$ against $c$ plots were linear, suggesting that the solution was stable, and that dilution had little effect on the aggregation.

Table 1

Heat aggregation of bovine serum albumin

| Initial concentration (g/100 ml) | $n_0 \times 10^{16}/cm^3$ | $\beta \times 10^{-20}$ | $\epsilon \times 10^{-9}$ | *$RD \times 10^{-14}$ |
|---|---|---|---|---|
| 0.928 | 4.21 | 0.356 | 1.2 | 23.6 |
| 1.86 | 13.1 | 0.725 | 1.2 | 48.5 |
| 3.17 | 19.6 | 0.96 | 1.2 | 64.6 |
| 3.85 | 35.0 | 1.04 | 1.2 | 69.5 |
| 4.83 | 44.0 | 7.0 | 1.2 | 467 |

* Values for $R = 40 \times 10^{-8}$ cm, $D = 5.9 \times 10^{-7}$ taken from Tanford (1961)

At the lower concentrations the result is reasonably close to Smoluchowski's predictions, though higher concentrations produce some curvature. Since $n_0$ is known, from the mol. wt. of albumin 66,000

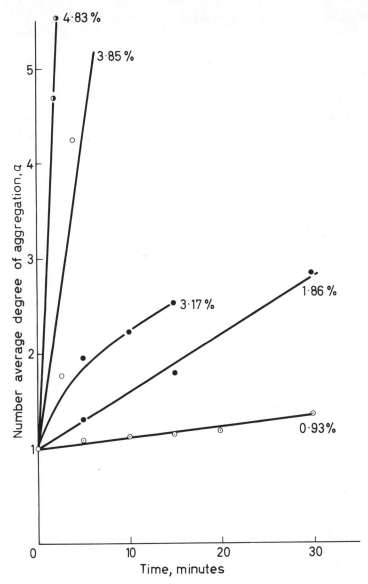

*Figure 1. Aggregation of bovine serum albumin: the concentrations indicated (all in g/100 ml solution) were heated at 69°C in sodium phosphate buffer pH 6.24. a is calculated from the molecular weight, determined by osmometry*

(Tanford, 1961) $\beta$ may be calculated. The results are shown in Table 1. $\beta$ was calculated for the lowest concentration and least aggregated case, by using available values for $R$ and $D$, and then $\epsilon$ assumed to remain constant at the other concentrations. $RD$ was plainly not a constant. The value of $\epsilon$ suggests that about one collision in $10^9$ leads to aggregation, and compares with a value of $1 \times 10^{-8}$ obtained by a very indirect method by Klecskowski (1949).

*Figure 2* shows a plot of $K$ and in effect the progress towards gelation of these solutions. Gelation times were measured independently and suggest that it does occur when $K$ is approaching $0.9-1.0$ (i.e. the degree of aggregation is ten or more).

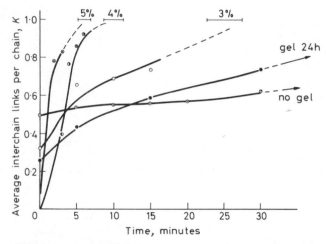

*Figure 2. Progress to gelation of bovine serum albumin. The bars at the top of the figure indicate approximate gelation times, at the concentrations indicated. Other conditions were as for Figure 1*

Finally, a relationship between intrinsic viscosity and molecular weights appeared, and is shown in *Figure 3*. Viscosity is often used to characterize solutions approaching gelation, and it is also sometimes assumed that the increase in viscosity on heating protein solutions is due to 'unfolding'. This result suggests that aggregation may also be a factor in such viscosity increase since

$$\log [\eta] = \alpha \log K + \alpha \log M \qquad (5)$$

$\alpha$ and $K$ being constants, for many polymers (Tanford, 1961). There is

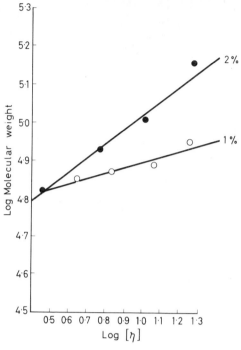

*Figure 3. Relationship between intrinsic viscosity and molecular weight for heated bovine serum albumin solutions, at* 1 per cent (w/v) *and* 2 per cent (w/v) *total protein*

however, no way of interpreting the value of α and K for mixtures of components of varying size and shape, and in this situation viscosity measurement can give little information on the structures involved (cf. Smoluchowsky, 1918).

## NATURE OF INTERCHAIN LINKS

Broadly, only two kinds of links occur between protein molecules, covalent of which the only probable kind is the disulphide bond, and non-covalent involving electrostatic, hydrogen bond and hydrophobic interactions. It is supposed that heating solutions of proteins brings about conformational change, which alters the way in which protein-protein interactions occur, usually in the direction of greater or more powerful interactions. Certainly, the thiol groups tend to become more reactive (Cecil, 1963).

Table 2

Molecular weight of albumin and arachin aggregates in various solvents

| Pre-treatment | Solvent | $\bar{M}_n$ | a | K |
|---|---|---|---|---|
| None | 4M GHCl | 74,100 | 1.12 | 0.107 |
| None | 4M GHCl 0.1M Na$_2$SO$_3$ | 68,000 | 1 | 0 |
| Heated 30 min 69° at 2% in phosphate pH 6.3 | 4M GHCl<br>Phosphate pH 6.3 | 189,470<br>252,000 | 2.87<br>3.81 | 0.65<br>0.74 |
| As above but 3.5% for 4-5 min | 4M GHCl<br>Phosphate pH 6.3 | 227,000<br>312,000 | 3.44<br>4.74 | 0.64<br>0.79 |
| 2.05% arachin 30 min at 70° in phosphate pH 9 | 4M GHCl<br>Phosphate pH 9 | 35,000<br>280,000 | 1*<br>8.0 | 0<br>0.87 |
| 1.35% arachin 30 min at 70° phosphate pH 9 | Phosphate pH 9 | 1,100,000 | 31 | 0.97 |

* relative to the sub-unit molecular weight
GHCl—abbreviation for guanidine hydrochloride

Dissociating solvents, such as urea or guanidine hydrochloride solutions disrupt all but covalent links, so that measurement of $\bar{M}_n$ in such solvents may be used to estimate what proportion of the links are covalent. Some data are given in Table 2. In the case of albumin aggregates the molecular weight drops slightly on adding guanidine hydrochloride, and a comparison of the $K$ values shows that about 85 per cent of the links must be covalent. There is good evidence that for albumin they are disulphides (Huggins, Tapley and Jensen, 1951). The results also show that simply adding guanidine does not produce significant aggregation. Arachin gives a quite different result, as isolated it has a molecular weight of 360,000, though forms of 180,000 and 720,000 also exist.

The time course of aggregation suggests that it partly dissociates to subunits before aggregates form from the dissociated fragments. The 'native' state contains 12 chains (Tombs and Lowe, 1967) and $a$ and $K$ are calculated on the basis of individual chains. The effect of guanidine also suggests that the bonds are non-covalent. It is probably more typical of proteins used in processing than is albumin, which is unusual in containing only one chain in its native form.

## SIZE, SHAPE AND NUMBERS OF AGGREGATES

The results discussed so far have been solely concerned with average properties and this is reasonable for a process such as the aggregation of globular proteins where reaction is due to random collisions between the molecules. However, to form a gel, strands must be formed by the aggregates. A random aggregation would presumably lead to more or less spherical particles, so that gelation must be the result of a fairly specific oriented interaction. It is at first sight improbable that gels could be formed from globular proteins at all because such orientation does not seem likely.

The aggregates are large enough to be easily visualized by electron microscopy. *Plate I* shows some examples of albumin aggregates obtained by heating at 70° and 100°C. At 70° the solution eventually gels, while at 100° it coagulates. *Figure 4* shows the way in which the proportion of chains to spheres varies with temperature. The spherical particles have a fairly sharp size distribution which is not consistent with entirely random aggregation, while the presence of chains implies orientation effects.

Pre-treatment with 4*M* guanidine hydrochloride before microscopy did not alter the appearance of either type of aggregate, while an unheated albumin solution showed no aggregates by the same technique.

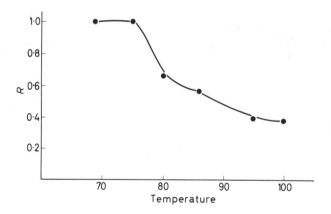

*Figure 4. Effect of temperature on particle shape.* 1 per cent (w/v) *bovine serum albumin heated* 10 minutes *in phosphate buffer* pH 6.24
$R$ = *number of chains/total number of chains + spheres*

133

The distribution of particle sizes was deduced by Smoluchowski (1918) as

$$n_a = \frac{n_0(\beta n_0 t)^{a-1}}{(1 + \beta n_0 t)^{a+1}} \qquad (6)$$

where $n_a$ is the number of particles of degree of aggregation $a$. Since $\beta$ had been obtained, this distribution was calculated and is shown in *Figure 5* along with the measured distribution.

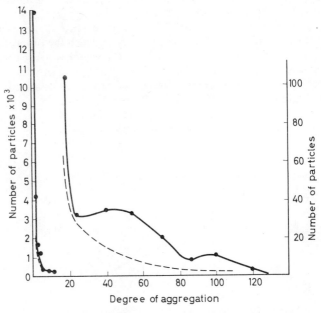

*Figure 5. Number-degree of aggregation distribution for albumin, 0.928 per cent (w/v) heated at 69° for 5 min. Note that the right-hand part of the curve is on the scale to the right. The broken line shows the approximate theoretical prediction from equation 6*

As might be expected, a theory which is based on the idea of random aggregation fails to predict the two peaks at high degrees of aggregation, which represent the chains. The shape of the distribution suggests a complex, and oriented aggregation.

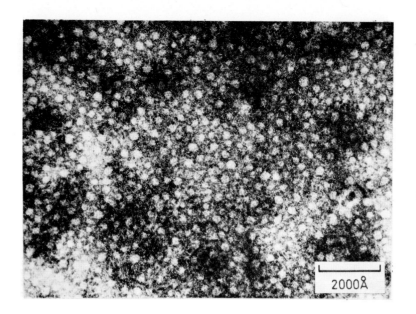

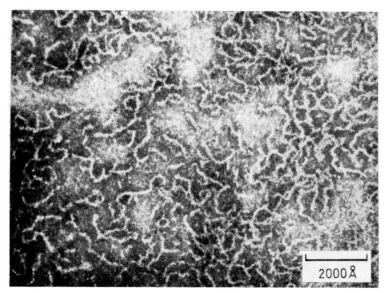

Plate I. *Electron micrographs of aggregated bovine serum albumin. The upper print shows 3 per cent (w/v) protein heated at 100°C for 8 seconds. The lower, the same solution heated at 69°C for 30 minutes. Both cases were negative stained with phosphotungstic acid on a carbon grid.*

*To face page 134]*

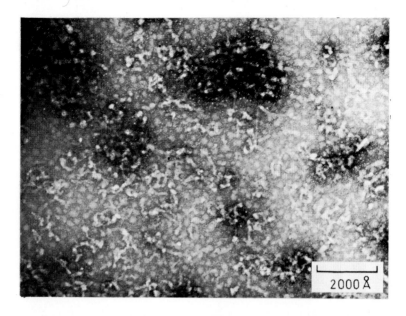

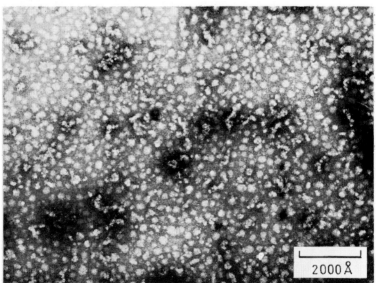

*Plate II. Electron micrographs of aggregated arachin : negative stained with uranyl formate. The upper print shows the results of 30 minutes at 69°C at pH 10, 1 per cent (w/v) protein, the lower at pH 9, 1 per cent (w/v) at 50°C for 30 minutes.*

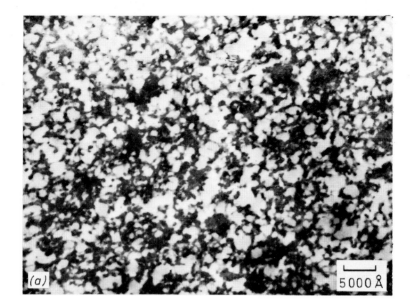

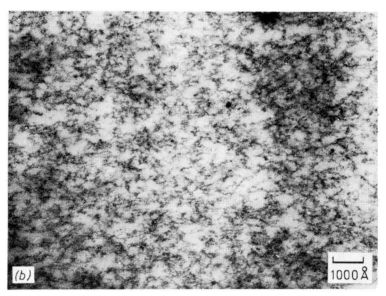

Plate III. Examples of protein gels. (a) Transverse section of a groundnut protein fibre. (b) Groundnut protein gel, 20 per cent protein pH 7, autoclaved 1 hour at 110°C, positive stain with uranyl acetate.

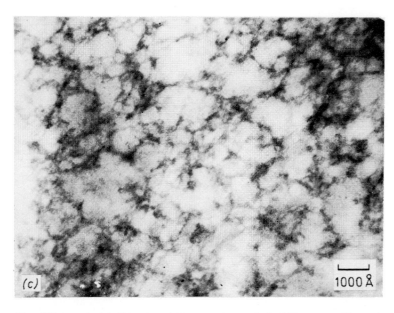

*Plate III (cont.). (c) Albumin gel, 2 per cent protein in 8 M urea, positive stain with uranyl acetate. All the samples were fixed, embedded and sectioned.*

*Plate II* shows some arachin aggregates and the same kind of difference can be seen; more or less spherical particles in a sample which coagulated and some indications of chain formation in conditions which can result in gelation.

## GEL STRUCTURE

It is possible to obtain some idea of gel structure by electron microscopy. *Plate III* shows some examples of an albumin gel, a groundnut protein gel, and a fibre, also from groundnut protein. All three, although prepared under very different conditions show the same type of structure, and it has two characteristic features, an average pore size $\bar{p}$ and a gel strand thickness $d$. These quantities must be related to the concentration of the gel forming agent which, although it is hardly in solution, can be described on either volume or weight scales (e.g. $cm^3/cm^3$ gel or $g/cm^3$ gel).

Suppose the gel strands are in a regular rectangular array. It can be shown that

$$p + d = \frac{1.53d}{\sqrt{c}}$$

where $c$ is the volume concentration.

They are obviously not in a regular array, but Ogston (1958) has derived an equation

$$\bar{p} = \frac{1}{\sqrt{4\nu L}}$$

where $\nu$ is the number of strands of length, $L$, for a random arrangement of fibres. If the strands are assumed to be made up of spherical particles, of diameter $d$ then it can be shown that

$$p = \frac{1.73}{\sqrt{nd}}$$

for a regular array, where $n$ is the number of molecules. Ogston's equation also converts to

$$\bar{p} = \frac{1}{\sqrt{nd}} \tag{7}$$

135

Both these expressions assume that $p$ is large ($p > 10d$ at least) compared with $d$, and also that the gel strands are of uniform diameter. These equations cannot therefore be precise, but no better ones are available.

The albumin gel illustrated in *Plate III* had an average pore size of about 330 Å. $d$ was estimated at about 100 Å, while $n = 18.2 \times 10^{16}$. This gives a value of $p = 230$ Å by equation (7).

The groundnut protein gel, although much more concentrated, had a pore size of about 200 Å. The approximations in equations (6) and (7) would be expected to lead to underestimates, so that the discrepancies are not surprising. It is of interest however, that changing the concentration tenfold has a much smaller effect on $\bar{p}$.

Preliminary results suggest that $p$ and $d$ correlate usefully with bulk mechanical properties. $p$ possibly relates to the hardness of a gel, while $d$ is connected with elasticity. The section of a fibre shown in *Plate III* illustrates that this too has a gel structure. There is no sign of orientated strands, and at least in this case it can be treated as a cylindrical gel. (This is not of course, true of all fibres, which may be slightly orientated.) Comparison of *Plates I* and *III* shows clearly that the gel strands obtained by heating albumin are nothing like those seen in urea gel, and could not be regarded as an intermediate stage in the formation of such a gel. The gels that were obtained had different mechanical properties and we hope to correlate these with the different types of aggregate in the two cases. The arachin strands, on the other hand, are similar to those in the gel, and could be regarded as intermediates.

## DISCUSSION

A number of investigations have shown (Privalov and Monaselidze, 1963; Barbu and Joly, 1953; Hospelhorn, Cross and Jensen, 1954; Kratochvil, Munk and Sedlacek, 1962) by a variety of techniques that albumin aggregates when its solutions are heated, and that this is responsible for a large part of the viscosity increase. It also aggregates in the presence of $8M$ urea (Huggins, Tapley and Jensen, 1951) by a chain reaction of the type,

$$P\text{--}SH \quad + \quad \begin{matrix} S \\ I \\ S \end{matrix}\!\!\!> P \longrightarrow P - S - S - P - SH \quad + \quad \begin{matrix} S \\ I \\ S \end{matrix}\!\!\!> P$$

$$\longrightarrow \quad P - S - S - P - S - S - P - SH \quad \longrightarrow$$

which can be catalysed by the addition of small amounts of thiol compounds, such as 2–mercaptoethanol. Bovine serum albumin contains seventeen intra-chain disulphides which, in the undisrupted molecule will possess different reactivities. Presumably one of them is so positioned that, in the relatively undisrupted state at 70°C, chain formation results. As the temperature is raised, the molecule unfolds, more of the disulphides become available for reaction, and the spherical aggregates which predominate at higher temperatures will tend to form This provides a partial explanation for the effect of temperature, but the spherical aggregates occupy too narrow a size distribution for this to be the whole reason. Kratochvil *et al.* (1962) have shown, also by electron microscopy, that ionic strength is also important in determining the shape of the aggregates.

The main conclusion is that, by slight variation of conditions, quite different types of aggregates may be obtained, and these lead to results varying from gels with a range of mechanical properties, to amorphous coagulates. This example suggests that temperature is an important variable when attempting to gel proteins, especially to make thermostable gels.

Smoluchowski's general theory of aggregation has not received much attention. More recently, Flory (1942) has briefly considered protein gelation in terms of statistical theories developed mainly for synthetic polymers using a parameter similar to the $K$ used here. There seems to be no reason why this approach cannot be used to follow the approach to gelation of protein solutions, although it is not possible at present to predict the appearance of, for example, the unexpectedly large chains seen in albumin. A possible explanation of these is that chains can grow more rapidly, the longer they are, producing an autocatalytic effect. Joly (1953) has produced some calculations to show that this may be general, for the aggregation of globular proteins, and could go far to explain the formation of chains.

The majority of globular proteins likely to be of interest in food processing contain more than one peptide chain: arachin has as many as twelve. This increases the possible modes of aggregation considerably, and in the arachin gel illustrated the strand thickness suggests that it is built up, not from the 'intact' native protein, but from its sub-units. Also the initial effect of heating appears to be not an aggregation but a dissociation towards the sub-unit. The groundnut fibre illustrated, made by the conventional extrusion of an alkaline solution into an acid bath, followed by stretching, shows that theories of 'unfolding' and 'alignment' of peptide chains may be unhelpful in some cases (e.g. Lundgren, 1945). Highly aligned fibres can exist, but the mechanical properties of this example, and similar casein and soy based fibres depend more on the gel mesh dimensions than on the possibilities of interaction between extended peptide chains.

There is now good evidence that proteins can be obtained, in solution, in a state which approximates to the random coil (Tanford, Kawahara and Lapanje, 1967) but under conditions (for example, $4M$ guanidine hydrochloride $0.1\ M$ mercaptoethanol) which are not similar to those encountered in food processing. Aggregation appears to be more important than unfolding in producing the gross changes which are made use of in protein processes. Aggregation is a consequence of conformational change in most cases, though there is no absolute dependence on it. For example, in the case of $\beta_A$ lactoglobulin polymerization, it is not the direct result of conformational change. On the other hand, the heat-induced aggregation of albumin is, though again it seems certain that the albumin molecules do not approach the random coil if only because they are held to shape by the intra-chain disulphides. These considerations suggest that it is important to distinguish clearly between the primary conformational alteration produced by heating protein solutions, and the secondary effects, mainly aggregations, which are probably responsible for the observed phenomena (such as viscosity increases) on which processes are based.

## ACKNOWLEDGEMENT.

I am much indebted to Mr. J.M. Stubbs for the electron micrographs.

## REFERENCES

Barbu, E. and Joly, M. (1953). *Discuss. Faraday soc.* **13**, 77
Cecil, R. (1963). *The Proteins.* Ed. by Neurath, H. New York; Academic Press
Flory, P. J. (1942). *J. Phys. Chem.* **46**, 132
Hospelhorn, V. D., Cross, B. and Jensen, E. V. (1954). *J. Am. Chem. Soc.* **76**, 2827
Huggins, C., Tapley, D. F. and Jensen, E. V. (1951). *Nature, Lond.* **167**, 592
Kleczskowski, A. (1949). *Biochem. J.* **44**, 573
Kratochvil, P., Munk, P. and Sedlacek, B. (1962). *Colln. Czech. Chem. Commun.* **27**, 788
Lundgren, H. P. (1945). *Tex. Res. J.* **15**, 335
Ogston, A. G. (1958). *Trans. Faraday Soc.* **54**, 1754
Privalov, P. L. and Monaselidze, D. R. (1963). *Biofizika,* **8**, 420
Rowe, D. S. and Abrahams, M. E. (1957). *Biochem. J.* **67**, 431
Smoluchowski, M. (1918). *Z. phys. Chem.* **92**, 129
Tanford, C. (1961). *The Physical Chemistry of Macromolecules.* New York; Wiley
Tanford, C., Kawahara, K. and Lapanje, S. (1967). *J. Am. Chem. Soc.* **89**, 729
Tombs, M. P. (1965). *Biochem. J.* **96**, 119
Tombs, M. P. and Lowe, M. (1967). *Biochem. J.* **105**, 181

# III. PROTEINS FROM ANIMAL
# SOURCES

# QUANTITATIVE AND QUALITATIVE CONTROL
# OF PROTEINS IN MEAT ANIMALS

## G.A. LODGE

*Department of Agriculture, Animal Research
Institute, Ottawa, Canada*

## INTRODUCTION

The distinction between quantity and quality of production in meat animals is not as clear as may seem at first sight, since at any given level of assessment 'quality' is merely the quantity evaluation of a deeper level Thus, the 'quality' of a dressed carcass may be assessed in terms of the relative quantities of bone, lean meat and fat; at a slightly deeper level, the 'quality' of the lean fraction may be defined in terms of the relative quantities of muscle, inter- and intracellular fat and connective tissue; at a still deeper level, the 'quality' of the muscle will depend upon its protein and water contents, and, ultimately the 'quality' of the protein depends upon its constituent amino acids.

To adhere rigidly to the subject of the title would implicate only the last two aspects, but, unfortunately, factual information on meat animals at these levels of detail is notable by its absence. Most experimental data stop short of even the first classification and provide evidence only in terms of liveweight change with, at best, some indirect and often poorly correlated superficial index of carcass 'lean'.

In the discourse which follows therefore, it is generally necessary to assume that in carcass assessment the part is indicative of the whole and that changes in 'lean' content are synonymous with changes in protein content. That these assumptions are not always valid, is indicated by the data presented in Tables 1 and 2.

As Reid *et al.* (1968) point out, the modern 'meat-type' pig may not necessarily have any more total protein in the carcass than its 'lard-type' predecessor of the same body weight but merely a different distribution of fat; indeed, a worse distribution of fat since it might be located where it is less readily removed in processing. These reservations should be borne

141

## Table 1

Some carcass measurements used as indices of lean and the actual
lean contents by dissection of Large White and Landrace pigs*
(From Cuthbertson and Pease, 1968 by courtesy of the Editor of the
Journal of the British Society of Animal Production)

| Breed | Midline backfat depth | | | Transverse section | | | Carcass lean |
|---|---|---|---|---|---|---|---|
| | Shoulder | midback | loin | fat at 'C' | fat at 'K' | 'eye' of lean area | |
| | mm | mm | mm | mm | mm | cm$^2$ | % |
| Large White | 42.8 | 18.3 | 23.9 | 19.1 | 25.7 | 27.0 | 53.8 |
| Landrace | 39.4 | 18.2 | 22.3 | 19.7 | 24.1 | 28.5 | 53.4 |

*From 637 Large White and 405 Landrace, matched for sex, from British
progeny testing stations in 1961 and 1962.

## Table 2

Composition of Poland China pigs of three distinct body types
as determined both by physical tissue separation and chemical
analysis (From Reid et al., 1968* by courtesy of Cornell
University)

| | | Type of pig | | |
|---|---|---|---|---|
| | | 'Chuffy' | Intermediate | 'Rangy' |
| Physical separation: | | | | |
| lean | (%) | 25.1 | 32.0 | 31.6 |
| fat | (%) | 43.4 | 31.9 | 30.9 |
| bone | (%) | 7.0 | 9.2 | 9.8 |
| skin | (%) | 3.1 | 3.8 | 4.0 |
| Chemical analysis: | | | | |
| water | (%) | 45.2 | 44.8 | 47.1 |
| protein | (%) | 12.9 | 12.4 | 13.1 |
| fat | (%) | 40.9 | 41.5 | 38.1 |
| ash | (%) | 2.3 | 2.2 | 2.4 |

*Derived from data of Mitchell and Hamilton (1929) on 61 pigs
chemically analysed and of Bull et al., (1935) on 30 pigs
physically dissected

in mind in the considerations which follow on the quantitative changes which may be effected in distribution of body tissues and, particularly, in protein content.

## GENETIC INFLUENCES

### Species differences in efficiency of meat production

In a situation where maximum protein output in the form of meat and edible offal is the reason for keeping livestock, uninfluenced by consideration of consumer preferences for meats of the different species, one way of influencing the quantity produced would be to concentrate on the species which converts its own feed most efficiently into meat.

Various estimates have been made in the past of efficiencies of the different forms of animal production (e.g. Brody, 1945; Godden 1948; Leitch and Godden, 1953) but these require recalculation because of the changes which have occurred in both animal performance and the nature of the desired end product with passage of time.

Revised estimates of relative efficiencies of conversion of dietary energy into muscle and of dietary protein into meat protein are presented both on the basis of the individual animal from birth (Table 3) and on the basis of complete systems which include the nutritional change of the breeding stock (Table 4).

The values shown in Table 3 indicate that no essential difference exists between species in conversion of dietary to muscle protein when comparison is made at a similar stage of development, except, perhaps that the pig shows a slight advantage over the ruminants when slaughtered at an early age. In the higher age categories this advantage shows to greater effect, with cattle killed at 18 months (still an early age by traditional standards) being the least efficient of the three species. Differences between species in efficiency of muscle growth per unit of energy intake are greater than for protein conversion and appear to be a direct reflection of relative growth rates, modified by differences in body composition Thus, the pig grows considerably faster than either lambs or calves in relation to initial weight, and, on the same basis, lambs grow faster than calves. However, the veal calf has appreciably less carcass fat (7 per cent; Hinks and Andersen, 1968) than has the conventional fat lamb (28 per cent; Wallace, 1955) and, therefore, a better energy return in terms of muscle growth. Similarly, the pork pig with 31 per cent carcass fat (Cuthbertson and Pomeroy, 1962) loses some of the advantage from its very rapid rate of growth but still remains the most efficient of the three species. The appreciable difference between age classes in cattle and

Table 3

Conversion efficiency of dietary energy to muscle gain and dietary protein to muscle protein for cattle, sheep and pigs from birth to slaughter

| | Age | Live weight at slaughter | Mean daily weight gain | Carcass weight | Energy intake (ME) | Muscle gain | Energy intake per kg muscle gain | Protein intake (CP) | Muscle protein gain | Protein intake per kg muscle protein gain |
|---|---|---|---|---|---|---|---|---|---|---|
| | month | kg | kg | kg | Mcal | kg | Mcal | kg | kg | kg |
| Cattle: veal * | 6 | 203 | 1.0 | 110 | 1624 | 64 | 25 | 103 | 14 | 7.5 |
| beef† | 18 | 455 | 0.8 | 260 | 6593 | 133 | 50 | 394 | 30 | 13.0 |
| Sheep: lamb ‡ | 4 | 30 | 0.25 | 18 | 242 | 8 | 30 | 13 | 1.7 | 7.5 |
| hogg ‡ | 9 | 64 | 0.2 | 32 | 732 | 13 | 56 | 28 | 2.8 | 10.0 |
| Pig: pork § | 5 | 68 | 0.5 | 50 | 441 | 25 | 18 | 33 | 5 | 6.5 |
| 'heavy' § | 7 | 118 | 0.6 | 92 | 1024 | 40 | 26 | 65 | 9 | 7.25 |

*Calculated from data of : Roy, 1959; Barton and Kirton, 1961; Lawrie, 1961; ARC, 1965; and Hinks and Andersen, 1968
†Calculated from data of: Roy, 1959; Lawrie, 1961; ARC, 1965; and Anonymous, 1966
‡Calculated from data of: Wallace, 1948; Palsson and Verges, 1952a and b; Wallace, 1955; Ulyatt and Barton, 1963; and ARC, 1965
§Calculated from data of: Lucas and Lodge, 1961; Hornicke, 1962; Cuthbertson and Pomeroy, 1962; Lawrie, Pomeroy and Cuthbertson, 1963; and ARC, 1967.

Table 4

Conversion efficiency of dietary energy to muscle gain and dietary protein to muscle protein for cattle, sheep and pigs, inclusive of dam's requirements

| | Age | Live weight at slaughter | Mean daily weight gain | Carcass weight | Energy intake from birth* (ME) | Energy intake of dam† (ME) | Total muscle gain‡ | Energy intake per kg muscle gain | Protein intake from birth* (CP) | Protein intake of dam† (CP) | Total muscle protein gain‡ | Protein intake per kg muscle gain |
|---|---|---|---|---|---|---|---|---|---|---|---|---|
| | month | kg | kg | kg | Mcal | Mcal | kg | Mcal | kg | kg | kg | kg |
| Cattle: | | | | | | | | | | | | |
| veal (c) | 6 | 203 | 1.0 | 110 | (a) 1624 (b) 651 | 265 5976 | 77 77 | 25 86 | 103 56 | 15 379 | 16 16 | 7 27 |
| beef (c) | 18 | 455 | 0.8 | 260 | (a) 6593 (b) 5488 | 265 5976 | 146 146 | 47 79 | 394 321 | 15 379 | 32 32 | 13 22 |
| Sheep: | | | | | | | | | | | | |
| lamb (d) | 4 | 30 | 0.25 | 18 | 120 | 568 | 11 | 63 | 7 | 40 | 2 | 24 |
| hogg (d) | 9 | 64 | 0.2 | 32 | 610 | 568 | 16 | 74 | 22 | 40 | 3 | 21 |
| Pig: | | | | | | | | | | | | |
| pork (e) | 5 | 68 | 0.5 | 50 | 316 | 181 | 25 | 20 | 30 | 10 | 5 | 8 |
| 'heavy' (e) | 7 | 118 | 0.6 | 92 | 870 | 181 | 40 | 26 | 62 | 10 | 9 | 8 |

\* Excluding energy or protein from milk

† Energy or protein consumed by dam during pregnancy, lactation and intervening period. In case of cattle excludes first 3 months of pregnancy as these are accounted for by previous lactation

‡ Muscle gain from conception to slaughter

a) Includes only additional needs of the dam for pregnancy

b) Includes all cow's requirements excepting first 3 months of pregnancy

c) Assumes lactation milk yield of 1,350 kg for a beef cow (see text)

d) Relates to ewe with twin lambs

e) Relates to sow with litter of 10 pigs

145

sheep, in contrast to the small difference in the pig, is due partly to the faster mean growth rate of pigs killed at the heavier weight, in contrast to the slower mean growth rates of the older cattle and sheep

On the basis of the comparison presented in Table 3, there is a clear advantage in favour of slaughter at young ages and light weights for all species, but particularly the ruminants. When, however, the feed requirements of the dams are taken into account (Table 4) the advantage in terms of protein conversion moves in favour of the heavier weights; only in the pig, where the overhead of the breeding stock is spread over a large number of offspring, does slaughter weight, over the range considered, make little or no difference.

These estimates show very clearly the influence of prolificacy and precise satisfaction of nutritional requirements for reproduction on the efficiency with which proteins are produced from meat animals. The ewe with an annual output of twin lambs is more efficient, if only marginally than the beef cow with a single calf, and the sow with 20 progeny per year is appreciably more efficient than either. The comparison between suckled calves (Table 4,b) and artificially reared calves from dairy cows (Table 4,a) poses the question whether beef from beef cattle is a luxury which can be afforded in a situation of protein shortage. The veal calf is nutritionally as efficient as the pig when from a dam whose essential purpose is the production of milk for human consumption, whereas the suckled calf returns protein via muscle with an efficiency of only some 5 per cent. Whether, in the production of beef from dairy cows, the beef or the milk be considered as the by-product is immaterial, the essential point is that the total return of human food for animal food consumed is appreciably greater than from any single-purpose form of meat production.

It should be emphasized, however, that nutritional and economic efficiency do not necessarily coincide and that a system which may be inefficient in the former terms, e.g. beef production from range cattle may be acceptable economically because no more efficient system is possible within the limit of the environment and an otherwise waste feed material is being utilized.

Of similar import is the ability of ruminants to utilize non-protein nitrogen sources, so that a lower efficiency of conversion of dietary to meat protein may be more than counterbalanced by the possible saving in true protein used in the animal's diet.

*Breed differences in muscle growth*

Although, unfortunately, our breeds of livestock are characterized mainly by differences in their superficial appearance rather than in their productive capacity, some broad differences between breeds do exist and breed comparisons reveal something of the genetic variation which occurs in meat-producing capacity.

The cattle data indicate breed differences in carcass muscle content when comparison is made at common weight or common age; but due primarily to differences in rate of maturity and, therefore, essentially to age. These differences are best illustrated by comparison between animals of a relatively small, early maturing 'beef' breed and those of a relatively large, later maturing 'dairy' breed, slaughtered at similar weight (Kidwell and McCormick, 1956) or similar age (Anonymous, 1966). Animals of the latter type, e.g. Holstein or British Friesian, grow some 20 per cent faster than those of the former type and have a higher percentage of muscle in the carcass. Kidwell and McCormick (1956) also reported 17· per cent more protein in sample muscle from Holsteins than from Herefords.

In general, the traditional beef breeds have a higher ratio of muscle: bone but a lower ratio of muscle:fat at common slaughter weights than do animals of the dairy breeds (Callow, 1961; Branaman et al., 1962; Carrol et al., 1964). The magnitude of these differences is influenced by age, however, and Herefords had more muscle at the expense of bone than Friesians in early life but less muscle in favour of fat than Friesians at 6 months of age and above (Anonymous, 1966).

In a comparison between traditional British beef breeds, which are small and early maturing, and the European beef breeds, larger and later maturing, as typified by the Charolais, Berg (1968) found that Charolais crosses had the heaviest carcasses and came between British beef-breed crosses and the Holstein dairy breed in muscle:bone ratio and carcass fat, indicating that muscle content is not influenced only by weight for age. That breed differences may exist even at a common stage of physiological development is indicated also by comparison between Shorthorn, Hereford and Aberdeen-Angus cattle grown under the same conditions (Tulloh, 1964b); at similar age and weight, steers of the former breed had significantly less muscle and more fat than those of the other two.

In addition to total muscle production, muscle distribution has considerable bearing on questions of meat quality. Certain muscles have not only a higher commercial value but also higher protein content than others (Lawrie, 1961; Lawrie et al., 1963), so any preferential growth of these would increase the total value of the carcass.

It has been established that certain muscles grow faster than others, that most of this difference occurs in early post-natal life and that the rate at which uniformity is achieved in growth rate of different muscles is influenced by plane of nutrition (Butterfield and Berg, 1966a and b). The question of particular relevance to beef quality is whether breeds differ in relative growth rates of different muscles so that some, notably the traditional beef breeds, might have better muscle distribution than other breeds not developed primarily for beef. Butterfield (1963) cites several reports in which differences in body conformation failed to influence yield of high-priced cuts (Willey *et al.*, 1951; Stonaker *et al.*, 1952; Carroll *et al.*, 1955; Riggs and Maddox, 1955; Butler *et al.*, 1956; Carpenter *et al.*, 1961) and others which showed that degree of fatness exerted the main influence on this characteristic (Butler, 1957; Kidwell *et al.*, 1959; Goll *et al.*, 1961). He, himself (Butterfield, 1963), presents data derived from several breeds and a wide range of environments which show negligible difference between types of cattle in the weights of various muscles in proportion to total muscle weight. He concludes that the total musculature of an animal is an anatomical system, which will resist very strongly attempts to upset its intrinsic balance, established to facilitate locomotion. Even such extreme animals as those displaying muscular hypertrophy, while having greater total muscle weight and muscle: bone ratio, show muscle weight distribution very similar to normal cattle (Pomeroy and Williams, 1962; Butterfield, 1966).

It is apparent, therefore, that breed differences in visual conformation are attributable primarily to differences in muscle: bone ratio and deposition of subcutaneous fat, which in turn reflect differences between genetic types in physiological relative to chronological age.

Sheep breeds range widely in mature size – in Britain alone from about 46 kg for Welsh ewes to about 90 kg for Lincolns – but in spite of this breeds showed little or no variation in rates of maturity; growth rates were such that all breeds reached their maximum weight at about 2 years of age (Wiener, 1967). There were appreciable differences between breeds in conformation, however; Southdowns, for example, had shortest legs but shoulder widths second only to the very much heavier Lincolns. The differences in daily growth rate but similarity in age at maturity would suggest that at any given slaughter age the muscle contents of carcasses would be similar but daily muscle growth to that slaughter age would be greater for the larger breeds. At any given weight however the larger breeds would be less mature and so be expected to have a lower muscle: bone ratio and less fat than the smaller breeds. That this is indeed so is indicated by data of Reid *et al.*, (1968) on chemical composition of sheep of various breeds and body weights; examples are give in Table 5.

The breeds are listed approximately in descending order of mature size and it is clear that at any given weight the tendency is for a smaller breed to have more fat and less water and protein in the body than a larger breed, that fat is a more variable component than water and that protein is the least variable of the three.

Table 5

Body composition of sheep of various breeds at
different weights
(From Reid *et al.*, 1968 by courtesy of Cornell University)

| Breed* | Body components according to EBW[†] (kg) | | | | | | | | |
|---|---|---|---|---|---|---|---|---|---|
| | 20 | | | 40 | | | 60 | | |
| | *Water* kg | *protein* kg | *fat* kg | *Water* kg | *protein* kg | *fat* kg | *Water* kg | *protein* kg | *fat* kg |
| Suffolk | 13.5 | 3.6 | 2.0 | 23.0 | 6.4 | 9.1 | 31.5 | 8.9 | 17.7 |
| Hampshire | 13.4 | 3.5 | 2.1 | 22.1 | 6.1 | 10.3 | 29.6 | 8.5 | 20.2 |
| Corriedale | 12.4 | 3.5 | 3.4 | 20.4 | 5.4 | 13.1 | 27.4 | 7.0 | 24.0 |
| Shropshire | 12.4 | 3.3 | 3.5 | 20.6 | 5.6 | 12.5 | 27.7 | 7.8 | 23.1 |
| Southdown (rams) | 12.7 | 3.3 | 3.2 | 21.0 | 5.9 | 11.9 | – | – | – |
| Southdown (ewes) | 11.8 | 3.2 | 4.3 | 18.0 | 5.1 | 15.8 | – | – | – |

*All animals except Southdowns were wethers (total 330)
†EBW=ingesta-free, wool-free body weight

Factual information on differences in muscle growth between breeds
of pig is sparse but comparisons involving diverse breeds are currently in
progress in the United Kingdom, preliminary results of which indicate
that wide differences do exist in rates of muscle growth The most
interesting breed in this respect is the Belgian Piétrain which appears to
defy the rules by being of small mature size and displaying the slow rate of
growth associated with the 'fatter' breeds but having, in fact, some 10 per
cent more lean in the carcass than the Landrace (Duckworth, *et al.*, 1966).
The answer probably lies in the interesting finding of Stant *et al.*, (1968)
that breeds may differ in the chemical composition of their muscle and fat
tissues at a common slaughter weight and similar age.

### Sex differences in muscle growth

Appreciable differences between sexes in rates of muscle growth have
been demonstrated in all farm species. The differences appear to be
associated with relative rates of maturity, in that females at birth are
about 7 per cent, whereas males are only 4–5 per cent, of mature weight
(Meyer, 1964), so that at any given age or weight, the female is relatively
more mature. The net result is that sex differences parallel those between
breeds of different mature size; the male, like the later maturing genetic
strains, has a faster growth rate and more muscle than the female,
equivalent to the earlier-maturing strains, at conventional slaughter
weights.

Although sex effects on growth and development of animals have been widely studied, the direct comparison between the bull and the heifer in terms of muscle growth does not appear to have been made. Comparisons have been made between castrates and females (Breidenstein *et al.*, 1963; Bradley *et al.*, 1966) and between bulls and castrates (Prescott and Lamming, 1964; Bailey *et al.*, 1966; Berg, 1968) which show that at a given weight the entire male is leaner than the castrate and that, in turn, the castrate is leaner than the female, from which it may be presumed that at a given weight the bull will have appreciably more lean and less fat than the heifer. This, coupled with the faster weight gain of the bull (Guilbert and Gregory, 1952), clearly indicates that the entire male has an appreciably faster rate of muscle growth than does the female.

Information on sex effects in sheep is more comprehensive than for the other species, since direct comparisons have been made between both intact and gonadectomized males and females (Everitt and Jury, 1966a and b; Bradfield, 1968). These studies showed that males were not only heavier at birth but grew muscle at a faster rate than females, and that intact animals grow muscle at a faster rate than those gonadectomized (Table 6). Beyond 12 weeks of age the 'sex' differences became appreciably greater and ratio of water to protein differed markedly between 'sexes', indicating that carcasses of gonadectomized lambs contained not only more fat than the intacts but that the muscle would contain relatively more water and less protein. These 'sex' differences may be defined in terms of rates of maturity in the order, ovariectomized female, entire female, castrated male and entire male.

The data of Reid *et al.* (1958), referred to in Table 5, show also the differences in growth of body components between entire males and females of the small, early maturing Southdown breed and illustrate that the differences increase with maturity.

Sex comparisons relevant to muscle growth in the pig are limited mainly to those between intact females and castrated males. These generally show that the intact female has a leaner carcass than the castrated male, in contrast to the reverse situation in cattle and sheep. The reason for this apparent species difference in the influence of sex on development of body tissues is not clear but could be related to differences in the physiological age at which comparisons are made. Thus, in sheep at 24 weeks of age, Everitt and Jury (1966a and b) found no differences between castrated males and entire females in carcass composition, whereas differences were apparent at younger ages. Evidence has been found also of nutritional interactions in the response of tissue growth to sex (Prescott and Lamming, 1967), so relative difference between species in nutritional status could account at least partially for apparent species

150

Table 6

Chemical composition of carcass weight changes in lambs
(From Everitt and Jury, 1966b by courtesy of Cambridge University Press)

| Carcass component percentage | Stage of growth | | | | | | | |
|---|---|---|---|---|---|---|---|---|
| | 0 – 12 weeks | | | | 12 – 24 weeks | | | |
| | Entire male | Castrated male | Entire female | Ovariectomized female | Entire male | Castrated male | Entire female | Ovariectomized female |
| Water | 45 | 41 | 39 | 36 | 43 | 15 | 24 | 22 |
| Fat | 36 | 41 | 44 | 48 | 42 | 80 | 66 | 74 |
| Ash | 4 | 4 | 4 | 4 | 5 | 4 | 3 | 4 |
| Protein | 15 | 14 | 13 | 12 | 11 | 3 | 7 | 0 |

differences in growth between sexes.

In a comparison with pigs between intact males, castrated males and intact females slaughtered at the relatively light weight of 60 kg (Lodge and Day, 1967), castrated males and intact females grew at a similar rate whereas intact males grew some 10 per cent faster. Physical separation of the carcasses into lean, fat and bone showed no significant difference between intact males and females in percentage lean but castrated males had some 5 per cent less. The data indicate a clear advantage for the entire male in rate of muscle growth and that the castrated male was inferior to the intact female in this respect.

Information on pigs slaughtered at heavier weights show the same trends (Charette, 1961; Blair and English, 1963; Calder, 1963; Lidvall *et al.*, 1964; Prescott and Lamming, 1964; Teague *et al.*, 1964) and add to the considerable volume of evidence that muscle growth is achieved more rapidly and efficiently in the intact male than in the female or, even more so, in the castrate. However, whereas arguments for the practise of castration in sheep are non-existent and in cattle are minimal, in the pig the problem of tainted meat from boar carcasses limits the abandonment of castration in practice to only those animals destined for slaughter at a very young age, and even then with some possible attendant risk.

It is clearly evident that the opportunity to select sexes, intact or gonadectomized, imparts a considerable degree of flexibility to the production of carcasses with predetermined contents of bone, muscle and fat. This degree of flexibility may be extended further by use of exogenous sex hormones or closely related chemical compounds. There is a considerable literature on this aspect of animal production including some comprehensive reviews (Hammond, 1957; Burgess and Lamming, 1957; Lamming, 1957 and 1958; Scarisbrick, 1960) which reveal that the modes of action are by no means clear and the effects of administration of exogenous hormones not readily predictable. Thus, while in general the administration of androgens and oestrogens may be expected to produce the same effects as in the intact animal, there are some anomalies. Oestrogen treatment increases carcass fatness in intact lambs and bulls (Casida *et al.*, 1959; Preston *et al.*, 1960), as might be expected, but increases bone and muscle growth in castrated animals, contrary to expectations from comparisons between castrates and intact females The effect of hormone treatment appears to be influenced by age for it would appear that response to hormonal supplementation is influenced by the relative rates of maturity of the animals concerned and their proximity to puberty (Bradfield, 1968).

Sex hormones, endogenous or exogenous, influence not only the proportions of the body tissues but also their value as meat. Reference has

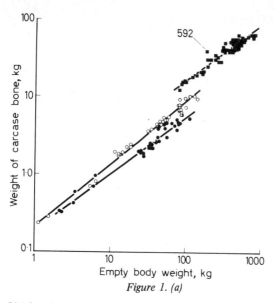

*Figure 1. (a)*

*Figure 1. Weight of dissected bone, muscle and fat in the carcass in relation to empty body weight for sheep (●), cattle (■) and pigs (○). The point designated 592 refers to a particularly emaciated animal. (From Tulloh, 1964a by courtesy of C.S.I.R.O., Melbourne)*

been made to the finding of Everitt and Jury (1966b) that ratios of carcass water to protein differed between sexes; similar differences have been reported as resulting from oestrogen administration, in that increased leanness was accompanied by increased water content of the muscle (Aitken and Crichton, 1956; Gee and Preston, 1957; Preston and Gee, 1958; Alder *et al.*, 1964).


## ENVIRONMENTAL INFLUENCES

*Age effects on muscle growth*

In the sense that age at slaughter is a factor which can be imposed upon the animal in contrast to its species, breed or sex, age effects on muscle growth are environmental in nature.

Although, clearly, changes in body composition do occur as an animal increases in age, it is not always apparent to what degree these are age or weight effects. Thus, while the younger animal generally has more bone

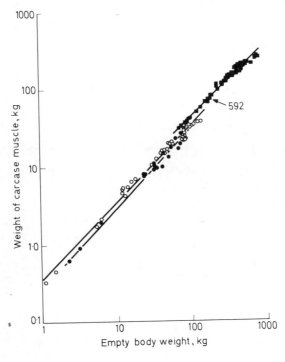

*Figure 1. (b)*

and less fat than the older one, with muscle content tending to remain relatively constant, Tulloh (1964a) concluded from a comprehensive study of carcass composition as a function of body weight in cattle, sheep and pigs, that carcass composition was mainly dependent on weight and independent of age and nutritional history *(Figure 1)*.

This suggestion that muscle growth is weight dependent rather than age dependent is supported by the data of Guenther *et al.* (1965), who slaughtered Hereford cattle at prescribed ages following two feeding regimes and found that total lean content differed significantly between cattle of the same age but different weight, but not between those of similar weight reached at different ages. However, it remained true that within any one nutritional group, the percentages of lean and of protein in the carcass tended to decline as the animals grew and aged (Table 7). Lean production reached its maximum daily rate within the first year of life and tended to subside as the animal matured and as the fattening period

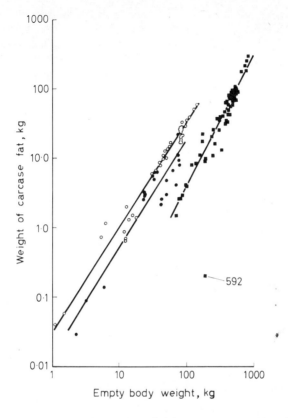

*Figure 1. (c)*

extended. Similar results were reported for both Hereford and British Friesian cattle (Anonymous, 1966), in which muscle percentage in the carcass increased from birth to about 5 months of age, remained relatively constant to 12 months of age and then declined with increase in fat content by 17 months of age.

Following a detailed appraisal of growth and body composition data for cattle, sheep and pigs, Reid *et al.* (1968) concluded that in early life the weights of water, fat, protein and ash increased as linear functions of body weight, but beyond a certain state of maturity, which appears to vary between species and is exemplified by concentration of body fat, the chemical components of the body are curvilinear functions of body weight. The sheep is cited as an example in which at a fat concentration

Table 7

Changes in lean and protein contents of carcass with increase in age
of Hereford steers on two planes of feeding from weaning to slaughter
at various ages
(From Guenther *et al.*, 1965 by courtesy of the Editor, *J. Anim. Sci.*)

|  | Treatment group* | | | | | |
|---|---|---|---|---|---|---|
|  | W | H1 | M1 | H2 | M2 | M3 |
| Age (month) | 7 | 10.8 | 10.8 | 14.3 | 14.3 | 15.6 |
| Weight (kg) | 236 | 355 | 320 | 425 | 394 | 440 |
| Carcass weight (kg) | 141 | 218 | 195 | 276 | 236 | 269 |
| Lean (kg) | 43 | 63 | 57 | 73 | 67 | 74 |
| Protein (kg) | 9.6 | 13.6 | 12.2 | 15.8 | 14.6 | 16.0 |
| Rate of lean deposition (kg/day) | – | 0.34 | 0.24 | 0.27 | 0.22 | 0.24 |
| Lean (%) | 31 | 29 | 29 | 26 | 28 | 28 |
| Protein (%) | 6.8 | 6.2 | 6.3 | 5.7 | 6.2 | 5.9 |

* *W,* weaning; *H,* high-plane feeding; *M,* medium-plane feeding

above 31 per cent, further deposition of fat occurs at an increasing rate
while weights of water and protein increase at a declining rate as body
weight increases.

Clearly, the points at which curvilinearity supersedes linearity, and the
factors which influence them, are of considerable importance in attempts
to control protein production and the efficiency with which it is achieved.
Existing data appear confusing, however, and preclude the drawing of any
firm conclusions. Thus, Wallace (1955) presents data which show a clear
and progressive decline in both carcass muscle and protein percentages
with increase in weight of lambs from 9 to 36 kg (Table 8).

Table 8

Changes in carcass composition of Suffolk lambs with increase in weight
(From Wallace, 1955 by courtesy of Cambridge University Press)

| Carcass Weight kg | Tissue in carcass | | | Protein in carcass | |
|---|---|---|---|---|---|
|  | bone % | muscle % | fat % | kg | % |
| 4.5 | 25.1 | 62.2 | 12.7 | 0.67 | 14.9 |
| 9.1 | 19.5 | 62.1 | 18.4 | 1.25 | 13.7 |
| 13.6 | 16.0 | 60.9 | 23.1 | 1.80 | 13.2 |
| 18.2 | 13.8 | 57.4 | 28.8 | 2.21 | 12.1 |
| 22.7 | 12.5 | 54.4 | 32.9 | 2.62 | 11.5 |
| 27.3 | 11.7 | 51.8 | 36.5 | 3.00 | 11.0 |
| 31.8 | 11.0 | 48.9 | 40.1 | 3.30 | 10.4 |
| 36.4 | 10.4 | 45.7 | 43.9 | 3.56 | 9.8 |

A similar trend, illustrating again the relative constancy of body protein in proportion to total weight and the reduction in water content of muscle with increase in age or weight, is evidenced for pigs (Clausen, 1953; Hornicke, 1962) and exemplified in Table 9.

Data for pigs on rates of tissue gain illustrate that even from birth lipid deposition exceeds that of protein and that most of the increase in rate of lipid deposition is at the expense of water (Brooks *et al.*, 1964). However, although percentage protein deposited by the pig declines from an early age, in genetic strains with a high capacity for muscle growth absolute amount of protein deposited did not decline over a weight range of 20–110 kg (Oslage and Fliegal, 1965). In continuous nitrogen metabolism trials, daily N retention was almost constant up to 100 kg liveweight, after which it declined.

Table 9

Changes in carcass composition of pigs with increase in liveweight
(From Clausen, 1953 by courtesy of the Dean, Queens University, Belfast)

| Liveweight kg | Protein % | Lipid % | Water % | Ash % |
|---|---|---|---|---|
| to     10 | 16.7 | 12.5 | 67.3 | 3.4 |
| 10 –   20 | 17.0 | 20.1 | 59.8 | 3.0 |
| 20 –   30 | 16.2 | 26.3 | 54.8 | 2.7 |
| 30 –   40 | 15.4 | 31.0 | 51.1 | 2.6 |
| 40 –   50 | 14.8 | 35.1 | 47.7 | 2.5 |
| 50 –   60 | 14.2 | 38.6 | 44.9 | 2.4 |
| 60 –   70 | 13.6 | 41.7 | 42.4 | 2.3 |
| 70 –   80 | 13.1 | 44.5 | 40.1 | 2.2 |
| 80 –   90 | 12.6 | 47.0 | 38.0 | 2.2 |
| 90 – 100 | 12.2 | 49.6 | 36.1 | 2.1 |
| 100 – 110 | 11.7 | 52.0 | 34.2 | 2.1 |
| 110 – 120 | 11.3 | 54.1 | 32.4 | 2.1 |
| 120 – 130 | 10.9 | 56.3 | 30.8 | 2.0 |
| 130 – 140 | 10.4 | 58.3 | 29.2 | 2.0 |
| 140 – 150 | 10.0 | 60.3 | 27.6 | 2.0 |

It would appear, therefore, that the most efficient production of protein as meat would be obtained by maintaining its deposition at the maximum rate up to the point of its natural decline, when the animal would be slaughtered, and by limiting deposition of fat to avoid energy wastage and the need to trim carcasses after slaughter.

Considerations so far have been in terms of total muscle or protein but the distribution of this is of relevance to meat quality and commercial value, if not to its nutritional value. While differences occur in the relative rates of growth of different muscles, it has been shown that most of this differential growth occurs in early post-natal life (Butterfield and Berg,

1966a; Butterfield, 1968). Subsequent differences in superficial conformation are more the result of variation in fat distribution. It is evident that the relative protein percentages of specific body parts may change with increase in age or weight of animal, due to changes in fat distribution Thus, sheep at high body weights had more subcutaneous than intermuscular fat, while at low body weights the reverse was true (Palsson and Verges, 1952a and b).

Age effects on meat quality in terms more meaningful than muscle and fat distribution, have been reported by Lawrie (1961). In cattle slaughtered over a range from birth to 40 months of age, total nitrogen content of longissimus dorsi muscle increased from 3.15 per cent at birth (fat-free basis) to reach the adult value of 3.62 per cent by about 10 months of age. In a similar study with pigs slaughtered at 68, 90 and 114 kg (Lawrie *et al.*, 1963), there was a progressive increase in the nitrogen content of muscles with increase in slaughter weight, resulting in a 5 per cent difference between the highest and the lowest levels. Recent American work (Usborne *et al.*, 1968) has shown also a linear relationship between slaughter weight and the protein content of longissimus dorsi of pigs.

Influences of age on meat characteristics are frequently difficult to interpret, however, because the younger age is achieved by reaching a given weight at a faster rate, so introducing complications from rate of growth and associated differences in proportion of fat and lean.

*Nutritional influences on muscle growth*

Considerable effort has been devoted to elucidation of the relationships between rate of growth, as determined by plane of nutrition, and development of the body tissues but these relationships are still by no means clear and there are at least three schools of thought surrounding the interpretation of the data.

The first of these, which (under the direction of the late Sir John Hammond) originated most of the data on which subsequent interpretations have been based, (McMeekan, 1940a, b and c; Pomeroy 1941; Palsson and Verges, 1952a and b), formulated the theory that bone muscle and fat tend to develop in that order, with the degree of overlap varying with growth rate, and that restriction in growth was manifest most severely on the tissue with maximum growth impetus at the time of its imposition. The implication of this would be that at any given weight, the animal which had grown most rapidly would have more fat and less bone than the slower growing animal, with the additional proviso that where overall mean growth rate was the same but one animal suffered restriction early in life while another received it later, the former would have particularly retarded bone growth and excess fat whereas the latter would approach the ideal of limited fat deposition without severe overall growth restriction.

The second school of thought, based largely on reappraisal of the original Cambridge data (Wallace, 1948; Wilson, 1954; Elsley *et al.*, 1964; Fowler, 1968) considers the true interpretation to be that restriction in total growth affects all tissues more or less equally with the exception of fat, which is accumulated when dietary energy exceeds the needs for organic growth and depleted when energy intake is inadequate for essential body function. The implication of this would be that as the plane of nutrition increased, the proportions of weight increment constituting bone and muscle would decrease at equal rates.

That this is a more probable explanation of events is indicated by McMeekan's (1940c) own data on tissue proportions of pigs following four different dietary regimes:

| Dietary regime* | High/high | High/low | Low/high | Low/low |
|---|---|---|---|---|
| Mean daily weight gain (kg) | 0.5 | 0.4 | 0.4 | 0.25 |
| Muscle/bone | 3.67 | 3.99 | 3.76 | 3.96 |
| Fat/bone | 3.48 | 2.97 | 4.56 | 2.22 |
| Fat/muscle | 0.95 | 0.74 | 1.21 | 0.51 |

*The changes in plane of feeding occurred at 16 weeks of age

These data show that while growth rate was influenced appreciably by dietary regime, muscle to bone ratio remained relatively constant and fat was the predominant variable. Nevertheless, Elsley *et al.*, (1964) stress that the theory of constant muscle:bone ratio should not be extrapolated to cover all possible feeding regimes and that extreme restriction of feeding levels, particularly during early growth, may upset the balance between the non-fat tissues. Evidence that this is so comes from experimental results with cattle which show that moderate degrees of feed and growth restriction failed to influence muscle:bone ratio (Callow, 1961; Hendrickson *et al.*, 1965), whereas severe restriction causing weight loss depleted muscle and fat but had little effect on bone, so narrowing muscle:bone ratio (Butterfield, 1966). The same effects were found in pigs under conditions of semi-starvation by Pomeroy (1941). Rehabilitation of the cattle in Butterfield's experiment resulted in recovery of muscle to near-normal muscle:bone ratio, whereas fat appeared to require a prolonged period of recovery to reach the level found in animals with uninterrupted growth.

The third school of thought (Tulloh, 1964a; Reid *et al.*, 1968) contends that carcass composition is weight dependent and largely uninfluenced by age or nutritional regime. The implication of this would be that at any given weight animals of the same sex and species would have equal proportions of bone, muscle and fat regardless of previous rate of growth, and, therefore, that weight increment must be of constant composition. This, however, would be too literal an interpretation of the postulation and all that it really implies is, perhaps, the simple fact that as the animal increases in weight so do its component tissues but not all in direct proportion; fat increases at a faster rate and bone at a slower rate than the total. Thus, with cattle slaughtered at similar ages but a variety of weights (Tulloh, 1964b), muscle weight increased with increase in body weight with a ratio close to 1.0, whereas fat increased at the rate of 1.5 and bone at the rate of 0.7–0.8, with the result that the proportion of muscle relative to body weight remained almost constant throughout life. This confirmed the earlier observations of Watson (1943) and Callow (1944) that carcass muscle always constituted about one-third of body weight.

That differences in growth rate, and perhaps other factors such as sex or breed, might upset the ratios of body tissues one with another are indicated, however, by Tulloh's own presentation of data (*Figure 1*) which shows very little individual deviation from the regression line for muscle on total body weight, but some deviation for bone and considerable deviation for fat. This supports the hypothesis of the second school of thought, that fat is the major variable in body composition and that to a much lesser degree some change in muscle:bone ratio might also occur.

Tulloh (1964b) concludes, from a detailed study of the data of Palsson and Verges (1952a and b) on plane of nutrition effects on body composition in sheep, that, 'perhaps effects of age and plane of nutrition do alter body composition but experiments designed to permit regression analyses over considerable weight ranges may be necessary to isolate these differences'. This view is diametrically opposed to that of our first school of thought and differs also, but to a much lesser degree, from our second whose hypothesis may be summarized in the words of Elsley *et al.* (1964) that 'restricted nutrition causes a more or less uniform retardation of development except in so far as fat tissue is concerned'.

When three such different postulations on the relationship between plane of nutrition and development of body tissues can be evolved from basically the same experimental data, perhaps the only safe conclusion to be drawn is that new experiments are required – designed with the specific object of measuring the influence of energy and nutrient intakes on the absolute growth of the major body tissues. However, from the standpoint of the subject of this symposium, a consoling aspect is that agreement is fairly general on the fact that, of the tissues considered, muscle is the most consistent and is relatively closely related to body weight under a variety of circumstances. That this is also true of protein is indicated by the work of Reid *et al.* (1968) who, from numerous experiments with sheep concluded that despite marked differences in energetic efficiency between certain treatments, body composition did not vary independently of total body mass *when the animals were maintained in at least a continously positive energy balance.* Only when they were allowed to lose weight at an average of 0.2 kg/day for 26 days and were then re-fed *ad lib.* so as to reach eventually the same weight as sheep on a continuous energy increment, did they contain less fat and more water and protein than the controls. In one experiment, Reid *et al.* (1968) compared lambs in groups of three at either equal weights or equal ages, with the results shown in Table 10.

Table 10

Relative influences of age and weight on body composition of sheep
(From Reid *et al.* 1968   by courtesy of Cornell University)

| Animal | Feed intake | Age | Weight | Body composition | | | | |
| | High or low | days | kg | water % | fat % | protein % | ash % | energy kcal/g |
|---|---|---|---|---|---|---|---|---|
| 1 | H | 270 | 28.2 | 57.4 | 24.4 | 15.0 | 2.9 | 3.10 |
| 2 | L | 270 | 19.9 | 61.5 | 18.5 | 15.6 | 3.9 | 2.61 |
| 3 | L | 349 | 28.7 | 56.6 | 23.9 | 15.8 | 4.0 | 3.10 |
| 4 | H | 381 | 49.6 | 46.1 | 38.1 | 13.1 | 2.6 | 4.30 |
| 5 | L | 381 | 27.7 | 54.5 | 27.7 | 14.3 | 2.8 | 3.38 |
| 6 | L | 583 | 47.5 | 46.1 | 38.5 | 12.6 | 2.7 | 4.32 |
| 7 | H | 374 | 58.3 | 46.2 | 38.4 | 12.8 | 2.4 | 4.38 |
| 8 | L | 374 | 31.8 | 56.3 | 24.1 | 15.8 | 3.3 | 3.13 |
| 9 | L | 613 | 56.0 | 46.0 | 38.5 | 12.7 | 2.8 | 4.42 |

These show clearly that a considerable difference in growth rate, through difference in feed intake, had virtually no effect on body composition in chemical terms when lambs were killed at equal weights. At equal ages, the slower growing animals had appreciably less fat, less ash, more water and a tendency for more protein; the latter two together indicating that they would have more muscle.

These results, of course, support Tulloh's hypothesis but express the results in chemical instead of physical terms and suggest, perhaps, that differences which have been found in proportions of body tissue of animals of equal weight but different age may be due to changes in location of water. Changes in water content of muscle with age have been referred to already (McMeekan, 1940a; Hornicke, 1962) and even greater differences have been found in the water content of separable fat from animals reared on different nutritional planes (Callow, 1948). A significant difference was found between breeds of pig in percentages of muscle, fat and bone but not in chemical composition of total carcass, indicating differences in location of water (Stant, et al., 1968). Such differences could explain why data, obtained from pigs fed diets of different energy value to an equal slaughter weight, indicate differences in weights of lean and fat. For example, Robinson and Lewis (1964) found the following with pigs slaughtered at 90 kg liveweight:

| | | |
|---|---|---|
| DE value of feed (kcal/kg) | 3340 | 2950 |
| Total DE intake (Mcal) | 832 | 746 |
| Carcass weight (kg) | 73 | 72 |
| % Lean | 43.5 | 47.1 |
| % Fat | 32.7 | 28.8 |
| Weight of lean (kg) | 31.8 | 33.9 |
| Weight of fat (kg) | 23.9 | 20.7 |

The situation with pigs tends to be complicated by the possibility of specific protein effects. Thus, data considered so far have been concerned with changes in total feed intake or energy value only; a different situation may exist in the pig when energy is maintained constant but protein intake varied. The influence of dietary protein on muscle development in the pig has not been fully elucidated, partly, perhaps, because there appear to be genetic interactions such that strains depositing little backfat respond with increased lean to higher protein intakes, whereas strains with a high propensity for fat deposition may not (Davey and Morgan, 1968). Response to higher protein intake is likely to show therefore, only in pigs with a high genetic capacity for muscle growth. Where such pigs have been fed diets with varying protein contents but a constant energy value, increases in carcass lean content have been obtained with increase in intake of dietary protein up to levels of 20–22 per cent crude protein in air dry feed (Lucas and Miles, 1967; Cooke et al., 1968; Chamberlain, 1968).

Where increases in intake occur equally in both energy and protein the result is more confusing but appears to indicate that energy effects override those of protein, so that while rate of muscle growth does increase, the rate of fat deposition increases even more and the end result is a fatter carcass (Cooke et al., 1968; Lodge, Cundy, Cooke and Lewis, unpublished).

The influence of nutrition on meat quality is difficult to assess because, as mentioned in relation to age effects, nutritional differences are commonly associated with age differences at a given weight. However, in a study to assess the relative nutrititive values of beef from 'intensive' and 'extensive' methods of production (Harries *et al.*, 1968) no differences were found between sample muscles from the two types of animal in contents of moisture, intramuscular fat, protein or non-protein nitrogen.

## CONCLUSIONS

The data presented above indicate the many complexities and inter-actions which occur in growth of farm livestock and the impossibility of generalizing about specific effects. Thus, while in general older and heavier animals have a higher proportion of carcass fat to lean than younger and lighter animals, rapid growth may counteract this so that the latter become the fatter. Again, slow average growth rate generally results in high bone and lean contents with relatively little fat, but if the period of slow growth is followed by one of concentrated rapid gain then excess fat may be deposited. At a common age animals of a larger breed produce a heavier and leaner carcass than those of a smaller breed, illustrating the important practical point that the correct animal, be it by breed or sex must be selected for a specific system and that the larger, later maturing types of animal are best suited to systems allowing rapid daily gain while the smaller, early maturing types are more suited to the less intensive systems, for which, indeed, they were developed. So while the weight of evidence presented indicates that muscle weight increases in proportion to total weight in a very simple fashion, the complexities arise from the degree of fat, and to a lesser extent bone, associated with the muscle which greatly influence the commercial value and consumer acceptability of the carcass.

## REFERENCES

Aitken, J.N. and Crichton, J.A. (1965). *Br. J. Nutr.* **10**, 220
Alder, F.E., Taylor, J.C. and Rudman, J.E. (1964). *Anim. Prod.* **6**, 57
Anonymous (1966). *Report of Major Beef Research Project.* London; The Royal Smithfield Club
A.R.C. (1965). *The Nutrient Requirements of Farm Livestock.* No.2 Ruminants. London; Agricultural Research Council
– (1967). *The Nutrient Requirements of Farm Livestock.* No.3 Pigs. London; Agricultural Research Council
Bailey, C.M., Probert, C.L. and Bohmann, V.R. (1966). *J. Anim. Sci.* **25**, 132
Barton, R.A. and Kirton, A.H. (1961). *Anim. Prod.* **3**, 41
Berg, R.T. (1968). In *Growth and Development of Mammals. Proc. 14th Univ.*

*Nottingham Easter School,* p.429  Ed. by G.A. Lodge and.G.E. Lamming. London; Butterworths

Blair, R. and English, P.R. (1963). *Anim. Prod.* **5**, 215 (abstr.)

Bradfield, P.G.E. (1968). In *Growth and Development of Mammals. Proc. 14th Univ. Nottingham Easter School,* p.92  Ed. by G.A. Lodge and G.E. Lamming. London; Butterworths

Bradley, N.W., Cundiff, L.V., Kemp, J.D. and Greathouse, T.R. (1966). *J. Anim. Sci.* **25**, 783

Branaman, G.A., Pearson, A.M., Magee, W.T., Griswald, R.M. and Brown, G.A. (1962). *J. Anim. Sci.* **21**, 321

Breidenstein, B.C., Breidenstein, B.B., Gray, W.J., Garrigan, D.S. and Norton, H.W. (1963). *J. Anim. Sci.* **22**, 1113 (abstr.)

Brody, S. (1945). *Bioenergetics and Growth.* New York; Reinhold

Brooks, C.C., Fontenot, J.P., Vipperman, P.E., Thomas, H.R. and Graham, P.P. (1964). *J. Anim. Sci.* **23**, 1022

Bull, S., Olson, F.C., Hunt, G.E. and Carroll, W.E. (1935). III. *Agr. Expt. Sta. Bull.* No.415

Burgess, T.D. and Lamming, G.E. (1957). *N.A.A.S. q. Rev.* No.35, 1

Butler, O.D. (1957) *J. Anim. Sci.* **16**, 227

— Warwick, B.L. and Cartwright, T.C. (1956). *J. Anim. Sci.* **15**, 93

Butterfield, R.M. (1963). *Symp. Carcase Composition and Appraisal of Meat Animals,* Paper 7, p.1  Ed. by D.E. Tribe. Melbourne; C.S.I.R.O.

— (1966). *Res. vet. Sci.* **7**, 168

— (1968). In *Growth and Development of Mammals, Proc. 14th Univ. Nottingham Easter School,* p.212  Ed. by G.A. Lodge and G.E. Lamming. London; Butterworths

— and Berg, R.T. (1966a). *Res. vet. Sci.* **7**, 326

— — (1966b). *Proc. Aust. Soc. Anim. Prod.* **VI**, 298

Calder, A. (1963). *Rhodesian agric. Jl.* **60**, 102

Callow, E.H. (1944). *J. agric. Sci. Camb.* **34**, 177

— (1948). *J. agric. Sci. Camb.* **38**, 174

— (1961). *J. agric. Sci. Camb.* **56**, 265

Carpenter, J.W., Palmer, A.Z., Kirk, W.G., Peacock, F.M. and Koger, M. (1961). *J. Anim. Sci.* **20**, 336

Carroll, F.D., Clegg, M.T. and Kroger, D. (1964). *J. agric. Sci. Camb.* **62**, 1

— Rollins, W.C. and Ittner, N.R. (1955). *J. Anim. Sci.* **14**, 218

Casida, L.E., Andrews, F.N., Bogart, R., Clegg, M.T. and Nalbandov, A.V. (1959). *Nat. Acad. Sci., Nat. Res. Comm.* No.714

Chamberlain, A.G. (1968). *Anim. Prod.* **10**, 236 (abstr.)

Charette, L.A. (1961). *Can. J. Anim. Sci.* **41**, 30

Clausen, H. (1953). *George Scott Watson Memorial Lecture.* Belfast; Queens University

Cooke, R., Lodge, G.A., Pappas, S. and Lewis, D. (1968). *Anim. Prod.* **10**, 237 (abstr.)

Cuthbertson, A. and Pease, A.H.R. (1968). *Anim. Prod.* **10**, 249

— and Pomeroy, R.W. (1962). *J. agric. Sci. Camb.* **59**, 215

Davey, R.J. and Morgan, D.P. (1968). *J. Anim. Sci.* **27**, 1139 (abstr.)

Duckworth, J.E., Edge, T.M., Harrison, G., Olaniyan, O. and Holmes, W. (1966). *Anim. Prod.* **8**, 356 (abstr.)

Elsley, F.W.H., McDonald, I. and Fowler, V.R. (1964). *Anim. Prod.* **6**, 141.

Everitt, G.C. and Jury, K.E. (1966a). *J. agric. Sci. Camb.* **66**, 1

— — (1966b). *J. agric. Sci. Camb.* **66**, 15

Fowler, V.R. (1968). In *Growth and Development of Mammals, Proc. 14th univ. Nottingham Easter School.* p. 195 Ed. by G.A. Lodge and G.E. Lamming. London; Butterworths

Gee, I. and Preston, T.R. (1957). *Brit. J. Nutr.* **11**, 329

Godden, W. (1948). *Agric. Prog.* **23**, 105

Goll, D.E., Kline, F.A. and Hazel, L.N. (1961). *J. Anim. Sci.* **20**, 260

Guenther, J.J., Bushman, D.H., Pope, L.S. and Morrison, R.D. (1965). *J. Anim. Sci.* **24**, 1184

Guilbert, H.R. and Gregory, P.W. (1952). *J. Anim. Sci.* **11**, 3

Hammond, J. (1957). *Outl. Agric.* **1**, 230

Harries, J.M., Hubbard, A.W., Alder, F.E., Kay, M. and Williams, D.R. (1968). *Br. J. Nutr.* **22**, 21

Hendrickson, R.L., Pope. L.S. and Hendrickson, R.F. (1965). *J. Anim. Sci.* **24**, 507

Hinks, C.J.M. and Andersen, B. Bech (1968). *Anim. Prod.* **10**, 331

Hornicke, H. (1962). *Z. Tierphysiol. Tierernähr. Futtermittelk* **17**, 28

Kidwell, J.F. and McCormick, J.S. (1956). *J. Anim. Sci.* **15**, 109

– Hunter, J.E., Ternan, P.R., Harper, J.E., Shelby, C.E. and Clark, R.T. (1959). *J. Anim. Sci.* **18**, 894

Lamming, G.E. (1957), *Agric. Progr.* **32**, 31

– (1958). *Jl. R. Agric. Soc.* **119**, 41

Lawrie, R.A. (1961). *J. agric. Sci. Camb.* **56**, 249

– Pomeroy, R.W. and Cuthbertson, A. (1963). *J. agric. Sci. Camb.* **60**, 195

Leitch, I. and Godden, W. (1953). *Tech. Commun. Commonw. Bur. Anim. Nutr.,* No.14

Lidvall, E.R., Burgess, C.R., Ramsay, C.B. and Cole, J.W. (1964). *J. Anim. Sci.* **23**, 851 (abstr.)

Lodge, G.A. and Day, N. (1967). *Rep. Univ. Nottingham.* 1966-67, p.62

Lucas, I.A.M. and Lodge, G.A. (1961) *The Nutrition of the Young Pig., Tech. Commun Commonw. Bur. Anim. Nutr.* No.22

– and Miles, K.L. (1967). *Anim. Prod.* **9**, 273 (abstr.)

Matthews, D.J. and Bennett, J.A. (1962). *J. Anim. Sci.* **21**, 738

McMeekan, C.P. (1940a). *J. agric. Sci. Camb.* **30**, 276

– (1940b). *J. agric. Sci. Camb.* **30**, 387

– (1940c). *J. agric. Sci. Camb.* **30**, 511

Meyer, H. (1964). *Zuchtungskunde.* **36**, 303

Mitchell, H.H. and Hamilton, T.S. (1929). *Bull. Ill. agric. Exp. Stn.* No. 323

Oslage, H.J. and Fliegel, H. (1965). *Proc. Symp. Energy Metab.* p.297 (Ed. by K.L. Baxter). *Publs. Eur. Ass. Anim. Prod.* No.11 London; Academic Press

Palsson, H. and Verges, J.B. (1952a). *J. agric. Sci. Camb.* **42**, 1

– – (1952b). *J. agric. Sci. Camb.* **42**, 93

Pomeroy, R.W. (1941). *J. agric. Sci. Camb.* **31**, 50

– and Williams, D.R. (1962). *Anim. Prod.* **4**, 302 (abstr.)

Prescott, J.H.D. and Lamming, G.E. (1964). *J. agric. Sci. Camb.* **63**, 341

– – (1967). *Anim. Prod.* **9**, 535

Preston, T.R. and Gee, I. (1958). *Brit. J. Nutr.* **12**, 158

– – and MacLeod, N.A. (1960). *Anim. Prod.* **2**, 11

Reid, J.T., Bensadoun, A., Bull, L.S., Burton, J.H., Gleeson, P.A., Han, I.K., Joo, Y.D., Johnson, D.E., McManus, W.R., Paladines, O.L., Stroud, J.W., Tyrrell, H.F., Van Niekerk, B.D.H., Wellington, G.H. and Wood, J.D. (1968). *Proc. Cornell Nutr. Conf. for Feed Manufacturers.* p.18

Riggs, J.K. and Maddox, L.A. (1955). *Bull. Tex. agric. Exp. Sta.* No.B809

Robinson, D.W. and Lewis, D. (1964). *J. agric. Sci. Camb.* **63**, 185
Roy, J.H.B. (1959). In *Scientific Principles of Feeding Farm Livestock.* p. 48-88. London; Farmer and Stockbreeder Publications
Scarisbrick, R. (1960). *J. Fmrs' Club.* (1)
Stonaker, H.H., Hazaleus, M.H. and Wheeler, S.S. (1952). *J. Anim. Sci.* **11**, 17
Stant, E.G., Martin, T.G., Judge, M.D. and Harrington, R.B. (1968). *J. Anim. Sci.* **27**, 636
Teague, H.S., Plimpton, R.F., Cahill, V.R., Grifo, A.P. and Kunkle, L.E. (1964). *J. Anim. Sci.* **23**, 332
Tulloh, N.M. (1964a). *Symp. Carcase Composition and Appraisal of Meat Animals.* Paper 5, p.1 Ed. by D.E. Tribe. Melbourne, C.S.I.R.O.
– (1964b). *Aust. J. agric. Res.* **15**, 333
Ulyatt, M.J. and Barton, R.A. (1963). *J. agric. Sci. Camb.* **60**, 285
Usborne, W.R., Kemp, J.D. and Moody, W.G. (1968). *J. Anim. Sci.* **27**, 584
Wallace, L.R. (1948). *J. agric. Sci., Camb.* **38**, 93
– (1955). *Proc. Nutr. Soc.* **14**, 7
Watson, D.M.S. (1943). *Emp. J. exp. Agric.* **11**, 191
Weiner, G. (1967). *Anim. Prod.* **9**, 177
Wilson, P.N. (1954). *J. agric. Sci. Camb.* **44**, 67
Willey, N.B., Butler, O.D., Riggs, J.K., Jones, J.H. and Lyerly, P.J. (1951). *J. Anim. Sci.* **10**, 195

# PROPERTIES OF MEAT PROTEINS

REINER HAMM

*Bundesanstalt für Fleischforschung, Kulmbach, Germany*

## INTRODUCTION

Most changes in the properties of meat occurring during storage and processing are due to alterations in the muscle proteins. Knowledge of muscle proteins and their reactions may thus contribute to an understanding of the factors which influence the quality of meat and meat products; and could possibly improve the methods of production, handling and processing of meats.

## STRUCTURE OF THE MUSCLE FIBRE

*(Bendall, 1964; Bennett, 1960; Cassens, 1964; Gergely, 1966; Huxley, 1966; Huxley and Hanson, 1960; Lawrie, 1966; Needham, 1960\* )*

Skeletal muscle consists of long, cross-striated muscle fibres. The fibre comprises the myofibrils, the sarcoplasmic matrix and some small structural elements including the sarcoplasmic reticulum, the mitochondria and the nucleus *(Figure 1)*. The (partially crystallized) protein gel of myofibrils, which presents the contractile substance, amounts to about 80 per cent of the fibre volume  The protein concentration ranges . between 15 and 20 per cent.

The protein of the myofibrils is not homogeneous. This lack of homogeneity causes the optical effect of cross-striation, i.e. an alternating sequence of anisotropic *(A)* and isotropic *(I)* bands. The *A*-band of the myofibrils consists of thick filaments which are parallel and arranged in a hexagonal system. The *I*-band consists of thin filaments. The *I*-bands are bisected by the *Z*-lines. The distance between two *Z*-lines is called 'the sarcomere' *(Figure 2)*. The thick filaments are identical with the muscle protein myosin (about 38 per cent of the total muscle protein), the thin

---

\*The papers quoted under the section headings are review articles. In the text only such references are given which are not quoted in the reviews.

filaments contain mainly F-actin (14 per cent) but also tropomyosin. These proteins take part in the process of muscular contraction. Therefore, they are called 'contractile proteins'.

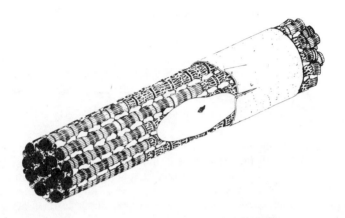

*Figure 1. A dissected skeletal muscle fibre, showing cylindrical myofibrils surrounded by mitochondria and enclosed in a sarcolemma. Individual myofibrils are organized as a series of sarcomeres 2-3 μ in length. A nucleus is seen in a typical position just beneath the sarcolemma. In the right part of the fibre, the sarcoplasmic reticulum surrounding the single fibrils is not removed. (From Dupraw, 1968, by courtesy of Academic Press)*

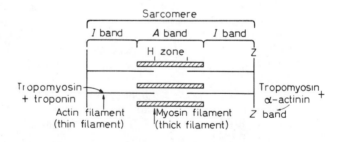

*Figure 2. Sketch of sarcomere model indicating probable location of several proteins. (By courtesy of Dr. E. J. Briskey)*

Six thin actin filaments are arranged around one thick filament. Both kinds of filaments are connected by cross-linkages *(Figure 3).*

168

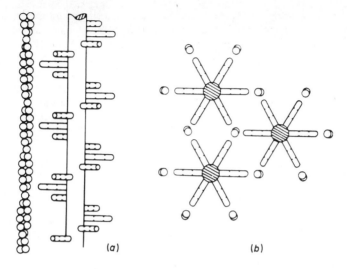

*Figure 3. Diagram to show the structure of the actin (thin) and myosin (thick)
filaments. Note (a) the double stranded beaded structure of actin, the pitch of the
spiral being about 350 Å; and the six staggered rows of feet on the myosin
filament; (b) the alignment of one actin filament, opposite each row of feet, in
cross-section. (From Bendall, 1964, by courtesy of AVI Publishing Co.)*

## PROTEINS OF SKELETAL MUSCLE

*(Bendall, 1964; Donelly et al., 1966; Pendl and Felix, 1960; Snyder,
1964; Szent-Györgyi, 1960 and 1964)*

*The contractile proteins (Seifer and Callop, 1966)*

The myofibril of skeletal muscle (rabbit) consists of 21 per cent actin,
54 per cent myosin, 15 per cent tropomyosin B and 10 per cent other
proteins ($\alpha$-actinin, $\beta$-actinin etc.).

After removing the water-soluble sarcoplasmic proteins from the
muscle tissue by extraction with salt solution of low ionic strength
($\mu \sim 0.1$), the contractile proteins of the myofibrils and the stroma
proteins of the connective tissue remain behind. Extraction of this
material by salt solutions of high ionic strength ($\mu \sim 0.6$) results in a
strongly viscous solution which contains, besides myosin and actin, also
actomyosin (a complex of actin and myosin). Pure myosin can be
obtained by stepwise lowering of the ionic strength.

*(a) Myosin*—Myosin (myosin A) is a thread-shaped molecule with a molecular weight (mol. wt.) of about 500,000. Myosin has enzymic properties: it breaks down adenosine triphosphate (ATP), the terminal phosphate group being split off, to yield inorganic phosphate and adenosine diphosphate (ADP) and releasing energy. This enzymic action of myosin is of great importance in the process of muscular contraction.

The adenosine triphosphatase (ATPase) activity of myosin is activated by calcium ions and inhibited by magnesium ions. Addition of actin changes the ATPase activity of myosin. This fact is very important with regard to the contractile system of muscle because in the presence of actin, magnesium ions – at low ionic strength – have no inhibition-effect but a strongly activating effect which is even greater than the activating effect of calcium ions. Here myosin ATPase is replaced by the actomyosin ATPase.

The myosin molecule is not a uniform substance. It consists of at least two subunits which can be separated by tryptic digestion. According to their behaviour in the ultracentrifuge, one unit, with a mol. wt. of about 380,000 is called 'heavy meromyosin' (H-meromyosin, HMM), the other, with a mol. wt. of about 120,000, 'light meromyosin' (L-meromyosin, LMM). Only the HMM shows ATPase activity and only this part of the myosin molecule is responsible for the binding of actin. As electron micrographs show, myosin has a 'head' formed by HMM and a 'tail' formed by LMM *(Figure 4)*. The heads of the myosin molecules serve as the cross bridges connecting the thick and thin filaments in muscle.

*(b) Actin*—Actin can be isolated from that material which is left after the partial extraction of myosin from muscle in the globular form

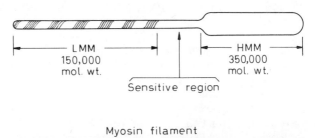

*Figure 4. Sketch of myosin molecule and portion of thick filament. (By courtesy of Dr. E. J. Briskey)*

(G-actin). The bead-shaped molecule of G-actin has a mol. wt. of 50,000. To remain in the G-form some ATP must be present in the solution and bound to the actin. The G-actin polymerizes on the addition of neutral salts to give chain-like molecules of fibrous actin (F-actin). This process is combined with simultaneous enzymic splitting of ATP to ADP and inorganic phosphate. In F-actin the globular particles are arranged side by side like the beads in a string of pearls *(Figure 5)*. Two of such strings are wound together to form a 'double helix'. The latter has no definite length and, therefore, no definite molecular weight. It consists of at least several million particles.

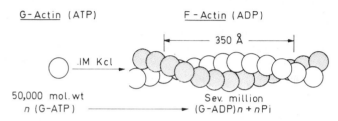

*Figure 5. Characteristics of G- and F-actin. (By courtesy of Dr. E. J. Briskey)*

*(c)  Actomyosin*—Mixing of solutions of F-actin and myosin results in a *solution* of high viscosity containing actomyosin. The addition of ATP, as well as inorganic polyphosphates, cause a drop of viscosity by dissociation of actomyosin into actin and myosin. When actomyosin is in the *gel* form, such as in the myofibril, then addition of ATP under specified conditions causes the protein system to synerase ('superprecipitation') or contract. In the latter case, pyrophosphate or tripolyphosphate are not able to simulate the action of ATP, which undergoes hydrolysis as syneresis or contraction occur.

Actomyosin, synthesized by adding together pure myosin and actin, is not identical with actomyosin preparations isolated from muscle fibres (myosin B). Myosin B or 'natural actomyosin' consists of actin, myosin, tropomyosin, troponin and $\alpha$- and $\beta$-actinin.

*(d)  Tropomyosin and Troponin*—Tropomyosin B represents a protein complex of tropomyosin and troponin. Tropomyosin shows neither any enzymic activity nor does it combine with myosin (Kominz and Maruyama, 1967). Tropomyosin probably regulates the interaction between myosin and actin (in the presence of ATP) in the process of muscular contraction (Endo *et al.*, 1966; Kominz, 1966; Ebashi *et al.*, 1967).

*(e) Muscular contraction and rigor mortis –(Bendall, 1966; Gergely, 1966; Huxley, 1965; Perry, 1966; Huxley and Hanson, 1960; Szent-Györgyi, 1966)* The myofibrillar proteins actin, myosin, tropomyosin and troponin are of basic importance for the living organism because contraction and relaxation of muscle are caused by interactions between these proteins. These proteins are also of particular interest for meat research because the drastic changes of meat *post mortem*, as in tenderness and water-holding capacity, are essentially due to changes in the actin-myosin system.

Contraction is induced by a release of very small amounts of calcium ions from the sarcoplasmic reticulum. These calcium ions activate myosin ATPase, causing a breakdown of ATP. As long as ATP is dephosphorylized, myosin and actin associate to actomyosin. This also happens after slaughter of the animal. The stiffening of the muscle fibre *post mortem*, which occurs as the ATP level falls and as actin and myosin associate, is called rigor mortis.

In resting, as well as in stretched muscle, the free end of the thin actin filaments do not adjoin each other in the centre of the sarcomere; the space remaining between them appears optically as the '*H*-band'. Contraction consists in a sliding of the actin filaments into the *H*-band. In the electron micrographs cross-bridges between the myosin and actin filaments appear. As already mentioned, these bridges, are formed by the HMM part of the myosin. It is not yet clear, however, what chemical reaction causes the linkage between HMM and actin *(Figure 6)*.

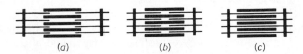

(a)                    (b)                    (c)

*Figure 6. Changes in the position of filaments associated with contraction (c) and extension (a) from resting length (b)*

### Proteins of the connective tissue

Besides the myofibrillar proteins, there exist other structural proteins in the muscle cell. These are the components of the connective tissue, namely collagen, elastin, reticulin, mucoprotein etc. There is no evidence as yet that they play any part in the contraction process of muscle.

*(a) Collagen–(Piez, 1966; Reich, 1966)* Collagen is the main constituent of connective tissue. It is characterized by its high content of the amino acids proline and hydroxyproline. The molecule shows a screw-shaped configuration; three of such helices are wound together like the

strings of a rope. There are cross-linkages within and between the helices providing the specific configuration of the molecule and the strength of the collagen fibril. It is well known that the toughness of meat is increased by collagen.

The toughness of meat from animals of different ages does not necessarily correlate with the total content of collagen. It is also dependent upon the molecular state of this protein. With increasing age of the animal the solubility of the collagen of muscle tissue in salt solutions or acid decreases; this phenomenon is due to an increase in cross links between the collagen molecules. With increasing cross-bridges, toughness rises (Carmichael and Lawrie, 1967; Herring *et al.*, 1967; Hill 1966).

*(b) Elastin–(Partridge, 1966)* Elastin is a protein which is highly resistant to acids, bases and proteolytic enzymes. It is present in muscle only in small amounts (less than 3 per cent of the total connective tissue) except in the *M. semitendinosus* which contains more elastin (up to 37 per cent of the total connective tissue) (Bendall and Voyle, 1967; Bendall, 1967). It is thus unlikely that elastin contributes much to the toughness of meat. The elastin molecule, the size of which is not defined, consists of long polypeptide chains which are cross-linked by internal bonds, probably formed by the two amino acids desmosine and iso-desmosine.

## Sarcoplasmic proteins

The structural proteins of muscle tissue (including the connective tissue proteins and the nuclei) can be separated from the other constituents by homogenizing the thoroughly minced tissue in dilute salt solution (ionic strength about 0.1) and centrifuging the homogenate at relatively low speed. The supernatant is usually called 'sarcoplasma'. The sarcoplasmic protein system contains hundreds of different proteins. Some of them can be separated electrophoretically. The supernatant which is obtained by centrifuging the watery extract at $100,000\,g$ is called 'the matrix'. In this matrix the globulins, which are soluble in salt solutions of low ionic strength, and the albumins, soluble in pure water (e.g. the muscle pigments as myoglobin, haemoglobin and cytochromes), are dissolved. The albumin fraction includes the 'myogens'. In this fraction most enzymes of the glycolytic process are found.

## TWO PROPERTIES OF MUSCLE PROTEINS OF PARTICULAR PRACTICAL IMPORTANCE

### Water-holding capacity (Hamm, 1960, 1963a and b)

The water-holding capacity of meat is closely related to taste, tenderness and colour and is influenced by treatment of the animal before slaughter. Furthermore, it affects the quality of meat during almost all processing operations after slaughter: storage, ageing, grinding, salting, curing, heating, drying, freezing and thawing. The binding of water within the muscle is effected by the muscle proteins.

Meat contains about 75 per cent water, but only about 4—5 per cent of the total water present in meat is bound tightly — as 'true hydration water' — to the muscle proteins. The amount of this 'hydration' water is scarcely influenced by the shape and electrical charge of the muscle proteins. Therefore, the marked changes in water-holding capacity which occur during storage and processing are determined by the extent to which physico-chemically 'free' water is immobilized within the microstructure of the tissue. The myofibrillar proteins, particularly myosin and actin, are responsible for binding hydration water and for immobilization of 'free' water in meat.

So far as the 'free' water is concerned, it seems to be a continuous transition from the tightly immobilized water within the protein network, which can only be expressed with difficulty, to the 'loose' water which can be squeezed out by very low pressure.

In contrast to the 'hydration' water, the amount of free water immobilized within the tissue is influenced by the spatial molecular arrangement of the myofibrillar proteins. Tightening the network of proteins (e.g. in rigor mortis, protein denaturation by heating, drying or freezing, effect of cations etc.) decreases immobilized water and increases the amount of expressible water. Loosening the protein structure (e.g. in ageing, salting etc.) has the opposite effect. Such structural changes may be caused by attraction or repulsion between the charged groups of adjacent protein molecules or by linking or loosening of cross linkages between the peptide chains. The strong influence of pH and of ions of certain salts (e.g. sodium chloride) on water-holding capacity can be explained by changes in the electrical charges of the myofibrillar proteins.

The salts dissolved in the sarcoplasma have a marked influence on the water-holding capacity of meat. About 50 per cent of the total water-holding capacity of beef muscle is due to the effect of the sarcoplasmic ions on myofibrillar proteins. Thus any loss of meat juice during storage, thawing etc. causes an undesirable decrease in water-holding capacity.

## Fat-emulsifying capacity (Saffle, 1968)

The capacity of muscle proteins for emulsifying fat is important for preparing meat emulsions. In the muscle-fat-water system of meat emulsions some of the muscle protein will be dissolved — particularly in the presence of salt — and exert an emulsifying effect by forming a thin protein layer around the fat droplets. A distinction has to be made between the emulsifying capacity of the proteins and the stability of the emulsion. Beef heart proteins, for instance, show a high emulsifying capacity but an emulsion prepared from heart tissue breaks down easily (Borton *et al.*, 1968). The emulsifying capacity of the muscle proteins decreases according to the series G-actin−myosin−actomyosin−sarcoplasmic proteins−F-actin. But in a sausage mixture the sarcoplasmic proteins may have a predominant effect because more of those proteins will be dissolved than myofibrillar proteins.

## INFLUENCE OF STORAGE AND PROCESSING OF MEAT ON THE MUSCULAR PROTEINS

*Post-mortem changes of muscle proteins (Bendall, 1960, 1964; Cassens, 1966; Lawrie, 1966; Newbold, 1966; Whitacker, 1959)*

(a) *Rigor mortis*−The most drastic changes which occur in meat as it passes into rigor mortis are the characteristic stiffening and loss of extensibility, the acidification (due to the production of lactic acid through the anaerobic glycolytic cycle) and, lastly, the loss of water-holding capacity. The details of the stiffening process and of the production of lactic acid cannot be discussed here. As already mentioned, rigor mortis consists in the formation of cross links between the actin and myosin filaments of the myofibril as the ATP supply of muscle becomes more or less rapidly exhausted after death to give a rigid and inextensible structure. The contraction model of the 'sliding filaments' (mentioned above) is also applicable to the process of rigor mortis. After 24 h the myofibrils of beef muscle are 'supercontracted' (Stromer and Goll, 1967).

Immediately after death and before the onset of rigor mortis, muscles are pliable and tender when cooked. The principal proteins of the myofibrils, actin and myosin, are dissociated. With the onset of rigor mortis, the sarcomere length decreases and the muscle becomes inextensible and is tough when cooked. During ageing, the sarcomere length increases (Gotthard *et al.*, 1966) and muscle becomes pliable again, and increasingly tender on cooking.

If the drop of pH after slaughter is unusually fast, a low pH value is reached when the temperature of tissue is still high ($>30°C$). Under such conditions, which lead to pale, soft, exudative pork ('PSE muscle'), the extractibility of sarcoplasmic and myofibrillar proteins is considerably lower than under normal conditions (Briskey *et al.*, 1966). The combination of low pH value and high tissue temperature results in a partial denaturation of sarcoplasmic proteins which are probably precipitated on the myofibrils.

(b) *Tenderness and muscle proteins−(Lawrie, 1967)* The more extensive the combination of actin and myosin during rigor mortis, the shorter is the sarcomere length of the myofibrils. It has been clearly demonstrated that the tenderness of cooked meat usually decreases with decreasing sarcomere length. As the temperature at which the post-mortem glycolysis proceeds is lowered, the degree of shortening decreases, reaching a minimum at about $15^o$. Thereafter, as the temperature during post-mortem glycolysis is lowered further, the degree of shortening increases once more, being nearly as great at $0^o$ as at $37^o$. This 'cold shortening' phenomenon has not yet been completely explained. 'Cold-shortening' also appears if only a little ATP is broken down (Busch et al., 1967; Cassens and Newbold, 1967). Therefore, this shortening cannot be identical with the physiological process of contraction.

As ageing of meat proceeds, the muscle becomes pliable once more and increasingly tender on cooking. It might be thought that this increase in tenderness during ageing is simply due to a dissociation of actomyosin into actin and myosin. But this cannot be the case because inextensibility of muscle remains and attempts to demonstrate a dissociation of acto-myosin have failed. Nevertheless, a certain weakening of the interaction between myosin and actin has been observed by several authors (Fujimaki et al., 1965; Okitani et al., 1967; Penny, 1967; Robson et al., 1967; Scharpf and Marion, 1966; Weidemann et al., 1967). There is now, however, considerable suggestion that the increased tenderness may be related to a detachment of actin filaments from Z-lines whereby the links formed with myosin during the onset of rigor remain unbroken (Davey and Gilbert, 1967). With increasing time of ageing, the structure of the Z-band is loosened and finally disintegrated (Davey and Gilbert, 1968; Fukazawa and Yasui, 1967). This may be due to proteolytic hydrolysis of tropomyosin (Penny, 1968).

Another type of reaction which could result in an increase in tender-ness is proteolytic breakdown of actomyosin by proteases of the muscle tissue. Several workers have been able to demonstrate the occurrence of proteolytic enzymes in muscle (Berman, 1967; Berman and Kotula, 1966; Noguchi and Kandatso, 1967; Iodice, 1967; Park and Pennington, 1967; Parrish and Baily, 1966; Randall and Macrae, 1967; Whitaker, 1964). There is no doubt that during ageing at low temperatures $(2-4^oC)$ some of the protein material is transformed into low-molecular nitrogen com-pounds, such as peptides and amino acids (Motoc and Banu, 1968; Suzuki et al., 1967). Up to $25^o$, temperature does not influence the proteolytic attack on myofibrils but at $37^o$ it does (Galloway and Goll, 1967). During 30 days ageing of beef at $2^o$ no correlation between breakdown of protein and tenderness was observed (Davey and Gilbert, 1966). Even after 312 h post-mortem storage a proteolytic breakdown of tropomyosin, which is most sensitive against proteolytic enzymes, is not detectable (Goll and Robson, 1967). These results suggest that enzymic proteolysis of muscle proteins cannot play a major part in the tenderization during normal meat ageing but could be a decisive factor during aseptic ageing at higher temperatures.

Generally there is no breakdown of connective tissue proteins by proteolytic muscle enzymes (Goll, 1965).

*Influence of freezing and frozen storage on meat proteins (Fennema 1966; Lawrie, 1968; Love, 1966; Partmann, 1968a)*

When meat is subjected to temperatures below its freezing point, the chemical changes effected depend on the rate at which freezing occurs and on the freezing temperature ultimately attained and its duration.

Freezing usually begins in extracellular spaces, thus increasing the concentration of solids in the extracellular fluid. In turn, this draws water osmotically from within the still-unfrozen cell which adds to the growing ice cystals and denatures muscle proteins. Slow-freezing of tissue results in large ice crystals which are located entirely in extracellular areas. There is extensive translocation of water and the slowly frozen cells have a shrunken appearance. Rapid freezing, on the other hand, results in numerous small crystals located uniformly throughout the specimen. The faster the transition from $0^\circ$ to $-5^\circ$, the less is the translocation during freezing and the less are protein damage and exudation.

The damage of muscle cells by freezing can be due *(a)* to a destruction of cells by the formation of ice crystals and *(b)* to a denaturation of muscle proteins by an increase of salts in the non-frozen cell fluid. The damage of cell walls by freezing can be demonstrated by the release of deoxyribonucleic acid into the press juice of the thawed meat. An increase in the time of frozen storage of meat usually leads to greater damage of cells (Crigler and Dawson, 1968). Freezing and thawing makes the muscle membranes permeable to proteins (Osner, 1966).

When meat is frozen before ATP is broken down, during subsequent thawing a strong contraction of the actomyosin system occurs which is probably due to damage of the sarcoplasmic reticulum whereby calcium ions are released and stimulate a high rate of ATP break-down (Kusmerick and Davies, 1968). This 'thaw-rigor' results in an undesirable drip forma tion.

The meat proteins – particularly the actomyosin – are much more stable to freezing than the fish muscle proteins. There is no doubt, however, that in meat and poultry frozen storage causes some protein denaturation and autolytic changes (Dzinleski *et al.,* 1967; Khan and Penz, 1965; Khan and Van den Berg, 1967; Partmann, 1967; Saffle and

177

Galbreath, 1964). During storage of frozen beef at -4°C, for instance, the amount of total extractable protein (sarcoplasmic proteins plus acto-myosin) decreases from 91 per cent to 51 per cent (Awad *et al.,* 1968). The proteolysis of meat proteins, however, seems to be quite small (Khan *et al.,* 1968; Linko and Nikkilä, 1963) although the proteolytic activity of the muscle tissue does not decrease much during frozen storage (Pavlov-ski, 1965). During frozen storage of chicken muscle at -3°C the free amino acid content increases remarkably within 2 months; at -8°C this increase is much smaller; and at -28°C almost no changes were observed (Partmann, 1967).

Denaturation of muscle proteins by freezing and frozen storage is reflected by decreasing solubility of sarcoplasmic proteins, increasing difficulty of extracting actomyosin, a loss of myosin ATPase activity (especially below -20°C), a decrease of titratable sulphydryl groups and a loss of contractibility of fibrils on addition of ATP (Partmann, 1968b). Two factors, namely increase in non-protein nitrogen and decrease in the content of free sulphydryl groups, during frozen storage, can be com-bined to provide an index which is closely related to the quality of the thawed meat (Khan, 1966).

The reddish exudation or drip which appears on thawing contains proteins, peptides and amino acids. Therefore, slow freezing can lead to some loss of the nutritive value of the meat unless the exudate is retained for incorporation during cooking. It is nevertheless true that only minor changes in the nutritive value of meat arise through freezing and frozen storage. Thus after frozen storage at -18°C for 7 months, the amino acid content of meat is not changed. After 2 years storage, however, it is decreased (Gordzierkie, 1967). A decrease of glutamic acid content of meat after storage at -35°C was observed (Pavlovski, 1966).

*Influence of freeze-drying on meat proteins (Hamm, 1964; Lawrie, 1968)*

The mildest method for drying meat is the sublimation of water from the frozen state under vacuum. Because of the low temperature and the high speed of operation the water-holding capacity of the proteins is not too much affected. But even under optimum operating conditions there is some evidence that proteins are altered. The result is a decrease in water-holding capacity of the rehydrated meat.

The decrease of water-holding capacity and increase in toughness of meat caused by freeze-dehydration might be due to a closer approach of the actomyosin molecules – rendered possible by the withdrawal of water and a certain unfolding of the peptide chains. This approach of myofibrillar protein molecules is accompanied by the formation of new inter-molecular salt and/or metal-bonds. However, contractility, ATPase activity and solubility of the myofibrillar proteins are not greatly influenced by freeze-dehydration. With chicken meat some decrease of protein solubility by freeze-drying has been found (Bolshakov *et al.*, 1964). The extent of denaturation of myosin A, myosin B and H—meromyosin preparations by freeze-drying is influenced by pH and ionic strength (Yasui and Hashimoto, 1966).

It can be demonstrated that denaturation of myofibrillar proteins during freeze-drying is caused only by the dehydration process itself, i.e. by the withdrawal of water, and not by the freezing process or by the increase in concentration of salts in the sarcoplasm during dehydration.

There is some evidence that the proteins of the sarcoplasmic reticulum are altered. As to the meat pigments, the bulk survives as bright red oxymyoglobin, especially at low plate temperatures. The concentration of brown metmyoglobin, however, increases with time and temperature of storage. Furthermore, non-enzymic Maillard type browning occurs by reactions between proteins and the carbohydrates of tissue which leads to bitter flavours.

The digestibility of meat and its content of essential amino acids are not changed by freeze-drying. During storage, however, essential amino acids can be destroyed by browning reactions.

*Influence of cooking and canning on the meat proteins (Hamm 1966; Hofmann, 1966; Lawrie, 1968)*

The most drastic changes in meat during heating are those that involve the muscle proteins. The shrinkage of the tissue and the release of juice (Rogers *et al.*, 1967; Tyszkiewicz and Tyszkiewicz, 1966; Tyszkiewicz *et al.*, 1966) are caused by changes in the myofibrillar proteins. The discoloration of the muscle and the loss of the activity of muscle enzymes are the result of denaturation of the sarcoplasmic proteins. The solubility of myofibrils and sarcoplasmic proteins decreases with increasing duration and temperature of heating (Cohen, 1966; Paul *et al.*, 1966; Rivenson *et al.*, 1966). When bound to actin, myosin in the myofibril is more resistant to heat denaturation (Penny, 1967) than in the unbound state.

It can be shown that the physical and chemical changes of muscle during heating occur in different steps:

*At 20 to 30°C*—No changes occur in the colloid-chemical properties of the tissue or in the solubility and ion-binding of muscle proteins. The ATPase activity of myosin decreases at 30°C.

*At 30 to 50°C*—Changes in myofibrillar proteins occur in this range of temperature which influence water-holding capacity and rigidity of the tissue. They include two steps: an unfolding of peptide chains and the formation of relatively unstable cross-linkages. This results in a tighter network of protein structure at the isoelectric range of pH. A small part of the sarcoplasmic proteins is also denatured (decrease of solubility). Heating of meat at 45–60°C for longer time (10 h) may lead to breakdown of muscle protein by tissue proteases (Paul *et al.*, 1966).

*At 50 to 55°C*—In this range of temperature a rearrangement of myofibrillar proteins occurs causing a delay in the changes of water-holding capacity. At this temperature new cross-linkages begin to form which are quite stable and cannot split by addition of weak acid or base. The denaturation of sarcoplasmic proteins is continued.

*At 55 to 80°C*—Most of the changes occurring between 40°C and 50°C continue to a lesser extent. At 65°C most of the myofibrillar and globular muscle proteins are coagulated. Collagen shrinks at temperatures around 63°C and may be partially transformed to gelatin at high temperatures.

*Above 80°C*—The formation of disulphide bonds by oxidation of the sulphydryl groups of actomyosin begins between 70°C and 90°C and is continued with increasing temperature. Above 90°C hydrogen sulphide is split off from the sulphydryl groups of actomyosin. A significant correlation between $H_2S$ developed and other volatile sulphur compounds and the flavour of canned meat has been found (Przezbiecka and Zoltowska, 1967). Maillard reactions begin at about 90°C and are continued with increasing temperature and time of heating. The browning of meat (Savic and Kepcija, 1966) is mainly due to a reaction of carbohydrates of muscle with the amino groups of proteins. To a lesser extent it is due to pyrolysis of carbohydrates (Pearson *et al.*, 1966). Thus the degree of browning increases with the amount of reducing sugar in the meat (Bowers *et al.*, 1968). Browning reactions lower the nutritive availability of amino acids of meat proteins as lysine (Dvorak, 1965). Collagen may be transformed to gelatin, causing an increase in tenderness.

The method of cooking will largely determine whether the toughening effect of heat on myofibrillar proteins will be offset by its tenderizing action on collagen; and the method of cooking, in turn will be determined by the relative amount of connective tissue in the meat.

Normal methods of cooking may have some influence on the digestibility of meat proteins but do not greatly change the amino acid content of meat. Heating at a higher temperature for a longer time, as it is often used for full sterilization of canned meats, damages essential amino acids (Zoldowsga, 1967) particularly cysteine, methionine and lysine. The result is a decrease in the nutritive value of the product. The pressure-cooking of meat, which is desirable from the point of view of tenderness, has disadvantages. Thus, when autoclaved at 112°C for 24 h, 45 per cent of the cysteine of pork may be destroyed and other amino acids made unavailable during digestion.

*Influence of curing on meat proteins (Hamm 1960; Lawrie, 1968)*

As already mentioned, the increase in the water-holding capacity of meat caused by the addition of salts (e.g. sodium chloride) is due to an electrostatic repulsion of adjacent peptide chains caused by binding of salt ions. A part of the NaCl effect can also be caused by an exchange of bivalent cations which are bound to myofibrillar proteins lowering their water-holding capacity, against sodium ions (Berman and Swift, 1964).

The high water-binding capacity of ground meat caused by the addition of inorganic polyphosphates in the presence of NaCl might be due to the combination of several effects, e.g. partial dissociation of actomyosin to actin and myosin, increase of protein charges by binding of polyphosphate anions to myofibrillar proteins and sequestering the calcium and magnesium ions of muscular tissue (Hellendoorn, 1962; Yasui *et al.*, 1964). With rising ionic strength of the added salt, and higher pH, in sausage mixes, increasing amounts of muscle proteins will be dissolved, improving the emulsion stability and water-holding capacity of the product. Excessive salt ($>8$ per cent) has a dehydrating effect on comminuted meat.

*Influence of ionizing radiation on meat protein (Lawrie, 1968)*

The changes in proteins produced by ionizing radiation are determined both by their individual nature and by the dose of radiation to which they are exposed. With a dose of 5 Mrad (approximately that required for microbial sterilizing) there is a marked loss of water-holding capacity (Jay, 1967). The oxidation of sulphydryl groups may be responsible for those changes.

Many enzyme proteins are relatively stable against radiation and require considerably more than 5 Mrad for inactivation. This can be a serious problem in the storage of irradiated meat. Irradiation may transform myoglobin to a bright red compound, similar in absorption spectrum to oxymyoglobin; or some of the meat pigment may be converted to green sulphmyoglobin. Most often brown metmyoglobin is formed.

As to the influence of irradiation on the nutritive value of meat proteins, the lysine, tryptophan, methionine, leucine, valine, threonine and histidine levels of meat are affected when doses of 1.4 Mrad are used. The decrease in the amino acid content of the treated meat is an exponential function of the irradiation dose (Curatola and Zaio, 1967). When comminuted beef is treated by either electron beam or gamma ray irradiation, the most sensitive amino acid is cystine. Approximately 50 per cent of cystine is destroyed under severe conditions, and tryptophan shows 10 per cent decrease. Other amino acids are little affected. The extent of destruction is not primarily related to the total dose but to dose rate and particularly to energy level of irradiating dose (Johnson and Moser, 1967).

## REFERENCES

Awad, A., Powrie, W. D. and Fennema, O. (1968). *J. Fd Sci.* **33**, 227

Bendall, J. R. (1960). In: *The Structure and Function of Muscle* Ed. by G. H. Bourne, Vol. III, p. 227. New York; Academic Press

– (1964). In: *Symposium on Food Proteins and Their Reactions* Ed. by H. W. Schultz, p. 225. Westport, Conn.; AVI Pub. Co.

– (1966). In: *The Physiology and Biochemistry of Muscle as a Food* Ed. by E. J. Briskey, R. G. Cassens and J. C. Trautman, p. 7. Madison; Univ. Wisconsin Press

– (1967). *J. Sci. Fd. Agric.* **18**, 533

– and Voyle, C. A. (1967). *J. Fd Technol.* **2**, 259

Bennett, H. S. (1960). In: *The Structure and Function of Muscle* Ed. by G. H. Bourne. Vol. I. p. 137. New York; Academic Press

Berman, M. D. (1967). *J. Fd Sci.* **32**, 568

– and Kotula, A. W. (1966). *Nature, Lond.* **210**, 1771

– and Swift, C. E. (1964). *J. Fd Sci.* **29**, 182

Bolshakov, A. S., Pugachev, P. I., Shabanova, V. A. and Ishukov, V. P. (1964). *Trudy vses. Nauchno. Inst.* **10**, 33; *Chem. Abstr.* **63**, 13940a (1965)

Borton, R. J., Webb, N. B. and Bratzler, L. J. (1968). *Fd Technol.* **22**, No. 4, 162

Bowers, J. A., Harrison, D. L. and Kropf, D. H. (1968). *J. Fd. Sci.* **33**, 147.

Briskey, E. J., Kastenschmidt, L., Forrest, J. C., Beecher, G. R., Judge, M. D., Cassens, R. G. and Hoekstra, W. G. (1966). *J. agric. Fd Chem.* **14**, 201

Busch, W. A., Parrish, S. C. and Goll, D. E. (1967). *J. Fd Sci.* **32**, 390

Carmichael, D. J. and Lawrie, R. A. (1967). *J. Fd Technol.* **2**, 299

Cassens, R. G. (1964). *Proc. 17th a. recipr. Meat Conf.* (Nat. Live Stock and Meat Board). 114

– (1966). In: *The Physiology and Biochemistry of Muscle as a Food* Ed. by E. J. Briskey, R. G. Cassens and J. C. Trautman, p. 181. Madison; Univ. Wisconsin Press

– and Newbold, R. P. (1967). *J. Fd Sci.* **32**, 269

Cohen, E. M. (1966). *J. Fd Sci.* **31**, 246

Crigler, J. C. (1968). *J. Fd Sci.* **33**, 248

Curatola, G. and Zaio, A. (1967). *G. Med. milit.* **117**, 397. Ref. *Chem. Abstr.* **68**, 86189g (1968)

Davey, C. L. and Gilbert, K. V. (1966). *J. Fd Sci.* **31**, 135

– – (1967). *J. Fd Sci.* **2**, 57

– – (1968). *J. Fd Sci.* **33**, 343

Davies, R. I. (1968). *Biochim. biophys. Acta* **153**, 279

Donelly, T. H., Rongey, E. H. and Barsuko, V. J. (1966). *J. agric. Fd Chem.* **14**, 196

Dupraw, E. J. (1968). *Cell and Molecular Biology,* p. 158. New York and London; Academic Press

Dvorak, Z. (1965). *Prům. Potravin* **16**, No. 4, 172

Dzinleski, B., Necev, T. and Ivocic, M. (1967). *Tehnologija Mesa* **8**, 43

Ebashi, S., Ebashi, F. and Kodama, A. (1967). *J. Biochem, Tokyo* **62**, 137

Endo, M., Nonomura, Y., Masaki, T., Ohtsuki, I. and Ebashi, S. (1966). *J. Biochem, To* **60**, 605

PROPERTIES OF MEAT PROTEINS

Fennema, O. (1966).*Cryobiology* 3, 197
Fujimaki, M., Arakawa, N., Okitani, H. and Takagi, O. (1965). *J. Fd Sci.* 30, 937,
  *Agric. Biol. Chem., Tokyo* 29, 700
Fukazawa, T. and Yasui, T. (1967). *Biochim. biophys. Acta* 140, 534
Galloway, D. E. and Goll, D. E. (1967). *J. Anim. Sci.* 26, 1302
Gergeley, J. (1966). *Biochemistry of Muscle Contraction.* Retina Foundation
  Monograph Vol. II. Boston
Goll. D. E. (1965). *Proc. 18th a. recipr. Meat Conf.* (Nat. Live Stock and Meat
  Board) 161
– and Robson, R. N. (1967). *J. Fd Sci.* 32, 323
Gordzierkie, L. N. (1967). *Izv. Vyssh. Vehed. Zaved., Peshch Technol.* 1967, No.
  22, 40; *Chem. Abstr.* 67, 20715y (1967)
Gotthard, R. M., Mullens, A. M., Boulware, R. S. and Hansard, S. L. (1966). *J. Fd
  Sci.* 31, 825
Hamm, R. (1960). *Adv. Fd Res.* 10, 355
– (1963a). *Recent Adv. Fd Sci.* 3, 218
– (1963b). *Fleischwirts.* 15, 298
– (1964). *Dt. Lebensmitt-Rdsch.* 60, 97
– (1966). In: *The Physiology and Biochemistry of Muscle as a Food.* Ed. by E. J.
  Briskey, R. G. Cassens and J. C. Trautman. p. 363. Madison; Univ. Wisconsin
  Press
Hellendoorn, E. W. (1962). *Fd Technol.* 16, 119
Herring, H. K., Cassens, R. G. and Briskey, E. J. (1967). *J. Fd Sci.* 32, 534
Hill, F. (1966). *J. Fd Sci.* 31, 161
Hofmann, K. (1966). *Fleischwirts.* 46, 1121
Huxley, H. E. (1965). *Scient. Am.* 213, No. 6, 18
– (1966). In: *Muscle* Ed. by W. M. Paul, E. E. Daniel, C. M. Kay and G. Monkton,
  p. 3. Oxford; Pergamon Press
– and Hanson, J. (1960). In: *The Structure and Function of Muscle* Ed. by G. M.
  Bourne. Vol. 1, p. 183. New York; Academic Press
Iodice, A. A. (1967). *Arch. Biochem. Biophys.* 121, 241
Jay, J. M. (1967). *J. Fd Sci.* 32, 371
Johnson, B. L. and Moser, H. (1967). *Adv. Chem. Ser. No.* 65, 171; *Chem. Abstr.*
  67, 10451v (1967)
Khan, A. W. (1966). *Nature, Lond.* 208, 204
– and Penz, C. (1965). *J. Fd Sci.* 30, 787
– and Van den Berg, L. (1967). *J. Fd Sci.* 32, 148
– Davidkowa, E. and Van den Berg, L. (1968). *Cryobiology* 4, 184
Kominz, D. R. (1966). *Arch. Biochem. Biophys.* 115, 583
– and Maruyama, K. (1967). *J. Biochem., Tokyo* 61, 269
Kushmerick, M. J. and Davies, R. E. (1968). *Biochem. biophys. Acta* 153, 279
Lawrie, R. A. (1966). *Meat Science.* Oxford; Pergamon Press
– (1967). In: *Rheology and Texture of Foodstuffs* S.C.I. Monograph No. 27,
  p. 134
– (1968). *J. Sci. Fd Agric.* 19, 233
Linko, R. R. and Nikkilä (1963). *Sci. Agric. Soc. Finland* 35, 92
Love, R. M. (1966). In: *Cryobiology* Ed. by H. T. Meryman, p. 317, New York;
  Academic Press.
Mommaerts, W.F.H.M. (1966). *J. mol. Biol.* 15, 377
Motoc, D. and Banu, C. (1968). *Fleischwirts* 48, 1045

Needam, D. M. (1960). In: *The Structure and Function of Muscle* Ed. by G. H. Bourne Vol. II. p.55. New York: Academic Press

Newbold, R. P. (1966). In: *The Physiology and Biochemistry of Muscle as a Food* Ed. by E. J. Briskey, R. G. Cassens and J. C. Trautman, p. 213. Madison; Univ. Wisconsin Press

Noguchi, T. and Kandatso, M. (1967). *Agric. biol. Chem. Tokyo* **30**, 199

Okitani, A., Takagi, O. and Fujimaki, M. (1967). *Agric. biol. Chem. Tokyo* **31**, 939

Osner, R. C. (1966). *J. Fd Sci.* **31**, 832

Park, D. C. and Pennington, R. J. (1967). *Enzym. biol. clin.* **8**, 149

Parrish, F. C. and Baily, M. E. (1966). *J. agric. Fd Chem.* **14**, 232

Partmann, W. (1967). *Fleischwirts.* **47**, 957

– (1968a). *Fleischwirts.* **48**, 1317

– (1968b). *Z. Lebensmittelunters. u.-Forsch.* **131**, 74

Partridge, S. M. (1966). In: *The Physiology and Biochemistry of Muscle as a Food.* Ed. by E. J. Briskey, R. G. Cassens and J. C. Trautman. p. 327. Madison, Univ. Wisconsin Press

Paul, P. C., Buchter, L. and Wierenga, A. (1966). *J. agric. Fd Chem.* **14**, 490

Pavlovski, P. E. (1965). *Mijasnaja Industrija SSR* **36**, No. 1, 50; *Abstr. Fleischwirts.* **45**, 1334 (1965)

– (1966). *Mijasnaja Industrija SSR 37,* No. 4, 45; *Chem. Abstr.* **66**, 11469x (1967)

Pearson, A.M., Tarladgis, B. G., Spooner, E. and Quinn, J.B. (1966). *J. Fd Sci.* **31**, 187

Pendl, I. and Felix, K. (1960). In: *Handbuch der physiologisch- u. pathologisch-chemischen Analyse* Ed. by K. Land and W. Lehnartz. Vol. V, Part 1, p 496. (Berlin)

Penny, I. F. (1967). *J. Fd Technol.* **2**, 325

– (1968). *J. Sci. Fd Agric.* **19**, 518

Perry, S. V. (1966). In: *Muscle* Ed. by W. M. Paul, E. E. Daniel, L. M. Kay and G. Monckton. p. 29 Oxford: Pergamon Press

Piez, K. A. (1966). In: *The Physiology and Biochemistry of Muscle as a Food* Ed. by E. J. Briskey, R. G. Cassens and J. C. Trautman, p. 315, Madison; Univ. Winconsin Press

Przezbiecka, T. and Toltowska, A. (1967). *Roczniki Institutu Przemysly Miesnego* **4**, 107

Randall, C. J. and Macrae, H.F. (1967). *J. Fd Sci.* **32**, 182

Reich, H. (1966). *Kollagen.* Dresden.

Rivenson, S., Zuolaga, G. and Szavini, L. M. (1966). *Rev. Invest. Agrotecuar.* Ser. 4, 3 No. 4, 37; *Chem. Abstr.* **67**, 42671h (1967)

Robson, N., Goll, D. E. and Main, M. J. (1967). *J. Fd Sci.* **32**, 544

Rogers, P. J., Goertz, G. E. and Harrison, D.L. (1967). *J. Fd Sci.* **32**, 298

Saffle, R. (1968). *Adv. Food Res.* **16**, 105

–and Galbreath, J. W. (1964). *Fd Technol.* **18**, 119

Savic, I. and Kepcija, D. (1966). *Acta vet. Beogr.* **16**, 3

Scharpf, L. G. and Marion, W. W. (1966). *J. Fd Sci.* **31**, 680

Seifer, S. and Gallop, P. M. (1966). In: *The Proteins* Ed. by H. Neurath, Vol. IV., p. 430. New York; Academic Press

Snyder, H. E. (1964). *Proc. 17th a. recipr. Meat Conf.* (Nat. Live Stock and Meat Board, Chicago) 138

Stromer, M. H. and Goll, D. E. (1967). *J. Fd Sci.* **32**, 329, 386

Suzuki, A., Nakazado, M. and Fujimaki, N.W. (1967). *Agric. biol. Chem. Tokyo,* **31,** 953

Szent-Györgyi, A. G. (1960). In: *The Structure and Function of Muscle* Ed. by G. M. Bourne, Vol II, p. 1. New York, Academic Press

–(1964). *Proc. 17th a. recipr. Meat Confer.* (Nat. Live Stock and Meat Board, Chicago), 131

–(1966). In: *The Physiology and Biochemistry of Muscle as a Food* Ed. by E. J. Briskey, R. G. Cassens and J. C. Trautman, p. 287. Madison, Univ. Wisconsin Press

Tyszkiewicz, St. and Tyszkiewicz, I. (1966). *Roczniki Instytutu Przemyslu Miesneg* **3,** No. 1, 39

– Tyszkiewicz, I. and Dukalwska, M. (1966). *Roczniki Instytutu Przemyslu Miesnego* **3,** No 1, 29

Whitaker, J. R. (1959). *Ad. Fd Res.* **9,** 1

–(1964). *Proc. 17th a. recipr. Meat Conf.* (Nat. Live Stock and Meat Board, Chicago), 153

Weidemann, J. G., Kaess, G. and Carruthers, C. D. (1967). *J. Fd Sci.* **32,** 7

Yasui, T. and Hashimoto, Y. (1966). *J. Fd Sci.* **31,** 293

–Sakanishi, M. and Hashimoto, Y. (1964). *J. agric. Fd Chem.* **12,** 392

Zoldowsga, A. (1967). *Roczniki Instytutu Przemyslu Miesnego* **4,** 91

# INTRINSIC AND EXTRINSIC FACTORS AFFECTING
# THE QUALITY OF FISH

G.H.O. BURGESS and J.M. SHEWAN

*Torry Research Station, Ministry of Technology, Aberdeen*

## INTRODUCTION

Fish spoils rapidly and the requirements for its proper handling and transportation are considerably more exacting than for other protein foods, except perhaps milk. The conditions imposed by nature and by the structure of fish catching and processing industries in many countries, however, generally make the application of good practice very difficult.

The needs of international trade have led to world-wide interest in the development of food standards, and the establishment of the Codex Alimentarius Commission springs directly from this interest (Davies, 1968). Within the next few years there will be an ever increasing number of Codex standards for fish products and although drawn up for international use, there is no doubt that Governments will also begin to apply them internally. Quite apart from legislative factors which are causing more attention to be paid to the quality of fish products, social and economic forces are compelling fish industries everywhere to attempt to maintain a more uniform product quality than in the past.

The difficulties of delivering to the consumer a fish or fish product which is, within predetermined limits, uniform in initial biological quality, its physiological condition and also its degree of freshness are formidable indeed. Some form of inspection, mainly to prevent stale fish from reaching the consumer, is practised in most countries; fish exporting countries, such as Canada, Denmark and Norway, have higher standards and more rigorous control. It remains true, however, that in the U.K. fish industry as a whole, in company with fish industries in most other countries, ' . . . very few firms practise anything remotely resembling "quality control" as understood in some industries' (Cutting and Burgess, 1960). This situation arises largely from the inherent difficulties of control, but these must nevertheless be solved if an acceptable product is to be marketed. This paper discusses some of these difficulties and suggests how they might be solved.

## BIOLOGICAL FACTORS AFFECTING QUALITY

The term 'fish' comprehends three classes of vertebrates, apart from members of two or three Phyla loosely called 'shellfish'. Of these three vertebrate classes, however, the Pisces (Teleosts or Bony Fishes) are of overwhelming importance; of the total world catch in 1967 of 60.6 million metric tons, more than 90 per cent were bony fishes and only 0.7 per cent were Elasmobranchs (FAO, 1968). Over 300 species of marine and freshwater teleosts are listed for British waters alone (Norman, 1935), of which about one sixth are eaten and many more are edible. U.K. official statistics give over 30 'kinds' of which about eight are of preponderating importance (Ministry of Agriculture, Fisheries and Food, 1968); FAO statistics list over 130 'kinds', many of which contain large numbers of species.

Where non-specific fishing methods, such as trawling, are employed, the species composition of catches varies widely with ground and season, and although skilled fishermen know how and where to search for the more highly prized species, even with modern navigational and fish-finding equipment, fishing remains a form of hunting with all the lack of control of feed, environment and conditions of slaughter that this implies. It is therefore characteristic of most fishing industries that the size of catches and their species composition fluctuate widely from season to season and often from day to day.

Proximate chemical composition differs considerably from species to species, perhaps particularly the lipid fraction. Gadoids, for example, never contain more than 1 per cent muscle lipid, all of which is non-depot fat, whereas some Clupeoids may contain 25 per cent or more, but within-species variation is often large (Stansby, 1962b). Lipid content in British herring varies with season and sexual condition (Lovern and Wood, 1937) and very considerable variations from year to year have been reported in Canadian Atlantic herring (Leim, 1958). The texture of the cooked flesh of fatty fish is greatly dependent on fat content, which varies considerably from one part of the musculature to another (Brandes and Dietrich, 1953; Thurston and Groniger, 1959; Mannan et al., 1961). Adipose tissue in fish, clearly differentiated from surrounding muscular tissue, is not generally apparent to the naked eye, although particularly high concentrations of fat are often found beneath the skin and at the bases of dorsal and ventral fins.

Water and muscle depot fat are, to a considerable degree interchangeable; thus a herring which is low in fat does not necessarily look thin (Brandes and Dietrich, 1954). The hydrodynamic properties of a fatty fish may hence be less affected by prolonged starvation than would otherwise be the case.

Total protein in the flesh tends to be more constant, but nevertheless can show considerable changes in extreme circumstances. These changes are of great importance to the fish processor, for they influence not only yields of edible flesh but also its suitability for processing, such as smoke curing. Insufficient is known about these biological changes to advise industry on how to avoid catching particularly unsuitable fish let alone how to deal with it satisfactorily when it is caught. There appear to be few systematic differences in proximate composition attributable to sex (Jacquot, 1961).

That seasonal changes occur in the plumpness of fish has long been known (Graham, 1923; Hickling, 1930); such changes in cod have been correlated with changes in liver weight and oil content (Love 1958; Jangaard et al., 1967). Prolonged starvation may produce a drastic increase in the percentage water content of the muscle. Templeman and Andrews (1956) reported a 'jellied' condition in large American plaice (Hippoglossoides platessoides) caught on the Grand Bank. They concluded that this was due to protein emaciation caused by development of the gonads and the inability of large fish in cold water to provide for body repair and growth at the same time. The composition of the remaining protein appeared somewhat changed in the jellied fish which had proportionately more non-protein and stroma nitrogen than normal. Average water content of the muscle was 88.2 per cent in 34 samples of jellied fish but 82.5 per cent in 32 samples of normal fish. Collagen content of herring rises during the period when muscle fat is falling (Hughes, 1963): it is well known that salmon kelts have very thick skins.

Similar phenomena have been reported for other species elsewhere; Lovern (1939) reported the surprising observation that starving freshwater eels (Anguilla anguilla) become depleted in protein rather than fat, but this could have been due to experimental factors. Bertin (1956) mentions 'rubber' congers caught on the continental slope after spawning, a condition perhaps caused by depletion of fat. Generally less severe, but industrially more significant, changes have been studied by Love, who has shown that in cod muscle water content rises during starvation and maturation of gonads (Ironside and Love, 1968; Love, 1960). Such seasonal changes no doubt account for processing difficulties familiar in the fish trade. Barents Sea cod, for instance, in April and May is sometimes impossible to smoke cure satisfactorily. Fillets have a slightly opaque, milky appearance and although the smoked product looks satisfactory immediately it is removed from the kiln, it soon begins to exude a milky fluid.

Filleting yields vary from season to season in fish caught on the same ground, and also in fish caught on different grounds at the same season. There is much trade lore on this subject, but little systematic work. Data are available on the length/weight relationship of various commercial marine fish from which it appears, for example, that there are considerable differences between Icelandic and North Sea haddock (Baader, 1965). Differences between cod caught in different areas have been known for over 100 years (Yarrell, 1836).

Besides gross changes in the degree of hydration of fish muscle, there are more subtle, but no doubt equally important, seasonal changes in the free amino acids (Jones, 1954; Hughes, 1959b). Individual variations may be significant; large differences in concentration of free amino acids have been reported in lemon sole caught in the same haul (Jones, 1959).

Amino acids and peptides possibly contribute to flavour. Of greater significance, perhaps, are the mononucleotides which, even if they themselves are not strongly flavoured, provide reaction products which are (Jones, 1967). These are discussed below. Fish may also develop flavours resulting from their feed; cod in certain areas may taste unpleasant through feeding on the pteropod *Clione limacina*. Such fish contain dimethyl sulphide in the flesh (Sipos and Ackman, 1964).

Mention may finally be made of the effects on quality of the nutritional condition and feed of fish. Too little is known to be able to say more than that these may on occasions be of overriding importance. Newfoundland trap-caught cod has a low muscle glycogen level at the beginning and end of the season. During the middle of the season from mid-July to mid-August, however, when the fish are gorged on capelin *(Mallotus)*, high glycogen values occur and result in low ultimate pH in the muscle with consequent quality problems (MacCallum *et al.,* 1968). It is well known in the U.K. industry that 'feedy' haddock, gorged with herring spawn, spoil rapidly; so also do early summer herring if feeding heavily on *Calanus*.

## INSTITUTIONAL FACTORS AFFECTING QUALITY

The quality of the catch as it lands on the deck is almost entirely dependent on, first, the biological factors outlined above and, secondly, the method and manner of fishing. Thereafter, the handling and preservation techniques used on board can in some circumstances be of overriding importance. Furthermore, practice which may be adequate for fish to be stowed in ice may prove inadequate if the catch is to be frozen at sea.

The catching method has considerable importance; it has, for instance, been shown that 'chalky' halibut, where the flesh is dull white, opaque, soft and flabby, is a pH phenomenon (Tomlinson *et al.,* 1965). Halibut exhausted at the end of a line have depleted their glycogen reserves and have entered a recovery period and in consequence the incidence of chalkiness an such fish will be less than in trawled specimens (Tomlinson *et al.,* 1966). Ultimate pH of cod correlates inversely with toughness after storage at -7°, -14° and -29°C (Cowie and Little, 1966, 1967); low ultimate pH is of much less practical importance for cod stowed in ice.

The best procedures for handling North Atlantic trawl-caught fish have often been stated (Lumley *et al.,* 1929; Cutting *et al.,* 1953; Burgess *et al.,* 1965) and it will be sufficient here to draw attention to a few of the more important factors affecting quality. Delays in gutting may allow proteolytic enzymes to migrate from the gut into the muscle, so causing softening of the flesh (Baalsrud, 1951; Siebert *et al.,* 1962). Such changes are highly temperature dependent. Templeman and Pitt (1954) showed that bruising was much more obvious in ungutted than gutted American plaice. During chill stowage of gutted fish in ice, bleeding through severed abdominal vessels will continue, producing characteristically white flesh; sufficient bleeding may have occurred in cod in 30 min (Jones, 1964). Fillets cut from whole gutted cod frozen at sea may be discoloured by blood because insufficient time to bleed has been allowed before freezing. Filleting at sea is attended by a number of problems characteristic of the freezing of very fresh fish. These include blood discolorations (Kelly and Little, 1966) which in some ways are more severe than in whole fish, and rigor (Jones, 1964).

## RIGOR MORTIS

Some time after death of a fish, the muscle becomes hard. This is the outward sign of destruction of the equilibrium of the metabolic system in a series of imperfectly understood and complex changes involving the carbohydrates, phosphagens and nucleotides of the tissue. In biochemical terms rigor involves, amongst other substances, nucleotides such as adenosine triphosphate (ATP), muscle glycogen and phosphagens such as creatine phosphate. After rigor is fully developed ATP disappears, being degraded enzymically through ADP, AMP, IMP, and subsequently to inosine, ribose—l—phosphate, ribose and hypoxanthine; while glycogen is broken down by the Embden—Meyerhof system to lactic acid, giving rise to pH effects mentioned above (Partmann, 1965; Jones *et al.,* 1965; Tarr, 1965).

The times taken for the onset and duration of rigor depends on species, nutritional and physiological state before death and the temperature of subsequent storage. For Gadoids such as haddock and whiting stored at

$0^{\circ}C$, rigor begins 1–2 h after death and resolves after 21–40 h. The corresponding figures for cod and coalfish are 2–9 h and 40–115h for complete resolution; for lemon sole 4–7 h and 44 h for resolution; and for redfish *(Sebastes* sp.) 5–7 h and 125 h for resolution (Partmann, 1965; Stroud, 1969). The extreme variability quoted in the literature is largely due to the varying amount of exercise that trawled fish undergo during capture.

At higher temperatures, and where fish have been exhausted during capture or are in a poor nutritional state, the onset of rigor may be sooner and its duration shorter.

Recent work on rigor occurring at temperatures above $0^{\circ}$ has suggested that the physical changes occurring in the muscle, such as stiffening, may not all derive from a common cause. Thus in cod at about $17^{\circ}C$, contraction at the onset of rigor may be so severe that the myocommata, the sheets of connective tissue between the muscle blocks, are torn; the muscle itself becomes toughened and considerable drip occurs on resolution of rigor. (Dyer and Fraser, 1961; Jones *et al.,* 1965; Jones, 1964, 1969).

These changes, briefly outlined here, have some very important technological consequences. Thus unfrozen fish in rigor can only be fresh and there is some evidence that bacterial activity is considerably delayed until after resolution. Fish in rigor is, however, difficult to handle and particularly to fillet by hand or machine. Attempts to straighten fish cause tearing of the tissue. Fish stowed in ice have normally passed through rigor by the time they are landed.

The more important technological problems are encountered in the freezing of fish at sea. Ideally, where the catch is to be frozen, this should be done immediately after gutting and adequate washing and before rigor has set in; it should then be stored at a low temperature $(-30^{\circ}C)$; no difficulties should then be encountered. In practice some delays before freezing are often unavoidable, for example during periods of heavy catching. If unchilled fish are allowed to lie on deck, they may enter rigor at a relatively high temperature with the undesirable effects mentioned above. Fillets cut from such high temperature rigor fish are commercially unacceptable for all but the lowest grade uses such as fish cake manufacture or pet food (Jones, 1964).

Experience has shown that the temperature must be kept below $12^{\circ}C$ at all stages before freezing if whole sea-frozen cod is to give satisfactory fillets. The higher the temperature and the longer fish are kept before freezing, the greater the opportunity for autolytic and bacterial spoilage to take place before freezing (Jones, 1964).

The problems of freezing fillets at sea are even more formidable than with whole fish. If fillets are cut from pre-rigor fish, the restraining effect of the axial skeleton is lost and when rigor occurs the muscle shrinks and the whole fillet becomes distorted. The texture becomes tough and rubbery, the cut surface looks rough and crinkled, while the effects of high temperature mentioned above are even more marked. Delay to allow rigor to be resolved before filleting would demand considerable storage space and the fish to be held at a relatively low temperature (Dyer and Fraser, 1961; Jones, 1969).

There are undoubtedly technological problems in the freezing of fish at sea which have not yet been solved; other difficulties, however, relate to the management of a factory operation on a vessel far from land and often in bad weather.

If fish or fillets are frozen before rigor has been resolved and are stored at a low temperature, changes associated with rigor may occur when they are thawed. Thaw rigor is most evident in small blocks or single fillets, but may also be seen in the tails of large fish. Gaping, shrinkage and excessive drip loss occurs, but may be avoided by a 'conditioning' period such that the biochemical changes take place while the muscle is still frozen and hence held rigid by ice. In some experiments, cod stored for 14 months at -30°C still showed signs of thaw rigor but storage for shorter periods suffice if storage temperature is higher and thawing rates are low (Stroud, 1969; Jones, 1969; Torry Res. Handl. Preserv. Fish, 1966).

## SPOILAGE

The flesh of normal healthy fish is sterile but the gills, gut and skin carry heavy bacterial loads, which may be significantly higher in trawled than in line-caught fish. In ungutted cod stored in ice within 2–3 days of death, some bacteria can be found in the heart blood, along the caudal vein, and possibly in the flesh along the lateral line. The peritoneum remains sterile until perforation of the gut which may occur within a few hours or up to 9 days after death (Shewan, 1961).

Once bacteria become established in the flesh they begin to utilize the wide variety of low molecular weight compounds which are present and which range from carbohydrates such as glucose and ribose to amino acids, and other nitrogenous compounds such are urea, betaines, trimethylamine oxide (TMO) and creatine and simple peptides such as anserine and glutathione. The nature and amount of these low molecular weight substances, sometimes loosely termed 'extractives', vary according to many factors including species, nutritional state, season and time after death. In freshly caught gadoids such as cod and haddock these substances generally amount to about 1,500 mg per cent of the flesh; the concentration of creatine is about 400 mg per cent, of TMO about 350 mg per cent, of taurine 300 mg per cent, of purine derivatives 200 mg per cent and anserine 150 mg per cent. The remainder consists of free amino acids, 70–75 mg per cent, and glucose, 9–35 mg per cent (Shewan, 1961).

In elasmobranchs such as skate and dogfish, the total concentration of 'extractives' may reach 3,000 mg per cent with urea (1,500–2,000 mg per cent), TMO (500–1,000 mg per cent), creatine (300–500 mg per cent) and betaine (100 mg per cent) predominating. In herring, on the other hand, where the total concentration of 'extractives' is about the same as in cod, anserine is absent but free amino acids reach concentrations of 300 mg per cent, the largest single component being histidine – up to 180 mg per cent in the white flesh (Hughes, 1959–64).

Post-mortem spoilage results of course from a combination of degradation by tissue enzymes and bacterial activity. In some species, such as cod, many of the predominant 'extractives', such as TMO, taurine and possibly creatine, are virtually unaffected by tissue enzymes, although most suffer from bacterial attack. Anserine, on the other hand, is split by the tissue enzyme anserianase to its constituents methyl histidine and $\beta$-alanine (Shewan and Jones, 1957).

The proteolytic activity of muscle enzymes, as measured by increase in the concentration of free amino acids and ammonia, is small and in a fish such as cod, particularly at $0^\circ$C, little or no softening of the muscle occurs but in more actively swimming species such as herring, mackerel and tunny, proteolysis may be much more significant.

Once bacterial action becomes predominant, the major changes occurring in cod and similar species are the increasing production of lower amines, such as dimethylamine and trimethylamine from TMO; some lower fatty acids, such as acetic acid, from the sugars, and ammonia from the free amino acids or possibly the proteins and creatine. In the later stages of spoilage, hydrogen sulphide, mercaptans and indole become increasingly apparent (Shewan, 1961, 1962).

The products of both autolytic and bacterial action very profoundly affect taste, smell and appearance of fish, that is, its organoleptic quality. Although leaching by water during storage in ice causes loss of both desirable and undesirable constituents, the relationship of the concentration of some extractives to certain sensory characteristics, has now been fairly well established. The pleasant sweetness of fresh muscle can be related to the glucose present. Some nucleotides, such as inosine, and in particular, inosine $5^1$-monophosphate, are known to be potent flavorous materials or, at the low levels normally present in cod, flavour enhancers (Hashimoto, 1965).

Some workers believe that the strong bitter flavours in spoiling fish are due to hypoxanthine (Jones, 1967) which others believe to be tasteless (Fraser *et al.*, 1968). The so-called 'fishy' odour of spoiling fish is probably due to trimethylamine linked with unsaturated fat (Stansby, 1962a) although pure TMA at the concentration in spoiling fish merely has a penetrating ammoniacal odour. Studies with sterile cod muscle inoculated with pure cultures of *Pseudomonas* sp. known to be implicated in spoilage, have indicated that it is the sulphur-containing constituents, and in particular methyl mercaptan, dimethyl sulphide and $H_2S$, which are implicated to the greatest degree in the odours and possibly the flavour of spoiling fish muscle (Shaw and Shewan, 1968; Herbert, 1968–69). Sensory studies have shown that methyl mercaptan need be present in a concentration of only $0.02/10^9$ parts for a solution to smell strongly of stale cabbage water, a term frequently used to describe the odour of spoiling fish (Guadagni *et al.*, 1963). It has been shown chromatographically that sulphur-containing compounds are present in at least these concentrations in spoiling fish.

Another group of flavorous compounds, the carbonyls, are known to develop during chill storage, but it is still uncertain what enzymes systems, if any, are involved in their production, possibly from lipid and/or amino acids (Jones, 1967; Mendelsohn and Steinberg, 1962; Wong *et al.*, 1967).

Finally, the temperature dependency of spoilage rate must be stressed. In cod and similar species, the spoilage rate at $5°C$ is roughly twice that at $0°C$ (Spencer and Baines, 1964).

## MODIFYING EFFECTS

Many of the undesirable changes described may be profoundly modified during processing; the quality of fish used in the manufacture of fish cakes, for example, is relatively much less important than that used in smoked fish which in turn is less important than that used for the wet fillet trade. Space does not allow discussion of this exceedingly important aspect. Freezing, however, is not a process in the same sense, since freezing and cold storage properly carried out should cause no significant change in the product, at least in so far as the consumer is concerned.

In practice, however, the product may be considerably affected; slow freezing is known to affect texture of fish such as cod and haddock, while during relatively high temperature storage, or prolonged low temperature storage, undesirable toughening of the myofibrillar proteins occurs and fat may become oxidized and rancid.

Although odour and flavour changes due to bacteria do not occur during frozen storage, some tissue enzyme systems, and perhaps bacterial ones also, are still active at fairly low temperatures. It has been suggested that the bitterness which develops in some frozen fish during storage is due to the liberation of hypoxanthine (Jones, 1967).

Moreover, fish which may be quite satisfactory when stored in ice may fall apart if frozen and subsequently thawed.

## INDUSTRIAL SIGNIFICANCE

In former times, when sea fish was mostly preserved by smoking, salting or drying, the quality of the raw material was often of relatively minor importance compared with the care with which the preservation techniques were carried out. Ironically, however, since the catches were often obtained near the shore, or processing was carried out at sea, very fresh fish was in fact generally used; relatively light fishing of the available stocks allowed some choice to be made of fish of the best biological quality.

In recent years, and particularly since 1945, excessive exploitation of available stocks of fish on grounds near at hand has reduced yields, so forcing many fishing nations to seek further afield and to accept whatever quality of fish can be caught. At a time, therefore, when man is obtaining better understanding of, and control over, the production of meat and poultry of uniform quality, the supplies of fresh fish of good biological quality have been diminishing. Some, but not all, of these problems may be solved by freezing at sea which, however, has been attended by a special crop of difficulties, largely physiological in character.

When catches are landed, however, they are frequently handled in ways that are less than ideal, with the result that fresh fish may be mediocre by the time it reaches the consumer, and mediocre fish may be stale (Burgess et al., 1959; Burgess and Cutting, 1959).

In most countries, the industries devoted to catching, processing and distributing fish for human food have been lagging behind other food industries in the application of techniques to maintain uniformity of quality. The formidable problems of control presented by fish are unlikely to be solved by highly traditional, small firms lacking the technical expertise necessary for innovation. Nevertheless, drastic and speedy changes in methods of handling and processing are essential if fish is to continue to be used, in the developed countries at least, for human rather than animal food.

195

## WHAT REQUIRES TO BE DONE

The problems reviewed here demonstrate the sketchy state of present knowledge. The processor is confronted by a variety of species, variation in size, biological and physiological quality, degree of freshness and superimposed on everything else, the modifying effects of processing. What advice can the fish technologist offer in the search for better control of quality? It is unfortunately true that although the technologist can offer some advice, this must at present be rather generalized.

It is, for example, impossible to describe in anything but the most general terms, the seasonal changes in biological quality likely to occur in even the commonest species of fish caught on a specified ground; to forecast these changes is currently impossible. Nevertheless, in the same way as the horticultural grower has become accustomed to being told when to harvest his crop, the fisherman of the future must be told where and when to go for a particular catch, and must perhaps be given the means to measure its biological quality. Although work in this field is being carried out in many places, it is highly questionable whether it is on an adequate scale  The significance of biological and physiological quality in fish processing is still, in any event, imperfectly understood.

Advice on methods of control of freshness quality, probably the most important single factor affecting acceptability, can again be given in only the most general terms. There is a need for much detailed work both in the laboratory and in industrial plants and again on methods of assessing significant quality factors and on the numerous statistical problems involved, before the technologist can advise the factory quality controller how to do much more than make random checks on the production line.

If what is known even now about control of freshness quality was applied in industry, perhaps backed by some statutory enforcement, some of the poorer quality fish now being landed would no longer reach the consumer. Nevertheless, even if the stalest fish was removed, the remainder would still have a wide range of quality; what industry urgently requires is a quick, cheap, foolproof and reliable method of objectively measuring the degree of freshness of fish.

Sensory (taste panel) methods, which have been developed in the laboratory to a high degree of sensitivity, are often too slow, cumbersome and costly for routine use on a production line; an experienced individual grader, as employed in other food industries such as the tea and wine trades, could, and indeed is, used, but his judgments must be accepted and cannot be scientifically checked or controlled. Moreover, the skilled wine or tea taster can make repeated comparisons with other samples, each of which can be truly representative of a large consignment; the sampling problems in a fish plant are much more difficult for reasons already discussed.

An instrument for measuring freshness based on a physical method has been developed (Hennings, 1963) and rapid chemical tests have been advocated and some are in use, but all suffer from some disadvantage.

Nevertheless, given the incentives, there appear to be no insuperable difficulties preventing adequate on-line control of the quality of at least some fishery products, including the raw material from which they are made.

With other animal protein foods, good husbandry including selective breeding has produced more suitable and desirable materials, both for the processor and the consumer, But until fish farming becomes a reality, it seems unlikely that such ideas can be applied to fish.

This paper was prepared as part of the programme of the Torry Research Station.

(Crown Copyright Reserved)

## REFERENCES

Baader, R. (1965). *Machines for the Fishing Industry.* Lubeck, Nordischer Maschinenbau
Baalsrud, K. (1951). *Tidsskr. Kjemi Bergv. Metall.* **11**, 71
Bertin, L. (1956). *Eels.* London; Cleaver-Hume Press
Brandes, C.H. and Dietrich, R. (1953). *Fette Seifen.* **55**, 533
− − (1954). *Fette Seifen Anstr-Mittel.* **56**, 495
Burgess, G.H.O., Cockburn, R.M., Cutting, C.L. and Robb, W.B. (1959). *Torry Tech. Pap.* No.1
− and Cutting, C.L. (1959). *Proc. Xth Int. Congr. Refrig. Inds.* **3**, 160
− and Cutting, C.L., Lovern, J.A. and Waterman, J.J. (eds.) (1965). *Fish Handling and Processing.* Edinburgh; H.M.S.O.
Cutting, C.L., Eddie, G.C., Reay, G.A. and Shewan, J.M. (1953). *Fd Invest. Leafl.* **3**.
− and Burgess, G.H.O. (1960). In *S.C.I. Monograph* No.8, p.59 London; Society of Chemistry and Industry
Cowie, W.P. and Little, W.T. (1966). *J. Fd. Technol.* **1**, 335
− − (1967). *J. Fd. Technol.* **2**, 217
Davies, J.H.V. (1968). *Chemy Ind.* 16 March. 337
Dyer, W.J. and Fraser, D.I. (1961). *Can. Fisherm.* August. p.17
F.A.O. (1968). *Yb. Fish. Statist.* 1967. Catches and Landings
Fraser, D.I., Simpson, S.J. and Dyer, W.J. (1968). *J. Fish. Res. Bd. Can.* **25**, 817
Graham, M. (1923). *Fishery Invest., Lond.* Ser. II. **6**, (6)
Guadagni, D.G., Buttery, R.G. and Okano, S. (1963). *J. Sci. Fd Agric.* **14**, 761
Hashimoto, Y. (1965). In *Technology of Fish Utilisation* Ed. by R. Kreuzer p.57. London; Fishing News (Books) Ltd.

Hennings, C. (1963). *Z. Lebensmittelunters. u. -Forsch.* **119**, 461
Herbert, R. (1968-69). *Unpublished data.* Torry Res. Station, Aberdeen
Hickling, C.F. (1930). *Fishery Invest., Lond.* Ser. II, **12**, (1)
Hughes, R.B. (1959a). *J. Sci. Fd Agric.* **10**, 431
– (1959b). *J. Sci. Fd Agric.* **10**, 558
– (1960a). *J. Sci. Fd Agric.* **11**, 47
– (1960b). *J. Sci Fd Agric.* **11**, 700
– (1961) *J. Sci. Fd Agric.* **12**, 475
– (1963). *J. Sci. Fd Agric.* **14**, 432
– (1964). *J. Sci. Fd Agric.* **15**, 293
Ironside, J.I.M. and Love, R.M. (1958). *J. Sci. Fd Agric.* **9**, 597
Jacquot, R. (1961). In *Fish as Food.* Vol. 1. Ed. by G. Borgstrom. Chapter 6.
    New York; Academic Press
Jangaard, P. M., Brockerhoff, H., Burgher, R. D. and Hoyle, R. J. (1967).
    *J. Fish. Res. Bd Can.* **24**, 607
Jones, N.R. (1954). *Biochem. J.* **58**, xlvii
– (1959). *J. Sci. Fd Agric.* **10**, 282
– (1964). In *Proc. Meeting on Fish Technology, Fish Handling and Preservation.*
    Scheveningen. p.31. Paris; O.E.C.D.
– (1967). In *Symposium on Foods – Chemistry and Physiology of Flavours.* Ed.
    by H.W. Schultz, F.A. Day and L.M. Libbey. Westport, Conn. Avi. Publishing
    Co. p.267
– (1969). In *Proc. F.A.O. Technical Conference on Freezing and Irradiation of
    Fish.* Madrid, 1967 (in press)
– Burt, J.R., Murray, J. and Stroud, G.D. (1965). In *The Technology of Fish
    Utilization.* Ed. by R. Kreuzer. London; Fishing News (Books) Ltd. p.14
Kelly, T.R. and Little, W.T. (1966). *J. Fd Technol.* **1**, 121
Leim, A.H. (1958). *J. Fish. Res. Bd Can.* **15**, 1259
Love, R.M. (1958). *J. Sci. Fd Agric.* **9**, 617
– (1960). *Nature, Lond.* **185**, 692
Lovern, J.A. (1939). *Salm. Trout Mag.* No.94, 56
– and Wood, H. (1937). *J. mar. biol. Ass. U.K.* **22**, 281
Lumley, A., Piqué, J.J. and Reay, G.A. (1929). *Fd Invest. Spec. Rep.* No.37
MacCallum, W.A., Jaffray, J.I., Churchill, D.N. and Idler, D.R. (1968). *J. Fish Res.
    Bd Can.* **25**, 733
Mannan, A., Fraser, D.I. and Dyer, W.J. (1961). *J. Fish Res. Bd Can.* **18**, 483
Mendelsohn, J.M. and Steinberg, M.A. (1962). *Fd. Technol., Champaign.* **16**, 113
Ministry of Agriculture, Fisheries and Food (1968). *Sea Fish. Statist. Tabl., Lond.*
    1967
Norman, J.R. (1935). In *List of British Vertebrates.* London, British Museum
    Natural History
Partmann, W. (1965). In *The Technology of Fish Utilization.* Ed. by R. Kreuzer,
    London; Fishing News (Books) Ltd. p.4
Shaw, B.G. and Shewan, J.M. (1968). *J. appl. Bact.* **31**, 89
Shewan, J.M. (1961). In *Fish as Food.* Vol. 1, Ed. by G. Borgstrom, New York;
    Academic Press. p.48
Shewan, J. M. (1962). In *Recent Advances in Food Science,* Ed. by J. Hawthorn
    and J. Muil Leitch. London; Butterworths p. 167
Shewan, J. M. and Jones, N.R. (1957). *J. Sci. Fd Agric,* **8**, 491
Siebert, G. Malortie, R. and Beyer, R. (1962). *Arch. FischWiss* **13**, 21
Sipos, J. C. and Ackman, R. G. (1964). *J. Fish Res. Bd Can.* **21**, 423

Spencer, R. and Baines, C. R. (1964). *Fd Technol., Champaign* **18,** 769

Stansby, M. E. (1962a). *Fd Technol., Champaign* **16,** 28

– (1962b). In *Fish in Nutrition.* Ed. by E. Heen and R. Kreuzer.
London; Fishing News (Books) Ltd

Stroud, G. D. (1969). *Torry Advis. Note No. 36*

Tarr, H. L. A. (1965). In *The Technology of Fish Utilization.* Ed. by R. Kreuzer.
London; Fishing News (Books) Ltd. p. 26

Templeman, W. and Pitt, T. K. (1954). *Fish. Res. Bd Can. Progr. Rep. Atlantic
Sta.,* No. 59

Templeman, W. and Andrews, G. L. (1956). *J. Fish. Res. Bd Can.* **13,** 147

Thurston, C. E. and Groniger, H. S. (1959). *J. agric. Fd Chem.* **7,** 282

Tomlinson, N., Geiger, S. E. and Dollinger, E. (1965). *J. Fish. Res. Bd Can.* **22,**
653

Tomlinson, N., Geiger, S. E. and Dollinger, E. (1966). *J. Fish. Res. Bd Can.* **23,**
925

*Torry Res. Handl. Preserv. Fish* (1966), p. 23

Wong, N.P., Damico, J.N. and Salwin, H. (1967). *J. Ass. off. agric. Chem.* **50,** 8

Yarrell, W. (1836). *A History of British Fishes.* London; Van Voorst

# PROPERTIES OF FISH PROTEINS

J.J. CONNELL

*Humber Laboratory, Ministry of Technology, Hull*

## INTRODUCTION

The contribution which fish make and are likely to make in the future to world protein supplies has been indicated in the previous papers. Summarizing a good many arguments there appears to be general agreement that this contribution, though important at the moment and likely to remain so, is very unlikely to become of dominating significance. The naively optimistic views expressed some years ago of an inexhaustible marine protein source have been dissipated. It is worth also remembering that, because of large variations in availability, the importance of fish protein in the diet necessarily already varies considerable from country to country and is likely to continue to vary. For example, one fairly recent survey in a number of countries (Rao, 1961) shows that fish protein contributes from 0.6 to 16.9 per cent of the total protein in Turkey and Japan, respectively. Another estimate (Borgstrom, 1962) puts the variation in fish protein contribution from 2.0 to 63.8 per cent of the animal protein eaten in Argentina and Japan, respectively. In the U.K. fish protein contributes at present about 5 per cent of the total protein and about 8 per cent of the animal protein eaten (Anonymous, 1968). These U.K. percentages have remained rather constant for several years and in the face of an apparently inexorable rise in the production of other forms of cheap animal protein, often under subsidy, it seems unlikely that the contribution which fish protein makes to the diet in this country will change much for a good many years.

The main purpose of this paper is to examine a number of properties specific to fish proteins which act as a limitation to the full exploitation of fish both in non-sophisticated and sophisticated products. Several factors operate to diminish the efficient utilization of fish which do not concern the proteins directly, but these will either not be covered or only touched on; such factors include unfamiliar or disliked flavour, toxicity, size, spoilage behaviour, difficulty in catching and processing, alternations of periods of glut and scarcity. Much of the treatment will of necessity generalize over a large number of species. There are hundreds if not thousands of fish species which are eaten, and because the proteins of fish are species specific, the properties of the proteins in different species will, in general, differ from one another. This situation may be contrasted with that for the proteins of all the other foods to be discussed at this School — each of these foods are covered by perhaps only four or five species, sometimes only one.

## NUTRITIVE PROPERTIES OF FISH PROTEINS

Perhaps the first factor which ought to be established when considering utilization is the nutritional value of fish proteins. Clearly, if nutritional value is low then this would be one reason for low or reduced exploitation. After the extensive publications and propaganda which have circulated on this subject, it is perhaps remarkable that the nutritional value of fish protein needs to be discussed at all. However, a surprising number of people who ought to know better continue to come up with the idea that the proteins of fish are somehow less valuable than those of land animals, and it is therefore worth reiterating that this idea is false. In fact, some evidence indicates that fish proteins, probably as a result of their ready breakdown by proteolytic enzymes, are nutritionally at a slight advantage over meat proteins. A fairly comprehensive justification for the view that fish proteins possess high nutritive value was given some years ago (Geiger and Borgstrom, 1962). More recent references have confirmed that the amino acid composition of fish flesh is very similar to that of carcass meat (Ellinger and Boyne, 1965; F.A.O, 1968). Admittedly the range of fish species analysed is very small in relation to the numbers of species exploited as food but it seems in principle highly unlikely that the nutritive value of different species will vary significantly (Connell and Howgate, 1959). The only exception would be a small number of instances where the fish was consumed with an appreciably high proportion of bone, gut or skin.

It is both the high nutritive value of fish protein and the possibility of fairly readily exploiting untapped fish sources which have in recent years focused interest on the potential use of fish in the alleviation of the world shortage of protein. The utilization of fish for mass feeding in developing countries depends, in the present state of knowledge, upon preservation by traditional or quasi-traditional methods, of which drying is the most important. It is therefore of considerable interest to know whether these traditional methods, in particular drying, reduce the nutritive value of the protein in the product. Of all methods of preserving fish, drying in the form of production of fish meal for animal feeding is by far the most important, and it is known that the nutritive quality of fish meal can vary quite considerably. However, it appears that for most of the methods employed in producing dried products for human use the nutritive value of the protein is relatively unaffected (Cutting, 1961; Geiger and Borgstrom, 1962; Aitken *et al.*, 1967). This is also true of the much canvassed solvent-dried fish flours or protein concentrates discussed below (Geiger and Borgstrom, 1962; Stillings, 1967). Canning, which has been suggested as an alternative to fish protein concentrate as a method of preservation for large-scale feeding (Lovern, 1968) when carried out properly also results in little impairment of nutritive value (Bramsnaes, 1961). In the case of sophisticated products used in highly developed countries, for example frozen fish, no significant alteration in nutritive value occurs (Bramsnaes, 1961); irradiation, at least with pasteurizing doses is also without significant effect (Shewan, 1961; Reber *et al.*, 1966).

It is worth noting that the place of fish as a source of protein in the diet of any given community is usually governed to a large extent by customary eating habits. Some fish species are familiar and find ready acceptance. In these instances the level of fish protein as a percentage of the total protein consumed could by probably increased to some extent merely by supplying increased amounts of these species in realistic competition with other proteinaceous foods. On the other hand, some species do not find ready acceptance and the increased availability of these species even at low cost would not necessarily lead to higher levels of fish consumption. Thus, in the United Kingdom fresh redfish, monk fish and mackerel are generally nothing like as readily acceptable as in other countries.

## FISH PROTEIN CONCENTRATES

A great deal has been written about this product and considerable development work has been accorded it. The concept of a cheap, stable, relatively easily transportable and handleable protein supplement of high nutritive value is an attractive one, and for some people fish protein concentrate (F.P.C.) seems to meet this concept because undoubtedly it fulfils many of these ideal requirements.

The most practical and possibly cheapest way of producing acceptable F.P.C. is by treating whole, comminuted fish with an organic solvent which removes water and lipid simultaneously. The protein-rich residue remaining can be dried free of organic solvent to give a product of high nutritive value. Although all the technological problems surrounding this kind of process have not been solved there seems no reason why, given the effort, they could not be. The United States Food and Drug Administration which is well known for its stringent rules governing the introduction of new food products, has nevertheless accepted F.P.C. as a food additive, although with certain very hampering restrictions including one which limits the species employed in the production process to hake or hake-like fishes. To be viable as a product for world feeding it is almost certain that F.P.C. would have to be made from the prolific and relatively under-exploited fatty, pelagic species, but so far F.P.C. acceptable to the Food and Drug Administration has not been prepared from such fatty species. Unfortunatley, present types of F.P.C., although promising, still fall short of being ideal and some experts (Lovern, 1968) are very doubtful about their future. In the first place, they cost much more than the original optimistic estimates suggested and it is difficult to see how the cost could be reduced significantly; in the second place, F.P.C. leaves something to be desired organoleptically, its very bland flavour and chalkiness being definite disadvantages.

As alternatives to F.P.C., fish silages or fermented fish products either left in a stable liquid form or subsequently dried, have been proposed but have not proceeded much beyond the initial stages of development. Ideas based on the selective extraction of protein direct from whole fish have not proved successful. For example, the use of salt, acid or alkaline solutions for extracting proteins from fish has been suggested, but such methods are likely to prove either inefficient because of low yield and difficulty in handling the large volumes of extractant, or costly. Some non-aqueous solvents are also good protein solvents and might possibly be used in a selective fashion. An attempt to use anhydrous formic acid in this way failed because of the low biological value of the recovered protein (Connell, 1966; Connell, 1967). Similarly, aqueous solutions of detergents have been tried, as selective protein solvents but their use failed because the detergent-free protein could not be recovered cheaply enough (Connell, 1967; Connell, 1968). It appears that any method which uses anything but the simplest and cheapest of plant is likely to increase the cost of F.P.C. beyond reasonable limits.

## PROPERTIES OF FISH PROTEINS WHICH INFLUENCE UTILIZATION

Although most methods of processing have little deleterious effects on their nutritive value, certain peculiar properties of fish proteins can reduce the value of fish as a food through their influence on processing characteristics or palatability to the consumer. The most outstanding peculiarity of fish proteins when compared to the proteins of carcass meat is their relatively high instability. By high instability is meant a propensity

203

to undergo denaturation, coagulation, degradation or minor chemical changes which result in large changes in overall physical properties. The practical effect of this high instability is that fish cannot be processed so readily as can meat; that is, it is often impossible to freeze, store in the frozen state or dry fish under conditions which with meat induce no or an acceptable degree of change. Conversely, if fish is to be processed to yield an acceptable product the conditions of production have generally to be more stringent than those adopted for meat.

In practical terms the changes in proteins of fish which are induced by processing manifest themselves as changes in physical properties associated with textural eating quality. Thus, processing by freezing and frozen storage or by drying can, and often does, result in fish which after cooking is firmer than normal or frankly tough, rubbery, woody or stringy in texture when eaten; associated with these changes is a diminution in the juicy succulence of fresh fish towards an altogether drier texture. Undoubtedly such changes are encountered occasionally in some types of processed meat, but in nothing like so severe a form. As will be discussed later there is good evidence that all these undesirable changes are caused predominantly by denaturation of the constituent muscle proteins, in particular the structural or myofibrillar group of proteins.

As far as frozen storage is concerned, undesirable textural changes can be kept in check for a practicable length of time by storing at a sufficiently low temperature, and temperatures in the region of $-30°C$ are recommended for long term commercial storage of fish. In large, new, cold storage warehouses in this country such temperatures are usual, but are not available in smaller distribution stores, retail cabinets or refrigerators in catering establishments. This latter group of installations are held at temperatures normally safe for most produce but the quality of fish is often at risk in them, and, in fact, throughout the cold chain, fish, because of its instability, is at a disadvantage compared with most other frozen products. The textural damage resulting from merely freezing some types of fish can, on subsequently thawing, cause loss of fluid called 'drip' or 'weep' which in some circumstances is so great as to be aesthetically unpleasant and uneconomical. This phenomenon had led to the development of measures aimed at controlling the loss of fluid in frozen and thawed fillets of fish by dipping them before distribution in solutions of polyphosphate. This reagent, by forming a layer of swollen protein round the fillet, acts to seal in the fluid which would otherwise escape.

On the other hand, drying even under the mildest conditions always results in significant and often unacceptable degrees of textural deterioration in ordinary fish flesh. This is true even of freeze drying in any of its forms. Some crustacea like shrimp are freeze dried commercially but some firming of texture in this product is evidently acceptable.

The nature and cause of these deleterious changes in fish proteins will now be considered in more detail.

*Changes in frozen fish*

It has been shown that the fish protein most sensitive to freezing and frozen storage is myosin, the principal myofibrillar protein making up about 50 per cent of the total protein in the muscle. During frozen storage of cod, the myosin gradually becomes inextractable in solvents like neutral 0.5—1.0 M salt which in the native muscle extract it completely (Connell, 1962b; King, 1966). On the other hand, under the same conditions of frozen storage actin, the other principal myofibrillar protein, remains virtually undamaged (Connell, 1960) as does the sarcoplasmic group of proteins. The change in extractability of myosin appears to be the result primarily of a denaturation reaction because the ATPase activity of this protein diminishes concurrently with diminution of extractability (Connell, 1960; Sawant and Magar, 1961). In addition, unusual forms of enzymically inactive myosin appear in extracts of frozen stored cod (Mackie, 1968), which have some of the properties expected of a denatured intermediate form of the protein. This denatured form of myosin appears to interact with the native actin in the muscle in some way because the extractability of the complex of actin and myosin (so-called actomyosin) diminishes in such a way that ultimately no more actin remains extractable in salt solutions. Presumably the interactions between denatured myosin molecules and between denatured myosin and actin molecules take the form of intermolecular cross links which result in the firming up of the muscle structure and the diminution of water-binding capacity of the three dimensional protein network making up the cells. Some clues about the nature of these cross links has been obtained from physico-chemical measurements on cod muscle stored in the frozen state until very tough. With such materials no change in charged groups (Connell and Howgate, 1964) or sulphydryl groups (Connell, 1960) occurs, indicating that relatively few covalent links are involved. In addition, the molecular weight of the fragments of myofibrillar protein produced when frozen stored cod muscle is dissolved in sodium dodecyl sulphate solutions is the same as the molecular weight of the fragments from fresh muscle dissolved in the same way (Connell, 1965). Sodium dodecyl sulphate splits secondary, non-covalent bonds but not covalent bonds, therefore this evidence shows that the types of cross link which give rise to tough fish muscle on frozen storage are largely if not entirely non-covalent. Non-covalent cross links are of course the predominant type of bond formed when denatured protein molecules interact, as in coagulation.

Whilst the formation of constraining and toughening cross links is undoubtedly the end reaction in frozen stored fish muscle, detailed ultracentrifugal analysis of the myofibrillar protein extracts obtained during the course of storage shows that the reaction is rather complex (King, 1966). It appears that as well as association, dissociation reactions may occur. In unfrozen muscle, weak bonds exist between the actin molecules making up the thin filaments, the molecules thereby being held in a highly ordered helical arrangement. It is possible that minor protein components such as actinin, which are associated with the actin molecules, may assist in providing the weak forces necessary to keep this helical structure intact. During frozen storage it seems as though the bonds between the actin molecules in the thin filaments are broken so that in extracts of frozen stored muscle fewer thin filaments are obtained than in extracts of fresh muscle prepared in the same way.

The location of the cross links between the myofibrillar proteins is of considerable interest but little direct information is available about cross linking sites. Normal, live muscle can stiffen merely as the result of reactions between the H-meromyosin heads of the myosin molecules at the surface of thick filaments and presumably additional cross links similarly located could explain toughening in frozen fish muscle. In addition, the possibility of additional bonds between myosin molecules in the thick filaments is conceivable.

The reason why freezing and frozen storage should damage the myofibrillar proteins in this way is still not clear though various theories have been proposed. The first of these supposes that the increased concentration of solutes, in particular of ions, consequent upon the dehydration induced by removal of water as ice, causes denaturation. There is some evidence to support this view in that by adding enough salt to unfrozen muscle evident denaturation of the myofibrillar proteins has been demonstrated. In addition, the existence of a maximum temperature of protein damage just below the freezing point of the muscle can be explained on the basis of increased salt concentration. The second theory is based on the observation that the amount of fatty acid increases during storage concomitant with the damage to the protein. Model experiments have shown that addition of unesterified fatty acid to unfrozen fish muscle can cause the myofibrillar protein to become inextractable in salt solutions, and that increasing the amount of fatty acid increases the amount of inextractability. Therefore, it is suggested that the fatty acid which develops during frozen storage of fish muscle reacts with proteins in a similar way causing them to become gradually inextractable. The third theory supposes that proteins are damaged by simple dehydration consequent upon ice formation; this view is based on the idea that water is essential for the integrity of some types of protein molecule. It has been recently proposed that freezing damage to erythrocytes is the result merely of shrinkage of cells as a result of ice dehydration (Meryman, 1968) and it is possible that similar mechanisms may apply to fish muscle.

*Changes in Dried Fish*

Much less work has been done on dried fish but enough is known to indicate that the changes in the protein are similar to those described for frozen fish. The textural characteristics of dried fish (even freeze-dried fish) resemble those of rather badly frozen stored fish.

Investigation of protein changes in dried fish have been mostly carried out on freeze-dried fish. With some types of freeze-dried cod only part of the myosin is denatured as indicated by loss of extractability in selective extractants, and by the retention of ATPase activity and contractility of the muscle. As with badly frozen stored fish, actin and the sarcoplasmic group of proteins appear to be relatively unchanged (Connell, 1962a). The nature of the reactions causing the textural changes in dried fish is even more obscure than in the case of frozen fish. Presumably the same types of bonds in the same types of location are likely. The extractability of the proteins in freeze dried fish can be increased when secondary bond breaking substances like sodium dodecyl sulphate and urea are added, which indicates that secondary bonds are important in stabilizing the structure of freeze-dried fish. Also, it has been found that addition of sulphydryl reagents like monothioglycol to extractants increases the extractability of the myofibrillar proteins of freeze-dried fish (Connell, 1958). These sulphydryl reagents are known to be specific disulphide bond breaking agents and the inference is that some disulphide bonds are present in freeze dried fish. Few if any such bonds exist in fresh fish and so the conclusion is that some oxidation of sulphydryl groups to inter-molecular disulphide bonds occurs during freeze drying. Judging from extractability measurements, the amount of damage in freeze dried fish is always greater than the amount of damage suffered by merely freezing and thawing the fish. Thus it seems that the additional damage is caused by the removal, during freeze drying, of water from the still unfrozen portions of the fish muscle (Connell, 1964). Possibly, collapse and disorganization of the protein structure occurs as a consequence of this further dehydration. Fatty acids have nothing to do with the case because, unlike the situation for frozen stored fish, fatty acids are not formed on freeze drying.

*Instability of Fish Myosin*

It is clear from the previous two sections on freezing and drying that the myofibrillar protein characteristically exhibiting most instability is myosin. This is not entirely unexpected because fish myosins in general are known from results of model studies to be peculiarly unstable relative to the myosins isolated from carcass meats (Connell, 1961). This instability reveals itself in a pronounced tendency for the molecules to aggregate in a side-by-side fashion when the isolated pure protein is stored in solution at O°C. Definite signs of aggregates are evident within 12—24 h under these conditions. Concomitantly the ATPase activity of the myosin declines to zero. In contrast, the myosins of rabbit or beef can be kept unchanged for up to a week under the same conditions. Evidence for a 'looseness' in the myosins of fish was obtained by studying the effect of the structure breaking substance urea on the molecule. It was found that much smaller concentrations of urea were necessary to produce evidence of unfolding of fish myosins than in the case of myosins from rabbit, beef and chicken (Connell, 1961). Thus, there is considerable evidence that the greater tendency of fish muscle to be damaged by processing can be traced back to the intrinsic instability of their myosins.

Even within the class of fishes there are differences in stability both of the proteins in the intact muscle and of the isolated myosins. Thus, the rate at which the myofibrillar proteins of different species becomes inextractable in the same solvent differs markedly; the rate for lemon sole, for example, being much less than that for cod (Love and Olley, 1965). This behaviour may be a reflection of inter-species differences in myosin stability because the rate at which isolated lemon sole myosin aggregates is less than that for cod myosin stored under the same conditions (Connell, 1961). If denaturation during frozen storage is caused by fatty acids or high concentrations of salts then it would be instructive to examine the relative rates of aggregation of myosins from different fish species in the presence of different concentrations of fatty acid or salt, perhaps in the frozen state, but no detailed studies of this kind have yet been made.

Not all fish myosins are extremely unstable. Tuna, striped bass (Richards *et al.*, 1967) sea mullet (Hamoir *et al.*, 1960) and tilapia (Hamoir, 1967) myosins appear to be almost as stable as rabbit or beef myosins. It is striking that differences in stability of myosins appear to be related to the body temperature of the animal from which the myosins were prepared. Thus, the myosins from all warm blooded animals are stable whilst those from cold-blooded fish inhabiting temperate or Arctic waters like cod and haddock are very unstable. The myosins of fish like tuna, striped bass, sea mullet and tilapia which inhabit warm or tropical waters are all more stable than the myosins of cod and haddock. In fact, it is known that the body temperature of tuna is several degrees higher than the enviornmental sea temperature (Carey and Teal, 1966). These inter-relationships suggest that the stability of myosin has become adapted to suit the body temperature of the animal. Supporting evidence for this view comes from work on the stability of myosin ATPase of different species of lizards which live at different temperatures (Licht, 1964).

*Miscellaneous properties of the proteins of different species or kinds of fish*

There are a number of specific peculiarities of fish proteins which sometimes limit the utilization of fish for processing. Usually these stem from biological variations in the properties of the constituent muscle proteins. Examples of this kind of thing are as follows:

*(a)* The collagen content of herring varies with season and this phenomenon can affect processing. Thus, the suitability of herring for canning may be affected because the tendency of some fish to break down into a mush in the can may be greater in those with low collagen contents as compared with those of high content. Also, taking an example from a more industrial process, the 'stick-water' produced during the reduction to fish meal of herring with high collagen content tends to be gluey, viscous or gel-like because of its high content of gelatin. In consequence the 'stick-water' is difficult to handle and dry.

*(b)* Difficulty has been experienced in some areas with the freezing of very fresh, heavily feeding cod at certain times of the year, as for example during the trap cod fishery of Newfoundland. Because of the high glycogen content of the flesh and the rapidity with which the fish are handled the pH falls to a low value during processing causing the texture to deteriorate and large amounts of water to form in pockets in the frozen blocks of cod (Dyer, 1961).

*(c)* With cod caught in the White Sea during summer some difficulty is experienced in obtaining as good a smoke cure as with most other cod. The difficulty stems from the fact that on pressing the finished product, moisture from the underlying muscle tends to exude through the glossy, smoked pellicle of the fillet. Any handling or packing of the product then gives rise to an unpleasant 'sweaty' appearance. The cause of this defect is unknown, but may be connected with a low intrinsic water-holding capacity or combination of high water content and low pH.

*(d)* One essential rheological property which the Japanese fish product Kamaboko has to possess in order to be classed as of good quality is the so-called 'Ashi'. This term denotes the capacity to give a sticky kind of firm gel when minced fish muscle is kneaded with salt, sugar and starch and then steamed. The ability of the flesh from different species of fish to give the desired property varies considerably and in fact some species are practically useless for the purpose of making Kamaboko (Simidu, 1944).

209

Since the gelling capacity of the flesh is entirely a function of the constituent myofibrillar proteins it is clear that, under the conditions employed, there must be a large difference in the network forming ability of these proteins in different species.

*(e)* Protein content varies seasonally in some species of fish (Love, 1960) and the variation can be so great that the actual physical properties of the flesh are affected. At certain times of the year fish can be so soft as a result of depletion of protein and consequent relatively low ratio between protein and water that the flesh is entirely unsuitable for processing. These variations give rise to the concept of 'condition' in fish; good condition represents that in which the protein content is relatively high.

*(f)* A somewhat analogous phenomenon to the previous one is that of gaping, a condition afflicting the cut surfaces of fish as in a fillet. Gaping takes the form of splits, tears or holes in the fillet which probably arise from separation of the muscle cells from one another or from the breakage of the connections between the connective tissue fascia (myocommata) and the ends of the muscle cells. The condition can be very serious because it effects commercial utilization very considerably; fish prone to gape often cannot be machine filletted or skinned because the fillets fall apart when handled. The factors affecting the incidence of gaping in fish fillets are still being elucidated (Love and Robertson, 1968) but, essentially, gaping is bound up with the properties of the protein components in the cell and their relationship to other biochemical components. Gaping varies in incidence from species to species and this variation is presumably a reflection of variations in the intrinsic properties of the proteins from different species. Of relevance to gaping of fillets and the low strength of connective tissue in fish is the low shrinkage and gelatinization temperatures of fish collagens relative to those of collagens from land animals. This further example of relatively low stability in fish proteins means in practical terms that treatments, especially those involving warming, which with meat can be used successfully, with fish lead to complete breakdown of the flesh structure.

*(g)* It was noticed in Japan (Noguchi, 1965) that irrigation with water of pre-rigor fish muscle promotes contraction. Such contractions are undesirable because they adversely affect appearance of texture. It is not uncommon to wash fillets of fish before further processing (a practice practically unknown with other edible flesh) and there is a risk that this practice may lead to textural defects in pre-rigor fish muscle.

(Crown Copyright Reserved)

PROPERTIES OF FISH PROTEINS

## REFERENCES

Aitken, A., Jason, A. C., Olley, J. and Payne, P. R. (1967). *Fishg News int.* 6, 42
Anonymous (1968). *Household Food Consumption and Expenditure, 1966.*
   London; Her Majesty's Stationery Office
Borgstrom, G. (1962). *Fish as Food,* Vol. 2, New York; Academic Press, p. 267
Bramsnaes F. (1961). *Fish in Nutrition.* London; Fishing News (Books) Ltd. p.183
Carey, F. G. and Teal, J.M. (1966). *Proc. natn. Acad. Sci.* 56, 1464
Connell, J. J. (1958). *Fundamental Aspects of the Dehydration of Foodstuffs.*
   London; Society of Chemical Industry. p. 167
– (1960). *J. Sci. Fd. Agric.* 11, 515
– (1961). *Biochem. J.,* 80, 503
– (1962a). *Freeze Drying of Foods.* Washington, D.C.; National
   Academy of Sciences–National Research Council. p.50
– (1962b). *J. Sci. Fd Agric.* 13, 607
– (1964). *Proteins and Their Reactions.* Westport, Connecticut: The
   Avi Publishing Co., Inc. p.255
– (1965). *J. Sci. Fd Agric.* 16, 769
– (1966). *Torry Research Station Annual Report.* Edinburgh; Her
   Majesty's Stationery Office
– (1967). *Torry Research Station Annual Report.* Edinburgh; Her
   Majesty's Stationery Office
– (1969). *Fd Technol., Champaign* 23, 72
– and Howgate, P. F. (1959). *J. Sci. Fd Agric.,* 10, 241
– and – (1964). *J. Fd Sci.* 29, 717
Cutting, C. L. (1961). *Fish in Nutrition,* London; Fishing News (Books) Ltd. p. 161
Dyer, W. J. (1961). *Can. Fisherm.* August, 2
Ellinger, G. M. and Boyne, A. W. (1965). *Brit. J. Nutr.* 19, 587
Food and Agriculture Organisation of the United Nations (1968). *Amino acids
   content of Foods and Biological Data on Proteins.* Rome; F.A.O.
Geiger, E. and Borgstrom, G. (1962). *Fish as Food.* Vol. 2, New York; Academic
   Press. p. 29
Hamoir, G. (1967). unpublished results
Hamoir, G., McKenzie, H. A. and Smith, M. B. (1960). *Biochim. biophys. Acta* 40,
   141
King, F. J. (1966). *J. Fd Sci.* 31, 649
Licht, P. (1964). *Comp. Biochem. Physiol.* 12, 331
Love, R. M. (1960). *Nature, Lond.* 185, 692
Love, R. M. and Olley, J. N. (1965). *The Technology of Fish Utilization,* London;
   Fishing News (Books) Ltd. p. 116
Love, R. M. and Robertson, I. (1968). *J. Fd Technol.* 3, 215
Lovern, J. A. (1969). *Proc. Nutr. Soc.* 28, 81
Mackie, I. M. (1968). unpublished results
Meryman, H. T. (1968). *Nature, Lond.,* 218, 333
Noguchi, E. (1965). *The Technology of Fish Utilization,* London; Fishing News
   (Books) Ltd. p. 70
Rao, K. K. P. N. (1961). *Fish in Nutrition,* London; Fishing News (Books) Ltd.
   p.237
Reber, E. F., Raheja, K. and Davis, D. (1966). *Fedn. Proc. Fedn. Am. Socs.* 25,
   No. 5, Part I

Richards, E. G., Chung, C.-S., Menzel, D. B. and Olcott, H. S. (1967). *Biochemistry* **6,** 528

Sawant, P. L. and Magar, N. G. (1961). *J. Fd Sci.* **26,** 253

Shewan, J. M. (1961). *Fish in Nutrition,* London; Fishing News (Books) Ltd. p.207

Simidu, W. (1944). *Kamaboko.* Tokyo; Seikatsusha Co. Ltd.

Stillings, B. R. (1967). *Activities Report, Food and Container Research and Development,* U.S. Army Natick Laboratory, Massachusetts, **19,** 109

# MILK AND MILK PRODUCTS

## J.A.B. SMITH

*The Hannah Dairy Research Institute, Ayr*

## INTRODUCTION

Before the nature and nutritive value of the proteins of milk and milk products are discussed, it may be of interest, by way of introduction, to consider what contribution these proteins make to the dietary of various countries. Table 1 has been prepared from data summarized by Samuelsson (1962) at a meeting organized by the International Dairy Federation, and although the figures in it apply to the period 1958–59, it is probable that the position has not changed much in the past 10 years. It will be seen from Table 1 that in the countries that are cited as representing the developed areas of the world, milk and milk products supply some 19–26 g protein per head per day. This is about 25 per cent of the total protein of the diet, and 40–70 per cent of the total protein from animal sources. In these countries, therefore, milk protein makes a very

Table 1

Estimates of the amounts of milk protein per head per day in the diets of the people of various countries, and the proportion of the total protein that appears to be supplied by milk protein

| | Protein from milk (g) (A) | Animal protein (g) (B) | Total protein in the diet (g) (C) | Milk protein as % of total protein $\left(\frac{A}{C} \times 100\right)$ | Animal protein as % of total protein $\left(\frac{B}{C} \times 100\right)$ |
|---|---|---|---|---|---|
| United Kingdom | 19 | 50 | 85 | 22 | 59 |
| Eire | 26 | 39 | 96 | 27 | 41 |
| Denmark | 22 | 57 | 92 | 24 | 62 |
| New Zealand | 26 | 72 | 106 | 25 | 68 |
| U.S.A. | 25 | 65 | 93 | 27 | 70 |
| Ceylon | 1 | 12 | 48 | 2 | 25 |
| India | 4 | 6 | 47 | 9 | 13 |
| Pakistan | 5 | 8 | 49 | 10 | 16 |
| Philippines | 2 | 11 | 36 | 6 | 31 |

213

significant contribution to the diet. On the other hand, the figures given in the lower part of Table 1 make it only too clear to what an extremely small extent milk protein and animal proteins generally are available in countries typical of developing areas of the world.

## THE PROTEIN CONTENT OF MILK AND FACTORS THAT AFFECT IT

The amount of protein in milk varies from one cow to another within any one breed, and it varies also from one breed to another. Typical mean values are 3.4 per cent for Friesian cows, 3.6 per cent for Ayrshires and 3.9 per cent or so for the Channel Island breeds. It is affected also by various factors such as the stage of lactation, the season of the year, the age of the cow, the type and amount of food it receives and whether the udder is affected by any form of mastitis, clinical or sub-clinincal.

The colostrum which is secreted immediately after the birth of the calf contains as much as 14 per cent of protein, but by the third day or so this value has declined to a normal value of 3–4 per cent. At the first few milkings after parturition the albumin and globulin contents of the colostrum or milk are very high, and together they exceed the amount of casein, but the contents of albumin and globulin rapidly decline, and the mixed proteins of the milk soon become established with the type of composition shown in Table 2.

Table 2

Typical values for the main constituents of milk protein expressed as a percent-age of the liquid milk and of the total protein

|  | Percentage of the milk | Percentage of the total protein |
|---|---|---|
| Caseins | 2.70 | 76 |
| $\beta$-lactoglobulin | 0.50 | 14 |
| $\alpha$-lactalbumin | 0.08 | 2 |
| Blood serum albumins | 0.03 | 1 |
| Immunoglobulins | 0.06 | 2 |
| Fat globule protein | 0.02 | 0.5 |
| Others | 0.14 | 4 |
| Total | 3.53 | 99.5 |

It will be seen from that table that the caseins make up almost 80 per cent of the total protein of normal milk, and that the next most abundant protein is $\beta$-lactoglobulin, which contributes about 14 per cent.

The caseins are phospho-proteins, and, as far as is known, caseins of some type occur in the milk of all mammals and yet they occur nowhere else in nature. They have the ability to coagulate with rennin at an optimum pH of about 5.4, a property which enables the liquid diet of the very young to be converted in the stomach into a coagulum of such a consistency that it passes along the alimentary tract at a rate suitable for efficient digestion and absorption to occur.

It has already been mentioned that the amount of protein in milk is affected by the stage of lactation. In fact the protein content tends to fall slightly for about 5 weeks after parturition, perhaps to a value of 3.1 per cent. It then continues to rise slowly, and by the end of lactation some 40 weeks later it may have reached 3.8 per cent. These values apply to cows for which the overall mean would be about 3.4 per cent.

For optimum protein content in milk the cow must be adequately fed, and it has been well established that it is easier to cause a reduction in protein content by giving insufficient 'energy' in the diet than by altering the intake of protein. Inadequate energy in the feed is one of the most common causes of sub-optimum protein levels.

Mastitis in its various forms results in decreased milk yields, and although the total protein content of the milk may not be significantly affected the proportion of casein in the total protein may be reduced from around 80 to 65 per cent, with a corresponding increase in proteins that pass more or less directly into the milk from the blood serum.

Although various factors, such as those that have just been mentioned, can affect the amount of protein in milk and even to some extent the proportions of the various types of protein in the total mixed proteins, they have little effect on the nutritive value of the whole protein, particularly in bulk milk. It is of great importance, therefore, in considering the production of milk protein for human food, to ensure that the amount of protein in the milk is not allowed to fall below a level that can readily be attained in practice. In the past two decades this fact has become increasingly appreciated, and in some countries milk is now paid for, not only according to the amount supplied, but also according to the amount of solids it contains. In this country the Milk Marketing Boards pay the farmer on a system which takes into account not only the amount of milk but also its content of total solids. In the Netherlands the authorities have gone a stage further, and take three criteria into consideration: the amount of milk, its fat content and its protein content. In addition to the basic amount of about 6 guilders (13s. 6d.) paid for 100 kg of milk, some 3½ guilders (8s. 0d.) is added for each one per cent of fat in the milk and some 2½ guilders (5s. 8d.) for each one per cent of protein. Adjustments in the milk price paid to the farmers are made at fortnightly

intervals. Schemes such as that for payment of milk are a great advance in
the milk industry, for they can do much to ensure that the nutritive value
of milk is not allowed to decline, and that the farmer becomes as
interested in the amount of protein produced as in the amount of milk
itself.

A simple calculation may stress the importance of maintaining satisfactory protein levels in milk. In Britain some 2,700 million gallons of
milk are produced in a year. If on average the level of protein in that milk
were to be only 3.2 per cent when it might just as easily be 3.4 per cent, it
would mean that the milk of this country would be supplying 24,000 tons
of first class protein less in a year than it could readily provide. This is
important not only where the milk is to be used for liquid consumption,
but also where it is to be converted into products such as cheese or dried
milk.

## THE NATURE OF MILK PROTEINS

In Table 2 the composition of milk protein is given in terms of the main
classes of protein, but it is important to note that each of these classes
may consist of several proteins. The casein fraction, for example, consists
of distinct caseins which can be separated by suitable precipitation
methods or by electrophoresis into α-, β- and γ-caseins which make up
some 67, 30 and 3 per cent of the total casein respectively. Again the
α-casein can be further fractionated into $\alpha_s$- and κ-caseins. Theories
have been put forward to explain the part played by these various
proteins in the formation and stabilization of the casein micelles in milk
and in the coagulation of milk protein by rennin, a process in which
calcium plays an important part, but much more research will be
required before this subject is fully elucidated.

Here again, as with the total amount of protein itself, the various
proportions of the different individual caseins in the mixture of caseins
vary slightly from animal to animal and from breed to breed, and they are
also affected by stage of lactation, by diet and by the presence of mastitis.
But again it is true to say that the differences that occur, certainly in bulk
milk, are by no means sufficient to have any significant effect on the value
of the total milk proteins in human nutrition.

## THE AMINO ACID COMPOSITION OF MILK PROTEINS

Typical figures for the amino acid content of whole milk protein, whole
casein, the three main constituents of casein, and of β-lactoglobulin are
given in Table 3. In nutritional studies designed to evaluate proteins,

whole egg protein is often used as the reference protein, so typical values for that protein have been included in Table 3.

Table 3

The phosphorus content (%) of the main proteins of milk, and the amino acid content (%)* of these proteins and also of egg protein for comparison

| | Whole egg protein | Whole milk protein | Whole casein | α-casein | β-casein | γ-casein | β-lacto-globulin |
|---|---|---|---|---|---|---|---|
| Phosphorus | – | 0.7 | 0.86 | 0.99 | 0.61 | 0.11 | None |
| *'Essential' amino acids and cystine* | | | | | | | |
| Isoleucine | 6.9 | 6.5 | 6.6 | 6.6 | 5.7 | 4.6 | 7.4 |
| Leucine | 9.4 | 9.9 | 10.1 | 8.2 | 12.1 | 12.5 | 15.0 |
| Lysine | 6.9 | 8.0 | 8.2 | 9.2 | 6.8 | 6.4 | 11.9 |
| Phenylalanine | 5.8 | 5.1 | 5.8 | 4.8 | 6.0 | 6.0 | 3.8 |
| Threonine | 5.0 | 4.7 | 4.5 | 5.1 | 5.3 | 4.6 | 5.2 |
| Tryptophan | 1.6 | 1.3 | 1.5 | 1.7 | 0.7 | 1.2 | 2.3 |
| Valine | 7.4 | 6.7 | 7.4 | 6.5 | 10.6 | 10.9 | 5.8 |
| Methionine | 3.3 | 2.4 | 3.3 | 2.6 | 3.5 | 4.3 | 3.3 |
| Cystine | 2.3 | 0.9 | 0.4 | 0.4 | 0.1 | 0.0 | 3.0 |
| *Other amino acids* | | | | | | | |
| Alanine | – | 3.6 | 3.1 | 3.8 | 1.8 | 2.4 | 6.8 |
| Arginine | 6.7 | 3.5 | 4.2 | 4.4 | 3.5 | 2.0 | 2.9 |
| Aspartic acid | 8.2 | 7.5 | 6.5 | 8.7 | 5.1 | 4.2 | 11.7 |
| Glutamic acid | 12.6 | 21.7 | 23.6 | 23.2 | 24.1 | 23.8 | 19.8 |
| Glycine | 3.6 | 2.1 | 2.1 | 2.9 | 2.5 | 1.6 | 1.7 |
| Histidine | 2.4 | 2.7 | 3.0 | 3.0 | 3.2 | 3.8 | 1.7 |
| Proline | 4.5 | 9.2 | 12.3 | 8.5 | 16.6 | 17.7 | 5.2 |
| Serine | 7.8 | 5.2 | 6.3 | 6.5 | 7.1 | 5.7 | 4.3 |
| Tyrosine | 4.1 | 4.9 | 6.3 | 8.4 | 3.3 | 3.8 | 4.0 |

*These values have been taken from a table published by Ling *et al.* (1961).

It is clear from that table how much the three main casein fractions differ in phosphorus content and also in their content of some of the amino acids such as leucine and valine.

When whole milk protein is compared with egg protein, the following points regarding the essential amino acids and cystine may be noted.

(1) The amounts of isoleucine, leucine, phenylalanine, threonine, tryptophan and valine are at much the same levels in both these proteins.

(2) The lysine content of milk protein is significantly higher than that of egg protein.

(3) The content of the sulphur-containing amino acids, methionine and cystine, is appreciably less in milk protein (3.3 per cent) than in egg protein (5.6 per cent).

In fact it has been shown by many experiments on the nutritive value of whole milk protein and of casein itself that while these proteins are of high biological value, the efficiency with which they are utilized can be still further increased in some animal species by the addition of small amounts (0.2 or 0.4 per cent, for example) of cystine or methionine. This has been shown to be true for rats by several workers, such as Henry *et al.* (1948), Henry and Kon (1953, 1956), Block (1949), Riesen *et al.* (1946) and Lewis and Fajans (1951), and for dogs by Wyzan *et al.* (1950). In experiments by Cox *et al.* (1947) it was found that while the addition of methionine to casein led to improved growth in the rat and to greater nitrogen retention in the dog, it was without effect in experiments with human adults and infants. There is therefore an important species difference here, and it was pointed out by Meuller and Cox (1947) that for man the proportions of the sulphur amino acids present in whole milk proteins could be expected to be adequate from the knowledge available regarding amino acid requirements.

As would be expected from the results given in Table 3, milk protein should be a valuable source of lysine, and it is probable that the supplementary value of milk protein, which is referred to in the next section, is due at least in part to its lysine content. It has been claimed that the human infant requires about six times as much lysine as tryptophan, and if this is correct, it is of interest to observe that according to the typical figures quoted in Table 3 the ratio of lysine to tryptophan in whole milk protein is just about 6.

## THE SUPPLEMENTARY VALUE OF MILK PROTEIN

One of the great nutritional advantages of including milk protein in the diet is that it can have a most valuable supplementary effect in enhancing the value of the protein of the rest of the diet. This is clearly shown by the work of Henry and Kon (1946) whose main results, summarized in Table 4, showed that the relatively low nutritive value of bread protein could be raised to the high value of that of cheese if half the bread protein were replaced by cheese protein. Similarly, the value of potato protein was very significantly increased when it was supplemented with the protein of dried milk, and it is important to note that for the greatest advantage to be obtained from these supplementation effects, the two sources of protein (bread and cheese, or potatoes and dried milk) had to be given at the same time. Several other workers, such as Hutchinson *et al.* (1959) and Howard *et al.* (1958) have confirmed that milk protein has this supplementary effect. One of the main reasons for it is the relatively high lysine content of milk protein.

Most of the work on the supplementary value of milk protein has been done with rats as the experimental animals, but there is no reason why the

Table 4

The supplementary value of milk protein in experiments with rats
(After Henry and Kon, 1946)

| | Biological value | | Biological value |
|---|---|---|---|
| White bread alone | 52 | Potato | 71 |
| Cheese alone | 76 | Dried skim milk | 89 |
| A mixture in which 50 per cent of the protein came from the bread and 50 per cent from the cheese | 75 | A mixture in which 50 per cent of the protein came from potato and 50 per cent from dried milk | 86 |
| When the two sources of protein were given on alternate days | 67 | When the two sources were given on different days | 81 |

results should not apply in principle to man. In fact in experiments with a young man as the subject, Kofrányi (1957) found that when only one-fifth of the protein of a purely vegetable diet was replaced by cheese the biological value of the total protein of the diet was greatly increased Similarly, Mitra and Verma (1947) in nitrogen balance experiments with Indian subjects found higher biological values for the proteins of rice-milk diets than for the proteins of rice-pulse diets. When they studied the effect of varying the proportion of milk to rice, they obtained maximum values when milk supplied 25 per cent of the protein of the mixture. Indeed, it can be calculated that since rice contains about 7.5 per cent protein with a lysine content of 4.4 per cent, and dried skimmed milk contains 36 per cent protein with a lysine content of 8.0 per cent, by supplementing rice with 7 per cent of its weight of dried skimmed milk, a quarter of the total protein in the mixture will be milk protein and the lysine content of the total protein will be about 5.3 per cent.

## CHEESE

One of the main forms in which milk protein is consumed in developed countries is in the form of cheese, which often contains some 20–30 per cent of protein, almost all of which is casein. The level of protein in different types of cheese depends, of course, on the method of manufacture. In the making and maturing of cheese the nutritive value of the protein is not significantly affected, so this particular milk product is an excellent source of most of the amino acids, particularly lysine, and it will be realized from what has already been said that although the content of sulphur-containing amino acids is low compared with that of egg protein, cheese can be a most valuable source of dietary protein for man.

## PRODUCTS INVOLVING THE HEAT TREATMENT OF MILK

Most of the milk produced in Britain today is subjected to some form of pasteurization before it reaches the consumer, and the milk used for making products such as evaporated milk and dried milk is subjected to varying degrees of heat treatment during the manufacturing processes. For ordinary high-temperature, short-time pasteurization, milk is heated to 72°C for about 15 s, and for the recently introduced 'long-life' milk, the raw milk is heated to about 140°C for 2 s and is then filled into sterile containers under aseptic conditions.

In the past 30 years much research has been done in several countries on the processing of milk with the result that a very high standard has been reached both in the manufacturing procedures themselves and in the quality and nutritive value of the products. Particular attention has been paid to the digestibility and biological value of the proteins in such products. Henry and Kon (1958) in summarizing much of their work on this subject, gave 84 as a typical figure for the biological value of the protein of raw, pasteurized and well-made spray-dried milk, compared with a value of 83 for that of roller-dried milk and one of 82 for that of evaporated milk. The effect of pasteurizing and processing was exceedingly slight and only in evaporated milk did it reach significance. It is now known that the decrease in biological value found in evaporated milks occurs mainly during the period when the product contained in sealed cans is sterilized at around 115°C for 15–18 min. Henry et al. (1939) showed also that only in evaporated milk was the true digestibility of the proteins significantly affected. They found it to be 91 for evaporated milk compared with 94 for spray-dried milk. In that same work with rats as the test animal, the gains in weight obtained when raw milk and reconstituted spray-dried, roller-dried and evaporated milks were given ad lib. did not differ significantly one from another, but it was observed that the rats ate somewhat more of the evaporated milk than of the other products. When the growth rates per 100 ml of milk or of reconstituted milk consumed were calculated it was found that the mean daily gains were 3.79, 3.71 and 3.70 g per rat for raw, spray-dried and roller-dried milks respectively, but only 3.31 g for evaporated milk. It is clear, therefore, that in well-made dried milks the nutritive value of the protein of the original milk is practically unimpaired, but that in evaporated milk it tends to be slightly affected. In later experiments with rats Henry et al. (1948) showed that the proteins of spray-dried milk had the same biological value as those of a sample of freeze-dried milk, and that with both these products the biological value was improved to the same extent by the addition of 0.18 per cent cystine, thus confirming that in the spray-drying process cystine had not been destroyed to any significant extent (*see also* Henry, 1957).

## HIGH PRE-HEATING TEMPERATURES

More than 20 years ago it was shown by Mattick *et al.* (1945), Findlay *et al.* (1946) and White *et al.* (1947) that the storage-life of dried whole milk could be greatly extended if the milk from which it was made was pre-heated to 88°C for a few seconds instead of to only 71°C which was the more usual pre-heating temperature at that time. Experiments by Henry and Kon (1947) with rats showed that the use of the higher temperature had no significant effect on the biological value and digestibility of the proteins of the resulting dried milk, and later White *et al.* (1952) found that even a temperature of 110°C for a few seconds had no deleterious effect. Some of the main findings of that work are summarized in Table 5.

Table 5

The effect of the temperature to which the raw milk is heated before processing and the effect of storage of the spray-dried milk produced on the biological value and digestibility of the proteins of the dried milk

| Pre-heating temp. (°C) | Freshly made powder | | After storage for 6 months at 37°C | | References |
|---|---|---|---|---|---|
| | Biological value | Digestibility | Biological value | Digestibility | |
| 71 | 89.0 | 91.8 | — | — | Henry and Kon (1947) |
| 88 | 87.7 | 90.3 | — | — | |
| 88 | 87.7 | 91.8 | 87.1 | 91.6 | White |
| 110 | 88.7 | 90.4 | 88.4 | 92.2 | *et al.* (1952) |

In fact it is now well established that treatment of milk at high temperatures for short times is much less harmful than treatment at lower temperatures for longer times, and it leads to the manufacture of dried milk of high nutritive value and extended storage life.

## THE STORAGE OF DRIED MILK

The results recorded in Table 5 show that storage of dried milk for as long as 6 months at 37°C had no ill-effect on the nutritive value of its proteins, but it has been found that this is true only if the moisture content of the powder is kept below about 5 per cent. The results in Table 6 show that when the moisture content of a powder was allowed to rise from 4.7 to 7.3 per cent the biological value of the proteins was considerably reduced after storage for only 2 months at 37°C, but when 1.25 per cent of lysine was added to the deteriorated powder, the biological value was restored.

Table 6

The effect of a high moisture content on the biological value of spray-dried skimmed milk during storage
(From Henry *et al.*1948 by courtesy of Cambridge University Press)

|  | Moisture content (%) | Period of storage at 37°C (months) | Biological value |
|---|---|---|---|
| Dried milk | 4.7 | 0 | 86 |
|  | 4.7 | 6 | 85 |
|  | 7.3 | 1 | 83 |
|  | 7.3 | 2 | 69 |
| Dried milk + 1.25 per cent lysine | 7.3 | 2 | 87 |

It is now known that during storage at moisture contents above 5 per cent a Maillard type of reaction occurs, in which the amino group on the end carbon atom of a lysine residue combines irreversibly with the aldehyde group of lactose, and in this way the availability of the lysine to the animal may be greatly impaired. In badly deteriorated powder some 40 per cent of the lysine may be rendered unavailable in this way. It is vitally important, therefore, that in the manufacture, packing, transport and storage of dried milk, a low moisture content is at all times maintained. If reasonable precautions are taken this can easily be achieved, but if through careless handling or storage the moisture content is allowed to rise, the protein of the resulting product will be of little value either in itself or as a dietary supplement. It is particularly important to note that dried milk which has been allowed to deteriorate in that way may well be practically useless in the treatment of protein deficiency diseases such as kwashiorkor, whereas well made dried milk which has been maintained at a low moisture content is excellent for that purpose.

## CONCLUSIONS

(1)  In discussing milk proteins as human food, reference has been made to the fact that in many developed areas of the world milk protein

supplies about 25 per cent of the total protein in the diet and some 40—70 per cent of the protein derived from animal sources. These values have been compared with corresponding figures for some of the developing areas.

(2) The percentage of protein in milk can be affected by environmental and managerial factors on the farm, and it is important that all reasonable steps should be taken in practice to maintain the protein content at as high a level as is reasonably possible. Payment for milk not only according to its amount but also according to its protein content can be a great help in this direction.

(3) As would be expected from its content of amino acids and from its high digestibility, the biological value of milk protein is high. For some animal species its content of sulphur-containing amino acids is limiting, but there is evidence to suggest that this does not hold for human adults and infants.

(4) Milk protein is an excellent supplement for cereal and other vegetable proteins, one of the main advantages here being its high lysine content of about 8.0 per cent.

(5) Heating milk to high temperatures, provided that it is only for very short times, has no deleterious affect on the nutritive value of the proteins. Pasteurization and the spray-drying of milk, therefore, do not result in any significant decline in digestibility or biological value.

(6) If during manufacture or storage the moisture content of dried milk is allowed to rise beyond 5 per cent, much of the lysine of the protein undergoes a Maillard type of reaction with lactose and is thereby rendered biologically useless. It is important therefore that the moisture content of dried milk products should always be kept below 5 per cent.

## REFERENCES

Block, R. J. (1949). *J. Am. diet. Ass.* **25,** 937
Cox, W. M., Mueller, A. J., Elman, R., Albanese, A. A., Kemmerer, K. S.,Barton, R. W. and Holt, L. E. (1947). *J. Nutr.* **33,** 437
Findlay, J. D., Higginbottom, C., Smith, J. A. B. and Lea, C. H. (1946). *J. Dairy Res.* **14,** 378
Henry, K. M. (1957). *Dairy Sci. Abstr.* **19,** 604
– and Kon, S. K. (1946). *J. Dairy Res.* **14,** 330
– and – (1947). *J. Dairy Res.* **15,** 140
– and – (1953). *Brit. J. Nutr.* **7,** 29
– and – (1956). *Brit. J. Nutr.* **10,** 39
– and – (1958). *Proc. Nutr. Soc.* **17,** 78
– Houston, J., Kon, S. K. and Osborne, L. W. (1939). *J. Dairy Res.* **10,** 272
Kon, S. K., Lea, C. H. and White, J. C. D. (1948). *J. Dairy Res.* **15,** 292

Howard, H. W., Monson, W. J., Bauer, C. D. and Block, R. J. (1958). *J. Nutr.* **64**, 151

Hutchinson, J. B., Moran, T. and Pace, J. (1959). *Br. J. Nutr.* **13**, 151

Kofrányi, E. (1957). *Hoppe-Seyler's Z. Physiol. Chem.* **309**, 253

Lewis, H. B. and Fajans, R. S. (1951). *J. Nutr.* **44**, 399

Ling, E. R., Kon, S. K. and Porter, J. W. G. (1961). In *Milk: The Mammary Gland and its Secretion.* Edited by S. K. Kon and A. T. Cowie. New York; Academic Press. p. 210

Mattick, A. T. R., Hiscox, E. R., Crossley, E. L., Lea, C. H., Findlay, J. D., Smith, J. A. B., Thompson, S. Y. and Kon, S. K. (1945). *J. Dairy Res.* **14**, 116

Mitra, K. and Verma, S. K. (1947). *Indian J. med. Res.* **35**, 23

Mueller, A. J. and Cox, W. M. (1947). *J. Nutr.* **34**, 285

Riesen, W. H., Schwiegert, B. S. and Elvehjem, C. A. (1946). *Archs. Biochem.* **10**, 387

Samuelsson, E. G. (1962). *A. Bull. int. Dairy Fed.* Part II, p. 27

White, J. C. D., Smith, J. A. B. and Lea, C. H. (1947). *J. Dairy Res.* **15**, 127

White, J. C. D., Waite, R., Hawley, H. B., Clark, J. G. and Henry, K. M. (1952). *J. Dairy Res.* **19**, 339

Wyzan, H. S., Kade, C. F. and Shepherd, J. R. (1950). *J. Nutr.* **41**, 347

# EGGS AND POULTRY

## D.H. SHRIMPTON

*The British Oil and Cake Mills Ltd., London, E.C.4.*

## INTRODUCTION

The poultry industry in the United Kingdom is both large and advanced. By 1962-3 it accounted for sales of £246 million, approximately 15 per cent of a total value of £1,600 million (Annual Abstracts of Statistics, 1964) and the relative situation is comparable today. Almost one quarter of the protein-rich foods consumed in the United Kingdom are from poultry meat and eggs. The consumption relative to other protein-rich foods has been summarized by Shrimpton (1965) and the relative comments are quoted in Tables 1 and 2. Thus nearly as much poultry meat is

Table 1

Annual consumption of protein-rich foods in the United Kingdom 1962-3

| Commodity | Amount (lb per head) | Proportion (% of total) |
|---|---|---|
| Fresh and frozen meat | 98.5 | 47.1 |
| Poultry meat and eggs | 48.4 | 23.2 |
| Bacon and Ham | 25.2 | 12.0 |
| Fish | 19.4 | 9.3 |
| Offal and canned meat | 17.6 | 8.4 |
| Total | 209.1 | 100.0 |

Table 2

Annual consumption of poultry meat, eggs and egg products in the United Kingdom 1962-3

| Commodity | Amount (lb per head) | Proportion (% of total) |
|---|---|---|
| Eggs in shell | 31.1 | 14.8 |
| Poultry meat | 14.9 | 7.2 |
| Egg products | 2.4 | 1.2 |
| Total | 48.4 | 23.2 |

eaten in the United Kingdom as fish, and more eggs (by weight) are consumed than bacon and ham.

The role of poultry products in world food supplies is less dramatic. The nutrient requirements of the fowl are essentially similar to those of the human and unlike the ruminant they share with humans an absolute demand for the essential amino acids and vitamin $B_{12}$. These nutrients can only come from other non-plant sources; and, economically only from fish or meat. The conversion ratio of essential amino acids into edible meat in poultry is 6:1. Although this is good compared with other domestic species, it is poor in relation to the economic use of World resources of essential amino acids. In this broad context the contribution made by eggs and poultry meat to the human dietary is primarily that of an acceptable source of essential amino acids. Consequently this review is primarily concerned with those properties of the proteins which might be expected to be responsible for the acceptability of poultry meat and eggs in the human dietary. Most especially is this of interest in communities such as those of Western Europe and North America where material prosperity makes possible the purchase of food as much for pleasure as for

Table 3

Nutritive value of eggs

| Dietetic characteristic | Units | Amounts per 100 g (excluding shell) | | |
|---|---|---|---|---|
| | | Whole egg | Yolk | White |
| Water | g | 74.0 | 49 | 87.8 |
| Ash | g | 0.7 | 2.0 | 0.3 |
| Crude protein | g | 12.9 | 16.0 | 10.9 |
| Gross energy | g | 163 | 347 | 50.9 |
| Carbohydrate | g | 0.9 | 0.6 | 0.8 |
| Fats: Total | g | 11.5 | 30.6 | 0.2 |
| sat. fatty acids | g | – | 10.3 | – |
| oleic acid | g | – | 14.7 | – |
| linoleic acid | g | – | 2.5 | – |
| Calcium | mg | 54 | 141 | 9.0 |
| Phosphorus | mg | 205 | 569 | 15 |
| Iron | mg | 2.3 | 5.5 | 1.1 |
| Sodium | mg | 122 | 52 | 146 |
| Potassium | mg | 129 | 98 | 139 |
| Thiamine | μg | 92 | 224 | 4.4 |
| Riboflavin | μg | 264 | 440 | 271 |
| Niacin | μg | 44 | 44 | 110 |
| Vitamin A | i.u. | 1,049 | 3,400 | 0 |

Calculated from original data of Brooks and Taylor (1955) and Watt and Merrill (1963)

## Table 4
### Nutritive value of roasting chickens (broilers)

| Dietetic characteristic | Units | Raw | | | | Cooked (fried in vegetable oil) | | | |
|---|---|---|---|---|---|---|---|---|---|
| | | Light meat | Dark meat | Skin | Giblets | Light meat | Dark meat | Skin | Giblets |
| Water | g | 77.2 | 77.3 | 66.3 | 78.4 | 59.5 | 57.5 | 32.5 | 51.7 |
| Ash | g | 0.8 | 0.8 | 0.5 | 0.5 | 0.9 | 1.3 | 1.2 | 1.6 |
| Crude Protein | g | 20.5 | 18.1 | 16.1 | 17.5 | 32.1 | 30.4 | 28.3 | 30.8 |
| Gross energy | kcal | 101 | 112 | 223 | 103 | 197 | 220 | 419 | 103 |
| Carbohydrate | g | 0 | 0 | 0 | 0.1 | 1.1 | 1.5 | 9.1 | 4.7 |
| Fat: Total | g | 1.5 | 3.8 | 17.1 | 3.1 | 6.1 | 9.3 | 28.9 | 11.2 |
| sat. fatty acids | g | — | 1.0 | 5.0 | — | — | 3.0 | 9.0 | — |
| oleic acid | g | — | 1.0 | 6.0 | — | — | 4.0 | 12.0 | — |
| linoleic acid | g | — | 1.0 | 3.0 | — | — | 1.0 | 5.0 | — |
| Calcium | mg | 11 | 13 | 9 | 14 | 12 | 14 | 8 | 18 |
| Phosphorus | mg | 218 | 188 | 174 | 220 | 280 | 235 | 186 | 336 |
| Iron | mg | 1.1 | 1.5 | 2.4 | 4.5 | 1.3 | 1.8 | 2.4 | 6.5 |
| Sodium | mg | 50 | 67 | — | — | 68 | 88 | — | — |
| Potassium | mg | 320 | 250 | — | — | 434 | 330 | — | — |
| Thiamine | μg | 50 | 60 | 30 | 160 | 50 | 70 | 70 | 170 |
| Riboflavin | μg | 170 | 340 | 130 | 1,360 | 250 | 450 | 710 | 2,180 |
| Niacin | μg | 7,600 | 5,300 | 2,000 | 4,900 | 12,900 | 6,800 | 7,000 | 8,000 |
| Vitamin A | i.u. | 50 | 120 | 550 | 4,530 | 50 | 130 | 490 | 5,760 |

Calculated from data of Watt and Merrill (1963)

necessity. It is in this very society that consumption of poultry meat has increased the most in the past two decades and where evaluation of quality in terms of desirability, or of 'food acceptability', is the most developed. Nutritive value is, of course, part of this evaluation, but it is dominated by characteristics of texture, primarily associated with the constituent proteins, flavour and appearance.

Before considering the biochemical characteristics of the proteins of eggs and poultry meat which determine their acceptability, it is relevant to discuss briefly their nutritive value. Tables 3 and 4 summarize the nutritive value of chicken eggs and of roasting chickens (Shrimpton, 1967). Values for the latter were calculated for cooked meat as well as for raw meat and, where frying in deep fat is customary, it is clearly demonstrated that the major contribution to energy comes from the frying oil rather than from the meat itself. The unique contribution of the meat is in its protein content, the major subject of this review.

## EGGS

The proceedings of the fourth symposium of the British Egg Marketing Board (Carter, 1968) have been recently published and contain ten chapters on the food science of the egg. Hence attention will be drawn here only to a few selected aspects of the protein constituents of the hen's egg as they contribute to the protein requirements in the human dietary and the reader is referred to the text of the B.E.M.B. symposium for further detail.

A characteristic of animal proteins, which is of major importance in their attractiveness as foods, is their ability to form structures and so to determine texture. Structure in the egg is commonly associated with the shell, the shell membranes and the vitelline membrane, less frequently with the white and only rarely with the yolk. Yet the shell and membranes, so far as food is concerned, are little more than wrappers for the major food elements of yolk and white and it is to these that most attention is required to understand organic organization and consequently structure.

### Yolk

Hardy (1936) drew attention to the presence of an organized structure in yolk in a note on a paper by Hale (1933) in which the measurement of the freezing points of the yolk and white of a hen's egg had been determined. This work revealed a paradox, the interpretation of which was the subject of Hardy's note. A difference in freezing point between

228

yolk and white was confirmed, -0.56 to -0.58°C for yolk compared with -0.41 to -0.42°C for white, and that implied a difference in osmotic pressure. Yet, and here was the paradox, there was no difference in hydrostatic pressure greater than a delicate, elastic, though possibly tough, membrane such as the vitelline membrane could bear. Hardy suggested that there was no sharp change of pressure at either of the surfaces of the vitelline membrane because there was a gradient from the centre of the yolk outwards. Only recently has study of the macro-molecular biology of the yolk, chiefly by Cook (1968) and his co-workers, provided a biochemical basis for Hardy's theory.

Table 5

Comparative chemical composition of yolk solids

| Chemical class or compound | Proportions of compounds | Proportions of classes |
|---|---|---|
| | Per cent of total yolk solids | |
| Proteins* | | 33 |
| livetins | 4–10 | |
| phosvitin | 5–6 | |
| vitellin (lipid-free) | 4–15 | |
| vitellenin | 8–9 | |
| Lipids† | | 63 |
| triglycerides | 41.0 | |
| phospholipids | | |
| lecithin | 14.8 | |
| cephalin | 3.2 | |
| sphingomyelin | 0.5 | |
| cholesterol | 3.5 | |
| Free glucose | | 0.4 |
| Inorganic elements | | 2.1 |
| Other compounds (namely, amino acids) | | 1.5 |

* Bernardi and Cook (1960); Fevold (1951); Parkinson (1966)
† Lea (1962); Privett et al. (1962)

The comparative chemical composition of yolk solids is shown in Table 5, approximately one third of the solids being proteins or lipo-proteins. The livetins are water soluble. The term was first used by Plimmer (1908). Kay and Marshall (1928) were the first to show that more than one protein was present. Phosvitin and the vitellins, as lipo-vitellins, are present in the granular components of yolk. Vitellenin, as lipo-vitellenin, is present in a low density fraction of yolk. Hence, on centrifugation the structure of yolk can be broken and classified into 3 parts: soluble (livetins), granular (phosvitin and vitellins) and a low density fraction (vitellenin). This facilitates biochemical study and is a necessary step towards understanding the biological role of these components when the vitellins and vitellenins are both associated with lipids and most probably play a key role in the structural organization of the yolk predicted by Hardy.

The water soluble livetins are serum proteins and Williams (1962a) has identified α-livetin as chick serum albumin, β-livetin as $\alpha_2$-glycoprotein and γ-livetin as γ-globulin.

Phosvitin is characterized by a high content of phosphorous (1.1 mmoles/g dry protein) and serine (3.45 mmoles/g dry protein) and the absence of sulphur and proline. The contents of methionine, tyrosine and tryptophan, each at 0.02 mmoles/g dry protein, are low compared with those in the other insoluble proteins of the yolk.

α and β vitellin are similar in amino acid composition and Cook *et al.* (1962) have demonstrated only one difference that is statistically significant, a lower content of histidine in β-vitellin (1.5 compared with 1.9 mmoles/g dry protein).

Vitellenin differs substantially in its quantitative content of amino acids from the vitellins, Cook *et al.* (1962) having shown statistically significant differences in 10 of the 15 amino acids which they examined. Compared with the vitellins, vitellenin has a lower content of nitrogen (14.5 per cent compared with 15.7–15.8 per cent), phosphorus (0.13 per cent compared with 0.30–0.53 per cent) and sulphur (0.87 per cent compared with 1.19–1.30 per cent).

### White

Water is the major component but protein accounts for nearly all of the solids content. Its composition is unusual in that it is one of the few naturally occurring proteins to provide all the amino acids that are essential for the growth of the human, in appropriate proportions. There

Table 6

Composition and properties of layers of egg white
(From Brooks and Taylor, 1955, by permission of the Controller, H.M.S.O.)

| | Outer thin | Thick | Inner thin | Chalaziferous |
|---|---|---|---|---|
| Content as percentage of total white | 23.3 (10–60) | 57.3 (30–80) | 16.8 (1–40) | 2.7 |
| Dry matter % | 10.70 | 12.85 | 13.80 | 15.82 |
| Content of Ovomucin % of dry weight (mucoprotein) | 0.25 | 2.13 | 0.27 | – |
| Specific gravity | 1.0315 | 1.0346 | 1.0369 | 1.0469 |
| Refractive index | 1.3509 | 1.3540 | 1.3578 | 1.3613 |

are four structurally identifiable regions of the white: outer thin, proximate to the shell, thick and inner thin, proximate to the yolk, and the chalaziferous layer from which the fibrous spindles emerge to support the yolk. The composition and physical properties of these layers are shown in Table 6.

The protein of egg white is in fact a mixture of many proteins and it is to their separate but complimentary properties that the structure of the white is due. The proportions of the major proteins, expressed as a percentage of total white solids, are summarized in Table 7.

Table 7

Proportions of proteins in egg white solids
(From Feeney, 1964, by courtesy of AVI Publishing Co.)

| Constituent | Per cent of egg white solids |
|---|---|
| Ovalbumin | 54 |
| Conalbumin | 13 |
| Ovomucoid | 11 |
| Lysozyme | 3.5 |
| Ovomucin | 1.5 |
| Uncharacterized globulins | 8 |
| Flavoprotein-apoprotein | 0.8 |
| Ovoinhibitor | 0.1 |
| Avidin | 0.05 |
| Non-protein | 8 |

Ovalbumin, the major protein of egg white, is a glycoprotein containing intra-molecular disulphide bonds. A heat-stable form of ovalbumin was observed by Smith and Back (1962) who suggested that the increased stability might be the result of an intra-molecular displacement of disulphide bonds, on the pattern of the sulphydryl-disulphide exchange of Huggins *et al.* (1951), which could be expected to lead to an increased stability of the tertiary structure with little or no change in the hydrodynamic or surface properties of the albumen gel. Subsequent work (Smith and Back, 1968) has failed to substantiate this hypothesis and there is, at present, no explanation for the heat stability of ovalbumin termed S-ovalbumin by Smith and Back (1965) who determined its apparent molecular weight as 45,500 compared with 46,700 for ovalbumin. It has been suggested by Meehan *et al.* (1962) that decreased baking quality of some egg albumen may be associated with an increase in the temperature of heat coagulation such as would be expected from an increased content of S-ovalbumin relative to ovalbumin.

Conalbumin is well known as a chelating agent and its strong affinity for iron enables it to play a major role in the microbiological defence of

231

the egg (Brooks, 1960a). A practical application of this property has been developed in the United States by Garribaldi and Bayne (1962) who have shown a decrease in the incidence of spoilage from *Pseudomonas spp.* in farm washed eggs when water was used which was low in iron compared with the water normally available. Under these conditions the small amount of iron in the albumen was all chelated by the conalbumin present so depriving the invading *Pseudomonas sp.* of iron, an essential metabolite for their multiplication.

The iron-binding property of conalbumin, first demonstrated by Alderton *et al.* (1964), stimulated comparative study and Williams (1962b) was able to demonstrate the identity of the protein moieties of conalbumins and transferrin, the metal-binding protein of vertebrate sera.

The characteristic property of ovomucoid is also that of inhibition, Lineweaver and Murray (1947) have demonstrated that ovomucoid is the trypsin-inhibitor of egg white. Interestingly subsequent work (Buck *et al.*, 1962) has shown that ovomucoid does not bind human trypsin.

Lysozyme and ovomucin were thought by Brooks (1960a) to be the proteins primarily responsible for the elasticity of the gel of the thick white. Later work by Brooks and Hale (1961) supported Brooks hypothesis that the thick white is a weak gel interpenetrated by a system of microscopic elastic fibres, a view contrary to the usual belief up to that time in which thick white was believed to be an entanglement network of microscopic fibres containing a liquid phase essentially similar to thin white (Romanoff and Romanoff, 1949). Brooks (1960b) explained the weakening of the gel of the thick white during storage by a gradual depolymerization of the cross-linked, three-dimensional networks which make up the fine structures of both the fibrous and the transparent phases and the simultaneous shrinking of the gel as a result of decreasing swelling volumes of a continuous series of chemically changed networks. Robinson and King (1964) continuing Brooks' work after his death have shown that ovomucin is the protein mainly responsible for the integrity of the fibres in the network of the thick white and current experience is in general support of Brooks' theory.

Much has been written of the anti-bacterial activity of lysozyme, now classified as a muramidase (Salton, 1964) with the specific function of a $\beta$-n-acetyl-hexosaminidase. It is doubtful if lysozyme is as important in the microbiological defence of the egg as was once thought. Under normal conditions gram-positive bacteria, especially *Micrococcus lysodeikticus*, are more sensitive than gram-negative bacteria, but even amongst the former many are resistant and Board (1968) has suggested that the occurrence of a predominently gram-negative microflora in rotten eggs is due only in part to the action of lysozyme.

The inhibitory action of avidin on biotin is well known and no other biological characteristic has been associated with this protein. The enzymes have no particular significance in relation to the food industry although the apparently chance presence of α-amylase has been used as a basis for a test for the adequacy of heat pasteurization of egg products (Brooks, 1962, Shrimpton *et al*., 1962).

## POULTRY MEAT

The relation of poultry muscle to poultry meat is the same in principle as that between mammalian muscle and meat and the principles of meat science which describe this relationship have been recently reviewed by Lawrie (1966).

Superficially the most striking difference between poultry meat and red meat is the whiteness of the breast meat of the former caused by its low content of myoglobin. The average diameter of the muscle fibres is $47.6 \pm 13.8 \mu$ and there are few mitochondria, which are short and arranged along the I bands between the myofibrils. The leg muscles have fibres which are smaller on average in diameter at $44.3 \pm 20.5 \mu$, but the areas between the fibres are filled out by mitochondria, often for seven or more sarcomeres. For comparison the mean diameters of the muscle fibres of mature sheep, cattle and pigs are 50.4, 73.3 and $90.9 \mu$ respectively (Lawrie, 1966).

Table 8

Chemical characteristics of chicken muscle

| Characteristic | Breast muscle | Leg muscle |
|---|---|---|
| Total N mg/g | 42.3 | 35.0 |
| Free amino N mg/g | 1.56 | 0.69 |
| Non-protein N | 5.85 | 3.65 |
| Anserine and Carnosine (arbit) | 72.9 | 28.7 |
| Thiamine | low | high |
| Riboflavin | low | high |
| Niacin | 10 | 5 |
| A.T.P. P mg/g | 0.8 | 0.3 |

The chemical characteristics of breast and leg muscle of the chicken are shown in Table 8. The presence of a relatively large amount of the dipeptide carnosine in breast muscle is of interest in relation to the requirement of this muscle to work under extreme pressure for short periods compared with the prolonged but regular activity of the leg muscles. Attention was first drawn to the biochemical consequences of this difference in function and the role of dipeptides in these situations by Davey (1960a,b).

The contents of nitrogenous fractions change in birds with age as in mammals and data for turkeys from Scharpf and Marion (1964) is shown in Table 9.

Table 9

Nitrogen values for light and dark muscle in turkeys in three age groups
(From Scharpf and Marion, 1964, by courtesy of the Institute of Food Technologists)

| Component | Amount* | | | | | |
|---|---|---|---|---|---|---|
| | 11 week | | 21-26 week | | 25-32 week | |
| | Light | Dark | Light | Dark | Light | Dark |
| Total nitrogen | 4.88† | 4.23 | 5.03 | 4.32 | 4.46 | 3.96 |
| Extractable nitrogen | 2.36 | 1.58 | 2.91 | 1.78 | 3.06 | 2.16 |
| Coagulable nitrogen | 1.77 | 1.16 | 2.20 | 1.32 | 2.53 | 1.68 |
| Non-protein nitrogen | 0.58 | 0.42 | 0.70 | 0.46 | 0.67 | 0.45 |

* g nitrogen per 100 g muscle (wet weight)
† Average of six birds representing 12 determinations

The major skeletal proteins, as in mammals, are actin and myosin. They are interdigitated and account for 60–65 per cent of the crude protein of the muscle. Like mammals, too, the connective tissue consists primarily of collagen and elastin. The skeletal muscle is a rich source of essential amino acids but, unfortunately from the standpoint of world food supplies, to elaborate it birds must be fed on similar amino acids in comparable proportions. Lysine is often the first limiting amino acid in poultry rations. The essential amino acid composition of chicken muscle in Table 10 has thus been calculated relative to lysine at 1.0; and compared with ideal diets, from natural sources or synthetic sources, in which the relative proportions of essential amino acids are similarly expressed. There is a general similarity and clearly no gain in quality from feeding such rations to birds. The significance for the human, as has been previously mentioned, lies in the palatability and acceptability of the product of poultry meat. The remainder of this discussion is consequently concerned with the changes in muscle structure and composition relative to palatability and acceptability.

## Changes during rigor mortis and ageing

Takahashi et al. (1967) have observed both a fragmentation of the myofibrils and a contraction of the sarcomeres. The fragmentation could proceed until units of 4 sarcomeres or less were left but in all cases a

Table 10

Proportions of essential amino acids relative to lysine in chicken muscle, a diet with native protein and a diet with free amino acids

| Amino acid | Chicken muscle | Diet with native protein | Diet with Free amino acids |
|---|---|---|---|
| Lysine | 1.0 | 1.0 | 1.0 |
| Glycine | – | 0.92 | 1.43 |
| Leucine | 1.11 | 1.27 | 1.07 |
| Isoleucine | 0.70 | 0.86 | 0.72 |
| Valine | 0.81 | 0.99 | 0.73 |
| Threonine | 0.69 | 0.71 | 0.58 |
| Methionine | 0.29 | 0.41 | 0.49 |
| Cystine | – | 0.27 | 0.31 |
| Arginine | 1.04 | 1.19 | 0.98 |
| Histidine | 0.29 | 0.45 | 0.27 |
| Tryptophan | 0.15 | 0.20 | 0.20 |
| Phenylalanine | 0.64 | 0.89 | 0.61 |
| Tyrosine | – | 0.62 | 0.56 |
| Total | – | 9.78 | 7.52 |
| C.F. Non-essential AA | 5.95 | 8.65 | 11.6 |

reversal of the initial contraction could be observed. Hence microscopic evidence is available to demonstrate the relaxation of rigor observed macroscopically although the concomitant biochemical changes have not yet been elucidated.

A large number of biochemical changes have been observed but as yet a complete explanation of the maturation process is not available. Fischer (1963) studied changes in the extractable protein during rigor and up to 24 h after death. The results of his experiments are shown in Table 11. The extractability of water soluble protein falls whilst that of salt soluble protein increases. The former was thought by Fischer to be the result of

Table 11

Extractable protein (mg/ml) from chicken muscle during rigor and ageing*

| Time after death (h) | Water soluble | Salt soluble (KCl in moles/litre) | | | |
|---|---|---|---|---|---|
| | | 0.05 | 0.2 | 0.5 | 1.0 |
| ½ | 4.6 | 1.3 | 2.4 | 1.7 | 1.0 |
| 2 | – | 2.0 | 1.6 | 3.0 | 1.2 |
| 4 | – | 1.8 | 2.1 | 3.2 | 1.5 |
| 5 | 3.7 | – | – | – | – |
| 24 | 2.9 | 1.7 | 2.4 | 5.5 | 0.6 |

* Calculated from data of Fischer (1963)

changes in molecular configuration and there is experimental evidence to support the view that the increase in salt-soluble protein results from changes in the actomyosin fraction. The relation of these changes to comparable situations in beef and pork have been studied by McIntosh (1967) who also extended the period of observation to 28 days.

A summary of her results is shown in Table 12 from which it can be seen that the rate of change in chicken muscle *post mortem* is very much more rapid than in either beef or pork muscle. Nevertheless, it must be stressed that there is not necessarily a direct and linear relationship between extractability of protein and of tenderness of meat. There may well be a discontinuous relation in one or more of the species so that direct quantitative prediction of comparative degrees of tenderness of the different meats from the protein-solubility data is not possible at this time.

Table 12

Post-mortem changes in extractability of water-soluble nitrogen in beef, pork, and chicken muscle

(From McIntosh, 1967, by courtesy of the Institute of Food Technologists)

| Time after death | Nitrogen (% of total N) | | |
|---|---|---|---|
| | Extractable | Protein | Actomyosin |
| Beef muscle | | | |
| 30 min | 68 | 53 | 23 |
| 24 h | 68 | 54 | 24 |
| 6 days | 71 | 65 | 34 |
| 14 | 82 | 82 | 50 |
| 28 | 82 | 81 | 52 |
| Pork muscle | | | |
| 30 min | 76 | 65 | 27 |
| 24 h | 43 | 31 | 3 |
| 4 days | 50 | 37 | 2 |
| 6 | 58 | 47 | 18 |
| 8 | 50 | 47 | 19 |
| 11 | 70 | 66 | 35 |
| 14 | 76 | 77 | 50 |
| Chicken muscle | | | |
| 30 min | 55 | 47 | 23 |
| 5½ h | 40 | 35 | 7 |
| 24 | 43 | 31 | 4 |
| 4 days | 72 | 63 | 32 |
| 6 | 71 | 73 | 43 |
| 8 | 78 | 78 | 44 |

Whilst it is clear that some proteins can be extracted into water under laboratory conditions, it does not necessarily follow that a comparable situation will exist in the ice-water chillers in the processing plant. Osner (1966) studied this situation, at first *in vitro* with isolated gastrocnemius

236

muscles immersed in Ringer's solution or in water and also in the same muscles after normal processing in a factory. Results from the *in vitro* studies are summarized in Table 13 and these are in general agreement with the predictions already made, there being little loss of protein when the muscle was immersed in an isotonic solution and so not damaged. However, in the processing plant there was evidence that intramuscular proteins could pass through the sarcolemma 20 h after slaughter, probably as a result of physical injury to the muscle membranes during muscular contraction on the carcass during the onset of rigor. It is, however, necessary to retain a perspective and Osner found that in spite of this post-morten permeability 98 per cent of the muscle protein remained in the muscle. The changes are clearly of no nutritional significance although they may be important in relation to changes in texture.

Table 13

Diffusion of soluble proteins from gastrocnemius muscles into surrounding media
(From Osner, 1966, by courtesy of the Institute of Food Technologists)

| Time of sampling (h) | Milligrammes of soluble protein per g muscle | |
|---|---|---|
| | Ringer's solution | Distilled water |
| 0 | 0.038 | 0.067 |
| 1 | 0.441 | 0.237 |
| 24 | 0.635 | 3.38 |
| Muscle* | 26.7 | 28.5 |

\* 24 h post-mortem

*Changes during holding at 0°C*

Khan and van den Berg (1964) have studied proteolysis in chicken muscle by following changes in stroma nitrogen and ATPase activity in asceptically stored chicken breast and leg muscle. The results of one of their experiments are shown in Table 14. The increase in nitrogen extract-ability was greatest in leg muscle and could not be accounted for by the small increase in solubility of the stroma-protein fraction. It was also observed by these workers that increase in protein breakdown products was accompanied by increased odour scores and that whilst the changes were quantitatively similar to those taking place during frozen storage their rate of occurence was of the order of 20–30 times as rapid.

*Changes during freezing*

Khan and van den Berg (1967) have also studied changes in muscular proteins consequent to freezing. Greater amounts of protein breakdown

Table 14

Change in stroma-protein fraction and myosin-adenosinetriphosphatase activity of actomyosin fraction after 4 to 5 weeks of storage at 0ºC (values are averages of three samples)
(From Khan and van den Berg (1964) by courtesy of the Institute of Food Technologists)

| Bird age | Kind of muscle | Storage time (weeks) | Stroma nitrogen (% of total N) | | ATPase activity (µg of P released/ mg N/min) | |
|---|---|---|---|---|---|---|
| | | | Fresh | Stored | Fresh | Stored |
| 10 weeks | breast | 5 | 10.0 | 9.8 | 240 | 230 |
| 10 weeks | leg | 5 | 19.6 | 19.0 | 200 | 210 |
| 4 months | breast | 4 | 10.6 | 9.3 | 190 | 180 |
| 8 months | breast | 4 | 13.6 | 11.4 | 180 | 170 |
| 8 months | leg | 5 | 25.7 | 23.4 | – | – |

products, expressed as tyrosine-N, were found after slow freezing (no air movement at -18ºC) compared with fast freezing (liquid immersion at -80ºC). The loss of ATPase activity in the myofibrillar proteins is consistent with the view that some deteriorative changes in these proteins has taken place and hence, by implication, some loss of eating quality also.

*Changes during frozen storage*

In birds these are small compared with changes in red meats. Khan and van den Berg (1965) observed a fall in sulphydryl content of chicken breast muscle of the order of 30 per cent during storage at -40ºC for 18 months, but a similar fall after only 6 months at -10ºC. That is to say, the effect of temperature on the rate of deterioration is real at sub-zero temperatures as well as at temperate ones even though the time scale in the former is substantially extended.

Pool (1967) has studied changes in the connective tissue during frozen storage and has determined the effect of freezing or freeze-drying on the

Table 15

Influence of cooking time and freeze-drying on the connective tissue tenacity (CCT) and shear force in fowl muscle
(From Pool (1967) by courtesy of the Institute of Food Technologists)

| Time cooked (min) | CTT in g-cm | | Shear force in lb | |
|---|---|---|---|---|
| | Frozen | Freeze-dried | Frozen | Freeze-dried |
| 10 | 88 | 77 | 8.6 | 11.1 |
| 20 | 62 | 51 | 6.8 | 9.5 |
| 40 | 39 | 29 | 7.9 | 8.4 |
| 80 | 19 | 13 | 7.7 | 8.3 |

'connective tissue tenacity', a measure of the work done in separating the sample. Pool also examined the changes in the force required to shear the samples and his results are summarized in Table 15. From these results it can be seen that the freeze-dried material compared with the frozen muscle has a higher shear value but a lower degree of cohesiveness. That is to say, it is relatively tough but without structure. Hence the connective tissue is disorganized, leaving the skeletal muscle fibres intact and giving a sensation of 'stringiness'.

White *et al.* (1964) amongst many workers have attempted to relate objective assessments of poultry muscle to preferences expressed by panels and their results from an experiment with turkeys are shown in Table 16. Compared with red meats none of the samples was tough and only when the shear values exceeded 25 lb was there any consistent down grading of the meat by the panel.

Table 16

Influence of shear resistance on tenderness, with other quality ratings for comparison (From White *et al.* (1964) by courtesy of the Institute of Food Technologists)

| Shear resistanc (lb) | Samples (No.) | Average ratings | | | |
|---|---|---|---|---|---|
| | | Tenderness* | Moisture | Flavour | Quality |
| Light meat | | | | | |
| 7-12 | 229 | 3.1 | 3.7 | 2.8 | 2.8 |
| 13-18 | 252 | 3.3 | 3.8 | 2.9 | 2.9 |
| 19-24 | 140 | 3.5 | 3.9 | 3.1 | 3.1 |
| 25+ | 72 | 3.8 | 3.7 | 2.8 | 2.9 |
| Dark meat | | | | | |
| 4- 6 | 228 | 3.2 | 3.4 | 2.8 | 2.7 |
| 7-12 | 112 | 2.9 | 3.7 | 2.9 | 2.9 |

* 1 = extremely tender; 8 = extremely tough

## Effect of growing conditions on meat quality

Little work has been reported in which pre-slaughter history is compared with post-slaughter quality, but it would be incomplete to close this review without reference to the obvious but sometimes overlooked fact that meat is only available after the bird or animal has been grown and that some attention should be given to the control of agricultural conditions if high quality food is to result.

Shrimpton and Miller (1960) studied the influence of good versus poor management during the rearing of chickens on the subsequent quality of their meat and found a wide range of textures, from tender to tough. Moreover, this wide range, and especially the occurence of toughness, contrasted sharply with the narrow range of textures of varying degrees of tenderness only, which resulted from previous studies of Shrimpton (1960) in which only the dead birds had been the subject of experiments during processing.

Whilst differences in toughness of poultry meat cannot be adequately explained by differences in the total amount of collagen present, it seems possible that its location within the overall structure of the muscle may be significant in relation to texture if one is to take account of the differences in tenderness and toughness which can result from different patterns of growth.

## REFERENCES

Alderton, G., Ward, W. H. and Fevold, H. L. (1946). *Archvs. Biochem* **11,** 9

*Annual Abstracts of Statistics* (1964). No. 10, 1964. London; H.M.S.O.

Bernadi, G. and Cook, W. H. (1960). *Biochim. biophys. Acta* **44,** 86

Board, R. G. (1968). *Proc. 4th Symp., Br. Egg Mkt. Bd.,* Edinburgh; Oliver and Boyd

Brooks, J. (1960a). *J. appl. Bact.* **23,** 499

– (1960b). *Texture in Food. Soc. Chem. Ind. Monogr.,* No. 7, London; Soc. Chem. Ind. p. 149

– (1962). *J. Hyg. Camb.* **60,** 145

– and Taylor D. J. (1955). *Spec. Rep. Fd. Invest. D.S.I.R.* London; H.M.S.O. No. 60

– and Hale H. P. (1961). *Biochim. biophys. Acta* **46,** 289

Buck, F. F., Bier, M. and Nord, F. F. (1962). *Archvs. Biochem. Biophys.* **98,** 528

Carter, T. C. (1968). *Proc. 4th Symp., Br. Egg Mkt. Bd.,* Edinburgh; Oliver and Boyd

Cook, W. H. (1968). *Proc. 4th Symp., Br. Egg Mkt. Bd.,* Edinburgh; Oliver and Boyd, p. 109

– Burley, R. W., Martin, W. G. and Hopkins, J. W. (1962). *Biochim. biophys. Acta.* **60,** 98

Davey, C. L. (1960a). *Archvs. Biochem. Biophys.* **89,** 296

– (1960b). *Archvs. Biochem. Biophys.* **89,** 303

Feeney, R. E. (1964). *Proteins and Their Reactions.* Ed. by Schultz, H. W. and Anglemier, A. F. Westport, Conn. AVI p. 209

Fevold, H. L. (1951). *Adv. Protein Chem.* **6,** 187

Fischer, R. L. (1963). *Proc. Meat Tenderness Symposium.* Camden, New Jersey; Campell Soup Co. p. 70

Garribaldi, J. A. and Bayne, H. G. (1962). *Poult. Sci.* **41,** 850

Hale, H. P. (1933). *Proc. R. Soc. (Lond).* **112B,** 473

Hardy, W. B. (1936). *Collected Scientific Papers of Sir William Bate Hardy.* Cambridge; University Press

Huggins, C., Tapley, D. F. and Jensen, E. V. (1951). *Nature, Lond.* **167,** 592

Khan, A. W. and van den Berg, L. (1964). *J. Fd. Sci.* 29, 49

– (1965). *J. Fd. Sci.* **30,** 151

– (1967). *J. Fd. Sci.* **32,** 148

Kay, H. D. and Marshall, P. G. (1928). *Biochem. J.* **22,** 1264

240

Lawrie R. A. (1966). *Meat Science.* Oxford; Pergamon Press

Lea, C. H. (1962). *Rec. Adv. Fd. Sci.* **1**, London; Butterworths. p. 92

Lineweaver, H. and Murray, C. W. (1947). *J. biol. Chem,* **171**, 565

McIntosh, E. N. (1967). *J. Fd. Sci.* **32**, 208

Meehan, J. J., Sugihara, T. F. and Kline, L. (1962). *Poult. Sci.* **41**, 892

Osner, R. C. (1966). *J. Fd. Sci.* **31**, 832

Parkinson, T. L. (1966). *J. Sci. Fd. Agric.* **17**, 101

Plimmer, R. H. A. (1908). *J. Chem. Soc.* **93**, 1500

Pool, M. F. (1967). *J. Fd. Sci.* **32**, 550

Privett, O. S., Blank, M. L. and Schmit, J. A. (1962). *J. Fd. Sci.* **27**, 463

Robinson, D. S. and King, N. R. (1964). *Biochim. biophys. Acta* **368**

Romanoff, A. L. and Romanoff, A. J. (1949). *The Avian Egg.* London; Chapman and Hall Ltd

Salton, M. R. J. (1964). *The Bacterial Cell Wall.* Elsevier, Amsterdam

Scharpf, L. G. and Marion, W. W. (1964). *J. Fd. Sci.* **29**, 303

Shenstone, F. S. (1968). *Proc. 4th Symp. Br. Egg Mkt. Bd.,* Edinburgh; Oliver and Boyd, p. 26

Shrimpton, D. H. (1960). *Br. Poult. Sci.* **1**, 101

– (1965). *Rep. Progr. appl. Chem* 1964, **49**, 406

– (1967). *Proc. XIV Mostra Internazionale Avicole,* Varese, II, 39

– and Miller, W. G. (1960). *Br. Poult. Sci.* **1**, 111

– Monsey, J. B., Hobbs, B. C. and Smith, M. E. (1962). *J. Hyg., Camb.* **60**, 153

Smith, M. B. and Back, J. F. (1962). *Nature, Lond.* **193**, 878

–– (1965). *Aust. J. biol. Sci.* **18**, 365

–– (1968). *Aust. J. biol. Sci.* **21**, 549

Takahashi, K., Fukazawa, T. and Yasui, T. (1967). *J. Fd. Sci.* **32**, 409

Watt, B. K. and Merrill, A. L. (1963). *Agric. Handbook No. 8,* U.S. Govt. Printing Office, Washington, D.C. 20402

White, E. C., Hanson, H. L., Klose, A. A. and Lineweaver, H. (1964). *J. Fd. Sci.* **29**, 673

Williams, J. (1962a). *Biochem. J.* **83**, 346

– (1962b). *Biochem. J.* **83**, 355

# IV. PROTEINS FROM PLANT

# SOURCES

# CONTROL OF PLANT PROTEINS:
## THE INFLUENCE OF GENETICS AND
## ECOLOGY OF FOOD PLANTS

W. SCHUPHAN

*Bundesanstalt für Qualitätsforschung
pflanzlicher Erzeugnisse,
Geisenheim/Rheingau, Germany*

## INTRODUCTION

Protein supply — in terms of quantity and quality — plays an important role in the human dietary regime. The specific symptoms and the origin of protein deficiency in man are well known. Quantitative and qualitative protein deficiency prevails in periods of famine, and in the tropics, where protein-calorie malnutrition causing kwashiorkor and marasmus, is of frequent occurrence. (Anonymous, 1952, 1954; Bressani, 1963; Narayana *et al.*, 1963). These failures in the supply of nutrients lead to severe ill-health and even to death. Quality in proteins depends upon a high biological value (Thomas, 1909), originating from the presence of essential amino acids in an adequate proportion, as found in whole egg or in mammalian milk (Schuphan *et al.*, 1965; Schwerdtfeger, 1965, 1968). An impression of the relative fluctuation in the biological value of protein (e.g. in food plants) as influenced by genetics and ecology may be obtained by calculating the Essential Amino Acid-Index (EAA-Index) (Oser, 1951) better than by other methods. Wünsche *et al.*, (1965) found highly significant correlations between the contents of essential amino acids, determined by microbiological methods, and the corresponding biological values in experiments with albino rats. Similar results were attained by Brune (1969) with growing pigs, in which metabolism is similar to that in human beings. Kofranyi *et al.* (1967) however, failed to get such correlations in human experiments using chemical methods (Moore and Stein) to determine the essential amino acids.

According to Oser (1968) the delegates of an International Symposium on the Evaluation of Novel Protein Products held at Stockholm (September 1968) 'were in general agreement that world protein requirements for the next decade would be met by fortification of low-protein cereals with essential amino acids, by genetic improvement of corn and other grains, by increased production of animal (including marine) sources of food, by imitation or extended milk foods, and by new protein beverages. Textured protein foods and microbially derived products were projected for the longer range future'.

The statement also considers sources of plant protein. It recommends genetic improvement of cereal protein. Protein of wheat and rye is deficient in lysine, protein of maize in lysine and in tryptophan (except in the case of some newly bred cultivars, e.g. opaque maize).

The question may be raised, why recommendations of sources of plant protein only involve cereals. We agree with the delegates in many, but not in all points. Dormant caryopses of cereals are relatively light in weight, and very handy in storing and shipping, affording relatively low costs of transportation. They can be milled and manufactured in or near the place of distribution. Protein contents of cereals are relatively high. Wheat grains yield about 9–14 per cent of crude protein and have a fairly low water content of 11–14 per cent (Watt et al., 1963). Cereals provide also vitamins of the B-group, minerals and trace elements, though they are chiefly deposited in the outer layer of the caryopsis (Hinton et al., 1953). Table 1 shows some details. The same is true in regard to proteins of high biological value which are stored mainly in the outer layers, as pointed out by my co-worker Postel (1957)*. Due to their site in the outer layers these substances may be removed more or less easily by milling techniques. It is well known that the amount of loss depends upon the intensity of grinding. This seems to be of great importance.

Table 1

Distribution of certain B-vitamins in the wheat grain
(Hinton et al., 1953 by courtesy of the Editor of *Nature*)

| Fraction of caryopsis | Total in fraction as percentage of that in whole grain | | | |
|---|---|---|---|---|
| | Vitamin $B_1$ (Thiamine) | Vitamin $B_2$ (Riboflavin) | Nicotinic acid | Pantothenic acid |
| *Outer layers* | | | | |
| Pericarp + Testa | 1 | ~5 | 4 | 8 |
| Aleurone | 31 | 37 | 84 | 39 |
| Embryo | 2 | 12 | 1 | 3.5 |
| Scutellum | 62.5 | 14 | 1 | 4 |
| *Inner layers* Endosperm (flour body) | 3 | 32 | 11.5 | 41 |

* *See also* Schuphan (1965) Figure 30, page 113 and Figures 31/2, page 131.

Sreenivasan (1963) pointed out that:

> 'in areas where protein malnutrition is widespread and where there co-exist deficiencies of vitamins and minerals as well, the influence of these latter will also have to be stated. It is well established that amino acid metabolism and utilization are profoundly modified by dietary vitamins and by certain minerals. With diets deficient in these, protein requirements may be higher'.

This statement leads one to survey sources of plant protein, where such suppositions mentioned by Sreenivasan could be realized. Green leafy vegetables (Weinmann *et al.*, 1958; Schuphan, 1958; Schuphan *et al.*, 1965; Busson, 1965) and potatoes (Schuphan, 1959; Schuphan *et al.*, 1959; Kofranyi *et al.*, 1965) are worth considering in this respect, though green leafy vegetables (e.g. kale) provide only about 4 per cent†, potatoes even less, (namely about 2 per cent‡) of crude protein on a fresh matter basis. Table 2 critically elucidates the situation in terms of biochemical data and physiological experience in human nutrition. Kale may be looked upon as representative of green leafy vegetables, eaten preferentially in North and middle Germany during the winter. Potatoes are a well known basic food mainly consumed in Central and Eastern Europe. Corresponding figures of bread, legumes, beef meat and whole eggs are given for comparison in Table 2. Apart from animal sources of protein, soybeans, which are valuable plant-food for undernourished people in the Far East, and potatoes, can be both considered high in protein quality (as indicated by the EAA-Index) and especially valuable because of the low minimum of protein required for nitrogen balance in human experiments (column 3 of Table 2). The reverse is true for bread (a cereal food) and the pea (a legume).

On the other hand the edible parts of kale – distinguished by a high EAA-Index – have proved the high biological value of its protein in experiments with adults (Weinmann *et al.*, 1958) and with growing pigs (Brune, 1969). In addition kale is rich in certain vitamins and minerals and has the highest protein-calorie value of all the foods mentioned in Table 2 (last column). This is due to the rather low calorie value of kale. By adding fat, as used in Germany, some more calories are provided for the meal and the taste of kale is improved. Simultaneously lipid soluble carotene, found in fair amounts in leaf blades of kale (Schuphan, 1940, 1958), will be better absorbed by addition of fat. Kale may be considered a model of the normal type of green leafy vegetable somewhat representative for similar types also in the tropics (*see* Busson, 1965).

---

†Mean of 53 determinations (Bundesanstalt für Qualitätsforschung, Geisenheim).
‡Mean of 260 determinations (Schuphan, 1959).

Table 2

Protein quality of different food

| Food | EAA-Index (8 EAA)‡ | Biological value of protein (human experiments)‖ | Daily intake of protein in g† for minimum protein balance‖ | Calories§ | Crude protein‡ | Crude protein per 100 calories |
|---|---|---|---|---|---|---|
| | | | | in 100 g fresh matter | | |
| Kale | 70 (53)* | — | — | 46 | 4.0 (53)* | 8.7 |
| Soyabean (seed) | 72 (7) | — | 25.4 (Soy flour) | 445 | 34.3 (7) | 7.7 |
| Peas (ripe) | 65 (41) | 56 | — | 370 | 23.4 (41) | 6.3 |
| Bread (50% rye, 50% wheat) | 67 § | — | 38.4 (wheat) | 256 | 7.3 § | 2.9 |
| Potatoes | 73 (258) | 71-79 | 23.7-29.6 | 85 | 2.0 (260) | 2.4 |
| Beef meat | 79 § | 67-105 | 19.2-26.0 | 213 | 18.8 § | 8.8 |
| Whole egg | 100 | 94 | 19.9-26.7 | 163** | 12.9** | 7.9 |

* Numbers in parenthesis ( ) denote numbers of analytical determinations
† Per adult of 70 kg body weight
‡ Schuphan et al. (1958); (1959); (1960)
§ Souci, Fachmann and Kraut (1962)
‖ Lang and Ranke (1950)
** Watt and Merril (1963)

## POTATO

It may be gathered from Table 2 that potatoes provide protein of very good quality. Since Rubner's experiments in 1902 we have known that nitrogen balance, and even nitrogen increment, in man can be achieved with low amounts of potato protein. Rubner* found a daily need as low as 20–30 g (and Abderhalden* (1915) 28.1 g), potato protein/70 kg of body weight. Kon and Klein* kept two persons (a male and a female) during a period of 167 days on a diet, of which the total amount of nitrogen required came exclusively from potato protein. According to the report (published in 1928) both persons felt well over the whole time of the nutritional experiment. The daily need for protein from potatoes was ascertained to be 35.6 g, and 23.8 g/70 kg b.w. for male and female respectively.

Recent nutritional experiments with 5 students carried out by Kofranyi and Jekat (1965) gave some surprising results. They examined the protein of animal food (beef, tunny, whole milk, whole eggs) and the protein of plant food (potatoes, wheat flour, maize, rice, sea weed, soya and kidney beans). The protein of potatoes was found to be equal to that of whole egg in terms of biological value and better than that of all other food examined. The protein of the whole egg is supposed to have the highest biological value of animal proteins. Some other results are worth mentioning. A mixture of 35 per cent protein of whole egg plus 65 per cent potato protein (in other words 500 g of potatoes plus one whole egg) was found to be exceptional, resulting in the lowest daily need of protein ever found by these workers (0.34 g/kg body weight = 24.2 g/70 kg b.w.). As shown in *Figure 1* no other mixture – egg-protein with that of soy, sea weed, rice, wheat – attained such a low value of minimum amounts of protein to cover the N-balance. Thus, neither the combination of milk protein with wheat, nor that of beet with potato were as effective.

Mitrovic *et al.* (1957) gave an account of the important role of potatoes as food in those areas where pellagra (caused by niacin-deficiency) is endemic. In the Yugoslavian district of Metomie, people live on maize almost exclusively. Maize is deficient in the two essential amino acids, tryptophan and lysine. Pellagra disappeared immediately when a daily supplement of 500 g of potatoes per head had been supplied. Potatoes are rich in lysine and in tryptophan, the latter serving as precursor of niacin.

The general deficiencies of maize diets for health made it desirable to replace currently used cultivars of maize – deficient in two essential

*Cited in Schuphan, 1959, Schuphan *et al.*, 1959.

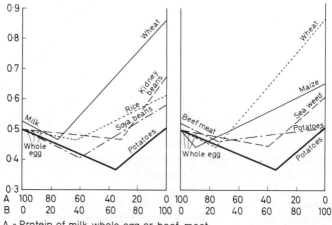

*Figure 1. Minimum amounts* of protein/kg *of* body weight/day *for maintaining nitrogen balance* (After Kofranyi *et al.,* 1967)

amino acids – by newly bred cultivars containing protein of high biological value. This is of great importance and essential for the health of maize-eating people in developing countries. The data in Table 2 clearly show markedly greater biological value of the protein of potato compared with that of bread. A comparison of both products, in terms of contents of vitamins and minerals, is shown (Tables 3 and 4). Vitamin C – not found in bread – has not been considered in Table 3, though cooked potatoes are a fairly good source of ascorbic acid. In order to allow a fair comparison between both foods it seemed that the data should be examined on a dry matter basis. The dry matter content of bread (62 per cent) is much higher than that of cooked potatoes (23–25 per cent). But even on a fresh matter scale most of the data for vitamins and minerals favour potatoes (except for thiamine, sodium and phosphorus).

Some questions – mentioned before – remain in regard to statements favouring cereals for use in developing countries. It has been said that cereals are preferred because of low transportation costs and good storing conditions, even in the tropics. Potatoes have not the same advantages.

There are many more difficulties in handling, transportation and keeping quality, mainly in the tropics (depending on temperature and moisture). We agree with this particular objection. Nevertheless, we recommend the introduction of potato growing in developing countries as far as the climatic conditions allow. It should be remembered that even in the tropics (but in higher altitudes) potatoes can be grown, e.g. in Kenya. Problems of potato pests in Kenya seem to be rather a problem of improvement of soil hygiene, of cultural methods and of rotation than a problem of breeding resistant cultivars of potatoes (Braun, 1968).

Investigations of the contents of essential amino acids in wild potato (Schuphan, 1959) and in potato cultivars (Schuphan *et al.*, 1959) were carried out between 1951 and 1958 in Geisenheim. They led us to the conclusion that contents of crude protein and EAA-Indices may be genetically fixed. In a wild species – native in South America *(Solanum stenotomum* Juz. et Buk.) – a relatively high content of crude protein of 2.6 per cent and a value of 69 (EAA-Index) were detected, the latter being within the limits observed in cultivars. In potato trials – comparing different German cultivars – contents of crude protein ranged between 1.5 and 2.1 per cent and EAA-Indices between 61 and 75. No genetical correlations could be detected between contents of crude protein and EAA-Indices, but positive correlations (highly significant) between protein-N as percentage of total-N and the EAA-Indices (Reissig, 1958; Schuphan *et al.*, 1959; Schick *et al.*, 1961) were found. *Such findings will facilitate the work in potato breeding. Determinations of total-N and pure protein-N can be carried out quickly. They are, by far, less expensive than determinations of essential amino acids.*

Another fact may be of interest both to nutritionists and plant breeders. Some German cultivars of potatoes were found as high in their contents of crude protein as in the EAA-Indices (Schuphan *et al.*, 1959). The potato cultivar 'Carmen' – grown in two different sites – represented contents of crude protein of 2.1 and 2.2 per cent and of EAA-Indices 88 and 82. We observed, in further experiments, a substantial difference in the contents of nitrogenous constituents depending on tuber weight, as shown in *Figure 2* (Schuphan *et al.*, 1959). Increasing tuber weight of potatoes is followed by a distinct reaction of nitrogenous compounds while practically no response is given by pure protein and isoleucine; the contents of crude protein, of lysine and threonine increase with higher weight of tubers. Methionine, tryptophan, phenylalanine and valine only show reactions with weight until tubers have reached a medium weight of 134 g. EAA-Indices decreased from 80 to 75. Small tubers, therefore, have a more favourable pattern of essential amino acids than big ones have. Here again a positive correlation between

Table 3

Contents of thiamine, riboflavin and niacin in potatoes* compared with bread†

| Food | Dry matter % | Thiamine mg/100 g | | Riboflavin mg/100 g | | Niacin mg/100 g | |
|---|---|---|---|---|---|---|---|
| | | Fr. M | Dr. M | Fr. M | Dr. M | Fr. M | Dr. M |
| *Potatoes* Raw peeled | 23.4 | 0.083 | 0.355 | 0.136 | 0.582 | 1.37 | 5.86 |
| *Cooked* peeled (salted) | 23.0 | 0.081 | 0.354 | 0.133 | 0.580 | 0.92 | 4.00 |
| *Cooked* in their jackets | 25.3 | 0.090 | 0.358 | 0.145 | 0.569 | 1.07 | 4.26 |
| *Bread* prepared by using (50% wheat, 50% rye) | 62 | 0.12 | 0.19 | 0.09 | 0.14 | 0.97 | 1.56 |

* Data obtained by own Analysis of 1967 grown potatoes stored till February 1968
† Data obtained by calculating data of Souci, Fachmann and Kraut (1962)
*Fr. M* = fresh weight basis
*Dr. M* = dry weight basis

Table 4

Contents of minerals in potatoes* compared with bread†

| Food | K mg/100 g | | Na mg/100 g | | Ca mg/100 g | | Mg mg/100 g | | P mg/100 g | |
|---|---|---|---|---|---|---|---|---|---|---|
| | Fr. M | Dr. M | Fr. M | Dr. M | Fr. M | Dr. M | Fr. M | Dr. M | Fr. M | Dr.M |
| *Potatoes* Raw peeled | 421 | 1800 | 13 | 55 | 35 | 150 | 29 | 125 | 59 | 251 |
| *Cooked* peeled (salted) | 357 | 1550 | 100 | 435 | 33 | 145 | 27 | 116 | 52 | 226 |
| *Cooked* in their jackets | 436 | 1725 | 9 | 35 | 53 | 210 | 10 | 40 | 59 | 235 |
| *Bread* prepared by using (50% wheat, 50% rye) | 118 | 174 | 302 | 487 | 39 | 63 | 15 | 24 | 111 | 179 |

\* Data obtained by own Analysis of 1967 grown Potatoes stored till February 1968
† Data obtained by calculating data of Souci, Fachmann and Kraut (1962)
*Fr. M* = fresh weight basis
*Dr. M* = dry weight basis

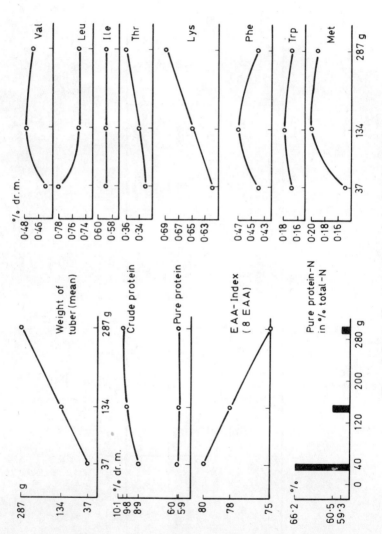

*Figure 2. Potato N-compounds in relation to tuber weight*

the EAA-Indices and the values of pure protein-N in percentage of total-N is obvious *(Figure 2)*.

There are further findings which may be of interest to plant breeders. The outer layers in potato tubers contain protein crystals. We have found that the outer layers of potato tubers, chiefly the so-called cortex, have a much higher concentration of essential amino acids (EAA-Index = 74) than the inner layers which constitute starch-storing tissues, including the pith (EAA-Index 61). The cortex — being within the vascular ring and the periderm with apical and lateral buds — may be compared, to a certain extent, with the outer layers of cereals. The observations and the analytical results in potato tubers are in full agreement with those observed in other plants, showing that the cell layers capable of division are favoured by higher EAA-Indices than the ordinary tissues which only serve storage and transport functions in the plant. Embryos, buds, tissues surrounding growing points, are generally found to have higher EAA-Indices (Schuphan, 1960).

The fact that essential amino acids are concentrated in the outer layers of potato tubers led us to take this phenomenon into account in breeding potatoes containing protein of high biological value, i.e. by increasing the outer layers in proportion to the whole tubers. It will be well understood that, before any practical application, genetical variation has to be tested in this respect. *Figure 3* indicates what may happen when the outer layers are increased in weight to an extent of 15 per cent by breeding. There would be a considerable augmentation of protein-N, of essential amino acids (e.g. of lysine and methionine) of ascorbic acid and also of nitrate-N. Nitrate in potatoes does not play a role, as the amounts occurring are not harmful to man.

It may be of interest to compare the results obtained with potato tubers with those in the caryopsis of cereals. As shown (*Figures 4* and *5*) we get a much greater effect with wheat and barley than in potato tubers. This may be even by a 10 per cent increase in the weight of the outer layers. This statement refers to nitrogenous compounds as well as to vitamins of the B-group (Schuphan, 1966; Schuphan *et al.*, 1968).

The effect of nitrogenous fertilizers, on yield and on the biochemical constituents of potatoes, can be seen in *Figure 6*. In long-term experiments with potatoes we were able to show that excessively heavy application of N causes an increase of crude protein and somewhat less of pure protein, but a decrease of the starch content and of the EAA-Indices. We found optimum EAA-Indices with application at the rate of 5–60 kg. In these investigations it was also found that cultivated virus-infected potatoes gave low yields, high contents of crude protein and relatively low EAA-Indices, while the optimum was displaced to 90 kg N/hectare.

255

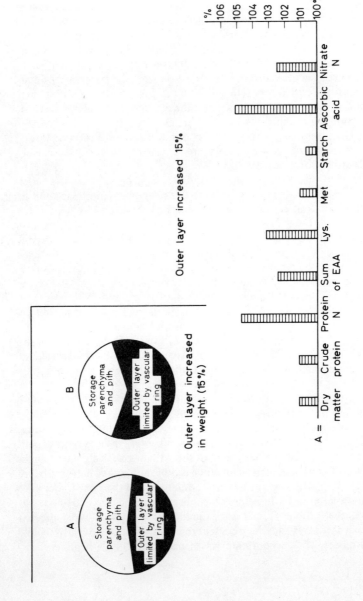

Figure 3. Potato (19.2.58)

3 years mean

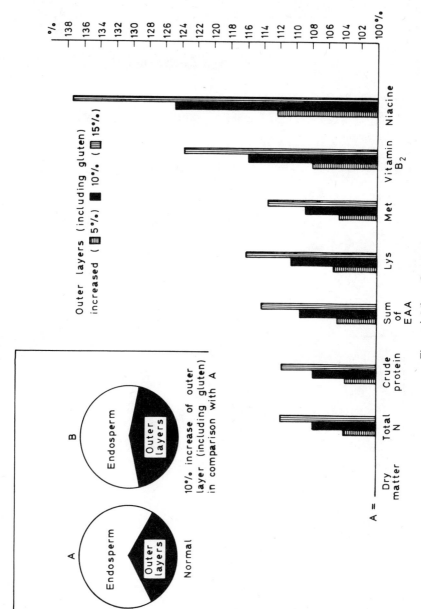

*Figure 4. Wheat Caryopsis*

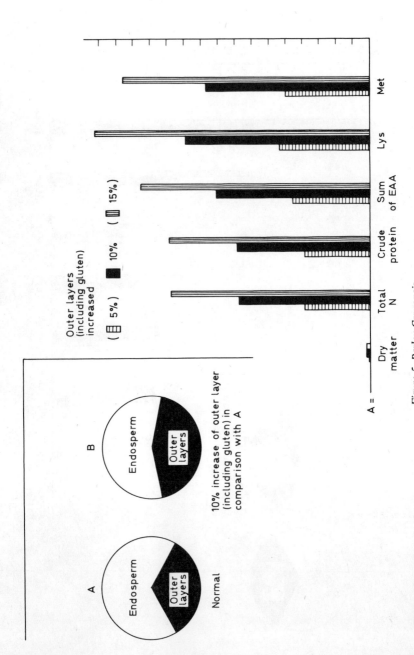

Figure 5. Barley Caryopsis

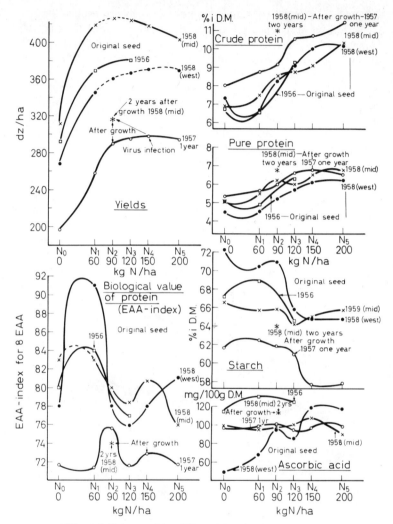

*Figure 6. Potato, cultivar 'Olympia', Geisenheim, 1956–8*

## GREEN LEAVES

Green leaves – to be precise their intercostal tissues – are most complicated centres of plant life, where a great number of differentiated biochemical reactions control processes essential for normal plant

259

metabolism. There is no doubt that this fact is able to explain the great concentration of so many substances important for life of the plant and animal, e.g. of proteins of high biological value and of practically all of the vitamins important for man. Long-term investigations on a large number of leafy food plants of normal and of anomalous type of growth (Schuphan, 1958, 1960) lead us to compare kale and cabbage — two types of the Brassicaceae which are extremely different in terms of morphology. The aim was to find out, firstly, which type might be especially valuable in respect of its leaf protein and, secondly, what could be done by selectors in plant breeding to improve the nutritive value of green leafy plants (especially the biological value of their protein).

## Kale

Kale — serving simultaneously as vegetable and as fodder-plant — represents a type bearing, on an erect stem of varying height, normally inserted leaves in alternate sequence with prominent and rather tough midribs and petioles which are not used for cooking *(Figure 7)*. The same is true for the fairly ligneous stem. Midribs, petioles and stems contain higher amounts of nitrates and isothiocyanate compounds, which are not

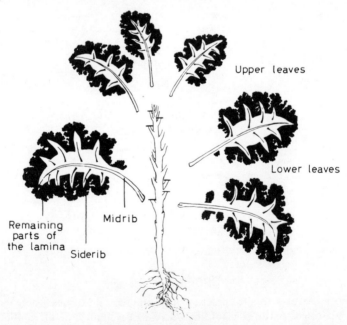

*Figure 7. Kale sampling:* 19.8.58.

wanted. The dark green leaves — more or less curled — have rather small cells, of which the size depends on the grade of curling (Schwanitz, 1967).

The transport system in kale — stem, petioles and ribs — are poor sources of nutrients — except of minerals. On the other hand, the leaves — deprived of main ribs — yield high contents of vitamins, of the provitamin A carotene, relatively high contents of crude protein (lower leaves 3.3 per cent, upper leaves 5 per cent) and a high biological value. The EAA-Indices are found to reach 85—86 (Schuphan, 1958, 1960). The contents of essential amino acids in kale — dry matter basis — show a well differentiated pattern between blades and ribs. There are much higher contents in the blades. Isoleucine, leucine, lysine and valine were present at higher concentrations than the remaining essential amino acids. (This refers both to blades and to ribs.)

*Cabbage*

What happens in terms of biochemical alterations, when plants of the normal type, such as kale are genetically transformed, e.g. when a giant bud, (head) is built up (as shown in *Figure 8*)? In cabbage, stems are shortened and somewhat swollen. Petioles and leaf blades are turned more or less inward becoming colourless and rather tender because of the entire exclusion of light and air in the head. This restriction, depriving the head-forming leaves of their natural metabolic functions, leads to a general levelling and to sharp reduction in the content of nitrogenous substances. Contents of protein and the EAA-Indices, e.g. in the leaf blades of cabbage, are reduced about 50 per cent in comparison with those of kale. These values of the EAA-Index are almost equal to those found in stem and midribs of cabbage, having

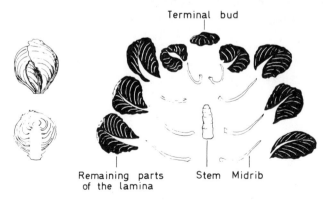

*Figure 8. Cabbage sampling*

261

been lowered because of exclusion of light. The decrease in essential amino acids is even more than that in EAA-Indices: lysine about 66 per cent, isoleucine, leucine and phenylalanine about 80 per cent. A peculiarity with heads of cabbage seems to be the formidable increase of arginine in the stem, and a slight one in leaf blades.

## CONCLUSION

I have been discussing improvement of green leafy vegetables and fodder-plants, in terms of nutritive value, by plant breeders. Kale and cabbage served as models to clarify the problems. I do hope that the negative results in respect of protein in cabbage may not be misunderstood. Cabbage has its merits as a food in another field; heading in cabbage gives rise to greater tenderness, and to rather high sugar contents, fostering effective fermentation in sauerkraut manufacture. As it is well known, sauerkraut supplies relatively high amounts of vitamin C to man.

Kale on the other hand may be considered a very valuable source of vitamins, minerals — and last but not least — of protein of high biological value. It therefore merits as much attention, regarding breeding for enhanced nutritional value, as potatoes. As seen in *Figure 9* kale can be improved by selection of types having the portion of leaf blades enlarged at the expense of petiole and midrib. Selecting those types having relatively thin, but wirelike petioles and midribs would certainly lead to a similar result. The improvement of kale on a nutritional basis can be seen in *Figure 9*. A remarkable increase in nitrogenous compounds, including lysine and methionine, in ascorbic acid and in carotene occur. Undesirable substances (e.g. mustard oil and nitrate-N) are notably decreased. The minerals potassium, iron, phosphorus and suphur increase also, due to a change in the proportions of petiole, midrib and the remaining parts of leaf blades in favour of the latter.

My views on green leafy vegetables in terms of plant breeding lead to some complementary considerations in regard to ecology. The influence of ecological conditions on nitrogenous substances seems to be not as effective as genetical variation does. This statement is true with one exception: nitrogen supply to the plant. As with potatoes, green leafy plants react to nitrogen given in excess by stagnation of yield production, by increasing amounts of undesirable nitrate (Schuphan, 1969), by a slight decrease in protein N in percentage of total-N, and by a very distinct depression of EAA-Indices. The latter is caused exclusively by a great decrease in the content of methionine. This has been shown to be highly significant (Schuphan, 1961).

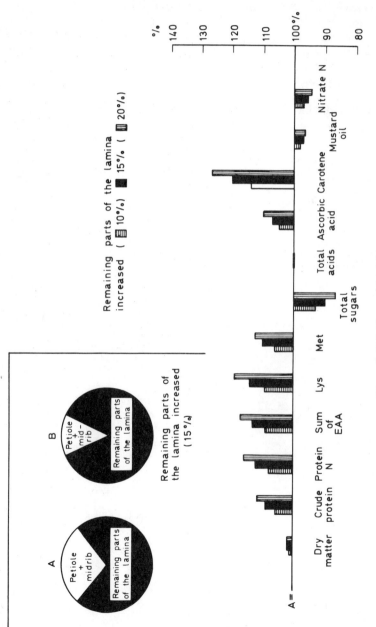

Figure 9. *Kale Harvested*: 20.12.54

It may be of special interest that the content of free essential amino acids in leafy vegetables (lettuce) – according to our findings – may increase considerably when stored for several days. This may signify a lowering of the biological value of the protein, since free essential amino acids will be available prior to the absorptive tract, unlike essential amino acids derived directly from the lettuce protein (Schwerdtfeger, 1969).

Finally, we may compare (Table 5) the annual per hectare yield of proteins, calories and vitamin C from animal production, cereal and arable crops including kale (Schuphan, 1965).

Table 5

| Source | Pure proteins kg/ha | Calories $10^6$/ha | Vitamin C kg/ha |
|---|---|---|---|
| A. *Animal husbandry* | | | |
| Pig keeping | 48 | 1.6 | – |
| Dairy cows | 107 | 2.2 | – |
| B. *Plant crops* | | | |
| Maize | 301 | 11.6 | 0.06 |
| Winter wheat | 329 | 10.8 | 0.06 |
| Kale | 600 | 10.0 | 25.25 |
| Early potatoes followed by kale | 720 | 24.6 | 26.53 |

REFERENCES

Anonymous (1952). *FAO-nutr. Stud.* No. 8
– (1954). *FAO-nutr. Stud.* No. 13
Braun, H. (1968). *Kartoffelbau* 19, H. 11
Bressani, R. (1963). *Qualitas Pl. Mater. veg.* 10, 73
Brune, H. (1969). *Qualitas Pl. Mater. veg.* (In press)
Busson, F. (1965). *Plantes alimentaires de l'ouest africain.* Impr. M. Leconte, Marseille
Hinton, J. J. C., Peers, F. G. and Shaw, B. (1953). *Nature. Lond.* 172, 993
Kofranyi, E. and Jekat, F. (1965). *Forschber Landes NRhein-Westf.*, Nr. 1582, 1
– –(1967). *Hoppe-Seyler's Z. physiol. Chem.* 348, 84.
Lang, K. and Ranke, O. F. (1950). *Stoffwechsel und Ernährung.* Springer Verlag, Berlin, Göttingen, Heidelberg
Mitrovic, M. et Gladilin, N. (1957). *Les diètes préventives et curatives de la pellagra endémique.* 4 ième Congrès intern. Nutr., Paris
Narayana, M., Swaminathan, M., Sreenivasan, A. and Subrahmanyan, V. (1963). *Qualitas Pl. Mater. veg.* 10, 133

Oser, B. L. (1951). *J. Am. diet. Ass.* **27**, 396
–(1968). *World Protein Situation Subject of Swedish Meeting. What's new in Food and Drug Research,* No. **54**, 2 and 4
Postel, W. (1957). *Z. Pfl Zücht* **37**, 113
Reissig, H. (1958). *Züchter* **28**, 51
Schick, R. and Klinkowski, M. (1961). *Kartoffel,* Bd. 1. (Schreibers: 193-301) D. Landw, Verl., Berlin
Schuphan, W. (1940). *Vorratspflege Lebensmitt Forsch,* **3**, 209
–(1958). *Z. Pfl Zücht.* **39**, 127
–(1959). *Qualitas Pl. Mater. veg.* **6**, 1
–(1959a). *Qualitas Pl. Mater. veg.* **6**, 16
–(1960). *Qualitas Pl. Mater. veg.* **6**, 199
–(1961). *Qualitas Pl. Mater. veg.* **8**, 261
–(1965). *Nutritional Values in Crops and Plants,* London; Faber & Faber
–(1966). *Qualitas Pl. Mater. veg.* **13**, 3
–(1969). *Bibl. Nutritio et Dieta* No. 11. S. Karger Verl., Basel (In press)
–and Weinmann, I. (1958). *Qualitas Pl. Mater. veg.* **5**, 23
–and Weinmann, I. (1959). *Nahrung* **3**, 857
–and Postel, W. (1960). *Z. Lebensmittelunters. u-Forsch,* **113**, 223
–and Schwerdtfeger, E. (1965). *Nahrung* **9**, 755
–Klink, M. and Overbeck, G. (1968). *Qulitas Pl. Mater. veg.,* **15**, 177
Schwanitz, F. (1967). *Die Evolution der Kulturpflanzen,* BLV-Verlag, Munchen
Schwerdtfeger, E. (1965). *Naturwissenschaften* **52**, 162
–            (1968). *Z. Lebensmittelunters. u.-Forsch.* **137**, 143
–            (1969). *Qualitas Pl. Mater. veg.* (In press)
Souci, S. W., Fachmann, W. and Kraut, H. (1962). *Die Zusammensetzung der Lebensmittel* (Nährwert-Tabellen). Wiss. Verl. Ges. Stuttgart.
Sreenivasan, A. (1963). *Discussional Remarks. Qualitas Pl. Mater. Veg.* **10**, 165
Thomas, K. (1909). *Arch. Anat. Physiol.* 219
Watt, B. K. and Merril, A. L. (1963). *Composition of Foods. Agr. Hdb.,* No. 8, U.S. Dept. Agr., Washington D.C.
Weinmann, I. und Schuphan, W. (1958). *Qualitas Pl. Mater. veg.* **5**, 85
Wünsche, J. und Bock, H. D. (1965). *Arch. Tierernähr.* **15**, 103

265

# ENRICHMENT OF PLANT PROTEIN

## D. ROSENFIELD

*High Protein Foods and Agribusiness Group,*
*Foreign Economic Development Service,*
*U.S. Department of Agriculture,*
*Washington, D.C.*

## INTRODUCTION

Substantial segments of the world's population do not receive adequate amounts of protein due to inequitable distribution of protein resources. (Abbott, 1966). It is now generally accepted that the primary cause of this uneven distribution and subsequent protein malnutrition is poverty. The classical approach has been to attempt to increase supplies of meat, eggs, milk, and other dairy products. However, since those suffering from protein deprivation cannot afford high-priced products, this approach has not had any significant impact in those areas of the world where the need is the greatest.

In this presentation, I will discuss enrichment of food staples, especially those of plant origin, with amino acids and/or protein concentrates and I will mainly direct my remarks towards fortification of cereals. Since they are currently the major contributor of protein to the human dietary (Altschul, 1967), I will try to show why additions of amino acids to cereals can have an immediate beneficial effect for great numbers of people. I will present the recent history of amino acid fortification, some economic considerations, the justifications advanced for field trials, an outline of the proposed Tunisian field trial and some world-wide fortification activities.

The concept of enrichment or fortification of plant proteins is not new. The observation that wheat protein can be nutritionally improved by the addition of lysine goes back over a half a century to the work of Osborne and Mendel (1914). In 1915 Harold H. Mitchell, one of the outstanding nutritionists of the first half of this century, advanced in his Ph.D. thesis the concept of suplementing a poor protein with another one which would supply the amino acids deficient in the first protein (Edan *et*

266

*al.,* 1968). The protein value of the resulting mixture would then be greater than the value of the component proteins due to complementary effects.

Since the time of Osborne, Mendel and Mitchell, there have been many studies investigating the myriad of technical, medical, and technological aspects of upgrading the biological quality of plant proteins in general, and cereal proteins in particular. A number of review papers detail the current state of our knowledge and thinking in this area (Jansen and Howe, 1964; Howe *et al.,* 1967; Altschul, 1967; Hegsted, 1968; Harris, 1968; Brooke, 1968; Hegsted, 1969; Jansen, 1969, and Rosenfield, 1969).

It can be unequivocally stated that the past half century's work with animals and humans shows that fortification of plant materials with amino acids and/or protein concentrates is beneficial in raising their protein quality. In view of this, it is reasonable to ask why fortification is not carried out on a large-scale, since protein malnutrition is such a serious world health problem. The issue related to this question is economic rather than medical. The health value of fortification is no longer the issue; it is accepted. Rather, more precise data on the costs of fortification and corresponding health benefits compared to alternative approaches to alleviating protein deprivation is needed.

## RECENT HISTORY OF AMINO ACID FORTIFICATION

Before exploring some of the economic aspects of fortification, a brief review of the recent history of fortification would be helpful. In 1952, it was demonstrated that U.S.-type commercial white bread could be substantially improved in protein quality by the addition of lysine (Rosenberg and Rohdenburg, 1952). However, the cost of lysine was so high that its commercial use was out of the question. By December 1954, research had led to the development of a chemical method for producing lysine on a commercial scale at a price of $ 12.00 per pound. Many considered this value to be sufficiently low to permit large-scale fortification of bread in the U.S. with lysine as an economically feasible proposition.

The DuPont Company together with Charles Pfizer and Merck initiated a vigorous campaign in the 1950s to convince the food processing and nutritional communities of the benefits to the U.S. population of adding lysine to a widely-consumed cereal product — white bread. DuPont was especially active and sponsored a series of animal experiments and a limited number of child feeding tests in the 1950s; the references to the results are given in the review articles previously cited. As in all fields of endeavour, all questions were not completely answered,

267

but it would not be misleading to state that the nutritional soundness of the amino acid fortification concept was verified.

In May, 1952, a Standard of Identity for white bread which did not include lysine as an optional ingredient had been issued by the Food and Drug Administration (FDA) after lengthy hearings in the late 1940s. During these hearings, lysine had not been considered as an optional ingredient because its high cost made its additon impractical. When its use became economically feasible in 1954, the situation was such that it could not be included in a bread which was to be labelled simply 'white bread'. If lysine were added, the product would have to have some special name such as 'protein bread' or 'body-building bread.' In essence, the use of lysine was (and is still) limited to speciality breads. With the backing of many members of the medical and nutritional communities, DuPont and the Huber Bread Company petitioned the FDA in 1958 to amend the Standard of Identity to permit the use of lysine in white bread.

In retrospect, it is difficult to appreciate the issues and emotions − pros and cons − which were raised by the petition to include lysine as an optional ingredient in white bread. The FDA indicated that they would disallow the petition. Their reasoning was as follows: U.S. citizens consume adequate amount of protein of high biological value from meat, milk, eggs and fish; there is no evidence of a protein shortage or deprivation in the U.S. and therefore, there is no need to improve the protein quality of wheat protein for the U.S. dietary. DuPont felt that a formal rejection could have detrimental implications concerning the biological efficacy of lysine and therefore, withdrew their petition in 1960.

This action for all intents and purposes halted commercial lysine fortification activities with a few exceptions. For example, lysine had been added to Kelloggs Special K breakfast food for a number of years. A & P and Safeway stores have been producing speciality breads containing lysine since the 1950s. While business activities were still negligible, much research went on to define the effects of amino acid fortification of cereals. Objectives of these experiments were varied: some were directed towards refining the methodology for measuring protein quality; others toward measuring lysine efficacy in human and animal feeding tests under closely controlled conditions. In particular, workers at the Institute of Nutrition for Central America and Panama (Bressani *et al.*, 1963) found that children responded to amino acid fortification as measured by increases in nitrogen retention in those fed cereals to which the appropriate limiting amino acids had been added.

*Historic Exchange of Letters*
It is paradoxical that about the same time as DuPont withdrew their

petition, the world-at-large began to concern itself with the interrelated public health problems of hunger, malnutrition, and uncontrolled population expansion. In nutrition, the possibilities and limits for amino acid fortification in alleviating protein malnutrition in developing countries were being discussed to a limited degree by the international scientific community and their policy-planning counterparts.

In the United States, special attention was given in 1966 to the feasibility of fortifying wheat initially, and then other cereals being shipped overseas as part of the Food For Peace Program. The subject was actively explored between staff of the U.S. Department of Agriculture and the Agency for International Development. The then Secretary of Agriculture, Orville Freeman, wrote in March, 1966 to the Food and Nutrition Board seeking 'The advice of the Food and Nutrition Board on a number of questions related to lysine fortification of wheat for shipment in our AID programs.' His letter and the Board's reply constitute an historical exchange (IADS Newsletter 1967). The Secretary asked the Board's opinion on the following specific questions:

(1) Would fortification of wheat flour with lysine bring about significant improvement in the nutritional value of wheat based diets of less developed countries?

(2) Are there particular situations in which lysine fortification of wheat flour could be expected to have merit?

(3) If so, what would be desirable or maximal levels of lysine addition to wheat flour to assure benefit to some and safety to all?

(4) Is there sufficient information to answer these questions, or if not, what studies should be undertaken?

(5) Does the present knowledge of protein nutrition and lysine fortification justify immediate pilot projects to gain practical experience preparatory to developing larger projects in the future?

(6) Are there any reasons that would mitigate the addition of lysine to wheat flour in our AID program for developing countries?

The Board's reply is as follows:

'At its meeting April 2, 1966, the Food and Nutrition Board considered the questions in Secretary Freeman's letter of March 11 concerning the possible nutritional advantages of adding lysine to wheat shipped in to aid programs.

The Board recognized the fact that the addition of lysine to wheat enhances the value of wheat protein for animals and might be expected to have similar effects in human population where the diet is largely wheat and deficient in protein.

Since little direct evidence of benefit under practical feeding situations is available, the Board judged that present knowledge of the effects of lysine fortifications of wheat on its protein value would justify and immediate large-scale pilot project to study, first, the practicality of providing lysine fortified wheat or wheat flour to people in need, and assuring that the lysine will be available to the ultimate consumer, and secondly, to study the measurable effects that might be observed on the well-being of the consumers, particularly undernourished pre-school children and pregnant or lactating women, that would justify extension of the program.

The Board agreed to continue its evaluation of the problem through its Committee on Amino Acids and will be pleased to co-operate further with the Department of Agriculture if requested.'

## SOME ECONOMIC CONSIDERATIONS

The economics as well as the technological and health aspects must be considered in any assessment of the value of fortification. It is readily agreed that the greater need of both total and higher quality protein is found in pre-school children and pregnant and lactating women. A major economic concern about wide-spread fortification is that in addition to the aforenoted target populations, others not in need will receive the improved food. Therefore, the cost of improving the protein dietaries for those in need must also include the cost of reaching those whose protein requirements are already being met. For the latter it might be asked how much of this is luxury. Do we have adequate knowledge to rule out the possibility that improved protein nutrition does not make any contribution to their ability to compete or undergo stress. In any event, the cost and benefits of fortification must take into account the reaching of those whose diets are deficient and those who may not be in need. And these costs and benefits must be compared to the economic and health benefits of other approaches.

One way to illustrate this is by considering food distribution within the family system. Figure 1 speculates on three different ways of improving the nutrition of the youngest child in the family suffering from inadequate protein quantity and quality (Altschul, 1969).

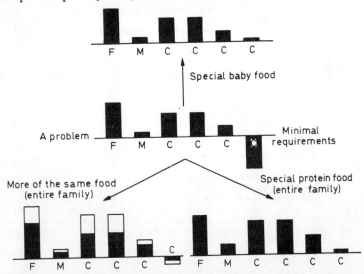

Figure 1. Alternative approaches to improving a child's protein nutrition

In one approach, the total supply of food reaching the family is increased. Every member of the family then eats better, including the malnourished child. The cost of improvement of the child's health is the cost of the total food in excess over that normally consumed by the family. One obviously cannot just calculate the extra food given to the malnourished child.

A second alternative is to provide the child's requirements in terms of a baby food. In the context of an impoverished family, this can be done by removing the child from his family environment to a special situation such as a school lunch programme. Otherwise, there is a good possibility that the special baby foods may go to the older children or even to the parents.

A third approach is to provide the family with a special protein food. A plant product whose utilisable protein has been increased by fortification meets the definition of a special protein food. As in the first approach all members of the family eat better. The cost of improving the nutrition of the child is the total cost of fortifying the plant-based food which is the staple of the diet.

A fourth approach is not directly illustrated in *Figure 1*. This is education of the family to redistribute the food so that the child gets an adequate amount of calories. But education cannot take place in a development vacuum. Those who have been involved in nutrition education in developing countries point out that this is a time-consuming process with minimal success up to the present time. It might be expected that nutrition education will be able to have more of an impact as the whole process of development proceeds.

The foregoing discussion only skims the surface of the economic factors which must be considered in any equation designed to evaluate costs of a nutrition system versus benefits. To me, the economist's term (infra-structure) refers to not-so-obvious components of the system and, thus, to indirect costs. For example, if a special baby food is developed, the total cost of the nutrition system must include the financial and human resources allocated to education and advertising to ensure the child gets the food. These infra-structure expenses are frequently overlooked.

It is always helpful to compare the costs of fortification with amino acids with the direct distribution of additional protein. The following illustrates one way of making this comparison. Tables 1 and 2 give the percentage of biologically available protein in unfortified wheat and that to which lysine has been added.

The percentage of utilizable protein from Hegsted's data and net protein value from Jansen's table are comparable ways to measure protein which is biologically available. There is a significant divergence between their values for unfortified wheat — 3.2 g utilizable protein for wheat flour according to Hegsted, 7.3 g net protein value for water bread according to Jansen. However, they agree quite well on the increment of protein achieved by fortification with lysine. Jansen shows an increase to 10 g NPV when 0.3 g lysine is added to water bread. This is equivalent to (10−7.3)/0.3 which equals 0.97 g increase in NPV per gramme lysine. Hegsted shows an increase to 5.3 g utilizable protein when 0.2 per cent

Table 1

Effect of lysine upon the nutritive value of protein (Hegsted, 1968)
(By courtesy of The American Society for Clinical Nutrition)

|  | Grammes of protein 100 g flour* | Percentage relative nutritive value† | Grammes utilizable protein‡ |
|---|---|---|---|
| Wheat flour | 13.75 | 24 | 3.20 |
| Wheat + 0.2 lysine HCl | 13.94 | 38 | 5.30 |

\* N x 6.25 (all assays are based on nitrogen content)
† Nutritive value relative to lactalbumin
‡ Protein content x RNV = utilizable protein

Table 2

Effect of lysine upon the nutritive value of protein (Jansen, 1969)
(By courtesy of the American Society for Clinical Nutrition)

|  | Grammes of protein 100 g bread (dry weight) | Protein retention Efficiency (PRE) | Net protein value in grammes (NPV) |
|---|---|---|---|
| Bread | 15 | 49 | 7.3 |
| Bread + 0.3% lysine HCl | 15 | 66 | 10.0 |
| Assay standards | PRE |  |  |
| ANRC Casein | 82 |  |  |
| Egg albumin | 95 |  |  |

The percentage of utilizable protein from Hegsted's data and net protein value from Jansen's table are comparable ways to measure protein which is biologically available

lysine is added to wheat flour. This is equivalent to (5.30−3.20)/0.2 which equals a 1.05 g increase in utilizable protein per gramme lysine. For ease of calculation, let us use the value of 1 g increase in utilizable protein per 100 g of grain per 0.1 per cent added lysine. If 100 g or more of wheat flour are fortified with lysine, the equivalent of an additional 1 g of wheat protein will be obtained for each gramme lysine added. If lysine monohydrochloride costs $1.00 per lb, it can be calculated that 0.1 g costs 0.022 cents and this is the cost for the additional gramme of wheat protein.

If non-fat dry milk cost 28.3 cents per lb and its protein content is 35% of which 80 per cent is utilizable*, then the cost per gramme of protein in non-fat dry milk is 22 cents. If fluid milk costs $6.55 per 100 lb and its protein content 3.5 per cent of which 80 per cent is utilizable*, then the cost per gramme of protein in fluid whole milk is approximately 52 cents.

Table 3 summarizes the comparative costs of supplying additional protein in the diet by fortification of wheat and direct distribution of milk products.

Table 3

Comparative costs of supplying protein

| Lysine fortification of wheat | Non-fat dry milk | Fluid milk |
|---|---|---|
| 1 | 10 | 24 |

These ratios are based on protein content alone and do not reflect the value of other nutrients in the milk products. Also, no attempt was made to correct for possible damage to the dry milk protein by improper drying.

## JUSTIFICATIONS ADVANCED FOR FIELD TRIALS

It might be appropriate at this point to reflect upon the role of field trials. Early in this presentation it was stated that enrichment of plant materials with amino acids and/or protein concentrates is beneficial in raising their protein quality. The reply of the Food and Nutrition Board to Secretary Freeman confirms this and goes on to say that since there is little direct evidence of benefit under practical feeding conditions, a large-scale pilot project is justified. The report of the Panel on the World Food Supply of the President's Science Advisory Committee cites evidence of the value of fortification and indicates there is a need for large-scale testing (1967). One of their recommendations concerning food aid clearly points out their feelings for field trials.

It is as follows:

'If the fortification of wheat with lysine being studied on a large-scale is found to be effective as a means of improving the protein supply to the target area, consideration should be given to fortification of all cereal grains and flours shipped from the United States.'

The Economic and Social Council of the Advisory Committee on the Application of Science and Technology of the United Nations (1968) has proposed that during the forthcoming 5 years, 2 million U.S. dollars per year 'will have to be made available through FAO, WHO, and UNICEF to

*Hegsted (1969) gives values of 100 per cent for lactalbumin and 75 per cent for casein; Jansen (1969) lists standard casein as having a protein retention efficiency of 82 per cent.

support demonstrations of the feasibility of these procedures in developing countries'. The procedures they refer to are the use of synthetic amino acids or protein concentrates to improve the nutritive value of cereal and other plant proteins.

Therefore, there should be no doubt that the vast majority of nutrition scientists feel that studies under the practicalities of life at village level are essential to determine in man the resultant health benefits in order to permit economic comparison with alternate methods of combating malnutrition. Let me emphasize that it is the reference to economic comparison which is responsible for the current discussion on the value of fortification with amino acids. There is confusion on this point as some believe the continuing discussion concerns the need for medical data. But this is not the case as few are questioning the medical value. This has been established in animal and small-scale testing with humans. Rather, the economic value of amino acid fortification, related to the expected health benefits from real life amino acid fortification, needs critical study. Until the health benefits in relation to costs are defined, it is not unreasonable to assume that amino acid fortification on a meaningful scale will not occur.

The field of heart disease, as it relates to dietary practices, is in a similar situation. It has been shown that serum cholesterol levels can be correlated with the incidence of coronary artery disease. Further, it has been shown that alterations in diet can reduce serum cholesterol levels. What remains to be done is to demonstrate, in large-scale field trials, that alterations of diet can reduce the incidence of heart disease. Such a study might cost 10 or even 20 million dollars a year for up to 10 years. It has been estimated that the economic cost in the U.S. of deaths from myocardial infarction before age 65 easily exceeds 1 billion dollars per year (Fredrickson 1968). Thus a field trial costing 200 million dollars which can lead to action to reduce this toll, will be proportionately worth it.

It is appropriate to note that information from amino acid fortification field trials would be related to genetic approaches in improving protein quality in cereals. From a nutritional standpoint there is no known difference between adding the deficient amino acid to the cereal or breeding it into the cereal. As the present yield of high lysine corn is at best 92 per cent of normal corn, it is not immediately clear that substitution is automatically warranted. While the nutritional value of high lysine corn is not questioned, the returns and comparisons of crop yield, protein quality, and nutritional benefits must be understood and defined. The conclusions derived from field studies such as that contemplated for Tunisia will be applicable to justifications for continuing to seek genetic solutions.

## PROPOSED TUNISIAN FIELD TRIAL

The foregoing indicated that high priority should be given to undertaking one or more studies to define the efficacy of amino acid fortification under real-life conditions. After a series of field trips by U.S. personnel to determine feasibility for such a large-scale test in a specific country, the U.S. and Tunisian goverments have agreed to undertake a co-operative test in Tunisia. (As of this writing, initiation of the project is awaiting arrangements for funds). It was determined that Tunisia is an ideal and probably unique place for undertaking a real-life technical and economic study on lysine fortification of wheat for the following reasons:

(1) Tunisians receive the largest part of their calories and proteins from wheat;

(2) The identified test area in the southern part of Tunisia does not grow any wheat;

(3) Other protein sources in this area are minimal;

(4) The Tunisian Goverment closely controls the shipments of wheat flour and processed products into this area from northern Tunisia.

The project is as follows: Three similar political-geographical sub-divisions of Southern Tunisia — Douz, Kebili, and Degache, representing more than 70,000 people will be investigated. In the first subdivision all wheat products entering the area will be fortified with vitamins, minerals and lysine. In the second subdivision, wheat products will be fortified only with vitamins and minerals. The third subdivision will receive its wheat products unfortified. Four villages of each subdivision will be selected in which to measure the clinical effects of fortification. These twelve villages will provide a population of more that 12,000 from which approximately 2,000 children, ages 1—5 years, will be measured for height, weight, skin fold, leg length, haemoglobin, haematocrit, and possibly serum protein, albumin, and globulin. Mortality statistics will also be obtained. The inhabitants of half the villages will be given basic immunizations and anti-helminth treatment.

This study is unique from other village-level tests in that the co-operation of the subjects is not required. In similar field studies to investigate the effects of nutritional supplements on physical and mental development, there have been feeding stations or special institutions such as orphanages in which test foods are distributed. Or there have been educational campaigns to inform the people of the tests and why their food habits and/or foods are being altered. A fundamental aspect of these studies is that the co-operation of the people is required. But in the Tunisian project, no such co-operation is involved. The villagers will receive the foods which they will proceed to consume in their normal manner. From an experimental point of view, this is desirable since no new variable is being introduced.

The conclusions drawn from this project will be valid for any country in which people derive the major part of their calories and protein from a single cereal source and where there is poverty. The conclusions need not be restricted to wheat-eating situations. They would be equally valid where rice or corn supply the bulk of a population's food energy and nutrient requirements.

### Evaluation of results

Much thought has been given to the criteria necessary for drawing conclusions from the project results. It has been suggested that the following effects will at least have to be found in order to conclude that lysine fortification of wheat can appreciably improve child health under the practicalities of life:

(1) A decrease in the mortality of pre-school children by a magnitude of 10–20 per cent.

(2) A 50–80 per cent decrease in the incidence of Kwashiorkor.

(3) A statistically significant reduction in child morbidity.

## WORLD-WIDE ACTIVITIES

A number of goals have been achieved and efforts launched within the past 3 years which collectively have advanced the potential for amino acid fortification. Some of these are below:

(1) *Lowered costs of amino acids:* The price of lysine has been lowered to $1 per lb. Reliable estimates suggest that manufacturing costs can be reduced to the vicinity of 40 cents per lb.

(2) *Animal feeding:* Use of lysine in animal feeds is now a practical reality even where soy bean protein concentrate is the major supplement to grain.

(3) *Modern Bread:* Modern Bakers, Ltd., an enterprise of the Goverments of India, inaugurated its first bakery unit in Bombay on January 2, 1968. Together with the technical assistance of USAID, the Goverments of Canada and Australia co-operated under the Colombo plan to provide India with automatic baking equipment and the training of personnel in its use. Modern Bread, the name of the product, is fortified with vitamin A, riboflavin, thiamine, niacin, iron, and lysine. The level of production is aimed for 80 million loaves (400 g) yearly. At this production level, it is the largest amino acid fortification programme in the world. The Dutch Government is supplying the lysine for the initial programme through a government to government donation. The

276

reception given to Modern Bread has exceeded all expectation. Competitive bakeries have approached Modern Bakeries for the fortification formula.

(4) *Incaparina:* The Central American high protein food ' Incaparina ' has been fortified with lysine for the past year and a half.

(5) *Decree by Peruvian Government:* In May 1968 President Fernando Belaunde Terry issued Supreme Decree No. D. S. 032–68–A6 which states that '. . .lysine enrichment of popularly consumed grains and their derivatives is of social interest and national necessity.' Initially, wheat milled in Peru will be fortified; then rice. Though there has been a government change, indications are that this will not affect implementation of the Decree.

(6) *Harvard Rice Fortification Project:* The Agency for International Development has recently awarded a research grant to the Department of Nutrition in the Harvard School of Public Health to establish levels of addition and to evaluate the quantitative and qualitative effects on infants and young children of fortifying rice with the limiting amino acids lysine and threonine. The rice will be fortified by adding 'synthetic rice grains' containing the amino acids, vitamins, and minerals to regular Thai rice. A second objective is to define marketing patterns by which fortification might be introduced into the usual Thai commercial channels of distribution.

(7) *INCAP-Rutgers Corn Fortification Project:* The Institute for Nutrition for Central America and Panama (INCAP) and the Food Science Department at Rutgers University have submitted to AID a research proposal entitled 'A Practical Approach to the Lysine and Tryptophan Supplementation of Lime-Treated Corn.' INCAP's prior research has shown that the protein quality of lime-treated corn can be easily improved by using only lysine and tryptophan or by using protein concentrates in combination with lysine. INCAP and Rutgers proposed to carry out research to determine how to put their finding into practice in Latin America where there are many small mills and only a few large central mills.

(8) *Small-Scale Human Feeding Studies – India:* There are a number of small-scale human feeding studies on amino acid fortification in India. Dr. Shelia Pereria at the Christian Medical College and Hospital in Vellore, South India is feeding lysine-fortified wheat to pre-school children to study effects on growth. The children receive 200 g of wheat per day which supplies nearly all the protein and about 70 per cent of the daily calorie intake. Dr. Pereria is undertaking a similar study with rice.

Drs. H. A. B. Papria and Gopalan are directing a number of human (and animal) feeding studies.

277

(9) *Human Feeding Studies – Japan and Iran:* There have been a number of testing projects in Japan. Active workers are Professor Tadataka Fuku of Tokushima University and Dr. Toshu Oiso.

A field trial to measure the value of lysine-fortified wheat in a school lunch programme has been planned for Iran. It will be undertaken by the Food and Nutrition Institute of Iran with the help of Dutch State Mines, CARE and the technical advise of the UN's Protein Advisory Group. Project Director is Dr. H. Hedayat.

(10) *Indonesian Workshop on Food:* The Indonesian Institute of Sciences – U.S. National Academy of Sciences sponsored a Workshop on Food in Djakarta in May, 1968. The Workshop recommended that all wheat flour imported into Indonesia be fortified with vitamins, minerals, and 0.2 per cent lysine. Under study is the possibility for the Japanese Government to donate to Indonesia a cost equivalent value of lysine in place of a specified amount of food under its Food Aid Convention Commitment.

In addition to conventional fortification approaches, there are others which are now being seriously considered. These are as follows:

(1) *Salt Fortification:* In order to distribute lysine to rural cereal-eating populations which do not utilize central mills, the suggestion has been made that lysine be added to 'common table salt' which is used as a condiment for cereals. Officials in India have shown an active interest in this approach as a result of positive experiences with iodized salt. A salt fortification conference which discussed iron and calcium as well as lysine addition was held in Hyderabad in the spring of 1968. A number of technological problems have been uncovered concerning methodology of lysine addition and product stability. Research is under way in the laboratories of companies such as Merck and Hoffman-LaRoche to solve these technical problems.

(2) *Nutricube:* An option to salt fortification in reaching rural areas (and urban also) is the concept of a 'pill' containing needed vitamins, minerals and amino acids. This would be added to the cooking utensil in which the major dietary staple for the family is prepared. Samples have been produced by Hoffman-LaRoche; they have been named nutricubes. Much work is still needed on determining the nutrients and their levels to be incorporated into a nutricube.

(3) *MSG Fortification:* In many countries monosodium glutamate (MSG) is widely used as a condiment for rice and other foods. Therefore, it is logical to consider this as a vehicle for amino acid distribution. A country being considered for study of the concept is the Philippines.

## CONCLUSIONS

It has been my intention to indicate why fortification of food staples with amino acids (and protein concentrates) is a practical approach for combating protein malnutrition and why its use can have an immediate large-scale beneficial effect. It can benefit people who derive their nourishment from one or two cereals, legumes and starchy foods. In theory, it is possible for combinations of cereals and legumes to have amino acid patterns which complement each other to upgrade the quality of total protein in the diet; but the simultaneous possibility of complementing food crops within a specific country or region occurs irregularly in real life. Thus, fortification is an economically and socially desirable method for overcoming this situation. Without changing eating habits and increasing crop acreage, it increases the amount of protein available for use by humans.

It is important that fortification should be considered in all programmes designed to overcome protein malnutrition. Its importance in any programme will be dependent upon the total economic system in which it will be used. There can be no doubt that it has a significant role to play in the solution of the world's protein problems.

## REFERENCES

Abbott, J.C. (1966). *Adv. Chem. Ser.* No.57, 1

Altschul, A.M. (1967). *Science, N.Y.* **158**, 221

– (1969). *Proc. Joint Annual Meeting of American Assoc. Cereal Chemists and American Oil Chemists Society*. April, 1968, Washington. p. 82

Anonymous (1967). *International Agricultural Development Newsletter*. No.31, 6-7, Wash., D.C.

Anonymous (1968). *International Action to avert the Impending Protein Crisis, Report to the Economic and Social Council of the Advisory Committee on the Application of Science and Technology to Development (1968)*, United Nations Document E/4343/Rev. 1, p.14, New York

Bressani, R., Wilson, D.L., Behar, M., Chung, M. and Scrimshaw, N.S. (1963). *J. Nutr.* **79**, 333

Brooke, C.L. (1968). *J. Agric. Food Chem.* **16**, 163

Edman, M., Forbes, R.M. and Johnson, B.C. (1968). *J. Nutr.* **96**, 1

Fredrickson, D.S. (1968). *Bull. New York Acad. Medicine.* **44**, 985

Harris, R.S. (1968). *J. Agric. Food Chem.* **16**, 149

Hegsted, D.M. (1968). *Amer. J. Clin. Nutr.* **21**, 688

– (1969). *Proc. Joint Annual Meeting of Am. Ass. Cereal Chemists and American Oil Chemists Society*. April, 1968, Washington, p. 38

Howe, E.E., Jansen, G.R. and Anson, M.L. (1967). *Am. J. Clin. Nutr.* **20**, 1134

Jansen, G.R. (1969). *Am. J. Clin. Nutr.* **22**, 38

– and Howe, E.E. (1964). *Am. J. Clin. Nutr.* **15**, 262

Osborne, T.B. and Mendel, L.B. (1914). *J. biol. Chem.* **17**, 325

Rosenberg, H.R. and Rohdenburg, E.L. (1952). *Archs. Biochem. Biophys.* **37**, 461

Rosenfield, D. (1969). *Proc. of Conference on Protein Foods in the Caribbean*, August, 1968, Georgetown, sponsored by Caribbean Food and Nutrition Institute, Jamaica, p.58

# STRUCTURAL AND NUTRITIONAL PROPERTIES
# OF CEREAL PROTEINS

## N.L. KENT

*Flour Milling and Baking Research
Association, St. Albans*

## INTRODUCTION

In their preface to the Proceedings of the 12th Easter School at Sutton
Bonington, in 1965, on 'The Growth of Cereals and Grasses', Professors
Milthorpe and Ivins enunciated an essential difference between these two
great groups of plants. Cereals, they said, are annuals grown for conveniently stored carbohydrate; grasses are perennials grown for a continued supply of carbohydrate and protein. It is perhaps a fallacy all too
widely held that cereal grains and their milled products are no more than a
source of carbohydrate; the allocation of two whole lectures in this
Symposium to a consideration of cereal proteins is evidence that those
responsible for the programme are of the opinion that the contribution of
cereal proteins to the human dietary is by no means insignificant.

According to the 1966 National Food Survey (Ministry of Agriculture,
1968), cereals contributed 28.2 per cent of the total protein consumption
in the U.K. in 1966. On a world-wide scale, cereals provided 47.5 per cent
of the proteins consumed by peoples of the world in 1960 (*Milling*, 1968).
Moreover, the proteins of cereals, besides being valuable nutrients in the
edible products, perform important functions, perhaps described as
'structural', in the grain and during its processing, which are dependent on
their chemical and mechanical properties. Proteins are largely responsible
for hindering the disruption of the endosperm cell contents during the
roller milling of hard wheat, and for conferring upon the endosperm a
texture which may be hard or soft; they have a lot to do with the precise
way in which the endosperm shatters during the milling process, and with
the sizes and types of particles that result. Their mechanical properties,
together with those of the starch granules, are paramount in the processes

280

of fine grinding and of protein shifting in flour by means of air classification; and, of course, they play an essential role in bread making, as my colleague, Dr. Chamberlain, will be telling you in the following paper.

I therefore intend to deal, in this contribution, first with the structural properties of the proteins of cereal grains, and particularly of those in the endosperm, and afterwards briefly discuss their nutritional properties.

## STRUCTURAL PROPERTIES

### Distribution of protein

The protein content of all the common cereals averages around 10 per cent at natural moisture content – although individual samples of particular cereals might contain as little as 6 per cent or more than 20 per cent.

The protein is distributed non-uniformly among the morphological tissues of the grain, the highest concentrations occurring in the outermost, or subaleurone, part of the so-called 'starchy endosperm' (Kent, 1966) and in the germ and the aleurone layer of the endosperm. The inner endosperm has a lower protein content than that of the whole grain, and there is very little in the pericarp.

By manual dissection of whole grains and microanalysis of the parts, Hinton (1953) mapped the distribution of protein in wheat and in maize (Table 1). For his dissection of wheat, Hinton used a soft English variety, Vilmorin 27, with a relatively low protein content, 8.75 per cent (N x 6.25). The low ratio of protein content, of the outer endosperm to that of the inner endosperm (2.2) was typical of low protein soft winter wheats. The staining of a transverse section of the grain of this type of wheat with a protein stain, such as Orange G, gives a semi-quantitative estimate of the protein gradient, and shows that the higher protein

Table 1

Distribution of protein in wheat and maize
(From Hinton, 1953 by courtesy of the American Asscn. of Cereal Chemists)

| Part of grain | Proportion of kernel | | Protein content* | | Proportion of total nutrient in kernel | |
|---|---|---|---|---|---|---|
| | Wheat % | Maize % | Wheat % | Maize % | Wheat % | Maize % |
| Pericarp | 8 | 6.5 | 4.4 | 3.0 | 4.0 | 2.2 |
| Aleurone | 7 | 2.2 | 19.7 | 19.2 | 15.5 | 4.7 |
| Endosperm | (82.5) | (79.6) | | | (72.5) | (71.0) |
| outer | 12.5 | 3.9 | 13.7 | 27.7 | 19.4 | 11.9 |
| middle | 12.5 | 58.1 | 8.8 | 7.5 | 12.4 | 48.2 |
| inner | 57.5 | 17.6 | 6.2 | 5.6 | 40.7 | 10.9 |
| Embryo | 1 | 1.1 | 33.3 | 26.5 | 3.5 | 3.2 |
| Scutellum | 1.5 | 10.6 | 26.7 | 16.0 | 4.5 | 18.9 |

*N x 6.25, 14.5 per cent moisture basis

content is restricted to the outermost single cell layer of the starchy endosperm (the 'subaleurone endosperm'). These cells, although of higher protein content than the inner endosperm cells, are still tightly packed with starch granules.

A different appearance is shown by a similarly stained section of a high protein hard wheat (e.g. U.S. Hard Red Winter). There is a much greater intensity of staining and concentration of protein in the subaleurone endosperm cells, many of which contain only a few, peripherally situated, starch granules and a large central mass of protein. The appearance of subaleurone endosperm cells from the two contrasting types of wheat is shown in *Plate I*. The protein contents (N x 5.7, 14 per cent moisture basis) of pure specimens of subaleurone endosperm and inner endosperm obtained from Hard Red Winter wheat averaged 45 per cent and 11 per cent, respectively (Kent, 1966). The subaleurone endosperm comprises some 11 per cent of the whole grain by weight (Kent and Jones, 1952), and the protein of this single cellular layer, in the case of the Hard Red Winter wheat, accounts for about 25 per cent of the total endosperm protein.

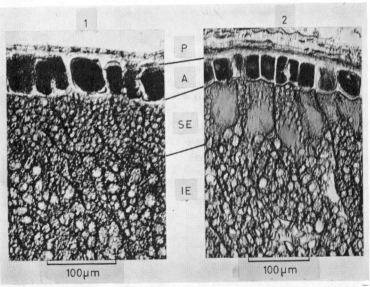

*Plate I. Part transverse sections of grains of a soft English wheat, Capelle Desprez (1) and of Hard Red Winter wheat (2). The subaleurone endosperm cells of Capelle are tightly packed with starch granules; those of HRW contain large protein deposits and fewer starch granules. P: pericarp; A: aleurone layer; SE: subaleurone endosperm; IE: inner endosperm*

*Protein in the endosperm cell*

The inner starchy endosperm of wheat consists of largish cells having a thin, flimsy cell wall, and a mass of cell contents which is comprised of starch granules in two size ranges (0.5–7.5 $\mu$m, 15–40 $\mu$m), and a matrix of protein in which the starch granules are embedded and which holds the cell contents together.

Proteins in cereal endosperm have been classified structurally in numerous ways. None of these classifications is entirely satisfactory, but all have made some contribution to our knowledge of cereal proteins. I shall try to reconcile some of the suggested classifications.

Treatment of wheat flour in succession with water, dilute salt solutions, 70 per cent aqueous ethanol, and dilute acid or alkali removes protein fractions that have been called respectively albumin, globulin, prolamin (gliadin), and glutelin (glutenin) since Osborne first carried out this fractionation in 1907. Since this early work, cereal protein chemists have shown that none of these fractions is a pure protein. The albumin and globulin, however, have lower molecular weights, and faster electrophoretic mobilities on starch gel, than the other fractions. The gliadin and glutenin, about 80–85 per cent of the total endosperm protein, together with small amounts of other proteins, lipids and starch, made up the 'gluten', or hydrated protein, that is obtained as a coherent mass when a flour-water dough is kneaded under running water to remove the starch and water-solubles. Although gliadin is soluble in aqueous alcohol, and glutenin in dilute acids and alkalis, these two fractions together are often referred to as 'insoluble protein', meaning insoluble in water and salt solutions; 'soluble' protein generally refers to the albumin and globulin.

When endosperm is ground finely enough to disintegrate the cell contents, the starch granules mostly separate one from another while remaining intact and unbroken, whereas the protein matrix breaks into tiny pieces which have an average size about half that of the larger starch granules. Fragmentation of endosperm is shown diagrammatically in *Figure 1*. Hess *et al.* (1952) observed particles of free protein in finely ground flour and called them 'Zwickel' or interstitial (wedge) protein, from their shape. Hess also postulated the existence of an exceedingly thin layer of protein around each starch granule, and described this as 'Haft' or adherent protein. He calculated the thickness of the adherent protein layer as 0.22 $\mu$m, and later showed, by electron microscopy, that it consisted of a series of fibrils (Hess *et al.*, 1955).

When finely ground wheat flour is fractionated into fairly sharply defined particle size fractions, a partial separation of protein from starch is effected. The critical particle sizes are in the sub-sieve zone, and the separation is carried out by means of air classification, a process of centrifugation in air. By classifying at about 17 μm and 35 μm in succession, flour is subdivided into three fractions, of which the finest, 0–17 μm, contains a concentration of particles of interstitial protein, the intermediate, 17–35 μm, a concentration of starch granules (carrying the

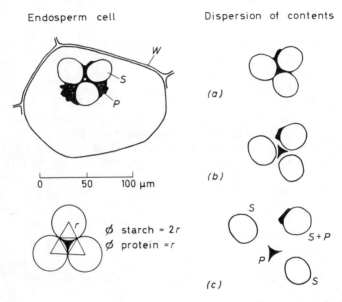

*Figure 1. Diagram showing the dispersion of the cell contents of wheat endosperm. The protein matrix fractures at points of weakness, or separates from the starch granules. S: starch granule; P: protein; W: endosperm cell wall. The small diagram, bottom left, shows that the dimensions of the interstitial protein particle are approximately half those of the large starch granules.*

thin layer of adherent protein on their surfaces), while the coarse fraction, over 35 μm, is undisintegrated endosperm particles (*see* Table 2).

The interstitial protein, being less dense than the starch-plus-adherent protein, can be separated from other constituents of finely ground flour by flotation in non-aqueous liquids. By this means, Hess (1954, 1954a) found that interstitial and adherent proteins differed in their properties: a cohesive ball of gluten could be washed out and recovered from interstitial protein, but not from adherent. Interstitial protein differs from adherent protein in having a higher ratio of aqueous alcohol-soluble gliadin to salt-soluble albumin (Gallenkov, 1952; Elton and Ewart, 1964; Coulson and Sim, 1965), and there are differences in amino acid composition (Rohrlich and Niederauer, 1965).

284

Table 2

Yield and protein content of air-classified fractions of flours with or without pinned disc grinding
(From Kent, 1966b by courtesy of the American Asscn. of Cereal Chemists)

| | Fine (0–17 μm) | | Medium (17–35 μm) | | Coarse (over 35 μm) | |
|---|---|---|---|---|---|---|
| | Yield % | Protein content* % | Yield % | Protein content* % | Yield % | Protein content* % |
| Hard wheat flour † | | | | | | |
| Unground | 1 | 17.1 | 9 | 9.9 | 90 | 13.8 |
| Ground | 12 | 18.9 | 41 | 10.0 | 47 | 14.7 |
| Soft wheat flour † | | | | | | |
| Unground | 7 | 14.5 | 45 | 5.3 | 48 | 8.9 |
| Ground | 20 | 15.7 | 71 | 5.0 | 9 | 9.5 |

*N x 5.7, 14 per cent moisture basis
† Protein content:  hard wheat flour 13.6 per cent,
    soft wheat flour 7.6 per cent.

*Structural classes of protein*

These observations suggest the existence in the endosperm of two fundamentally different structural classes of protein, and supporting evidence was advanced by the late Professor Morton and his associates at the Waite Agricultural Institute, Australia, who studied the changes in the main chemical constituents of wheat endosperm during maturation of the kernel. This work was reviewed by my colleague, Dr. J.J.C. Hinton, in his lecture on 'Biochemical Aspects of Quality in Cereals', given at the 12th Easter School on 'The Growth of Cereals and Grasses' (Hinton, 1966).

In the Australian work referred to (Jennings and Morton, 1963), the protein was fractionally extracted from endosperm of developing wheat grains in a modified Osborne fractionation by successive treatment with sodium pyrophosphate – which gave the so-called 'soluble' fraction – and with dilute acetic acid and dilute sodium hydroxide – which gave the gliadin/glutenin, or 'insoluble' fraction. The ratio of insoluble to soluble fractions steadily increased from 14 to 46 days after flowering because, although each type of protein was accumulating in the grain, the insoluble protein was accumulating at a greater rate (*see* Table 3). Amino acid compositions of the soluble and insoluble fractions also differed.

Another kind of fractionation was also achieved. Endosperm of the developing grain was homogenized and fractionated by density gradient centrifugation, obtaining denser and lighter fractions. The amino acid composition of the denser fraction agreed with that of the fraction extracted with acetic acid, and that of the lighter fraction with that of the pyrophosphate-soluble fraction. Moreover, the denser fraction was

Table 3

Nitrogen in protein fractions of developing wheat endosperm
(From Jennings and Morton, 1963 by courtesy of C.S.I.R.O.)

| Protein fraction | Days after flowering | | | | Rate of increase 14–46 days ($\mu$g/grain/day) |
|---|---|---|---|---|---|
| | 14 | 18 | 32 | 46 | |
| | | ($\mu$g/grain) | | | |
| Pyrophosphate soluble | 4 | 36 | 51 | 81 | 2.4 |
| Acetic acid soluble | 19 | 57 | 163 | 318 | 9.3 |
| Sodium hydroxide sol. | 28 | 56 | 116 | 220 | 6.0 |

found, upon examination by electron microscopy, to consist of particles having a definite structure, and resembling particles seen in the electron micrographs (Graham *et al.*, 1963).

Using radioactive tracers, the utilization of sulphur by the endosperm in developing ears of wheat was followed. Radioactivity appeared first in the insoluble fraction of the protein, although the final level of radioactivity was higher in the soluble fraction, which contained the greater proportion of sulphur-containing amino acids. When the two protein fractions separated by centrifugation were incubated with tagged amino acids, it was found that each was capable of synthesizing its own type of protein (Graham and Morton, 1963; Graham *et al.*, 1963). These findings led to the conclusion that soluble and insoluble protein are different entities, formed separately and existing independently in the endosperm cell.

Electron micrographs of developing endosperm were re-examined in the light of these findings, and it was concluded that certain particles were protein-forming bodies, or proteoplasts, and that these comprised the dense fraction of insoluble protein from the centrifugation.

It has been known for a long time that much of the protein in the endosperm of maize is localized in granules (Harz, 1885), and development of the granules has been studied (Weatherwax, 1930; Duvick, 1955, 1961). Protein granules can easily be seen in the endosperm of maize and of sorghum, using the light microscope. Similar protein granules probably exist in the endosperm of all cereals.

The structure of the developing endosperm cell is now seen as a cell wall enclosing a general ground substance of protoplasm corresponding to the soluble protein, in which various organelles are embedded. The most prominent are amyloplasts in which starch is synthesized, and proteoplasts in which protein is synthesized. The endoplasmic reticulum present in the cell, is also a site of protein synthesis. Amyloplasts and proteoplasts have bounding membranes of lipoprotein (Buttrose, 1963).

The type of protein synthesized in the proteoplasts is generally referred to as 'storage' protein, perhaps not the most suitable term as it implies the absence of any metabolic function in the cell.

The proteoplasts, which may measure up to $20\,\mu m$, in the immature grain (Morton *et al.*, 1964), become compressed and distorted by contraction of the grain during the dehydration that accompanies maturation, and finally appear in the milled flour as the major constituent in the particles of interstitial protein described by Hess.

Turning to a brief consideration of the distribution of protein species within the endosperm cell, there is evidence in the case of maize that the protein granules are composed largely of the prolamin zein, while most of the matrix protein surrounding the granules is of the alkali-soluble, glutelin type of protein (Duvick, 1961; Christianson *et al.*, 1968).

In the case of wheat, the protein bodies have been shown (Graham *et al.*, 1963) to be the sites of accumulation of the acetic acid-soluble proteins (primarily gliadin and glutenin) and contain the principal storage protein of the endosperm. Further fractionation of the homogenized endosperm material by density gradient provided Jennings and Morton (1963) with a fraction of 'small protein bodies' (ranging $0.1–0.3\,\mu m$ in diameter) which had a composition closely resembling that of the alkali-soluble proteins. They concluded that the protein bodies are not necessarily uniform in composition, and suggested that their composition might change during growth. An alternative explanation of these results is that the fraction of small protein bodies, with a relatively large surface area, would contain a larger proportion of lipoprotein membrane, the protein moiety of which differs in composition from that of the storage protein deposit.

The soluble protein, in the supernatant fraction from centrifugation of homogenized endosperm was identified by Graham *et al.* (1964) with the cytoplasmic ground substance of the developing endosperm cell, and more specifically by Morton *et al.* (1964) with the endoplasmic reticulum and other organelle membranes. At maturity the adherent protein of Hess, situated on the surface of the starch granules, would become part of this 'soluble protein' fraction.

There is thus experimental evidence for the existence in wheat endosperm cells of two functionally different types of protein, formed in different ways, and having different chemical constitutions, although these two types do not correspond exactly with Hess's interstitial and adherent protein fractions. It would seem that storage protein, formed in the proteoplasts, predominates in interstitial protein, but that the latter will contain, besides, a proportion of membrane protein and cytoplasmic protein. Hess's adherent protein, however, is likely to consist largely of

287

membrane and/or cytoplasmic protein. To this extent, then, Hess's sub-division of the endosperm protein into interstitial and adherent portions does appear to represent the concentration of two distinct protein species into one or other of his fractions. An attempt to relate the various schemes for classifying endosperm protein fractions is shown diagram-matically in *Figure 2*.

*Texture of endosperm*

The physical appearance or texture of the endosperm of wheat grain may take one or other of two forms, described as 'vitreous', or 'mealy'. Vitreous endosperm is translucent, glassy and physically hard; mealy

| *Basis of classification* | *Protein fractions* | | | |
|---|---|---|---|---|
| Starch gel electrophoretic mobility | Fast moving | Fastest moving | Slow moving | Immobile |
| Protein species (Osborne) | Albumin | Globulin | Gliadin | Glutenin |
| Solubility | Aqueous sol. | Salt sol. | 70% aq. EtOH sol. | Alkali sol. |
| Location in cell | Cytoplasm (attached to membranes) | Cytoplasm (membranes & endoplasmic reticulum) | Granules (protein bodies) | |
| Function in cell | Metabolic (enzymic) | Structural | Storage | |
| Amino acid composition: basic amino acids | more | | less | |
| glu + pro | less | | more | |
| Endosperm fragmentation (Hess) | Haft (adherent) | | Zwickel (interstitial) | |

*Figure 2. Various schemes proposed for the classification of the proteins of wheat endosperm, and their relationship*

endosperm is opaque, floury-looking, and physically soft. The opacity of mealy endosperm is due to the presence of innumerable tiny cracks or fissures in the endosperm which constitute refractive surfaces. Vitreous and mealy portions of endosperm, dissected from mosaic grains of Hybrid 46 wheat, differed in protein content: vitreous 9.12 per cent, mealy 5.76 per cent (McDermott and Pace, 1960).

All immature wheat grains are vitreous; as maturation proceeds, some grains remain vitreous, while others become mealy. Duvick (1961), describing the situation in maize, has suggested that the vitreous or mealy condition is related to the ratio of viscous protein (clear cytoplasm) to granular inclusions (starch granules, protein granules). The viscous protein in immature endosperm is plastic and plentiful enough to encase all the granular inclusions. As the endosperm dries out during maturation, the viscous protein loses volume and elasticity; it shrinks and sometimes becomes insufficient in volume to encase all the granules completely; in such cases it ruptures. The cells in which the viscous protein has thus been shattered become the mealy endosperm cells. The relative proportions of soluble and storage proteins thus influence the texture of the endosperm, and this affects the milling quality of the grain.

The endosperm of the mature wheat kernel has both plastic and brittle properties, the one or the other being exhibited during grinding according to the moisture content of the endosperm and the method of grinding (Kent, 1966a). When grinding of endosperm is effected by means of a roller mill, a machine in which pressure is applied relatively slowly to the particles, so that compression takes a measurable time, the particles exhibit plasticity, and become increasingly disorganized as moisture content of the material at the moment of grinding is increased; this is so because plasticity increases with moisture content. If the same material is pulverized in a pin mill, in which the particles are fragmented instantaneously, the particles exhibit brittleness, and the degree of fragmentation increases as moisture content at the moment of grinding is reduced. It seems probable that the protein, rather than the endosperm cell walls (which are flimsy and weak) or the starch granules (which remain intact during fragmentation of the endosperm), is responsible for the phenomena of brittleness and plasticity; the protein is thus important as a structural element in the endosperm cell, governing the manner in which the endosperm becomes fragmented during milling.

## NUTRITIONAL PROPERTIES

Protein in food is required to provide amino acids from which new protein can be synthesized, to permit growth in the developing organism, to make good that lost in metabolism, and to resist infection and aid recovery from sickness and injury. Certain of the amino acids cannot be synthesized by the organism, and these, the so-called 'essential amino acids', must all be supplied as such in the food and, moreover, they must all be present simultaneously, at the sites of synthesis of the proteins. Some of the vegetable proteins differ from the proteins of meat, milk and eggs in having a lower content of one or more of the essential amino acids, in which they are therefore said to be 'deficient'.

## Variation among cereals

Ewart (1967) determined the amino acid composition of the protein in the flours of five cereals (wheat, rye, barley, oats, maize) under comparable conditions (Table 4), and concluded that the overall similarity of amino acid composition among the cereals suggested a common ancestor. Greater variation can be tolerated, and is found, among the storage proteins than among the albumins and globulins of the soluble fraction, which consists largely of enzymes having metabolic functions (Ewart, 1968). The average molecular weight of an amino acid is greatest in wheat and lowest in maize; this may indicate that wheat is more highly evolved than maize (Ewart, 1967).

Table 4

Amino acid residues in $10^5$ g of recovered anhydro amino acids from cereal flours
(From Ewart, 1967 by courtesy of the Society of Chemical Industry)

| Amino acid | Wheat | Rye | Barley | Oats | Maize |
|---|---|---|---|---|---|
| Cystine (half) | 25.7 | 28.7 | 28.0 | 45.3 | 30.6 |
| Methionine | 10.2 | 12.9 | 13.0 | 14.3 | 15.6 |
| Aspartic acid | 31.4 | 48.5 | 41.0 | 66.1 | 54.3 |
| Threonine | 27.1 | 33.3 | 32.4 | 36.3 | 38.8 |
| Serine | 63.0 | 58.4 | 54.2 | 64.2 | 61.5 |
| Glutamic acid | 281.3 | 227.4 | 226.7 | 173.7 | 149.0 |
| Proline | 124.2 | 123.6 | 123.2 | 59.8 | 100.5 |
| Glycine | 51.6 | 53.2 | 51.3 | 71.1 | 59.7 |
| Alanine | 35.1 | 50.9 | 47.4 | 66.8 | 97.7 |
| Valine | 37.2 | 44.0 | 46.2 | 50.1 | 49.3 |
| Isoleucine | 31.9 | 32.1 | 32.2 | 33.8 | 32.0 |
| Leucine | 59.6 | 59.4 | 63.3 | 68.0 | 102.8 |
| Tyrosine | 15.9 | 13.1 | 16.7 | 16.1 | 14.4 |
| Phenylalanine | 34.5 | 33.5 | 37.2 | 35.5 | 33.2 |
| Lysine | 15.4 | 25.4 | 24.0 | 34.7 | 27.5 |
| Histidine | 15.8 | 15.3 | 14.1 | 15.3 | 23.1 |
| Arginine | 21.9 | 28.3 | 29.7 | 43.3 | 31.7 |
| Tryptophan | 6.0 | 9.5 | 10.7 | 10.5 | 5.0 |
| Total | 887.8 | 897.5 | 891.3 | 904.9 | 926.7 |

*Nutritive value of wheat protein*

The value of wheaten flour as a source of amino acids was strikingly demonstrated in the studies of Widdowson and McCance (1954) with undernourished German Children of 5–15 years of age. In their trials at Duisburg, wheaten flour provided 75 per cent of the total calories, and the average protein intake was 61–73 g per day, of which about two-thirds came from bread and only about 8 g were obtained from animal sources. This diet, maintained for 18 months, provided all the nutrients required for a high rate of growth and development. About this investigation, Davidson and Passmore (1963) commented: "McCance and Widdowson's only firm deduction from this experiment was that wheat in any form is an excellent food for growing children. Their results show that wheat proteins are capable of maintaining high rates of growth for a long period. Bread indeed is a good source of protein and has been wrongly condemned as a 'starchy food'."

Nevertheless, wheat protein is deficient in lysine, in the sense that lysine is the amino acid that limits its nutritive value when its growth-promoting potential is compared with that of animal protein at lower levels of protein intake. Data quoted by Moran and Pace (1967) show that bread and flour contributed 16 per cent or more of the dietary intake of every one of the essential amino acids except lysine in the average British diet in 1964, but contributed only 7.6 per cent of the total lysine intake. In an average mixed diet, wheat protein is an important and cheap contributor to the nutritive value of the diet; its relative deficiency of lysine is obscured because of lysine supplementation by other constituents of the diet.

The effect of the correction of lysine deficiency is strikingly shown in feeding trials with weanling rats, whose lysine requirements are high because of their rapid potential growth in relation to their food intake. The growth rate of weanling rats fed on bread containing 12 per cent protein as the sole source of protein was approximately trebled by the addition of 0.2–0.3 per cent of *L*-lysine (Rosenberg and Rohdenburg, 1952; Hutchinson *et al.*, 1959), and with the addition of 0.5 per cent *L*-lysine plus 0.1 per cent *L*-threonine (the next limiting amino acid) became comparable with that obtained with a good quality protein such as casein (Hutchinson *et al.*, 1959).

Comparison of the amino acid compositions of the protein of wheat and of the white flour milled from it (*see* Table 5) shows that the flour protein has less of the basic amino acids arginine and lysine but more glutamic acid and proline than the whole grain protein. This is a consequence of the removal, during the milling process, of the aleurone layer of the endosperm, which forms part of the milling product bran, and of the germ, both of which are poor in storage protein, but rich in a type of protein characterized by particularly high contents of arginine and lysine (Table 5). It thus appears that a highly nutritious portion of the protein of the wheat grain is being diverted from white flour to the milling by-products, which are normally used as animal feed. Attention is now being paid, at the Flour Milling and Baking Research Association, to means whereby the aleurone protein can be utilized. The desirability of including aleurone protein in bread-baking flour, although this would be nutritionally advantageous, is questionable; its content of gluten proteins (glutenin and gliadin) is negligible, and the presence of sulphydryl groups could possibly lower bread-baking quality of the flour.

These amino acid data indicate that the nutritive value of the protein in 100 per cent wholemeal should be superior to that in white flour of 70 per cent extraction rate, as the lysine is less limiting in the former than in the latter. This is indeed the case when fed to rapidly-growing, weanling rats,

Table 5

Amino acid composition of protein in grain, flour, germ and aleurone cell contents of wheat

| Amino acid | (g *amino acid* N/ 100 g *total* N) | | | | |
| | Grain* | Flour* (patent) | Germ* | Flour† | Aleurone† |
| --- | --- | --- | --- | --- | --- |
| Alanine | 4.2 | 3.3 | 6.5 | 2.8 | 4.6 |
| Arginine | 10.6 | 8.4 | 15.4 | 6.8 | 21.1 |
| Aspartic acid | 3.7 | 3.0 | 5.7 | 2.4 | 4.8 |
| Cystine | 1.5 | 1.5 | 0.9 | – | 1.2 |
| Glutamic acid | 20.0 | 22.9 | 9.5 | 20.0 | 8.9 |
| Glycine | 6.1 | 4.6 | 8.0 | – | – |
| Histidine | 4.1 | 3.7 | 4.3 | 3.4 | 6.1 |
| Isoleucine | 2.9 | 3.0 | 2.7 | 2.2 | 1.9 |
| Leucine | 5.1 | 5.1 | 4.5 | 4.6 | 3.6 |
| Lysine | 3.7 | 2.7 | 7.2 | 2.2 | 5.0 |
| Methionine | 1.2 | 1.2 | 1.3 | 1.0 | 0.8 |
| Phenylalanine | 2.6 | 2.8 | 2.0 | 2.7 | 2.0 |
| Proline | 9.0 | 10.6 | 4.6 | 9.0 | 2.7 |
| Serine | 5.3 | 5.5 | 4.7 | 3.9 | 3.4 |
| Threonine | 2.4 | 2.3 | 3.0 | 1.8 | 2.1 |
| Tryptophan | 1.1 | 0.9 | 0.9 | – | – |
| Tyrosine | 1.7 | 1.8 | 1.5 | 1.4 | 1.3 |
| Valine | 4.2 | 3.8 | 4.4 | 3.1 | 3.7 |

*From Hepburn *et al.* (1960), recalculated. Original data are given as g amino acid /16g N. The patent flour and germ were two mill streams obtained from the wheat (50 per cent HRS, 50 per cent HRW)

†From Stevens *et al.* (1963). Flour and aleurone obtained from Manitoba (HRS) wheat

whose rate of growth is better on wholemeal bread than on white bread (Chick, 1942; Widdowson and McCance, 1954; Hutchinson *et al.*, 1956). However, 8-week old rats, with a lower growth rate:food intake ratio, grow equally well on either bread (Widdowson and McCance, 1954), because their requirements for lysine are less exacting, and the same is true for human adults. Indeed, Widdowson and McCance, in their German experiments, found that the children grew equally well on diets containing flours of 70 per cent, 85 per cent or 100 per cent extraction rates, and the explanation is that, in the circumstances of this trial, bread formed so large a part of all the diets that each supplied adequate lysine. That is to say, each diet contained sufficient lysine to build as much body protein as was needed by the children.

In synthesizing this protein, the body would have taken in other amino acids in excess of requirements. It is here implied that because lysine is 'limiting', other amino acids are super-abundant, and a proportion of them cannot be utilized for the synthesis of protein. Such surplus amino acids are metabolized in the body to provide energy. Improvement of the lysine status of cereal proteins, by supplementation or by plant breeding, would thus lead to their more economical use in diets of lower protein content, and particularly in diets based largely on cereal products, upon which the less developed countries often depend.

*Lysine content of protein*

The amino acid composition of the proteins of developing wheat endosperm undergoes a change, the content of basic amino acids decreasing, that of glutamic acid and proline increasing, with degree of maturation (Pomeranz *et al.*, 1966). In the case of maize, the aqueous alcohol-soluble fraction, zein, is absent from the immature kernel; the proportion of zein increases with maturity, and eventually it becomes the predominant protein. At the same time, the amino acids found in significant amounts in zein (isoleucine, leucine, phenylalanine, arginine) increase, while those present in small amounts in zein (lysine, tryptophan, methionine) decrease, both on a nitrogen basis and on a kernel basis (Bressani and Conde, 1961).

McDermott and Pace (1960) found generally similar amino acid compositions for the proteins of flours from such dissimilar wheats as soft English and hard Manitoba, although increase in protein content of the endosperm was associated with relatively greater increase in glutamic acid and proline than of the basic amino acids lysine and arginine in the protein. Differences in amino acid composition of this nature were found between high protein vitreous and low protein mealy endosperm from mosaic grains (McDermott and Pace, 1960), and between high protein subaleurone and low protein inner regions of the endosperm (Kent and Evers, 1969) *see Figure 3*. These results reflect the higher proportion of the gluten proteins in endosperm of high protein content and, in general, the increase in ratio of storage to cytoplasmic protein, and of insoluble to soluble protein, with increasing protein content. Further explanation of the previous statement comes from consideration of the amino acid composition of the various types of protein in the wheat grain (Table 6), from which it is apparent that glutenin and gliadin (the storage proteins) contain relatively much more glutamic acid and proline and less lysine and arginine than are contained in albumin and globulin, typical of the soluble, cytoplasmic proteins.

Increasing the protein content of wheat endosperm by nitrogenous fertilizing produces a similar increase in ratio of storage to soluble types of protein, and a corresponding shift in amino acid composition. Lawrence *et al.* (1958) examined 142 wheats with protein content below 13.5 per

Table 6

Amino acid composition of fractions of wheat protein
(moles of anhydro amino acids per $10^5$ of recovered anhydro
amino acids)

| Amino acid | Glutenin* | Gliadin* | Albumin† | Globulin‡ |
|---|---|---|---|---|
| Cystine (half) | 23.2 | 29.0 | 58.5 | 123.4 |
| Methionine | 12.6 | 10.9 | 0 | 3.3 |
| Aspartic acid | 32.5 | 24.8 | 61.8 | 55.6 |
| Threonine | 30.7 | 21.3 | 25.0 | 44.5 |
| Serine | 61.8 | 53.6 | 46.3 | 102.0 |
| Glutamic acid | 256.8 | 301.1 | 125.7 | 47.0 |
| Proline | 105.9 | 142.0 | 76.3 | 33.6 |
| Glycine | 67.0 | 26.8 | 43.2 | 87.5 |
| Alanine | 39.0 | 28.6 | 65.2 | 56.3 |
| Valine | 42.8 | 41.6 | 72.6 | 21.7 |
| Isoleucine | 33.0 | 38.0 | 32.9 | 12.6 |
| Leucine | 58.1 | 60.6 | 85.5 | 83.0 |
| Tyrosine | 22.1 | 16.0 | 19.4 | 15.0 |
| Phenylalanine | 32.4 | 37.5 | 31.9 | 22.6 |
| Lysine | 17.6 | 5.0 | 78.4 | 98.0 |
| Histidine | 16.9 | 16.3 | 28.8 | 16.3 |
| Arginine | 26.5 | 17.4 | 45.0 | 98.1 |
| Tryptophan | 11.2 | 3.8 | n.d. | n.d. |
| Hydroxylysine | n.d. | n.d. | 1.6 | 0 |
| Total | 890.1 | 874.3 | 898.1 | 920.5 |
| Amide N | 236.1 | 198.7 | 23.8 | n.d. |

*From Ewart (1967a)
†From Waldschmidt-Leitz and Hochstrasser (1961)
‡From Fisher et al. (1968)

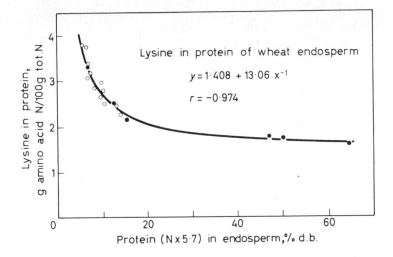

*Figure 3. The relationship between protein content of wheat endosperm and lysine content of the protein. The shape of the curve indicates that at quite low protein contents the protein has a relatively high lysine content, and that additional protein in the endosperm beyond the first 5 per cent or so contains only about 1.4 per cent lysine (on nitrogen basis). Hollow circles: data from McDermott and Pace (1960) for white flour and dissected endosperm; solid circles: data from Kent and Evers (1969), with other unpublished data, for inner and subaleurone endosperm*

cent and found a highly significant inverse correlation ($r = -0.73**$) between grain protein content and lysine content of the protein.

Inverse correlations between grain protein content and the content of certain essential amino acids, particularly lysine, in the protein have been found for other cereals also. Thus, for rice, Juliano *et al.* (1964) reported highly significant negative correlations of $-0.64$ for lysine, $-0.65$ for threonine, and $-0.72$ for methionine contents of the protein, respectively, with grain protein content.

In the case of sorghum, an increase in protein content was associated with a decrease in percentage of lysine in the protein (Virupaksha and Sastry, 1968); the protein increase was represented by an increase in the relative proportion of kafirin (a prolamin, soluble in 60 per cent aqueous ethanol) compared with glutelin, albumin and globulin fractions of the sorghum protein. Kafirin has a high content of glutamic acid, but is extremely low in lysine content. Hence, an increase in the kafirin portion of high protein sorghums explains the actual decrease in the percentage of lysine in the protein (Rooney and Clark, 1968).

In the case of maize, it is recognized that the grain is inadequate as a source of proteins for human and monogastric animals. Grain protein contents are low, and the protein has an unbalanced pattern of amino acids. Attempts to improve the nutritive value of maize by increasing the protein content, e.g. by selection, or by nitrogenous fertilizing, have failed because, as protein content increases, the storage prolamin, zein, becomes an increasing proportion of the total protein (Frey, 1951). Zein is practically devoid of lysine and tryptophan; thus, increase in total protein content is accompanied by decrease in lysine and tryptophan contents of the protein, and by a lowering of its food value. Correlation coefficients calculated from data published by Flynn *et al.* (1954) were −0.71 for lysine content of the protein, −0.85 for tryptophan content of the protein, respectively, with grain protein content.

It is therefore of considerable interest that the recent introduction of new breeding material for hybridization has led to the production of strains of maize, wheat and sorghum in which the lysine content of the protein is higher than that expected on the basis of the known inverse relationship between grain protein content and lysine content of the protein. Maize grains homozygous for the gene opaque-2 are now commercially available: they have endosperm protein with nearly 70 per cent higher lysine and 20 per cent higher tryptophan than normal, probably as a consequence of a change in ratio of proteins synthesized, since the zein to glutelin ratio is reduced (Mertz *et al.*, 1964). Solubility fractionation of the so-called 'gluten' obtained by Watson and Yahl (1967) in the wet-

Table 7

Protein, lysine and tryptophan contents of opaque-2 and normal maize, and fractionation of 'gluten' from wet-milling
(From Watson and Yahl, 1967
by courtesy of the American Assn of Cereal Chemists)

|  | *Opaque-2* | *Normal* |
|---|---|---|
| *Content in grain:* | | |
| Protein, % | 13.6 | 10.4 |
| Lysine, % | 0.49 | 0.25 |
| Tryptophan, % | 0.10 | 0.06 |
| *Content in protein:* | | |
| Lysine, % | 3.6 | 2.4 |
| Tryptophan | 0.74 | 0.6 |
| *Content in 'gluten'* | | |
| Salt-soluble (globulin) | 2.8 | 1.5 |
| Alcohol-sol. (zein) | 32.8 | 65.0 |
| Alkali-sol. (glutelin) | 51.0 | 30.4 |
| Insoluble | 12.0 | 2.8 |

milling of opaque-2 showed a shift from zein to glutelin in comparison with a normal maize (*see* Table 7).

The dwarf wheat variety Sharbati Sonora bred by Swaminathan at the Indian Agricultural Research Institute by γ-irradiation of the Mexican variety Sonora 64, is a good yielder, has 16.5 per cent protein content, and, according to preliminary reports, contains 3 g of lysine per 100 g of protein, a higher figure than that expected for wheat with so high a level of protein (Agrawal, 1968).

An Indian variety of sorghum, 160-Cernum, has been found to deviate from the normal relationship by being high in lysine content of the protein and in addition containing 17–18 per cent protein content (Virupaksha and Sastry, 1968).

These discoveries have raised hopes that further improvement in the nutritional quality of cereals can be achieved by selective breeding.

Amino acid imbalance may be important in the pathogenesis of pellagra, a nutritional deficiency disease affecting people who subsist on diets based predominantly on maize. The traditional view is that pellagra is brought about because maize is deficient in free nicotinic acid, the greater part of this vitamin in maize being present in a bound form. However, the occurrence of pellagra has sometimes been attributed to the low tryptophan content of maize, tryptophan being linked metabolically to nicotinic acid. But pellagra is known also to occur in populations whose staple is 'jowar' (a millet, *Sorghum vulgare*), which has a tryptophan content higher than that of maize and close to that of rice, and in which nicotinic acid is present in an available form (Gopalan, 1969). Both jowar and maize have an abnormally high content of leucine, and this amino acid has been found to interfere with tryptophan and nicotinic acid metabolism. Thus, according to Gopalan (1969), pellagra may be thought of as a human nutritional deficiency disease mediated by leucine imbalance. For jowar-eating peoples, the disease could be controlled by selective propagation of strains of jowar which are low in leucine content.

## REFERENCES

Agrawal, H. (1968). *New Scient.* 438
Bressani, R. and Conde, R. (1961). *Cereal Chem.* **38,** 76
Buttrose, M. S. (1963). *Aust. J. biol. Sci.* **16,** 305
Chick, H. (1942). *Lancet,* p. 405
Christianson, D. D., Nielsen, H., Khoo, U., Wolf, M. J. and Wall, J. S. (1968). *Cereal Sci. Today* **13,** 118
Coulson, C. B. and Sim, A. K. (1965). *Nature, Lond.* **208,** 583
Davidson, S. and Passmore, R. (1963). *Human Nutrition and Dietetics.* 2nd edn. Edinburgh; Livingstone

Duvick, D. N. (1955). *Am. J. Bot.* **42**, 717
–(1961). *Cereal Chem.* **38**, 374
Elton, G. A. H. and Ewart, J. A. D. (1964). *J. Sci. Fd Agric.* **15**, 119
Ewart, J. A. D. (1967). *J. Sci. Fd Agric.* **18**, 548
–(1967a). *J. Sci. Fd Agric.* **18**, 111
–(1968). *J. Sci. Fd Agric.* **19**, 241
Fisher, N., Redman, D. G. and Elton, G. A. H. (1968). *Cereal Chem.* **45**, 48
Flynn, L. M., Zuber, M. S., Leweke, D. H., Grainer, R. B. and Hogan, A. G.
    (1954). *Cereal Chem.* **31**, 217
Frey, K. J. (1951). *Cereal Chem.* **28**, 123
Golenkov, V. F. (1962). *Soobshch. vses. Nauchno-issled. Inst. Zerna* **2**, 8
Gopalan, C. (1969). *Lancet*, p. 197
Graham, J. S. D. and Morton, R. K. (1963). *Aust. J. biol. Sci.* **16**, 357
– – and Raison, J. K. (1963). *Aust. J. biol. Sci.* **16**, 375
– – – (1964). *Aust. J. biol. Sci.* **17**, 102
Harz, C. O. (1885). *Landwirtschaftliche Samenkunde.* Berlin; Paul Parey
Hepburn, F. N., Calhoun, W. K. and Bradley, W. B. (1960). *Cereal Chem.* **37**, 749
Hess, K. (1954). *Kolloidzeitschrift* **136**, 84
–(1954a). *Fette Seifen Anstr-Mittel* **56**, 393
–, Kiessig, H. and Hanssen, E. (1952). *Naturwissenschaften* **30**, 135
–, Mahl, H., Gutter, E. and Dodt, E. (1955). *Mikrospokie* **10** (1/2), 6
Hinton, J. J. C. (1953). *Cereal Chem.* **30**, 441
– (1966). In: *The Growth of Cereals and Grasses.* Proc. 12th Easter School in Agric.
    Sci., University of Nottingham 1965, p. 272. Ed. by Milthorpe, F. L. and
    Ivins, J. D. London; Butterworths
Hutchinson, J. B., Moran, T. and Pace, J. (1956). *Proc. Ry. Soc.* B **145**, 270
– – – (1959). *Br. J. Nutr.* **13**, 151
Jennings, A. C. and Morton, R. K. (1963). *Aust. J. biol. Sci.* **16**, 384
Juliano, B. O., Bautista, G. M., Lugay, J. C. and Reyes, A. C. (1964). *J. agric. Fd Che.*
    **12**, 131
Kent, N. L. (1966). *Cereal Chem.* **43**, 585
– (1966a). *Cereal Sci. Today* **11**, 91
– (1966b). *Technology of Cereals.* Oxford; Pergamon Press
– and Evers, A. D. (1969). *Cereal Chem.* **46**, 243
– and Jones, C. R. (1952). *Cereal Chem.* **29**, 383
Lawrence, J. M., Day, K. M., Huey, E. and Lee, B. (1958). *Cereal Chem.* **35**, 169
McDermott, E. E. and Pace, J. (1960). *J. Sci. Fd Agric.* **11**, 109
Mertz, E. T., Bates, L. S. and Nelson, O. E. (1964). *Science, N.Y.* **145**, 279
*Milling* (1968). **150** (9), 31
Ministry of Agriculture, Fisheries and Food (1968). 'Household Food Consumption
    and Expenditure 1966'. *Ann. Rpt of the National Food Survey Committee.*
    London; H.M.S.O.
Moran, T. and Pace, J. (1967). *J. Fd Technol.* **2**, 17
Morton, R. K., Palk, B. A. and Raison, J. K. (1964). *Biochem. J.* **91**, 522
Pomeranz, Y., Finney, K. F. and Hoseney, R. C. (1966). *J. Sci. Fd Agric.* **17**, 485
Rohrlich, M. and Niederauer, Th. (1965). *Ber. Getreide-Chem. Tag., Detmold,* 1
Rooney, L. W. and Clark, L. E. (1968). *Cereal Sci. Today* **13**, 258
Rosenberg, H. R. and Rohdenburg, E. L. (1952). *Archs. Biochem. Biophys.* **37**, 461
Stevens, D. J., McDermott, E. E. and Pace, J. (1963). *J. Sci. Fd Agric.* **14**, 284
Virupaksha, T. K. and Sastry, L. V. S. (1968). *J. agric. Fd Chem.* **16**, 199
Waldschmidt-Leitz, E. and Hochstrasser, K. (1961). *Hoppe-Seyler's Z. physiol.
    Chem.* **324**, 243

Watson, S. A. and Yahl, K. R. (1967). *Cereal Chem.* **44,** 488
Weatherwax, P. (1930). *Am. J. Bot.* **17,** 371
Widdowson, E. M. and McCance, R. A. (1954). *Med. Res. Coun., Spec. Rep. Ser.* No. 287, London, H.M.S.O.

# BAKING: THE SIGNIFICANCE OF MODERN PROCESSING METHODS

## N. CHAMBERLAIN

*Flour Milling and Baking Research Association,
Chorleywood, Herts*

## INTRODUCTION

Attention has already been drawn to the considerable importance of cereal, and in particular wheat, protein in the diet. In Great Britain, the most recent National Food Survey (Ministry of Agriculture, Fisheries and Food, 1968) reveals that in 1966 bread and flour contributed 21.7 per cent of the total protein consumption of all households, and cakes, biscuits and other cereal products a further 6.5 per cent. It should not be forgotten also that, as the same source shows, these foods supplied 30.3 per cent of total calories and, partly as a result of the legally enforced supplementation of flour with other nutrients (Great Britain, Parliament, 1963), 22.8 per cent of total calcium, 31.3 per cent of iron, 33.2 per cent of thiamine and 28.6 per cent of nicotinic acid.

By far the largest proportion of all the nutrients derived from wheat flour is taken in the form of bread made by commercial bakers, and bread is a staple item of diet in Europe, including the Soviet Union, the Middle East, North America and many countries colonized by Europeans. The consumption of bread is beginning to rise rapidly among the native populations of former colonies such as Africa and India and competing with other staple cereals such as rice in Japan.

The function of baking is to present cereal flours to the consumer in an attractive, palatable and digestible form. At its simplest this consists of baking portions of a kneaded mixture of the crushed grain and water, usually with salt added to give flavour, but since the discovery of leavening in the time of the Egyptian Pharaohs it has become normal to add yeast to the mixture and allow it to ferment before baking. This simple art has become the subject of a complex technology but its essence has remained unchanged through centuries which have seen the breeding of new wheats, the development of advanced milling techniques, the introduction of mixing and processing machinery and the provision of standardized compressed yeast especially suitable for panary fermentation.

However, a fundamental revolutionary change in the basic breadmaking method is now taking place. It began in the early 1950s in the United States of America, has been greatly extended in application in Great Britain and is gradually gaining a foothold in many other countries. In view of the great nutritional significance of bread it is my purpose in this paper to describe this new technology, examine its impact on the properties of bread as a food, and to see whether the new techniques offer any hope of applications which may help to alleviate any local or world shortages of protein.

## BREADMAKING METHODS

### Bulk dough fermentation

In British practice the traditional breadmaking method involves mixing a dough from the ingredients, basically flour, yeast, salt and water and usually a little fat, and setting it aside to ferment for a period of about 3 h. The mixing is often carried out in a low speed machine designed to imitate the action of the human hand and arm, consuming a total quantity of energy of about 1–2 Wh/kg (0.5–1.0 Wh/lb) and taking about 15–20 min. At the end of the fermentation period, during which the dough is expanded by gas and is said to 'ripen' or 'mature', the dough is divided into pieces of the correct weight, moulded into a ball shape and allowed to rest for 15–20 min at about 27°C (80°F) in what is known as first or intermediate proof. The dough piece is then remoulded into its final shape, placed in a baking tin if desired, and allowed to ferment for a further 45–60 min at a temperature in the range 38–48°C (100–120°F) and high relative humidity. This final proof is followed by baking for about 30 min at about 220–230°C (430–450°F). The end product is a loaf with a specific volume usually in the range 3.6–4.0 ml/g.

Details of traditional practice vary widely. For instance, in the U.S.A. the recipe contains relatively high levels of fat, milk powder and sugar, the dough is made up and fermented in two stages known as the sponge and dough, taking together perhaps 4.5–5.5 h, and the end product may have a specific volume as high as 7 ml/g.

### Mechanical dough development

Looking at such a traditional process it is natural for anyone wishing to make bread more rapidly to turn their attention to the bulk fermentation stage. It occupies about 60 per cent of the total time taken to convert the raw materials into bread and accommodation of the fermenting doughs takes up a great deal of space. Moreover, it is wasteful of the principal raw material, flour, as a proportion of its carbohydrate content is the substrate for the fermentation and is lost in the form of volatile products, principally ethyl alcohol and carbon dioxide. This loss may account for 1–2 per cent of total dough weight.

As far back as 1926 it was demonstrated (Swanson and Working, 1926), using a specially designed laboratory-scale mixer, that the application of intense mechanical work during the mixing of dough would permit the omission of the bulk dough fermentation from the traditional bread-making process without loss of bread quality. They suggested that this could be the basis of a rapid commercial process and discussed the potential savings of time, space and raw materials. However, the suggestion was later withdrawn by Working (1928) and the process was never exploited. Kohman (1927) took out a patent for a method of bread-making in which bulk fermentation was replaced by a combination of 'overmixing' and the use of high levels of oxidizing agents in the dough.

(1) *The 'Do-Maker' process:* It was not until the early 1950s that the principle of mechanical development was successfully applied commercially in the U.S.A. as a result of research by Baker (1954), the machinery and process used being now well-known under the trade name of the 'Do-Maker' (Wallace and Tiernan Process Co., 1955).

The dough making stage of the 'Do-Maker', and closely related 'Amflow' (American Machine and Foundry Co., 1959), process is continuous and in two steps. The first step involves pre-fermenting a sugar solution for 2–4 h with yeast to form a brew or broth. The brew also contains the salt, oxidizing agents and additional materials such as milk powder and often, in current practice, a large proportion of the flour. This brew is then metered into a pre-mixer where it is combined continuously with the rest of the flour and melted fat to form the dough. In the second step, the dough is pumped at a constant, controlled rate through a closed developer chamber, full of dough, in which revolve two impellers driven by a 50–60 h.p. motor at speeds of up to 200 r.p.m. During its passage through the developer chamber the dough absorbs a considerable quantity of energy and this, together with rapid oxidation due to added agents such as iodate, azodicarbonamide (azobisformamide) and bromate, brings the dough into such a condition that it can be extruded directly into the baking tins ready for final proof and baking.

Such a process clearly offers considerable savings in time and space and 'Do-Maker' and 'Amflow' plants are now reputed to be responsible for 30–40 per cent of American bread output.

The first 'Do-Maker' was introduced into Britain in 1956, but considerable experimentation was necessary to find the best operating conditions for producing bread more European in character than American. In particular, there was no simply quantitative basis for controlling the all-important mechanical development step at that time.

The 'Do-Maker' loaf had a characteristically fine and even crumb structure, due to subdivision of bubbles of entrained gas in the closed developer chamber and its partial dissolution under pressure and re-emergence in fine bubble form when the dough was extruded into the tin. This bread did not prove widely popular with the British consumer, and though the equipment has now been modified to allow a considerable degree of control of crumb structure, only a few 'Do-Makers' are currently operating in Britain. This experience has been repeated to some extent in other countries such as Australia. The plant is of high capacity and expensive, and the relative absence of large, centralized bakeries in many European countries has also restricted the application of the 'Do-Maker' process.

(2) *The Chorleywood Bread Process:* Stimulated by the difficulties being experienced in adapting the 'Do-Maker' process to British bread production, the Flour Milling and Baking Research Association (then the British Baking Industries Research Association) began work in 1958 to identify the factors of importance in controlling the mechanical development of bread doughs. This resulted in the introduction in 1961, under the name of the Chorleywood Bread Process (CBP), of a mechanical dough development system of breadmaking which was defined quantitatively and linked to a number of other requirements in such a way that it could be carried out in batch as well as continuous mixers of suitable design.

The CBP has been described on a number of occasions (Chamberlain *et al.*, 1962; Axford *et al.*, 1963; Elton, 1965; Chamberlain *et al.*, 1965; Chamberlain *et al.*, 1965a; Chamberlain *et al.*, 1967) but its characteristic features are as follows:

*(a)* Intense mixing of the dough to a fixed work level of 11 Wh/kg (5 Wh/lb) in a time of less than 5 min, preferably between 2 and 4.

This quantity of energy is about 5–8 times that employed in mixing a dough destined for bulk fermentation and is applied in about a quarter of the time. This necessitates the use of a specially designed, high-powered batch or continuous mixer.

*(b)* The presence in the dough of ascorbic acid as an oxidizing improver at a constant level of 75 p.p.m. of flour. Combinations of ascorbic acid and potassium bromate to a similar total level are also widely and successfully used.

*(c)* The presence of fat in the recipe at a level of 0.7 per cent of flour, or somewhat less if special high melting point fats are used (Chamberlain *et al.*, 1965b).

*(d)* The absence of any brew or pre-ferment.

*(e)* The addition of about an extra 3.5 per cent of water, based on flour. This is a consequence of the retention of flour solids normally lost during bulk fermentation and the absence of the dough softening which takes place during that period. Such softening is due largely to the release of absorbed water from starch by the action of alpha and beta amylases present in the flour.

*(f)* The yeast is fermenting less rapidly at the beginning of final proof due to the absence of bulk fermentation and therefore it is usually necessary to raise its level to maintain normal proof times. In British practice it is raised by a factor of 1.5 to 2.

Apart from these special requirements and the absence of bulk dough fermentation the rest of the traditional breadmaking process remains unchanged, except for a contraction of the first proof period to about 10 min.

The first commercial scale batch mixer for the CBP only began operating in England in early 1962, yet adoption of the method has been so rapid that already about two-thirds of British bread is made in this way. About ten British manufacturers have designed and are selling suitable mixers and the CBP is in use in about fourteen other countries. The advantages which led to this rapid change from traditional methods are discussed later.

### Chemical or activated dough development (ADD)

A second approach to rapid breadmaking is the use of a balanced blend of reducing and oxidizing agents. First introduced by Henika and Zenner (1960) as 'instant dough development', the process is now in commercial operation in the U.S.A. using a proprietary dough additive with the trade name of 'Reddi-Sponge' (Foremost Dairies Inc., 1962).

This contains the amino acid cysteine as the reducing agent, potassium bromate as the oxidant and a large proportion of whey powder. 'Reddi-Sponge' is added to the dough recipe, the dough is mixed on a carefully controlled time basis, allowed a short period of about 30–40 min bulk fermentation and processed immediately. The 4–5 h of sponge fermentation conventional in American breadmaking is entirely omitted.

Though the legal situation does not at present permit its commercial use in Britain, studies have been made of the applicability of the principle to the manufacture of British bread using cysteine (Chamberlain *et al.*, 1966; Coppock, 1966) or sodium metabisulphite (Pace and Stewart,

1966) as the reducing agent, in combination with mixtures of potassium bromate and ascorbic acid as oxidant.

Chamberlain *et al.* (1966) concluded that the whey powder of 'Reddi-Sponge', which replaces the milk solids normally present in American bread recipes, served no useful purpose in British practice and could be omitted. Acceptable bread could be obtained by adding to the dough recipe 35 p.p.m. (based on flour) of *L*-cysteine hydrochloride, corresponding to about 27 p.p.m. of cysteine itself, in combination with 50 p.p.m. of ascorbic acid and 25 p.p.m. of potassium bromate. These results were obtained with flours in the approximate range of 11–12 per cent protein content which had already been treated at the mill with up to 20 p.p.m. of potassium bromate. Ascorbic acid alone was not satisfactory as the oxidizing agent.

Low-speed, conventional bakery mixers can be used, with a mixing time similar to that of doughs intended for bulk fermentation. The dough is taken direct from the mixer to the mechanical divider and processed exactly as for the CBP. Other features of the CBP are equally important in ADD; for instance, fat is necessary and extra water and yeast are required.

## MECHANISMS OF DOUGH FORMATION AND DEVELOPMENT

Before proceeding to examine the practical implications of these new breadmaking methods it is of interest to pause and consider why such varied techniques as bulk fermentation, intense mechanical work and the combined action of reducing and oxidizing agents should all be capable of maturing the dough to the point where it can be divided into pieces and processed further into bread.

The terms 'maturing' and 'ripening' are applied to the marked changes which occur in the physical properties of a dough as bulk fermentation proceeds. When first mixed the dough is inextensible and inelastic, being incapable of inflation by gas; as fermentation proceeds, the dough becomes more extensible and exhibits marked elastic properties when moulded. At optimum maturity the dough can be inflated by gas, which it can hold in the form of finely dispersed bubbles, even during the rapid expansion which occurs in the oven. If fermentation is allowed to proceed too far the dough becomes overripe, being then too soft and extensible and too permeable to gas to make a bold, well-risen loaf.

These vital changes in physical properties are firmly associated with the properties and reactions of the proteins present. Thus, in the same way that wheat proteins have structural and nutritional roles in grain and flour, as described by my colleague Dr. Kent, so they have similar dual roles in terms of bread.

The protein molecules present in the flour particles are held in a closely packed, tightly coiled form by a variety of physical forces, including hydrogen bonding and salt links. Probably the most important however are intra-molecular covalent disulphide bonds between cysteine residues.

When the flour is wetted with water, the proteins hydrate and swell and some of the cohesive forces contributing to the contracted conformation begin to weaken. There is also initiated the series of reactions known as thiol-disulphide or disulphide interchange. This mechanism, first suggested by Goldstein (1957) and Bloksma (1958), and elaborated by Mecham (1959), Frater *et al.* (1960), Mauritzen and Stewart (1963), Redman and Ewart (1967, 1967a) and others, occurs when a disulphide bond under stress comes into close proximity to a thiol group carried on the same or another molecule. The disulphide bond breaks and one half forms a new thiol group while the other forms a new disulphide bond with the original thiol group in such a way as to relax the stress. Two adjacent thiol groups may also be linked oxidatively into a new disulphide bond.

The net effect of these reactions is to uncoil the original protein molecules and bring them into contact with each other under conditions where linking reactions between them can take place. The whole process is accelerated by the stirring action of the mixer and the end result is the three-dimensional mass of protein with visco-elastic properties known as gluten.

During 'ripening' by fermentation further rearrangement and orientation of the protein network proceeds under the gentle influence of the growing gas bubbles and the chance exposure and coming together of suitable reactive groups. Stresses within the network gradually relax and 'ripeness' represents the optimum condition for expansion by gas and ability to hold gas without breakdown.

Clearly such a system will be sensitive to the presence of oxidizing and reducing agents because of their effect on the thiol-disulphide interchange system. In fact, it is common practice in bulk fermentation to add low levels of an oxidant, for example potassium bromate at 10–20 p.p.m. of flour, which will slowly take thiol groups out of circulation and help stabilize the final network.

In the case of mechanical dough development the above processes will be greatly speeded up as a result of the intense mixing, but it has been suggested by Axford and Elton (1960) that in addition there is actual mechanical scission of disulphide bonds. The thiyl radicals probably revert immediately to thiol groups by abstraction of hydrogen from water and the whole process of thiol-disulphide interchange is greatly accelerated. It is of interest that Axford and Elton (1960) supported their hypothesis with the observation that the optimum work input in mechanical dough development was reduced by the addition of the reducing agent bisulphite, which would break disulphide bonds, and that this has now found practical application in the U.S.A. (Henika, 1965), where addition of cysteine is recommended as reducing work input requirements in the 'Do-Maker' process.

Ewart (1968) has suggested that the optimum rate and quantity of work input in the CBP are a reflection of the increasing rapidity of normal reactions which is beneficial up to the observed levels but tends to be irreversibly destructive beyond these points due to mechanical scission of disulphide bonds. The optimum work input may also be associated with the observation of Axford *et al.* (1962) that the disulphide group content of flour changes only slowly relative to protein content, and thus the energy needed for disulphide scission remains roughly constant over a wide range of flours.

The need for rapid stabilization of the gluten network in mechanical development explains the need for relatively high levels of oxidation in the CBP. This can be met by the use of low levels of rapid acting agents such as iodate (10–15 p.p.m.) or azodicarbonamide (20–25 p.p.m.), or higher levels of slower agents such as potassium bromate or ascorbic acid. It is to be noted that ascorbic acid though chemically a reducing agent, acts as an oxidizing agent in dough due to its rapid conversion to dehydroascorbic acid by ascorbic acid oxidase present in flour (Melville and Shattock, 1938; Kuninori and Matsumoto, 1963; Tsen, 1965).

It is relatively easy to suggest a plausible mechanism for activated dough development. The added reducing agent acts rapidly during dough mixing to accelerate normal thiol-disulphide interchange reactions and the slower acting oxidants stabilize the final network. The choice of oxidant is important as a fast-acting agent such as iodate fails to form a suitable combination with cysteine, probably due to rapid interaction between the two instead of acting sequentially on the flour proteins.

Those interested in mechanisms of dough formation and development are recommended to read Ewart (1968), where the subject is discussed in the context of a new hypothesis that the major fraction of glutenin is a linear polymer of polypeptide sub-units linked difunctionally by disulphide bonds.

## ADVANTAGES OF MECHANICAL DEVELOPMENT

*General*

As an example of mechanical development the CBP offers a number of advantages over bulk dough fermentation, many of which are obvious and predictable though others are more subtle and unexpected.

The CBP clearly saves a considerable amount of time in converting batches of raw materials into bread. Almost any common variety of bread can be produced in less than 2 h from the start of mixing to the end of baking, a reduction of 60 per cent compared with traditional British practice.

Areas previously allocated to mixers and fermenting doughs can be reduced by about 75 per cent. Temperature and humidity control of such areas is less necessary.

At any time, about 75 per cent less dough is in the course of processing than in traditional British practice, and potential losses due to machinery breakdown and other causes are correspondingly reduced.

The process is very flexible, especially in batch mixers. These have capacities ranging from about 5 to 250 kg of dough, the largest having outputs of up to about 3000 kg/h. Thus the CBP can be applied to any scale of production and to any variety of fermented wheat flour breads.

The CBP is simple to operate by virtue of the substitution of precise automatic control for the subjective judgement of dough ripeness which depends heavily on craft skills which are in increasingly short supply. Each batch mixer is fitted with a watt hour meter and counter unit and the circuitry is arranged in such a way that the no-load power consumption is not recorded. The total dough weight in kg is multiplied by 11 (or the weight in lb multiplied by 5) and the figure arrived at is set on the counter unit. When the mixer is switched on, the watt hour meter counts down to zero as energy is absorbed by the dough and the mixer is then automatically switched off. The dough is then in optimum condition for further processing. Continuous mixers are controlled by maintaining constant pre-determined values on wattmeters.

Another factor operating where the weight of the final loaf needs to be strictly controlled is that mechanical dividers, which operate on a volume basis, give increased accuracy with the denser, more uniform CBP doughs.

*Yield*

An important feature of the CBP is that it gives rise to an extra yield of about 4 per cent of bread as a result of the elimination of bulk fermentation loss and dough softening, and the addition of extra water and yeast. In British practice the fermentation loss may amount to about 1.5 per cent of flour solids, largely made up of starch granules which have suffered some form of mechanical damage during the milling process and are capable of absorbing up to twice their own weight of water (Greer and Stewart, 1959). The dough softening referred to results partly from the release of absorbed water from damaged starch granules which are being digested by diastatic enzymes during the course of bulk dough fermen-

308

tation, and this sets a limit to the proportion of water added to the flour at doughmaking in order to avoid handling difficulties during later moulding operations.

*Flour properties*

Just as wheats can be classified as 'hard' or 'soft' according to their milling characteristics, as Dr. Kent has already explained, so can flours be classified by bakers as 'strong' or 'weak' depending on their baking characteristics. Strong flours are capable of giving loaves of large volume, fine texture and good keeping quality, whereas weak flours are not. Strength is a reflection of the quantity and properties of the wheat protein and strong flours are most frequently, though not invariably, obtained from hard wheats. Canadian and some North American wheats give typically strong flours, whereas most Western European wheats are soft milling and give weak flours. The protein content of a good Canadian wheat may be 14 per cent while that of a typical English wheat may be only 9 per cent.

The CBP had been largely developed, and was first used commercially, with typical British bread flours of about 12 per cent protein content milled from grists containing about 60 per cent imported strong Canadian wheat and a mixture of weak wheats, much of which was also imported. Commercial experience, followed by detailed experimental work, led to the conclusion that the CBP could produce better bread in terms of volume, keeping properties and other characteristics, than could bulk fermentation, especially with weaker flours (Collins, 1966). The effect was such that when changing from bulk fermentation to the CBP the baker could simultaneously switch to a flour containing 1.0–1.5 per cent less protein without significant loss of bread quality. This meant that, given good parent wheats, the milling grist for British bread flour need only contain about 35 per cent of imported strong wheat together with 65 per cent of weak wheats, of which in good harvest years domestic wheat could form an appreciable proportion, giving a flour of about 10.5 per cent protein. In practice, many millers now provide a flour for the CBP which averages about 11.3 per cent protein content compared with about 12 per cent for bulk fermentation.

Collins (1966) has discussed these findings in more detail and also pointed out that weaker flours usually have lower water absorbing powers, due to lower protein and damaged starch contents, and frequently have higher levels of diastatic activity. The water absorption can be restored to normal levels by careful adjustment of milling techniques to bring about a judicious increase in damaged starch, but a high level of alpha amylase is at least as detrimental to the quality of CBP bread as it is to bulk fermented bread because the major attack on the starch takes place as it is being gelatinized during baking, a feature common to both processes.

This ability of the CBP to make better, more attractive bread from weaker wheats is of considerable significance. It means that countries such as Great Britain can reduce their dependence on imported wheat from dollar sources and increase the proportion of domestic wheats in the grist, given good harvest weather, and that countries currently making bread entirely from domestic wheats can make a product which is bigger in volume, softer, whiter in colour, finer in crumb structure, of better keeping quality and generally a more attractive and palatable food by the standards of many people.

A further important possibility is that this property of the CBP might be exploitable by diluting imported strong flour with native starches such as cassava, or non-gluten forming cereals such as maize, millet and sorghum, while raising the nutritional value of the reduced protein content by supplementation with oilseed or other proteins. Pringle *et al.* (1969) have reported encouraging experiments in the production of bread from a composite flour made from 64 per cent Canadian wheat flour, 30 per cent cassava starch and 6 per cent defatted soya flour, and that a demonstration project is in progress in Brazil under the auspices of the Food and Agriculture Organization of the United Nations.

*Comparison with ADD*

The advantages of ADD compared with bulk fermentation should be the same as those of the CBP in terms of time, space and yield, though mixing times are of similar duration. The baker can avoid the necessity of buying a special CBP mixer but must pay for the reducing agent. However, it is proving difficult to make British bread by ADD of the same high quality as that from the CBP, and a large question mark hangs over the ability of ADD to permit the use of weaker flours without loss of desirable bread characteristics.


# BREAD PROPERTIES AND THE CHORLEYWOOD BREAD PROCESS

The CBP has strong economic attractions in that the extra yield and the ability to use weaker, cheaper flours more than offset the extra costs of yeast, oxidizing improver and electrical power, but it would not have been adopted so rapidly in Great Britain if it had not been capable of producing bread of high quality. Though the basic features of the process remain constant the operating conditions can be adjusted so that varieties of bread can be made which are entirely conventional in appearance and eating quality. In fact, the British public is generally quite unaware that such a drastic change in production methods has taken place in recent years.

It might have been expected that CBP bread would have lacked flavour due to the absence of the bulk dough fermentation, with its production of volatile and aromatic compounds, but this has turned out not to be the case. Cornford (1962) showed that taste panels could not distinguish between bread made by the CBP and that from processes involving up to 18 h of bulk dough fermentation. Collyer (1966) showed additionally that the use of pre-fermented sugar brews in place of water in the dough recipe had no beneficial effects on bread flavour. Collyer (1966) concluded that the role of yeast fermentation in bread flavour is very much less important than is generally supposed. It is likely that reactions taking place in the crust of the loaf during baking are a dominating influence in the development of bread flavour.

The composition of bread made by the CBP and bulk fermentation from the same flours has been examined by Chamberlain *et al.* (1966a). They found that the breads were indistinguishable in their content of protein, fat, ash and nicotinic acid, and in protein quality as indicated by net protein utilization value. In those particular tests the contents of thiamine and moisture were slightly higher and of carbohydrate slightly lower in CBP than in conventional bread. No ascorbic or dehydroascorbic acid could be detected in any of the bread. A much more comprehensive survey of the nutrient content of CBP and fermented bread at point of sale is currently in progress in Great Britain as a collaborative exercise between the Flour Milling and Baking Research Association, the Ministry of Agriculture, Fisheries and Food and the Laboratory of the Government Chemist.

Axford *et al.* (1968) have shown that both the rate and extent of staling of CBP bread are lower than those of bulk fermented bread. The phenomenon was studied by following changes in crumb elastic modulus and the conclusion reached that the beneficial effect of the CBP was independent of its tendency to give bread of higher specific volume, a factor which would itself lead to a reduction in rate and extent of staling.

It has been shown (Collyer, 1968), however, that CBP bread is slightly more susceptible to mould growth than bulk fermented bread, most of the effect being attributable to a somewhat higher residual ethanol concentration in the fermented bread which exerts a delaying effect on the appearance of mould.

## CONCLUSION

The merits of rapid breadmaking processes such as mechanical and activated dough development must be judged in the context of traditional procedures and products in each country where their use is contemplated. The Chorleywood Bread Process seems likely to be adopted on a very wide scale as a result of the advantages outlined in this paper. However, its economic attractions are somewhat reduced where the traditional methods include only a very short period of bulk fermentation and there is thus less possibility of achieving higher yields by avoidance of fermentation loss. It is also most suitable for bread based on wheat flour and some modification of its basic features may be desirable when dealing with cereals such as rye with reduced abilities to form coherent gluten structures. In the broad, long term view, it is to be hoped that methods such as the Chorleywood Bread Process will lead to a more economical use of world wheat resources, enhancing the ability of bakers to produce palatable, attractive and nutritious bread from a wider range of raw materials.

### REFERENCES

American Machine and Foundry Co. (1959). *British Patent* No. 808, 836
Axford, D. W. E. and Elton, G. A. H. (1960). *Chemy Ind.* 1257
–, Campbell, J. D. and Elton, G. A. H. (1962). *J. Sci. Fd Agric.* **13**, 73
–, Chamberlain, N., Collins, T. H. and Elton, G. A. H. (1963). *Cereal Sci. Today* **8**, 265
–, Colwell, K. H., Cornford, S. J. and Elton, G. A. H. (1968). *J. Sci. Fd Agric.* **19**, 95
Baker, J. C. (1954). *Bakers' Wkly.* **161**, (11), 55
Bloksma, A. H. (1958). *Getreide Mehl* **8**, (9), 65
Chamberlain, N., Collins, T. H. and Elton, G. A. H. (1962). *Bakers' Dig.* **36**, (5), 52
– – – (1965). *Proc. 1st Int. Cong. Food Sci. and Technol.* (London, 1962), **4**, 553 London: Gordon and Breach
– – – (1965a). *Cereal Sci. Today* **10**, 412
– – – (1965b). *Cereal Sci. Today* **10**, 415
– – Dodds, N. J. H. and Elton, G. A. H. (1966). *Milling* **146**, 319
– – – Hollingsworth, D. F., Lisle, D. B. and Payne, P. R. (1966a). *Br. J. Nutr.* **20**, 747
– – – (1967). *Brot und Gebäck*, **21**, (3), 53
Collins, T. H. (1966). *Milling* **146**, 296
Collyer, D. M. (1966). *J. Sci. Fd Agric.* **17**, 440
– (1968). *J. Fd Technol.* **3**, 95
Coppock, J. B. M. (1966). *Milling* **146**, 317
Cornford, S. J. (1962). *Milling* **138**, 224
Elton, G. A. H. (1965). *Proc. R. Aust. Chem. Inst.* **32**, (3), 25
Ewart, J. A. D. (1968). *J. Sci. Fd Agric.* **19**, 617

Foremost Dairies Inc. (1962). *United States Patent* No. 3,053,666

Frater, R., Hird, F. J. R., Moss, H. J. and Yates, J. R. (1960). *Nature, Lond.* **186,** 451

Goldstein, S. (1957). *Mitt. Geb. Lebensmittelunters. u. Hyg.* **48,** 87

Great Britain, Parliament (1963). *The Bread and Flour Regulations, 1963.* Stat. Instrum. No. 1435

Greer, E. N. and Stewart, B. A. (1959). *J. Sci. Fd Agric.* **10,** 248

Henika, R. G. and Zenner, S. F. (1960). *Baker's Dig.* **34,** 3, 36

– (1965). *Cereal Sci. Today* **10,** 420

Kohman, H. A. (1927). *British Patent* No. 244,489

Kuninori, T. and Matsumoto, H. (1963). *Cereal Chem.* **40,** 647

Mauritzen, C. A. M. and Stewart, P. (1963). *Nature, Lond.* **197,** 48

Mecham, D. K. (1959). *Cereal Chem.* **36,** 134

Melville, J. and Shattock, H. T. (1938). *Cereal Chem.* **15,** 201

Ministry of Agriculture, Fisheries and Food: National Food Survey Committee (1968). *Household Food Consumption and Expenditure: 1966,* London; H.M. Stationery Office

Pace, J. and Stewart, B. A. (1966). *Milling* **146,** 317

Pringle, W., Williams, A. and Hulse, J. H. (1969). *Cereal Sci. Today* **14,** 114

Redman, D. G. and Ewart, J. A. D. (1967). *J. Sci. Fd Agric.* **18,** 15

– – (1967a). *J. Sci. Fd Agric.* **18,** 520

Swanson, C. O. and Working, E. B. (1926). *Cereal Chem.* **3,** 65

Tsen, C. C. (1965). *Cereal Chem.* **42,** 86

Wallace and Tiernan Process Co. (1955). *British Patent* No. 735, 184

Working, E. B. (1928). *Cereal Chem.* **5,** 223

# V. UNCONVENTIONAL PROTEIN SOURCES

# HYDROCARBON-GROWN YEASTS IN NUTRITION

## C.A. SHACKLADY

*Research and Technical Development Department*
*The British Petroleum Company Limited, London*

## INTRODUCTION

The fact that various hydrocarbon fractions can be used as substrates for yeast production is now well known. Somewhat naturally, details of the processes involved have not been published since most of the relevant work has been carried out by organizations with a view to establishing industrial scale plants. Nonetheless BP workers have given accounts of general process aspects in a number of papers, (Champagnat *et al.* 1963a, 1963b; Champagnat 1964, 1966; Vernet 1965, Vernet *et al.* 1966; Lainé *et al.* 1967, 1968; Llewelyn 1967; Evans 1967; Todd 1968). Japanese workers have also been active in the field of hydrocarbon fermentation and Yamada (1968) lists over 145 papers plus a number of patent specifications and reviews as emanating from Japan in 1967 and 1968.

It would seem that, in general, the quantities of material produced by various workers have been insufficient to permit extensive testing with farm animals although the Russians have been able to do so. A general account of the work at the Kuban Institute has been published by Tkačev and co-workers (1967). Apart from this it is difficult to find references in the literature to such work. There has been some account given, in general terms, of a joint Esso/Nestlé essay into hydrocarbon fermentation in a paper by McNab *et al.* (1966) to the American Association for the Advancement of Science in December, 1966. However, one might deduce from this that their interest was primarily directed towards human nutritional uses and that they were concentrating on bacterial rather than yeast proteins.

BP's efforts have been directed towards the manufacture of an animal feed ingredient as the first objective. Even though the topic of this Symposium is 'Proteins as Human Food', it is hoped the reader will not regard this paper as irrelevant. The fact that the yeast will be used for humans indirectly, that is via the animal, should not obscure the immense potential contribution which it can make to improve human nutrition even though this could and, eventually, may be done more efficiently by direct administration to man.

## OBJECTS OF THE EXPERIMENTS WITH ANIMALS

Once the technical feasibility of the processes had been demonstrated, there were four general questions to be answered.

(1) Are the processes economically viable?

(2) How are the products intended to be used?

(3) Are they safe for the purpose for which they are intended?

(4) If they are toxicologically safe, what is their value in nutrition?

The announcement that commercial units are to be built in Scotland and France provides the answer to the first question. As to the second one, it was stated at an early stage of development of the project that the primary objective was to produce an animal feed component.

At this time, a categorical answer cannot be given to the third question but it should not be long delayed. The procedures which have been adopted to determine the safety of the materials have been based on those recommended for radiation-pasteurized foods. Acute sub-chronic and chronic toxicity tests have been carried out over 6 weeks, 3 months and 2 years respectively using a single dietary level of 40 per cent of yeast in the first case and levels of 10, 20 and 30 per cent in the other cases. The animals employed in these tests have been, for the most part, rats but occasionally other species have been used and, in the carcinogenicity studies, mice have also been used.

Approximately 500 samples have undergone the 6 week rat feeding test. In the early days of the project some samples depressed growth when compared with control diets and also produced a liver enlargement without any specific pathogenic features. The reason for this behaviour was traced and eliminated so that, of recent years, there has been no evidence of any toxicity in the short term at levels up to 40 per cent of the diet.

When it was evident that acute toxicity was no problem, tests were extended to 3 months and then to 2 years. The first of these chronic tests ended in January, 1969 and the various organ and tissue sections are now undergoing histopathological examination but with something like 85 observations to be made on 26 or more tissues, results are not immediate. Until they are available, therefore, the material cannot be said to have passed, successfully, the chronic toxicity test.

However, a sample number of rats killed after 1 year on test showed no treatment-related abnormalities which gave an 85–90 per cent probability that the situation would be the same after 2 years. Furthermore, biochemical tests on blood, urine and various organ functions did not show deviations from normal, up to the time of slaughter, that could be attributed to the treatments.

In anticipation of a favourable result of the long term toxicity studies, work commenced late in 1965 on the fourth problem, that of demonstrating the utility of the material in animal feeds. A consideration of the amino acid composition of yeast grown on gas oil — and of that grown on normal paraffins which is almost identical — suggested that it might be expected to behave in a similar way to solvent-extracted soya bean meal or, with the addition of DL-methionine, to fish meal. This is shown in Table 1.

Table 1

| Amino acid | Content gramme per 16 g N | | |
| --- | --- | --- | --- |
| | BP protein concentrate | Fishmeal | Soya bean meal |
| Isoleucine | 5.3 | 4.6 | 5.4 |
| Leucine | 7.8 | 7.3 | 7.7 |
| Phenylanine | 4.8 | 4.0 | 5.1 |
| Tyrosine | 4.0 | 2.9 | 2.7 |
| Threonine | 5.4 | 4.2 | 4.0 |
| Trytophan | 1.3 | 1.2 | 1.5 |
| Valine | 5.8 | 5.2 | 5.0 |
| Arginine | 5.0 | 5.0 | 7.7 |
| Histidine | 2.1 | 2.3 | 2.4 |
| Lysine | 7.8 | 7.0 | 6.5 |
| Cystine | 0.9 | 1.0 | 1.4 |
| Methionine | 1.6 | 2.6 | 1.4 |
| Cystine + methionine | 2.5 | 3.6 | 2.8 |

The unique ability of the ruminant to use urea and other relatively cheap sources of protein made it appear that hydrocarbon-grown yeast would be more attractive economically in those rations in which soya and fish meal were the proteins of choice. This meant, in broad terms, pig and poultry feeds and for this reason the farm animal work has been confined to these species.

It was considered that the use of merely token quantities of yeast in the rations would do little to demonstrate its suitability as a major contributor of protein. Consequently, and because of its similarity to fish meal in total protein content, it was decided to use rations in which the

319

level of yeast was about the same as would have been used for fish meal. When enough animals were available, a high level of yeast which was twice that of the basic level was included in one of the rations. The object of this was to see what margin of safety could be expected in normal commercial conditions.

In the case of both pigs and poultry the scheme of experiments consisted of repeating relatively short term experiments over two or three generations so as to determine long term effects.

## EXPERIMENTS WITH POULTRY

Digestibility coefficients and metabolizable energy were determined for yeast, grown on gas oil and normal paraffins, with chicks at 3 and 5 weeks of age. Percentage digestibility coefficients for nitrogen, organic matter and total dry matter were found to be 80, 74 and 72 respectively for yeast grown on gas oil and 77, 63 and 64 for n-paraffin yeast. Metabolizable energy was 2,550 and 2,540 kcal/kg.

Since these figures were obtained the protein content of n-paraffin grown yeast has been increased quite substantially so it is now thought desirable to repeat the determinations for this material.

A number of short term trials with broilers has been carried out and the results, of which the following are typical, were very similar in all cases.

Table 2

| Group 1 | Control ration with 10 per cent fish meal |
| Group 2 | Ration with 7½ per cent LL 360 plus 2½ per cent fish meal |
| Group 3 | Ration with 10 per cent LL 360, no fish meal |
| Group 4 | Ration with 15 per cent LL 360, no fish meal |
| Group 5 | Ration with 7½ per cent BRG 3053 plus 2½ per cent fish meal |
| Group 6 | Ration with 15 per cent BRG 3053, no fish meal |

LL 360 – Gas oil substrate    BRG 3053 – n-paraffin substrate

Table 3

Average weight in grammes of birds at 3 and 5 weeks of age

| Age | 3 weeks | | 5 weeks | |
|---|---|---|---|---|
| Group No. | Actual | As percentage of control | Actual | As percentage of control |
| 1 Control | 315 | 100 | 739 | 100 |
| 2 | 327 | 103.8 | 748 | 101.2 |
| 3 | 316 | 100.3 | 730 | 98.8 |
| 4 | 314 | 99.7 | 715 | 96.8 |
| 5 | 320 | 101.6 | 742 | 100.4 |
| 6 | 316 | 100.3 | 714 | 96.6 |

Table 4

Feed conversion (kilogramme per kilogramme weight gain)
and mortality at 5 weeks

| Group No. | Feed conversion | | Mortality |
| | Actual | As percentage of control | Actual |
|---|---|---|---|
| 1 Control | 1.79 | 100 | 1 |
| 2 | 1.80 | 100.6 | 3 |
| 3 | 1.81 | 101.1 | 1 |
| 4 | 1.86 | 103.9 | 4 |
| 5 | 1.81 | 101.1 | 4 |
| 6 | 1.80 | 100.6 | 3 |

It was found, in general, that the performance of the ration decreased as the level of yeast was increased to 15 and 20 per cent of the feed. A similar, but less marked, effect was observed also when the level of fish meal was increased to the same extent.

By its nature, an experiment with broilers is both a short term one and incapable of being repeated with successive generations. For longer term studies it was necessary to determine the effect of yeast on the laying and breeding performance of birds. The first experiment in this category was carried out on heavy hybrids so it too was restricted to a single generation. After this, the experiment was repeated with a pure strain, Rhode Island Reds being chosen in preference to White Leghorns because of the need to use artificial insemination and the resultant frequent handling of the birds. It was felt that the Rhodes would endure this with a greater degree of equanimity than the Leghorns.

The intention was to use two levels of yeast, 10 and 20 per cent contributing approximately 6.5 and 13 per cent of protein respectively to the ration. In these circumstances it became advisable to use two control rations, one having a protein level around 15–16 per cent, the other 20–21 per cent. The control rations were of the normal commercial type based on fish and soya bean meal as the main protein sources (Table 5).

Table 5

Laying/breeding rations

| Ingredient % | Control 1 | Experimental 1 | Control 2 | Experimental 2 |
|---|---|---|---|---|
| Cereal | 77.9 | 78.2 | 65.5 | 67.0 |
| Fish meal | 7.0 | – | 12.0 | 2.0 |
| Extracted soya meal | 6.5 | 2.5 | 14.5 | 2.0 |
| BP yeast | – | 10.0 | – | 20.0 |
| Mineral/vitamin mixture | 8.6 | 9.3 | 8.0 | 9.0 |
| DL-methionine | – | 0.053 | – | 0.07 |

The major characteristics of these rations were calculated to be as shown in Table 6.

Table 6

| Group | | 1 | 2 | 3 | 4 |
|---|---|---|---|---|---|
| Metabolizable energy kcal/kg | | 2,610 | 2,615 | 2,610 | 2,625 |
| Calcium | % | 3.0 | 3.0 | 3.1 | 3.1 |
| Phosphorus | % | 0.76 | 0.77 | 0.85 | 0.85 |
| Methionine + cystine | % | 0.53 | 0.53 | 0.69 | 0.69 |
| Lysine | % | 0.74 | 0.81 | 1.07 | 1.22 |
| Arginine | % | 0.83 | 0.77 | 1.11 | 1.0 |

In the first experiment which ran for 32 weeks from March to October, 1966 the general conclusion was that, a level of 10 per cent yeast had no influence on egg production or feed conversion efficiency but had a slight adverse effect on egg weight (1.7 per cent below the control). The 20 per cent yeast level gave nearly 7 per cent fewer eggs than the control at 1.7 per cent lower weight. Even though, due to an interaction effect, the difference in egg production was said not to be significant it was probable that this did represent an inferior performance.

The next experiment was with the Rhode Island Reds. These were reared from 1 day of age to point of lay on control rations or on rations with 10 and 20 per cent of yeast. As in the previous experiment the laying birds were caged individually and fed *ad libitum.*

After 52 weeks in lay, egg production in the 10 per cent yeast group was 2.5 per cent better and in the 20 per cent yeast group 15 per cent better than the control but this latter figure is due partly to an unexplained drop in production by the high protein control group in the eighth month.

Towards the end of the period, eggs were hatched to produce chicks to repeat the experiment on the next generation. These birds have now been in lay for 9 months and the up-to-date figures for egg production and egg weight are:

Table 7

| | Eggs/100 hen days | | Egg wt. (grammes) | |
|---|---|---|---|---|
| | Actual | Relative | Actual | Relative |
| Low protein control | 66.6 | 100% | 63.2 | 100% |
| 10 per cent yeast ration | 64.0 | 96.1% | 63.0 | 99.7% |
| High protein control | 63.3 | 100% | 62.5 | 100% |
| 20 per cent yeast ration | 64.8 | 102.4% | 61.0 | 97.6% |

Towards the end of January the chicks, which will form the next generation to go into the batteries (in May/June) were hatched.

In the first experiment the fertility of eggs on the control diet was from 4 to 7 per cent higher than those on the yeast diets. This difference was less marked in the second experiment and in the third, i.e. current one, there is virtually no difference between treatments. At no stage has the hatchability of fertile eggs been affected.

## EXPERIMENTS WITH PIGS

Starting with the parent generation of 16 sows in each of two groups, it was the intention to produce the F1, F2 and F3 generations and compare the performance of those which had been bred and reared on rations containing yeast with the controls which were on fish/soya based rations.

In the first generation, three litters were produced, the 1a and 1b litters being taken to slaughter weight and the 1c litter to weaning only. From the F1a boars and F1b gilts were bred the F2a litters and the gilts are now in pig for the second time to produce the F2b litters which should be born in March/April. It is intended to breed the F2b gilts to produce an F3 litter but it is unlikely that this series of experiments will be taken beyond that stage.

For the breeding sows there have been two treatments only, a control and a ration with 10 per cent BP yeast. Sucking pigs have also been on two treatments only, control and 15 per cent yeast. The growing/fattening pigs have generally been subjected to three treatments, control, 7.5 and 15 per cent yeast though on one occasion an additional treatment, in which 20 per cent of yeast was incorporated in the ration, was included.

In addition, determinations of digestibility coefficients for nitrogen, organic matter and total dry matter were made. These showed an encouragingly high level of digestibility for pigs at 35 and 65 kg liveweight being in all cases between 85 and 90 per cent.

All the litters have been produced as the result of artificial insemination. For the first, i.e. the F1a and F1b litters, the conception rate of the yeast fed sows was somewhat lower than that of the controls but there was no difference in the case of the F1c, F2a and F2b litters. In view of the somewhat limited number of sows used originally it is not possible to state with certainty whether these results are fortuitous or treatment related. Tkačev claims that the use of yeast in breeding pig rations positively increased fertility and conception rate and particularly the potency of the boars.

Litter size and birth weights for the first 4 litters were:

Table 8

| Litter | Number of pigs | | Wt. of pigs in grammes | |
|---|---|---|---|---|
| | Controls | Yeast fed | Controls | Yeast fed |
| Fla | 10.25 | 10.85 | 1244 | 1231 |
| Flb | 11.3 | 12.4 | 1326 | 1271 |
| Flc | 12.4 | 13.7 | 1191 | 1164 |
| F2a | 10.3 | 8.7 | 1398 | 1284 |

The performance of the pigs in the growing/fattening stage has generally been to the advantage of the yeast fed groups in liveweight gain and invariably in feed conversion efficiency. The F1b litters on yeast treatments got away to a slower start than the controls but, as can be seen, most of this effect had disappeared at the time of slaughter.

Table 9

Mean daily liveweight gain over 8 and 17 weeks feeding periods (Fla)

| Group | 0–8 weeks | | 0–17 weeks | |
|---|---|---|---|---|
| | Grammes/day | Percentage of control | Grammes/day | Percentage of control |
| Control | 623 | 100 | 679 | 100 |
| 7.5 per cent BP protein | 643 | 103.2 | 691 | 101.8 |
| Control | 620 | 100 | 670 | 100 |
| 15 per cent BP protein | 645 | 104.0 | 695 | 103.7* |

*Significant $p < 0.05$

Table 10

Feed conversion efficiency over 8 and 17 weeks feeding periods (Fla)

| Group | 0–8 weeks | | 0–17 weeks | |
|---|---|---|---|---|
| | Absolute | Percentage of control | Absolute | Percentage of control |
| Control | 2.63 | 100 | 3.17 | 100 |
| 7.5 percent BP protein | 2.60 | 98.9 | 3.14 | 99.1 |
| Control | 2.60 | 100 | 3.15 | 100 |
| 15 percent BP protein | 2.50* | 96.2 | 3.07* | 97.5 |

*Significant $p = 0.05$

Table 11

Mean daily liveweight gain over 8 and 17 week feeding periods (Flb)

| Group | 0−8 weeks | | 0−17 weeks | |
|---|---|---|---|---|
| | Grammes/day | Percentage of control | Grammes/day | Percentage of control |
| Control 1 | 589 | 100 | 646 | 100 |
| 7.5 per cent BP protein | 562 | 95.4 | 641 | 99.2 |
| Control 1 | 612 | 100 | 666 | 100 |
| 15 per cent BP protein | 584 | 95.4 | 657 | 98.6 |
| Control 2 | 621 | 100 | 674* | 100 |
| 20 per cent BP protein | 627 | 101.0 | 691* | 102.5 |

*after 14 weeks

Table 12

Feed conversion efficiency over 8 and 17 weeks feeding periods (Flb)

| Group | 0−8 weeks | | 0−17 weeks | |
|---|---|---|---|---|
| | Absolute | Percentage of control | Absolute | Percentage of control |
| Control 1 | 2.46 | 100 | 3.07 | 100 |
| 7.5 per cent BP protein | 2.41 | 98.0 | 2.98 | 97.1 |
| Control 1 | 2.35 | 100 | 2.99 | 100 |
| 15 per cent BP protein | 2.33 | 99.1 | 2.94 | 98.3 |
| Control 2 | 2.28 | 100 | 2.73 | 100 |
| 20 per cent BP protein | 2.27 | 99.6 | 2.68* | 98.2 |

*at 14 weeks

For the F2a litters the latest figures available are those after 10 weeks of the growing period. Starting weight was 37 kg for each treatment and weight gains over 10 weeks were 46.8 kg for the control group, 48.1 for the 7½ and 48.9 for the 15 per cent yeast groups. Corresponding feed conversion figures were 2.86, 2.80 and 2.75.

In contrast to some reports on torula yeasts there has been no indication of unpalatability and indeed one pig ate a ration containing 65 per cent of BP yeast for 11 weeks and appeared to relish it.

Commercial evaluation of the carcasses has indicated no difference between control and experimental groups.

## ANIMAL PRODUCTS

Meat from yeast fed pigs and poultry, as well as eggs produced in the experiments described, have had the same texture and flavour as correͻμεͺͺding products from control animals. Meat, fat liver, kidney and eggs from the experimental animals have produced no toxic symptoms when fed to rats.

## OTHER CRITERIA OF NUTRITIVE VALUE

Samples of yeast which are being produced from gas oil or normal paraffins have a Net Protein Utilization Value in rats of 50—55 when unsupplemented with methionine. Addition of 0.3 per cent DL-methionine to the test diets increases this to a value around 90, three recent samples giving 99, 89 and 93. Digestibility, again measured with rats is consistently over 90 so that Biological Values are between 50 and 60 for the unsupplemented but 90 to 100 for the methionine supplemented yeast.

## CONCLUSION

The general conclusion that seems to be justified from the experiments described is that yeast grown on hydrocarbon fractions can form a satisfactory alternative to fish/soya mixtures in pig and poultry feeds provided that adjustment is made to the methionine content of the ration where appropriate. The experiments indicate that all the fish meal and part of the soya bean meal can be replaced by BP yeast in pig rations with no disadvantage accruing. Complete, as distinct from major, replacement of fish meal in poultry rations by yeast may be practicable but this has not yet been attempted in these experiments.

Nevertheless, the results so far achieved encourage the view that yeast grown on hydrocarbons in closely controlled and specific conditions is both a safe and useful feed ingredient.

## REFERENCES

Champagnat, A. (1964). *U.N. Inter-Regional Conference of the Development of Petrochemical Industries in Developing Countries,* Tehran
— (1966). *7th Int. Cong. Nutr.,* Hamburg
— Vernet, C., Lainé, B. and Filosa, J. (1963a). *Nature, Lond.* 197, 13
———— (1963b). *Proc. 6th World Petr. Congr.* Sect. IV, Paper 4, PD 10, 259
Evans, G. H. (1967). *Symposium on Single Cell Protein,* M.I.T.
Lainé, B., Levi, J. D. and Cox, R. E. (1968). *3rd Int. Fermentation Conf.* Rutgers University
Lainé, B., Vernat, C. and Evans, G. H. (1967). *Proc. 7th World Petr. Congr.* 8, 197
Llewelyn, D. A. B. (1967). *Proc. Inst. Pet. Symp. on Microbiology,* p. 63
McNab, J. G. and Rey, L. R. (1966). *Meeting Am. Ass. Adv. Sci.,* Washington D.C.

Tkačev, I. F., Petunin, F. A., Tarenenko, G. A. and Bachikalo, A. P. (1967). *Vest. Sel'Skohoz, Nauki* **12**, 44
Todd, J. R. (1968). *Br. Ass. Meeting,* Dundee
Vernet, C. (1965). *Ind. Chem. Belge,* **30** (3), 213
– Lainé, B. and Evans, G. H. (1966). *Congr. Int. de Chimie Ind.,* Brussels, September, 1966
Yamada, K. (1968). *Res. Ass. of Petroleum Ferm.,* Tokyo, Japan

# ALGAL PROTEINS AND THE HUMAN DIET

## J.F. GORDON

*Unilever Research, Colworth/Welwyn Laboratory,*
*The Frythe, Welwyn, Herts.*

## INTRODUCTION

In recent years much has been said and written (Food and Agriculture Organization, 1963; Gould, 1965; Boyd Orr, 1968) on the present and future inadequacy of man's food supply, particularly in regard to the supply of edible protein. The protein problem in human nutrition is twofold. Firstly, malnutrition, currently a critical dietary problem in many areas of the world, is widely forecast to become more acute in the future; and secondly, taking into account expected population increases, the total protein demand by the end of the present century could conceivably be two and a half times that of the present day (UNFAO, 1963). There is therefore an urgent need to step up both the production and supply of edible protein, with particular emphasis being laid on the increased production of good quality, low-cost, locally-available plant proteins.

We can of course look to conventional agriculture to fulfil this requirement, and at the present time much research is directed towards this end. However, even with improved agricultural practices, land reclamation schemes, the use of better fertilizers and pesticides, and the wider application of plant genetics, there is little evidence to date of any substantial improvement in the protein production situation. As a result, an increasing number of people are questioning the ability of conventional agriculture to meet these enormous requirements *in toto*. It is largely for this reason that nowadays so much interest is being shown in examining the feasibility of protein production from unconventional sources such as bacteria, yeasts, fungi and the unicellular algae.

Over the past twenty years a considerable amount of research has been undertaken in examining the potential of unicellular algae, particularly members of the Chlorophyceae (green algae) and Cyanophyceae (blue-green algae), as producers of edible protein. Progress has been made in this area, but it has been steady rather than spectacular. In this paper I will discuss selected aspects of this work on unicellular algae, with particular reference to the potential of algal protein as a supplement in the human diet, and will explore the reasons why the early promise of algal protein has not yet been fulfilled.

## THE POTENTIAL OF ALGAE AS A PROTEIN SOURCE

Interest in the use of algae as a protein supplement for human and animal diets arose in the early years of the Second World War, out of researches being conducted in the United States of America and Germany on photosynthesis. For a long time, it had been recognized that sunlight is the prime factor which sets the absolute limit to primary food production on the earth's surface, and that the photosynthetic step, in which the sun's energy is transformed into chemical bond energy, is the rate-determining factor in this process. Much attention was therefore directed to investigating the basic mechanism of photosynthesis, since it was considered essential to obtain this knowledge before any attempt to optimize the process, and thereby apply it in primary food production, could be undertaken. Because the unicellular algae were at this time thought to be much more efficient than higher plants in their inherent capacity to utilize the energy of sunlight, they were often chosen as the model system in such studies. The net result was that, in addition to furthering our knowledge on photosynthesis, much valuable information was obtained on the large scale culture of algae (Burlew, 1953).

Probably the most significant result emerging from this work was that obtained by Spoehr and Milner (1949), who showed that the chemical composition of an organism such as *Chlorella pyrenoidosa* was influenced by the cultural conditions employed, and that furthermore it was possible to control these conditions so that a protein content of about 50 per cent could regularly be attained. This finding, and the favourable results obtained subsequently by Fisher and Burlew (1953) in animal feeding experiments with *Chlorella pyrenoidosa,* gave rise to the idea that unicellular algae might be grown on a large scale as a food source.

The primitive character of their cellular organization gives the microscopic green and blue-green algae a number of advantages over higher plants as a means of producing protein:

(1) Owing to the unicellular nature of the algal biomass, there is no differentiation of the cells into inedible mechanical tissues such as roots and stems. Essentially the whole plant is nutritious.

(2) When grown under suitable conditions, algal cells can contain up

to 65 per cent protein on a dry weight basis. The average protein content of most algae examined to date is somewhat lower than this, but nevertheless it is still higher than that found in the edible parts of most higher plants. In Table 1, the average protein contents for a number of green and blue-green algae are listed and, for comparison, those from a number of traditional human foodstuffs are shown; protein content of the algae is, in most cases, considerably higher. Furthermore, these proteins should be suitable for inclusion in the human diet for, as discussed later, several studies have revealed that they have a favourable overall amino acid composition.

Table 1

Protein content of algae compared with that of various food sources

| Product | Average protein content (%) |
|---------|------------------------------|
| Skim milk powder | 36 |
| Fish flour | 80 |
| Beef | 12 |
| Chicken | 15 |
| Egg | 11 |
| Chick peas (gramme) | 20 |
| Dry beans | 22 |
| Wheat flour | 12 |
| | |
| *Green algae* | |
| *Chlorella pyrenoidosa* | |
| *Chlorella vulgaras* | 50 |
| *Scenedesmus obliquus* | |
| *Scenedesmus quadricauda* | |
| *Uronema gigas**  | 50 |
| *Stigeoclonium spp** | 48 |
| *Hormidium spp** | 46 |
| *Ulothrix spp** | 42 |
| | |
| *Blue green algae* | |
| *Spirulina maxima*† | 62 |
| *Plectonema boryanum*‡ | 34 |
| *Mastigocladus laminosus*‡ | 34 |
| *Gloeocapsa alpicola*‡ | 36 |
| *Fremyella diplosiphon*‡ | 38 |

* Hindak and Pribil, *Biologia Pl.* 1968, **10** (3), 234
† Clément, Giddey and Menzi, *J. Sci. Fd. Agric.* 1967, **18**, Nov., 497
‡ Hopkins, Day and Gordon—previously unpublished results

(3) The algae have an intrinsically higher rate of growth than higher plants. The high growth rate of algae stems from the microscopic size of the individual cells. Only a small proportion of the surface of a higher

plant is available for uptake of essential nutrients and thus complex transport systems for the distribution of materials are needed within the body of the organism The algal cell, on the other hand, is able to take in nutrients over its entire surface area which is high in proportion to the mass of the cell.

(4) Being predominantly aquatic organisms, the algae are not as a rule subjected to such wide fluctuations in climatic conditions as conventional crop plants. They are not seasonal, and thus the potential growing season is unlimited.

(5) They have relatively simple cultural requirements.

(6) In terms of production efficiency and capacity, algal culture is several orders of magnitude better than conventional agriculture. Traditional agricultural methods for plant and animal production require the use of vast areas of land for relatively low yields. Unicellular algae can be cultivated in compact units such as fermenters which, although complex, occupy only a relatively small area. The cultivation of algae in fermenters under artificial light confers other advantages. The growth of algae in such a system is predictable and independent of climatic conditions and of infestation by insects and other spoilage organisms. By the use of suitable control equipment, such as pH and temperature regulators, and proper lighting regimes, environmental conditions optimum for growth can be achieved and maintained. Additionally, in such a system, the chemical composition of the algal biomass, and therefore presumably its nutritive value, can be varied by modifying the environmental parameters.

Lagoon culture of algae under sunlight likewise has potential advantages over conventional agricultural methods in terms of production efficiency and capacity. If we assume, for example, that half the human daily requirement of 70 g of protein was to be obtained from algae, an

Table 2

Protein productivity (theoretical) for algae as compared to other sources
(After W. A. Vincent, 1969)

| Source | Protein dry weight/acre/year (lb avoirdupoids) |
|---|---|
| Spirulina platensis | 21,700 |
| Chlorella pyrenoidosa | 14,000 |
| Fish | 560 |
| Peanuts | 420 |
| Peas | 353 |
| Wheat | 269 |
| Milk | 90 |
| Eggs | 54 |

area no greater in size than the County of Essex would be required to fill the requirements of the present world population. ✓

Some indication of what these advantages of algal culture could theoretically add up to in terms of protein yields has recently been presented by Vincent (1969), whose estimates are shown in Table 2. The figures quoted for milk, meat, fish, etc. represent yields known to be attainable in practice, whilst those quoted for the two algal species were obtained by extrapolating laboratory results. As Vincent himself points out, for all kinds of reasons we cannot hope to attain such high annual protein yields from algae, but even if it were one order of magnitude less, the protein yield from these algae would still be appreciably higher than that obtained from traditional sources.

Thus, taking all these factors into account, it would seem that the mass culture of algae offers greater potential than conventional agriculture as a means of producing protein. How then do these advantages stand up in practice? Can protein be produced economically by mass culture techniques and, if so, can such protein be used satisfactorily as a supplement in the human diet?

## TECHNICAL AND ECONOMIC ASPECTS

It is essential that if we are to achieve our stated objective of producing nutritionally-adequate, low-cost protein from algae we must have the facility to produce large quantities of algal biomass. Additionally, for commercial viability, we must be able to produce algal protein at a cost which competes favourably with the cost of producing protein from conventional sources.

In the main, there are five requirements for achieving good growth of algae:

(1) A supply of carbon dioxide.

(2) Mineral elements in adequate concentrations.

(3) Illumination with light of the appropriate wavelength and intensity.

(4) Maintenance of optimum temperature for the particular organism concerned.

(5) Adequate agitation of the algal cells to prevent sedimentation, and to ensure even distribution of carbon dioxide, nutrients and light.

Over the years a large number of techniques for the mass culture of algae have been devised. All these techniques take into account the above requirements, and vary in complexity from culturing in bottles and trays (Davis *et al.*, 1953), to culturing in chambers (Matthern and Koch, 1964; Leone, 1963) and columns, through to tanks and lagoons (Golueke and

Oswald, 1965). Additionally a wide range of techniques for harvesting and processing algae has been investigated. Methods proposed for harvesting the algal biomass from the culture medium include centrifugation (Geoghegan, 1951), sedimentation (Davis *et al.*, 1953), coagulation (Kott and Wachs, 1964) and froth flotation. After harvesting, other processing treatments are required. Processing treatments can be divided into two categories,

*(a)* Drying for preservation and storage.

*(b)* Processing to render the dried material more digestible and palatable.

Some form of drying is essential, since storage of the harvested algae in the wet state could lead to heavy spoilage losses. A wealth of information is now available on mass culture techniques for growing and processing algae and detailed discussion of these techniques is outside the scope of this article. For further details, the reader is referred to articles by Burlew (1953), Tamiya (1957), van Swaaij (1964) and Uesaka (1965).

Considering the generally simple cultural requirements of algae, one might expect that it would be an easy task to produce protein at an economic rate on an industrial scale. After all, sunlight is free, carbon dioxide is free and readily available from the atmosphere, and water and mineral elements are present in abundance on the earth's surface. In practice however, it has proved exceedingly difficult to produce protein economically from algae, and as far as is known to the author, no one has as yet succeeded in achieving this objective.

Essentially, three fundamentally distinct methods have been investigated for feasibility of protein production on an industrial scale:—

*(a)* cultivation of algae in an enclosed system (e.g. fermenters) under artificial light or sunlight, with the cells being grown in a completely autotrophic medium;

*(b)* cultivation of algae in an identical system to *(a)*, but in this case the cells are grown in heterotrophic media (e.g. media supplemented with an organic carbon source such as glucose and a nitrogen source such as urea) and

*(c)* cultivation of algae in open lagoons under sunlight with either autotrophic or heterotrophic culture media.

In all such investigations it has been found that algal growth rates obtained in practice are always considerably lower than theoretical calculations predict. The net result is that the yields obtained are low. There are many reasons for this discrepancy between practice and theory and a penetrating analysis of these has been presented by Thacker and Babcock (1957). There are many limitations imposed by nature on the growth rate and yield of algae. Most of these are concerned with the photosynthetic process *per se,* which is a very inefficient process in energy conversion (light → chemical bond) terms. It is now known (Wassink *et al.,* 1953) that algae are no more efficient than higher plants in their inherent capacity to utilize the energy of visible light. The major factor affecting yield is 'light saturation' and to the present it has not proved possible to overcome this by improved culture vessel design. Other factors affecting yield include auto-inhibition of the algal cells and toxicity effects exerted by essential micro-elements when such elements are present in too high a concentration.

The overall result is that, although growth on a large scale under factory-type conditions (methods *(a)* and *(b)*) is possible, the process is extremely expensive:

*(i)* because of the low efficiency of all artificial light sources (conversion of electrical energy to usable light energy is low),

*(ii)* the necessary sterile growth conditions require heavy capital outlay,

*(iii)* the necessity for maintenance of high partial pressures of oxygen and carbon dioxide for high growth rates.

Table 3

Prospective economic characteristics of blue-green algae production
(After Meier, 1966)

Estimated for a location in an underdeveloped area.

*Assumption as to yield*
    50 tons/ hectare (45,000 lb/acre) dry wt.

| *Capital costs* | |
|---|---|
| Land levelling | $ 1,000/hectare |
| Pump units (50/hectare) | 10,000 |
| Piping and valves (300 m/hectare) | 2,000 |
| Frames, channels, etc | 2,000 |
| Central facilities | 1,000 |
| | $16,000/hectare |

| *Operating costs* | |
|---|---|
| Labour (50 workers/1000 hectares, $1000 p.a.) | $    50/yr/hectare |
| Water and minerals | 200 |
| Power (at 1-2c/kwh) | 300 |
| Replacements + repairs | 150 |
| | $   700/yr/hectare |

*Total costs*
    (10 year amortization, 8 per cent interest on capital) = $3,500/yr/hectare
        + $70/ton or £28/ton*

* Before drying, and protein extraction (if needed)

334

Thacker and Babcock (1957) estimated that production costs in fermenter grown cells to be at least 110c/kg. This figure compares favourably with that obtained in practice by Japanese workers who are finding that algae cannot be produced for less than 84c/kg (Tannenbaum and Mateles, 1968). In my estimation, growth of algae under these conditions would result in a final price for extracted protein of approximately £800/ton, which is obviously uneconomic.

There appear to be two possible routes to the economic culture of algae. Both are based on lagoon culture. One would aim at developing a process that would require an investment as low as possible per unit of output. It would depend little upon by-products as a source of income, and would use easily available raw materials, standard pieces of equipment and require no advanced operating skills. One such process has recently been postulated by Meier (1966), whose cost estimates are shown in Table 3.

Only one possibility remains — the use of lagoon culture of algae on sewage to assist in the purification of water. This is applicable only in those areas of the world giving rise to a large volume of sewage, where the supply of water is critical, where the intensity of sunlight over the whole year is adequate and where temperatures of 70–80° are obtained throughout the year. The belt of latitude running through California represents such a compromise. Sites such as the U.K. are hopeless because of low light intensities and low temperatures during the winter. One such system has recently been described by Mattoni *et al.*, (1965).

# THE NUTRITIONAL VALUE OF ALGAL PROTEINS

Protein foods in the human diet are of many different kinds and their nutritional values vary considerably depending on their actual content of protein, the amino acid composition of the protein and the availability of the protein for utilization. We have already seen in Table 1 that in terms of average protein content unicellular green and blue-green algae compare very favourably with some of Man's more conventional food sources. It is also known that both the level and the composition of such protein can be controlled by variations in the cultural conditions. (Taub and Dollar, 1965; Spoehr and Milner, 1949).

Results of amino acid analyses by various workers for a number of Chlorella species and for a number of species of blue-green algae are shown in Tables 4 and 5. The recommended essential amino acid content for an ideal protein for human consumption as defined by the World Health Organization and the Food and Agriculture Organization is tabu-

## Table 4

### Amino acid composition of a number of chlorella (g/100 g protein)

| Amino acids | FAO standard combination | Chlorella species | | | |
|---|---|---|---|---|---|
| | | Chlorella vulgaris (Fowden, 1954) | Chlorella pyrenoidosa (Combs, 1952) | Chlorella pyrenoidosa (Dam et al.,1965) | Chlorella ellipsoidea (Uesaka, 1965) |
| Isoleucine* | 4.2 | 3.5 | 1.69 | 2.20 | 4.5 |
| Leucine* | 4.8 | 6.1 | 1.99 | 4.41 | 9.3 |
| Lysine* | 4.2 | 10.2 | 2.43 | 3.50 | 5.9 |
| Phenylalanine* | 2.8 | 2.8 | 2.14 | 2.65 | 4.2 |
| Tyrosine* | 2.8 | 2.8 | | | 1.7 |
| Cysteine/cystine* | 4.2 | 0.2 | | | 0.7 |
| Methionine* | 2.2 | 1.4 | 0.57 | 0.81 | 0.6 |
| Threonine* | 2.8 | 2.9 | 1.91 | 2.02 | 4.9 |
| Tryptophan* | 1.4 | 2.1 | 0.41 | | |
| Valine* | 4.2 | 5.5 | 2.67 | 3.01 | 7.9 |
| Alanine | | 7.7 | | | 12.2 |
| Glutamic acid | | 7.8 | | | 10.5 |
| Glycine | | 6.2 | 2.20 | | 10.4 |
| Aspartic acid | | 6.4 | | | 8.8 |
| Arginine | | 15.8 | 2.39 | | 5.8 |
| Serine | | 3.3 | | | 5.2 |
| Proline | | 7.2 | | | 5.0 |
| Histidine | | 3.3 | 0.65 | | 1.7 |
| Protein content (% dry weight) | — | — | 40 | 56.5 | ~ 50 |

* Essential amino acids

## Table 5

### Amino acid composition of species of blue-green algae (g/100 g protein)

| Amino acids | FAO Standard Composition | Spirulina maxima (Clément et al., 1967) | Phormidium uncinatum (Rzhanova et al., 1965) | Blue-green algae: Anabaena flosaquae (Pakhomova, 1963) | Anabaena cylindrica (Fowden, 1954) | Anabaena cylindrica (Hopkins & Gordon) (prev. unpub.) | Gloeocapsa alpicola (Hopkins & Gordon) (prev. unpub.) |
|---|---|---|---|---|---|---|---|
| Isoleucine* | 4.2 | 6.03 | 2.20 | } 7.7 | 3.9 | 5.8 | 6.2 |
| Leucine* | 4.8 | 8.02 | 5.95 | } | 6.1 | 9.7 | 10.9 |
| Lysine* | 4.2 | 4.59 | 7.83 | 4.2 | 6.6 | 5.3 | 4.9 |
| Phenylalanine* | 2.8 | 4.97 | 4.0 | 1.72 | 2.9 | 4.4 | 2.2 |
| Tyrosine* | 2.8 | 3.95 | 1.77 | 1.82 | 1.6 | | |
| Cysteine/cystine* | 4.2 | 0.4 (Cystine) | 3.53 | | | | |
| Methionine* | 2.2 | 1.37 | 2.64 | 1.44 | 1.2 | 0.8 | 1.2 |
| Threonine* | 2.8 | 4.56 | 11.03† | 4.88 | 5.7 | 2.1 | 2.7 |
| Tryptophan* | 1.4 | 1.40 | | 0.68 | 1.0 | 5.8 | 6.3 |
| Valine* | 4.2 | 6.49 | 7.94 | 3.61 | 7.0 | 6.8 | 6.6 |
| Alanine | | 6.8 | 8.83 | 8.09 | 6.0 | 10.6 | 10.5 |
| Glutamic acid | | 12.6 | 9.71 | 5.50 | 5.6 | 13.0 | 13.8 |
| Glycine | | 4.75 | 3.09 | 7.00 | 5.5 | 6.3 | 6.2 |
| Aspartic acid | | 8.6 | 2.2 | 5.28 | 6.9 | 14.0 | 13.8 |
| Arginine | | 6.5 | 26.40 | 21.95 | 11.7 | 9.6 | 8.6 |
| Serine | | 4.2 | | 3.83 | 2.4 | 4.6 | 5.6 |
| Proline | | 3.9 | | | 5.0 | | |
| Histidine | | 1.77 | 3.09 | 5.88 | 2.5 | 1.6 | 1.1 |
| Protein content (% dry weight) | | 62 | 31.73 | — | | 26.25 | 36 |

\* Essential amino acids
† Also serine

lated for comparison. From the results presented both in Table 4 and by other workers (Leveille *et al.*, 1962; Tamura *et al.*, 1959), it is evident that whilst all the essential amino acids are present in Chlorella species, the protein is low in sulphur-containing amino acids and is particularly deficient in methionine. This seems to be a common feature of all green algae examined to date, for low levels of sulphur-containing amino acids have also been reported for Scenedesmus species (Tamura *et al.*, 1959; Mitsuda *et al.*, 1961) and for a number of filamentous green algae, including *Uronema gigas,* Stigeoclonium, Hormidium and Ulothrix (Hindak and Pribil, 1968). Green algae are not alone in showing low methionine levels, for the same deficiency is found regularly in other vegetable foods, particularly in soya beans.

On the whole, all species of blue-green algae which have been examined to date (Table 5) show slightly higher levels of essential amino acids than green algae; as in the green algae, however, the levels of sulphur-containing amino acids are low, but in this case methionine levels are much more favourable. The level of cysteine/cystine in *Phormidium uncinatum* seems incredibly high and this result probably merits re-examination.

Whilst a large number of animal feeding trials with algae have now been reported, relatively few studies have been conducted on the nutritional adequacy of this material for man. Much of the research on human subjects has been limited to taste tests and rough estimates of nutritive value. Protein efficiency ratios (Table 6) quoted by Ribbons (1968), on the basis of feeding trials with rats, show that Chlorella protein is clearly adequate, in the sense that it can provide the essential amino acids; additionally, the protein efficiency ratio is higher than for most vegetable and cereal proteins. On this basis, we are reasonably safe in assuming that the nutritive value of Chlorella protein is relatively high and that other things being equal the protein could be used as a supplement in human food.

The earliest recorded human feeding trial with algae was conducted by Jorgensen and Convit (1953) who fed a green algal 'Plankton soup' in amounts up to 35 g per man daily to patients in a Venezuelan leper colony. The trials were conducted over a 3 year period. In many patients acceptability was good, and increased energy, weight gain and improved general health was noted. No adverse side-effects were described at that time. In later reports, however, adverse factors, particularly from the human acceptability standpoint, were mentioned (Tamura *et al.*, 1958; Hayami and Shino, 1958).

Powell, Nevels and McDowell (1961) attempted to determine the maximum quantity of algae which could be added to the diet of man without causing pathological symptoms. Five volunteers were fed with

Table 6

Protein Efficiency Ratios (PER) of known foods and Chlorella*

| Food | PER |
|---|---|
| Whole egg | 3.5 |
| Fish flour | 3.0 |
| Whole milk | 2.7 |
| Chlorella | 2.17 |
| Soya flour | 2.04 |
| Whole wheatbread | 1.1 |
| Cereal protein | 0.03 |
| Gelatin | Negative |

$$PER = \frac{Weight\ gain}{weight\ of\ available\ protein\ consumed}$$

* After D. W. Ribbons, *Chem. and Ind.*, 1968, No. 26, 867

increasing amounts of a mixture of Chlorella and Scenedesmus, which had been blanched, vacuum-dried and autoclaved before incorporation into their diet. The algae, which contained 59 per cent protein, were given alone, mixed into milk, or added to baked products such as cakes and pastries before cooking, at levels in the diet of 10, and then 20, 50, 100, 200 and finally 500 g per day for each subject. All five men tolerated the diets supplemented with algae below the 100 g level, although even early in the study there were some adverse gastro-intestinal symptoms. Above this level, some subjects suffered nausea, vomiting and abdominal pain. Two of the five subjects tolerated algae at the 500 g level as the only source of food, but not without symptoms. All the symptoms noted were more pronounced at the start of each experimental period and disappeared within 48 h of returning to an ordinary diet. During the course of the experiment, all subjects lost weight from 1 to 2 kg. Faecal analysis led the authors to conclude that the digestibility of protein, fat and carbohydrates decreased with the increase of algae in the diet. Blood counts and urine analyses were normal for all subjects and follow-up examinations after the experiment failed to reveal toxicity.

More recently, Dam and his colleagues at the University of Nebraska (1965) have examined the feasibility of using algae as the principle source of nitrogen for human subjects. Two separate experiments were conducted in which algal protein contributed over 90 per cent of the total nitrogen intake. In the first experiment, whole green lyophilized *Scenedesmus obliquus* was fed in various forms over a 5 day period at a level of 7.1 g N/day to five volunteers. At the end of the trial, the mean nitrogen balance for the subjects was +0.20 g N/day. In the second experiment, using five different subjects, two levels of an ethanol-extracted commercial strain of *Chlorella pyrenoidosa 71105* were fed

(6.0 and 10.0 g N/day), each for a period of 10 days. The mean nitrogen balance for the 6.0 g algae nitrogen was negative, whilst that in subjects fed 10 g N/day was positive (0.84 g N/day). High faecal excretion of nitrogen was characteristic of all levels of algal diet in both experiments. As a result, Dam concluded that the algae used in these studies had low apparent nitrogen digestibility, 68 per cent for dried green *Scenedesmus obliquus* and 58 per cent for ethanol-extracted *Chlorella pyrenoidosa*. Digestibility was the major factor contributing to positive or negative nitrogen balances.

In a further series of experiments, these same workers have reported on the supplementary value of *Chlorella pyrenoidosa* protein in the human diet (Lee *et al.*, 1967). They successfully demonstrated that algae can replace one-third of the protein of egg and up to two-thirds of the protein of fish without any impairment in the nitrogen retention of human adults. The protein quality of rice was definitely improved by partial replacement with Chlorella protein, and a similar result has recently been reported by Kofranyi and Jekat (1967) for *Scenedesmus obliquus* protein. Since cereal proteins in general are deficient in lysine, Lee and her colleagues consider that Chlorella protein may prove to be a useful supplement.

Poor digestibility is one of the most undesirable characteristics of algal protein, certainly as far as Chlorella and Scenedesmus species are concerned. A number of workers have studied this problem in human feeding trials, and widely different digestibilities have been reported (Tamura *et al.*, 1959; Miyoshi, 1960; Dam *et al.*, 1965). The reason for the poor digestibility of Chlorella and Scenedesmus species by the human digestive processes is normally ascribed to the presence of a chemically inert cell wall, but it could well be that the non-protein nitrogen (amides, purines, pyrimidines and amino sugars) content of these species is excessively high. It should be emphasized that improved methods for processing algae may render the final product more digestible, and it is also possible that other species of algae will be more digestible.

There is evidence to suggest that when the pigment component of algae is extracted with methanol, ethanol, butanol or ether, the remaining decolorized algal biomass is improved in digestibility (McDowell and Leveille, 1963). Similarly, the digestibility of algae can be improved by the use of suitable drying procedures (Theriault, 1965) or by the use of enzymes such as trypsin, pepsin and cellulase, etc. (Hindak and Pribil, 1968: King and Shefner, 1962; Leveille *et al.*, 1961). All such processing treatments, however, are certain to appreciably increase the cost of algal protein production, and thus the stated objective of producing low-cost protein will almost certainly be lost.

One possible approach to overcome this problem would be to use thin-walled, more readily-digestible species such as the blue-green algae *Spirulina maxima*. The latter is known (Clément *et al.*, 1967) to be rich in protein and vitamins, has a long history of use as a staple item in the human diet of certain tribes in Central Africa, is easily harvested, and is known to be readily digestible. Several species of blue-green algae, particularly *Anabaena flosaquae* and *Microcystis aeruginosa,* are known to produce potent toxins (Schantz, 1967), and thus the choice of a suitable species for nutritional studies would need to be carefully vetted. Animal feeding trials to assess possible toxicity could add substantially to the cost of such a development.

In summary, feeding algae to humans as a major dietary item has been a virtually unexplored field of investigation to the present and many questions remain to be answered. What effects do species and culture conditions have on digestibility? What processing conditions will yield the most acceptable and nutritious product, consistent with favourable economics? Can some higher organism be profitably inserted in the food chain between algae and man? All these questions set a formidable challenge to future researchers.


## ACCEPTABILITY OF ALGAL PROTEIN

The value of algal proteins as a supplementary protein source in the human diet will be related not only to their nutritional properties, but also to the extent to which they can be used in conventional and non-conventional foods, and additionally to the extent to which such foods are acceptable to the consumer.

In recent years, many attempts have been made to introduce novel or unfamiliar foods into the diet of both sophisticated and unsophisticated peoples alike. With few exceptions, however, these have failed. Food yeast, for example, failed to gain acceptance in the U.K. during World War II despite grave food shortages, while Incaparina, initially distributed in a developing country by a governmental agency, has achieved only limited success as a commercial venture, largely because it has come to be identified as 'poor man's food'. Until recently, surprisingly little consideration had been given to algal proteins from the standpoint of palatability and acceptability and this could be one of the main reasons why the algae have made such little impact in the human diet; and yet the precedent had already been set.

The use of algae as human food goes back to very early times. Johnston (1968) has referred to the consumption of red and brown seaweeds by

341

early Chinese, Greek and Roman civilizations. Here in Britain seaweeds such as Dulse *(Rhodymenia palmata)*, Irish Moss *(Chondrus crispus)* and Laverbread *(Porphyra lacinata)* have been eaten for generations. In western countries, however, the use of seaweed for human food is trivial when compared with that in the S.E. Asian countries, especially Japan, where very large tonnages of *Porphyra* and *Laminaria* are farmed annually to produce the foods known respectively as 'Amonori' and 'Kombu' (Oishi *et al.,* 1961). Even the unicellular algae have found a place in the human diet. Farrar (1966) records that certain species of blue-green algae probably formed an important and essential element in the diet of the ancient Aztecs. It is also known that other blue-green algae such as Nostoc have been consumed for centuries in China and South America (Echlin, 1966), and likewise that species of Spirulina are consumed in appreciable quantities as a meat substitute by people in the Republic of Chad (Leonard, 1966). These examples aside, however, there is little evidence to suggest that the algae have, at any time, formed more than a minor constituent in Man's diet.

The real problem in increasing the popularity of algal protein is the divergence in the thinking of the nutritionist and the consumer. When he talks of protein, the nutritionist is speaking of a basic constituent derived from innumerable foods available in many forms. Normally he cares little from which particular food man obtains these constituents or whether they are obtained by direct synthesis or via plants and animals. But the consumer does care. He is a complex amalgam of soma and psyche, who eats food for its own sake and for the pleasure and satisfaction it provides, rather than for its physiological value. Moreover, he has food prejudices and habits which condition his attitudes to foods and cause him to approve or reject a particular food. New foods can be highly digestible and nutritious, but if the appearance is unwholesome, or the consumers' image of the food is unfavourable, or some other attribute such as taste or texture is unappealing, then such foods will not be consumed.

The acceptability of any food thus poses a complex problem in which many factors are involved. Palatability and consumer appeal are the major ones. Each of these in turn is also complex. Palatability, for instance, covers the sensory properties or stimuli coming from the food, which include appearance, taste, odour, aroma or flavour, texture, consistency, mouth feel and so on. Of all these properties, taste is probably the most important, since it conditions the subsequent attitude or behaviour of the consumer towards the food.

In consumer appeal terms, a whole range of criteria interact to determine the acceptability of foods. Cost, availability, ease of preparation, digestibility, keeping quality, packaging, capacity to fit into the consumers diet pattern, nutritive quality and advertising are all included amongst such criteria.

When viewed against these requirements, and aside from any cost considerations, it is not difficult to understand why proteins from mass-cultured unicellular algae have not as yet found acceptance in the human diet. On the face of it, algae such as Chlorella and Scenedesmus have little to commend them. They have no previous history of usage in human dietary regimes, their texture is slimy and uninviting, they have an objectionable colour and flavour and, in the unprocessed state, they tend to have a strong and bitter taste, variously described as bearing resemblance to 'pumpkin' (Burlew, 1953), 'powdered green tea' (Morimura and Tamiya, 1954) or 'forage' (Dam *et al.*, 1965). Additionally, many of the earlier protagonists for algal proteins showed a remarkable lack of imagination in the way in which they set up their taste tests, the algal samples being presented for consumption in an unattractive form and without any of the adornments capable of being given to them by the food technologists of the day.

It is now known that algae such as Chlorella and Scenedesmus can be made palatable, and hence more acceptable, by incorporating them into standard items of the diet (Jorgensen and Convit, 1953; Morimura and Tamiya, 1954; Powell *et al.*, 1961; Lee *et al.*, 1967; Matsunaga and Tsuchiya, 1968). Such results signify the ways in which the barrier of human acceptability can be overcome. Another way is to select any organism which has already found a place in the diet of certain communities, such as *Spirulina platensis,* and in this context the work of Clément and her colleagues at the Institut Français du Pétrole has much to commend it.

In the long run, the wider human acceptability of algal proteins could be made possible by the application of appropriate processing treatments, or by incorporation into the standard items of existing diets. In this regard, a better understanding of the financial, sociological and psychological background which governs the existing dietary habits of the consumer in various regions of the world, is vital.

REFERENCES

Boyd Orr, Lord J. (1968). *Science J.* **4,** 3
Burlew, J. S. (1953). In *Algal Culture from Laboratory to Pilot Plant,* Ed. by J. S. Burlew. Washington D.C.; Carnegie Inst. of Washington Publ. 600, p. 2
Clément, G., Giddey, C. and Menzi, R. (1967). *J. Sci. Fd. Agric.* **18,** 497
Combs, G. F. (1952). *Science, N.Y.* **116,** 453

Dam, R., Lee, S., Fry, P. C. and Fox, H. (1965). *J. Nutr.* **86,** 376

Davis, E. A., Dedrick, J., French, C. S., Milner, H. W., Myers, J., Smith, J. H. C. and Spoehr, H. A. (1953). In *Algal Culture from Laboratory to Pilot Plant,* Ed. by J. S. Burlew. Washington D.C.; Carnegie Inst. of Washington Publ. 600 p. 105

Echlin, P. (1966). *Scient. Am.* **214,** 74

Farrar, W. V. (1966). *Nature, Lond.* **211,** 341

Fisher, A. W. and Burlew, J. S. (1953). In *Algal Culture from Laboratory to Pilot Plant.* Ed. by J. S. Burlew. Washington D.C.; Carnegie Inst. of Washington Publ. 600, p. 303

Food and Agriculture Organization, United Nations, *Third World Food Survey,* Rome, 1963

Fowden, L. (1954). *Ann. Bot.* **18,** 257

Geoghegan, M. J. (1951). *Nature, Lond.* **168,** 426

Golucke, C. G. and Oswald, W. J. (1965). *U.S.A. Patent* 3,195,271

Gould, R. F. (Ed.) (1965). *World Protein Resources* in *Advances in Chemistry Series No. 57,* Washington D.C.; American Chemical Society

Hayami, H. and Shino, K. (1958). *Ann. Rep. Natn. Inst. Nutr., Tokyo,* 59.

Hindak, F. and Pribil, S. (1968). *Biologia Pl.* **10,** 234

Johnston, C. S. (1968). *Process Biochemistry,* October, 11

Jorgensen, J. and Convit, J. (1953). In *Algal Culture from Laboratory to Pilot Plant.* Ed. by J. S. Burlew. Washington D.C.; Carnegie Inst. of Washington Publ. 600

King, M. E. and Shefner, A. M. (1962). *U.S. Air Force Tech. Doc. Rep.* AMRL-TDR-62-91, p. 1

Kofranyi, E. and Jekat, F. (1967). *Hoppe-Seyler's Z. Physiol. Chem.,* **348,** 84

Kott, Y. and Wachs, A. M. (1964). *Appl. Microbiol.* **12,** 292

Lee, S. K., Fox, H. M., Kies, C. and Dam, R. (1967). *J. Nutr.* **92,** 281

Leonard, J. (1966). *Nature, Lond.* **209,** 126

Leone, D. E. (1963). *Appl. Microbiol.* **11,** 427

Leveille, G. A., Sauberlich, H. E. and Edelbrock, J. A. (1961). *U.S. Army Med. Res. and Nut. Lab. Rep.* **259**

Leveille, G. A., Sauberlich, H. E. and McDowell, M. E. (1962). *U.S. Air Force Tech. Doc. Rep.* AMRL-TDR-62-116, p. 405

McDowell, M. E. and Leveille, G. A. (1963). *Fed. Proc. Fedn. Am. Soc. exp. Biol.* **22,** 1431

Matthern, R. O. and Koch, R. B. (1964). *Fd. Tech.,* **18,** 652

Mattoni, R. H. T., Keller, E. C. and Myrick, H. N. (1965). *Bioscience,* June, p. 403

Matsunaga, N. and Tsuchiya, K. (1968). *Japan Patent* No. 6,965/68

Meier, R. L. (1966). *Science and Economic Development,* Cambridge, Mass.; MIT Press

Mitsuda, H., Shikanai, T., Yoshida, K. and Kawai, F. (1961). *J. Jap. Soc. Fd. Nutr.* **13,** 401

Miyoshi, T. (1960). *Shikoku Acta med.* **16,** 76

Morimura, Y. and Tamiya, N. (1954). *Fd Tech.* **8,** 179

Oishi, K. (1961). In *Industrial Uses of Algae,* C. S. Johnston, *Process Biochemistry,* October 1968, p. 11

Pakhomova, M. V. (1963). *Biochemical Investigations of some Algae,* Diss. MGU

Powell, R. C., Nevels, E. M. and McDowell, M. E. (1961). *J. Nutr.* **75,** 7

Ribbons, D. W. (1968). *Chemy. Ind.* No. 26, 867-870

Rzhanova, G. N. and Goryunova, S. V. (1965). *Mikrobiologiya* **34,** 268

Schantz, E. J. (1967). In *Biochemistry of Some Foodborne Microbial Toxins,*
   Ed. by Richard I. Mateles and Gerald N. Wogan. Cambridge, Mass.; M.I.T. Press
   p. 51
Spoehr, H. A. and Milner, H. W. (1949). *Pl. Physiol.* **24,** 120
van Swaaij, W. P. M. (1964). *Ph. D. Thesis,* Technical University, Eindhoven.
Tamiya, H. (1957). *A. Rev. Pl. Physiol.,* **8,** 309
Tamura, E., Baba, H., Tamura, A., Matsuno, N., Kobatake, Y. and Morimoto, K.
   (1958). *Ann. Rep. Natn. Inst. Nutr.,* Tokyo, Japan, 20
Tamura, E., Nishihara, A., Isobe, S. and Matsuno, N. (1959). *Eiyogaku Zasshi,* **17,**
   19
Tannenbaum, S. R. and Mateles, R. I. (1968). *Science J.,* **4,** 87
Taub, F. B. and Dollar, A. M. (1965). *J. Fd. Science,* **30,** 359
Thacker, D. R. and Babcock, H. (1957). *J. solar Energy Sci. Engng.* **1,** 37
Theriault, R. J. (1965). *Appl. Microbiol.* **13,** 402
Uesaka, S. (1965). *Wld Rev. Anim. Prod.,* (4), Oct-Dec., 11
Vincent, W. A. (1969). *Process Biochemistry* **4,** (6), 45
Wassink, E. C., Kok, B. and van Oorschot, J. L. P. (1953). In *Algal Culture from
   Laboratory to Pilot Plant,* Ed. J. S. Burlew. Washington D.C.; Carnegie Inst. of
   Washington Publ. 600, p. 55

# SOYA PROTEIN ISOLATES FOR FOOD

EDWIN W. MEYER

*Central Soya Company, Chicago, U.S.A.*

## INTRODUCTION

A 1968 report to the United Nations stresses, in one policy objective, the need to increase the direct food use of oilseeds and oilseed protein concentrates by a broader segment of the human population (United Nations, 1968). More recently, Scrimshaw (1969) stated in his Trulson Memorial Lecture that 'among the unconventional sources of protein, the highest priority must go to oilseed meals'.

Over the years, numerous publications have described the potential of the soya bean as an additional source of food protein. In spite of its long history of use for food in the Orient, and its position as a primary protein source for the feeding of livestock and poultry, the further adoption of the soya bean as a protein food or food ingredient for direct human consumption has been slow. It is recognized that the technological problems involved are often overshadowed by sociological, psychological and economic factors.

Much promise has been held out for the newer soya protein concentrates and isolates as a source of dietary protein because of their higher protein content, improved flavour and ease of incorporation into a broader variety of food systems as compared to the traditional soya flours (Anson, 1958). Whether these can have a significant near-term impact on the food protein shortage is highly problematical. This paper presents a review of the commercial preparation of soya protein isolate, a description of certain basic features of its composition and properties, and finally, a short discussion of its utilization in processed foods, particularly in relation to functional and nutritional contributions. Perhaps progress in this area can provide a useful reference point in the development and utilization of other oilseed isolates.

For purposes of trade in the U.S.A., isolated soya protein has been defined as the major proteinaceous fraction of soya beans prepared from high-quality, sound, clean, dehulled soya beans by removing a preponderance of the non-protein components and shall contain not less than 90 per cent protein (N x 6.25) on a moisture-free basis (*Soybean Blue Book*, 1966). Although this definition is quite loose, it has served a useful purpose in commercial channels. At this stage of development and introduction to the food industry, a more rigid definition could be premature. I am certain that we will witness the development of various isolates designed to meet the needs of individual food systems.

## PROCESSING OF SOYA PROTEIN ISOLATE

*(a) Source material*—Sound, mature field-run soya beans of No. 1 or No. 2 yellow grade are the source material for the production of isolate in the U.S.A. These grades have been carefully defined, and grading is supervised by the U.S.A. Department of Agriculture for commodity trading purposes (*Soybean Blue Book*, 1968). At present there is no segregation as to variety. Such a practice must await fuller appreciation of the influence of varietal characteristics upon the qualities of the isolate that are of significance in food manufacture. Up to the present, the incidence of aflatoxin contamination of soya beans in the U.S.A., has been very low, and has been restricted to low grade beans (Shotwell *et al.*, 1969). These beans are cleaned to remove foreign matter of field origin, dried to less than 14 per cent moisture, and stored in such manner as to prevent infestation by insects and rodents, and to prevent the growth of micro-organisms.

For processing, the beans are again cleaned, then cracked, dehulled and flaked for oil extraction. The extraction is done in a continuous counter-current manner with a selected lower hydrocarbon fraction by well established procedures. The defatted flakes are then 'desolventized'. This is a critical stage and must be done with limited moist heat to produce flakes having a maximum nitrogen dispersibility (Smith *et al.*, 1966).

*(b) Protein processing*—The basic elements of protein-isolation from defatted soya bean flakes are relatively simple *(Figure 1)*, and are well documented in the literature (Smith, 1958; Meyer, 1967; Cogan *et al.*, 1967). However, there exists little published information on the specifics of the design and operation of processing plants since large-scale know-how is limited currently to a few industrial organizations.

The defatted flakes are extracted with an aqueous medium which may vary in pH from near neutrality to a moderately alkaline pH. pH adjustment is usually accomplished with common food-grade alkalies such as sodium and calcium hydroxides. Extraction variables such as particle size, liquids-to-solids ratio, pH, agitation, temperature and time are selected to give optimally economic yields. These have recently been discussed by

DEFATTED SOYA BEAN FLAKES

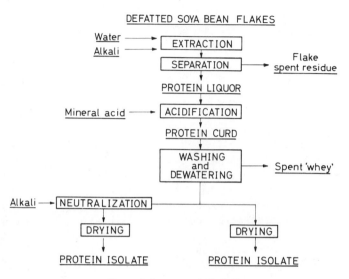

*Figure 1. Soya protein isolation*

Cogan *et al.* (1967), and so there is no need to dwell on them here. It should be pointed out, however, that certain of these extraction conditions, together with subsequent processing conditions, have an important bearing on the functional and nutritional qualities of the isolated protein. For example, at very high pH there is a gradual destruction of cystine and a marked alteration in the gelation properties of the protein.

After extraction, the protein-containing extract is separated from the insoluble flake residue by appropriate mechanical devices. The major globulins are then precipitated by the addition of food-grade acid, usually hydrochloric acid. The pH of the clarified extract is lowered to about pH 4.5, at which pH the solubility of the globulins is near a minimum. The major protein fraction separates as a finely-divided white curd. This curd is then separated to remove the soluble constituents present in the whey. Because of the presence of soluble oligosaccharides, proteins, peptides and amino acids, salts and minor constituents, washing the curd increases the purity of the separated protein. The washed curd can than be concentrated to a heavy slurry or cake containing from 15 to 30 per cent solids.

The concentrated and washed protein can be either dried as such or neutralized and subsequently dried. Neutralization of the curd is accomplished with food-grade alkali with adjustment of the pH to about 7 prior to drying. The isolate is available in several forms, including the so-called 'isoelectric form' or as sodium, potassium or calcium derivatives. Most often, drying is done in a spray drier. The temperature of drying, by whatever means, is an important factor since excessive heat can result in loss in solubility, loss of water absorption on rehydration, discoloration and even degradation in nutritional quality. At present, the sodium derivative is the most important, commercially, in the U.S.A. because of its ready water dispersibility.

Sound process design requires sanitary construction in stainless steel with manual or automatic clean-in-place systems. Critical attention must be given to sanitary process control to prevent microbial growth and contamination thereby assuring that the product meets food-grade standards (Meyer, 1967).

Various literature references indicate that the yield of isolated soya protein, in a process such as described here, may vary considerably. One pilot plant study reported yields of 33–43 per cent based upon defatted, dehulled flake weight (Alderks, 1949). Another study employing ideal laboratory conditions reported a yield of about 42 per cent, but it was stated that 30 per cent was good for commercial operations (Smith, 1958). The yield is directly dependent upon the protein content of the

Table 1

By-Products

---

PROTEIN ISOLATION FROM OIL SEEDS

OIL SEED MILLING

Foreign matter,

seed coats, etc.

PROTEIN ISOLATION

Insoluble residues

Soluble solids

---

source material (Smith *et al.*, 1966), the extent of protein denaturation in the production of the source material, the extraction conditions, and the efficiency of various unit operations (Cogan *et al.*, 1967).

*(c) Processing by-products*—The isolation of soya protein results in the generation of by-products, both liquid and solid, which must be dealt with (Table 1). The solid by-products formed in seed milling and those arising from the drying of spent insoluble residue from protein extraction are not difficult to handle, but they must be disposed of economically so as to improve the cost of the protein operation. These have been used in animal feeds, principally ruminant feeds, because of their higher fibre content. Smith (1958) *et al.* (1962) discussed the more troublesome whey problem, but approaches to the resolution of this processing problem have been described (Smith *et al.*, 1962; Circle *et al.*, 1968). The solids in the whey can also be used in the feeding of ruminants for the energy values contained in the oligosaccharide fraction.

## COMPOSITION OF SOYA PROTEIN ISOLATE

*(a) Proximate analysis*—The proximate analyses of samples of several commercially-available soya protein isolates are given in Table 2. Two of the isolates, *C* and *D,* are of the isoelectric form and hence are not dispersible in water. The soluble forms show good nitrogen solubility.

Table 2

Proximate Analyses of Commercial Soya Protein Isolates

|  | A | B | C | D |
|---|---|---|---|---|
| Moisture % | 4.7 | 6.4 | 7.6 | 3.7 |
| Protein (N x 6.25), % | 92.8 | 92.2 | 92.9 | 94.7 |
| Protein, mfb., % | 97.4 | 98.7 | 100.0 | 98.4 |
| Crude Fibre, % | 0.2 | 0.1 | 0.1 | 0.2 |
| Ash, % | 3.8 | 3.5 | 2.0 | 2.7 |
| Nitrogen Solubility Index, % | 8.5 | 95 | — | — |
| pH (1:10 aq. disp.) | 7.1 | 6.8 | 5.2 | 5.5 |

It should be pointed out that high nitrogen solubility is not a critical factor in many food systems and may be undesirable in some. These isolates have high protein (N x 6.25) and low crude fibre contents, indicative of good flake residue separation and adequate curd washing. The soluble forms are slightly higher in ash content because of neutralization of the protein curd before drying.

*(b)  Amino acid composition*—The essential amino acid compositions of several commercially-available isolates are shown in Table 3 (Meyer, 1967). These isolates show very similar patterns with some minor differences. These differences may be due to variations in source material and processing conditions. Rackis *et al.* (1961) have pointed out that the isolates, as a rule, are lower in the growth-limiting sulphur amino acids than the source flakes or meal. In contrast, the total whey proteins, those not recovered in isolation, are higher in these amino acids than either the isolates or the meal. This is important in nutritional considerations and will be discussed later in this report.

Table 3

Amino acid composition of soya protein isolates
Essential Amino Acids, g/16 g N*

|  | A | B | C |
|---|---|---|---|
| Lysine | 6.0 | 6.0 | 5.8 |
| Methionine | 1.2 | 1.0 | 1.0 |
| Cystine † | 1.2 | 0.9 | 0.9 |
| Tryptophan ‡ | – | 1.3 | 1.3 |
| Threonine | 3.6 | 3.7 | 3.8 |
| Isoleucine | 4.6 | 4.9 | 4.8 |
| Leucine | 7.7 | 8.1 | 7.8 |
| Phenylalanine | 5.2 | 5.6 | 5.5 |
| Valine | 4.6 | 5.0 | 4.6 |

*Ion-exchange chromatography
†Determined as cysteic acid (Schram *et al.*)
‡Colorimetric method (Spies and Chambers)

*(c)  Minor components*—It is obvious that a soya protein isolate may contain a number of minor components arising from flake constituents or introduced in processing. These can be eliminated, for the most part, with sufficient protein purification; however, this is limited by the practical aspects of economics and of technology. These may include some residual fibre, salts, phytic acid (Smith *et al.*, 1957), carbohydrates (Wolf *et al.*, 1966), bound lipid material, other minor organic components of the flake (Nash *et al.*, 1967) and those proteins of the whey not removed in curd separation and washing. Most commercial isolates contain about 0.7 per cent phosphorus, present chiefly as phytic acid or phytates.

## PROPERTIES OF SOYA PROTEIN ISOLATE

The protein isolates of commerce are derived from the major reserve globulins of the soya bean (Table 4) and thus are of heterogeneous origin. During commercial isolation, these proteins are subjected to conditions of

Table 4

Major reserve gobulins of the soya bean*

| Ultra-centrifuge fraction | Percentage of water-extractable protein | Sedimentation constant $S^o_{20,w}$ | Molecular weight | Isoelectric point |
|---|---|---|---|---|
| 2S | 18 | – | 26,000 | – |
| 7S† | 27 | 7.9S | 330,000 (180,000, 210,000) | 4.9 |
| 11S† | 34 | 12.2S | 350,000 | ∿5 |
| 15S | 6 | – | – | – |

*Adapted from Wolf (1969)
†Evidence indicates that the 7S fraction contains three immuno-chemically homogeneous proteins, β-conglycinin, γ-conglycinin and glycinin monomer; and the 11S fraction is composed of glycinin dimer (Catsimpoolas *et al.*, 1969, 1969a)

Table 5

Major proteins of soya bean whey (Albumins)*

| Ultra-centrifuge fraction | Percentage of water-extractable protein | Purified protein | Sediment-ation constant $S^o_{20,w}$ | Molecular weight | Isoelectric point |
|---|---|---|---|---|---|
| 2S | 9 | Trypsin Inhibitor | 2.3S | 21,500 | 4.5 |
| | | Chalcone Flavanone Isomerase | 1.6-2S | – | – |
| 6S | 6 | Haem-agglutinin(s) | 6.15S | 89,000–110,000 | 6.1 |
| | | Lipoxidase | 5.6S | 102,000 | 5.4 |
| | | β–Amylase | 4.67S | 61,700–69,100 | 5.85 |

*Adapted from Wolf (1969)

pH, temperature and salt concentration which are conducive to protein dissociation-association reactions, and hence the product is a complex mixture of altered proteins (Nash *et al.*, 1967a; Wolf *et al.*, 1964). Nonetheless, a more detailed knowledge of the character of the individual protein entities of the source material will provide a foundation for understanding the nature and behaviour of the commercial isolates. In recent years, much basic information on the major globulins and bio-logically-active proteins (Table 5) of the soya bean has been reported; however, an adequate review of this unfolding area of endeavour is not within the scope of this discussion.

Isolated soya protein is customarily merchandized in the U.S.A. as a spray dried powder having a cream-white colour. The neutral product, which is the major factor in the market, has a low flavour intensity as compared to the available soya flours and soya protein concentrates (Circle *et al.*, 1958). Its flavour has often been described as slightly cooked cereal-like with off notes. Although the isolate is now used in the manufacture of certain processed foods wherein its flavour is not incompatible with the flavour profile of the food product, there is intensive development effort in progress to produce a blander product which will permit its incorporation in a broader variety of processed foods. Even so, it stands to reason that the design of intentional flavouring is necessary to match established flavour images (Anson, 1958). It is important to recognize that a bland isolate may alter flavour characteristics in food products of established composition by interaction with other components in the food system. Obviously, the problem is less critical in the design of new foods which have no established and accepted flavour patterns.

Several past reviews have mentioned the various physical and chemical properties of soya protein isolates which can be of significance in the design of foods from a functional standpoint (Anson, 1958; Johnson *et al.*, 1959; Ziemba, 1966). These functional properties include gelling, emulsifying, emulsion stabilizing, foaming, texture and fibre forming, thickening, moisture and fat binding, and the like. In spite of the importance of these characteristics in processed food design, very few of these are the subject of reported studies. Certainly these merit further investigation to develop the full value of soya protein as a food ingredient.

Circle *et al.* (1964) have reported on the rheological properties of relatively concentrated dispersions of soya protein isolate. In particular, these authors discuss the properties of protein gels which are of value in developing chewy structures desirable in certain food items. These gels, which are thermosetting, are concentration, pH and temperature dependent. Common food ingredients, such as starches and fats, may be incorporated in these gel structures to provide prototypes of textured food systems. The chewy gel concept has been described in a number of patents (Anson, 1958).

Another characteristic of isolated soya protein which has received much attention is its fibre-forming properties. The resulting fibres form the matrix for a variety of formulated analogues which are surprisingly meat-like in quality (Odell, 1967). The technology of food-fibre spinning is based upon earlier efforts in developing regenerated protein filaments for textile use. In the process, soya protein isolate in caustic dispersion, is maintained at high pH to develop good fibre-forming properties. Subsequently, the dispersion is spun into an acidic coagulating-precipitating bath. The fibres are collected into tows, washed, and finally combined with other food ingredients to form meat analogues. *Figure 2* shows a patented device for food-fibre spinning.

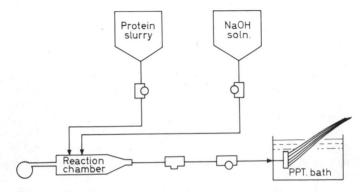

*Figure 2. Soya protein food fibre (U.S. Patent 3, 118,959)*

Recently, Kelley *et al.* (1966) described the changes in protein during the alkaline 'ripening' process. They conclude that there is a dissociation and unfolding of the protein and the generation of new inter-chain linkages through sulphydryl-disulphide interchange. In addition, they point out the role of both hydrogen and ionic bonding in fibre formation. However, further basic information is needed to clarify molecular changes in fibre formation.

Another area which has been the subject of some investigation is the foaming qualities of isolated soya protein (Eldridge *et al.*, 1963). After alcohol washing, soya protein forms very stable foams either above or below its isoelectric point. It was found that heating the whipping dispersion before aeration or increasing the protein concentration enhances foam stability. The alcohol treatment of the protein removes a small quantity of lipid-like material. The denaturation of the soya bean globulins by aqueous isopropanol has been described (Wolf *et al.*, 1964).

## FOOD USES OF SOYA PROTEIN ISOLATE

The major current food uses and areas of potential use for soya protein isolate are given in Table 6.

*(a) Processed meat and meat-like products*—The largest single area of current food utilization in the U.S.A. is in certain processed comminuted meat products (Meyer, 1967). Here it is employed as a minor additive for

Table 6

Food uses of soya protein isolates

Comminuted meat products
    Frankfurters
    Bologna
    Miscellaneous sausage
    Luncheon loaves
    Canned luncheon loaves
    Poultry products

Bakery Products
Dairy-Type products
    Coffee whiteners
    Whipped toppings
    Frozen dessert
    Beverage powder
    Cheeses

Dried Meat Bits
Infant Formulations

its moisture-binding, fat-emulsifying and meat emulsion stabilizing properties (Rock *et al.*, 1966). Pearson *et al.* (1965) found isolated soya protein to be a poorer emulsifier than the milk proteins using a model system. However, this could not be confirmed, and was indeed reversed in actual sausage production tests as reported by Inklaar *et al.* (1969). These authors discussed the influence of variable parameters, such as time, temperature, concentration, etc., on the stability of a model emulsion system. This general area was also explored by Schut (1968) who concluded that a non-coagulating protein is the most suitable one for emulsifying ability and stability. However, in view of the coagulating power of myosin, this needs further clarification. In tests on canned frankfurters and luncheon meat, processed under sterilizing conditions, Bocksch (1965) found that by inclusion of isolated soya protein, there was a considerable reduction in fat and jelly desposits. Certain discrepancies in the evidence from meat product tests and from model systems indicate that more information is needed on the practical applicability of the model system for processed meat products.

In recent years, dehydrated meat bits comprised of cooked shredded meat, both red meat and poultry, and soya protein isolate have appeared in the U.S.A. market place (Coleman *et al.*, 1966). These meat bits are a part of convenience foods such as dry soup mixes and dry casserole food mixes.

Although meat-like foods derived from fibre and other textured soya proteins (Frank *et al.*, 1959) are on the market, I do not foresee any major displacement of meat and dairy foods where these are available. We can

355

look for evolutionary changes wherein the consumer will be presented with new convenience items containing vegetable proteins. It is also apparent that there exists a much broader potential in combining meat, fish and dairy proteins with vegetable proteins to produce food items having consumer appeal. In speaking of meat products, Call (1968) stated that the extended meat products can fill a market gap as the costs of producing red meat slowly rise.

*(b)  Bakery products*—At present, soya protein isolate is not used in significant quantity in the production of commercial bread in the U.S.A. Nevertheless, the use of the protein in bread has been studied by a number of workers with a view toward improvement of nutritional value of the wheat product (Finney *et al.*, 1963; Ehle *et al.*, 1965; Mizrah *et al.*, 1967). Isolated soya protein does not have the characteristic extensibility of wheat gluten. When added to leavened bread, particularly at higher levels, it results in decreased loaf volume with concomitant decrease in certain aesthetic values. However, this is true of many protein additives. It has been pointed out that the isoelectric and calcium forms cause less loaf volume reduction than the sodium derivative. A recent report by Mizrah *et al.* (1967) indicates that the inclusion of lecithin in the bread formulation counteracts the volume depressant effect. However, this is true only if the loaf formulation has either no shortening or is very lean in shortening. Nevertheless, with correct moisture addition, reasonably acceptable bread with good nutritional value can be made with the proper isolate at a level of addition up 6 per cent. In contrast to the isolate, significant quantities of soya flour and soya protein concentrate are used in bakery products.

*(c)  Dairy-type products*—Although isolated soya protein offers much potential in the manufacture of dairy-type products, these products are not produced in the U.S.A. in significant volume. A few such as liquid coffee whitener, liquid whip topping and an imitation milk enjoy limited distribution in selected geographical areas. However, there is considerable development effort being devoted to a broad variety of dairy-type foods. These include coffee whiteners, whip toppings, imitation milks, convenience beverage powders, frozen desserts, sour cream and cheese-like products.

Very little has been published on the use of soya protein isolate in dairy-like foods. Recently there has been much interest and grave concern in the U.S.A. over the introduction of filled and imitation milks (Hetrick, 1969). In part, the interest has centred on the utilization of soya protein isolate, together with vegetable fat, sugars, minerals, vitamins and flavouring, to produce a beverage having milk-like qualities. There is much concern that such imitation milks will not fill the nutritional needs of the consumer. I think we would all agree that because of the importance of fluid milk in milk-consuming areas of the world, any substitute should provide equivalent nutrition.

In the development of acceptable bland-flavoured dairy-like products, the flavour contribution of soya protein isolate will be most critical. Properly processed and stored milk products have a complex flavour profile which is desired by consumers in milk-drinking areas of the world. At present, flavour is a deterrent to the fuller utilization of soya protein isolate in certain simulated milk foods, but flavour improvements will be forthcoming because of the current emphasis in identifying the flavour components and flavour precursors in the source material (Arai *et al.*, 1967).

Soya bean curd or Tofu, often referred to as soya bean cheese, has been a prominent source of food protein in certain Oriental diets. However, this is not truly a cheese since it is a bland product and is eaten either cooked or fried. Recent efforts in Israel were devoted to exploring the utilization of isolated soya protein in fermented cheeses (Zimmerman *et al.*, 1967). These included soft cheeses, hard cheeses and surface-ripened semi-hard cheeses. Some progress was made in all classes, but it is obvious that more work is necessary to develop commercial items having consumer acceptability.

*(d) Miscellaneous food uses*—In the last several years, two hypoallergenic infant formulations containing isolated soya protein have appeared on the U.S.A. market. For many years, soya flour products dominated this market. Recently, Cherry *et al.* (1968) have reported on a clinical study comparing a properietary milk formula and an isolate-containing formula. Although some differences in performance were observed, with usually higher values in the milk-fed group of infants, these authors noted that "higher values of course, do not necessarily mean 'better values'". In contrast to the commercial products, the soya formulation of Cherry *et al.* (1968) did not contain added DL-methionine. The lack of methionine could be responsible for the observed differences in the cited clinical study (Harkins *et al.*, 1967).

A rather unusual and interesting use of isolated soya protein has been found in the spray drying of banana puree (Mizrahi *et al.*, 1967a). It was concluded that isolated soya protein at levels ranging from 4 to 20 per cent, on a dry basis, may be used as an aid in drying the sticky banana mass, as an anti-caking agent in the resulting powder, or as a nutritional supplement in banana powder for infant feeding.

357

## NUTRITIONAL PROPERTIES OF SOYA PROTEIN ISOLATE

An examination of the current food usage of soya protein isolate reveals that it is employed, in the main, for its functional values in processed food rather than for its nutritional contribution. These values are of importance to the food manufacturer in processing control, in the improvement of product quality, in product economy and in the design of new foods. Yet this division in role is not a clear one since nutritional value cannot be divorced from food design, and food of good nutritional value must be presented in a form having consumer-acceptable structure and flavour patterns.

Much has been written about the nutritional value of soya protein products, including meals and flours, and hence this discussion will be limited to selected comments concerning the nutritional properties of soya protein isolate. In general, the isolate has shown lower nutritional value in rat feeding studies than either properly-processed soya flour or soya protein concentrate (Meyer, 1967). Indeed, the protein efficiency ratio values for commercial isolates, as cited in the literature, are quite variable (Longenecker *et al.*, 1964; Meyer, 1967) as illustrated in Table 7. This variation may be due, in part, to variations in the critical sulphur amino acid content as influenced by source material and processing conditions, other deleterious changes through heat processing (Osner *et al.*, 1968), or the presence of growth inhibitory substances including the trypsin inhibitors and haemaglutinins (Cogan *et al.*, 1968; Wolf, 1967). Both Rackis (1966) and Cogan *et al.* (1968) found some antitryptic activity in various soya protein isolates. This suggests the need for adequate separation of the whey proteins during isolation and controlled moist-heat processing to inactivate remaining growth inhibitory material. Supplementation of the isolate with up to 1.5 per cent of DL-methionine on protein weight results in an improved nutritional response (Meyer, 1967).

Table 7

Nutritional value of isolated soya protein
Rat feeding studies: 10% protein diet; 28 day

| Protein product | Percentage protein | Methionine, g/16g N | Available lysine, g/16g N | PER |
|---|---|---|---|---|
| Isoelectric protein (Spray dried)* | 82.7 | 1.10 | 4.81 | 2.06 |
| Ca-coagulated protein (Spray dried)* | 83.9 | 1.05 | 4.58 | 1.94 |
| Commercial isolates† | 86–90 | – | – | 1.4–1.9 |
| Soya protein concentrate‡ | 66 | 1.3 | – | 2.3–2.5 |

*Cogan *et al.* (1968); Casein *PER* – 2.83
†Longenecker *et al.* (1964); Casein *PER* – 3.00
‡Meyer (1967). Casein *PER* – 2.65

Although this nutritional data is important for diets wherein the isolate is the sole source of dietary protein, in processed foods containing other protein sources it is necessary to consider the value of the composite protein.

Because of our interest in meat products, we have evaluated processed comminuted meat-isolated soya protein mixtures ranging up to 25 per cent soya protein in rat feeding studies. In this study, there was no significant decrease in protein efficiency ratio *(Figure 3)*.

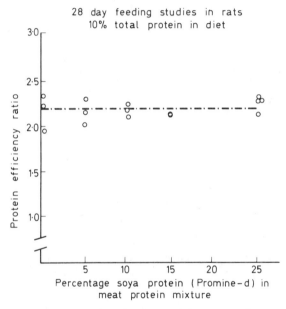

*Figure 3. Nutritional value of meat protein – soya protein mixtures*

More work has been done on the supplementary effect of isolated soya protein in wheat bread (Jansen *et al.,* 1965; Jansen, 1969; Mizrahi *et al.,* 1967). This work shows that the increase in the *PER* of bread, as a result of protein supplementation, is proportional to the lysine content of the bread. Jansen *et al.* (1965) reported that with non-fat dry milk supplementation there is more destruction of lysine in the baking process. There appears to be no significant difference in the *PER* of bread containing the isolate and that of bread containing soya flour at isonitrogeneous levels (Mizrahi *et al.,* 1967). Obviously there is a bread quality advantage in using the more concentrated protein form. It has been reported that above 6 per cent, and up to 10 per cent addition of the isolate, the increase in *PER* of bread is not significant.

There has been some concern about the use of soya flour in certain foods because of the presence of flatulence-producing factors (Steggerda *et al.,* 1966). These could be important in diets where the daily intake of the flour is high. It has been demonstrated that the causative factors, which are associated with the oligosaccharide fraction, are removed during the isolation of soya protein.

## ECONOMICS AND OUTLOOK

The volume of soya protein isolate now being sold for food use in the U.S.A. is estimated to be about 15 million pounds per year. This is 50 per cent higher than an estimate reported in 1967 (Meyer, 1967). The isolate is now selling at about 35–40 cents per pound. This price has not changed materially within the past several years, nor do I foresee any downward trend in the near term in view of rising costs and supported crop prices.

However, the use of soya protein isolate for food will continue to increase, not dramatically, but steadily. In the U.S.A., there is a deterring factor in archaic food product regulations, particularly those of a recipe type. With revision of these, the utilization of soya protein isolate would be stimulated.

In closing, I would suggest that the selected extension of existing animal proteins with vegetable proteins is an area of food technology which merits attention in the development of acceptable and nutritious processed food items. Although the vegetable protein isolates will contribute in a selective way in increasing our food protein supply, I do not feel that these proteins, in contrast to the less refined protein products, will make a significant contribution to lessening the critical world shortage of food protein.

### REFERENCES

Alderks, O. (1949). *J. Am. Oil Chem. Soc.* **26,** 126
Anson, M. (1958). *Processed Plant Protein Foodstuffs.* Ed. by A. Altschul, New York; Academic Press. Chap.11
Arai, S., Koyanagi, O. and Fujimaki, M. (1967). *Agr. Biol. Chem.* **31,** 868
Bocksch, W. (1965). *Fleischwirts.* **45,** 779
Call, D. (1968). *Meat* **35,** 34
Catsimpoolas, N. and Eckenstam, C. (1969). *Archs. Biochem. Biophys.* **129,** 490
– Campbell, T. and Meyer, E. (1969a). *Archs. Biochem. Biophys.* (in press)
Cherry, F., Cooper, M., Stewart, R. and Platou, R. (1968). *Am. J. Diseases Children* **115,** 677-692

Circle, S. and Johnson, D. (1958). *Processed Plant Protein Foodstuffs*. Ed. by
    A. Altschul, New York; Academic Press. Chap.15
– Meyer, E. and Whitney, R. (1964). *Cereal Chem.* **41**, 157
– and Whitney, R. (1968). *U.S. Patent.* 3, 365, 440
Cogan, U., Yaron, A., Berk, Z. and Mizrahi, S. (1967). *J. Am. Oil Chem. Soc.* 321
– – – and Zimmermann, G. (1968). *J. Agric. Fd. Chem.* **16**, 196
Coleman, R. and Creswick, N. (1966). *U.S. Patent.* 3, 253, 931
Ehle, S. and Jansen, G. (1965). *Fd. Technol.* **19**, 129
Eldridge, A., Hall, P. and Wolf, W. (1963). *Fd. Technol.* **17**, 120
Falanghe, H., Smith, A. and Rackis, J. (1964). *Appl. Microbiol.* **12**, 330
Finney, K., Rubenthaler, G. and Pomeranz, Y. (1963). *Cereal Sci. Today.* 8, 166, 183
Frank, S and Circle, S. (1959). *Fd. Technol.* **13**, 307
Harkins, R. and Sarett, H. (1967). *J. Nutr.* **91**, 213
Hetrick, J. (1969). *J. Am. Oil Chem. Soc.* **46**, 58A, 60A, 62A
Inklaar, P. and Fortuin, J. (1969). *Fd. Technol.* **23**, 103
Jansen, G. and Ehle, S. (1965). *Fd. Technol.* **19**, 1439
– (1969). *Am. J. clin. Nutr.* **22**, 38
Johnson, D. and Circle, S. (1959). *Fd. Process.* **36**, 36
Kelly, J. and Pressey, R. (1966). *Cereal Chem.* **43**, 195
Longenecker, J., Martin, W. and Sarrett, H. (1964). *J. Agric. Fd. Chem.* **12**, 411
Meyer, E. (1967). *Proc. Int. Conf. Soybean Protein Foods.* Agr. Res. Ser., USDA,
    Publication ARS-71–35, p. 142
Mizrahi, S., Zimmermann, G., Berk, Z. and Cogan, U. (1967). *Cereal Chem.* **44**, 193
– – – – (1967a). *Cereal Sci. Today.* **12**, 322, 325
Nash, A., Eldridge, A. and Wolf, W. (1967). *J. agric. Fd. Chem.* **15**, 102
– and Wolf, W. (1967a). *Cereal Chem.* **44**, 183
Odell, A. (1967). *Proc. Int. Conf. Soybean Protein Foods.* Agr. Res. Ser., USDA,
    Publication ARS-17–35, p. 163
Osner, R. and Johnson, R. (1968). *J. Fd. Technol.* **3**, 81
Pearson, A., Spooner, M., Hegarty, G. and Bratzler, L. (1965). *Fd. Technol.* **19**, 1841
Rackis, J., Anderson, R., Sesame, H., Smith, A. and Van Etten, C. (1961). *J. Agric.
    Fd. Chem.* **9**, 409
– (1966). *Fd. Technol.* **20**, 1482
Rock, H., Sipos, E. and Meyer, E. (1966). *Meat* **32**, 52
Schut, J. (1968). *Fleischwirts.* **48**, 1030
Schram, E., Moore, S. and Bigwood, E. (1954). *Biochem. J.* 33-37
Scrimshaw, N. (1969). *J. Am. diet. Assoc.* **54**, 94
Shotwell, O., Hesseltine, C., Burmeister, H., Kwolek, W., Shannon, G. and Hall, H.
    (1969). *Cereal Chem.* (in press)
Soybean Blue Book. (1966). *Soybean Dig.* **26**, 20
– (1968). *Soybean Dig.* **28**, 18
Smith, A. and Rackis, J. (1957). *J. Am. Oil Chem. Soc.* **79**, 633
Smith, A. (1958). *Processed Plant Protein Foodstuffs.* Ed. by A. Altschul.
    New York; Academic Press. Chap.10
– Nash, A., Eldridge, A. and Wolf, W. (1962). *J. Agric. Fd. Chem.* **10**, 302
– Rackis, J., Isnardi, P., Cartter, J. and Krober, O. (1966). *Cereal Chem.* **43**, 261
Spies, J. and Chambers, D. (1949). *Anal. Chem.* **21**, 1249 – 1266
Steggerda, F., Richards, E. and Rackis, J. (1966). *Proc. Soc. exp. Biol. Med.*
    **121**, 1235
United Nations. (1968). Publication No. E-68 x 111.2
Wolf, W., Sly, D. and Babcock, G. (1964). *Cereal Chem.* **44**, 328

Wolf, W. and Kwolek, W. (1966). *Cereal Chem.* **43,** 80
− (1967). *Proc. Int. Conf. Soybean Protein Foods.* Agr. Res. Ser., USDA,
    Publication ARS-71−35, p.112
− (1969). *Cereal Sci. Today.* (in press)
Ziemba, J. (1966). *Fd. Engng.* 38, 82
Zimmermann, G. and Berk, Z. (1967). *Final Rep. U.S. Dep. Agric.* Project No.
    UR-A10-(40)-30

# VI. PRESENTATION

# THE ORGANOLEPTIC QUALITIES OF PROTEIN FOODS (WITH SPECIAL REFERENCE TO COOKING PROCEDURES)

## DOREEN A. PARRY

*College of Domestic Science, Edinburgh*

## INTRODUCTION

At this stage, it seems appropriate to stress that people eat foods rather than diets. It would be of little value if adequate supplies of high quality proteins were to become available if such proteins proved unacceptable. Hence, between supplying foods and their physiological utilization lies the problem of presenting them in attractive form so that people will enjoy eating them. It should be added that the importance of food acceptance is increasingly recognized in nutrition studies.

Securing acceptance of foods, even of the highest nutritive value, cannot be taken for granted. Since people are extremely suspicious and conservative in their attitudes to foods to which they are unaccustomed, establishing new dietary habits is inevitably a slow process, although, on a long term basis, feasible. Unfortunately, relatively few people are adventurous where foods are concerned. Both in prosperous Western countries and in less wealthy communities, foods may be rejected solely because of unfamiliar appearance, flavour or texture.

As well as fulfilling nutritional requirements, eating foods normally elicits pleasurable responses. These responses, which attain their highest development in man, are greatest when food is attractively prepared and presented. In most cultures, an important aspect of celebrating a festal occasion is to cook special foods and to serve them with attractive accompaniments.

Factors, other than familiarity, which exert strong influences on food acceptance and hence choice, are economic, social, cultural and religious. The significance of social and economic factors was indicated by Tremolieres (1962). Within this framework, strong elements of individual

365

preference combine with subjective assessments of appearance, flavour and texture, to produce acceptance or rejection of a particular food. Appearance, flavour and texture are all qualities which can be modified by cooking procedures and which can be assessed by sensory methods. This sensory appraisal is a reflection of the organoleptic qualities of a food. Because of its apparent simplicity, sensory evaluation is the method by which palatability is usually assessed. Possible nutritive value usually plays a comparatively minor role in food acceptance.

The problems of food acceptance have been studied by many workers in the fields of Nutrition, Physiology and Psychology often in collaboration with those concerned with physical sciences. It is increasingly clear that, initial choice accomplished, it is inherent sensory qualities as foods are eaten which are of fundamental importance (Caul, 1957; Caul and Sjorstrom, 1959).

## THE ORGANOLEPTIC ASSESSMENT OF FOODS

Some knowledge of the sensory mechanisms concerned in the organoleptic appraisal of foods enables the effects of cooking procedures to be assessed on a sound scientific basis. Several specialized textbooks have become available in recent years. Detailed studies are therefore possible, but, for those unfamiliar with the problems of food testing, a brief summary of the more important aspects is included.

*Visual stimuli – appearance*

Visual stimuli of colour and form are important in organoleptic appraisal. Many authors stress the importance of colour (Mackinney and Little, 1962; Judd and Wyszecki, 1963). Colour and flavour anticipation are associated to the extent that colour distortion may cause confusion in interpreting flavour (Hall, 1958; Pangborn, 1960; Pangborn *et al.*, 1963). The effects of lighting, food dyes and foods and serving dishes of contrasting colours are of significance. Colour changes which parallel development of 'off' flavours cause food rejection. Undesirable flavour and texture are predicted if foods are dried or shrunken.

*Auditory stimuli*

Sounds associated with attractive foods are well recognized. The characteristic sizzling of frying bacon, meat and fish and noises associated with food preparation and service are known to create pleasurable anticipation. Raw fish and meats may be unattractive merely because they 'squeak' as they are chewed. Meats and fish served uncooked are usually modified so that 'squeaking' is less likely. Raw meats are pounded or served in thin slices. Oysters are swallowed whole (Woodworth and

Schlosberg, 1954). Many people have such profound aesthetic objections to eating these foods raw that it is difficult to separate the effects of purely auditory stimuli from psychological and kinaesthetic responses.

*The flavour of foods – olfactory and gustatory stimuli*
Of all organoleptic assessments, flavour is the most complex. The flavour of a food is a fully integrated blend of its odour and taste. Responses to olfactory and gustatory stimuli, are influenced by a variety of factors including personal preference, emotional state, pleasant or unpleasant association and appetite. In addition, a food may be considered to have good flavour when combined with some foods but not with others.

*The influence of olfaction on flavour*—The aroma of foods, although making the major contribution to flavour, has so far proved the more difficult to study. The olfactory receptors discriminate with great sensitivity between a seemingly infinite variety of compounds. Relatively little is understood of the mechanism of olfaction. Diffusion and solution of volatile compounds may be of significance (Amoore, 1952; Amoore *et al.*, 1964). Odour characteristics may be governed by the number of molecules stimulating the receptors in unit time rather than by total number and are probably linked to volatility and molecular size and configuration (Le Magen, 1956).

Considerable practical difficulties arise in assessing the contribution of odour to flavour. In earlier experiments, Amoore suggested seven primary olfactory stimuli but later increased odour descriptions to fourteen. Despite masking and interaction, humans can analyse the most complex aromas. Although GLC is used in investigations, research is handicapped by the problem of securing consistent results.

*Taste*—On the other hand, it has been recognized for many years that there are four primary tastes—sweet, bitter, sour and salt. (Shore, 1892; Skramlik, 1926; Pfaffman, 1954; 1956). Areas where the taste receptors of the tongue are located are known. Tastes described as 'metallic', 'biting', 'burning' and 'cooling' are presumably the result of stimulation of chemoreceptors of the mouth tissues.

Recently, considerable progress in the field of taste perception appears to have been achieved. Common structural characteristics of sweet tasting compounds and ability to form complexes with a protein of the taste buds have been reported. A similar bitter-sensitive protein has also been isolated (Shallenburger, 1964 and 1967; Dastoli and Price, 1966). Sour tastes are principally a response to hydrogen ions. The acids present and their concentration affect the sourness of foods. Saltiness is conferred by electrolytes. Certain ions exert modifying and synergistic effects.

Flavour appraisal of foods is far more complicated than in solutions designed to test primary tastes. Effects of colour have been noted. Variations in texture influence taste – detection is more difficult in gels than in liquids, with foams in an intermediate position* (Mackey and Valassi, 1956). Mackey (1958) reported lower sweet and bitter taste thresholds in aqueous than in oily media. Temperature and contrasts alter sensory responses.

Interaction between the four basic tastes is inevitable. The cook aims to achieve a satisfactory blending of the basic tastes and uses sugar to suppress bitterness, acidity and saltiness and salt to suppress sweetness. Salt and sugar are used to enhance, intensify or modify flavour. In processed foods, monosodium glutamate and nucleotide derivatives – in particular inosine $5'$ monophosphate – are used to enhance meaty and broth flavours, to increase 'mouthfilling' properties and to suppress undesirable flavour notes. (Caul and Raymond, 1964; Kawamura et al., 1964; Yoshimo and Suzuki, 1965). It is generally reported that taste panel scores are higher when small amounts of these additives are used – a finding of greater commercial significance than to the housewife.

*Food texture – sensory evaluation in the mouth*

Before foods are eaten, the cook will usually have pressed, prodded or stirred them, perhaps have broken a portion or noted viscosity in an attempt to ensure an attractive consistency or texture. Effects on cutlery

Table 1
Relations between textural parameters and popular nomenclatures

| Primary parameters | Secondary | Popular terms |
|---|---|---|
| Mechanical characteristics | | |
| Hardness | | Soft → firm → hard |
| Cohesiveness | Brittleness | Crumbly → crunchy → brittle |
| | Chewiness | Tender → chewy → tough |
| | Gumminess | Short → mealy → pasty → gummy |
| Viscosity | | Thin → viscous |
| Elasticity | | Plastic → elastic |
| Adhesiveness | | Sticky → tacky → gooey |
| | | |
| Geometrical characteristics | | |
| Particle size and shape | | Gritty, grainy, coarse, etc. |
| Particle shape and orientation | | Fibrous, cellular, crystalline, etc. |
| Other characteristics | | |
| Moisture content | | Dry → moist → wet → watery |
| Fat content | Oiliness | Oily |
| | Greasiness | Greasy |

*Temperature variation would be inevitable and it was not indicated if volume concentration of a component were constant.

368

and crockery are noted. But it is the touch receptors of the mouth which allow accurate appraisal of texture. Kinaesthetic sensations may also be of importance. Texture is a composite property. Because almost every characteristic of texture requires different measuring instruments, Matz (1962) considered that only sensory methods could yield reliable assessments. Several techniques have been described.

Szczesniak *et al.* (1963) suggested that the texture of foods could be evaluated mainly on the basis of mechanical and geometric characteristics. Her analysis scheme is set out in Table 1.

Brandt *et al.* (1963) developed texture profiles using scales which had been devised by Szczesniak. His techniques are indicated in Table 2.

Table 2

Procedure for evaluating textures

INITIAL
(perceived on first bite)

MECHANICAL

hardness    viscosity    brittleness

GEOMETRICAL

any, depending upon product structure

MASTICATORY
(perceived during chewing)

MECHANICAL

gumminess    chewiness    adhesiveness

GEOMETRICAL

any, depending upon product structure

RESIDUAL
(changes made during mastication)

rate of breakdown    type of breakdown    moisture absorption    mouthcoating

Although — apart from taste — texture is the most important sensory appraisal made in the mouth, quantitative data on the degree of pain produced by 'hot' foods such as curries and foods eaten at low or high temperatures is lacking. Temperature variation alters texture often to a greater extent than flavour.

## THE POSSIBILITIES OF REPLACING ORGANOLEPTIC APPRAISAL BY OBJECTIVE TESTS

Assessing the organoleptic qualities of foods is such a complex process, that positive correlation with objective tests — except for a particular quality – seems unlikely. Although good correlation has been reported, difficulties may be so great as to make objective methods mainly of value in quality control (Blanchard and Maxwell, 1941; McCarthy, 1963; Szczesniak, 1963). Objective measurements of flavour by GLC is, as yet, unsatisfactory (Kendall and Nielson, 1964) but objective measurements of the texture of bread and meat have correlated well with sensory methods (Sperring et al., 1959).

*Comparing subjective and objective assessments*

Although individuals may give different ratings to the same food, correlation between the results achieved by different taste panels is good. Panel members are selected by ability to recognize odours and tastes, and to distinguish slight differences of concentration sufficient to allow ranking on a numerical scale. Olfactory and taste thresholds should be low. With training, they learn to construct odour and flavour profiles and to describe textures with great accuracy. It is usual for them to test only a limited range of foods.

At present it seems that they are more likely to achieve an accurate assessment of foods than can instruments.

## PROPERTIES OF PROTEINS OF PARTICULAR SIGNIFICANCE IN COOKING PROCEDURES

Many of the important characteristics of the proteins of foods are a consequence of the colloidal dimensions of their molecules. Their ability to form sols, gels, foams and emulsions indicates an important influence on appearance and texture and, indirectly, on flavour.

Even in a given foodstuff, dispersion of proteins is variable. That the gluten of cake flours is more dispersed than in bread flours contributes to their different baking qualities. Mechanical treatments prior to cooking may influence dispersion – whisking egg white decreases dispersion by promoting partial protein coagulation. Heating has a similar effect. Depending on isoelectric point, variation of pH causes changes in dispersion. Alkalinity increases gluten dispersion (IEP 6.1), inhibits gel formation in gelatine mixtures and raises the coagulation temperatures of egg proteins. Acids exert similar effects to an extent which depends on proximity to the IEP of the protein concerned.

Enzymes also influence dispersion. Rennin decreases the dispersion of casein thus causing clotting whilst proteolytic enzymes in flour and in unheated milk increase gluten dispersion.

Subjecting protein dispersions to various treatments – many commonly used in cooking – causes denaturation of protein molecules.

Heat, alcohol, alkaloids, tannins, mechanical agitation and radiant energy cause this frequently irreversible change. Colvin (1964) considered that the resulting alteration in chemical, physical and biological properties is not caused by disruption of primary protein structure. Denaturing of proteins is said to make them more digestible in that the 'unfolding' of the protein chain allows easier access of hydrolytic enzymes.

Apart from their colloidal properties, protein molecules are amphoteric. In foods they can, therefore, act as buffers and bind ions at pH values other than their IEP.

The viscosity of protein hydrophilic sol/gel systems, like denaturation, is influenced by concentration, temperature, dispersion, solvation, charge, hysteresis and the presence of other colloids, sugar and salts. Thus the cook may alter the consistency of an egg custard by varying the proportion of eggs and sugar, whisking, and by regulating the temperature and speed of cooking. It is therefore scarcely a matter of surprise that replication is difficult if not impossible!

In cooking foods containing protein, the Maillard reaction is of considerable importance. Melanoidin pigments produce characteristic changes of colour and flavour (Ellis, 1959), combined with possible reduction in biological value (Clegg, 1960). Increased temperatures and high pH favour this reaction.

## METHODS OF COOKING PROTEIN FOODS

Most cooking procedures are likely to influence dispersion, denaturation, viscosity and thus texture, protein/aldose sugar interaction and intermolecular and decomposition reactions to a greater or lesser extent.

There are two main methods of cooking — dry and moist. The most important differences between the two methods arise as a result of higher external temperatures and the greater possibility of surface evaporation of moisture in dry methods. Dry methods include grilling (broiling), baking, frying and roasting. Moist methods include steaming, boiling, braising, stewing, poaching and pressure cooking. In the future, micro-wave cookery may become more common but at present costs are prohibitive for the housewife and the method has serious limitations in large scale catering. Modern practice is to encourage the use of dry methods of cookery whenever practicable and many cooking techniques have been modified to this end.

For those whose experience in the field is restricted and as an illustration of the practical difficulties in controlling variables a short summary of the main cooking procedures is included.

## Grilling

Rapid cooking by radiant heat produces marked surface changes. Infra-red grills make the cooking process even speedier. Foods which do not contain reasonable proportions of fat, should previously be coated with oil or fat to prevent charring and excessive moisture loss.

## Baking and roasting

Baking combines the effects of radiant heat and convection currents. Foods acquire an attractive, crisp, brown surface. Baked meats are often described as roasted — provided evaporation of moisture is possible from all surfaces — although roasting originally implied cooking on a spit by radiant heat. The modern rotisserie or revolving spit fitted in grills or ovens resembles traditional roasting more closely. Meats 'pot roasted' or foil-wrapped cannot be said to have been cooked by a 'dry' method since evaporation of surface moisture is impeded.

Baking and roasting are flexible methods of cooking. Temperature and hence cooking period may be adjusted to give considerable variation in results. These possibilities will be discussed in more detail with special reference to meats.

## Frying

Foods are cooked in varying quantities of fat or oil at temperatures between $160^\circ$ and $200^\circ$C. Moisture evaporates as steam. The selected fat should impart no unpleasant aroma or taste to the foods and its smoke (decomposition) point should be considerably above the required cooking temperatures.

## Stewing, boiling and poaching

In these moist methods of cooking, both the temperature and the quantity of liquid vary. To improve colour and flavour, stewed foods may first be fried before being simmered in a small amount of liquid. (Cooking temperature approximately $88^\circ$C). The cooking liquid is served with the food. Boiling, as such, is not used for protein foods except pasta when rapid bubbling prevents adhesion to the pan base.

Foods like fish and eggs can be successfully cooked in liquid below simmering temperatures and are said to be poached. The gentler bubbling maintains the food's structure. To minimize flavour losses, in both stewing and poaching the amount of liquid should be small.

## Braising

Meat, poultry and fish are cooked on a base of fried vegetables in a minimum of liquid. Preliminary browning may be carried out. Evaporation should be limited. The process combines stewing, steaming and pot roasting.

*Steaming*

This moist method is used mainly in fish and egg cookery. The food at no stage comes into direct contact with water.

*Pressure cooking*

The domestic pressure cooker is based on similar principles to the autoclave. The high temperature achieved and efficient heat transmission shorten the cooking period to an extent which, for foods which cook rapidly, may make the exact timing required impracticable. Even for meats, results can be disappointing. Excessive fibre shrinkage and collagen hydrolysis, may cause the dry fibres to fall apart.

## WHY PROTEIN FOODS ARE COOKED

Protein foods are cooked for reasons which include making them more digestible, increasing their keeping qualities and for safety. Eggs, meat and fish may be cooked for aesthetic reasons. But above all, for the majority, foods are cooked to make them more appetizing, that is to increase their organoleptic appeal. Many techniques — simple and elaborate — are used to secure a highly attractive appearance, flavour and texture. It is always salutary to remember that, whilst maintaining the highest standards of food hygiene and ensuring good nutritive value, the primary aim of cooking procedures must be to improve eating quality, in itself such an important prerequisite to satisfactory assimilation.

Variation in individual preference, in food quality as well as in cooking expertise combine to influence organoleptic appraisal but it is hoped to show that by modifying cooking methods and altering the proportions of added ingredients, foods may achieve desirable characteristics.

Although most protein foods are cooked primarily to enhance their eating quality, some, notably cheese, may be eaten either raw or cooked. Milk is usually considered to have deteriorated when 'cooked'. Eggs, meat, poultry, fish and cereals are seldom eaten raw. In this context, it should be recognized that protein concentrates, however nutritionally satisfactory, may lack desirable texture — although patents to produce textured protein supplements have been awarded (Boyer, Anson and Pader).

## THE EFFECTS OF HEATING MILK

'Raw' milk has a bland flavour and smooth texture. Some workers note a drying effect on the palate. Various flavouring compounds have been isolated (Jenness and Patton, 1959; Josephson, 1954).

Heating milk — even moderately — causes loss of volatile components. Sulphides are formed from the globulin fraction and the fat globule membrane. Above 74° C — approximately 2° C higher than pasteurization temperature — caramelization and Maillard reactions and the production of methyl ketones from milk fat combine to cause changes in colour and flavour (Richter, 1952). The extent to which 'cooked' flavour develops is dependent on length of heating and temperature attained. (Josephson, 1954; Parks and Patton, 1961).

Subtle and gradual changes on heating may cause rejection of pasteurized milk by those accustomed to 'raw' milk. Many people are unable to accept the 'sulphury' aroma and flavour of hot milk. Despite superior keeping qualities, evaporated, sterilized and ultra-heat treated (UHT) milks may be tolerated only in emergency.

After rennet coagulation, milk may be used as a dessert. The nature of gel formation is not fully understood. It has been suggested that partial casein hydrolysis causes the formation of an insoluble calcium/casein complex to produce an unstable gel. Simple experiments can be carried out to demonstrate the effects of pH, temperature and calcium ions on gel characteristics. Optimum pH for gel formation appears to be between 5.7 and 5.9. Gel stiffness is increased if rennet is added at higher temperatures and as rennet and calcium ion concentration increase. Because the colour and texture may be considered unattractive and rennet flavour obtrudes, colouring and flavouring can be added to increase palatability.

## CHEESE — ORGANOLEPTIC QUALITIES

Whereas most people consider 'cooked' milk unacceptable, cheese is eaten cooked or uncooked according to variety and personal preference. Despite variations in the milk used, method of curd separation and conditions of ripening, there are several qualitative characteristics in common.

During ripening, protein hydrolysis exerts marked effects on aroma and flavour. It is likely that the softer, creamier texture of ripened cheeses, their behaviour on heating and their ability to blend with other foods is a reflection of this hydrolysis. Fragmentation produces a wide variety of compounds (Kosikowski, 1951; Ali and Mulder, 1961). Addition of chelating agents to processed cheeses loosens the paracasein structure thus softening texture and increasing spreading and blending qualities (Hamm, 1962). The lipids of cheese influence texture and exert a modifying effect on flavour. Fat hydrolysis during ripening produces a variety of compounds. (Anderson and Day, 1965; Bills and Day, 1964).

Fermentation of traces of lactose provides flavour precursors. Some correlation between the organoleptically detectable hydrogen sulphide/ free fatty acid ratio and Cheddar flavour has been recorded (Krisofferson and Gould, 1960; Bills and Day, 1965).

Because there are so many variables, cooking qualities show considerable differences. Cooking may involve merely melting or incorporating with other ingredients as in sauce and soufflé making. It is desirable that melted fat should not separate from cooked cheese since it promotes tenderness by preventing the formation of a compact protein mass.

To illustrate differences in cooking quality, three samples can be toasted under identical conditions. Processed cheese browns well, does not separate but tends to toughen. Scotch cheddar browns less rapidly and shows marked fat separation which leaves a rather rubbery layer. Lancashire cheese gives a soft creamy mixture of good sensory appeal. Differences in cooking quality are most obvious in comparative tests such as these and indicate possible difficulties in cooking. Preparing cheese dishes is easier if cheese of good cooking quality is used: although gelatinized starch may absorb separated fat, the use of certain varieties requires a higher degree of manipulative skills.

To the author's knowledge, there are few accounts of rigorous tests. Experience shows that well ripened, high fat and processed cheeses possess superior cooking qualities. In the latter, increased moisture content and adjustment of pH to 5.6–6.0 are of benefit (Voss, 1954). Low temperatures and short cooking periods are less likely to cause fat separation, stringiness and toughness. The effects of excessive heat were studied by Personius *et al.*, (1944). Samples heated at 100°C were inferior to those heated at 75°C, as were those exposed to longer periods of direct heat of 177°C. Temperatures between 40° and 50°C are preferable to 60–70°C for blending cheese with other ingredients (Lowe, 1955).

## EGGS – ORGANOLEPTIC QUALITIES

Most people do not enjoy eating raw eggs. Appearance, aroma and flavour are uninviting. Organoleptic qualities are much enhanced by cooking.

Eggs are especially valuable for their coagulating and gel-forming properties and their ability to form foams and emulsions; qualities which are retained when they are blended with other foods.

During cooking, the proteins of the white coagulate – a process which begins at 62°C and is completed at 65°C, the latter being the temperature at which the coagulum no longer flows. Stiffness increases until 70°C when the texture becomes progressively more tough and rubbery (Romanoff, 1949). Egg yolk begins to coagulate at 65°C and no longer flows at 70°C. Thus when eggs are cooked whole, there is a stage at which the white is firm while the yolk is still liquid.

Because blended egg coagulates at higher temperatures than either yolk or white separately, some interaction must be assumed. Coagulation temperature rises with rate of heating and with additions of water, milk, fat and sugar. pH exerts an effect which varies with deviation from isoelectric point. Practically speaking, it is the difference between coagulation and curdling temperatures which is of importance.

Used alone, eggs are boiled, poached, fried, scrambled and served as omelets. Soft boiled eggs are easily cooked to personal preference. To prevent a dark ring forming at the yolk border of hard boiled eggs excessive heat should be avoided. Rapid cooling also minimizes reaction between iron and the hydrogen sulphide released from denatured yolk proteins. The egg white provides the high pH conducive to ring formation (Salwin *et al.*, 1953). Ring formation is thus more pronounced in stale eggs.

The appearance of poached eggs varies according to whether they are cooked in water or in water containing salt or vinegar. A well shaped glossy egg can be obtained using water alone. The addition of salt or vinegar to speed surface coagulation may improve shape but reduces glossiness and makes the white firmer. For fried eggs, cooking temperatures of 125–137°C have been recommended to avoid excessive spreading or overcooking (Andross, 1940). Eggs are scrambled using varying amounts of fat, milk and stirring according to the consistency preferred.

*Practical applications of the coagulating properties of eggs*

The ability of egg proteins to coagulate allows them to be used for thickening sauces and for pouring custards. Excessive heating – that is beyond coagulation temperature – causes curdling. Slow heating and increased proportions of egg lower coagulation temperature and reduce risk of curdling. Higher proportions of sugar raise coagulation temperature and reduce viscosity. Despite lower coagulation temperature, egg white is inferior in thickening power and produces a less attractive colour and texture than yolk.

In baked custards, a relatively stable gel forms. After coagulation of the outer edge, overcooking – with consequent syneresis – may be avoided by surrounding the container with water. An oven temperature of 177°C is recommended. Although partly decided by individual preference, optimum sweetness and gel stiffness are influenced by the temperature at which custards are eaten. When they are served at refrigeration temperatures, a higher proportion of sugar is required. The effects on texture may be counteracted by increased proportions of egg. During cooking, Maillard and caramelization reactions and changes in the proteins alter appearance, aroma and flavour.

*Practical applications of the foaming properties of eggs*

The proteins of egg form an aqueous dispersion of sufficient viscosity to allow foam formation which is accompanied by partial — and irreversible — coagulation. A layer of denatured protein molecules at the air/liquid boundary inhibits evaporation. Their charge prevents coalescing. Conditions favouring coagulation will therefore increase foam stability.

Perhaps because of lowered surface tension, foam formation in egg whites is more readily achieved at room than at refrigeration temperatures. Thin white foams more readily than thick white. The type of whisk used — apart from obvious effects on speed — influences both volume and stability. Salt lowers foam quality and increases whisking time. Water, whilst increasing speed of formation and foam volume, reduces stability. Fat inhibits foam formation as does egg yolk. Hence, whole egg foams — used in the making of fatless sponges and zabaglione — form more readily at higher temperatures.

Because of its retarding effects on protein coagulation, addition of sugar is usually postponed until foam formation is established. The added sugar gives a white elastic foam of great stability and has a tenderizing effect on cooked mixtures. The addition of acid substances, such as Cream of Tartar, whilst slightly delaying foam formation, increases stability, reduces sweetness and lowers pH which inhibits browning reactions during cooking.

*Practical applications of emulsifying properties*

The emulsifying properties of eggs are of value in almost every recipe in which they are used. The emulsifying and stabilizing power of the yolk, which does not depend solely on proteins, is superior to that of whole egg. For simplicity, most studies of emulsions have been made on mayonnaise. Because the emulsifiers are hydrophilic colloids tending to be adsorbed on the water phase, oil in water emulsions are more commonly produced although in creamed cake mixtures the water in oil emulsion persists until flour is added.

## MEAT — ORGANOLEPTIC QUALITIES

The effects of cooking on the eating quality of meats have been extensively studied. Considerable changes, capable of modification by cooking procedures, occur. Whereas it was formerly considered that dry methods of cooking should be reserved for tender cuts, it is now accepted that they may be used for all meats. Alterations in appearance, flavour and texture will be discussed separately.

*Colour*

Of all results of cooking, colour change is the most obvious and probably exerts the greatest influence on aesthetic and sensory appeal.

As meat is heated, its colour alters from red to brown or grey/brown according to species. The colour achieved depends on temperature attained, age of the animal at slaughter and carcass ripening. Colour changes occur at lower temperatures in younger animals, with short ripening periods and at lower cooking temperatures. In beef cooked by dry methods, there are three well defined stages in cooking — rare, medium rare and well done. In recommending cooking procedures, the internal temperatures quoted will usually achieve the following results:

| | |
|---|---|
| Rare | $60^{\circ}C$ |
| Medium rare | $71^{\circ}C$ |
| Well done | $77^{\circ}C$ |

In meats cooked rare, the colour is still red, reddish brown juice escapes freely and shrinkage is minimal. Medium rare meat is pinkish grey or brown. Rather less juice of a deeper red colour escapes. Colour change should be complete in well done meats with only small quantities of brown juice exuding. Thus adjustment of internal temperature allows variation in colour. In moist methods of cooking, although internal temperatures are higher, colour is little altered.

The brown colour of cooked meats, although principally an effect of heat on myoglobin, is also a result of Maillard and caramelization reactions and browning of surface fat.

*Shrinkage and fibre separation*

If matched pieces of raw and cooked meat are compared, considerable shrinkage and weight loss are obvious. Although factors influencing water holding properties of raw meats affect moisture loss during cooking (Hamm and Deatherage, 1960), internal temperature is of greater significance. Sanderson and Vail (1953) observed that shrinkage increased with rise in internal temperature. Losses are greatest between temperatures of 80–100°C, usually attained only in moist methods of cookery. Greater collagen hydrolysis, whilst promoting fat and water retention, cannot compensate for fibre moisture loss. Thus stewed and pressure cooked meats show greater shrinkage.

378

Meats cooked to identical internal temperatures may shrink to varying extents depending on cooking procedures. Long roasting periods at lower temperatures reduce shrinkage and weight loss. Preliminary searing causes rapid surface protein coagulation to give partial sealing. Contrary to findings reported by Andross (1949), shrinkage is greater when meat is seared (Alexander and Clark, 1939) as it is with meats 'roasted' in a covered tin or wrapped in foil (Cline and Swenson, 1939; Cover, 1941a; Hood, 1960). Hoke (1968) has reported greater yields when poultry was roasted to constant internal temperature at 163°C than at 191°C.

To minimize shrinkage, constant roasting temperatures of 163°C have been recommended for meat and poultry (added advantages are increased juiciness and tenderness). Surface browning – if insufficient – can be achieved by short exposure to high temperatures at the end of the cooking period. For those who prefer a crisp brown edge, a roasting temperature of 204°C gives good results.

Fibre separation, caused by collagen hydrolysis, is influenced by length of cooking, internal temperature and pH. Addition of acids promotes conversion of collagen to gelatine, increasing fibre separation.

Whilst colour changes increase sensory appeal, the extent to which shrinkage and fibre separation do so is more difficult to assess.

*Changes in aroma and flavour*

Raw meat has a faint aroma and insipid flavour. Aroma – characteristic of species – is influenced by fat content (Hornstein *et al.*, 1963; Wassermann and Talley, 1968). Most people consider neither the aroma nor the flavour of uncooked meats to be acceptable.

Much effort has been devoted to explaining the changes in aroma and flavour of cooked meats. Changes in proteins, fat and various interactions have been suggested. Many flavouring compounds indicative of decarboxylation, deamination, cysteine decomposition, lipolysis and oxidation have been isolated (Pippen and Nonaka, 1960; Bender and Balance, 1961; Mecchi *et al.*, 1964; Minor *et al.*, 1965). Addition of monosodium glutamate and nucleotide derivatives to processed meats increases fullness of flavour and succulence (Sjostrom *et al.*, 1955; Kurtzman and Sjostrom, 1964).

Dry methods of cooking such as grilling and roasting produce meats of superior flavour. Evaporation of moisture produces a highly concentrated surface layer of compounds which the cook knows as 'extractives'. Browning of fat and Maillaird reactions also improve flavour.

In moist methods of cooking, with minimal surface evaporation, the drip leaks into the cooking liquid so that its flavour masks any lack of flavour in the meat itself. Brown stews and braised meats improve in flavour as a result of preliminary browning. Pressure cooked meats are reported to have superior flavour to those cooked by other moist methods possibly because of greater chemical changes.

Cuts from heavily used muscles, meats from older animals and well ripened meats show more pronounced flavour irrespective of cooking procedure. Statistically significant differences in flavour between breeds are more difficult to establish (Vandore, 1967; Jackson, 1968).

*Effects of cooking on texture*

In assessing texture, tenderness and juiciness should be considered. Slender muscle fibres are associated with tenderness (Hiner *et al.*, 1953). Although the change in texture increases sensory appeal, coagulation of fibre proteins causes toughening. Denaturation begins at $40^{\circ}$C and is almost complete at $65^{\circ}$C (Hamm, 1960).

The amount of connective tissue also influences tenderness (Ramsbottom *et al.*, 1945 and 1948). Constant use produces muscle in which there is more collagen and larger elastin fibres. Significant correlation between objective tenderness rating of the cooked muscle and previous histological rating has been noted. Connective tissue softens at $61^{\circ}$C – that is, almost at the temperature of meat cooked rare. Denaturation begins between 35 and $40^{\circ}$C. At $63^{\circ}$C, when new cross-links form, shrinkage occurs and there may be considerable resistance to biting and chewing. Gelatine formation does not always occur. Therefore meats cooked to internal temperatures exceeding $63^{\circ}$C may still be tough. Elastin is little affected by cooking (Bendall, 1964).

Thus, during cooking, whereas connective tissue usually becomes tender as a result of hydrolysis, fibre proteins toughen. Weir (1960) suggested that the length of time meat remains at $57^{\circ}-60^{\circ}$C is important in that collagen is softened without corresponding toughening of the fibre proteins. This is in line with the observation that long cooking periods are required to make meats, in which connective tissue is abundant, tender.

Juiciness of meat is also considered desirable. Low internal temperatures and minimal cooking periods inhibit moisture loss and prevent excessive dryness. Loss of juiciness is also associated with decreasing fat content (Gaddis *et al.*, 1950). By inhibiting moisture loss, intramuscular fat reduces drying (Hamm, 1960). (Much of the emulsified fat remains within the tissues). Well marbled meats are therefore juicier.

Most of the earlier papers describing the effects of cooking procedures were published in the United States of America. Following the work of Sprague and Grindley (1907) experiments became more methodical and indicated the toughening effects of high temperatures over long periods.

If roasted to constant internal temperatures, lower oven temperatures give meats of superior tenderness and juiciness (reduced shrinkage has already been described). To avoid excessively long cooking periods, roasting temperatures of 163°C and 175°C were recommended for normally tender cuts (Cline *et al.*, 1930). For less tender meats, lower oven temperatures with consequent slow heat penetration promote tenderness. Tougher cuts previously considered suitable only for moist methods of cooking may thus be successfully roasted to produce greater tenderness and juiciness combined with good flavour and lower shrinkage. Frying and grilling are, of course, impracticable. That slower heat penetration − rather than lower oven temperatures − is of significance was demonstrated by Cover (1941b). Because of speed of heat penetration, 'roasting' meats enhanced and other moist methods reduce tenderness (Cover, 1938).

It should be noted that attainment of the same internal temperature in grilling produces juicier meat than roasting (Bramblett and Vail, 1964). In grilled meats it may be significant that 25 per cent collagen hydrolysis has been reported (Irvine and Cover, 1959). In moist methods of cookery, palatability scores are highest when an internal temperature of 85°C is reached. Greater tenderness is achieved when meats are simmered rather than boiled.

As a result of increased protein hydrolysis, meats cooked in the presence of acids − lemon juice, vinegar, tomatoes and other fruits, and wine are all used in various recipes − are more tender. Certain proteolytic enzymes are also used as tenderizers. They vary in ability to promote collagen hydrolysis but all are effective for fibre proteins. Because optimum temperatures may be fairly high, immediate cooking after enzyme application is satisfactory and often more convenient (Tappel *et al.*, 1956). Adequate ripening, mechanical treatments and salt, within the limits of palatability, improve tenderness. It will be noted that many experiments were carried out some years ago but Dr. Ruth Leverton, U.S. Department of Agriculture, has supplied detailed and recent references in general agreement with these findings.

## FISH − ORGANOLEPTIC QUALITIES

Although so many species of fish are used as human food, there has been much less investigation of the effects of cooking procedures than with meats. Except for fish reared at fish farms, there can be little control of intrinsic quality. As with meat, the muscle proteins influence appearance, aroma, flavour and texture of cooked fish. The fibres are inserted into sheets of connective tissue to give the typical flaky texture. Short fibre length and small amounts of easily softened connective tissue combine to allow a wide choice of cooking procedures. Cooking times are short. Heating should cease as soon as the fibre proteins have coagulated. Fish containing a high proportion of intramuscular fat can be grilled or baked without becoming dry. Those containing less than 5 per cent fat should first be coated with oil or fat. Most types can be successfully fried.

Possibly the low fat content of so many fish has influenced cooking techniques in that it is usually preferred fried or served with a rich sauce as a coating or an accompaniment. Since flavour is not pronounced, dry methods of cookery which allow surface evaporation with resulting concentration of flavouring compounds, are preferable.

## Effects of cooking on appearance

Most people find raw fish unattractive. Cooking improves eating quality. Coagulation of fibre proteins changes translucency to whiteness. Loose flakiness creates anticipation of tenderness. Appearance is enhanced by a crisp brown outer layer or a coating of sauce. Shrinkage, which increases with cooking beyond the optimum, occurs but there is little gradation of colour change.

## The flavour of cooked fish

When cooked, really fresh fish acquires a delicate flavour characteristic of variety. Later fish may be described as flavourless unless it is fried, poached in well flavoured stock or served with sauce. Storage causes flavour deterioration. Many substances which could contribute to the flavour of fresh fish have been isolated. (Hashimoto, 1964; Hughes, 1964; Jones and Burt, 1964).

Prolonged cooking increases loss of volatile flavouring compounds. This loss, combined with leaching effects in moist methods of cookery, tends to make fish insipid. The predominantly oily flavour of certain fish, may be counteracted by the use of vinegar or lemon juice.

## The effects of cooking on texture

Shrinkage and softening of fish collagen occurs at lower temperatures than in meat (45°C). Because the proportion of connective tissue is less, fish has a more open texture. Raw fillets may be ragged, tending to fall apart and flakes may be separated at only 30°C (Gustavson, 1956).

Coagulation of fibre proteins tends to make texture firmer. Fibre length and relatively high moisture content ensure tenderness. Overcooking causes excessive fibre shrinkage and increased moisture loss producing dryness. The work of Charley (1952) and experiments by students of Griswold (1962) suggest that optimum internal temperature rises as fat content of fish increases.

Different cooking temperatures for salmon steaks brought to a constant internal temperature of 75°C did not affect either tenderness or palatability, but, below 204°C white material oozed from the surface and above this cooking temperature, drip increased. A cooking temperature of 204°C was therefore recommended.

When salmon steaks were cooked – at the recommended temperature – to different internal temperatures, those which reached 80° C and 85° C were judged to be equally tender and more palatable than those cooked to internal temperatures of 70° C and 75° C. Since weight loss is greater at 85° C, an internal temperature of 80° C appears preferable.

## PROTEINS FROM VEGETABLE SOURCES

The Household Food and Expenditure Survey (HMSO, 1968) indicates that between one third and one quarter of the protein in the average diet is derived from seeds. Although changing food habits have increased the use of legumes, cereal proteins make the major contribution.

In the United Kingdom, wheat is the cereal of greatest importance in all aspects of cooking. It is the only cereal to yield protein fractions which, when hydrated, possess sufficient cohesiveness, elasticity and tenacity to form the framework of batters and doughs at room temperatures. These fractions, collectively known as gluten, vary in quality and quantity in flours from different wheats. The enzymes of flour – present in the albumin/globulin fraction – are important in yeast cookery.

Cooking qualities of flour samples are mainly linked with the visco-elastic properties of the gluten fraction. (Elton and Ewart, 1967). On addition of liquid to flour, whereas starch granules swell by approximately 15 per cent, the proteins swell by up to 200 per cent. Subsequent manipulations allow the swollen particles to form a network, that is to become attenuated. Thus, although initially present in smaller proportion, it is the gluten rather than the starch which is chiefly responsible for the texture of precooked mixtures.

During cooking, gases present cause stretching of the gluten framework so that the mixture becomes porous. Gelatinization of the starch (65°–85°C) and coagulation of egg proteins – usually completed by 85° C – influence the structure of the cooked product. Although time of heating, cooking temperature and ionic concentration affect heat denaturation, coagulation of gluten is seldom detected below 75°C (Baker and Mizel, 1939). Denaturation is considered to begin at 70°C and to increase progressively as internal temperature rises to 90°C (Pence *et al.*, 1953). Thus coagulation of gluten is not complete until late in the cooking period. The location of the glutelins and gliadians in the endosperm cells has been studied (Jennings *et al.*, 1963).

Simple experiments with gluten help to explain the behaviour of different flours in cooking and the effects of added ingredients. Glutens – freed from starch – vary in colour but generally resemble chewing gum. Their faint flour-like aroma soon disappears and gluten is tasteless when chewed. Its rubbery texture alters very little. After baking, increased size and attractive brown colour are misleading since flavour is lacking and texture tough and hard.

Fortunately other ingredients modify these effects. The isoelectric point of gluten is 6.1 (Kent-Jones and Amos, 1947). 0.5 per cent $NaHCO_3$ increases dispersion and the baked gluten is more compact. 0.5 per cent citric acid increases elasticity but reduces tenacity so that, on baking, considerable expansion is followed by collapse. Salt – within acceptable flavour limits – causes slight loss of extensibility and toughening. Sugar and fat exert tenderizing effects. Phosphates, used as acid salts in self-raising flours, act as gluten improvers. Studies of the properties of gluten enabled the Chorleywood breadmaking process to be developed (Axford et al., 1963; Chamberlain et al., 1965; Elton and Ewart, 1965).

Many studies of cooked flour products have been made. Maillard, caramelization and dextrinization reactions are important in their contribution to flavour but analyses suggest flavour to be a blend of many components. (Wiseblatt, 1957; Cole et al., 1962; Coffman, 1967). Texture is influenced by the recipe and preparation techniques used.

## ACKNOWLEDGEMENTS

I acknowledge with gratitude the assistance of Mrs. A. King, C.B.E., Principal of the Edinburgh College of Domestic Science, Miss P.M. Cousland, Head of the Science Department and Miss H.Y. Mitchell, Head of the Department of Food and Nutrition, and members of her staff, in particular Mrs. J. Murray. I should also like to thank Dr. A.Z. Baker, formerly of the Nutrition Information Centre, Mr. C.L. Copeland of the Flour Advisory Bureau, Miss M. Dixon of the Arthur D. Little Research Association, Dr. R. Leverton of the U.S. Department of Agriculture and many others who have helped in the preparation of this paper.

## REFERENCES

Alexander, L.M. and Clark, N.G. (1939). U.S. Dept. Agric. Tech. Bull. No.676
Ali, L.A.M. and Mulder, H. (1961). Dairying Lab. Agric. Univ. Wageningen, 15, 377
Am. Soc. Testing of Materials (1968).
    STP 433 Basic Principles of Sensory Evaluation.
    STP 434 Manual of Sensory Testing Methods.

STP 440 *Correlation of Subjective – Objective Methods in the Study of Odour and Taste.*

Amerine, M.A., Pangborn, R.M. and Roessler, E.B. (1965). *Principles of the Sensory Evaluation of Food.* New York; Academic Press

Amoore, J.E. (1952). *Perfum. essent. Oil Rec.* **43**, 321-330

– Johnston, J.W.Jr. and Rubin, M. (1964). *Scient. Am.* **210**, 42

Anderson, D.F. and Day, E.A. (1965). *J. Dairy Sci.* **48**, 248

Andross, M. (1940). *Chem. Indy.* **59**, 449

– (1949). *Br. J. Nutr.* **3**, 396

Anson, M.L. and Pader, M. *U.S. Pat.* 2,830, 902; *Brit. Pat.* 746,859

Axford, D.W.E., Collins, T.H. and Elton, G.A.H. (1963) *Cereal Sci. Today.* **8**, No.8

Baker, J.D. and Mizel, M.D. (1939). *Cereal Chem.* **16**, 517, 582

Bendall, J.R. (1964). *Symp. Proteins and their Reactions.* Westport, Connecticut; AVI Publ. Co. p.225

Bender, A.E. and Ballance, P.E. (1961). *J. Sci. Agric.* **12**, 683

Bills, D.D. and Day, E.A. (1964). *J. Dairy Sci.* **47**, 733

– – (1965). *J. Dairy Sci.* **48**, 1168

Blanchard, E.L. and Maxwell, M.L. (1941). *Fd. Res.* **6**, 105

Boyer, R.A. *Brit. Pat.* 699, 692

Bramblet, V.D. and Vail, G.E. (1964). *Fd. Tech., Champaign.* **18**, 123

Brandt, M.A., Skinner, E.Z. and Coleman, J.A. (1963). *J. Fd. Sci.* **28**, 404

Caul, J.F. (1957). *Adv. Fd. Res.* **7**, 5

– and Raymond, S.A. (1964). *Fd. Tech., Champaign.* **18**, 253

– and Sjorstrom, L.B. (1959). *Second Inter-American Food Congress.* Miami, Florida. 10th June, 1959. Paper No. 19. *(Perfum. essent. Oil Rec.* London, Nov. 1959)

Chamberlain, N., Collins, T.H. and Elton, G.A.H. (1965). *Cereal Sci. Today.* **10**, 273

Charley, H. (1962). *Fd. Res.* **17**, 136

Clegg, K.M. (1960). *Br. J. Nutr.* **14**, 325

Cline, J.A., Trowbridge, E.A., Foster, M.T. and Fry, H.E. (1930). *Missouri Univ. Agric. Exp. Stat. Bull.* No.293

– and Swenson, A.C. (1934). *Missouri Univ. Exp. Stat. Bull.* No.340

Coffman, J.R. (1967). *Chemistry and Physiology of Flavour.* Ed. by H.W. Schultz, E.A. Day and L.M. Libbey. Westport, Conn.; AVI Publ. Co. p. 182

Cole, E.W., Hale, W.S. and Pence, J.W. (1962). *Cereal Chem.* **39**, 114

Colvin, J.R. (1964). In *Symposium on Food Proteins and their Reactions.* Ed. by H.W. Schultz and A.E. Anglemier. Westport, Conn.; AVI Publ. Co. p.79

Cover, S. (1938). *J. Home Econ.* **30**, 386

– (1941a). *J. Home Econ.* **33**, 596

– (1941b). *Fd. Res.* **6**, 233

Dastoli, F. and Price, S. (1966). *Science.* N.Y., **154**, 905

Ellis, G.P. (1959). *Adv. Carbohyd. Chem.* **14**, 63

Elton, G.A.H. and Ewart, J.A.D. (1965). *Proc. R. Aust. chem. Inst.* **32**, No.2. Feb. 1965

– – (1967). *Bakers' Dig.* Vol. 41. No.1., 36, 42, Feb. 1967

Gaddis, A.M., Hankins, O.G. and Hiner, R.L. (1950). *Fd. Tech. Champaign.* **4**, 498

Griswold, R. (1962). *The Experimental Study of Foods.* London; Constable

Gustavson, K.H. (1956). *The Chemistry and Reactivity of Collagen.* New York; Academic Press

Hall, R.L. (1958). *Flavour Research and Food Acceptance.* Arthur D. Little Inc. Cambridge, Mass; p.224

Hamm, R. (1960). *Adv. Fd. Res.* **10**, 356

− (1962). In *Recent Advances in Food Science.* Vol.3. p.228 London; Butterworths

− and Deatherage, F.E. (1960). In *Food Science.* Vol. 3 Ed. by J. M. Leitch and D.N. Rhodes. London; Butterworths. p.218

− − (1960). *Fd. Res.* **25**, 387

Hashimoto, Y. (1964). *F.A.O. Symposium. Utilisation of Fish.* Paper WP/II/6

Hiner, R.L., Hankins, O.G., Sloane, H.S., Fellers, C.R. and Anderson, E.E. (1953). *Fd. Res.* **18**, 364

Hoke, I.M. (1968). *J. Home Econ.* **60**, No.8. Oct. 1968

Hood, M.P. (1960). *J. Am. diet. Ass.* **37**, 363

Hornstein, I., Crowe, P.E. and Sulzbacher, W.L. (1963). *Nature, Lond.* **199**, 1252

*Household Food Consumption and Expenditure.* 1968. London; H.M.S.O.

Hughes, R.B. (1964). *J. Sci. Fd. Agric.* **15**, 290

Irvine, L and Cover, S. (1959). *Fd. Tech.* **13**, 655

Jackson, T.H. (1968). *Personal Communication*

Jenness, R. and Patton, S. (1959). *Principles of Dairy Chemistry.* New York; John Wiley

Jennings, A.C., Morton, A.K. and Palk, B.A. (1963). *Aust. J. biol. Sci.* **16**, 366

Jones, N.R. and Burt, J.R. (1964). *F.A.O. Symposium. Utilisation of Fish.* Paper WP/I/5

Josephson, D.V. (1954). Borden Award Address. *J. Am. diet. Ass.* **30**, 855

Judd, D.B. and Wyszecki, G. (1963). *Colour in Business, Science and Industry.* 2nd ed. New York; Viking Press

Kawamura, Y., Adachi, A., Chara, M. and Ikeda, S. (1964). *Aminosan Kakusan.* **10**, 168

Kendall, D.A. and Nielson, A.J. (1964). *Ann. N.Y. Acad. Sci.* **116**, 567

Kent-Jones, D.W. and Amos, A.J. (1947). *Modern Cereal Chemistry.* Liverpool; Northern Publish. Co.

Kosikowski, F.W. (1951). *J. Dairy Sci.* **34**, 235

Kristofferson, K. and Gould, I.A. (1960). *J. Dairy Sci.* **43**, 1202

Kurtzman, C.H. and Sjostrom, L.B. (1964). *Fd. Tech.* **18**, 221

Lowe, B. (1955). *Experimental Cookery.* New York; Wiley. p.316

McCarthy, K. (1963). *J. Fd. Sci.* **28**, 379

Mackey, A.V. (1958). *Fd. Res.* **23**, 580

Mackey,A.V. and Valassi, K. (1956). *Fd. Tech.* **10**, 238

MacKinney, G. and Little, A.C. (1962). *Colour in Foods.* Westport, Conn.; AVI Publ. Co. p.308

Le Magnen, J. (1956). *C. r. Seanc. Soc. biol.* **145**, 800

Matz, S.A. (1962). *Food Texture.* New York; AVI Publ. Co. p.286

Mechi, E.P., Pippen, E.C. and Lineweaver, H. (1964). *J. Fd. Sci.* **29**, 393

Minor, L.J., Pearson, A.M., Dawson, L.E. and Schweigert, B.S. (1965). *J. Fd. Sci.* **30**, 686

Moncrief, R.W. (1967). *The Chemical Senses.* London; Leonard Hill

Pangborn, R.M. (1960). *J. Psychol.* **73**, 229

− Berg, H.W. and Hansen, B. (1963). *Am. J. Psychol.* **76**, 492

Parks, O.W. and Patton, S. (1961). *J. Dairy Sci.* **44**, 1.

Pence, J.W., Mohammed, A. and Mecham, D.K. (1953). *Cereal Chem.* **30**, 115

Personius, C., Boardman, E. and Ausherman, A.R. (1944). *Fd. Res.* **9**, 304

Pfaffman, C. (1954). *Abstr. Pap. Am. chem. Soc.* 17A

Pfaffman, C. (1956). *Ann. Rev. Psychol.* **7**, 391

Pippen, E.L. and Nonaka, N. (1960). *Fd. Res.* **25**, 764

Ramsbottom, J.M., Strandine, E.J. and Koonz, C.H. (1945). *Fd. Res.* **10**, 497

– – (1948). *Fd. Res.* **13**, 315

Richter, G.H. (1952). *Textbook of Organic Chemistry.* New York; Wiley

Romanoff, A.L. and Romanoff, A.J. (1949). *The Avian Egg.* New York; Wiley

Salwin, J.H.Jr. (1953). *Fd. Tech.* **7**, 447

Sanderson, M. and Vail, G.E. (1963). *J. Fd. Sci.* **28**, 590

Schultz, H.W., Day, E.A. and Libbey, L.M. (1967). *The Chemistry and Physiology of Flavours.* Westport, Conn; AVI Publ. Co.

Shallenburger, R.S. (1964). *New Scient. Lond.* **23**, 259

(1967). *Nature.* **216**, 480

Shore, L.E. (1892). *J. Physiol.* **13**, 191

Sjostrom, L.B., Cairncross, S.E. and Caul, J.F. (1955). *Monosodium Glutamate – a Second Symposium.* Camb. Mass; Arthur D. Little

von Skramlik, E. (1926). *Handbuch der Physiologi der neideren.* Sinne. Vol.1

Sperring, D.D., Platt, W.T. and Hiner, R.L. (1959). *Fd. Tech.* **8**, 201

Sprague, E.C. and Grindley, H.S. (1907). *The University Studies II.* No.4. Chicago; Univ. Chicago Press

Szczesniak, A.S. (1963). *J. Fd. Sci.* **28**, 385

– Brandt, M.A. and Friedman, H.H. (1963). *J. Fd. Sci.* **28**, 397

Tappel, A.L., Miyada, D.S., Sterling, C. and Maier, V.P. (1956). *Fd. Res.* **31**, 275

Tremolieres, J. (1962). *Proc. 1st. Int. Congr. Fd. Sci. & Tech.* London

Vandore, J.F. (1967). *M. Sc. Thesis.* Dept. of Agric. Univ. of Edin.

Voss, R. (1954). cited by Griswold, R.M. in *The Experimental Study of Foods.* 1962. London; Constable

Wasserman, A.E. and Talley, F. (1968). *J. Fd. Sci.* **33**, 219

Weir, C.E. (1960). in *The Science of Meat and Meat Products.* Ed. by Am. Meat Inst. Foundation. New York; Reinhold. p.212

Wiseblatt, L. (1957). *North West Miller Milling Prod.* Sect. 258, No.11. p.1A

Woodworth, R.S. and Schlosberg, H. (1954). *Experimental Psychology.* New York; Holt. p.948

Yoshino, H. and Suzuki, M. (1965). cited by A. Kuninaka in *Physiology and Chemistry of Flavours.* Westport, Conn; AVI Pub. Co.

387

# PROTEIN PROBLEMS IN LARGE-SCALE CATERING

EILEEN TELFORD

*Catering Division, J. Lyons & Co. Ltd, London*

## INTRODUCTION

In dealing with the problems of large-scale catering, I am approaching the end of a chain of events which have been the subjects of papers by the previous speakers at this symposium. By now you have heard a great deal about the sources of the protein foods, their properties, the processing which some of them receive and the attacks upon them by bacteria and larger pests. Now we have come to the stage of actually feeding the result to the consumer, and Mrs. Parry has given you mouth-watering illustrations of the ways in which some of the protein foods can be made attractive to Western European inhabitants and to many in North America. It is my task to deal with the way in which the information we have acquired already can be applied to the operations of feeding large numbers of people, and what is likely to be the fate of the proteins in their breakfasts, lunches and dinners in the process. Although it is obvious that the types of food involved and the general methods by which they are treated must be the same as those used in most of your homes, translation of these to large-scale operations brings in problems which often have no parallel on the domestic scene.

Among the problems posed by protein foods I shall make little mention of the cereal proteins. Though in bulk they feature largely among the supplies used in catering, in the form of bread, rolls, cakes and pastries, the principal difficulty they create is one of staling. The effects of this are straightforward and easily recognized, so it is comparatively easy to control. When the cereal exists in combination with other protein sources, such as cream, fruit or meat, the complications are usually due to the presence of these substances and are dealt with hereafter.

I am also spending little time on the vegetable proteins, which are used on a large scale in the form of potatoes, green vegetables, root vegetables and various types of beans. While these are important and are used extensively, they are also simple in the problems they raise compared with the animal proteins, and in addition one must not overlook the sordid commercial fact that those used in the greatest bulk are relatively cheap.

This brings me to the animal proteins and the problems they create in large-scale catering, and these stem from two of their properties which have already been dealt with by previous speakers. These are their suitability as media for microbial growth and their changes in physical properties when subjected to temperature increases sufficient to cause coagulation.

## MICROBIAL SPOILAGE AND THE
## FOOD HYGIENE REGULATIONS

The first of these problems encompasses not only the waste which accompanies microbial spoilage but also the legal involvement of caterers with the Food Hygiene Regulations. Perishable foods, as legally defined, consist in fact of the animal protein foods, meat, fish, eggs, milk and cream, and foods consisting mainly of these ingredients or containing significant quantities of them. The Regulations are designed, among other things, to ensure that perishable foods are kept by caterers at temperatures such that either bacterial growth is inhibited by cold or else that the bacteria themselves are destroyed by heat.

The concern of the Public Health authorities in these matters is wholly understandable. Although there has been a decrease in the number of instances of food poisoning reported to them in recent years, this is likely to be but the tip of the iceberg, the main body of which consists of the vast number of upset stomachs which seldom appear in the form of actual statistics. A Gallup poll conducted on behalf of the Jeyes Group in 1967 indicated that as high a proportion of the adult population as 22 per cent had suffered from these in one month, but the number of cases that could be attributed to some form of food poisoning could not accurately be estimated. The large majority of known instances of food poisoning are associated with the animal protein foods, and in particular with poultry, processed meats and fish, and milk. Although caterers are involved in only a limited number of these, the fact that their stock-in-trade contains such potentially dangerous foods is a matter of considerable concern, particularly to the large-scale operators.

The Food Hygiene Regulations provide for the storage of these foods at temperatures either below 50°F or above 145°F. (Reference to temperatures on the Fahrenheit scale is made throughout this paper because these are in current use both in the Regulations and among the majority of caterers in this country. The Centigrade equivalents of the above temperatures are 10°C and 62.5°C. The upper temperature limit is above that of 60°C mentioned by Professor Mossel as being sufficient to inhibit the growth of most spoilage bacteria.) The transition between these temperatures must be as rapid as possible, whether it consists of a heating or a cooling process. The foods in question are not covered by a temperature proviso during the periods when they are exposed for sale, and this provides a loophole for caterers on the many occasions when the provision of heated or refrigerated display equipment would impose an impossibly expensive burden both on themselves and on retailers.

## PROBLEMS CREATED BY DIFFERENT TYPES OF CATERING

The caterer is still expected to possess equipment capable of storing his perishable foods within the required temperature ranges, and also to satisfy his own requirements for the production of an acceptable range of foods for his business. The large-scale caterer is in an especially complicated position, as the extent of his difficulties varies according to the particular type of business with which he is involved. Three broad categories of such catering can be defined:

A. Catering for a large number of people all of whom have to be served simultaneously. The actual number to be fed will be known in advance. This category would include banquets, receptions and parties.

B. Catering for a large number of people over limited periods during the day, when the number of people is known with reasonable accuracy. This would cover works canteens, school meals, hospital catering and other institutional catering.

C. Catering for a problematical number of people over a variable period of time, i.e. normal commercial catering in restaurants and cafeterias.

In each of these categories certain general problems regarding perishable protein foods, both animal and vegetable, will have to be solved. The extent of these will vary considerably with the type of catering involved, but in all cases will necessitate the provision of food supplies, equipment and labour, and the cost of providing these. As in nearly all the aspects of modern existence, the cost factor is the first which has to be taken into account, because the basic rule applies in catering as in most other things, that the customer gets what he pays for. There is probably no problem even in cases of large functions requiring the highest quality that could not be solved if unlimited money were available to pay for the supplies, the equipment and the labour when and where they were needed, but it is rarely possible even to contemplate such a situation nowadays. The most that can be said is that a very limited number of special occasions in category A will be labelled 'Expense no object' and will thus be able to approach ideal conditions. For the rest, the limits imposed on the finished result will be determined by the money available, and the lower the cost of the operation is to be kept, the less ideal will be the final product in terms of culinary quality. Even here there will be some variation according to which type of catering is concerned, for it is obviously far easier to plan exactly the supplies, equipment and labour needed if the number of meals to be produced is known with some accuracy, as in categories A and B, than if this number is liable to fluctuate according to conditions outside the caterers' control, and the cash return on the operation is to vary accordingly.

## PROBLEMS OF SUPPLY AND STORAGE

The first problem to be tackled is one of supply. Perishable foods will have to be obtained in fairly large quantities, but the form in which these are received will be dictated by their availability and the facilities at hand for storage, including cold storage.

If the foods in question are out of season, or if it is necessary to obtain them in a semi- or totally-processed form to save labour, they may well be in the frozen state. Frozen foods are relatively expensive, and criticisms are often levelled at their quality when it is compared with the best possible fresh foods. It is true that the quality of many protein foods can be reduced by slow freezing, with the accompanying damage to cellular structure and loss of water, salts and vitamins from the damaged cells during defrosting. Also, bacteriologically a frozen food is only in as good a condition as the raw material before freezing. But from the caterer's point of view frozen foods have a number of advantages. By using them it is possible to achieve standardization, both of quality and price, availability regardless of seasonal or regional difficulties, and flexibility, in that a reserve stock may be held to counteract any variation in the delivery of supplies or the requirements of the business.

To cope with frozen foods it is necessary to have the appropriate equipment, and large-scale storage of frozen foods requires relatively expensive and bulky cabinets, or even cold rooms. It is also necessary to control the storage temperature and the length of time perishable foods are kept, as these two factors are interdependent, and are also affected by the efficiency or otherwise of the wrapping of the food in question. Not only are such foods liable to slow bacteriological deterioration and corresponding protein breakdown, but inadequate packaging will involve risks of freezer burn. This phenomenon, which has a particularly bad effect on meat and fish, also gives rise to a condition in which oxidation of flesh fats can occur very easily. Where fish is concerned, particularly cod and plaice fillets, denaturization of the protein takes place fairly rapidly at the usual temperature of small-scale commercial cold storage equipment, around $5^{\circ}$F, so that it can cause a serious deterioration in the quality of the products if they are kept for a long storage period, of the order of 15 weeks. This condition will become much worse if the storage equipment is not operating efficiently and allows the temperature to rise above $5^{\circ}$F.

The length of time foods may be stored in suitable equipment in the deep frozen condition is considerably longer than the period for which they can be held under mild refrigeration. Whereas frozen raw meat and fish or pre-cooked convenience foods, including vegetables, can be held for several weeks in this state, once defrosted their condition deteriorates much more rapidly. Although it is probably true that such foods can be and are kept under domestic conditions in the family refrigerator for longer periods, it is usually necessary for caterers to plan for a maximum cool storage period of two, or at the most three days for meat and fish, whether raw or cooked, and often one day only for fresh cream and products containing eggs and milk such as custards and sauces. It is thus necessary to control the stocks of such goods very carefully, to use them in the order in which they have been obtained or prepared and to regulate the quantities kept as closely as possible to the requirements of the business if expensive waste is to be avoided.

As mentioned previously, perishable foods displayed for sale or service are to a large extent exempt from the temperature restrictions of the Food Hygiene Regulations, but they are not at all free from the deterioration caused by exposure to warm, moving air. In addition to the microbial spoilage, these conditions produce in the animal protein foods in particular a darkening and discoloration associated with drying which enables one to identify meat, fish and cream products, both raw and cooked, which have been exposed to the air for any considerable length of time. These factors are naturally extremely limiting in the cafeteria-type service, where the appearance of the food constitutes its principal sales appeal. They also limit the extent to which pre-preparation for a large-scale single occasion such as a banquet can be carried out, unless precautions can be taken to reduce the damage by covering foods to be served cold with damp cloths, bedding their containers in crushed ice or providing other temporary conditions for cool, damp storage. This treatment would be suitable for sandwiches, salads, cold custards and fruit dishes, portions of butter, cheese and cold meats, and other cold foods which have to be laid out on plates or dishes.

This is a suitable point at which to mention ice-cream, which has some claim to be regarded as a food containing animal and vegetable proteins. It is, however, the subject of such stringent manufacturing regulations that the microbial spoilage problems are principally the concern of the manufacturer. The caterer has to provide enough equipment at the correct temperatures for storage and service to hold his requirements, and to make sure that strict hygienic precautions are taken if any portioning or unwrapping of the product is necessary. Nowadays much ice-cream is supplied pre-portioned and separately packaged by the manufacturers, and this practice tends to reduce considerably the risks of contamination during storage and service. The caterer still has to cope with the physical damage to ice-cream caused by shrinkage, which is the result of temperature variations after manufacture and can also ruin the colour and texture of the product. Prevention of this damage is a matter of strict attention to storage temperature from the time the ice-cream is first delivered to the point of service.

Between the atmospheric temperature conditions produced in the kitchen, restaurant or larder and those temperatures at which a food becomes indisputably hot lies a range, between about $90°F$ and $145°F$, which is usually described as warm and which is anathema to the food hygiene expert, be he caterer or Public Health official. Not only does bacteriological spoilage take place very rapidly between these temperatures, but also the drying and discoloration of the food is considerably speeded up.

There are, however, one or two awkward foods that can only exist in the form required for palatability while they remain within this range, and to which the Food Hygiene Regulations turn a conveniently blind eye. These are foods which depend for their appeal on their protein being heated to a point below coagulation temperature, usually to not more than $135°F$, and consist of under-done beef in the form of roast meat or steaks, of eggs and egg dishes, and of sauces such as Hollandaise.

The cooking of these foods, whether on a large or small scale, can be left to the skill of the chef, or controlled by the use of a thermometer. In the case of joints of beef the guesswork can be taken out of the cooking by using a probe thermometer to establish accurately the centre temperature of the joint, and this method is employed as one of the controls in the production of roast meat of consistent quality. The cooking of individual eggs and egg dishes is controlled visually and is usually arrested before the protein reaches the coagulated state, unless there is a demand for a

hard-cooked or fully-set egg. The problems arise when it is necessary to prepare these dishes in advance and store them in bulk until required. Technically this is easy enough, and poached eggs, for instance, can be stored in a soft-cooked condition for 2 h or more in a small steamer with the temperature controlled at 130–135°F. It would be possible to design equipment capable of keeping rare steaks or underdone beef at the same temperature and in very good condition for as long as needed, but as matters stand at present this would undoubtedly contravene the Food Hygiene Regulations. Caterers faced with this problem thus have the alternatives of serving overcooked food or storing it under illegal conditions!

## LARGE-SCALE PRODUCTION AND STORAGE OF HOT FOOD

Once we reach the temperature range above 145°F we are dealing with protein foods in a coagulated condition, and while they are maintained at such temperatures the bacteriological problems mostly cease to exist, the bacteria having a protein-coagulation problem of their own. The purely catering problems then concern the difficulties firstly of raising large quantities of animal and vegetable protein foods to these temperatures in a uniform manner and then keeping them hot for a period of time which will vary with the type of business concerned.

The nature of the various cooking processes, boiling, frying, roasting, grilling, steaming, baking, etc., has already been dealt with in the preceding paper. Expansion of these to large-scale operations requires different equipment and techniques, and it is here that the labour problem is of considerable importance. One man can stir a large steam-kettle of stew or curry nearly as easily as a small saucepan, and can supervise the cooking of a number of 20-pound joints of beef or turkeys with little more effort than one joint in a domestic oven. But the operations of grilling and frying, to say nothing of pie and pudding making and many others, involve the handling of a number of pieces of food, amounting each to one up to a dozen or so portions, each unit of which has to be prepared, cooked and stored individually. Production departments of food factories can mechanize these processes and give them the benefit of bulk treatment, but the caterer has only limited scope for mechanization. He must generally rely either on a large labour force to produce many items over a short period, or on being able to accumulate the limited output of a small number of staff until it is required. This may mean building up quantities of food for one mass service, and the meat or fish part of the food might have to be stored for one or even 2 h, although if it were combined with a

starchy or fatty coating this might necessitate a shorter storage period because of its own deterioration. This limitation would apply, for instance, to fish with a fried batter coating, or to food with a pastry or suet crust. There is also the complication that 145°F is too low a temperature for serving food if it is to be subjected to cooling from delays in transit between kitchen and customer, and a higher temperature for actual service will probably be needed if the food is to be regarded as satisfactorily hot on the plate. Deterioration at this higher temperature, about 160–170°F, tends to occur rather rapidly.

Animal foods of a more liquid nature, such as milk itself and milk puddings, egg custards and sauces containing eggs, milk and cheese all show unfortunate tendencies when kept hot for any length of time. The deterioration principally arises from the tendency of these foods to form a dried and coagulated skin on their surfaces, which is an object of detestation to a large number of people. If stirred it disintegrates into lumpy pieces, and these will spoil the texture of the product. There are various ways of minimizing this effect, such as covering the surface of sauces with a sheet of wet greaseproof paper until required, or using a lidded container, but the success of these methods is dependent on the food being left undisturbed until required for use, and they are not in general applicable to the cafeteria or canteen-type service. The formation of skin can be delayed by holding the foods at a lower temperature, but this is usually undesirable for the reasons given previously.

Vegetable protein foods fall into two categories from the catering point of view. Green vegetables, both leaf types such as cabbage and seeds and seed pods, such as peas and runner beans, lose their green colour when kept hot over periods longer than about half an hour, and thereafter look most unattractive. It is therefore necessary to store them in the hot state for as short a time as possible. Root vegetables, such as carrots, potatoes and the favourite British stand-by, baked beans, are more good-tempered and can often survive a hot storage period of up to 2 h, though it cannot be said that they are improved by it.

## REHEATING OF PRE-COOKED FOODS

So far, mention has been made of situations where the cooking, storage and service of food has been carried out as a continuous process. One way of coping with the labour problem when staff have to be kept to a minimum is to cook as many hot foods as possible during periods of little or no business, to cool them rapidly, to refrigerate overnight, or even for periods of up to 36 h and then to reheat the foods when required for

service. This process goes half-way to the convenience food situation without the expense of buying the completely prepared foods, and makes the maximum use of the labour already available. On the other hand, it must be pointed out that a considerable public health hazard can exist if the cooling is not rapid, or the storage is overlong or at too high a temperature, and the process should only therefore be carried out if all concerned are aware of the dangers involved.

Although such food is open to the criticism that it is twice cooked, the double process can, if carried out carefully, produce a result superior to that of the freshly cooked article which has in fact been freshly over-cooked by prolonged hot storage. Hygienically it is necessary to transfer the food in both directions through the thermal danger-zone between 50°F and 145°F, but if this transfer is carried out rapidly there need be little harm done from a culinary point of view provided the foods have been selected with an eye to their suitability for reheating. Equipment for reheating will also be required, and although some of the ovens, etc., already used for cooking may be utilized for this purpose, modern developments have provided the caterer with a range of units designed for reheating and for carrying out this process as rapidly and efficiently as possible. The time factor is important, because if it can be reduced sufficiently there will be little need for storing food in the hot condition, and a continuous supply of freshly heated food will be available.

Most of this specialized equipment makes use of conventional cooking processes which have been speeded up by various devices. For instance, convector ovens still use gas or electricity as a source of heat, but by efficient circulatory systems this heat is dispersed evenly throughout the oven cavity and is continuously applied to the surface of the food, instead of being allowed to act only through radiation and natural convection currents. The effects of this heating on animal protein foods, both flesh and semi-liquid, are therefore the same as in an ordinary oven, and conventional baking and roasting results are obtained, albeit more rapidly than in the older type of oven. It is possible to use such equipment to reheat pre-prepared foods from the frozen state in as little as 10 min for individual portions or 20 min for bulk containers of 6–8 portions. This operation can incorporate the baking of raw pastry which has encased a pre-cooked filling, e.g. a meat or fruit pie or a sausage roll. Comparable results for foods requiring a moist atmosphere can be obtained in a unit operating on super-heated steam.

## THE MICROWAVE OVEN FOR COOKING
## AND REHEATING

Efforts have been made to cook and reheat foods in a totally unconventional manner by making use of their dielectric properties. Various applications of this principle have been utilized by food manufacturers, but from the catering angle the available equipment for the purpose consists of the much-publicized microwave oven. Without digressing into the methods whereby these ovens actually convey energy to the food, it is sufficient to say that they break away completely from the principle of all other cooking processes, which involve the application of heat to the outside of the food and the conduction of such heat through the food bulk to its centre. The rate of cooking by conventional means is therefore dependent on the quantity of heat applied and the rate at which the food material can conduct it to the interior.

Microwave heating takes place by the application of electrical energy, not heat, and this can be applied throughout a mass of food with conducting properties, the only limitation of penetration being the wavelength of the microwaves used, commonly about 12 cm. The principal energizing effect in foodstuffs becomes apparent in the form of a rapid rise in temperature and vaporization of the water contained in them, which results in cooking or heating by a process which might be described as steaming in depth. The advantage of the microwave process is said to be the extremely rapid rate at which this heating takes place. The amount of energy applied to the food is large, the most usual output of a single magnetron being 2–2½ kW, but the rapidity of action is inversely proportional to the bulk of food treated, so that a large mass is heated relatively slowly, though still faster than by conventional methods. This feature alone limits the usefulness of microwave ovens in large-scale catering, as a large output of food can only be obtained by having a battery of such ovens, or a conveyer-type oven with several sources of energy. Both these are extremely expensive ways of obtaining a rapid result.

An equally serious disadvantage is the small number of operations that can be carried out successfully in such equipment. Since the heating process is essentially one of steaming it is not possible to obtain results such as those achieved by conventional baking, roasting, frying or grilling. But as far as animal protein foods are concerned, serious complications are introduced by the violence of the heating effect when carried out rapidly, i.e., on a fairly small bulk of material at a time. With a liquid or semi-liquid food, such as a milk pudding or a raw egg in its shell, the effect is literally explosive, and the food is liable to be distributed throughout the oven cavity in a matter of seconds. With raw red meat the contraction of the fibres is violent and results in rapid distortion and tough and inedible meat. Raw fish, on the other hand, reacts most favourably, and cooks rapidly in its own juice to give a result of excellent flavour. With such violent processes the time factor is obviously critical, and microwave oven manufacturers provide a variety of timing devices to enable the energy to be supplied for the exact time required for each type or quantity of food. If this time is exceeded, in addition to the results mentioned above, dehydration of the parts of the food containing least moisture or attracting most microwave energy takes place rapidly, and the effect on the protein is not just one of ordinary drying. A gummy hardness develops in portions of the food which renders them unchewable and inedible, and this effect is quite different in character from the drying, burning or shrinking produced by conventional over-cooking. This is particularly liable to appear with irregularly shaped portions, such as at the tail of a fish or near the bone of a chicken drumstick.

Since the microwave oven produces these effects on raw protein foods, it might be expected to behave similarly when used to reheat pre-cooked food. This is true to some extent, but if the process is controlled very carefully by accurate timing or by the use of comparatively large masses of food which will therefore react more slowly, it is possible to reheat both semi-liquid foods and red meat protein to an extent which will pass muster. Thus, carefully prepared fried eggs, omelettes, steaks and slices of roast beef can be reheated successfully in times varying from 5 to 45 s, and beef stews, curries or minced products can also be reheated. In the case of these items, and equally of such products as white meat or fish, another limitation of the microwave oven shows itself, i.e., the uneven distribution of the energy within the oven cavity which results in uneven heating. If, however, it is possible to hold the food subsequently for a few minutes to allow normal convection to distribute the heating effect more evenly throughout the bulk of the food, this disadvantage becomes minimal, except where portions of the food have become overheated to the extent of being dehydrated and tough. It is not possible, however, to use this oven for reheating foods direct from the frozen state, as the presence of ice crystals produces complications in the distribution of energy. This can result in the extreme condition of parts of a dish reaching boiling point while others are still frozen. The oven can be used for defrosting frozen foods quickly if they are given a short exposure followed by a resting period at room temperature to allow ordinary heat conduction to take place within the food mass.

It will thus become apparent that the microwave oven will be an effective tool for the large-scale caterer only in situations where its peculiar properties create a definite advantage to justify the expense involved, and where sufficient conventional equipment is also available to undertake the cooking processes of which it is incapable.

## CONCLUSIONS FOR THE CATERER

Although this paper has dealt mainly with the animal protein foods, these are in fact the items upon which caterers rely to provide the backbone of their menus and, incidentally, their most expensive products. It therefore follows that the success of any large-scale catering operation depends on the ability of a caterer to cope with the problems of animal protein in such a way that the results justify the price he expects his customers to pay for them or so that they will satisfy both the customers and the authority bearing the expense of providing the catering service. Solution of these problems will be simplified by expenditure on skilled labour and specialized equipment, but the most important factor will be the appreciation by management and staff of the processes which cause damage to all their protein foods. The successful caterer will be the one who can best harmonize his financial limitations with this knowledge, and who can produce the most satisfactory methods of dealing with the protein problems within the scope and limits of his operations.

Indeed, to conclude I would go further than this, and say that unless the large-scale caterer can cope with these problems to a satisfactory extent, a great deal of the trouble taken by all those concerned in production and processing to provide good quality protein foods will be wasted if these are presented to the consumer in an unappetising condition.

## REFERENCES

Gallup Poll (1967/8). *Br. Fd. J.* July/August 1968, p. 110
Surkiewicz, R. F., Groomes, R. J. and Shelton, L. R., Jnr. (1968). *J. Appl. Microbiol.* **16,** 147
Vernon, E. (1967). *Monthly Bulletin* of the Ministry of Health and Public Health Laboratory Service. **26,** 235

# VII. ASSIMILATION

# REGULATORY MECHANISMS IN
# MAMMALIAN PROTEIN METABOLISM

## H. N. MUNRO

*Physiological Chemistry Laboratories,*
*Department of Nutrition and Food Science*
*Massachusetts Institute of Technology, U.S.A.*

## INTRODUCTION

Animals are metabolic machines endowed with the capacity to adapt to changes in both the internal and the external environment. Adaptation occurs in response to such internal factors as activity versus rest and sleep, the transition from growth to maturity, and the menstrual cycle in the case of the female. Metabolism must also respond to variations in the external environment, such as heat and cold, and especially the intermittent intake of food. Consequently, the body has to be equipped to make short-term and long-term adaptive metabolic reactions. The regulatory mechanisms through which the animal makes these adjustments in metabolism usually involve changes both at the subcellular level and also through integrated co-operation between tissues, often including secretion of hormones. This implies that a comprehensive description of the metabolic responses to an internal or an external stimulus could be a formidable task.

In order to classify regulatory responses affecting protein metabolism, it can be considered that the free amino acids of the body can follow three different pathways: (1) protein synthesis, (2) synthesis of a variety of compounds of low molecular weight, such as creatine and the non-essential amino acids, and (3) degradation through the pathways of amino acid catabolism. These competing uses of amino acids are in equilibrium, so that a change in one route of disposal is compensated by reciprocal changes in others. For example, the new-born animal shows intense protein synthesis but limited degradation of circulating amino acids (McCance and Widdowson, 1964). Similarly, the administration of hydrazine to animals impedes amino acid degradation by interfering with transamination (McCormick and Snell, 1961). This reduction in amino acid catabolism is accompanied by increased tissue amino acid levels and by augmented protein synthesis in the liver (Amenta and Johnston, 1963), a clear case of cause and effect.

In the course of a single presentation, it is not possible to do justice to the many regulatory processes that have been identified in the area of mammalian protein metabolism, and indeed, a volume surveying such mechanisms is available (Munro, 1969). In view of this, the present article will be limited to some recent studies in my laboratory of the regulation of protein synthesis in the liver of the mammal, particular attention being paid to the response to nutritional and hormonal stimuli.

## SITES OF REGULATION OF LIVER PROTEIN SYNTHESIS

The structural complexity of the animal cell accounts for some of the problems inherent in studying control of protein synthesis. *Figure 1* represents some of the relevant features in the liver cell. All forms of RNA, with the probable exception of mitochondrial RNA, are formed in the nucleus but function in the cytoplasm. Consequently, regulation may be exercised at several points in the life-cycle of the RNA molecule. Thus the rate of synthesis of RNA is subject to regulatory variation, as will be discussed below. Several authors (e.g. Georgiev, 1968) have described a nuclear protein that probably transports messenger RNA to the cytoplasm, and this is obviously a candidate for regulatory control, though as yet no data on such control have been provided. Once in the cytoplasm, there is a dichotomy of function in protein synthesis. An important cytoplasmic feature of protein-secreting cells such as the hepatocyte is that part of the polysome population engaged in protein synthesis occurs attached to the membranes of the endoplasmic reticulum, and part occurs as free polysomes in the cytoplasm. It has been assumed for some years that membrane-attached polysomes are engaged in making proteins secreted from the cell (plasma proteins in the case of the liver cell), whereas the free polysomes fabricate protein that is retained within the cell. Recently, several investigators have attempted to verify this thesis, by examining the proteins made by the membrane-attached polysomes and by the free polysomes. In the case of plasma albumin, it has been demonstrated fairly conclusively, both by *in vivo* and *in vitro* studies, that this protein is made mainly or exclusively by membrane-attached polysomes (Redman, 1968; Takagi and Ogata, 1968).

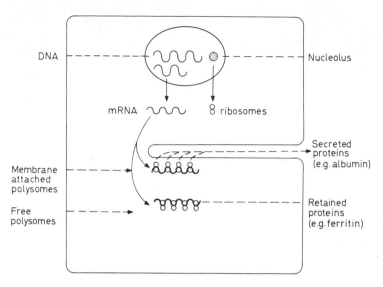

*Figure 1. Diagram of synthesis of secreted and retained cell proteins*

We have recently compared the efficiency of the free polysome population and the total (free and membrane-bound) polysome population of
the liver cell to make ferritin and also plasma albumin in a cell-free
protein-synthesizing system (Hicks *et al.*, 1969). Table 1 shows that the
total population is more efficient for albumin synthesis, presumably
because it includes the membrane-bound polysomes. On the other hand,
labelled amino acids are incorporated more efficiently into ferritin by the
free polysome fraction than by the mixture of free and attached polysomes. These results favour the view that retained proteins such as ferritin
are probably exclusively made by polysomes free in the cytoplasm of the
cell, whereas synthesis of secreted proteins such as albumin is likely to be
confined to membrane-bound polysomes. Consequently, in cells that
contain both types of polysome in their cytoplasm, there must be some
undescribed mechanism for directing messenger RNA coded for secreted
proteins towards the ribosome population attached to membranes.
Finally, the RNA of mammalian cells is subject to turnover, and as will be
demonstrated below, rate of RNA degradation is under regulatory control.

Many inhibitors of mammalian RNA and protein synthesis have been
described, and several have been frequently used to dissect out regulatory
processes in the overall mechanism of protein synthesis. Low doses of

405

Table I

Relation of incorporation of $^{14}$C-leucine by a cell-free protein-synthesizing system
into ferritin and into serum albumin using free polysomes and total polysomes
isolated from rat liver

(From Hicks *et al.*, 1969 by courtesy of the American Asscn. for Adv. of Science)

| Protein isolated | No. of expts | Uptake into Protein as percentage of total peptide incorporation | | Difference (%) |
| --- | --- | --- | --- | --- |
| | | Total polysomes | Free polysomes | |
| Ferritin | 5 | 0.08 | 0.13 | +65 |
| Albumin | 2 | 0.35 | 0.16 | −56 |

actinomycin D specifically inhibit ribosomal RNA formation (Perry, 1962), while moderate doses prevent formation of messengers for some proteins, such as tryptophan pyrrolase (Greengard *et al.,* 1963). There is some evidence, however, that some messengers may continue to be formed in response to stimuli even after very large amounts of actinomycin D are administered (Korner, 1964). Inhibition of cytoplasmic protein synthesis by puromycin is due to premature termination of peptide chains before they reach the end of the messenger, whereas cycloheximide at high concentrations inhibits the enzyme transferase II (translocase) and thus prevents movement of the ribosome along the messenger (Baliga *et al.,* 1969).

## REGULATION OF NUCLEAR MECHANISMS INVOLVED IN PROTEIN SYNTHESIS

It has already been pointed out that we know nothing about processes that may affect the rate of transport of different species of RNA out of the nucleus. However, some information has been gathered about regulation of RNA synthesis within the nucleus. Two types of control are exercised. First, there must be some means by which specific messengers are turned on when required. For example, when the hen starts to lay eggs, its liver begins to manufacture large amounts of three new proteins that are secreted into the blood and are then transported to the oviduct to form part of the complement of egg proteins. This process represents formation of new species of messenger RNA in the liver and can be suppressed by administration of actinomycin D (Greengard *et al.,* 1965). The signal for this new messenger formation is the secretion of oestrogen by the hen at the start of the laying period. In addition to specific activation of selected genes, hormones can also cause generalized changes in RNA synthesis. This occurs in the liver of the rat following corti-costeroid administration (Kenney, 1969). We have examined the changes produced in liver RNA polymerase a few hours after administering cortisol to adrenalectomized rats (Jacob et al., 1969). This polymerase is commonly assayed in the form of an 'aggregate enzyme', which contains not only the enzyme protein but also the chromosomal DNA template from which the polymer is copied. Consequently, changes in activity of the isolated aggregate polymerase could be due to an increase in the amount of enzyme or to an increase in the amount of active template. The enzyme can be assayed in the presence of either $Mg^{2+}$ or $Mn^{2+}$ along with $(NH_4)_2SO_4$. The latter activity is usually much higher and is thought to represent greater exposure of the DNA template due to stripping off of the chromosomal proteins by the high salt concentration. Table 2 shows that the aggregate enzyme assayed in the presence of $Mg^{2+}$ has much greater activity when prepared from cortisol-treated rats than when prepared from uninjected animals. However, activity in the presence of $Mn^{2+}$ and $(NH_4)_2SO_4$ is not affected by hormonal treatment. This has been interpreted as evidence that the amount of template exposed to the enzyme is increased by the hormone (Mg activity), but that the total activity of the enzyme is not altered (Mn-ammonium sulphate activity). This has recently received confirmation by solubilizing RNA polymerase using a new technique which extracts more than 80 per cent of the enzyme activity from liver nuclei without any accompanying DNA (Jacob et al., 1968). When the enzyme was extracted in this way from the nuclei of rats treated with cortisol, the amount of polymerase activity in the extract was no greater than that obtained by extracting the nuclei of control rats (Jacob, Sajdel, and Munro, unpublished data). It has been concluded that the hormone changes the amount of DNA available for transcription.

## CYTOPLASMIC REGULATION OF PROTEIN SYNTHESIS

It has been frequently assumed that regulation of rate of synthesis of a given protein can only be achieved by varying the amount of messenger secreted into the cytoplasm from the nucleus. While this mechanism undoubtedly accounts for many of the changes in liver enzyme levels observed in response to stimuli, the means available to the liver cell for varying its protein content are much more subtle than this simple model would imply. Two examples of responses of liver protein synthesis to nutrients will now be considered, each of which appears to occur through an exclusively cytoplasmic regulatory process. This is not unexpected

Table 2

Effect of hydrocortisone administration *in vivo* to adrenalectomized rats
on nucleolar RNA polymerase activities
(From Jacob *et al.*, 1969 by courtesy of the Editor,
European Journal of Biochemistry)

| Animals | Specific activity of RNA polymerase | |
| --- | --- | --- |
| | $Mg^{2+}$ –*activated* | $Mn^{2+}/(NH_4)_2 SO_4$ –*activated* |
| | $\mu\mu$moles $^{14}$C-UTP incorporated/mg DNA x $10^{-3}$ | $\mu\mu$moles $^{14}$C-UTP incorporated/mg DNA x $10^{-3}$ |
| Adrenalectomized | $4.7 \pm 0.1$ | $13.8 \pm 1.1$ |
| Adrenalectomized + hydrocortisone | $13.1 \pm 1.1$ | $15.4 \pm 1.0$ |

since in each instance, the stimulus demands a rapid response, so that a mechanism involving synthesis of more messenger RNA and its passage into the cytoplasm would not be appropriate.

First, we have examined the response of the iron-binding protein ferritin to an overload of iron (Drysdale and Munro, 1965a, 1966). This liver protein can be isolated by chemical or immunological procedures (Drysdale and Munro, 1965b) and its uptake of radioactive amino acids compared with that of other liver proteins. When ferric ammonium citrate is injected into rats, followed by injection of $^{14}$C-leucine, the uptake of the radioactive precursor into ferritin protein a few hours later has increased several-fold above the incorporation observed in untreated animals, whereas iron treatment does not influence incorporation of leucine into general liver proteins (Table 3). Some hours later there is an absolute increase in the amount of ferritin in the liver. Table 3 also shows the effect of iron administration to rats previously treated with actinomycin. Although this agent suppresses messenger RNA synthesis, it did not diminish the response of ferritin incorporation when iron salts were injected. This suggests that administration of iron may increase ferritin uptake of $^{14}$C-leucine by a cytoplasmic mechanism, and we have provided some evidence that the presence of excess iron in the cell may do so by stabilizing newly formed ferritin protein subunits against proteolytic degradation (Drysdale and Munro, 1966).

The second example of a cytoplasmic adjustment of liver protein synthesis is the response to an influx of amino acids. We have been examining the influence of amino acid supply on the mechanism of liver protein synthesis. It is well known that the liver responds rapidly to a

Table 3

Effect of actinomycin D on ferritin protein synthesis after
injection of iron
(From Drysdale and Munro, 1965a by courtesy of Elsevier)

| Dosage/100 g body weight | | $^{14}C$ Incorporation counts/min/mg protein | | | |
|---|---|---|---|---|---|
| Actinomycin | Iron | Into ferritin protein | Into mixed liver protein | Ratio: | Ferritin / Mixed protein |
| – | – | 305 | 190 | 1.6 | |
| – | 300 µg | 1050 | 165 | 6.5 | |
| 70 µg | – | 400 | 155 | 2.6 | |
| 70 µg | 300 µg | 1100 | 160 | 7.2 | |

change in protein intake; if an increased intake of protein (providing a balanced mixture of amino acids) is fed, the protein content of the liver increases. On the other hand, less protein is found in the liver after giving less dietary protein or after giving a dietary protein partially deficient in one of the essential amino acids (Munro, 1964). Along with these changes in liver protein content go parallel alterations in the amounts of RNA and of phospholipid in the liver, and it can be concluded that the quantity and quality of amino acid supply regulates the metabolism of at least three major constituents of the liver cell. We have chosen to examine the mechanism by which amino acid supply regulates the RNA content of the liver. In an early series of experiments (Clark et al., 1957), we concluded that amino acid supply regulates the rate of breakdown of liver RNA, probably ribosomal RNA. It was subsequently shown (Munro and Clark, 1959) that liver RNA metabolism is sensitive to the type of amino acid mixture fed to the rat; within an hour of giving an amino acid mixture lacking tryptophan, RNA metabolism is different from that of a rat receiving a similar amino acid mixture containing tryptophan.

These earlier experiments led us to examine the effect of feeding nutritionally complete or tryptophan-deficient amino acid mixtures on the ribosome population of the liver cell (Fleck et al., 1965). The response was evaluated by homogenizing the liver and examining the spectrum of polyribosomes (polysomes). As shown in Figure 2, the membrane-attached polyribosomes were detached with deoxycholate so that they could mingle with the polysomes free in the cytoplasm, and then the total polysome population was separated into different sizes by sucrose density gradients.

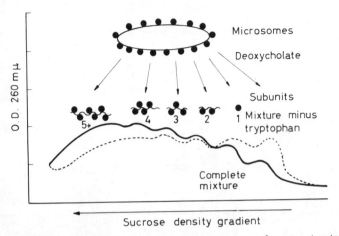

*Figure 2. Polysome patterns at 1 h after feeding a complete or a tryptophan-deficient amino acid mixture*

The diagram shows that animals fed 1 h before death with the amino acid mixture lacking tryptophan had fewer heavy polysome aggregates and more monosomes and disomes than had rats given the nutritionally complete amino acid mixture. In later experiments (Wunner *et al.*, 1966; Drysdale and Munro, 1967), this rapid response to lack of tryptophan was confirmed and was shown to be quickly reversible by feeding the animal with the missing tryptophan. Furthermore, it was demonstrated that the lack of tryptophan caused an increase in the number of ribosome subunits free in the liver cell cytoplasm; since dissociation of ribosome subunits has been shown to activate their latent ribonuclease, it was concluded that such an increase in the subunit population due to tryptophan deficiency would result in more rapid loss of RNA from the cell. We can thus conclude that a complete supply of amino acids engages large numbers of ribosomes with messenger RNA to form polysomes and that, because of the consequent depletion of the free ribosome pool, fewer ribosomes dissociate into subunits and thus less RNA is degraded. If, however, a mixture lacking the essential amino acid tryptophan is fed, the formation of polysomes from messenger and ribosomes is retarded, the free ribosomes accumulate, more dissociate into subunits, and RNA catabolism is accelerated. Consequently, we can construct a picture of the influence of amino acid supply on both protein content and RNA content of the liver cell *(Figure 3)*. As an influx of amino acids passes to the liver after each meal containing protein, more ribosomes are engaged with messenger to form polysomes, protein formation accelerates, and in addition there is diminished turnover of existing enzyme molecules by the influx of substrates. These changes result in a rapid increase in the protein content of the liver. At the same time, the reduction in the free ribosome and subunit pool restrains RNA breakdown and in consequence of continuing synthesis of RNA by the nucleus, there is an accumulation of liver RNA which parallels the increment in liver protein caused by the arrival of amino acids from the gut.

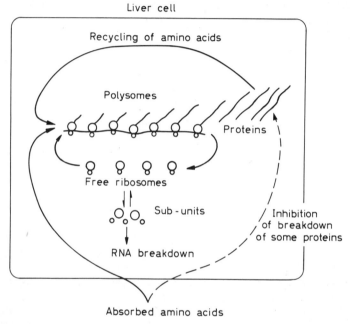

*Figure 3. Effect of absorbed amino acids on the synthesis of protein and breakdown of RNA in the liver cell. Note that the influx of amino acids increases synthesis of liver proteins and simultaneously reduces breakdown of some enzymes. It also reduces degradation of RNA by limiting the ribosome subunit population. (From Munro, 1968 by courtesy of the Federation of American Societies for Exp. Biology)*

We must now consider the site within the liver cell at which the incoming amino acids have their first action. If it involves secretion of messenger RNA from the nucleus, it can be blocked by prior treatment with effective doses of actinomycin D. In fact, animals treated in this way and then fed with nutritionally complete or tryptophan-deficient amino acid mixtures still show different polysome profiles (Fleck *et al.*, 1965), thus indicating that the response to amino acid supply is dependent on cytoplasmic mechanisms only. If this is so, then it should be possible to reconstruct such a system and study the factors affecting polysome formation *in vitro*. Accordingly, we have recently examined the effect of amino acid supply on protein synthesis and polysome formation in a cell-free protein-synthesizing system (Baliga *et al.*, 1968). This was prepared using liver polysomes, an energy source, cell sap dialysed to remove free amino acids, tRNA stripped of amino acids, and $^{14}$C-leucine. This cell-free system was consequently extensively depleted of available amino acids for protein synthesis, and ceased to incorporate $^{14}$C-leucine after a few minutes of incubation at 37°. *Figure 4* shows the polysome profile in this system after 20 min of incubation under these conditions. There are few remaining polysomes but there is instead a large peak of monosomes on the left of the profile. When a complete mixture of amino acids was now added to the incubation medium and the polysome profile again examined 2 min later, it is seen from *Figure 4* that the monosome peak has diminished extensively and heavy polysomes have now accumulated. Thus, polysomes have been synthesized from ribosomes and surviving messenger in response to an increased amino acid supply. By preparing a series of amino acid mixtures each lacking in one amino acid, it was possible to show that omission of any amino acid (except for isoleucine) results in failure of the polysomes to aggregate.

These experiments using a reconstructed cell-free system for protein synthesis confirm that changes in polysome profile can be brought about by alterations in amino acid supply, and that the participation of the nucleus in the mechanism of response is not required. Furthermore, the system requires all amino acids to be present simultaneously in order to allow polysomes to aggregate. However, in the case of the intact animal, it was found (Pronczuk *et al.*, 1968) that amino acid mixtures deficient in essential amino acids other than tryptophan did not cause disaggregation of polysomes in the way that tryptophan deficiency did. It is believed that this special sensitivity of polysomes in the intact animal to available tryptophan occurs because tryptophan is the least abundant amino acid in the free amino acid pool of the liver, and consequently becomes the rate-limiting factor in protein synthesis. By feeding imbalanced amino acid mixtures under circumstances that might be expected to reduce some other free amino acids in the liver to very low levels, it has been possible to demonstrate liver polysome responses that are sensitive to threonine or isoleucine deficiency (Pronczuk, Rogers and Munro, unpublished data).

412

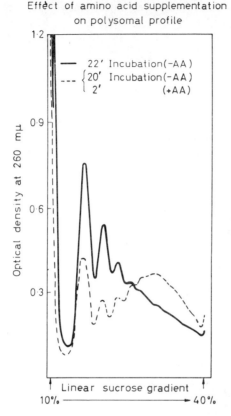

Effect of amino acid supplementation
on polysomal profile

*Figure 4. Changes in polysomes following addition of a complete amino acid mixture to a cell free protein-synthesizing system previously incubated for 20 min without amino acids. The monosome peak is on the left and the polysomes are towards the right of the profile*

## DIURNAL FLUCTUATIONS IN LIVER PROTEIN METABOLISM

The liver is subject to an intense bombardment with amino acids intermittently throughout the day, as each meal containing protein is delivered via the portal vein. Elwyn (1969) has recently measured the amino acid flux across the livers of dogs bearing cannulas on the blood supply going to the liver and coming from the liver. He finds that, after feeding a meal consisting of one pound of meat, the greater part of this amino acid load

413

does not pass through the liver, but is transformed within the liver into urea (about 60 per cent), liver protein (about 20 per cent) and plasma proteins (about 10 per cent), leaving only some 10 per cent for distribution to other tissues by way of the systemic circulation. This means that the liver is constantly undergoing phases of intense protein synthesis followed by periods of accelerated protein catabolism in order to regain its former protein content. Much work attests to the correctness of this picture. For example, breakdown of liver protein during the early stages of fasting in the post-absorptive period is so intense that endogenous amino acids released from the disintegrating proteins flood the hepatocyte and prevent penetration of the liver cell by labelled lysine infused into the blood-stream (Gan and Jeffay, 1967). This concept of variations

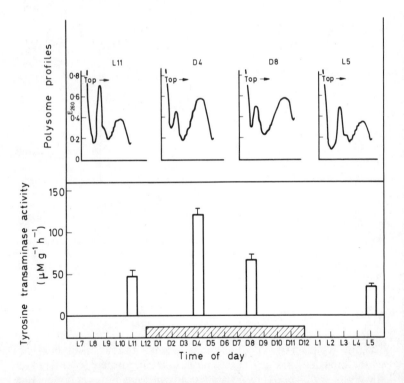

*Figure 5. Diurnal rhythms in polysome profile and tyrosine transaminase activity in rats subjected to 12 h of darkness and 12 h of light. Note that spontaneous eating occurs towards the end of the light period and terminates in the middle of the dark period. (Fishman et al., unpublished data.)*

in endogenous recycling of amino acids in the hepatocyte is incorporated in *Figure 3.*

We have recently examined the diurnal cycles in polysome aggregation and disaggregation, and in the level of the enzyme tyrosine transaminase in the livers of rats subjected to a 12 h cycle of light and darkness (Fishman, Wurtman and Munro, unpublished data). Rats living under these conditions adopt a feeding cycle which begins towards the end of the lighting period, reaches a maximum during the early hours of darkness, and terminates before the light comes on again. *Figure 5* shows that polysome aggregation is least in the middle of the period of light, starts to increase shortly after feeding begins, and is maximal in the middle of the dark period, and by the start of the next light period has begun to disaggregate again. The activity of tyrosine transaminase, an enzyme initiating degradation of tyrosine, follows a somewhat similar diurnal pattern. A more detailed discussion of diurnal changes in liver protein metabolism has recently been provided by Wurtman (1969)

From these and other studies, we may conclude that adaptation of the liver to variations in amino acid supply occurs after each meal and is of considerable magnitude. Furthermore, the fate of a large proportion of the incoming amino acids is decided by the hepatic response, so that it must play a significant role in utilization of dietary protein. So far, the experiments of Elwyn on amino acid metabolism in the liver of the dog, and our own studies on diurnal rhythms in polysome aggregation have been conducted at one (adequate) level of protein intake. It will be necessary to extend both types of experimental approach to animals receiving different levels of protein intake, including subnormal intakes, before it will be possible to assess the role of the liver in determining the utilization of dietary protein.

## ACKNOWLEDGEMENT

Some of the work reported in this contribution was supported by Grant CA 08893–03, and by Grant P 472, of the American Cancer Society.

## REFERENCES

Amenta, J. S. and Johnston, E. H. (1963). *Lab. Invest.* **12,** 921
Baliga, B. S., Pronczuk, A. W. and Munro, H. N. (1968). *J. mol. biol.,* **34,** 199
 − − − (1969). *J. biol. Chem.* 244, 4480
Clark, C. M., Naismith, D. J. and Munro, H. N. (1957). *Biochim. biophys. Acta* **23,** 581

Drysdale, J. W. and Munro, H. N. (1965a). *Biochim. biophys. Acta* **103**, 185
— — (1965b).*Biochem. J.* **95**, 851
— — (1966). *J. biol. Chem.* **241**, 3630
— — (1967). *Biochim. biophys. Acta* **138**, 616
Elwyn, D. (1969). In *Mammalian Protein Metabolism,* Vol 4, Ed. by H. N. Munro. New York; Academic Press (In press)
Fleck, A., Shepherd, J. and Munro, H. N. (1965). *Science, N. Y.* **150**, 628
Gan, J. C. and Jeffay, H. (1967). *Biochim. biophys. Acta* **148**, 448
Georgiev, G. P. (1968). In *Regulatory Mechanisms for Protein Synthesis in Mammalian* Cells, Ed. by A. San Pietro, M. R. Lamborg and F. T. Kennedy. New York; Academic Press p. 25
Greengard, O., Smith, M. A. and Acs, G. (1963).*J. biol. Chem.* **238**, 1548
Greengard, O., Gordon, M., Smith, A. and Acs, G. (1965).*J. biol. Chem.* **239**, 2079
Hicks, S. J., Drysdale, J. W. and Munro, H. N. (1969). *Science, N.Y.* **164**, 584
Jacob, S. T., Sajdel, E. and Munro, H. N. (1968).*Biochem. biophys. Res. Commun.* **32**, 831
— — — (1969). *Eur. J. Biochem.* **7**, 449
Kenney, F. T. (1969). In *Mammalian Protein Metabolism,* Vol. 4. Ed. by H. N. Munro. New York; Academic Press (In press)
Korner, A (1964). *Biochem. J.* **92**, 449
McCance, R. A. and Widdowson, E. M. (1964). In *Mammalian Protein Metabolism,* Vol. 2. Ed by H. N. Munro and J. B. Allison. New York; Academic Press p. 225
McCormick, D. B. and Snell, E. E. (1961). *J. biol. Chem.* **236**, 2085
Munro, H. N. (1964). In *Mammalian Protein Metabolism,* Vol. 1, Ed. by H. N. Munro and J. B. Allison. New York; Academic Press p.381
— (1968). *Fedn. Proc. Fedn. Am. Socs. exp. Biol.* **27**, 1231
— (Editor) (1969), *Mammalian Protein Metabolism,* Vol. 4. New York; Academic Press (In press)
—and Clark, C. M. (1959). *Biochim. biophys. Acta* **33**, 551
Perry, R. P. (1962). *Proc. nat. Acad. Sci. U. S. A.* **48**, 2179
Pronczuk, A. W., Baliga, B. S., Triant, J. W. and Munro, H. N. (1968). *Biochim. biophys. Acta* **157**, 204
Redman, C. M. (1968). *Biochem. biophys. Res. Commun.* **31**, 845
Takagi, M. and Ogata, K. (1968). *Biochem. biophys. Res. Commun.* **33**, 55
Wunner, W. H., Bell, J., and Munro, H. N. (1966). *Biochem. J.* **101**, 417
Wurtman, R. J. (1969). In *Mammalian Protein Metabolism,* Vol. 4, Ed. by H. N. Munro. New York; Academic Press (In press)

# EFFECTS OF DISPROPORTIONATE AMOUNTS OF AMINO ACIDS

A. E. HARPER and N. J. BENEVENGA

*Departments of Biochemistry,*
*Nutritional Sciences and Animal Science,*
*University of Wisconsin, Madison*

## INTRODUCTION

The thesis we should like to present is based on the assumption that plasma free amino acid concentrations are subject to homeostatic regulation (Harper, 1969). The thesis is that the responses of organisms to disproportionate amounts of amino acids in a diet are either normal homeostatic responses that tend to prevent drastic deviations in plasma amino acid concentrations; or are responses that occur because the capacity of the homeostatic mechanisms has been exceeded. In addition, we should like to propose that regulation of food intake represents an integrated response in which the animal as a whole serves as a complex feed-back mechanism contributing to homeostasis of circulating, free amino acid concentrations.

## TYPES OF AMINO ACID DISPROPORTIONS

If disproportion is taken to mean any change in the pattern or content of amino acids in the diet from the pattern and content that just meet the requirements of the organism, unlimited varieties and degrees of disproportion are possible. We shall group the types of disproportion under four general headings and shall talk about two examples in which characteristic responses are observed.

At the outset it is important to recognize: first, that organisms tolerate a measure of disproportion among the amino acids in a diet without showing evidence of adverse effects; second, that the tolerance of an organism for disproportionate amounts of amino acids depends upon its physiological and nutritional state; and third, that there is a continuous gradation of effects of disproportionate amounts of amino acids from innocuous to toxic, depending upon the degree of disproportion. All generalizations about effects of disproportionate amounts of amino acids are subject to these limitations.

*Amino acid deficiency* is the most obvious type of disproportion. An inadequate supply of one or more amino acids results in retarded growth and food intake in proportion to the degree of deficiency. The high correlation observed between amino acid content of the diet and both food intake and growth indicate that food intake, as well as growth, is a function of the content of the limiting amino acid (Boctor and Harper, 1968; Hegsted and Haffenreffer, 1949). However, the relationship is not constant; it depends upon the amounts of other amino acids in excess in the diet (Harper, 1967).

Effects of deficiencies are not the subject of this paper but we would like to emphasize that the effects of a severe amino acid deficiency are magnified when an animal is forcibly fed a greater amount of a severely deficient diet than it will eat freely (Sidransky and Farber 1958). Pathological signs develop that do not occur in animals fed *ad libitum* and the animals survive a shorter time. This is also true of diets low in protein (Sidransky and Verney, 1965) and as Platt and associates (1964) have shown, the effects of a protein deficiency are more severe if the carbohydrate intake alone is increased. These observations suggest that depressed food intake is an adaptive response with survival value for the organism that is consuming a severely inadequate diet.

*Amino acid imbalance* represents a variant of amino acid deficiency. The response in this condition is to a dietary surplus of amino acids other than the one that is growth-limiting. The effect is most clearly seen in comparisons involving two diets equally deficient in the limiting amino acid but with one containing more of the other indispensable amino acids. The main effects are depressed food intake and growth rate, the depressions being greater than would be predicted from the degree of amino acid deficiency (Harper, Leung, Yoshida and Rogers, 1964; Harper and Rogers, 1965). The degree of imbalance can vary greatly but such effects are readily demonstrated with animals fed on diets in which none of the individual amino acids is present in an amount that by itself, would be toxic.

The distinction between a simple deficiency and an amino acid imbalance is illustrated in *Figure 1*. The effects of a deficiency are attributable to an inadequate supply of the amino acid that limits growth. The effects of an imbalance are attributable to a surplus of amino acids other than the one that limits growth. Animals adapt to amino acid imbalances, and growth rate and food intake gradually improve without further treatment if the imbalance is not too severe (Leung, Rogers and Harper,

1968a). Treatments such as cold exposure (Harper and Rogers, 1966) and injections of cortisol (Leung, Rogers and Harper, 1968b) reduce the time required for adaptation and forced-feeding, instead of increasing the severity of the condition, tends to alleviate it (Leung *et al.*, 1968a).

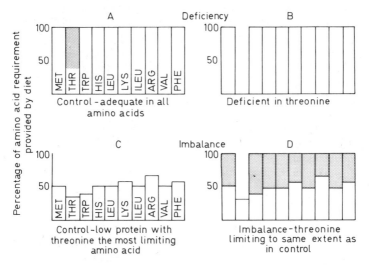

*Figure 1. Comparison of amino acid patterns of amino acid-deficient and amino acid-imbalanced diets. (Harper, 1967 by courtesy of executive editor, American Physiological Society)*

*Excesses of individual amino acids,* especially in low protein diets, retard growth and depress food intake; and, depending on the degree of excess, may result in signs of toxicity (Harper, 1964). The effects vary with the individual amino acid in excess and with the adequacy of the diet; most amino acids are tolerated in greater excess by animals receiving an adequate diet.

Animals will also adapt to excessive intakes of individual amino acids, if the amino acid is not in too great excess, and food intake and growth will gradually improve. The mental deterioration that so commonly accompanies high concentrations of individual amino acids in the body fluids of human subjects with inherited metabolic defects of amino acid metabolism indicates that the body has only a limited tolerance for excessive amounts of individual amino acids (Nyhan, 1967).

*A high protein intake* represents a disproportionate intake of amino acids frequently in a well-balanced pattern. This too results in depressed food intake and growth but usually the effects are only transitory as animals adapt readily to a high protein intake (Harper, 1965; Anderson, Benevenga and Harper, 1968). The adaptation is accompanied by liver and kidney hypertrophy but the adapted animal grows well and eats well although its life span may be shortened (Ross, 1959).

All of these effects are associated with changes in the pattern or concentrations of circulating free amino acids or metabolic products of them. The specificity of the effects presumably depends upon the specific metabolic inter-relationships among the amino acids or upon the chemical nature of the individual amino acids, and the severity of the effects depends upon the nutritional and physiological state of the animal.

Efforts to classify the different types of disproportions of amino acids according to certain characteristics of the responses of animals to them have been presented previously (Elvehjem and Harper, 1955; Harper, 1964, 1956, 1958; Elvehjem, 1956), and will not be discussed further here.

## REGULATION OF PLASMA AND TISSUE CONCENTRATIONS OF FREE AMINO ACIDS

Evidence that plasma amino acid concentrations are subject to homeostatic regulation comes from observations that fasting plasma amino acid concentrations for an individual are quite constant over time (Adibi, 1968) and fasting patterns within a species are similar (Munro, 1969). Restoration of plasma amino acid concentrations toward normal after they have been perturbed owing to ingestion of a meal is further evidence for such regulation. This occurs whether the amino acid intake is small and plasma concentrations fall during the post-absorptive state or whether the meal is large and plasma concentrations rise in the post-absorptive state. Further, plasma amino acid concentrations do not fall drastically during periods of prolonged starvation (Adibi, 1968).

The processes that contribute to regulation of free amino acid concentrations include tissue protein synthesis and degradation, amino acid degradation and excretion, and food intake regulation (*Figure 2*).

Amino acids are the building blocks of proteins; so, in the growing animal, amino acids are removed from the circulation as tissue proteins are synthesized. In the mature animal a supply of amino acids is required continuously for the replacement of amino acids that are being continuously degraded.

Amino acids in surplus cannot be stored as can surpluses of energy sources such as carbohydrate and fat. Amino acids in surplus are rapidly degraded and used as sources of energy. Clear evidence of this is obtained

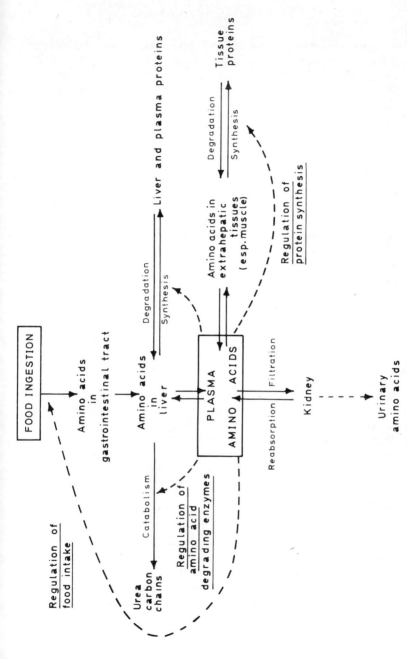

Figure 2. Schematic representation of the metabolic fate of plasma amino acids

from experiments in which diets devoid of an amino acid are fed, and the missing amino acid is provided later (Greiger, 1948). Provision of the missing amino acid even a few hours later results in growth failure; the exact time interval that can elapse before supplementation is ineffective and differs with the individual amino acid, indicating that degradative rates for the various amino acids are different.

This is not to deny that circulating amino acid concentrations can be maintained as a result of tissue protein degradation during periods of protein deprivation, and that the more essential tissue proteins can be synthesized from amino acids released as a result of breakdown of less essential proteins during such times (Harper, 1965; Munro, 1964). Nevertheless, organ and tissue protein concentrations of animals fed a high protein diet rise very little above the values for animals fed a standard diet (Mayer and Vitale, 1958; Maramatsu and Ashida, 1962), a further indication that tissue protein stores are limited; if they exist at all, as such. Also, survival during periods of deprivation is not improved by the prior feeding of a high protein diet (Holt, Jr., Halac, Jr. and Kajdi, 1962).

Changes in the rate of amino acid degradation represent the major means available for regulation of the concentrations of circulating free amino acids. There is a renal threshold for amino acids as indicated particularly by the amino acidurias observed in subjects lacking certain specific amino acid-degrading enzymes (Nyhan, 1967). However, in normal subjects and animals, even a very high protein intake does not lead to a substantial amino aciduria. The amino acid-degrading enzymes of the liver are adaptive and their activities tend to respond to changing protein intake, most falling to very low activities in animals with low protein intakes and rising to high activities in animals with high protein intakes. Thus the capacity for amino acid degradation tends to be proportional to amino acid intake (Harper, 1965). Only a few such enzymes, respond in animals with high intakes of individual amino acids (Knox and Greengard, 1965), so the animal fed a low protein diet and having only low activities of amino acid-degrading enzymes generally is ill-prepared to contend with a large surplus of one or a few individual amino acids.

When the capacity of an animal for protein synthesis or amino acid degradation is limited and it is fed a diet containing a large amount of protein or amino acids, since amino acids cannot be stored, they will tend to accumulate in the body fluids. One remaining mechanism is available to such an animal to prevent or reduce amino acid accumulation — that is to reduce its amino acid intake. Ordinarily an animal eats in proportion to its need for energy; many studies show a close relationship between energy intake and energy output (Mayer, 1964). However, despite the need for energy by animals fed a high protein diet or a diet high in one or more individual amino acids, their food intake usually falls. This suggests that under conditions of amino acid excess food intake regulating mechanisms are responsive to amino acid intake and that food intake regulation represents an important homeostatic mechanism for the regulation of body fluid amino acid concentrations.

## RESPONSES TO INGESTION OF DISPROPORTIONATE AMOUNTS OF AMINO ACIDS

Responses to ingestion of disproportionate amounts of amino acids, according to this thesis, should, then, be the result of homeostatic responses of regulatory mechanisms or the result of exceeding the capacity of these mechanisms, or of some combination of the two.

Several amino acids are clearly toxic when consumed in large quantities, particularly if the protein content of the diet is low. This is true of methionine (Benevenga and Harper, 1967), tyrosine (Alam, Becker, Stucki, Rogers and Harper, 1966) and tryptophan in particular (Sauberlich 1961). The tolerance of the rat for different amino acids varies greatly as shown in Table 1.

Table 1

Effect of addition of 5 per cent of various amino acids to a low protein diet on growth of weanling rats
(From Sauberlich, 1961, by courtesy of the American Institute of Nutrition)

| Amino acid added to diet | Percentage depression in growth |
|---|---|
| DL-Alanine | 0 |
| L-Glutamic acid | 8 |
| L-Proline | 16 |
| L-Lysine | 37 |
| L-Arginine | 44 |
| Glycine | 50 |
| L-Tyrosine | 73 |
| L-Histidine | 73 |
| DL-Methionine | 123 |

Although adverse effects of many individual amino acids in excess were documented 35–40 years ago and although means of alleviating some of these adverse effects have been discovered, for not a single one has the specific nature of the lesion and the underlying basis for it been established. Amino acids fed in excess, without exception, depress food intake and growth and these depressions are accompanied by substantial elevations in the plasma concentration of the amino acid in excess. Alleviation of the food intake and growth depression appears to be accompanied by a fall in the plasma concentration of the amino acid fed in excess or at least in the animal being able to consume more of it without any further increase occurring. This is evidence that the ability to remove it has increased.

## EFFECTS OF A DIETARY EXCESS OF METHIONINE

Some recent studies in our laboratory on methionine toxicity (Benevenga and Harper, 1967) will illustrate some of these points with respect to individual amino acids fed in excess. The studies were done with young white rats. The basic diet contained 10 per cent of casein but was otherwise complete. The diets were prepared as agar gels with a water content of 50 per cent.

*Figure 3* shows the weight gains of rats fed different amounts of L-methionine in the basic diet. This is essentially a recapitulation of studies reported earlier by several investigators. A small supplement of methionine stimulated growth greatly but quantities much in excess of 1 per cent depressed growth; with 3 per cent or more L-methionine, growth was severely depressed. This amount was used routinely in subsequent studies.

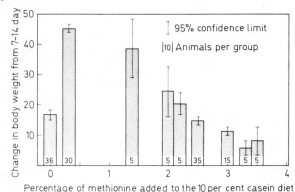

*Figure 3. Weight gain of rats fed a 10 per cent casein diet containing various amouts of methionine. (Benevenga and Harper, 1969 by courtesy of the Editor, Journal of Nutrition and the American Institute of Nutrition)*

Table 2 shows that the growth depression due to excess methionine is alleviated but not prevented by additional glycine. The quantities tested represent one, two and three times the molar quantity of methionine. Table 3 shows that serine also alleviated the growth depression. It would appear to be less effective than glycine but it should be noted that the

Table 2

Effect of Glycine levels on weight gain of rats fed 10 per cent casein diets plus 3 per cent L-methionine[1]
(From Benevenga and Harper, 1967, by courtesy of the American Institute of Nutrition)

| L-Methionine[2] % | Glycine[2] % | Weight gain (7-14 day) g |
|---|---|---|
| 0.3 | – | 46.6 + 2.0[3] |
| 0.3 | 1.5 | 49.4 ∓ 1.3 |
| 0.3 | 3.0 | 46.0 + 1.7 |
| 0.3 | 4.5 | 41.3 ∓ 1.3 |
| 0.3 | 6.0 | 38.1 ∓ 3.2 |
| 0.3 | 7.5 | 30.5 ∓ 4.1 |
| 3.0 | – | 2.0 + 2.1 |
| 3.0 | 1.5 | 14.8 ∓ 1.8* |
| 3.0 | 3.0 | 21.3 ∓ 1.2* |
| 3.0 | 4.5 | 27.3 ∓ 1.7* |
| 3.0 | 6.0 | 21.1 ∓ 0.9 |
| 3.0 | 7.5 | 24.3 ∓ 1.6 |

[1] Six animals/group except for* which have 16 animals/group
[2] Three per cent methionine equals 0.2 moles/kg diet and 1.5, 3.0, 4.5, 6.0 and 7.5 per cent glycine equals 0.2, 0.4, 0.6, 0.8 and 1.0 moles/kg diet
[3] SE of mean

Table 3

Effect of L-serine level on weight gain of rats fed on 10 per cent casein diets plus 3 per cent L-methionine[1]
(From Benevenga and Harper, 1967, by courtesy of the American Institute of Nutrition)

| L-Methionine[2] % | L-Serine % | Weight gain (7-14 day) g |
|---|---|---|
| 0.3 | – | 45.0 ± 4.3[3] |
| 0.3 | 2.1 | 42.5 ± 2.8 |
| 0.3 | 4.2 | 33.6 ± 2.4 |
| 0.3 | 6.3 | 32.0 ± 0.7 |
| 3.0 | – | 2.3 ± 1.0 |
| 3.0 | 2.1 | 12.8 ± 1.6 |
| 3.0 | 4.2 | 15.8 ± 1.3 |
| 3.0 | 6.3 | 17.5 ± 1.0 |

[1] Six animals/group
[2] Three per cent methionine equals 0.2 moles/kg diet and 2.1, 4.2 and 6.3 per cent L-serine equal 0.2, 0.4 and 0.6 moles/kg diet
[3] SE of mean

higher quantities of serine, equivalent on a molar basis to those of glycine, caused severe growth depressions. Other experiments have indicated that this effect is quite specific for glycine and serine, several other amino acids being ineffective (Benevenga and Harper, 1967).

The nature of the growth response with time, shown in *Figure 4*, indicates that there is a lag in the growth response of rats fed additional glycine with an excess of methionine. This suggests that the animal must undergo some adaptation before the glycine becomes effective. The results obtained when the diets were switched after 14 days indicates that animals fed the high methionine diet undergo this adaptation since there was no lag in their response to glycine. As well, glycine must be continued in the diet to alleviate the toxicity because immediately after it was withdrawn growth rate fell.

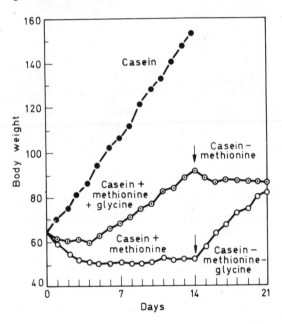

*Figure 4. Effect of methionine* (3 per cent) *and glycine* (4.5 per cent) *on weight gain of rats fed a* 10 per cent *casein diet. Arrows indicate time at which diets were alternated. (Benevenga and Harper, 1969 by courtesy of the Editor, Journal of Nutrition and the American Institute of Nutrition)*

*Figure 5* shows that the food intake patterns resemble closely the growth-response patterns.

The implication of the nutritional experiments is that glycine and serine in some way facilitate the metabolism of the excess of methionine. The effect of glycine on the plasma methionine concentration was clearly evident from measurements of plasma amino acids (Table 4). Glycine in

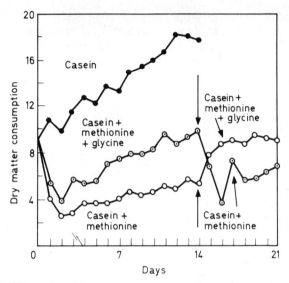

*Figure 5. Effect of methionine* (3 per cent) *and glycine* (4.5 per cent) *on food intake of rats fed a* 10 per cent *casein diet (as for Figure 4). (Benevenga and Harper, 1969 by courtesy of the Editor, Journal of Nutrition and the American Institute of Nutrition)*

Table 4

Effect of glycine levels on plasma glycine and methionine in rats fed 10 per cent casein diets plus 3 per cent L-methionine*

| Dietary | | Amino acid level in $\mu$m/100ml *plasma* | |
|---|---|---|---|
| L-Methionine % | Glycine % | Glycine | Methionine |
| 0.3 | — | 15 | 15 |
| 0.3 | 1.5 | 145 | 12 |
| 0.3 | 3.0 | 321 | 14 |
| 0.3 | 4.5 | 401 | 12 |
| 0.3 | 6.0 | 505 | 16 |
| 0.3 | 7.5 | 732 | 22 |
| 3.0 | — | 26 | 483 |
| 3.0 | 1.5 | 76 | 315 |
| 3.0 | 3.0 | 101 | 230 |
| 3.0 | 4.5 | 310 | 112 |
| 3.0 | 6.0 | 577 | 226 |
| 3.0 | 7.5 | 484 | 116 |

* Plasma from 6 rats pooled for each sample

excess had little effect on the plasma methionine concentration of rats fed the low methionine diet but greatly reduced plasma methionine concentration of those fed the high methionine diet. Also glycine concentration of animals receiving high glycine diets rose less when the diet was also high in methionine.

These observations suggested that oxidation of an excess of methionine was stimulated by a high intake of glycine. To investigate this, rats were trained to eat a single meal daily, then were fed a meal of the high methionine diet containing L-methionine $^{14}$C-methyl or this diet with additional glycine or serine. Groups of rats were continued on these diets for one week, during which they should have adjusted to the diets, then they too were fed a meal of their respective diets containing the labelled methionine. The expired air was collected and the radioactivity in carbon dioxide was measured.

From *Figure 6* it can be seen that on the first day the quantity of carbon dioxide expired was not influenced by additions of glycine or serine. After 7 days the capacity for methionine oxidation had increased greatly regardless of the diet and values for groups fed the diets containing additional glycine and serine were above those for the group receiving only excess methionine. Although these differences were significant the

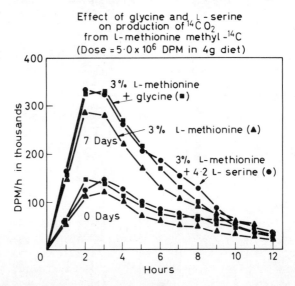

Figure 6. *Effect of glycine and L-serine on production of* $^{14}CO_2$, *from L-methionine methyl-*$^{14}C$ *by rats fed a diet containing* 10 per cent *of casein and* 3 per cent *of L-methionine*

amount of diet fed in this experiment was small so in a subsequent experiment the size of the meal was increased in an effort to increase the total methionine pool and to prolong the period over which differences might be observed.

In *Figure 7* are the results of an oxidation study with L-methionine-1-$^{14}$C indicating that high intakes of glycine and serine substantially increased the capacity of the rat to oxidize an excess of L-methionine.

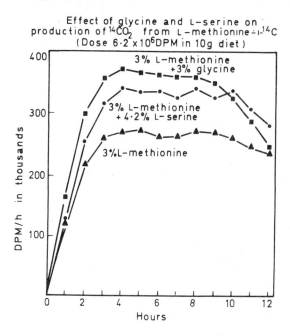

Figure 7. *Effect of glycine and L-serine on production* $^{14}CO_2$ *from L-methionine-1-$^{14}$C by rats fed a diet containing* 10 per cent *of casein and* 3 per cent *of L-methionine*

The metabolic pathway for methionine odixation is outlined in *Figure 8.* After removal of the methyl group, the homocysteine remaining reacts with serine to form cystathionine. When this is split it yields cysteine and homoserine. Oxidation of homoserine results in C-1 of methionine being converted to carbon dioxide. The main point here is that serine is required for this oxidation and the implication of our observations is that this becomes the limiting step in methionine oxidation when methionine is

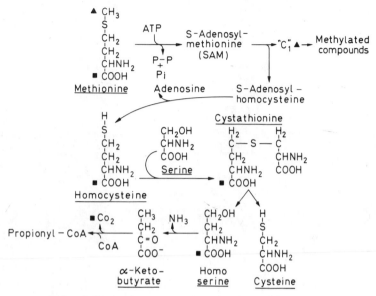

*Figure 8. Schematic representation of methionine metabolism*

fed in great excess. As serine can be formed from glycine, this will also account for the effectiveness of glycine.

This is obviously not the entire answer to methionine toxicity as serine and glycine do not completely prevent the growth depression due to excess methionine. Serine seems to be more effective in alleviating homocysteine toxicity which suggests that there is a further problem in relation to the metabolism of the methyl group. This remains to be unravelled.

A further study of plasma amino acids, in an experiment resembling the metabolic study, indicates that excess glycine and serine cause plasma methionine of rats fed excess methionine to fall, coincident with the stimulation observed in methionine oxidation (Table 5). Associated with

Table 5

Effect of 3 per cent glycine and 4.2 per cent L-serine on plasma methionine levels of rats fed 10 per cent casein diets plus 3 per cent L-methionine*

| Diet | Plasma methionine levels $\mu$m/100 ml | | | |
|---|---|---|---|---|
| | 3 h | 6 h | 9 h | 12 h |
| Cas. + Met. | 245 | 244 | 222 | 278 |
| Cas. + Met. + Gly. | 205 | 143 | 137 | 56 |
| Cas. + Met. + Ser. | 165 | 243 | 159 | 47 |

*Each rat was fed 10 g of the diet in agar gel form (5 rats/time period)

the more rapid rate of oxidation and lowering of plasma methionine is an increased rate of stomach emptying (Table 6).

Table 6

Effect of 3 per cent glycine and 4.2 per cent L-serine on stomach emptying rate of rats fed 10 per cent casein diets plus 3 per cent L-methionine[1]

| Diet | Percentage of dry matter consumed in stomach | | | |
|---|---|---|---|---|
| | 3 h | 6 h | 9 h | 12 h |
| Cas. + Met. | 61 | 37 | 28 | 6 |
| Cas. + Met. + Gly. | 58 | 34 | 15*[2] | 3 |
| Cas. + Met. + Ser. | 57 | 41 | 16* | 2** |

[1]Each rat was fed 10 g of the diet in agar gel form (10 rats/time period)
[2]Means different from casein + methionine group, $*P < 0.05$, $**P < 0.01$

From these associations it would appear that a high methionine intake results in greatly elevated plasma methionine concentration, that at some point of increase this leads to a reduced rate of stomach emptying and depressed food intake, both of which would tend to prevent further consumption of methionine by an organism already loaded beyond its metabolic capacity to remove methionine.

If glycine or serine are provided with excess methionine, oxidation is stimulated and a greater amount of food can be consumed before the maximum tolerable rise in plasma methionine concentration occurs. Although plasma methionine may still rise abnormally, it remains high for a shorter time, food intake is depressed less and the condition of the organism is improved.

## EFFECTS OF AN AMINO ACID IMBALANCE

The term 'amino acid imbalance' as we use it is not synonymous with the term 'amino acid disproportion'. As mentioned earlier, we use it specifically to describe a particular type of disproportion, in which amino acids other than the limiting one are in excess in diets that are low in protein, but with no individual amino acid in sufficient excess to be toxic by itself. Two degrees of amino acid imbalance are illustrated in *Figure 9*. In one the imbalance has been created by a small supplement of the second limiting amino acid; in the other the imbalance has been created by supplementation of a low protein diet with a mixture of all of the indispensable amino acids except for the one that is growth-limiting. The lower part shows correction of the imbalance by a supplement of the limiting amino acid.

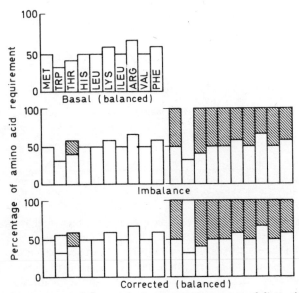

*Figure 9. Schematic representation of amino acid patterns of diets with amino acid imbalances and correction of the imbalances. (Harper, in The Chemical Senses and Nutrition, 1967 by courtesy of the John Hopkins Press)*

*Figure 10* illustrates the most obvious effects of amino acid imbalances — depressions of growth and food intake. These depressions, caused by adding a mixture of amino acids devoid of histidine to a diet containing 6 per cent of fibrin, occur within a short time but if the imbalance is not too severe, as was mentioned, the animal undergoes adaptation to the imbalanced diet and growth and food intake gradually increase with time.

Another effect is illustrated in *Figure 11*. Rats offered a choice between a protein-free diet and a diet with an imbalance also created by adding an amino acid mixture devoid of histidine to a 6 per cent fibrin diet show a distinct preference for the much more inadequate protein-free diet over the diet with the imbalance. The degree of preference depends upon the degree of imbalance (Leung, Rogers and Harper, 1968c). If the amino acid imbalance is corrected rats select exclusively the corrected diet and reject the protein-free diet.

Accompanying the food intake depression and aberrant food preference are changes in plasma amino acid pattern and concentrations of the type shown in *Figure 12*. The plasma concentration of the growth-limiting amino acid, in this case histidine, falls; and concentrations of

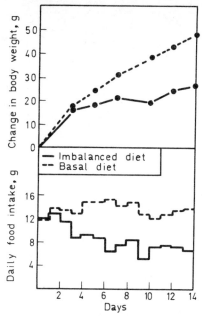

*Figure 10. Changes in body weight and food consumption of protein-depleted rats fed a 6 per cent fibrin diet imbalanced by addition of 6 per cent of a mixture of indispensable amino acids devoid of histidine. (Sanahyja and Harper (1962) Am. J. Physiol. 202, 165 by courtesy of the executive editor, American Physiological Society)*

amino acids added to create the imbalance rise. The control value is shown as a line = 100 per cent. Histidine concentration falls considerably below that of rats fed a diet containing exactly the same amount of histidine but to which no amino acids have been added to create an imbalance. The pattern resembles that observed in rats fed a diet with a more severe histidine deficiency, with a low concentration of histidine and elevated concentrations of other amino acids.

Unlike effects of excesses of individual amino acids, which are specific and unique, effects of amino acid imbalances are more truly effects of amino acid disproportion as such. The effects are due to a surplus of amino acids other than the growth-limiting one. They can be demonstrated with diets in which different amino acids are growth limiting; the severity of the effect depends on both the quantity and the composition of the mixture of amino acids added to create the imbalance but is usually more severe when the mixture contains the second limiting amino acid. It can be caused by a supplement of the second limiting amino acid alone,

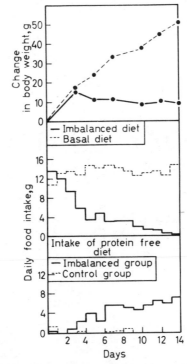

*Figure 11. Changes in body weight and food consumption of rats offered free choice of a protein-free diet and a 6 per cent fibrin diet or a 6 per cent fibrin diet with an imbalance created by addition of a mixture of indispensable amino acids devoid of histidine. (Sanahyja and Harper (1962) Am. J. Physiol. 202, 165 by courtesy of the executive editor, American Physiological Society)*

frequently in rather small amounts. It is thus a general and largely predictable phenomenon.

What is the basis for these marked alterations in plasma amino acid pattern? First, the diets commonly used in studies of amino acid imbalances are low in protein. Enzymes of amino acid catabolism usually fall to quite low activities under these conditions as shown for threonine dehydratase in *Figure 13*. With low activities of these enzymes a surplus of amino acids in body fluids cannot be cleared rapidly. Thus the amino acids added to create the imbalance tend to accumulate.

The fall in the concentration of the limiting amino acid in the diet cannot be attributed to an enhanced rate of amino acid oxidation, as was originally thought, for the limiting amino acid is, at least initially, oxidized as rapidly by control animals as by those fed a diet with an

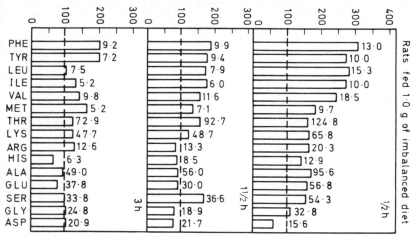

*Figure 12. Changes with time in plasma amino acid pattern of rats fed a 1.0 g meal of a diet containing 6 per cent of casein and a similar amount of a mixture of amino acids devoid of histidine. Dotted line indicates control values set at 100 per cent*

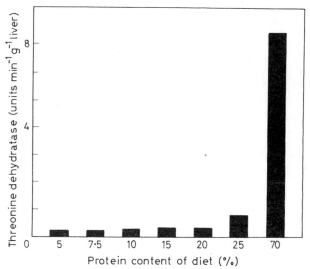

*Figure 13. Influence of protein content of diet on hepatic threonine dehydratase activity (Harper (1968) Am. J. Clin. Nutrition 21,358 by courtesy of the Editor Am. J. Clin. Nutr.)*

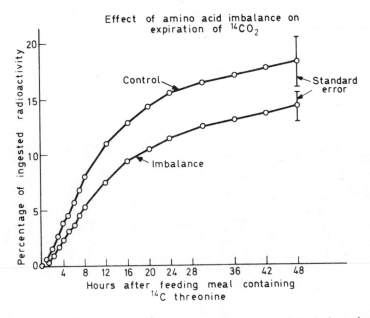

*Figure 14. Radioactivity from $^{14}$C-Threonine expired by rats fed a single meal of a diet containing 6 per cent of casein or the same diet containing a mixture of amino acids devoid of threonine to create an imbalance (Yoshida et al. (1966) by courtesy of the Editor, Journal of Nutrition and The American Institute of Nutrition)*

imbalance. *Figure 14* illustrates this. The curves show the lack of influence of a mixture of amino acids devoid of threonine on the expiration of $^{14}$C-carbon dioxide from U-$^{14}$C-threonine by rats fed a meal of a 6 per cent casein basal diet or a threonine-imbalanced diet (Yoshida, Leung, Rogers and Harper, 1966).

On the other hand, ingestion of a low protein diet to which a mixture of amino acids devoid of histidine has been added to create an amino acid imbalance results in increased retention of histidine in the liver (Benevenga, Harper and Rogers, 1968) and enhanced incorporation of histidine into liver proteins (Table 7). This should result in increased removal of histidine from plasma and hence in less histidine circulating to peripheral tissues. Thus, the surplus of amino acids causing an imbalance presumably stimulates protein synthesis in the liver. The combination of this with the slow rate of removal of other amino acids results in the plasma amino acid pattern resembling that of an animal fed a diet that is severely deficient in histidine (McLaughlan and Morrison, 1968).

436

Table 7

Effect of amino acid imbalance on incorporation of radioactivity from limiting amino acid into liver protein

|  |  | Radioactivity in liver protein dpm/mg N |
|---|---|---|
| A. | Control (6% casein) | 20,485 |
| B. | Imbalance (A + 6% A.A. mix-his) | 32,157 |
| C. | Corrected (B + 0.1% L-his . HCl) | 38,165* |

*Corrected for dilution by extra dietary histidine: values are significantly different from each other

Reference was made earlier to the observation that force-feeding rats a diet completely deficient in a single amino acid shortens the time they survive. When they are fed *ad libitum* they survive longer despite a severe reduction in food intake and do not show drastic histopathologic changes. Almquist (1954) and Frazier *et al.* (1947) have suggested that the circulating plasma amino acid pattern or concentrations are monitored in rats fed amino acid deficient diets, and that the response to abnormality is reduced food intake. This would be a homeostatic response with survival value. Since an amino acid imbalance can result in a plasma amino acid pattern resembling that caused by a more severe amino acid deficiency, the signal, if it arises from the plasma pattern, would resemble that arising from a deficiency and the response would be the same — reduced food intake. It is tempting to speculate that greatly elevated concentrations of plasma amino acids indicate that protein synthesizing mechanisms are saturated and that sensitivity to this signal increases when the limiting amino acid is in short supply.

There have been several suggestions that plasma amino acid patterns and concentrations influence food intake. Almquist (1954) and Frazier *et al.* (1947) suggested this in relation to amino acid deficiencies, Mellinkoff (1957) suggested it in relation to pathological states in man. Observations from our own laboratory support the idea for animals fed a high protein diet (Anderson *et al.*, 1968). A high protein intake results in greatly elevated plasma amino acid concentrations and depressed food intake. However, within a few days, activities of amino acid-degrading enzymes become greatly elevated, plasma amino acid concentrations are rapidly restored to normal and food intake increases. Here the food intake depression would appear to be a homeostatic response that reduces the influx of amino acids until the metabolic capacity of the animal increases sufficiently to control the surplus of amino acids ingested.

These observations are of particular interest in relation to the preference of rats offered a choice between an imbalanced diet and a protein-free diet, for the protein-free diet. The selection for a nutritionally inadequate diet seems anomalous but it is selection for a diet that tends to restore the plasma amino acid pattern to 'normal'.

The food intake depression of rats fed a diet with an amino acid imbalance can be prevented, or adaptation to it can be speeded, by such treatments as cortisol administration, prior feeding of a high protein diet or cold exposure – treatments that tend to increase the metabolic capacity of the animal. In recent studies in our laboratory we have examined changes occurring in rats fed a diet with an imbalance with respect to histidine during cold exposure (Anderson *et al.*, 1969a) and during adaptation to such a diet at room temperature (Anderson *et al.*, 1969b).

Rats exposed to a cold environment, $4° - 7° C$, and fed a diet with an imbalance of this type eat well, and depending upon their previous treatment, may show no food intake depression below that of controls fed a balanced diet, or only a transitory depression as is evident from *Figure 15*. They grow as well as or better than the controls (*Figure 15*), indicating that the effects of the imbalance are not due to toxicity which should increase in severity with increasing food intake. Interestingly, however, despite their greatly enhanced food intake, their plasma amino acid patterns resemble those of animals fed this diet at room temperature and whose food intake is depressed (*Figure 16*).

Also, with time, rats maintained at room temperature adapt to a diet with an imbalance, their food intake gradually increases and they begin to

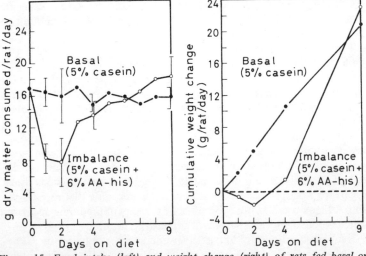

*Figure 15. Food intake (left) and weight change (right) of rats fed basal or imbalanced diet at 5°C*

438

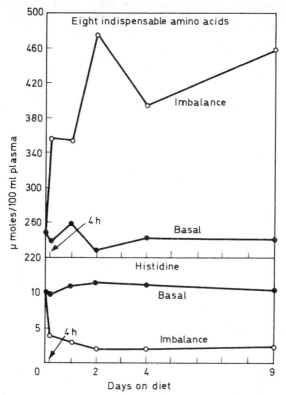

*Figure 16. Changes with time in plasma histidine and indispensable amino acid concentrations of rats fed basal or imbalanced diets as for Figure 15*

grow quite well (*Figure 17*). Nevertheless, their plasma amino acid pattern is also as abnormal at the end of the adaptation period as it was earlier when their food intake was depressed (*Figure 18*).

Examination of threonine dehydratase activity, as an example of the activities of amino acid degrading enzymes, in these two conditions indicates that amino acid-degrading activity increases, although not nearly as much as in animals fed a high protein diet. This is shown for cold exposure in *Figure 19*. Capacity for amino acid degradation is enhanced. This is accompanied by an increase in food intake and increased growth rate and tissue protein synthesis so total body capacity for removal of amino acids is enlarged.

These observations support the idea that calorie need is, as is generally believed, the major determinant of food intake but, with the restriction,

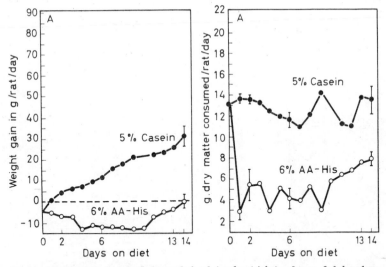

Figure 17. Weight change (left) and food intake (right) of rats fed basal or imbalanced diets (as for Figure 15) at room temperature (Anderson et al. (1969b) by courtesy of the Editor, Journal of Nutrition and the American Institute of Nutrition)

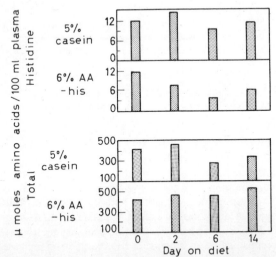

Figure 18. Changes with time in plasma histidine and indispensable amino acid concentrations of rats fed basal or imbalanced diets (as for Figure 15) at room temperature (Anderson et al. (1969b) by courtesy of the Editor, Journal of Nutrition and the American Institute of Nutrition)

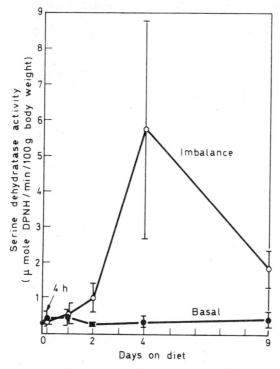

*Figure 19. Changes with time in hepatic threonine dehydratase of rats fed basal or imbalanced diets (as for Figure 15) at 5°C*

that if amino acids are ingested in excess of the metabolic capacity of the organism to remove them, food, and hence, calorie intake may be depressed in order to prevent too drastic a deviation in circulating plasma amino acid pattern and concentrations from the standard state. The organism can obviously withstand some considerable deviation from the standard state and function well, as indicated by observations on cold-exposed animals fed an imbalanced diet and on those adapted to such a diet at room temperature. Presumably, then, an animal will eat a diet that causes such changes in plasma amino acid pattern in an effort to satisfy its calorie need until it can tolerate no greater change in plasma amino acid pattern or concentrations. Whether it can satisfy its calorie need before this stage is reached will depend upon its capacity to dispose of amino acids. Thus food intake is obviously not a direct function of plasma amino acid concentrations and pattern but the resultant of the combination of this and metabolic capacity.

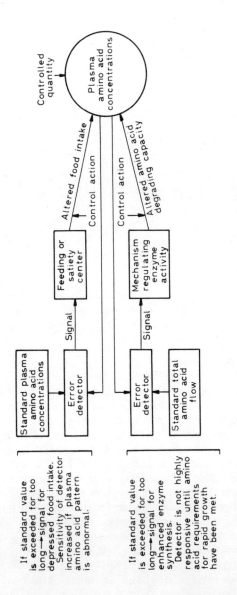

Figure 20. Schematic representation of homeostatic regulation of plasma amino acid concentrations

The influence of glycine on food intake and plasma methionine concentration of rats fed a high methionine diet (Table 8) also illustrates this. The elevation of plasma methionine was not quite as great for the group fed the high methionine diet with glycine as it was for the high methionine group: nevertheless it was substantial. However, the group receiving the additional glycine ate almost twice as much food as that receiving methionine alone, 9.1 *vs.* 5.2 g, the elevated food intake presumably being the result of the increased capacity for methionine degradation.

Table 8

Effect of glycine supplementation on plasma glycine and methionine levels O, 3 and 8 hours after feeding*

| | 10% *casein supplemented with* | | | | | |
| | *0.3% L-Met* | | *3% L-Met* | | *3% L-Met + 3% Gly* | |
| | *Plasma amino acid concentration in* $\mu$m/100 ml | | | | | |
| Hours | *Gly* | *Met* | *Gly* | *Met* | *Gly* | *Met* |
|---|---|---|---|---|---|---|
| 0 | 74 | 9 | 27 | 9 | 78 | 3 |
| 3 | 27 | 14 | – | 198 | 142 | 136 |
| 8 | 32 | 11 | 15 | 123 | 66 | 59 |

*Animals fed 2 h each day

The regulatory mechanisms envisioned have been summarized in *Figure 2.* Plasma amino acid concentrations will be determined primarily, then, by the capacity of the organism for protein synthesis and amino acid degradation, and by food intake. In turn each of these, for homeostatic regulation to be effective, must be responsive to changes in plasma amino acid pattern and concentrations or something closely related to them.

*Figure 20* shows this schematically in terms of feed-back regulation with plasma amino acids as the controlled quantity and with a double feed-back loop indicating sensitivity of both food intake and animo acid degrading activity to changing, circulating amino acid concentrations. According to this model an influx of amino acids that exceeded the capacity of the homeostatic mechanisms of the organism would initiate responses resulting in increased amino acid-degrading enzyme activity. If the capacity were sufficiently exceeded, food intake would be depressed to reduce the amino acid influx until the amino acid-degrading response was great enough to prevent excessive amino acid accumulation. This would be the situation when the amino acid disproportion consists of a large influx of well-balanced protein. Then food intake depression is transitory and catabolic activity increases rapidly.

With amino acid imbalances of the type discussed, the influx of amino acids is insufficient to cause a rapid and large response in amino acid-degrading activity, hence, food intake depression is more prolonged. Only gradually does the degrading activity rise sufficiently so that further

443

influx of amino acids will not exceed the tolerable limits. Hence food intake rises only gradually. The adaptive process can be greatly enhanced by treatments such as cold exposure or glucocorticoid injections. On the other hand, if the amino acid mixture causing the imbalance is infused intravenously, the depression in food intake does not prevent the influx, the capacity of the homeostatic mechanisms is exceeded, and the organism deteriorates *(Figure 21)*.

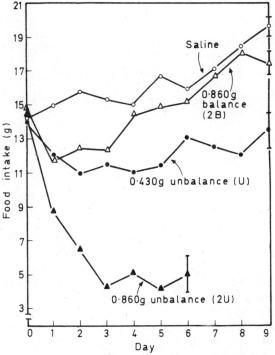

*Figure 21. Food intake of rats fed 6 per cent casein diet and infused with amino acid mixture devoid of histidine to create imbalance. Rats of group 2U did not survive beyond 7 days (Peng and Harper (1969) Am. J. Physiol 217, 1441 by courtesy of the Executive Editor, American Physiological Society)*

A somewhat similar situation can be envisioned with animals ingesting excessive quantities of individual amino acids. Here the response of the degrading capacity is also very slow and can readily be greatly exceeded if the intake is very high. Even the depression of food intake may not reduce the influx sufficiently to prevent the amino acid from accumulating to an extent that will cause adverse effects. At the point where the capacity of the homeostatic mechanisms is exceeded some additional treatment is required to prevent deterioration of the organism. The provision of glycine or serine for animals fed toxic amounts of methionine falls into this category. Such treatments supplement the normal homeostatic response just as treatment by a physician is directed toward supplementing the normal homeostatic responses of the body to disease agents which result in changes that exceed the body's capacity to respond.

Does all of this have any practical importance? First, it gives us some idea of the tolerance of an animal for disproportionate amounts of amino acids. Animals fed on diets that satisfy their amino acid requirements tolerate considerable deviations from the ideal pattern. Homeostatic mechanisms and enzymatic adaptations tend to counteract deviations in the concentrations of free amino acids in blood and body fluids. These homeostatic mechanisms are much less effective in animals fed a low protein diet and such animals tolerate disproportionate amounts of amino acids less well.

This raises some questions – one, in supplementation of a low protein diet is the amino acid being added the one that is limiting? Is it possible that imbalances occur in children? At INCAP in some experimental studies, a supplement of methionine caused some adverse effect in children fed a vegetable protein diet – they regurgitated, failed to gain weight normally – but did so when the same amino acid was added with two others. With a food supplement all amino acids would be added together and the likelihood of an amino acid imbalance occurring would be slight. Is it possible that some of the amino acid patterns of some diets in poor countries are enough out of balance to depress food intake and contribute to the development of protein-calorie malnutrition? I do not know, and it would be very difficult to prove, but it is a possibility deserving consideration.

If the intake of an individual amino acid is excessive there is a very real possibility of exceeding the capacity of homeostatic mechanisms. These quantities would never be used for supplementation of diets but they might be used pharmacologically. Also, subjects with metabolic defects of amino acid degradation are examples of just this situation and special treatments are needed to protect them from adverse effects.

## ACKNOWLEDGEMENT

The research reported in this paper was supported by Public Health Service grants AM10748 and AM10747 from the National Institute of Arthritis and Metabolic Diseases and by a grant from the National Live Stock and Meat Board, Chicago, Illinois.

REFERENCES

Adibi, S.A. (1968). *J. appl. Physiol.* **25**, 52
Alam, S.Q., Becker, R.V., Stucki, W.P., Rogers, Q.R. and Harper, A.E. (1966). *J. Nutr.* **89**, 91
Almquist, H.J. (1954). *Archs. Biochem. Biophys.* **52**, 197
Anderson, H.L., Benevenga, N.J. and Harper, A.E. (1968). *Am. J. Physiol.* **214**, 1008
Anderson, H.L., Benevenga, N.J. and Harper, A.E. (1969a). *J. Nutr.* **99**, 184
– – – (1969b). *J. Nutr.* **97**, 463
Benevenga, N.J. and Harper, A.E. (1967). *J. Nutr.* **93**, 44
– – and Rogers, Q.R. (1968). *J. Nutr.* **95**, 434
Boctor, A.M. and Harper, A.E. (1968). *J. Nutr.* **94**, 289
Elvehjem, C.A. (1956). *Fedn. Proc. Fedn. Am. Socs. exp. Biol.* **15**, 965
– and Harper, A.E. (1955). *J. Am. med. Ass.* **158**, 655
Frazier, L.E., Wissler, R.W., Steffee, C.H., Woolridge, F.L. and Cannon, P.R. (1947). *J. Nutr.* **33**, 65
Geiger, E. (1948). *J. Nutr.* **34**, 97
Harper, A.E. (1956). *Nutr. Rev.* **14**, 225
– (1958). *A. N.Y. Acad. Sci.* **69**, 1025
– (1964). Ch. 13 In *Mammalian Protein in Metabolism.* Vol. II, Ed. by H.N. Munro and J.B. Allison. New York; Academic Press. p.87
– (1965). *Can. J. Biochem. Physiol.* **43**, 1589
– (1967). In *Handbook of Physiology.* Section 6: Alimentary Canal, Vol. 1 Control of food and water intake. Washington; The American Physiological Society. p.399
– (1969). Amino acid balance and food intake regulation. *Conference on Parenteral Nutrition.* Vanderbilt University. In press
– and Rogers, Q.R. (1965). *Proc. Nutr. Soc.* **24**, 173
– – (1966). *Am. J. Physiol.* **210**, 1234
– Leung, P. M-B., Yoshida, A. and Rogers, Q.R. (1964). *Fedn. Proc. Fedn. Am. Socs. exp. Biol.* **23**, 1087
Hegsted, D.M. and Haffenreffer, U.K. (1949). *Am. J. Physiol.* **157**, 141
Holt, L.E. Jr., Halac, E. Jr. and Kajdi, C.N. (1962). *J. Am. med. Assoc.* **181**, 699
Knox, W.E. and Greengard, O. (1965). *Adv. Enz. Regulation.* **3**, 247
Leung, P. M-B., Rogers, Q.R. and Harper, A.E. (1968a). *J. Nutr.* **95**, 474
– – – (1968b). *J. Nutr.* **96**, 139
– – – (1968c). *J. Nutr.* **95**, 483
McLaughlan, J.M. and Morrison, A.B. (1968). In *Protein Nutrition and Free Amino Acid Patterns.* Ed. by J.H. Leatham. New Jersey; Rutgers University Press. p.3
Maramatsu, K. and Ashida, K. (1962). *J. Nutr.* **76**, 143
Mayer, J. (1964). In *Nutrition: A Comprehensive Treatise.* Vol. II, Ed. by Beaton and McHenry. New York; Academic Press. p.1
– and Vitale, J. (1958). *Am. J. Physiol.* **189**, 39.
Mellinkoff, S. (1957). *A. Rev. Pysiol.* **19**, 193
Munro, H. N. (1964) In *Mammalian Protein Metabolism,* Vol. II, Ed. by H. N. Munro and J.B. Allison. New York; Academic Press. p. 3.
– (1969) Ch. 34. In *Mammalian Protein Metabolism,* Vol. IV, Ed. by H. N. Munro. In press.
Nyhan W. L. (1967) (Editor). *Amino Acid Metabolism and Genetic Variation.* New York; McGraw-Hill.

Platt, B. S., Heard, C. R. C. and Stewart, R. J. C. (1964). In *Mammalian Protein Metabolism*. Vol. II, Ed. by H.N. Munro and J.B. Allison. New York; Academic Press. p.446.

Ross, M. H. (1959). *Fedn. Proc. Fedn. Am. Secs exp Biol.* **18,** 1190

Sauberlich, H. E. (1961). *J. Nutr.* **75,** 61

Sidransky, H. and Farber, E. (1958), *Archs Path.* **66,** 135

– and Verney, E. (1965). *J. Nutr.* **86,** 73

Yoshida, A., Leung, P. M-B., Rogers, Q. R. and Harper, A. E. (1966). *J. Nutr.* **89,** 80

# PROCEDURES OF PROTEIN EVALUATION

D. LEWIS and K. N. BOORMAN

*Dept. Applied Biochemistry and Nutrition,*
*University of Nottingham*

## INTRODUCTION

Attempts to evaluate protein are concerned with efforts to ascribe to any particular protein a single numerical index to represent its nutritional worth. This becomes an impossible task with any degree of precision once it is recognized that the protein component is a complex of several different nutrients (amino acids) and that the relative needs for these nutrients varies from one physiological circumstance to another. The single value that is sought can never represent anything but a compromise between a series of approximations.

Dietary proteins serve to supply the needs of the animals in terms of essential amino acids and materials necessary (amino groups) for the synthesis of those amino acids individually regarded as non-essential. Since the amino acid requirements of different species vary and also since the needs of different physiological states within the same species (e.g. laying hen or broiler chick) cover a wide range it is only possible to visualize a concept of evaluating a protein as a whole by using different numerical values for each physiological circumstance. Even if this were possible the single numerical values so derived can only be regarded as meaningful if animals receive diets containing only a single protein: all indices of protein quality are not additive. This can be exemplified by considering two proteins each of poor quality but particularly deficient in different amino acids: upon mixing the two proteins a product of good value might be obtained, each protein in effect compensating for the relative inadequacy of the other.

A further indication of the inadequacy of attempting to ascribe to proteins single numerical indices of value comes when the use of such indices is considered. The values could be regarded as a means of discarding certain proteins, or they might be used to step up quantitatively the usage of a protein if its quality is sub-standard. These approaches are both

448

most unsatisfactory developments since they can only perpetuate inefficiency and add to potential problems of imbalance. It must be possible to develop systems whereby certain amino acid inadequacies in one protein are met by the judicious use of other proteins relatively rich in these nutrients. Concepts of evaluating a protein as a whole preclude such developments and are in fact valueless as a foundation for precise dietary formulation.

There is, however, a considerable volume of information which has been collected using the standard procedures of protein evaluation and it is relevant to review these methods briefly. Fuller descriptions of these procedures can be found elsewhere (Anonymous, 1963; Mitchell, 1964).

## EVALUATION AS PROTEIN

Apart from any practical considerations biological methods of protein evaluation have made a large contribution to the understanding and conceptual development of protein nutrition. It is, for example, difficult to separate the development of the idea of biological value from that of partition of protein metabolism. It should also be remembered that certain of the essential amino acids (e.g. threonine) had not been identified at the time when initial ideas on protein evaluation were developing, and that methods for the determination of individual amino acids were not readily available.

The most commonly used biological methods of protein evaluation are of two types; those which depend upon growth rate as a criterion of adequacy and those based upon assessment of the nitrogen economy of the animal. The growth index, protein efficiency ratio (PER), was proposed over 50 years ago (Osborne and Mendel, 1917) as the weight gain supported per unit of protein ingested by rats. This procedure has been standardized since its inception such that the test material is fed to provide 10 per cent protein in the ration and the PER obtained is expressed as a percentage of the PER obtained for casein. A further modification has been used in which the growth rate of animals on a protein free diet is subtracted from the growth rate of animals receiving the test protein, this index is termed the net protein value (Bender and Doell, 1957).

Growth methods have been criticized on the basis that they involve the measurement of a parameter that is not solely dependent upon the quality of the protein in the diet. It should also be noted that in such methods it is usual to ensure that protein is the nutrient which primarily limits growth and, as such, growth methods are essentially biological assays. It is recognized, for example, that gross protein value (Heiman, Carver and

449

Cook, 1939), a modified form of PER used in assessing the quality of proteins for poultry rations, is in fact a measure of the available lysine content of the test material. In that growth methods are biological assays the standard conditions for a valid assay should be met. This fact has been recognized by Hegsted, Neff and Worcester (1968) who have used a regression analysis method for assessing protein quality.

Procedures for the evaluation of protein quality by nitrogen balance have been in existence for 50 years. The original method of Thomas, modified by Mitchell (1923), determined the proportion of the absorbed nitrogen which was retained by the animal. This index, biological value, represents an attempt to express the efficiency with which the pattern of amino acids, provided by a particular protein, can be utilized in the body. Allison and Anderson (1945) developed an alternative procedure for determining the proportion of absorbed nitrogen which is retained, by measuring the gradient of the line relating nitrogen balance to absorbed nitrogen. This gradient was termed the nitrogen balance index. Retained nitrogen has also been estimated by carcass analysis in the derivation of net protein utilization (Miller and Bender, 1955).

In a conceptual sense the nitrogen balance methods have contributed much to the understanding of protein utilization: they have, however, been subject to repeated examination and criticism. This criticism has usually been concerned with the methods of measuring what is called the endogenous compartment of nitrogen metabolism and the assumption that the size of this compartment is not influenced by the quality or quantity of protein in the diet. As has been pointed out previously, from a practical viewpoint nitrogen balance methods and growth methods can be criticized in that they do not provide information that can be used for devising diets. It should also be noted that while it can be assumed that the growth or nitrogen balance achieved is determined primarily by the concentration of the most limiting amino acid in the protein, these methods do not identify the most limiting amino acid.

Considerations of the chemical composition of protein have led to the development of various indices of protein quality which relate the amino acid composition of a test protein to the composition of a protein thought to meet the requirements of the animal. Chemical score (Block and Mitchell, 1946) was derived by expressing the concentration of each amino acid in a test protein as a percentage of the concentration of each amino acid in whole egg protein and using the lowest value so obtained. Other indices have been used, including the complex geometric mean of Oser (1959). Such methods have been criticized in that no account is taken of the biological availability of the amino acids in the protein and that any possibility of temporary withdrawal from reserves is overlooked.

450

These methods also emphasize that there has been a continuing desire to express the quality of a protein in the form of a single value. With respect to the chemical methods of protein evaluation it would seem to be particularly relevant to question whether the indices obtained are of greater value than the separate amino acid concentrations used in their derivation.

## EVALUATION AS AMINO ACIDS

For an assessment of the value of the protein component in the diet in terms of amino acids, there are three basic needs: knowledge of the amino acid composition of the protein, information on the extent to which the constituent amino acids are available to the animal and data on the amino acid needs of the animal in a particular situation. These issues can each be considered briefly, emphasizing some of the important points of principle.

*Amino acid composition*
Automated ion-exchange systems for amino acid analysis have totally changed the situation concerning amino acids in nutrition. The comparative ease of operation of the systems that are available has, however, led to some neglect of problems that still exist. Although the reproducibility obtained with a single system is usually adequate there are still problems of variability using different systems (Porter, Westgarth and Williams, 1968), there is considerable variation in a standard biological material and there are special difficulties concerning the methods of protein hydrolysis used. Loss of amino acids during hydrolysis, especially of sulphur amino acids, still presents a problem and systems of tryptophan measurement are relatively inadequate. Gas chromatography is not sufficiently developed, as yet, for routine use in amino acid analysis.

*Availability*
The data that is usually collected concerning the amino acids in food ingredients is restricted to values of the total amino acid content, generally by chemical determination. On the other hand, the proportion of each amino acid that is available for useful metabolism is usually not known. Such information is particularly valuable in view of the considerable effects of processing and storage methods upon availability. Though a bio-assay procedure is the most likely one to supply meaningful information the methods are rather complex for use under routine circumstances, especially for batches of ingredients. An indication of the proportion of dietary lysine that is available to the animal is given by the

chemical test developed by Carpenter, Ellinger, Munro and Rolfe (1957), based upon a measurement of the terminal amino group of lysine that is not chemically bound. This method does not take into account lack of availability for other reasons and must therefore be considered to represent a maximum value. The procedure seems to be unique for lysine and similar methods for other amino acids have not been developed.

Bio-assay procedures have a distinct advantage in terms of a direct relationship to a physiological situation: it must, however, be remembered that this is largely lost if it becomes necessary to extrapolate findings from one species to another or if the appropriate parameter of response for the stated nutritional objective is not selected. It might, for example, be inappropriate to use maximum growth rate as the parameter of response in a bacon pig. In devising a bio-assay procedure, there are standard conditions that must be recognized or satisfied. Thus the response measured must be a function only of the amino acid to be assayed. The degree of response must be linearly related to the dose of supplementary material added. Since the aim of the assay is to evaluate the full potential availability of the test amino acid within the protein it is essential to create conditions such that maximum rates of the response measured can be attained. Failure to achieve this would indicate that the effective value of the protein to supply the test amino acid has not necessarily been established. Furthermore, attainment of the maximum response demonstrates as far as is possible that no secondary factors are modifying availability.

In an assessment of amino acid availability which involves the measurement of rate of growth in relation to graded inclusions of standard amino acids and test protein, all responses to the test protein, other than those due to its contribution of the amino acid being assayed, must be eliminated. In this respect, it is essential to avoid the differentials in dietary protein levels that generally result from the addition of graded levels of test protein. Furthermore, conditions of relative amino acid imbalance in basal diets, and the varied changes imposed on these by adding test protein will only serve to distort the response to the amino acid being assayed. Failure to eliminate these so-called protein effects considerably reduce the value of assay procedures. It is important to ensure that a good overall nutrient balance is maintained — for poor amino acid balance will adversely affect utilization just as will incomplete digestion and absorption.

Several satisfactory bio-assay procedures are available using the chick or the rat as test animals.

*Amino acid needs*

In devising efficient diets every effort must be made to supply each nutrient at a level supporting optimum growth or production. This means that within the diet each constituent is allocated its own appropriate proportion and that all the components fit into an ideal balance one with the other. Procedures to determine amino acid requirements must be established upon such an outlook. The method usually employed involves the recording of growth performance in relation to a graded addition of the particular nutrient to a basal diet known to be deficient in terms of that nutrient but entirely adequate in every other respect. This does not imply that a casual experimental programme can be devised.

There are numerous pitfalls that may be encountered in developing a satisfactory experimental situation for establishing amino acid needs. It is essential to be able to show that adequate growth performance can be achieved — and so establish that other nutrient levels are satisfactory. It is also necessary to ensure that an appropriate parameter of response is used in evaluating nutritional adequacy, whether it be growth, efficiency of food utilization, lean meat production, some index of reproductive capacity, health or even the attainment of longevity.

It is unfortunate that experimental studies designed to determine requirements have given somewhat variable results. It is likely that some of the lack of uniformity in recommended values is due to the fact that determinations have been carried out under circumstances of relative amino acid and energy-protein imbalance and without due attention being given to the differences in amino acid availability in the various ingredients used. It is also apparent that the technique usually employed, of adding graded supplements of a single amino acid, only serves to define the relative level of the next limiting amino acid. In general, little attention has been given to defining the allocation, within the protein component, of an appropriate proportion for the synthesis of amino acids which are individually dispensable

A few of the particular pitfalls that can be encountered in establishing amino acid needs can be exemplified. In establishing a methionine requirement it is essential to ensure that the importance of the cystine level is recognized. A relationship can be calculated for what would appear to be the methionine requirement of the chick at different dietary cystine levels (*Figure 1*). If the diet is inadequate in respect of cystine, methionine will be required to satisfy the need for cystine. The value obtained for the requirement of methionine at sub-optimal cystine levels would therefore be dependent upon the cystine content of the diet. It is also possible to illustrate the fact that the value obtained for the requirement of an amino acid can depend upon the level of another in the diet when no obvious metabolic relationship exists between the two amino acids (*Figure 2*). If the sulphur amino acid requirement is determined in a ration in which lysine is the second limiting nutrient the maximum performance that can be achieved by methionine supplementation will be determined by the extent to which lysine is limiting. It is evident that a relationship of this nature is not specific for amino acids, the estimation of a requirement can be influenced by the level of any limiting nutrient in the diet.

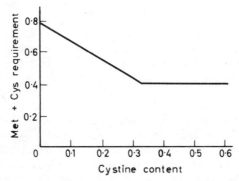

*Figure 1. Methionine requirement in relation to dietary cystine level* (Met = methionine, cys = cystine)

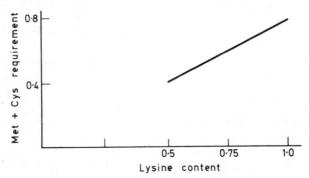

*Figure 2. Methionine requirement in relation to dietary lysine level*

Some relationships specific for amino acids have also been observed. It is established that increased lysine in the diet of chicks and rats can cause a 'wastage' of arginine (Jones, Petersburg and Burnett, 1967). D'Mello and Lewis (1967) have shown that nutritionally this relationship between lysine and arginine can be demonstrated as a dependence of the arginine requirement upon the lysine content of the diet (*Figure 3*). It should be noted that this differs from the non-specific effects referred to above in that lysine was not the second limiting nutrient in the diets used to determine the arginine requirement. Bearing these complications in mind

454

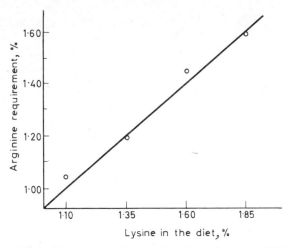

*Figure 3. Effect of lysine on requirement for arginine* (Lewis and D'Mello, 1967)

it is understandable that there is still considerable uncertainty about amino acid needs; but the groundwork for establishing requirement is now well recognized. The complications should not be allowed to undermine the fact that definition of the protein component in nutritional terms must be separately effected for each essential amino acid and the non-essential component. It is too easy to assume that the problems in establishing amino acid requirements represent a basic defect in defining the protein component of the diet in terms of its amino acid constitution.

## AMINO ACID NEEDS IN THE HUMAN SUBJECT

The establishment of requirements in the human subject presents problems which do not occur with other species. Experimental circumstances are severely limited, replication is difficult to achieve, and criteria of adequacy are extremely difficult to define. The establishment of nutritional objectives is probably best achieved in physiological terms rather than in the form of productivity-plasma amino acid patterns and not liveweight gain.

A procedure for determining the amino acid needs of children was recently described by identifying the point at which a physiological defect could be seen (Holt and Synderman, 1967). A crystalline amino acid mixture was fed and normal growth and nitrogen-balance was recorded. The level of each amino acid was then dropped in turn until growth or nitrogen retention was impaired and then increased until the two criteria

455

were restored to the normal level. The intake of each amino acid at this point was taken as the requirement.Another procedure recently described (Fomon and Filer, 1967) involved the use of a simulated milk of known composition. This was offered to children allowed to eat to appetite, and records of growth and N-balance made. They were compared with a control group receiving their mother's milk and only when the performance on both criteria were equal to the control group was it considered that requirements were met. Both these yardsticks can probably be claimed to have a very prominently empirical foundation – analogous to the chemical score that is arbitrarily related to whole egg as the reference product.

## Plasma amino acid levels

The prosposition can be made that by judicious interpretation of patterns of plasma amino acids a physiologically founded pattern of ideal dietary amino acids can be identified. The actual amino acid level at any one time – as with all intermediates in a dynamic system – merely represents a small balance between major entries and withdrawals. It is therefore difficult to accord to a single value an absolute meaning but it may still be appropriate to draw conclusions from relative changes. Relative amino acid patterns might be used to identify an ideal amino acid balance through the ability to recognize the metabolic consequences of imbalance or deficiency. It has been shown repeatedly that when there is a surplus of a particular amino acid in the diet its level within blood plasma tends to increase. As a corollary it is possible that when there is an ideal

Table 1

Amino acid inadequacy and plasma levels

(leu = leucine, val = valine, arg = arginine, thr = threonine, lys = lysine; all values given as mg/100 ml; data of Hill and Olsen, 1963 by courtesy of the Editor, *Journal of Nutrition)*

|  | Leu | Val | Arg | Thr | Lys |
|---|---|---|---|---|---|
| Basal diet (9.5% protein) | 2.3 | 1.9 | 4.3 | 1.0 | 2.8 |
| + Amino acids (– leucine) | 0.6 | 13.6 | 6.2 | 15.1 | 11.0 |
| + Amino acids (– valine) | 2.8 | 1.0 | 3.8 | 15.7 | 9.2 |
| + Amino acids (– arginine) | 3.6 | 7.4 | 1.2 | 25.5 | 10.9 |
| + Amino acids (complete) | 3.3 | 6.6 | 8.7 | 10.6 | 7.9 |

dietary amino acid balance and when the overall protein intake is held at a relatively low level the individual plasma amino acid levels and the total plasma amino acid nitrogen concentration would be minimal (see Lewis, 1967). It has repeatedly been possible at least to identify the limiting amino acid by means of an appraisal of plasma amino acid levels (e.g. Longenecker and Hause, 1959). The metabolic consequences of amino acid inadequacy were clearly shown by Hill and Olsen (1963): a selection of the data in Table 1 shows the effect of adding to a basal low-protein diet a supplement devoid of a particular amino acid. Sequential evaluation of limiting amino acids or the consequencies of inadequacy whilst various patterns of supplementation are made will surely allow of a progression towards defining a satisfactory dietary amino acid balance in physiological terms.

## REFERENCES

Allison, J. B. and Anderson, J. A. (1945). *J. Nutr.* **29**, 413

Anonymous (1963). *Evaluation of Protein Quality.* Natl Acad. Sci., Natl. Res. Counc., Washington D. C. Publication No. 1100

Bender, A. E. and Doell, B. H. (1957). *Br. J. Nutr.* **11**,140

Block, R. J. and Mitchell, H. H. (1946).*Nutr. Abstr. Rev.* **16**, 249

Carpenter, K. J., Ellinger, G. M., Munro, M. I. and Rolfe, E. J. (1957). *Br. J. Nutr.* **11**, 162

D'Mello, J. P. F., Hewitt, D. and Lewis, D. (1967). *Proc. Nutr. Soc.* **26**, vii

Fomon, S. J. and Filer, L. J. (1967). In *Amino Acid Metabolism and Genetic Variation,* Ed. by W.L. Nyham. London: McGraw-Hill Book Co.

Hegsted, D. M., Neff, R. and Worcester, J. (1968). *J. agric. Fd Chem.* **16**, 190

Heiman, V., Carver, J. S. and Cook, J. W. (1939). *Poult. Sci.* **18**,464

Hill, D. C. and Olsen, E. M. (1963). *J. Nutr.* **79**, 296

Holt, Jr., L. E. and Snyderman, S. E. (1967). In *Amino Acid Metabolism and Genetic Variation.* Ed. by W. L. Nyham. London: McGraw-Hill Book Co.

Jones, J. D., Petersburg, S. J. and Burnett, P. C. (1967). *J. Nutr.* **93**, 103

Lewis, D. (1967).In *Protein utilization by Poultry.* Ed. by R. A. Morton and E. C. Amoroso. London: Oliver & Boyd

— and D'Mello, J. P. F. (1967). In *Growth and Development of Mammals.* Ed. by G. A. Lodge and G. E. Lamming. London: Butterworths

Longenecker, J. B. and Hause, N. L. (1959). *Arch. Biochem. Biophys.* **84**, 46

Miller, D. S. and Bender, A. E. (1955). *Br. J. Nutr.* **9**, 382

Mitchell, H. H. (1923). *J. biol. Chem.* **58**, 873

— (1964). In *Comparative Nutrition of Man and Domestic Animals,* Vol. II, London: Academic Press p.575

Osborne, T. B. and Mendel, L. B. (1917). *J. biol. Chem.* **32**, 369

Oser, B. L. (1959). In *Protein and Amino Acid Nutrition.* Ed. by Albanese, A. A. New York: Academic Press

Porter, J. W. G., Westgarth, D. R. and Williams, A. P. (1968). *Br. J. Nutr.* **22**, 437

457

# ABNORMALITIES IN PROTEIN METABOLISM

## NINA A. J. CARSON

*Nuffield Department of Child Health*
*Queen's University, Belfast*

## INTRODUCTION

Many diverse aspects of proteins for human consumption have been discussed at this symposium. The supply and demand, the quality, the various sources of protein for human consumption and the economics of production have been considered. We have also heard how best to preserve proteins in an uncontaminated and edible state, and how best to cook this expensive and indispensable item of our diet.

However, all this is to no avail if through disorders in protein metabolism we cannot assimilate the protein we ingest. In the normal healthy infant and adult, proteins are assimilated in a speedy and orderly manner. Ingested protein plus a considerable amount of endogenous protein, which is normally secreted into the gastrointestinal tract, is hydrolysed to small polypeptides and to free amino acids by the action of pancreatic and, to a lesser extent, gastric proteases. The mucosal cells of the small intestine possess dipeptidases and hydrolysis of the dipeptides occurs at or within the luminal border of the cell. The resulting amino acids are then transported across the intestinal cell by a specific, energy-dependent, active transport system. From there they pass via the portal blood stream to the liver, where they undergo further metabolism by the action of specific enzymes. Any prolonged interference with these physiological processes will cause disease in man, the severity of which varies from minor inconvenience in health, to severe and incapacitating illness and death.

Inability to assimilate ingested protein may result from a variety of causes and I wish to consider these protein disorders under the following headings: disorders in the intestinal digestion of protein; disturbances of transport of amino acids across the intestinal mucosal cell, and inborn errors of amino acid metabolism. Also to be considered are the protein-losing states, the role of the intestinal bacterial flora in disease and, lastly, protein 'intolerance'.

458

## DISORDERS OF DIGESTIVE ENZYMES

In man, protein digestion starts when food enters the stomach. Stimulation of the vagus nerve endings in the stomach wall through the act of eating, the distension of the stomach wall with food and the contact of the products of protein digestion with the gastric mucosal cells, produce a flow of proteolytic enzymes (of which the pepsins are the most important), acid, and the hormone gastrin. The latter stimulates the secretory cells to produce more acid and pepsinogen, the activator of the pepsins. However, gastric digestion of protein is expendable and patients with atrophy of the gastric mucosa, where there is failure to secrete proteases and acid, can remain in positive nitrogen balance. At best, gastric digestion of protein is probably only 10–15 per cent efficient.

The pancreas is probably the most important source of digestive enzymes. Its function is unusual in that it produces both an internal and an external secretion, although only the latter (exocrine) function will be considered here. Pancreatic juice is excreted directly into the duodenum and contains two major components, an alkaline fluid (bicarbonate) and enzymes. The enzyme component consists of three major groups having amylolytic, lipolytic and proteolytic functions. The most important of the proteolytic enzymes is trypsin, which is secreted in the form of an inactive precursor, trypsinogen. This is activated by enteropeptidase (enterokinase) secreted by the cells of the duodenal mucosa. Chymotrypsin and the carboxypeptidases are also secreted by the pancreas; they in turn are activated by trypsin in the duodenum. Trypsin and chymotrypsin are very powerful proteolytic enzymes whose activity is optimal at an alkaline pH.

As the absence of pancreatic juice greatly impairs protein digestion, any pathological process which inhibits the secretion of pancreatic enzymes or prevents their entry into the duodenum will interfere with the normal digestive processes and result in malabsorption. Typical of such processes are infection, fibrosis of the glandular secretory tissue or the inherited deficiency of one of the enzymes. In man, the most common disorder of exocrine pancreatic function is cystic fibrosis of the pancreas.

### Cystic fibrosis of the pancreas

This is an hereditary disease involving not only the pancreas but all other exocrine glands, such as sweat and salivary glands, and the mucus glands of the bronchial tree. The complex pathology arises from the increased viscosity of mucus secretion throughout the body and raised levels of sodium and chloride in the sweat.

In the pancreas the absence of trypsin, lipase and amylase leads to poor digestion and absorption of food. Symptoms may be noticed shortly after birth with failure to gain weight in spite of a good appetite and good food intake. The stools are foul smelling due to undigested protein and greasy in appearance because of unabsorbed fat. Respiratory complications, due to the viscosity of mucus from the bronchial tubes and secondary infections, are of serious consequence, eventually leading to destruction of lung tissue and interfering with the natural development of the lungs. Children with fibrocystic disease lose excessive amounts of both sodium and chloride in the sweat due to the failure to reabsorb salt from the sweat in the sweat ducts and during hot weather, periods of excessive physical exercise, or feverish spells, the addition of salt to the diet is necessary.

No permanent cure is known for this disease and treatment is by dietary means and by attempted alleviation of symptoms. A high protein, low fat diet with the use of commercially prepared oral pancreatic extracts, will keep the malabsorption under control. Respiratory complications are treated by antibiotic aerosol sprays together with physical means; and these children must have continuous physiotherapy.

Although evidence of protein malabsorption is present in this disease as seen by the stunted growth of these patients and the high content of unabsorbed amino acids in the faeces, yet it is not of primary importance and is overshadowed by the more serious respiratory complications and electrolyte disturbance of the sweat glands. The basic defect remains unknown and a unified explanation must be found to account for the involvement of all the exocrine glands.

As opposed to the more serious disease of cystic fibrosis of the pancreas, the syndrome of pancreatic insufficiency has only recently been recognized (Bodian et al., 1964). In this condition (unlike cystic fibrosis) no sweat abnormality and no chronic respiratory infections are found. It does, however, appear to be associated with haematological abnormalities; a reduced rate of blood cell production in bone marrow, with anaemia and reduced numbers of circulating white blood cells, have been described. This also has a familial incidence, as described by Shwachman et al. (1964). The common features of the syndrome are diarrhoea with failure to thrive in infancy and childhood. Samples of fluid from the duodenum show reduced levels — or the absence — of trypsin, lipase and amylase.

A very rare disease involving the specific deficiency of trypsinogen has been reported in two infants (Townes, 1965; Townes et al., 1967). The infants presented with severe hypoproteinaemia, oedema, anaemia, and growth failure. Treatment with protein hydrolysates produced a marked improvement with the disappearance of oedema, a rise in plasma proteins, increase in weight and improvement of the anemia. Diagnosis was made by enzyme assays on aspirated duodenal fluid and the results indicated a complete lack of trypsinogen, with normal levels of lipase and amylase.

No primary deficiencies in the intestinal peptidase enzymes have yet been discovered in man, although these enzymes may be secondarily inhibited through other destructive lesions of the small bowel.

## DISTURBANCES IN INTESTINAL AMINO ACID TRANSPORT

Amino acid transport was once thought to be due to a simple mechanism of diffusion shared by all amino acids. It is now apparent that it is a much more complicated and active process with specificity the rule not the exception. We know that transport proceeds against an energy gradient, and is thus energy-dependent. It proceeds at a high rate but its activity can be decreased by low temperatures. The transport mechanism is subject to a saturation phenomenon and can be inhibited by other amino acids and metabolic inhibitors. It is also subject to competitive inhibition by other materials which have a similar common pathway.

Just as there is more than one catabolic pathway in the metabolism of a specific amino acid, so now we know that there is more than one transport mechanism for each amino acid. One type has the capacity to transport the substrate in higher concentration than is present in the plasma and is shared by a specific group of chemically related amino acids, i.e. group transport. An alternative type of transport is also present for the same amino acid in the same or different tissue from the group transport system. This is usually a very specific system not shared by other amino acids. Therefore a transport disorder affecting one tissue will allow activity in another. These transport systems are genetically controlled and the integrity of each specific system is probably dependent on one single gene locus. The number of specific amino acid transport mechanisms is as yet undefined but at least five group systems have been described. Four of these transport $\alpha$-amino acids and are present in both kidney and intestine. They are concerned with (1) neutral amino acids and tryptophan, (2) dibasic amino acids and cystine, (3) iminoacids, glycine and N methylated amino acids, (4) the dicarboxlyic acids (acidic). It appears that the $\beta$-amino acids have a separate transport system, and this has only so far been reported in kidney tissue. (Scriver *et al.*, 1966). Many disorders concerned with the group specific transport of amino acids appear to be benign in comparison with single specific transport defects and other types of aminoacidopathy.

461

Typical of group transport disorders in man are the following conditions:

## Cystinuria

In this disorder there is a transport defect across the renal tubule and the jejunal epithelial cell for the dibasic amino acids, lysine, ornithine, arginine, and for cystine. In the kidney this results in loss into the urine of large quantities of these amino acids. Due to its insolubility in urine, cystine tends to precipitate and form stones in the urinary passage. The continual formation of these calculi results in severe damage and may reduce life expectancy. The intestinal defect appears not to have any serious untoward effect apart from causing malabsorption of the amino acids concerned. Enough of these amino acids are absorbed to allow normal plasma levels. When the unabsorbed amino acids reach the colon, they are further metabolized by bacteria to diamines such as putrescine and the cyclical compounds piperidine and pyrolidine. These are absorbed from the colon and are also found in the urine.

## Hartnup disease

This was first described by Baron *et al*. in 1956 and is characterized by defective transport of the neutral amino acid group (involving most of the monoamino-monocarboxylic acids) across the jejunal and the renal tubule cell. The clinical symptoms involve a pellagrous skin rash, neurological and psychological effects. There appears to be no intellectual deterioration with these attacks and the clinical manifestations improve with age. This is an hereditary disease and appears to have an autosomal recessive type of inheritance. The renal tubule defect results in a greatly increased quantity of the neutral amino acids in the urine (although the levels in the plasma are normal). The amount of amino nitrogen lost in the urine is of no nutritional importance, and no symptoms result from this generalized amino-aciduria. In Hartnup disease, unlike cystinuria, it is the associated intestinal transport defect which causes the symptoms of the disorder. In 1960 Milne *et al*. demonstrated an intestinal defect for tryptophan and thus solved the problem of at least one of the clinical symptoms, namely, the pellagrous rash. As can be seen in *Figure 1*, tryptophan is the precursor of nicotinamide, the 'anti-pellagra' vitamin. In this disorder, a considerable amount of tryptophan is lost in the urine and faeces or is degraded by bacteria in the colon, thus causing deficiency of this vitamin. It has been suggested (but not yet proven) that the neurological symptoms may be due to the effects of bacterial decarboxylation of the other neutral amino acids with the production of amines such as histamine derived from histidine, phenylethylamine from phenylalanine, tyramine from tyrosine, and indole from tryptophan. Provided these patients are given an adequate supply of nicotinamide they usually remain symptom free.

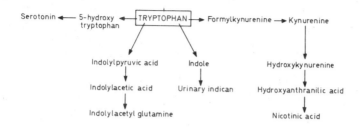

*Figure 1. Schematic summary of tryptophan metabolism*

The following are examples of specific amino acid transport defects:

*Tryptophan malabsorption*

An isolated malabsorption of tryptophan known as 'Blue Diaper Syndrome' was described by Drummond *et al.* (1964) in two siblings, both presenting clinically with failure to thrive. The blue staining of the napkins was due to indigotin derived from urinary indican. There was specific intestinal malabsorption of tryptophan and an increased absorption of calcium. Indole derivatives, derived from bacterial breakdown of the malabsorbed tryptophan were present in faeces and urine. The main pathology was, however, due to the increased calcium absorption which resulted in high levels of blood calcium and deposits of calcium in the kidney. Treatment with a low calcium diet resulted in some clinical improvement.

*Methionine malabsorption*

A specific intestinal malabsorption of methionine was described by Hooft *et al.* in 1964. The patient had white hair, was mentally retarded and suffered attacks of over-breathing with generalized convulsions and episodes of diarrhoea. The urine had a peculiar odour. Methionine and the branched chain amino acids were present in excess in the faeces with a normal amino acid excretion. The urine and faeces contained excess $\alpha$-hydroxybutyric acid produced by bacterial degradation of unabsorbed methionine; it was this acid which caused the unpleasant smell.

A low methionine diet resulted in improvement in the clinical state and the disappearance of $\beta$-hydroxybutyric acid from the urine and faeces.

## INBORN ERRORS OF AMINO ACID METABOLISM

Amino acids are used for protein synthesis and are therefore vitally necessary for growth in infancy and childhood and for the repair of the general wear and tear of body tissues. For their metabolism specific enzymes are required. These are manufactured mainly by the liver but are also present in other tissues such as kidney and brain. There exists a group of amino acid disorders in which these specific enzymes are either deficient or abnormal and therefore inactive. They are commonly known as the 'inborn errors of amino acid metabolism'. These are all very rare inherited diseases, usually with an autosomal recessive type of inheritance with both parents carriers of the abnormal gene. The most common of these disorders is that due to a disturbance in phenylalanine metabolism, called phenylketonuria, first described in 1934 by Fölling, where the specific enzyme phenylalanine hydroxylase is inactive, thus preventing the formation of tyrosine (Figure 2). This results in a marked rise in the level of phenylalanine in the blood and tissues with overflow into the urine when the renal tubule transport mechanism becomes saturated. In an attempt to lower the high levels of phenylalanine, the body develops other subsidiary pathways, such as the ketoacid pathway, by which phenylalanine is deaminated with the production of ammonia and the phenylketone, phenylpyruvic acid, hence the name given to the disease. Clinically, this disorder is characterized by mental retardation and the classical appearance of blond hair and blue eyes. The lack of pigmentation is thought to be due to competitive inhibition (by the high blood levels of phenylalanine) of the enzyme tyrosinase, which is situated in the pigment producing cells of the skin (melanocytes). This effect is reversible and

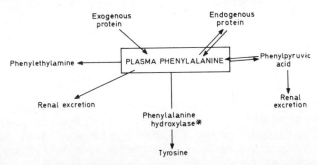

Figure 2. Diagram illustrating pathways involved in phenylalanine activity
*Enzyme inactive in phenylketonuria

pigmentation can be increased by either giving a diet low in phenylalanine or by increasing the dietary tyrosine. The brain damage is progressive and the mental defect is usually evident within the first six months of life. The actual cause of the cerebral damage is not known. Most workers do not feel that the damage is due to the high levels of phenylalanine *per se* but that there may exist competitive inhibition between the excess phenylalanine and some other vital enzyme system in the brain. Other work suggests that the toxicity is due to a high concentration of a metabolite of phenylalanine metabolism not normally present in high concentration, such as the amine phenylethylamine. Although the aetiology of the brain damage remains unknown, it has been shown that if the affected infants are treated with a low phenylalanine diet at an early age, near normal mental development results.

As 'first class proteins' contain approximately 5 per cent by weight of phenylalanine, infants with this specific enzyme deficiency are therefore exposed from birth to phenylalanine from milk protein. Commercial amino acid mixtures, low in phenylalanine, made into balanced formulae with the addition of lipids, carbohydrates, electrolytes and vitamins are now available for treatment of this disorder.

The incidence of phenylketonuria varies in different countries from 1 in 5,000 to 1 in 10,000 of the general population. In most countries of the world widespread screening of newborn infants for the detection of this disease is in operation. As this inborn error of amino acid metabolism is one of the few causes for brain damage that is preventable, these measures are deemed justified.

Many other examples of specific amino acid disorders resulting from enzyme defects have been described and many are associated with brain damage. These include inborn errors in the metabolism of homocystine, histidine, glycine, lysine, citrulline and the imino acids proline and hydroxyproline. However, the situation existing in phenylketonuria serves as an example for others.


## PROTEIN-LOSING GASTROENTEROPATHY

It has been observed for many years that hypoproteinaemia occurs in some patients which can neither be explained by excessive loss via the kidney nor by inadequate hepatic synthesis. Citrin *et al.* in 1957 focused attention on the fact that lesions in the gastrointestinal tract could be responsible for excessive leakage of endogenous protein molecules into the gut, resulting in hypoproteinaemia. It is only since development of radioisotope techniques that the important role played by the gastro-intestinal tract in the physiological degradation of endogenous proteins has been fully appreciated. An average man will break down approximately 12 g of endogenous albumin daily, and according to Wetterfors *et al*. (1960) 75 per cent of this will be degraded in the stomach and small intestine (10–30 per cent in the stomach and 33–50 per cent in the duodenum and jejunum). This endogenous protein is catabolized in the same manner as that of exogenous origin. It is enzymically broken down to amino acids, absorbed into the blood stream and resynthesized to body protein once again by the liver. Hypoproteinaemia results when the rate of protein loss and degradation exceeds the body's maximum rate of protein synthesis. In patients with gastrointestinal protein loss, all serum proteins, including the macroglobulins, are lost at the same rate irrespective of their molecular size. The actual mechanism whereby the whole protein molecule enters the gastrointestinal tract is not understood although it is thought that the lymphatic channels in the gut are involved in the process. The level of those proteins with the longest normal survival, such as albumin and $\gamma$-globulin proteins, are the most severely depressed. By the use of isotope techniques it has been shown that iron, copper, calcium and lipids may also be lost to the body.

Clinically, hypoproteinaemia and oedema may be the only initially discernible symptoms. In those more severely affected, failure to thrive with growth retardation, gastrointestinal symptoms, tetany due to excess loss of calcium, iron deficiency anaemia, eosinophilia, lymphopenia and amino-aciduria may occur.

Protein-losing gastroenteropathy is not a single disease entity but may complicate many other gastrointestinal disorders, and has been demonstrated in association with more than 40 diseases (Waldmann, 1966).

One of the most severe disorders associated with the protein-losing syndrome and one of the most common on record is intestinal lymphangiectasia (Waldmann, 1965). Over 40 such patients have so far been described. The disease affects children and young adults. All patients have oedema and generally mild gastrointestinal symptoms, some only having diarrhoea but a few patients have been reported with severe diarrhoea, fatty stools, nausea, vomiting and abdominal pain. Hypoproteinaemia is severe, and there is always a low level of circulating lymphocytes. The diagnosis of this condition is made on examination of a jejunal biopsy. There is dilation of the lymphatic vessels of the intestinal wall often causing distortion of the normal mucosal architecture. The pathogenesis of this condition remains obscure. In some patients it appears to be due to a congenital malformation of the lymphatic vessels and in others appears to be an acquired defect. There is no satisfactory treatment although localised lesions can be removed surgically and some patients benefit from a low fat diet.

## THE ROLE OF INTESTINAL BACTERIA IN PROTEIN METABOLISM

Except during acute infections, a healthy man lives in a state of symbiosis with bacteria. This is particularly noticeable when flora from the gastro-intestinal tract are involved, where physiological equilibrium has long been suspected in man and higher animals. As quoted by Francois and Michel (1964), over 80 years ago Pasteur raised the question of whether the bacterial flora is of use to the host, is harmful to the host or is a matter of indifference. He suggested that germ-free animals should be grown to study the relationship. Some 10 years later the first documented attempts were made to produce germ-free animals. During the past 10 years it has been clearly demonstrated that germ-free life is possible. It has been shown that under stress these animals show an increased mortality and morbidity compared with conventional animals under the same conditions. The relationship between protein metabolism and digestive flora has been studied by Levenson and Tennant (1963). These authors conclude that given isocaloric diets, germ-free rats excrete more faecal nitrogen but less urinary nitrogen than conventional animals; the overall retention of nitrogen appears to be the same in both groups. The study of the total body composition of nitrogen in germ-free rats compared with conventional rats killed at the same age showed that the quantity of nitrogen retained is identical in both groups, although the germ-free group had less body fat.

The relationship of antibiotics and increased retention of nitrogen in animals has been given much publicity in recent years. In pigs, Zelter *et al.* (1961) and Delort-Laval *et al.* (1963) have shown that chlortetracycline allows an increase in the biological value of proteins, the retention of nitrogen being increased by about 15 per cent. Antibiotics in general tend to produce a different bacterial flora, with the rapid disappearance of the lactobacilli and a rapid increase in enterococci and gram-negative bacilli.

In healthy individuals the small intestine contains a very low concentration of bacterial organisms. The stomach and jejunum may contain bacteria from the mouth and throat. Higher concentrations of organisms are recovered from the lower ileum and a colonic type flora may exist. The factors controlling the growth of bacteria in the small intestine are unknown. Gastric acidity or peristaltic action which propels the small intestinal contents rapidly to the caecum and colon, may play a part. Some workers have suggested that the mucosal cell may be capable of secreting a substance which will inhibit bacterial growth. Any lesion of

467

the small intestine which results in stasis of intestinal contents will favour overgrowth by clonic type bacteria. *Figure 3* illustrates the different clinical disorders of the small intestine in man which favour overgrowth of abnormal intestinal bacterial flora.

The enzymic activities of the gut bacteria under certain conditions can have a detrimental effect on the products of protein digestion. Unabsorbed amino acids can follow abnormal pathways of degradation as the result of bacterial enzymes in the bowel. Species of *E. coli, streptococci, clostridia* and *proteus* have well known capacities to decarboxylate amino acids; the amines formed can be reabsorbed into the blood stream and may cause toxic symptoms. If the dibasic amino acids, lysine, ornithine, and arginine are not completely absorbed and pass into the colon, they are decarboxylated to the diamines, cadaverine and putrescine. Tryamine is formed from unabsorbed tyrosine and histamine from histidine. As already stated elsewhere, the excretion of indican in the urine of patients with malabsorption is largely due to bacterial breakdown of indole derived from unabsorbed tryptophan. The quantity of indican excreted is a crude but useful indication of the activity of indole-producing intestinal bacteria in malabsorption states. Deamination of unabsorbed amino acids can also occur with the production of ammonia which is then absorbed into the blood stream. Jones *et al.* (1968) have

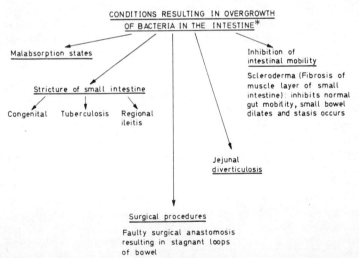

*Figure 3.\** *In these conditions the overgrowth of organisms is confined to the lumen of the gastrointestinal tract. However, in acute gastroenteritis organisms may migrate into the mucosal epithelial causing transient malabsorption*

described a patient in which this situation exists due to the overgrowth of bacteria in the stagnant loop of bowel produced as a result of surgery for partial removal of the stomach. In this patient excessive bacterial de-amination and production of ammonia caused a large proportion of dietary protein nitrogen to be directed into urea production by the liver and become unavailable for protein anabolism, resulting in a state of protein calorie malnutrition.

Irrespective of the pathogenesis, malabsorption states can occur as a result of bacterial overgrowth in the small intestine. The extent of the malabsorptive process will depend on the anatomical site of the lesion and the length of intestine involved. The nearer to the stomach the lesion, the more varied the unabsorbed products will be, involving amino acids, lipids, disaccharides, minerals, vitamins and electrolytes, whereas if the pathology is confined to the terminal ileum, only the absorption of vitamin $B_{12}$ may be affected. The fact that treatment with broad spectrum antibiotics may correct the malabsorptive states in the above cited lesions, has been proof of the aetiological role played by the overgrowth of bacteria. The most commonly used antibiotics are tetracycline and chlortetracycline. Neomycin is ineffective in these disorders probably because the species bacteroides are resistant to its action and the antibiotic itself is reported to cause malabsorption. (Hvidt and Kjeldsen, 1963).

## PROTEIN 'INTOLERANCE'

Rare disorders in the assimilation of protein in man are the protein intolerance states. These diseases are usually first noted in infancy and childhood. Some are specific, i.e. milk protein, while others act indirectly from protein breakdown.

### Coeliac disease

This is a familial disorder with specific intolerance to wheat and rye protein causing structural alteration to the small intestinal mucosa with impaired absorption. In the untreated patient there occurs atrophy of the villi of the duodenum and proximal jejunal mucosa, with lymphocytic and plasma cell infiltration and degenerative changes in the surface epithelial cells. The absorptive and digestive activity of the upper small intestine is markedly impaired and a severe malabsorption results with a wide range of deficiency states. The introduction of cereals into the diet of affected infants is often followed after a few weeks or months by diarrhoea and vomiting, and as cereals are now introduced at a very early

469

age the symptoms of coeliac disease may occur from 5–6 months on-wards. The initial illness can take the form of an acute gastroenteritis which responds slowly to treatment and relapses when the infant is given a normal diet. Malabsorption results and these children have diarrhoea with bulky, offensive, fatty stools, anaemia unresponsive to oral iron, and stunted growth. Diarrhoea may not be conspicuous in the older children. As toddlers, these children present a typical physical appearance with a large protuberant abdomen, wasting of buttocks and limbs and oedema of the feet. A complication only recently recognized in association with the coeliac syndrome is deficiency of the disaccharide enzymes, especially lactase and sucrase. This is not unexpected as these enzymes act in the brush border lining of the intestinal epithelial cell, which is atrophied in coeliac disease.

Dicke demonstrated in 1950 that coeliac disease was due to an intoler-ance to the protein gluten of wheat and rye. When wheat and rye gluten was excluded from the diet, patients with this disease made complete clinical recoveries with a return to normal intestinal function and normal or near normal intestinal structure. Failure to adhere strictly to this diet will be revealed by a return of the clinical symptoms. While there is no doubt of the efficacy of the gluten-free diet in the treatment of coeliac disease (now also known as gluten sensitive enteropathy) the basic defect remains unknown. Gluten and its alcohol soluble fraction, gliadin, are complex mixtures of different proteins and when fed in pure form to coeliac patients will reproduce the disease process. Peptic and tryptic digests of gluten and gliadin still retain their toxicity but further digestion with extracts of small intestinal mucosa are non-toxic. This suggests that the offending protein is a polypeptide of low molecular weight and that intracellular peptidases may be concerned with the normal digestion of gluten. It has been postulated that in coeliac disease there may be a deficiency of intestinal peptidase – this would result in an intracellular accumulation of non-digested peptides derived from gluten, which might have a direct toxic effect on the intestinal cell. Recent work by Douglas and Booth (1967) suggests that this does in fact occur, but that it appears to be a secondary effect.

A number of recent observations suggest that an immunological process may be of importance in coeliac disease, e.g. the plasma cell infiltration in the intestinal mucosa could reflect the local production of antibodies in response to the absorption of antigens, the resulting antigen-antibody complex causing mucosal cell damage. The pathogenesis of this disease remains unproven and a fertile field for investigation.

As stated above, treatment is dietary with the complete exclusion of wheat and rye gluten. Theoretically, this should be simple but practically is difficult owing to the number of canned foods which have wheat added to them. Gluten-free starch and substitutes such as rice flour can be used to provide bread and cakes. As already mentioned, a disaccharide deficiency may complicate treament and intially a diet also low in disaccharides and starch may be necessary for the first few months of treatment. If a child is acutely ill when first seen, dietary management should be more gradual. A high protein, low fat diet should be given, until the diarrhoea has settled, with the gradual addition of meat and starches. Vitamins, minerals and calcium supplements should be added to the diet.

Much divergence of opinion exists on the subject of allergy to cows' milk in the first few years of life. It is thought most likely to be due to the lactalbumin fraction; symptoms occur after starting feeding cows' milk. Clein (1954) reports that 89 per cent of affected infants develop symptoms during the first year of life. The symptoms attributed to milk allergy vary widely but include vomiting and/or diarrhoea, colic, asthma and eczema, recurrent rhinorrhoea or urticaria: the infants are irritable and generally unhappy. Diagnosis of this condition can only be considered if symptoms appear within a reasonable time of ingestion of the offending protein and must disappear when the allergen is excluded from the diet, with reappearance of symptoms when the allergen in reintroduced.

Milk intolerance associated with protein-losing enteropathy has recently been reported. (Waldmann *et al.*, 1967, and Bookstein *et al.*, 1965). A milk-free diet resulted in marked clinical improvement in the patients with return of symptoms when milk was reintroduced.

Recently, a familial protein intolerance associated with an amino acid transport defect in kidney and intestine has been described in 10 infants from Finland by Kekomaki *et al.* (1967). In this disorder, the intolerance was not confined to milk protein but all 'first class' proteins caused symptoms. There was a family incidence with three pairs of siblings among the 10 patients. All infants tolerated breast milk without symptoms but a few months after weaning, vomiting and diarrhoea appeared with failure to thrive. They were unable to tolerate full strength cows' milk, meat, fish, liver and eggs, and the diarrhoea tended to disappear on this naturally selected low protein diet. On physical examination, the children showed retarded growth, with body weight silightly below average and reduced muscle mass. Two patients had had multiple fractures and all had enlarged livers at some stage in the disease. Biochemical investigation revealed high levels of ammmonia after a protein meal, accompanied by a delayed fall in plasma amino nitrogen and impaired urea production. This suggested an impairment in the urea cycle but the enzymes responsible for the normal working of this cycle were all present in normal concentration. A transport defect for lysine, and to a smaller extent arginine, has been demonstrated in the renal tubule and the intestine. Oral supplements of arginine could prevent the post prandial hyperammonaemia. The pathogenesis of this disorder has not been defined.

## CONCLUSION

Only a few of the many diseases resulting in malassimilation of ingested protein in man have been discussed but these examples serve to show how many and varied are the defects and illustrate the deficiencies still existing in our knowledge of the aetiology, diagnosis and treatment of these conditions. The mystery surrounding allergic reaction to polypeptides is still unsolved and the basic defect in many of the hereditary protein abnormalities remains unknown. Diagnosis has been made easier by the elaboration of more refined biochemical and pathological techniques. One of the greatest steps in aiding diagnosis, especially in the malabsorption states, has been the availability of per oral biopsies of the gastric and intestinal mucosa. These small fragments of mucosa can now be examined not only for histopathology and histochemistry, but also by micro-techniques for quantitative enzyme studies. It is now also possible to study amino acid transport defects using these small quantities of living tissue.

With such techniques we can look forward to a better understanding of the complex physiology and pathology of the gastrointestinal tract.

## REFERENCES

Baron, D.N., Dent, C.E., Harris, H., Hart, E.W. and Jepson, J.B. (1956). *Lancet,* 2, 421
Bodian, M., Sheldon, W. and Lightwood, R. (1964). *Acta paediat, Stockh.* 53, 282
Bookstein, J.J., French, A.B. and Pollard, H.M. (1965). *Am. J. dig. Dis.* 10, 573
Citrin, Y., Sterling, K. and Halsted, J.A. (1957). *New Engl. J. Med.* 257, 906
Clein, N.W. (1954). *Pediat. Clin. N. Amer.* 1, 949
Delort-Laval, J., Charlet-Lery, G. and Zelter, S.Z. (1963). *Ann. Biol. anim. Biochem., Biophys.* 3
Dicke, W.K. (1950). *Utrecht M.D. Thesis*
Douglas, A.P. and Booth, C.C. (1967). *Gut* 8, 629
Drummond, K.N., Michael, A.F., Ulstrom, R.A. and Good, R.A. (1964). *Am.J. Med.* 37, 928
Fölling, A. (1934). *Hoppe-Seyler's physiol. Chem.* 227, 169
Francois, A.C. and Michel, M. (1964). in *Role of the Gastrointestinal Tract in Protein Metabolism.* Oxford; Blackwell. p.239

Hooft, C., Timmermans, J., Snoeck, J., Antener, I., Oyaert, W. and Van Den Hende, Ch. (1964). *Lancet*, **2**, 20

Hvidt, S. and Kjeldsen, K. (1963). *Acta. med. scanda.* **173**, 699

Jones, E.A., Craigie, A., Tavill, A.S., Franglen, G. and Rosenoer, V.M. (1968). *Gut* **9**, 466

Levenson, S.M. and Tennant, B. (1963). *Fedn Proc. Fedn Am. Socs Exp. Biol.* **22**, 109

Kekomaki, M., Visakorpi, J. K., Perheentupa, J. and Saxen, L. (1967). *Acta paediat. Stockh.* **56**, 617

Milne, M. D., Crawford, M. A., Girao, C. B. and Loughridge, L. W. (1960). *Q. Jl. Med.* **29**, 407

Shwachman, H., Diamond, L. K., Oski, F. A. and Khawk, T. (1964). *J. Pediat.* **65**, 645

Scriver, C. R., Pueschel, C. M. and Davies, E. (1966). *New Eng. J. Med.* **274**, 635

Townes, P. L. (1965). *J. Pediat.* **66**, 275

– Bryson, M. F. and Miller, G. (1967). *J. Pediat.* **71**, 220

Waldmann, T. A. (1965). *Ross Conference on Macromolecular Aspects of Protein Absorption and Excretion in the Mammalian Intestine.* Columbus, Ohio. p.94

– (1966). *Gastroenterology* **50**, 422

– Wochner, R. D., Laster, L. and Gordon, (Jr.) R. S. (1967). *New Eng. J. Med.* **276**, 761

Wetterfors, J., Gullberg, R., Liljedahl, S. O., Plantin, L. O., Birke, G. and Olhagen, B. (1960). *Acta. med. scand.* **168**, 347

Zelter, S. Z., Charlet-Lery, G., Durand-Salomon, M. and Vaz-Portugal, A. (1961). *Ann. Biol. anim.* **1**, 222

# CONCLUDING REMARKS

## P. BROWN

*British Nutrition Foundation Ltd.*

We have been told of the international recognition of the need and urgency for finding some solution to the world protein problem. Apart from producing more protein, there are problems of wastage and faulty distribution and a general lack of education. The wastage of food due to pests and other forms of spoilage is appalling and if it could be prevented would go a significant way toward closing the protein gap. There needs to be more extensive work in developing countries on insecticides and rodenticides and improved agricultural practices. It has been estimated that the preventable loss of protein during grain storage alone is greater than the current world production of oil-seed protein. Mould attack on crops is also significant and may be implicated in the high incidence of liver cancer in tropical Africa.

## BETTER DISTRIBUTION

Effective distribution is often difficult, it adds to the cost of the food and the poor and dependent are the main sufferers. The most successful methods for producing an extra supply of protein are likely to be those in which the protein is produced at or near the site of need.

A key factor which has been emphasized in this symposium is that of acceptability. However effective the technological contributions are, they will be frustrated if the sociological problems are not overcome; and experience has shown that people suffering from protein deficiency do not necessarily welcome an added supply of protein even if it is made available cheaply.

The difficulties of persuading a tradition-bound, illiterate people to accept a food on the basis that it is nutritious are highly complex, as was mentioned by Miss Hollingsworth in her paper and as is also described in the report by the Harvard Business School personnel, 'The Protein

474

Paradox'. Such a situation is likely to call for all the marketing skills exerted in a sophisticated environment and new attention must be paid to local food habits, particularly in regard to taste, texture and colour, culture and taboos. Local resources must be utilized and if unconventional sources of protein are to be used it is still necessary from a cost standpoint that they be produced locally.

The status of local technology — both in terms of production and of cooking technology — must be considered. Though any product introduced must take into account the maximum price that low income groups can afford to spend on food, the product must nevertheless avoid giving the appearance of being a poor man's food: the presentation of the product must be attractive. The skills of product development in terms of taste, texture and appearance are as necessary in an unsophisticated environment as in other markets. All these factors need to be studied and modified to suit the palate of the potential customer if full acceptance is to be gained. Above all there is a great need for education: people must be educated to want proteins before they will spend money on them.

One of our large industrial concerns, when considering the acquisition of a malted milk product, found two large areas of marketing potential. One was in the affluent society of the United States where people who had fed too well were anxious to restrict their intake — and were seeking a product which was highly nutritious in small bulk. The other was in India, where spending power was the limiting factor and people were seeking a concentrated product providing relatively inexpensively a wide range of nutrients. The fact that the same product can satisfy two extremes of requirement is significant and may have lessons for the marketing side.

Finally, on the question of acceptability, many protein products have been devised with the aim of simulating products normally derived from more expensive protein (the simulated meats from soya and groundnut protein, for instance). Is there not scope for the food technologist to derive entirely new foods — not necessarily simulating existing products? Products do not always have to resemble ham and beef. This has been done successfully in the confectionery area, e.g. ice cream.

We have been told of the urgency of the problem for some areas of the world. Which is the best way in which to deploy the existing resources? Dr. Rosenfield made a claim that effort should be concentrated on the supplementation of cereals with essential amino acids, and he concentrated solely on the use of lysine to increase the protein value of wheat. His reasons for urging this step were that the measures could be applied immediately and on a massive scale and was attractive on a cost basis. Professor Harper doubted that this course was the right one to follow, partly because of the difficulty of always being able to identify the limiting amino acid in a given situation, but more gravely, because in a situation of protein-calorie malnutrition, lack of calories and of vitamins and minerals may be a more serious problem. Replacement of existing supplies of protein by lysine, as had been offered by Japan, might worsen the situation rather than improve it. M. Autret also spoke on the complex nature of this problem. Deficiencies in terms of the limiting amino acid may vary from place to place within a country or region, and may also vary seasonally at the same place, depending on the availability of different local foods. He also showed that lysine was not usually the limiting amino acid and the sulphur-containing amino acids, methionine and cysteine, or isoleucine were more often crucial. Professor Munro, in pointing out the existing discrepancy of opinion as to which amino acid was most likely to be limiting, also drew attention to the unsatisfactory state of our criteria for judging this factor. He made a plea for more work to be carried out to devise methods of identifying the physiologically limiting amino acid.

In the longer term there can be no doubt of the desperate need for attack on the problem of producing more protein from all possible sources. More proteins need to be produced both for sophisticated and unsophisticated markets. Increased production must come from conventional plant and livestock sources.

We heard from Dr. Schuphan of the possibility of producing new strains of plants by genetic control which could lead to better sources of vegetable protein. Oilseeds appear to be inadequately exploited at the present time. One difficulty is that much oilseed protein is produced as a by-product of the oil-milling industry and the treatment that the oilseed meal receives is not optimal for the production of best quality protein. We heard from Dr. Meyer of the details of the processing necessary to produce a soya protein isolate of the highest quality; but this is intended primarily for processed foods in a sophisticated market.

Non-conventional sources of protein have attracted a great deal of attention in recent years and we heard details of two such sources. The British Petroleum Company's protein concentrate, from yeast grown on gas oil, and algal proteins from both green and blue green algae. Clearly there is hope, but no certainty, that these sources will provide a useful contribution directly for human food, and the possibility that they will open up new avenues of supply at an economically viable price will attract much interest. A conference on single cell protein was held at M.I.T. in 1967 and the proceedings are now published. Unfortunately, for commercial reasons, most industrial concerns engaged in this area are unwilling to divulge information about the processes they operate.

If new proteins are produced for human food their safety-in-use is of paramount importance. Often too simple a view is taken of this. There are a number of toxic amino acids, e.g. those in ackee fruit; and there are toxic polypeptide antibiotics. Proteins formed by single cell proteins may cause complex problems from the presence of unusual amino acids. Dr. Gordon sounded a note of caution here. Chemical contamination from the use of petroleum products could be troublesome; it was reassuring to hear from Mr. Shacklady of the low level of polycylic aromatic hydrocarbons in the B.P. concentrate. Dr. Elias presented an excellent and comprehensive paper on the subject of toxic agents in relation to protein availability. He omitted one somewhat bizarre example, of an exotic source of protein, the green quail. The green quail has a remarkable degree of indifference to hemlock, on which it sometimes feeds. It can accumulate quite a lot of hemlock alkaloids in its tissues and should be eaten only with caution.

Finally, there is a need to attract workers of high quality into the fields of nutrition, food science and food technology and to use them effectively in all the areas relating to human food. Our Foundation is anxious to play a part in this.

Easter Schools of this type help by focusing attention on the interesting problems and areas that exist. These four days have been a most enterprising undertaking both with regard to scope and timing.

There has recently been an intensified interview in the subject of protein as human food. Within the last year several meetings have been organized on an international basis and the organizers of this meeting are to be congratulated on the particularly distinguished array of speakers who have addressed this meeting and on the comprehensive coverage and practicality in approach to the subject that has been achieved. Finally, I would like to thank the organizers for the excellent arrangements which they made for the comfort of all who attended.

# LIST OF REGISTRANTS

| | |
|---|---|
| Airey, Mr. J.M. | H.J. Heinz Co. Ltd., Hayes Park, Hayes, Middx. |
| Andah, Mrs. A. | Food Research Institute, P.O. Box M20, Accra, Ghana. |
| Autret, Dr. M. | Nutrition Division, F.A.O., Via delle Terme Caracella, Rome, Italy. |
| Aylward, Prof. F. | Department of Food Science, The University, Reading, Berks. |
| Banfield, Dr. F.H. | C. Shippam Ltd., East Walls, Chichester, Sussex. |
| Banigo, Mr. E.W. | Federal Institute of Industrial Research, Oshodi, Lagos, Nigeria. |
| Bews, Dr. A.M. | Imperial Chemical Industries Ltd., Nobel Division, Research Department, Stevenston, Ayrshire. |
| Blanchfield, Mr. J.R. | Bush Boake Allen Ltd., Wharf Road, London, N.1. |
| Blanshard, Mr. J.M.V. | Department of Applied Biochemistry and Nutrition, University of Nottingham. |
| Blair, Dr. R. | A.R.C. Poultry Research Centre, King's Buildings, West Mains Road, Edinburgh 9. |
| Bolton, Dr. W. | A.R.C. Poultry Research Centre, King's Buildings, West Mains Road, Edinburgh 9. |
| Bon, Mr. J. | Instituut voor Visserijprodukten TNO, Postbus 68, IJmuiden, The Netherlands. |
| Boorman, Dr. K.N. | Department of Applied Biochemistry and Nutrition, University of Nottingham. |
| Briskey, Prof. E.J. | Muscle Biology Laboratory, College of Agriculture and Life Sciences, University of Wisconsin, Madison, Wisconsin 53706, U.S.A. |
| Brown, Mr. P. | British Nutrition Foundation Ltd., Alembic House, 93, Albert Embankment, London, S.E.1. |
| Burgess, Dr. G.H.O. | Torry Research Station, Ministry of Technology, Aberdeen. |

| | |
|---|---|
| **Burleigh, Dr. I.G.** | A.R.C. Meat Research Institute, Langford, Nr. Bristol, BS18 7DY. |
| **Carson, Dr. Nina** | The Nuffield Department of Child Health, Queen's University, Belfast. |
| **Chamberlain, Dr. N.** | Flour Milling and Baking Research Association, Chorleywood, Herts. |
| **Chandler, Mr. R.** | Bovril Group Central Laboratories, Sunleigh Road, Alperton, Middx. |
| **Christian, Mr. W.F.K.** | Food Research Institute, P.O. Box M20, Accra, Ghana. |
| **Chubb, Dr. L.G.** | Spillers Ltd., Kennett Nutritional Centre, Bury Road, Kennett, Suffolk. |
| **Collison, Mr. V.** | British Soya Products Ltd., The Grange, Puckeridge, Nr. Ware, Herts. |
| **Connell, Dr. J.J.** | Torry Research Station, Ministry of Technology, Wassand Street, Aberdeen. |
| **Cooper, Miss S.L.** | H.J. Heinz Co. Ltd., Gayes Park, Hayes, Middx. |
| **Coton, Mr. S.G.** | Milk Marketing Board, Thames Ditton, Surrey. |
| **Curtis, Mr. J.** | Dragoco (G.B.) Ltd., Lady Lane, Hadleigh, Nr. Ipswich, Suffolk. |
| **Cuthbertson, Sir David** | Department of Pathological Chemistry, Royal Infirmary, Glasgow, C.4. |
| **Das, Mr. T.K.** | Dr. Bernard Dyer & Partners Ltd., Peek House, London, E.C.3. |
| **Davis, Dr. J.G.** | 9, Gerrard Street, London, W.1. |
| **Deatherage, Prof. F.E.** | Biochemistry, The Ohio State University, 2121, Fyffe Road, Columbus, Ohio 43210, U.S.A. |
| **Delaney, Mr. R.A.** | National College of Food Technology, University of Reading, St. George's Avenue, Weybridge, Surrey. |
| **D'Mello, Dr. J.P.F.** | Edinburgh School of Agriculture, West Mains Road, Edinburgh, 9. |
| **Duckworth, Dr. R.B.** | Department of Food Science, University of Strathclyde, Glasgow C.1. |
| **Duthie, Dr. I.F.** | Lord Rank Research Centre, Lincoln Road, High Wycombe, Bucks. |
| **Elias, Dr. P.S.** | Department of Health and Social Security, Alexander Fleming House, Elephant and Castle, London, S.E.1. |

| | |
|---|---|
| Fazakerley, Dr. S. | Biological Research Division, BP Refinery Ltd., Grangemouth, Scotland. |
| Frazer, Dr. A.C. | British Nutrition Foundation Ltd., Alembic House, 93, Albert Embankment, London, S.E.1. |
| Giddey, Dr. C. | Institut Battelle, Route de Drize 7, 1227 Carouge-Geneve, Switzerland. |
| Gordon, Dr. J.F. | Unilever Research Laboratories, The Frythe, Welwyn, Herts. |
| Greaves, Dr. J.P. | Ministry of Agriculture, Fisheries and Food, Great Westminster House, Horseferry Road, London, S.W.1. |
| Green, Dr. E. | Milk Marketing Board, Thames Ditton, Surrey. |
| Greenfield, Prof. A.D.M. | Medical School, University of Nottingham. |
| Hacking, Mr. A. | Bacteriology Department, NAAS/MAFF, Shardlow Hall, Shardlow, Derby. |
| Hamm, Prof. Dr. R. | Bundesanstalt für Fleischforschung, Kulmbach, W. Germany. |
| Harper, Prof. A.E. | Department of Biochemistry, University of Wisconsin, Madison, Wisconsin 53706, U.S.A. |
| Hawley, Mr. H.B. | Bernard Hawley & Associates, Marston Road, Sherborne, Dorset. |
| Hawley, Mrs. | Bernard Hawley & Associates, Marston Road, Sherborne, Dorset. |
| Hawthorn, Prof. J. | Department of Food Science, University of Strathclyde, Glasgow. |
| Herringa, Dr. L.G. | Instituut voor Visserijprodukten TNO, Postbus 68, IJmuiden, The Netherlands. |
| Henry, Dr. Y. | Institut National de la Recherche Agronomique, Station de Recherches sur l'Elevage des Porcs, C.N.R.Z., 78 Jouy-en-Josas, France. |
| Hewitt, Dr. D. | National Institute for Research in Dairying, Shinfield, Berks. |
| Hollingsworth, Miss D.F. | Ministry of Agriculture, Fisheries and Food, Great Westminster House, Horseferry Road, London, S.W.1. |
| Holmes, Dr. A.W. | British Food Manufacturing Industries Research Association, Leatherhead, Surrey. |

| | |
|---|---|
| Johnson, Dr. R.M. | Department of Applied Biology & Food Science, Borough Polytechnic, Borough Road, London, S.E.1. |
| Jul, Mr. M. | FAO/WHO/UNICEF Protein Advisory Group, United Nations, New York, 10017, U.S.A. |
| Keay, Mr. P.J. | Luton College of Technology (Science Dept.), Park Square, Luton, Beds. |
| Kent, Dr. N.L. | Flour Milling and Baking Research Association, St. Albans, Herts. |
| Kihlberg, Dr. R. | Applied Microbiology, Kerolinske Institutet, Tomtebodavagen 17, 17164 Solna 1, Sweden. |
| Lawrie, Dr. R.A. | Department of Applied Biochemistry & Nutrition, University of Nottingham. |
| Lewis, Prof. D. | Department of Applied Biochemistry & Nutrition, University of Nottingham. |
| Lewis, Mr. W. | MAFF, NAAS, Shardlow Hall, Shardlow, Derby. |
| Lister, Dr. D. | A.R.C. Meat Research Institute, Langford, Nr. Bristol, BS18 7DY. |
| Lodge, Dr. G.A. | Animal Research Institute, Ottawa, Canada. |
| Londahl, Mr. G. | Frigoscandia AB, Fack, S251–01 Helsingborg, Sweden. |
| McMurray, Mr. T.A. | H.J. Heinz Co. Ltd., Hayes Park, Hayes, Middx. |
| McNab, Dr. J.M. | Poultry Research Centre, King's Buildings, West Mains Road, Edinburgh 9. |
| Marwood, Miss H.K. | Van Den Berghs Ltd., Kildare House, Dorset Rise, London E.C.4. |
| Maughan, Miss A. | Bovril Group Central Laboratories, Sunleigh Road, Alperton, Nr. Wembley, Middx. |
| Meyer, Dr. E.W. | Central Soya Company, 1825 North Laramie Avenue, Chicago, Illinois 60639, U.S.A. |
| Moran, Dr. F. | Societe Internationale de Recherche BP, Rue des 4-Filles, 28 Epernon, France. |
| Mosha, Mr. A.C. | Research and Training Institute, Ilonga, Kilosa, Tanzania. |

| | |
|---|---|
| Mossel, Prof. D.A.A. | Department of Microbiology, Central Institute for Nutrition & Food Research, Utrechtseweg 48, Zeist, The Netherlands. |
| Munden, Dr. J.E. | Lord Rank Research Centre, Rank Hovis McDougall Ltd., Lincoln Road, High Wycombe, Bucks. |
| Mundy, Mr. D. | Rose, Downs & Thompson Ltd., Cannon St., Hull. |
| Munro, Dr. D.N. | Petfoods Ltd., Melton Mowbray, Leics. |
| Munro, Prof. H.N. | Physiological Chemistry Laboratories, Department of Nutrition & Food Science, Massachusetts Institute of Technology, Cambridge, Mass. 02139, U.S.A. |
| Murrells, Mr. D.F. | National College of Food Technology, St. Georges Avenue, Weybridge, Surrey. |
| Myres, Mr. A.W. | National Institute for Research in Dairying, Shinfield, Reading, Berks. |
| Neal, Mr. W.T.L. | Ministry of Agriculture, Fisheries & Food, Great Westminster House, Horseferry Road, London, S.W.1. |
| Newman, Mr. D.G. | White Fish Authority, 2/3 Cursitor Street, London E.C.4. |
| Newport, Dr. M.J. | Pig Husbandry Department, National Institute for Research in Dairying, Shinfield, Reading. |
| Nilsson, Prof. T.E. | Frigoscandia AB, Fack, S 251–01 Helsingborg, Sweden. |
| Osner, Mr. R.C. | Department of Applied Biology and Food Science, Borough Polytechnic, Borough Road, London S.E.1. |
| Page, Mr. J.F. | Van Den Berghs & Jurgens Ltd., Purfleet, Essex. |
| Parker, Mr. C.G.S. | J.Bibby Agriculture Ltd., Nutrition Research and Advisory Department, Weatherstones, Neston, Wirral, Cheshire. |
| Parnell, Mr. C. | Bayer Chemicals Ltd., Kingsway House, 18-24 Paradise Road, Richmond, Surrey. |
| Parry, Mrs. D.A. | College of Domestic Science, Edinburgh. |
| Pirie, Mr. N.W. | Biochemistry Department, Rothamsted Experimental Station, Harpenden, Herts. |
| Raistrick, Mr. A.S. | The Lord Rank Research Centre, Lincoln Road, High Wycombe, Bucks. |

| | |
|---|---|
| Richardson, Mr. I.D. | White Fish Authority, 2/3 Cursitor Street, London, E.C.4. |
| Roberts, Dr. D.G. | Chemistry Department, Belfast College of Technology, Belfast, BT1 6DJ. |
| Robinson, Mr. A.A. | Department of Dairy Technology, West of Scotland Agricultural College, Auchincruive, Ayr. |
| Rolfe, Prof. E.J. | National College of Food Technology, Weybridge, Surrey. |
| Rolls, Mr. B.A. | Nutrition Department, National Institute for Research in Dairying, Shinfield, Reading, Berks. |
| Rosenfield, Dr. D. | High Protein Foods & Agribusiness Group, Foreign Agricultural Service, U.S.D.A., Washington, D.C. 20250, U.S.A. |
| Salmon, Miss J.A. | Birds Eye Foods Ltd., Station Avenue, Walton-on-Thames, Surrey. |
| Salter, Dr. D.N. | National Institute for Research in Dairying, Shinfield, Reading, Berks. |
| Schaffer, Dr. A.G. | Department of Science, Luton College of Technology, Park Square, Luton, Beds. |
| Shaw, Mr. D. | Simon Engineering Ltd., Research Division, Cheadle Heath, Stockport. |
| Shearer, Mr. G. | Ministry of Agriculture, Fisheries & Food, Food Science Unit, Food Research Institute, Colney Lane, Norwich, Norfolk, NOR.70F. |
| Schuphan, Prof. Dr. W. | Bundesanstalt für Qualitätsforschung pflanzlicher Erzeugnisse, Geisenheim, W. Germany. |
| Shacklady, Mr. C.A. | British Petroleum Co. Ltd., Britannic House, Moor Lane, London, E.C.2. |
| Shewan, Dr. J.M. | Torry Research Station, Ministry of Technology, Aberdeen. |
| Shrimpton, Dr. D.H. | British Oil & Cake Mills Ltd., Reading, Berks. |
| Smith, Dr. J.A.B. | Hannah Dairy Research Institute, Ayr, Scotland. |
| Smith, Dr. R.H. | Protein Biochemistry Department, Rowett Research Institute, Bucksburn, Aberdeen. |
| Smith, Mr. R.J. | Meat and Livestock Commission, P.O. Box 44, Queensway House, Bletchley, Bucks. |

| | |
|---|---|
| Southgate, Dr. D.A.T. | Dunn Nutritional Laboratory, University of Cambridge and Medical Research Council, Cambridge. |
| Spensley, Dr. P.C. | Tropical Products Institute, 127 Clerkenwell Road, London, W.C.1. |
| Stein, Dr. M. | Department of Applied Biochemistry and Nutrition, University of Nottingham. |
| Symons, Mr. H.W. | Birds Eye Foods Ltd., Walton-on-Thames, Surrey. |
| Shepherds, Dr. I.S. | Unilever Research Laboratory, The Frythe, Welwyn, Herts. |
| Telford, Miss E. | J. Lyons & Co. Ltd., Cadby Hall, London, W.14. |
| Tombs, Dr. M.P. | Unilever Research Laboratory, Colworth House, Sharnbrook, Bedford. |
| Tuck, Prof. R.H. | Department of Agricultural Economics, The University, Whiteknights Road, Reading, Berks. |
| Vincent, Dr. W.A. | Institut Battelle, Route de Drize 7, 1227 Carouge-Geneve, Switzerland. |
| Wakerley, Dr. S.B. | Boots Pure Drug Co. Ltd., Lenton Research Station, Nottingham, NG7 2QD. |
| Ward, Prof. A.G. | Procter Department of Food & Leather Science, The University, Leeds, 2. |
| Wilson, Mr. B.J. | A.R.C. Poulty Research Centre, West Mains Road, Edinburgh 9. |
| Wood, Mr. F. | Brown & Polson Ltd., Claygate House, Esher, Surrey. |
| Wood, Mr. J.C. | British Soya Products Ltd., The Grange, Puckeridge, Nr. Ware, Herts. |

# AUTHOR INDEX

Abbott, D. C., 81, 82
Abbott, J. C., 266
Abrahams, M. E., 128
Ackman, R. G., 189
Acs, G., 406
Adachi, A., 368
Adams, R., 91
Adibi, S. A., 420
Agrawal, H., 297
Aitken, J. N., 153
Ajmal, M., 103
Alam, S. Q., 423
Albanese, A. A., 218
Alder, F. E., 153,163
Alderks, O., 349
Alderton, G., 232
Alexander, L. M., 379
Ali, L. A. M., 374
Allison, J. B., 450
Almquist, H. J., 437
Altschul, A. M., 266, 267, 270
Amenta, J. S., 404
Amerine, M. A., 366
Amoore, J. E., 367
Amos, A. J., 109, 384
Andersen, B., 143, 144
Anderson, D. F., 374
Anderson, E. E., 380
Anderson, H. L., 420, 437, 438, 440
Anderson, J. A., 450
Anderson, R., 351
Andrews, F. N., 152
Andrews, G. L., 188
Andross, M., 376, 379
Anson, M. L., 267, 346, 353, 373
Antener, I., 463
Aoki, Y., 92
Arai, S., 357
Arakawa, N., 176
ARC, 144
Arcisz, W., 92
Asatoor, A. M., 98
Ashida, K., 422

Ashton, D. H., 90
Auclair, J., 90
Ausherman, A. R., 375
Autret, M., xvi, 3-19, 39, 41
Avery, G. B., 98
Avison, R. N., 69
Awad, A., 178
Axford, D. W. E., 303, 306, 307, 311, 384
Ayres, J. C., 91, 108

Baader, R., 189
Baalsrud, K., 190
Baba, H., 338
Babcock, G., 351, 352, 354
Babcock, H., 333, 335
Bachikalo, A. P., 317
Bachrach, U., 98
Back, J. F., 231
Bailey, C. M., 150
Bailey, M., 115, 176
Baines, A. H. J., 36
Baines, C. R., 194
Baird, T. T., 92
Baird-Parker, A. C., 101
Baker, J. C., 302
Baker, J. D., 382
Baliga, B. S., 406, 412
Ballance, P. E., 379
Banu, C., 176
Barber, M. A., 97
Barbu, E., 137
Barclay, G. R., 120
Barnell, H. R., 36
Barnes, J. M., 68, 69, 80
Baron, D. N., 462
Baross, J., 92
Barsuko, V. J., 169
Bartley, C. H., 92
Barton, R. A., 144
Barton, R. W., 218
Basel, F. C., 110

487

Bassir, O., 54
Bates, L. S., 296
Battey, Y., 94
Bauer, C. D., 218
Baumgart, J., 92
Bautista, G. M., 295
Bayliss, W. M., 33
Bayne, H. G., 232
Becker, K., 423
Becker, R. V., 101
Bedarf, E., 59
Beecher, G. R., 176
Behar, M., 268
Belden, G. C., 42
Bell, J., 410
Bell, R. H. V., 56
Bendall, J. R., 167, 169, 172, 173, 175, 380
Bender, A. E., 379, 449, 450
Benevenga, N. J., 417-445
Bennett, H. S., 167
Bennett, R. W., 94
Benoki, M., 92
Bensadoun, A., 141, 148, 150, 155, 160, 161
Berendsen, H. J. C., 122
Berg, H. W., 366
Berg, R. T., 147, 150, 157
Berg, W., 83
Bergdoll, M. S., 94
Bergère, J. L., 102
Berglund, F., 84
Berk, Z., 347, 348, 356, 357, 358, 359
Berman, M. D., 176, 181
Bernadi, G., 229
Berry, W. T. C., 36
Berthelot, A., 96
Bertin, L., 188
Bertrand, D. M., 96
Bettelheim, K. A., 97
Beyer, R., 190
Bhatia, D. S., 53
Bidstrup, L. P., 85
Bier, M., 232
Bigwood, E., 351
Bills, D. D., 374, 375
Birke, G., 466
Bissett, H. M., 111
Blackwell, B., 74, 98
Blackwell, R. Q., 49
Blair, R., 152

Blanchard, E. L., 370
Blanche-Koelensmid, W. A. A., 101
Blank, M. L., 229
Blaxter, K. L., xv
Block, R. J., 218, 450
Bloksma, A. H., 306
Board, R. G., 90, 232
Boardman, E., 375
Bock, H. D., 245
Bock, J. H., 101
Bocksch, W., 355
Boctor, A. M., 418
Bodian, M., 460
Bogart, R., 152
Bohmann, V. R., 150
Bolshakov, A. S., 179
Bookstein, J. J., 471
Boorman, K. N., 448-457
Booth, C. C., 470
Borgstrom, G., 200, 201, 202
Borton, R. J., 175
Boulware, R. S., 175
Bowers, J. A., 180
Boyd Orr, Lord J., 328
Boyer, A., 53
Boyer, J., 97
Boyer, R. A., 373
Boyne, A. W., 201
Bradfield, P. G. E., 150, 152
Bradley, N. W., 155
Bradley, W. B., 292
Brady, D. E., 119
Braham, E., 54
Bramblet, V. D., 381
Bramsnaes, F., 202
Branaman, G. A., 147
Brandes, C. H., 187
Brandt, M. A., 369
Brandts, J. F., 120
Bratzler, L. J., 175, 355
Braun, H., 251
Breidenstein, B. B., 150
Breidenstein, B. C., 150
Bressani, R., 54, 245, 268, 293
Brieger, L., 96
Briggs, M. H., 55
Briskey, E. J., 173, 175
British Nutrition Foundation, 76
Brock, J. F., 39
Brockerhoff, H., 188
Brody, S., 143

Brooke, C. L., 267
Brooks, C. C., 157
Brooks, J., 119, 226, 230, 232, 233
Brooks, R. F., 119
Brown, G. A., 147
Brown, P., 474-477
Brozek, J., 49
Brune, H., 245, 247
Bryson, M. F., 460
Buchanan, R. A., 53
Buchter, L., 179, 180
Buck, F. F., 232
Buechner, H. K., 56
Bull, L. S., 141, 142, 148, 150, 155, 160, 161
Burgess, C. R., 57
Burgess, G. H. O., 114, 186-197
Burgher, R. D., 188
Burkholder, L., 102
Burkholder, P. R., 102
Burlew, J. S., 329, 333, 343
Burley, R. W., 115, 230
Burmeister, H., 347
Burnett, P. C., 454
Burt, J. R., 190, 191, 382
Burton, J. H., 141, 148, 150, 155
Busch, W. A., 176
Bushman, D. H., 154, 156
Busson, F., 247, 249
Busta, F. F., 90
Butler, O. D., 148
Butterfield, R. M., 147, 148, 157, 158, 159, 160, 161
Butterworth, M. H., 53
Buttery, R. G., 194
Buttiaux, R., 92
Buttrose, M. S., 286
Byers, M., 53
Byrne, J. L., 100


Cahill, V. R., 152
Cairncross, S. E., 379
Calder, H., 152
Calhoun, W. K., 292
Call, D., 356
Callow, E. H., 147, 159, 160, 162
Campbell, C. C. R., 93
Campbell, J. A., 69
Campbell, J. D., 307
Campbell, T., 352

Cannon, P. R., 437
Carey, F. G., 208
Carmichael, D. J., 173
Caroline, L., 90
Carpenter, K. J., 53, 452
Carpenter, J. W., 148
Carroll, F. D., 147, 148
Carroll, W. E., 142
Carruthers, C. D., 176
Carson, N. A. J., 458-472
Carter, T. C., 228
Cartter, J., 347
Cartwright, T. C., 148
Carver, J. S., 449
Casida, L. E., 152
Casman, E. P., 94
Cassel, K., 93
Cassens, R. G., 167, 173, 175, 176
Catsimpoolas, N., 352
Caul, J. F., 366, 368, 379
Cecil, R., 131
Ceh, L., 68
Chalmers, T. C., 93
Chamberlain, A. G., 162
Chamberlain, N., 300-312, 384
Chambers, D., 351
Chambers, R., 121
Champagnat, A., 317
Chandrasekaran, A., 53
Chang, H., 93
Chara, M., 368
Charette, L. A., 152
Charlet-Lery, G., 467
Charley, H., 382
Cherry, F., 357
Chick, H., 293
Chow, B. F., 49
Christian, J. H. B., 107
Christianson, D. D., 287
Chu, A., 102
Chun, D., 92
Chung, C.-S., 208
Chung, M., 268
Churchill, D. N., 189
Circle, S., 353, 355
Citrin, Y., 465
Clark, C., 28
Clark, C. M., 409
Clark, J. G., 221
Clark, L. E., 295
Clark, N. G., 379

Clark, R. T., 148
Clausen, H., 157
Clegg, K. M., 371
Clegg, M. T., 147, 148, 152
Clein, N. W., 471
Clement, G., 330, 337, 341
Cline, J. A., 379, 381
Cline, J. D., 100
Coffman, J. R., 384
Cogan, U., 347, 348, 356, 357, 358, 359
Cohen, E. M., 179
Coin, L., 92
Cole, E. W., 384
Cole, J. W., 152
Coleman, J. A., 369
Coleman, R., 355
Collet, R. A., 113
Collins, T. H., 303, 304, 309, 384
Collyer, D. M., 311
Colwell, K. H., 311
Colvin, J. R., 371
Combs, G. F., 336
Condé, C., 293
Congleton, W. L., 42
Connell, J. J., 200-210
Connors, T. J., 102
Convit, J., 338, 343
Cook, J. W., 449
Cook, W. H., 115, 229, 230
Cooke, R., 162
Coomes, T. J., 36
Cooper, M., 357
Coppock, J. B. M., 304
Cori, C. F., 118
Cori, G. T., 118
Cornford, S. J., 311
Coulson, C. B., 284
Coulson, J. C., 74
Cover, S., 379, 381
Cowie, W. P., 190
Cox, R. E., 317
Cox, W. M., 218
Crabtree, A. N., 74
Craigie, A., 468
Crawford, M. A., 462
Creamer, B., 50
Cresta, M., 41
Creswick, N., 355
Crichton, J. A., 153
Crigler, J. C., 177

Cross, B., 137
Crossley, E. L., 221
Crowe, P. F., 379
Culbert, K. H., 100
Cundiff, L. V., 150
Cunningham, F. E., 110
Curatola, G., 181
Cuthbertson, A., 142, 143, 147, 158
Cuthbertson, D. P., xiii-xvii
Cutting, C. L., 114, 186, 190, 195, 202
Cybulska, J., 90

Dack, G. M., 97
Dakin, J. C., 102
Dalrymple, D. G., 40
Dam, R., 336, 339, 340, 343
Damice, J. N., 194
Daniel, V. A., 53
Dastoli, F., 367
Davey, C. L., 176, 177, 234
Davey, R. J., 162
Davidkowa, E., 178
Davidson, S., 291
Davies, E., 461
Davies, J. H. V., 186
Davies, R. E., 178
Davis, D., 202
Davis, E. A., 332, 333
Davis, J. G., 114
Davis, S. D., 90
Davys, M. N. G., 53
Dawson, L. E., 177, 379
Day, E. A., 374, 375
Day, K. M., 294
Day, N., 152
Deatherage, F. E., 378
Dedrick, J., 332, 333
Del Valle, F. R., 91
Delort-Laval, J., 467
Dent, C. E., 462
Denys, J., 97
Depierre, F., 97
Dept. Education and Science, 38
Dept. Health and Social Security, 37
Devoto, W. R., 42
Dewar, H. A., 93
Diamond, L. K., 460
Dicke, W. K., 470
Dickerson, J. W. T., 48

490

Dietrich, R., 187
D'Mello, J. P. F., 454, 455
Dobbing, J., 48
Dodds, N. J. H., 304, 305, 311
Dodt, E., 283
Doell, B. H., 449
Dollar, A. M., 102, 335
Dollinger, E., 190
Dolman, C. E., 93, 97
Donelly, T. H., 169
Donoso, G., 41
Dooren de Jong, L. E. den, 97
Doraiswamy, T. R., 53
Dorsey, A. E., 94
Douglas, A. P., 470
Dreosti, G. M., 116
Druckrey, H., 68
Drummond, K. N., 463
Drysdale, J. W., 405, 406, 408, 409, 410
Dubos, R., 50
Duckworth, J. E., 149
Duggan, R. F., 81
Dukalowska, M., 179
Duncan, C. L., 101
Dungal, N., 70
Dunn, W. E., xv
Durand-Saloman, M., 467
Duvick, D. N., 286, 287, 289
Dvorak, Z., 180
Dyer, W. J., 187, 191, 192, 194, 209
Dzinleski, B., 177

Ebashi, S., 171
Echlin, P., 169, 342
Eckenstam, C., 352
Eddie, G. C., 190
Eddy, B. P., 108
Edelbrock, J. A., 338, 340
Edge, T. M., 149
Edman, M., 266
Edwards, P. R., 92
Egan, H., 81, 82
Ehle, S., 356, 359
Ehrenbaum, E., 114
Eijgelaar, G., 102
Eklund, M. W., 93, 113
El-Bisi, H. M., 110
Eldridge, A., 351, 352, 354
Elias, L. J., 54

Elias, P. S., 65-87
Ellinger, G. M., 201, 452
Elliott, R. P., 108
Ellis, G. P., 371
Elman, R., 218
Elsley, F. W. H., 159, 160
Elton, G. A. H., 284, 294, 303, 304, 305, 306, 307, 311, 383, 384
Elvehjem, C. A., 69, 218, 420
Elwyn, D., 413
Ender, F., 68
Endo, M., 171
English, P. R., 152
Erichsen, I., 102
Esty, J. R., 110
Evans, G. H., 317
Everitt, G. C., 150, 151, 153
Evers, A. D., 294, 295
Ewart, J. A. D., 284, 290, 294, 306, 307, 383, 384

Fachman, W., 248, 252, 253
Fajans, R. S., 218
Farber, E., 418
Farber, L., 91
Farrar, N. V., 342
Feeney, R. E., 231
Felix, K., 169
Fellers, C. R., 115, 380
Fennema, O., 177, 178
Ferreira, G., xiii
Feudale, E. L., 69
Fevold, H. L., 115, 229, 232
Filer, L. J., 456
Filosa, J., 317
Findlay, J. D., 221
Finney, K. F., 293, 356
Fischer, R. L., 235
Fisher, A. W., 329
Fisher, N., 294
Fleck, A., 409, 411
Fleming, A., 90
Flewett, T. H., 120
Fliegel, H., 157
Flory, P. J., 137
Floyd, T. M., 92
Flynn, L. M., 296
Folinazzo, J. F., 93, 105
Fölling, A., 464
Fomon, S. J., 456

Fontenot, J. P., 157
Food and Agriculture Organization, 32, 38, 49, 53, 56, 67, 77, 80, 83, 84, 86, 187, 201, 328, 335
Forbes, J. J., 94
Forbes, R. M., 266
Ford, J. E., 53
Forrest, J. C., 175
Fortuin, J., 355
Foster, E. M. 101
Foster, M. T., 381
Fowden, L., 336, 337
Fowler, V. R., 159, 160
Fox, H., 336, 339, 340, 343
Fox, H. C., 53
Fox, J. B., 119
Foy, J. M., 75
François, A. C., 467
François, P. J., 8
Franglen, G., 468
Frank, S., 355
Fraser, D. I., 187, 190, 191, 194
Frater, R., 306
Frazer, A. C., 67, 68
Frazier, L. E., 437
Freame, B., 101
Fredrickson, D. S., 274
French, A. B., 471
French, C. S., 332, 333
Frey, K. J., 296
Friedman, H. H., 369
Fry, H. E., 381
Fry, P. C., 306, 339, 343
Fujimaki, M. W., 176, 177, 357
Fukazawa, T., 176, 234
Fukumi, H., 92
Fung, J., 100

Gaddis, A. M., 380
Galbreath, J. W., 178
Gallop, P. M., 169
Galloway, D. E., 176
Galton, M. M., 92
Gan, M. M., 414
Garribaldi, J. A., 232
Garrigan, D. S., 150
Garrow, J. S., 48
Gee, I., 153
Gehring, F., 102

Geiduschok, P., 121
Geiger, E., 98, 201, 202, 422
Geiger, S. E., 190
Geoghegan, M. J., 333
Georgiev, G. P., 404
Gergeley, J., 167, 172
Gerke, C. W., 119
Gery, I., 98
Giddey, C., 330, 337, 341
Gilbert, J. H., 49
Gilbert, K. V., 176
Gillespy, T. G., 110
Girao, C. B., 462
Girard, P., 97
Gladilin, N., 249
Gleeson, P. A., 141, 148, 150, 155, 160, 161
Godden, W., 143
Goertz, G. E., 179
Goldblith, S. A., 112, 113
Goldstein, S., 306
Golenkov, V. F., 284
Goll, D. E., 148, 175, 176, 177
Golley, F. B., 56
Golueke, C. J., 332
Gonet, P., 102
Good, R. A., 463
Gooding, E. G. B., 116, 117
Gopalan, C., 297
Gordon, J. F., 328-343
Gordon, J. N., 57
Gordon, M., 406
Gordon, R. S., 471
Gordzierkie, L. N., 178
Goresline, H. E., 112
Goryunova, S. V., 337
Gotthard, R. M., 175
Gould, I. A., 90, 375
Gould, R. F., 328
Goulding, R., 81, 82
Grady, G. F., 93
Graham, G. G., 48
Graham, J. S. D., 286, 287
Graham, M., 188
Graham, P. P., 157
Grainer, R. B., 296
Grant, E. M., 94
Gray, W. J., 150
Greathouse, T. R., 150
Greaves, J. P., 32-44
Green, S. H., 53

Greengard, O., 406, 422
Greer, E. N., 308
Gregory, P. W., 150
Grifo, A. P., 152
Grindley, H. S., 380
Griswald, R. M., 147
Griswold, R., 382
Groniger, H. S., 187
Groomes, R. J., 399
Guadagni, D. G., 194
Guenther, J. J., 154, 156
Guezennec, J., 97
Guggenheim, K., 50
Guilberg, R., 466
Guilbert, H. R., 150
Gulasekharam, J., 92
Gunderson, M. F., 108
Gustavson, K. H., 121, 382
Gutter, E., 283
Guttman, A., 116
Gwynne, M. D., 56


Hadjimarkos, D. M., 75
Haffenreffer, U. K., 418
Hagelberg, G. B., 55
Haines, R. B., 91, 102
Halac, E., 422
Hale, H. P., 121, 228, 232
Hale, W. S., 384
Hall, H., 347
Hall, H. E., 94
Hall, P., 354
Hall, R. L., 366
Hall, W. H., 90
Halsall, H. B., 120
Halstead, B. W., 73
Halsted, J. A., 465
Hamaguchi, K., 121
Hamilton, T. S., 142
Hamm, R., 167-182, 374, 378, 380
Hammerle, O. A., 116
Hammond, J., 152
Hammond, R. J., 36
Hamoir, G., 208
Han, I. K., 141, 148, 150, 155, 160, 161
Hankins, O. G., 380
Hannan, R. S., 112

Hansard, S. L., 175
Hansen, B., 366
Hansen, P. I. E., 113
Hanson, H. L., 114, 239
Hanson, J., 167, 172
Hanssen, E., 283
Hardy, W. B., 228
Harkins, R., 357
Harper, A. E., 417-445
Harper, J. E., 148
Harries, J. M., 163
Harrington, R. B., 149, 162
Harris, H., 462
Harris, R. S., 267
Harrison, D. L., 179, 180
Harrison, G., 149
Hart, E. W., 462
Harz, C. O., 286
Hashimoto, Y., 179, 181, 193, 382
Hasseltine, C., 346
Hauge, S., 92
Hauschild, A. H. W., 92
Hause, N. L., 457
Havre, G., 68
Hawley, H. B., 221
Hay, J. M., 117
Hayami, H., 338
Hazel, L. N., 148
Hazeleus, M. H., 148
Heard, C. R. C., 418
Heckelmann, H., 92
Hegarty, G., 355
Hegsted, D. M., 267, 272, 273, 418, 450
Heiligman, F., 113
Heiman, V., 449
Heiss, R., 101
Helgebostad, A., 68
Hellendoorn, E. W., 181
Heller, C. L., 109
Henika, R. G., 304, 307
Hennings, C., 197
Henrickson, R. L., 119, 159
Henry, K. M., 53, 218, 219, 220, 221, 222
Hepburn, F. N., 292
Hepburn, W. R., 53
Herbert, R., 194
Hermier, J., 102
Herring, H. K., 173
Hess, K., 283, 284

Hesseltine, C., 347
Hetrick, J., 356
Hickling, C. F., 188
Hicks, S. J., 404, 406
Higginbottom, C., 221
Hill, D. C., 456, 457
Hill, F., 173
Hindak, F., 330, 338, 340
Hiner, R. L., 380
Hinks, C. J. M., 143, 144
Hinton, J. J. C., 246, 281, 285
Hird, F. J. R., 306
Hiscox, E. R., 221
Hobbs, B. C., 92, 97, 109, 233
Hobbs, G., 90, 91
Hochstrasser, K., 294
Hodgkiss, W., 90, 91
Hoekstra, W. G., 175
Hofmann, K., 50, 179
Hogan, A. G., 296
Hoke, I. M., 379
Holdsworth, S. D., 102
Hollingsworth, D. F., 32-44
Holme, J., 120
Holmes, W., 149
Holt, L. E., 53, 218, 422, 455
Holzapffel, D., 91, 102
Hood, M. P., 379
Hooft, C., 463
Hopkins, J. W., 230
Hornicke, H., 144, 157, 162
Hornstein, I., 379
Hoseney, R. C., 293
Hospelhorn, V. D., 137
Houston, J., 220
Howard, H. W., 218
Howe, E. E., 267
Howgate, P. F., 201, 205
Hoyle, R. J., 188
Hsu, S., 92
Hubbard, A. W., 163
Huey, E., 294
Hughes, R. B., 188, 189, 193, 382
Huggins, C., 132, 137, 231
Hulse, J. H., 310
Hunt, G. E., 142
Hunt, S. M. V., 117
Hurlbut, T. A., 42
Hutchinson, J. B., 218, 291, 293
Huxley, H. E., 167, 172
Hvidt, S., 469

Idler, D. R., 189
Ikeda, S., 368
Indira, K., 53
Ingham, H. R., 94
Ingraham, J. L., 108
Ingram, M., 89, 90, 93, 101, 108, 111, 112
Inklaar, P., 355
Iodice, A. A., 176
Ironside, J. I. M., 188
Irukayama, K., 85
Irvine, L., 381
Ishukov, V. P., 179
Isnardi, P., 347
Isobe, S., 338, 340
Issa, J. A., 94
Ito, T., 92
Ivankovic, S., 68
Ivocic, M., 177
Iwanami, S., 92

Jackson, T. H., 380
Jacob, J., 97
Jacob, S. T., 407, 408
Jacquot, R., 188
Jadin, J., 92
Jaffray, J. I., 189
Jangaard, P. M., 188
Jansen, G., 356, 359
Jansen, G. R., 267, 272
Jansen, J. D., 97
Jay, J. M., 181
Jeffay, H., 414
Jekat, F., 245, 247, 249, 250, 340
Jeljaszcwicz, J., 90
Jenness, R., 373
Jennings, A. C., 285, 287, 383
Jensen, E. V., 132, 137, 231
Jensen, L. B., 90, 91
Jepson, J. B., 462
Jesudion, G., xv
Joffe, A. Z., 94
Johar, D. S., 53
Johnels, A., 83
Johnson, B. C., 266
Johnson, B. L., 182
Johnson, D. 353
Johnson, D. E., 141, 148, 150, 155, 160, 161
Johnson, R., 358

Johnson, V. A., 51
Johnston, B., 42
Johnston, C. S., 341
Johnston, E. H., 404
Johnston, J. W., 367
Jojo, W., 52
Joly, M., 137, 138
Jones, E. A., 468
Jones, C. R., 282
Jones, G. B., 92
Jones, J. D., 454
Jones, J. H., 148
Jones, N. R., 189, 190, 191, 192, 193, 194, 195, 382
Joo, Y. D., 141, 148, 150, 155, 160, 161
Joos, R. W., 90
Jorgensen, J., 338, 343
Josephson, D. V., 373, 374
Judd, D. B., 366
Judge, M. D., 149, 162, 175
Juliano, B. O., 295
Jury, K. E., 105, 151, 153

Kade, C. F., 218
Kaess, G., 176
Kajdi, C. N., 422
Kamer, J. H. van de, 98
Kandatso, M., 176
Kastenschmidt, L., 175
Katz, D. P., 42
Kawahara, K., 138
Kawai, F., 338
Kawamura, Y., 368
Kay, H. D., 229
Kay, M., 163
Kazemsaru, B., 102
Kekomaki, M., 471
Keller, E. C., 335
Kelley, J., 354
Kelly, C. B., 92
Kelly, T. R., 190
Kemmerer, K. S., 218
Kemp, J. D., 150, 158
Kendall, D. A., 370
Kennay, F. T., 407
Kennedy, G. C., 48
Kent, N. L., 280-297
Kent-Jones, D. W., 384
Kepcija, D., 180

Kerr, D. E., 93
Khan, A. W., 177, 237, 238
Khawk, T., 460
Khoo, U., 287
Kidwell, J. F., 147, 148
Kies, C., 340, 343
Kiessig, H., 283
King, F. J., 205, 206
King, K. W., 53
King, M. E., 340
King, N. R., 232
Kirk, W. G., 148
Kirton, A. H., 144
Kjeldsen, K., 469
Klezskowski, A., 130
Kline, F. A., 148
Kline, L., 231
Klink, M., 255
Klinkowski, M., 251
Klose, A. A., 239
Klotz, I. M., 121
Knobl, G. M., 116
Knox, W. E., 422
Kobalake, Y., 338
Koch, R. B., 332
Kodama, A., 171
Koff, R. S., 93
Kofranyi, E., 219, 245, 247, 249, 250, 340
Koger, M., 148
Kohman, H. A., 302
Kok, B., 334
Kominz, D. R., 171
Kon, S. K., 217, 218, 219, 220, 221, 222
Koonz, C. H., 380
Koppang, N., 68
Korner, A., 406
Kosikowski, F. W., 374
Kostyk, N., 102
Kott, Y., 333
Kotula, A. W., 176
Koyanagi, O., 357
Krakoff, I., 69
Kratochvil, P., 137
Kraut, H., 248, 252, 253
Kristofferson, K., 375
Krober, O., 347
Kroger, D., 147, 148
Kropf, D. H., 180
Kudo, Y., 92

Kuipers, F. C., 93
Kuninori, T., 307
Kunkle, L. E., 152
Kurtzman, C. H., 379
Kushmerick, M. J., 177
Kwolek, W., 347

Lainé, B., 317
Laing, W. B., 93
Lamming, G. E., 150, 152
Landman, W. A., 119
Lang, K., 248
Lanteaume, M. T., 97
Lapanje, S., 138
Larkin, J. M., 102
Laster, L., 471
Lataste-Dorolle, C., 113
Latuasan, J. M., 97
Lavers, C. G., 115
Lawes, J. B., 49
Lawrence, J. M., 294
Lawrie, R. A., 118, 144, 147, 158, 167,
    173, 175, 176, 177, 178, 179, 181,
    233
Lea, C. H., 119, 218, 220, 221, 222,
    235
Lechowich, R. V., 93, 105
Ledger, H. P., 56
Lee, B., 294
Lee, S. K., 336, 339, 340, 343
Legroux, R., 97
Lehman, A. J., 80
Lein, A. H., 187
Leistner, L., 90, 92
Leitch, I., 36, 143
Le Magnen, J., 367
Leonard, J., 342
Leone, D. E., 332
Lerke, P., 91
Leung, P. M. B., 418, 419, 432, 436
Levaditi, J., 97
Leveille, G. A., 338, 340
Levenson, S. M., 467
Levi, A. J., 98
Levi, J. D., 317
Levine, B. B., 66
Leweke, D. H., 296
Lewin, E., 116
Lewis, D., 162, 448-457
Lewis, H. B., 218

Lewis, J., 31
Lewis, K. H., 93
Licht, P., 209
Lidvall, E. R., 152
Lie, J. L., 96
Lightbody, H. D., 115
Lightwood, R., 460
Lijinsky, W., 70
Liljedahl, S. O., 466
Lilley, J. R., 98
Lindgren, D. L., 80
Lineweaver, H., 110, 114, 232, 239,
    379
Ling, E. R., 217
Ling, G. N., 122
Linko, R. R., 178
Lisle, D. B., 303
Liston, J., 92, 102, 113
Little, A. C., 366
Little, H., 114
Little, W. T., 190
Llewelyn, D. A. B., 57, 317
Lodge, G. A., 141-163
Loebel, W., 54
Lofröth, G., 84, 86
Loken, K. I., 100
Long, F. E., 101
Longenecker, J., 358, 457
Looy, G. van, 92
Lopez, A., 114, 115
Loughridge, L. W., 462
Love, R. M., 96, 177, 188, 208, 210
Lovelock, J. E., 114
Lovern, J. A., 114, 187, 188, 190, 202,
    203
Lowe, B., 375
Lowe, M., 126, 128, 132
Lucas, I. A. M., 144, 162
Lugay, J. C., 295
Lumley, A., 190
Lundgren, H. P., 138
Lusena, C. V., 114
Luyet, B. J., 121
Lyerly, P. J., 148

Mabbitt, L. A., 98
McCallum, W. A., 189
McCance, R. A., xvi, 39, 48, 291, 293,
    403
McCarthy, K., 370

McCollum, J. P. K., 94
McConnell, J. D., 59
McCormick, D. B., 404
McCormick, J. S., 147
McDermott, E. E., 289, 292
McDonald, I., 159, 160
McDowell, M. E., 338, 340, 343
McIntosh, E. N., 236
McKenzie, H. A., 208
Mackey, A. V., 368
Mackie, I. M., 205
McKinney, G., 366
McLaughlan, J. M., 436
McLean, W. R., 93
McLeod, N. A., 152
McManus, W. R., 141, 148, 150, 155, 160, 161
McMeekan, C. P., 158, 159, 162
McNab, J. G., 317
Macrae, H. F., 176
Macuch, P., 112
Maddox, L. A., 148
Madsen, R., 68
Magar, N. G., 205
Magee, P. N., 68, 69
Magee, W. T., 147
Magwood, S. E., 100
Mahl, H., 283
Mahmoud, S. A. Z., 102
Maier, V. P., 381
Maillard, L. C., 107, 119
Main, M. J., 176
Maloiy, G. M. O., 56
Malortie, R., 190
Mameren, J. van, 93
Mannan, A., 187
Maramatsu, K., 422
Marion, W. W., 176, 434
Marquardt, P., 77
Marshall, P. G., 229
Marth, E. H., 96
Martin, H. H., 90
Martin, T. G., 149, 162
Martin, W., 358
Martin, W. G., 230
Maruyama, K., 171
Masaki, T., 171
Mason, J. O., 9
Masurovsky, E. B., 113
Matches, T. R., 113
Mateles, R. I., 57, 335

Matheson, N. A., 117
Matsumoto, H., 307
Matsunaga, N., 343
Matsuno, N., 338, 340
Mattern, P. J., 51
Matthern, R. O., 332
Mattick, A. T. R., 221
Mattoni, R. H. T., 335
Matz, S. A., 369
Maxwell, M. L., 370
Mayer, J., 422
Mecham, D. K., 306, 383
Mechi, E. P., 379
Meehan, J. J., 231
Meesemaecker, R., 111
Mehrlich, F. P., 102
Meier, R. L., 334, 335
Mellinkoff, S., 437
Melville, J., 307
Mendel, L. B., 266, 449
Mendelsohn, J. M., 194
Menzel, D. B., 208
Menzi, R., 330, 337, 341
Merrill, A. L., 226, 227, 246, 248
Merritt, C., 112
Mertz, E. T., 296
Meryman, H. T., 114, 207
Meyer, E. W., 346-360
Meyer, H., 149
Meyer, K. F., 110
Michael, A. F., 463
Michel, M., 467
Michelson, J. T., 42
Michener, H. D., 108
Mickelsen, O., 71
Miles, K. L., 163
Miller, D. S., 9, 41, 450
Miller, G., 460
Miller, W. G., 239
Milne, M. D., 98, 462
Milner, H. W., 329, 332, 333, 335
Ministry of Health, xiii, 38
Minor, L. J., 379
Misani, F., 69
Mitchell, H. H., 142, 449, 450
Mitra, K., 219
Mitrovic, M., 249
Mitsuda, H., 338
Miyada, D. S., 381
Miyoshi, T., 340
Mizel, M. D., 383

Mizrahi, S., 347, 348, 356, 357
Mocquot, G., 102, 112
Mohammed, A., 383
Mol, J. H. H., 102
Mommaerts, W. F. H. M., 183
Monaselidze, D. R., 137
Moncrief, R. W., 386
Monier-Williams, G. W., 75
Monsey, J. B., 233
Monson, W. J., 218
Moody, W. G., 158
Moore, S., 351
Moran, T., 115, 218, 291, 292
Morgan, D. P., 162
Morgan, P. M., 93
Moriamez, J., 92
Morimoto, K., 338
Morimura, Y., 343
Morrison, A. B., 69, 436
Morrison, R. D., 154, 156
Morton, R. K., 285, 286, 287, 383
Moser, H., 182
Mosher, A. T., 30
Mosley, J. W., 93
Mosovich, L., 54
Moss, H. J., 306
Mossel, D. A. A., 89-103
Motoc, D., 176
Mouton, R. F., 113
Mueller, A. J., 218
Mulder, H., 374
Mullens, A. M., 175
Munk, P., 137
Munro, H. N., 403-415
Munro, M. I., 452
Murphy, H. C., 51
Murray, C. W., 232
Murray, J., 190, 191
Muschel, L. H., 90
Muster, M. J., 94
Myers, J., 332, 333
Myrick, H. N., 335

Nagasaki, M., 92
Naismith, D. J., 409
Nakanishi, H., 92
Nakazado, M., 176
Nalbandov, A. V., 152
Nank, W. K., 105
Narayana, M., 245

Nash, A., 351, 352
Neale, G., 48
Necev, T., 177
Needham, D. M., 167
Neff, R., 450
Nelson, O. E., 296
Nemethy, G., 120
Nevels, E. M., 338, 343
Newbold, R. P., 175, 176
Nickerson, J. T. R., 91, 113
Nicodemus, Z., 52
Niederauer, Th., 284
Nielsen, H., 287
Nielson, A. J., 370
Nikkila, R., 178
Nikodemusz, I., 92
Niles, G. R., 92
Nishihara, A., 338, 340
Niven, C. F., 112
Noguchi, E., 210
Noguchi, T., 176
Nonaka, N., 379
Nonomura, Y., 171
Nord, F. F., 232
Noren, K., 86
Norman, J. R., 187
Norton, H. W., 150
Nyhan, W. L., 419, 422

Odell, A., 353
Oftebro, T., 94
Ogata, K., 404
Ogston, A. G., 135
Ohtsuki, I., 171
Oishi, K., 342
Okano, S., 194
Okitani, H., 176
Olaniyan, O., 149
Olcott, H. S., 208
Olhagen, B., 466
Olley, J., 208
Olsen, E. M., 456, 457
Olson, F. C., 142
Oram, J. D., 90
Orillo, C. A., 102
Osborne, L. W., 220
Osborne, T. B., 266, 449
Oser, B. L., 245, 450
Oski, F. A., 460
Oslage, H. J., 157

Osner, R. C., 177, 236, 237, 358
Oswald, W. J., 332
Overbeck, G., 255
Oyaert, W., 463

Pace, J., 218, 289, 291, 292, 293, 295, 304
Pader, M., 373
Pakhomova, M. V., 337
Paladines, O. L., 141, 148, 150, 155, 160, 161
Palk, B. A., 287, 383
Palmer, A. Z., 148
Palsson, H., 144, 158, 160
Pangborn, R. M., 366
Pao, B. R. H., xv
Pappas, S., 162
Pariser, E. R., 116
Park, D. C., 176
Parkinson, T. L., 229
Parks, O. W., 374
Parratt, J. R., 75
Parrish, F. C., 176
Parry, D. A., 365-384
Partmann, W., 177, 178, 190, 191
Partridge, S. M., 173
Passmore, R., 291
Patton, S., 373, 374
Paul, P. C., 179, 180
Pavlovski, P. E., 178
Payne, D. R., 9, 303
Payne, W. J. A., 56
Peacock, F. M., 148
Pearce, J. A., 115
Pearson, A. M., 147, 180, 355, 379
Pease, A. H. R., 142
Pederson, S. S., 91, 102
Peers, F. G., 246
Peeters, E. M. E., 97
Pelroy, G. A., 101, 113
Pence, J. W., 383, 384
Pendl, I., 169
Pennington, R. J., 176
Penny, I. F., 118, 176, 179
Penz, C., 177
Perheentupa, J., 471
Perigo, J. A., 101
Périssé, J., 41
Perry, R. P., 406

Perry, S. V., 172
Personius, C., 375
Perutz, M. F., 120
Petersburg, S. J., 454
Peterson, A. C., 108
Petunin, F. A., 317
Pfaffman, C., 367
Pflug, I. J., 101
Piez, K. A., 172
Pike, M. C., 48
Pipkin, A. P., 42
Pippen, E. L., 379
Piqué, J. J., 190
Pirie, N. W., 46-60
Pitt, T. K., 190
Pivnick, H., 101
Plank, R., 114
Plantin, L. O., 466
Platou, R., 357
Platt, B. S., 9, 49, 418
Platt, W. T., 370
Plimmer, R. H. A., 229
Plimpton, R. F., 152
Pollard, H. M., 471
Pomeranz, Y., 293, 356
Pomeroy, B. S., 100
Pomeroy, R. W., 143, 144, 147, 158, 159
Pool, M. F., 238
Pope, L. S., 154, 156, 159
Popov, V. I., 78
Porter, J. W. G., 217, 451
Postel, W., 246, 248
Potts, G. R., 74
Powell, R. C., 338, 343
Powrie, W. D., 114, 115, 178
Poysky, F. T., 93
Prescott, J. H. D., 150, 152
Pressey, R., 354
Preston, T. R., 55, 92, 152, 153
Preussmann, R., 68
Pribl, S., 330, 338, 340
Price, S., 367
Pringle, W., 310
Privalov, P. L., 137
Privett, O. S., 229
Probert, C. L., 150
Pronczuk, A. W., 406, 412
Przezbiecka, T., 180
Pueschel, C. M., 461
Pugachev, P. I., 179

Quinn, J. B., 180

Rackis, J., 347, 351, 358, 360
Radouco-Thomas, C., 113, 118
Raheja, K., 202
Rainier, L., 69
Raison, J. K., 286, 287
Ramamurti, K., 53
Ramanatham, G., 53
Ramel, P., 97
Ramsay, C. B., 152
Ramsbottom, J. M., 380
Randall, C. J., 176
Randolph, H. E., 90
Randolph, J. G., 98
Ranke, O. F., 248
Rao, G. R., 53
Rao, K. K. P. N., 200
Rao, U. S. B., 53
Raymond, S. A., 368
Raymond, W. D., 52
Reay, G. A., 190
Reber, E. F., 202
Redman, C. M., 294, 404
Redman, D. G., 306
Reich, H., 172
Reid, J. T., 141, 148, 150, 155, 160, 161
Reimann, H. A., 93, 109
Reissig, H., 251
Reiter, B., 90
Resseler, J., 92
Reuter, K., 114
Revusky, S., 59
Rey, L. R., 317
Reyes, A. C., 295
Reynolds, T. M., 119
Rhee, R. van, 101
Rhodes, D. N., 111
Ribbons, D. W., 338, 339
Richards, E., 360
Richards, E. G., 208
Richardson, A., 74
Richter, G. H., 374
Riedel, L., 114
Riemann, H., 111
Riesen, W. H., 218
Riggs, J. K., 148
Ritchie, E. D., 97
Ritchie, J. A. S., 35

Ritchie, J. M., 97
Rivenson, S., 179
Roberts, R. C., 109
Roberts, T. A., 93, 100
Robertson, I., 210
Robinson, D. S., 232
Robinson, D. W., 162
Robinson, T., 74
Robson, N., 176
Robson, R. N., 177
Roburn, J., 81, 82
Rock, H., 355
Roeder, G., 90
Roels, O. A., 102
Rogers, P. J., 179
Rogers, Q. R., 418, 419, 422, 432, 436
Rohdenburg, E. L., 267, 291
Rohrlich, M., 284
Rolfe, E. J., 107-122
Romanoff, A. J., 232, 276
Romanoff, A. L., 232, 276
Rongey, E. H., 169
Ronsivalli, L. J., 102
Rooney, L. W., 295
Roos, B., 93
Rosenberg, H. R., 291
Rosenfield, D., 266-279
Rosenoer, V. M., 468
Rosham, R. Th., 93
Ross, M. H., 420
Rowe, D. S., 127
Rowinski, P., 113
Roy, J. H. B., 144
Rozansky, R., 98
Rubenthaler, G., 356
Rubin, M., 367
Rudman, J. E., 153
Russell, F. E., 94
Ruys, A. C., 92
Rzhanova, G. N., 337


Sadanaga, K., 51
Saffle, R., 174, 177
Saisithi, P., 102
Sajdel, E., 407, 408
Sakai, S., 92
Sakanishi, M., 181
Sakazaki, R., 92
Salton, M. R. J., 232
Salwin, H., 194, 376

Samuelsson, E. G., 213
Sanderson, M., 378
Sandford, S., 31
Sarrett, H., 357, 358
Sastry, L. V. S., 295, 297
Sauberlich, H. E., 338, 340, 423
Savic, I., 180
Sawant, P. L., 205
Saxen, L., 471
Scarisbrick, R., 152
Schade, A. L., 90
Schantz, E. J., 341
Scharpf, L. G., 176, 234
Schick, R., 251
Schlosberg, H., 366
Schmahl, D., 68
Schmidt, C. F., 93, 105
Schmidt, J. W., 51
Schmit, J. A., 229
Schram, E., 351
Schuphan, W., 245-264
Schut, J., 355
Schwanitz, F., 260
Schweigert, B. S., 218, 379
Schwerdtfeger, E., 245, 247, 264
Scott, W. J., 90, 107
Scrimshaw, N. S., 268, 346
Scriver, C. R., 461
Seaman, J. P., 101, 113
Sedlacek, B., 137
Seifer, S., 169
Selmi, F., 96
Sesame, H., 351
Shabanova, V. A., 179
Shacklady, C. A., 317-326
Shallenburger, R. S., 367
Shannon, G., 347
Sharp, J. G., 116, 119
Shattock, H. T., 307
Shaw, B. G., 194, 246
Shea, K. G., 112
Shearer, A. R., 93
Shefner, A. M., 340
Shelby, C. E., 148
Sheldon, W., 460
Shelton, L. R., 399
Shepherd, J., 409, 411
Shepherd, J. R., 218
Sherwood, H. P., 92
Shewan, J. M., 90, 91, 113, 190 192, 193, 194, 202

Shikanai, T., 338
Shino, K., 338
Shore, L. E., 367
Shotwell, O., 347
Shrimpton, D. H., 225-240
Shubik, P., 70
Shwachman, H., 460
Sidransky, H., 418
Siebert, G., 190
Siegel, B., 66
Silverman, M. P., 57
Sim, A. K., 284
Simidi, W., 209
Simpson, S. J., 194
Sinclair, W. B., 80
Singh, N., 53
Sipos, E., 189
Sipos, J. C., 354
Sizaret, F., 41
Sjorstrom, L. B., 366, 379
Sjöstrand, B., 83
Skinner, E. Z., 369
Slanetz, L. W., 92
Slavin, J. W., 102
Sloane, H. S., 380
Sly, D., 351, 352, 354
Smith, A., 347, 349, 351
Smith, J. A. B., 213-223
Smith, J. H. C., 332, 333
Smith, M. A., 406
Smith, M. B., 208, 231
Smith, M. E., 109, 232
Smith, R. T., 146
Smoluchowski, M., 127, 131, 134
Snell, E. E., 404
Snoeck, J., 463
Snyder, D. G., 116
Snyder, H. E., 169
Snyderman, S. E., 53, 455
Sohier, Y., 111
Solee, R. E., 100
Souci, S. W., 248, 252, 253
Spencer, R., 194
Sperring, D. D., 370
Spies, J., 351
Spiher, A. T., 102
Spoehr, H. A., 329, 332, 333, 335
Spooner, E., 180
Spooner, M., 355
Spragg, S. P., 120
Sprague, E. C., 380

501

Squires, B. T., 50
Sreenivasan, A., 245, 247
Stanley, K. W., 92
Stansby, M. E., 187, 194
Stant, E. G., 149, 162
Steffee, C. H., 437
Steggerda, F., 360
Steinberg, M. A., 194
Steiniger, F., 92
Sterk, V. V., 98
Sterling, C., 381
Sterling, K., 465
Stevens, D. J., 292
Stevenson, J. A. F., 50
Stewart, B. A., 304, 307
Stewart, P., 306
Stewart, R., 357
Stewart, R. J. C., 49, 418
Stillings, B. R., 202
Stokes, J. L., 102, 108
Stolk, A. C., 102
Stonaker, H. H., 148
Strandine, E. J., 380
Street, G., 53
Stromer, M. H., 175
Stroud, G. D., 190, 191
Stroud, J. W., 141, 148, 150, 155, 160, 161
Stucki, W. P., 423
Subrahamanyan, V., 245
Sugihara, T. F., 231
Sulzbacher, W. L., 379
Surkiewicz, R. F., 399
Sutton, R. G. A., 92
Suzuki, A., 176
Suzuki, M., 368
Swaminathan, M., 245
Swanson, C. O., 302
Swartz, B. L., 93
Swecker, F. F., 100
Swenson, A. C., 379
Swift, C. E., 181
Szavini, L. M., 179
Szezesniak, A. S., 369, 370
Szent-Györgyi, A. G., 169, 172
Szmelcman, S., 50

Takagi, M., 404
Takagi, O., 176
Takahashi, K., 234

Talbot, L. M., 56
Talbot, M. H., 56
Talley, F., 379
Tamiya, H., 333, 343
Tamura, A., 338
Tamura, E., 338, 340
Tamura, K., 92
Tanford, C., 128, 130, 138
Tannenbaum, S. R., 57, 335
Tansy, M. F., 98
Tapley, D. F., 132, 137, 231
Tappel, A. L., 381
Tarenenko, G. A., 317
Tarladgis, B. G., 180
Tarr, H. L. A., 111, 190
Tatton, J. O'G., 81, 82
Taub, F. B., 335
Tavill, A. S., 468
Taylor, D. J., 119, 226, 230
Taylor, J., 97
Taylor, J. C., 153
Taylor, W., 85
Teague, H. S., 152
Teal, J. M., 208
Tejning, S., 84
Telford, E., 388-399
Templeman, W., 188, 190
Tennant, B., 367
Terayama, T., 92
Ternan, P. R., 148
Terra, G. J. A., 52
Terracini, B., 69
Terrell, E. E., 51
Thaker, 333, 335
Thatcher, F. S., 101, 112
Theil, P. H. van, 93
Theriault, R. J., 340
Thomas, A. W., 115
Thomas, H. R., 157
Thomas, K., 245
Thompson, S. Y., 221
Thomson, J. S., 119
Thomson, S., 92
Thornley, M. J., 90, 113
Thurston, C. E., 187
Tibbets, C. D., 42
Timmermans, J., 463
Tissier, M., 97
Tkačev, I. F., 317
Todd, J. R., 317
Tolstowska, A., 180

Tombs, M. P., 126-138
Tomlinson, N., 190
Tomsich, M., 93
Tonge, J. I., 94
Townes, P. L., 460
Townsend, C. T., 110
Tremolieres, J., 365
Triant, J. W., 412
Trochou, P., 92
Trowbridge, E. A., 381
Tsen, C. C., 307
Tsuchiya, K., 343
Tuck, R. H., 20-31
Tulloh, N. M., 147, 154, 161
Tyrrell, H. F., 141, 148, 150, 155, 160, 161
Tyszkiewicz, I., 179
Tyszkiewicz, St., 179

Uesaka, S., 333, 336
Ulstrom, R. A., 463
Ulyatt, M. J., 144
United Nations, xiv, 39, 43, 55, 273, 346
Usborne, W. R., 158

Vail, G. E., 378, 381
Valassi, K., 368
Van den Berg, L., 177, 178, 237, 238
Van den Brock, C. J. H., 111
Van den Hende, Ch., 463
Van der Leuval, F. A., 116
Van der Merue, R. P., 116
Vandore, J. F., 380
Van Etten, C., 351
Van Niekerk, B. D. H., 141, 148, 150, 155, 160, 161
Van Oorschot, J. L. P., 334
Van Swaaij, W. P. M., 333
Vas, K., 112
Vaz-Portugal, A., 467
Veen, A. G. van, 97, 102
Velaudapillai, T., 92
Venturella, V. S., 98
Verdcourt, L. D., 56
Verges, J. B., 144, 158, 160
Verma, S. K., 219
Vernet, C., 317
Verney, E., 418

Vernon, E., 399
Villavicencio, O., 98
Vincent, L. E., 80
Vincent, W. A., 331, 332
Vipperman, P. E., 157
Virupaksha, T. K., 295, 297
Visakorpi, J. K., 471
Vitale, J., 422
Viteri, F., 54
Voit, C., xiv
Von Hippel, P. H., 120
Von Scramlik, E., 367
Voss, R., 375
Voyle, C. A., 118, 173

Wachs, A. M., 333
Wagner, J. R., 69
Waite, R., 221
Waldmann, T. A., 466, 471
Waldschmidt-Leitz, E., 294
Wall, J. S., 287
Wallace, L. R., 143, 144, 156, 159.
Ward, B. Q., 92
Ward, W. H., 232
Warwick, B. L., 153
Wasserman, A. E., 379
Wassink, E. C., 334
Waterlow, J. C., 48, 53
Waterman, J. J., 114, 190
Watson, D. M. S., 160
Watson, S. A., 296
Watt, B. K., 226, 227, 246, 248
Weatherwax, J. R., 81, 286
Webb, N. B., 175
Wedgwood, R. J., 90
Weidemann, J. G., 176
Weijers, H. A., 98
Weiner, G., 148
Weinmann, I., 247, 248, 249, 251
Weir, C. E., 380
Weiss, K. F., 94
Wellington, G. H., 141, 148, 150, 155, 160, 161
Wender, I., 57
Westerdijk, J., 89
Westermark, T., 83
Westgarth, D. R., 451
Weston, D. R., 42
Westöo, F., 86
Westöo, G., 85

Wetterfors, J., 466
Wheeler, S. S., 147
Whitaker, J. R., 175, 176
White, E. C., 239
White, J. C. D., 218, 220, 222
Whitney, R., 353
Widdowson, E. M., xvi, 39, 48, 291, 293, 403
Wieler, D. I., 93
Wierenga, A., 179, 180
Willey, N. B., 148
Williams, A., 310
Williams, A. P., 451
Williams, D. R., 148, 163
Williams, J., 90, 230, 232
Wilson, B. J., 94
Wilson, D. L., 269
Wilson, P. N., 159
Wiseblatt, L., 384
Wissler, R. W., 437
Witzenhausen, R., 90
Wochner, R. D., 471
Wogan, G. N., 70
Wolf, J., 102
Wolf, M. J., 287
Wolf, W., 351, 352, 354, 358
Wong, K. Y., 120
Wong, N. P., 194
Wood, H., 187
Wood, J. D., 141, 148, 150, 155, 160, 161
Wood, P. C., 94
Woodham, A. A., 53
Woodworth, R. S., 366
Woolridge, F. L., 437

Worcester, J., 450
Working, E. B., 302
Wunner, W. H., 410
Wünsche, J., 245
Wurtman, R. J., 415
Wyszecki, G., 366
Wyzan, H. S., 218

Yahl, K. R., 296
Yamada, K., 317
Yang, M. G., 71
Yaron, A., 347, 348, 358
Yarrell, W., 189
Yasui, T., 176, 179, 181, 234
Yates, J. R., 306
Yoshida, A., 418, 436
Yoshida, K., 338
Yoshimo, H., 368

Zahgi, S. de, 54
Zaio, A., 181
Zeller, M., 102
Zelter, S. Z., 467
Zender, R., 113
Zenner, S. F., 304
Zen-Yoji, H., 92
Ziemba, J., 353
Zillinsky, F. J., 51
Zimmermann, G., 356, 357, 359
Zoltowska, A., 180
Zuber, M. S., 296
Zuolaga, G., 179

# SUBJECT INDEX

Aberdeen Angus, as meat producer, 147

Abnormalities, protein metabolism, 458-472

Absorption,
  amino acids, protein synthesis, 410-412, 415
  proteins, 458

Accelerated Freeze-Drying (AFD), 117, 118

Acceptability,
  of algal protein, 338, 341-343
  enhanced by cooking, 373
  of novel foods, 59, 338
  of protein foods, 365-384
  simulated proteins, 475

Actin, 168-171, 174-176, 179, 181, 205-206, 234

Actinins, 171, 206

Actinomycin, D, inhibition of ribose nucleic acid synthesis, 406, 411

Actomyosin, 169, 171, 176, 177

Adrenalin, inducer of high pH, 113, 118

Advantages, of unicellular algae in protein production, 329-332

Aflatoxin, 94, 96, 347

Age,
  animal, and collagen structure, 173
  and growth rate, 143-146, 153-158, 161
  and poultry composition, 234

Ageing,
  and meat toughness, 175-177, 381
  in poultry, 234-237

Agene, 69

Aggregates, of protein in processing, 119-122, 126-131, 133-135, 137, 209

Aggregation, spherical, of protein, 137

Air-drying, 115, 116

Albumin,
  bovine serum, 126, 135, 136

Albumin–*cont.*
  bovine serum and gel structure, 135, 136
  of cereals, 283, 294
  egg, 272
  in milk, 214
  serum, loss in gastro-intestinal diseases, 466
  mode of synthesis, 404-406
  soya, 352

Algae, unicellular,
  difficulties of cultivation, 333
  digestibility, 340, 341
  growth control factors, 329-332
  mass culture, 332, 333
  as protein source, 328-343
  toxicity, 341

Allergies, proteins, 469-472

Alpha-ice, 121

Aluminium, salts, egg protein stabilizers, 110

Amines,
  toxic, intestinal bacteria, 468
  toxicity, 74, 75

Amino acids,
  absorbed, protein synthesis, 411, 412, 415
  in algal protein, 330, 335-338
  availability, 451, 452
  in cereal fortification, 266-269, 272, 273, 275-277
  in cereals, variability, 290
  of cereals, and nitrogenous fertilizers, 294, 295
  combination with pesticides, 80
  composition of soya protein, 350, 351
  content in various dietaries, xvi, 6, 15, 249, 250
  convertibility by poultry, 226
  costs lowered, 276
  criteria of value, 451
  decarboxylation, and toxicity, 98

Amino acids—*cont.*
 deficiency and imbalance compared, 418, 419
 deficiency,
  and inhibition of protein synthesis, 410, 411
  and mortality, 437
 degradation rate, 422
 dietary evaluation difficulties, 448
 difficulties in evaluating needs, 453-455
 in egg proteins, 230
 evaluation of human needs, 456
 evalued as protein, 447-451
 evalued as such, 451-455
 excess, type of disproportion, 419
 excess ingestion, toxicity, 444, 445
 fortification, 41, 246
 free, variation in fish, 189, 193
 high protein intake, type of disproportion, 419, 420
 higher yields, from plants, 250
 homeostasis control scheme, 421, 442
 in hydrocarbon produced protein, 319
 imbalance, 297, 431-445, 449
  and excess compared, 433, 434
  offset by corticosteroids, 438
  offset by low temperature, 438-441
  type of disproportion, 418, 419, 431, 432
 inborn errors of metabolism, 464, 465
 increased by cultivar selection, 262, 263
 index, 245, 247-249, 251, 261
 interrelationship, and requirement, 454, 455
 limiting, sequential evaluation, 457
 lowered availability, in heated meat, 184, 185
 metabolic pathways, 463
 in milk proteins, 216-218
 needs in human dietaries, 455-457
 non-essential, 6
 in plant tissues, xiv, xv, 15, 249, 250
 plasma,
  homeostatic control, 417, 420-423, 435, 437, 442, 443

Amino acids—*cont.*
 plasma—*cont.*
  index of requirement, 456, 457
  and tissue levels, regulation, 420-423
 potato tuber, 255
 in poultry, 234, 235
 radioactive, elucidation of protein synthesis, 406, 408
 requirements, evaluation, 453-455
 surplus to requirement, 293
 toxicity, 423, 424, 431, 465, 477
 transport, diseases, 461-463
 wheat and flour compared, 291, 292
Amino aciduria, 422
α-Amylase,
 and dough formation, 304, 309, 310
 and pasteurization of egg, 233
Androgens, administration, and carcass composition, 152, 153
Animals,
 age, effect on growth rate, 143-146
 growth, on hydrocarbon produced protein, 318
 as protein converters, 55, 141-163
 relative growth rates, 143
 wild species under-exploited, 56
Anserine, in fish muscle, 192, 193
Antibiotics,
 in food preservation, 102
 and intestinal flora, 467
 as toxins, 65, 66, 69
Appearance,
 and eating quality of food, 366
 fish, in cooking, 382
 of food, in catering, 392, 393
Arachin, 126
Arginine, 262, 294, 454, 462, 468
Aromatics, in bread manufacture, 311
Ascorbic acid, as oxidizing improver of dough, 303, 305, 307
ATPase,
 of muscle, 170, 178, 205, 207, 237
 retention in freeze-drying, 117, 207
Autolysis, in fish, 192, 193
Avidin, 233
$A_w$, 90, 99, 100, 107, 108
Ayrshires, 214
Aztecs, algae as food for, 342

Bacteria,
    overgrowth in intestine, 468
    producing toxic amines, 97
Baking, 300-312
    eggs, used in, 109, 231
    flour quality, 292
    soya protein and flour, 356
Barley,
    amino acid content, 290
    nutrient yields, 258
Beans, soya, processing, 347-350
Beef, from range cattle, 146
Benzpyrene, 69
Beverages,
    protein enriched, 43, 246
    soya protein, 356, 357
Bioassay, in amino acid evaluation, 452
Biochemical individuality, 37, 48, 70
Biological value,
    cereal proteins, 291-297
    of hydrocarbon-produced protein, 326
    milk protein, 218-222
    plant proteins, 245, 249, 260, 261, 267
    proteins, general, 449-451
    soya protein, 358-360
Birth Control, 46
Birth rate, and protein shortage, 28, 29, 46
Bitterness,
    of algal protein, 343
    in fish, due to hypoxanthine, 194, 195
Blood,
    antimicrobial activity, 90
    composition, as nutritional index, 48
'Boar-taint', 152
Botulism, 93
Bran, 292
*Brassicaceae,* as protein source, 260-264
Bread,
    composition, produced by different methods, 311
    crumb structure, 303, 311
    fortification, 267, 268, 276, 277
    overworking, 307
    properties, by Chorleywood process, 310-312
    soya protein additives, 359

Bread—*cont.*
    widespread dietary, 300
Bread-making,
    Chorleywood process, 303, 304
    'Do-Maker' process, 302, 303
    methods, 301-305
    protein changes involved, 306
    simplified by Chorleywood process, 308
Breed,
    and meat production, 146-149
    and muscle growth, 146-149
Breeding, plant, high-yielding cultivars, 250, 251
Breeds, 'beef' v. 'dairy', as meat producers, 147
Bromate, in bread manufacture, 302, 304, 306
Browning,
    of heated meat, 180
    non-enzymic, 107, 111, 117, 119, 179, 222, 371
    factors affecting, 119
Bulk fermentation, in bread manufacture, 301
By-products, of soya protein isolates, 350

Cabbage,
    as protein source, 260-264
    structure, 261
Calories, relation to protein, 8, 10, 32, 33, 35, 38, 47, 418, 439-441
Calves, carriers of *salmonellae,* 92
Canning,
    fish, heat susceptibility, 111, 209
    and meat proteins, effect on, 179, 180
    of proteinaceous foods, 100
Carcass,
    composition, weight effects, 153-156, 161
    of cattle, chemical composition, 142-147, 152-156
    of pig, chemical composition, 141, 142, 157
    sheep, chemical composition, 148, 149
Carcinogens, 68, 69
Carnosine, in poultry muscle, 233

Caryopses, cereal, protein content, 246, 255-258
Casein, 214, 215, 216, 217, 269, 272
Cassava, potential use for bread-making, 310
Castration, and carcass lean, species difference, 150
Catering,
    advance preparation, 392, 393
    protein foods, 388-399
    types of, problems with proteins, 390, 391
Cattle,
    as protein producer, 56, 143-146
    sex effect on development, 150
Cell, cereal endosperm structure, 286, 287
Cereals,
    coeliac disease, 469, 470
    fortification, 266, 273, 277
    non-gluten, use for bread-making, 310
    protein properties, in cooking, 383
    protein, staling in catering, 388
    protein value, 14, 15, 38, 40, 41, 51, 246, 251, 255-258
    proteins, nutritional and structural properties, 280-297
Chain/sphere ratio, in protein aggregation, 133
Charollais, as meat producers, 147
Cheese, 219
    eating quality, 374, 375
    soya protein, 357
    tyramine toxicity, 74
'Chemicals', as food poisons, 67
Children, protein requirements, 9, 33, 35, 36, 41, 42, 47
Chilling,
    of poultry, 237
    as preservative process, 113
China, algae as food in, 342
Chlorella,
    amino acic composition, 336, 338
    growth conditions, 329
*Chlorophyceae,* protein producers, 328, 336, 338
Cholera, food-borne, 98
Ciguatera, poisoning, 73
Classification, by air, of flour particles, 284

*Cl. botulinum,* 93, 100, 102, 108, 110, 112
Clupeoids, chemical composition, 187, 188
Coconuts, source of protein, 53
Cod,
    composition, seasonal changes, 188
    myosin, processing susceptibility, 205
Codex Alimentarius, fish products, 186
Coeliac disease, 469-471
Cohesiveness, in freeze-dried poultry meat, 239
'Cold-shortening', in meat, 176
Collagen, 121, 172, 173, 180, 234, 235, 236, 238
    in cooking, 378-380, 381, 382
    in herring, 188, 209
Colostrum, composition, 214
Colour,
    and eating quality of foods, 366
    loss, in hot stored vegetable foods, 395
    of meat,
        in cooking, 378
        in freeze-drying, 179
        on irradiation, 181
Commercial sterility, 109
Conalbumin, 109, 231, 232
Concentrates, protein, in fortification, 266, 346
Connective tissue,
    fish, torn in *rigor mortis,* 191
    and meat toughness, 173
    proteins of, 172, 173, 177, 180
Contamination, of sea, 72
Contraception, and population increase, 46
Contraction,
    muscular, mechanism, 172
    *rigor mortis,* in fish, 191
Convenience foods, catering problems, 390, 394-396
Cooking,
    cheese texture, 375
    and enzyme inactivation, 113
    of fish, 381-383
    and meat proteins, effect, 179, 180
    protein properties important in, 370, 371
    of protein foods, 365-384

Cooking—*cont.*
  microwave, 396-398
    disadvantages in catering, 397, 398
    mode of action, 397
  partial, in food preparation, 393-395
  protein foods, methods, 371-373
Corn,
  fortification, 277
  high lysine varieties, 274
Corticosteroids,
  and amino acid imbalance, 438, 444
  and protein synthesis, 407, 408
Costs,
  of algal protein production, 334, 335, 340
  in catering, 390, 391
  of fish protein concentrates, 203
  of protein supplements, 273
Cottonseed, as protein source, 42, 54
Covalent links, in protein dissociation, 132
Crotoxin, 115
Cultivars,
  maize, protein value, 250
  potato, protein value, 251, 254
Curd, soya protein, 348, 357
Curing,
  changes of microflora, 91
  and meat proteins, 181
  and microbial spoilage, 100
  by smoke, and fish condition, 188, 209
Custards, egg protein involvement, 376, 377
*Cyanophyceae,* as protein producers, 328, 337, 338
Cysteine, 180, 181, 304-306, 338, 379
Cystic fibrosis, of pancreas, 459, 460
Cystine, 181, 217, 218, 221, 348, 453, 454, 461
Cystinuria, 462

Dairy products, soya protein, 356, 357
DDT, metabolism of, 81
Decimal reduction, value, 110
Defence mechanisms, against toxins, 70, 71

Deficiency,
  amino acids, as type of disproportion, 418
  mixed, protein/mineral, 247
  proteins, resistance to innovation, 474, 475
Dehydration,
  as preservative process, 115-118, 202
  in microwave cooking, 398
Demand, changing, for high quality protein, 21, 23
Denaturation,
  of fish proteins, 203-208
  of proteins, in cooking, 370, 371
  of proteins in processing, 119-122, 177, 178, 179
  reversibility, 120
Deoxyribosenucleic acid, hormonal control, 407
Desmosine, in elastin, 173
Deterioration, high temperature, in stored food, 395
Developing regions, stimulating production in, 27, 30, 52
Development,
  economic, protein production, 27, 30
  mechanical, advantages in breadmaking, 307-310
Diastase, in flours, 308, 309
Dielectrics, in cooking, 397
Diet,
  balanced, 8, 32, 37
  fortified, clinical assessment, 275
  supplementation, 14, 41, 218, 219
  U.K.,
    poultry in, 225
    variability, 37
Dietaries,
  amino acid requirements, 455-457
  contribution of cereal proteins, 280
  deficient, survival time, 437
  national, fish in, 200
  resistance to change, 365
  staple, fortification by amino acids, 266-279
Dietary habits, change of, xv, 36, 59, 202
Digestibility,
  of algal protein, 339, 340

Digestibility—*cont.*
  of hydrocarbon-produced protein, 323
  of meat, and processing, 179, 180
  of milk, after processing, 220, 221
Digestion, of proteins, 458, 459
Discoloration, in food storage, 392, 393
Diseases,
  amino acid transport, 461-463
  gastro-enteric, from proteinaceous foods, 92, 93
  microbial, 92-98
  protein-calorie deficiencies, 38, 39
  protein digestion, types, 458
  protein-losing, 465, 466
  protein metabolism, 458-472
Disorders, digestive enzymes, 459-461
Disproportion, amino acids, 417-445
  responses to, 423, 424
Distribution, proteins, improved, 474
Disulphide,
  in albumin aggregates, 132, 137
  and fibre formation by soya protein, 354
  interchange, in bread doughs, 306, 307
  in ovalbumin, 231
  in processed fish, 207
  in processed meat, 180
Dough,
  bulk fermentation, 301
  chemical development, 304, 305, 310
  factors in mechanical development, 303, 304
  mechanical development, 301-304
  mechanisms of formation and development, 305-307
  rheological features, 305-307
  softening, 305, 308
Dried foods, *salmonellae* content, 100
Drip, and frozen meat, 113, 114, 177, 178
Drying,
  of algal protein, 333, 339, 340
  in fish preservation, 201, 204, 207
  of milk, 220-222
  of protein foods, 372
  of soya protein, 349
Dulse, as food, 342

Eating quality,
  of algae, 341, 343
  and catering costs, 391
  in fish, 203
  in frozen storage, 392
  in meat, 141, 173, 174, 180
  in poultry, 236-240
  protein foods, 365-384
  in reheated foods, 396
  retention problems in catering, 394, 395
Ecology, and plant proteins, 245-264
Economics,
  of algal protein production, 332-335
  of hydrocarbon fermentation, 318
  of mechanical dough development, 308, 310, 312
  of production, 20-31
  and protein fortification, 267, 270-274
  of soya protein isolation, 351, 360
Efficiency, of protein production, unicellular algae, 329
Egg,
  proteins, differential heat susceptibility, 109, 110, 120
  substitute, 118
Eggs, 225-240
  anti-microbial defences, 90, 91, 232, 233
  blending, and cooking properties, 376
  chemical composition, 226, 228-233
  cooking methods, 376
  consumption in U.K., 225
  eating quality, 375-377
  freezing damage, 114, 115
  liquid, pasteurization, 109, 110
  mercury content, 85
  nutritive value, 226, 230
  production,
    pesticide effect, 80
    and protein from hydrocarbon, 322, 323
  protein, synthetic mechanism, 406
  washed, 232
  white of, 370
Elasticity, of bread doughs, 305
Elastin, 173, 234, 380

Electron microscopy,
  of cereal endosperm particles, 286
  for visualization of protein aggregates, 133
Emulsification, egg proteins, 377
Emulsion, stability and soya protein, 353, 355
Emulsions, from meat proteins, 174, 175, 181
Endosperm,
  fragmentation, 283-286
  mealy and vitreous, 289
  protein, 283, 284
Energy,
  animal intake, and usage, 159
  in diet, interaction with protein, 162
  level in diet, and pig growth, 162
Energy-protein interdependence, 8, 10, 32, 35, 39, 47
Enzymes,
  activation during freezing, 114
  amino acid degradation, 422, 434, 437, 439-441, 443
  digestibility of algal protein, 340
  digestive, disorders, 459-461
  in post-mortem fish spoilage, 190, 193
  in protein synthesis, 407
  proteolytic, 113, 115, 175-177
    in fish, 190, 193, 201
    in meat cooking, 381
  radiation resistance of, 112, 113, 181
Equilibrium, of amino acids, 403, 404
Equipment, for reheating food in catering, 396-398
Ethylene bromide, selective toxicity, 80
Evaluation, of amino acids, 448-457
Exploitation, of fishing grounds, 195
Extenders, soya protein, of meat products, 355
Extraction, of leaf protein, 53
Extractives, of fish, relation to spoilage, 192, 193

Fabricated foods, texture, 126-138, 246
Family, types, and diet, 38

FAO, 3, 9, 39, 40, 53, 67, 77, 86, 187, 273, 274, 310, 328
Fat,
  carcass of, and joint yield, 148
  carcass, relation to water, 157
  in carcass, species effect, 143
  depot distribution, with age and weight, 158
  emulsifying capacity, of meat, 174, 175, 181
Fattening, and plane of nutrition, 158, 159
Fatty acids,
  cheese flavour, 375
  in fish spoilage, 193, 206
Fecundity, animal, and protein production, 146
Feed, animal,
  conversion efficiency, 146
  direct, amino acid addition, 276
  from hydrocarbon, 317, 320-325
  sophisticated control, 24
Feed-back, in plasma protein control, 442-444
Feed, conversion, with hydrocarbon product protein, 321, 324, 325
Fermentation,
  algal, 331
  in cheese, 375
  dough, in bread-making, 301, 304
  hydrocarbon, toxicity tests, 318, 319
  and nutritive enhancement, 54, 118
  as preservative method, 102, 118, 203
Ferritin, synthesis, 405, 408, 409
Fertilizers,
  importance, 40
  nitrogenous,
    and cereal proteins, 294, 295
    protein yield from potato, 255, 259
Fibres,
  formation, soya protein, 353, 354
  muscle, in poultry, 233
Field trial, of enriched protein, Tunisia, 275, 276
Filleting,
  of fish, and eating quality, 190
  pre-rigor, and fish quality, 192

Fish,
   chemical composition, 187, 188
   classification, 187
   dehydrated, 116
   eating quality, 381-383
   factors affecting catch, 187
   fermented, 203
   freezer burn, 392
   freezing at sea, 191, 192, 195
   handling, and eating quality, 190
   marine biotoxins in, 73, 85
   meal, 96, 202
   microbial toxins in, 92, 93
   microwave cooking of, 397
   in national dietaries, 200
   nitrosamine in cured, 59
   preservation
      by canning, 111
      by chilling, 101
      by fermentation, 118
   protein concentrate, 73, 116, 118,
      202, 205
   proteins, and eating quality, 381,
      382
   as protein source, 19, 56, 57, 200
   quality, 186-197
   *salmonellae* in, 92
   smoked, carcinogens in, 70
   species variability of proteins, 201,
      209, 210
   unstable proteins, 203-208
   world catch, 187
Fishing, control needed, 195-197
Flakes, soya protein, 347
Flatulence, factor, in soya flour, 360
Flavour,
   of algal protein, 343
   of bread, 311
   of cheese, 375
   and eating quality of food, 367,
      368
   of fish, 189, 193-195, 382
   of meat, in cooking, 379, 380
   of soya protein, 353, 357
Flour,
   enzymes, in yeast cookery, 383
   extraction rate, and nutritive value,
      291, 292
   fish, solvent-extracted, 202, 203
   properties, 309, 310
   weak, utilized by Chorleywood
      process, 309

Flour—*cont.*
   wheat, particle size fractionation,
      283, 284
Fluctuations, daily, protein metabolism, 413-415
Foams,
   egg proteins, in cooking, 377
   soya protein, 354
Food additives, relative toxicity, 66,
   67, 96
Food, consumption, surveys, 6, 36, 226
Food poisoning, 89-102
Foods,
   frozen,
      equipment for handling, 391,
         392
      quality in catering, 391, 392
   intake,
      depression by excess amino
         acids, 423
      in methionine toxicity, 427
      plasma amino acid patterns,
         437, 438
   low allergen, 357
   part-cooked, in catering, 393, 394,
      395, 396
   protein, in different types of
      catering, 390, 391
   protein, organoleptic quality,
      365-384
   protein-rich, consumed in U.K.,
      225
   and protein synthesis, 410, 411,
      415
   spoilt by specific micro-organisms,
      89
   stock control in catering, 392
   textured, 353
Fortification, 41, 246, 266-279
   by amino acids and protein
      comparison, 271, 272
   of bread, resistance to, 268, 269,
      275
   dangers of, 476
   by soya protein, 359
Free Trade, and protein consumption,
   9
Freeze drying, 117, 118
   in fish preservation, 204, 205, 207
   fish protein changes, 207
   and meat protein, effect on, 178,
      179

Freeze drying—*cont.*
　of poultry, 238
Freezer burn, stored foods, 392
Freezing,
　of egg yolk, 228, 229
　fish, 191, 192, 194, 206
　and meat protein, effect on, 177,
　　178
　of poultry, 237-239
　as preservative process, 113-115,
　　177, 178
　protein foods, and standardization,
　　391
　rates of, 114, 177
Freezing damage, cause of, 114, 177,
　206
Freshness, fish, instrumental measure-
　ment, 197
Friesian, as meat producer, 147, 155,
　214
'F' value, 110

Gadoids, chemical composition, 187,
　188
'Gaping', of fish fillets, 192, 210
Gelatin, 380
Gelling,
　of egg proteins, 228, 232, 375-377
　of milk, 374
　of proteins, 126, 135, 136, 209,
　　370, 371
　of vegetable proteins, in cooking,
　　383
Gels, soya protein, 353
Genetics, and meat production, 143
Germany,
　kale as protein source, 247
　nitrite poisoning, 77
Gliadins (Prolamins), 283, 287, 383
Globulins,
　of cereals, 283, 294
　milk, sulphide formation, 374
　soya, 351, 352, 354
Glucose, enzymic removal from food,
　119
Glutamate, monosodium, 278, 379
Glutamic acid, 178, 293, 295
Gluten, 283, 284, 292, 294, 306, 307,
　312, 383, 384
　in cooking, 370

Gluten—*cont.*
　intolerance, 470
Glutenins (Glutelins), 283, 287, 307,
　383
Glycine, in methionine toxicity, 424,
　425, 428-430, 443, 445
Glycogen, reserves, and fish quality,
　189, 190, 209
Glycolysis, post-mortem,
　in fish, 190
　and meat proteins, 176
Gossypol, 54, 71
Grain, cereal, protein distribution,
　281-284
Grilling, of protein foods, 372
Groundnut, EM structure of gel and
　fibre, 135
Growth,
　algal, requirements, 332, 333
　amino acid imbalance, 418, 432,
　　433
　animal,
　　conflicting interpretation,
　　　158-160, 163
　　on hydrocarbon protein, 318,
　　　320
　　linear and curvilinear relation-
　　　ship, 156
　conditions, and poultry quality,
　　239, 240
　in methionine toxicity, 426, 443
　rate, in protein evaluation, 449,
　　450
Gutting, and fish quality, 190

Hake, in production of fish protein
　concentrate, 203
Halibut, 'chalky', 199, 200
Hartnup disease, 462, 463
Harvesting, of algal protein, 333
H-band, of muscle, 172
Heat, as antimicrobial agent, 100, 101,
　109-111
　on cheese, 375
　on eggs, 375-377
　on egg proteins in cooking, 375-377
　on meat, effect on toughness of,
　　380, 381
　on meat colour, 378
　on meat proteins, 179, 180

Heat—*cont.*
  on meat shrinkage, 379
  on micro-organisms, 109-111
  on milk, 374
  on milk products, 220, 221
Heating, microwave, 396-398
Hereford, lean content, age x weight effect, 154-156
Herring,
  nematodes in uncooked, 93
  meal, nitrosamines in, 68
Histamine, and food poisoning, 97, 462
Histidine, 97, 181, 433, 436, 444
Holstein, as meat producer, 147
Homeostasis, amino acids, upset by excessive intake, 445
Hong-Kong, soya beverage, 43
Hormones,
  administration and carcass composition, 152
  and amino acid imbalance, 438, 444
  and protein synthesis, 407
HTST, 110, 220
Hybrid maize, 296
Hydration,
  of biopolymers, 121
  in fish muscle, 189
Hydrocarbon, yeast growth, 317-326
Hydrogen sulphide,
  in fish spoilage, 193, 194
  in heated meat, 180
'Hydrotactoids', 121
Hygiene, Food Regulations for, 389, 390, 392
Hypoproteinaemia, 465, 466
Hypoxanthine, production in fish *post mortem*, 190

Ice-cream, 393
Iceland, carcinogenic, smoked food, 70
Ichthyosarcotoxism, 73
Imbalance, of amino acids, 297, 431-445
  correction, 432
  defined, 431
  preference pattern, 432
  protein synthesis, 412
Incaparina, 42, 277, 341

India,
  food fortification, 277
  protein concentrate, 43
  protein requirements in 1985, 12, 18
Indonesia, food fortification, 278
Infants,
  cystic fibrosis in, 460
  protein deficiency diseases, xv, 38
Infection, protein deficiency, 50
Infrastructure, and improved nutrition, 271
Inhibitors, of microbial growth, 102, 108, 109
Inosine, 193, 368
Insufficiency, pancreatic, 460
Intellect, impaired by protein deficiency, 49
Intestines,
  atrophy, in coeliac disease, 469
  defective amino acid transport, 462
Ionizing radiation,
  appropriate dose levels, 111, 112
  combination processes, 112, 113
  in food preservation, 87, 102, 103, 111-113
  and high-yielding wheat, 297
  and meat proteins, 181, 182
  potential toxin production, 87
Iraq, mercury intoxication, 84
Iron, in egg, 109

Japan,
  food fortification, 278
  use of seaweed, 342
'Jellied flesh', in fish, 188
Jelly, formation, reduction by soya protein, 355
Juiciness, meat, on cooking, 384

Kale,
  protein source, 247-249, 260-264
  structure, 260, 262-264
Kamaboko, gell strength affects quality, 209
Kernel, wheat, maturation changes, 285, 289
Kwashiorkor, xv, 49, 245, 276

514

Lactalbumin, intolerance, 471
Lactation, stage of, and milk protein, 215
Lactic acid, egg protein stabilizer, 110
*Lactobacillacae,* in cured foods, 91
β-Lactoglobulin, 214, 216
Lagoons, algal culture, 331, 332, 334
Landrace, growth rate, 149
Laverbread, as food, 342
Leaves, protein, 52, 53, 260-264
Legumes, 15, 42
Lettuce, amino acid increment, 264
Leucine/Isoleucine, 217, 254, 261, 406, 409, 411
Light,
    exclusion, and cabbage structure, 261
    on protein synthesis, 415
    wavelength, algal growth, 332, 334
Limestone, as carbon source, 57
Lipids,
    of eggs, 229, 230
    variability between fish species, 187
Lipovitellins, 229, 230
Low acid foods, 110
Lysine, 15, 40, 96, 180, 181, 217, 218, 222, 234, 246, 249-251, 256-258, 261, 262, 271, 272, 274, 276, 291, 295, 296, 359, 414, 450, 451, 454, 468, 476
    transport disease, 471
Lysozyme, 232

Madagascar, food consumption survey, 8
Maillard, reaction, 107, 111, 117, 119, 179, 222, 371, 384
Maize,
    amino acid content, 249, 290, 293, 296
    endosperm cell proteins, 287, 289
    grain, distribution of protein, 281
    high yielding hybrids, 15, 40
    potential use in bread-making, 310
Malabsorption,
    of amino acids, and deamination, 468, 469
    in coeliac disease, 469
    proteins, 459, 460
Marasmus, 245

Marketing, importance of, 35
Mastitis, 215, 216
Maturation,
    of bread doughs, 305
    of wheat grain, 285, 289
Maturity,
    age at, sex differences, 149, 150
    animal, and carcass composition, 148-150
Meat,
    analogues, soya protein, 353-356
    'bits', dehydrated, 355
    colour, in cooking, 378
    composition, 142, 144, 145, 149
    cured, alleged nitrosamine content, 69
    dehydrated, 116
    eating quality, 378-381
    fat-emulsifying capacity, 174, 181
    freeze-dried, 117
    freezer burn, 392
    freezing damage, 113, 114, 121, 122
    lean, index of, 141, 142
    off-odours in, 112, 152
    'pale, soft, exudative', 175
    parasite irradiation, 111
    preservation by chilling, 101
    production of,
        age effect, 143-146, 153-158, 161
        breed effect, 146-149
        sex effect, 149, 150
    as protein source, 18
    proteins of, mechanism of heat damage, 179, 180
    proteins, properties of, 167-182
    quality,
        and animal age, 158
        and muscle function, 172
        and muscle proteins, 175, 176
        and nutritional plane, 163
    shrinkage on cooking, 378-379
    spoilage by micro-organisms, 90, 91, 96, 100
    texture, and hydrocarbon-produced feed, 326
    toughness, in microwave cooking, 397
    water-holding capacity, 173, 174, 175, 178, 179, 181

Membrane,
    endoplasmic, protein synthesis, 405
    vitelline, 229
Mercaptans, in fish, spoilage, 194
Mercury,
    in dressed grain, 84
    traces in foodstuffs, 82-86
Meromyosin, 170, 179, 206
Messenger RNA, role in protein synthesis, 404, 405, 411, 412
Metabisulphite, in bread manufacture, 305, 307
Metabolism,
    proteins, 403-415
    tryptophan, 463
Methionine, 69, 180, 181, 217, 218, 230, 251, 256-258, 262, 319, 326, 338, 351, 357, 358, 423, 424-431, 453, 454, 463
    excess, effects, 424-431
    malabsorption disease, 463
    metabolism of, 430
    oxidation, stimulation by glycine, 428-430
Methylmercury, in Baltic fish, 86
Microbial spoilage, control principles, 98-103, 107, 108
Microflora,
    digestive, protein metabolism, 467
    of rotten eggs, 232
Micro-organisms,
    and food spoilage in catering, 389, 390
    fish, origin, 192
    hydrocarbon utilization, 56
    intestinal, protein metabolism, 467-469
    as protein formers, 56
    in reheated foods, 396
    and soya protein spoilage, 349
    susceptibility to $a_w$, 99, 100, 107, 108
Microwaves,
    in cooking, 396-398
    for reheating foods, in catering, 398
Milk, 213-223
    allergy, 471
    antibiotic residues, 66
    antimicrobial properties, 90, 108
    'artificial', 356, 357

Milk—cont.
    buffalo, utilization, 43
    heat treatment, 220, 221, 373, 374
    in national dietaries, 213
    nutritive value, 215, 218-221
    price, related to consumption, 215, 216, 223
    protein, compared with fortified cereal, 273
    protein content, variability, 214-216, 223
    as protein source, 33, 36, 43
    skimmed and dried, imported, 36
Milling,
    flour, influence of cereal proteins, 280
    loss of starch, 308
Minimata disease, 85
Moisture, in dried milk, 222
Monoamine oxidase, 65, 74, 98
Mortality,
    affected by protein, 27, 48, 49
    decrease by fortification, 276
    germ-free animals, 467
Mould, growth on bread, 311
Muscle,
    composition,
        age effect, 153-158, 162
        factors affecting, 142-163
    fibres,
        ice formation in, 121, 122
        structure, 167-169
    differential growth, 147, 157-158
    growth,
        age effect, 143-146, 153-158
        breed effect, 146-149
        nutritional effects, 158-163
    proportion of body weight, 160
    ratio to fat and bone, 147-148, 155-156, 159
Mutton, carcinogens in smoked, 70
Mycotoxins, 94-96, 100
Myofibrils, 167-169
Myosin, 168, 169, 170, 174-176, 179, 181, 205-208, 234
    fish,
        freezing damage, 205-208
        variation in stability, 208
    stability, and body temperature, 208-209

Nausea, and algal protein, 339
Nematodes, in fish, 93
Net Protein Utilization (NPU), 9, 14, 272, 326
Net protein value, 449
Nitrate, curing agent, 68, 77
    increase in plants, from excess nitrogen, 262
    in plants, 76, 77
    in potato, 255
Nitrogen,
    non-protein, used by ruminants, 146
    in potato, 249, 254
    retention during pig growth, 157
    in turkey muscles, 234
Nitrogen balance,
    index, 450
    potato protein, 249
Nitrosamines, 68
Nitrites,
    as preservatives, 69, 77
    in ruminants, 77
    toxicity in babies, 77
Non-covalent bonds,
    in protein aggregation, 132
    responsibility for fish toughness, 205, 206
Nucleotides, and meat flavour, 379
Nutrients,
    bread, comparison of production methods, 311
    in eggs and poultry, 226-228
    in food, effect on spoilage, 90
    in milk, 215, 218-221
    recommended levels, 37
    soya protein, and processing effect, 348
Nutrition,
    of animals, feed conversion efficiency, 146
    of fish, and eating quality, 189
    infant, methods of improvement within family, 270, 271
    physiological standards, 48
    plane of, and muscle growth, 158, 163
    policy, 32-45
    resistance to improved, 271
    and sex, interaction, 150, 151
Nutritive value, algal protein, 335-341
Nuts, as protein source, 15

Oats, amino acid content, 290
Objective assessment, of foods, 369, 370
Oceans, source of protein, 72
Odour,
    'boar taint', 152
    and eating quality of foods, 367
    of poultry, 237
    'wet dog', in meat, 112
Oestrogens,
    administration, and carcass composition, 152, 153
    protein synthesis control, 406, 407
Off-flavour, fish, 189, 193
Oil, extraction from soya beans, 347
Oilseed,
    concentrate, 43
    as protein source, 52
Opaque 2, 15, 296
Organochloride pesticides, 81, 82
Organoleptic assessment, of foods, 366-369
Organomercurials, 82-86
Organomercurial pesticides, classification, 83
Organophosphorus pesticides, 80
Osmometry, investigation of protein aggregates, 128
Ovalbumin, 110, 120, 231
Ovomucin, and gel elasticity in egg, 232
Oxidizing agents, in bread manufacture, 303, 304, 306
Oxygen, effect on micro-organisms, 108

Palatability,
    of hydrocarbon-produced protein, 325
    of low protein diets, 37
Panama, Nutrition Institute, 42, 268, 277, 445
Pancreas,
    cystic fibrosis, 459, 460
    diseases, protein metabolism, 459, 460
Pasteurization,
    of egg, 233
    of milk, 220, 374
    in preservation, 109, 110
Pellagra, 297

Penicillin, allergy, 66
Pesticides, 78-86
    accumulation in body, 81, 82
    chronic exposure, 82
    classification, 78
    nature of hazards, 80
    residues in foodstuffs, 82
    residues in marine life, 74, 76
    value of, 78, 79, 81
Pests, of potato, 251
pH,
    algal growth, 331
    in cooking, 371, 374, 375
    in fish, 189-190, 209
    and microbial spoilage, 90, 91, 108, 110
    rate of fall, and meat exudation, 175
    soya protein isolation, 347-349, 353
    and water-holding capacity of meat, 118, 181
Phenylalanine, 37
    metabolism, 464
Phenylketonuria, 464
Philippines, high-yielding rice, 41
Phosvitin, 229, 230
Photosynthesis, and protein production, 329, 330, 334
Physiological status, and protein needs, 49
Phytic acid, in soya protein, 351
Pietrain, growth rate, 149
Pigs,
    growth rate, 143, 152, 157, 159
    growth on hydrocarbon-produced protein, 323-325
    as protein producer, 143-146
    sex effect on development, 150, 151
    weight, and muscle growth, 150
Pigment, algal, and digestibility, 340
'Plankton soup', 338
Plants, proteins of, 245-264
Plastic pouches, heating of, 101
Poisoning, type of food involved, 389
Polypeptides, allergicity, 472
Polyphosphate, for drip control in fish, 204
Polyphosphates, in ground meat, 181

Polysomes,
    dissociation, inhibition of protein synthesis, 410, 411
    free and membrane bound, 404, 405
    polymerization, degree controlled by amino acid availability, 410-412, 415
    protein synthesis, 404-406
    spectrum, and amino acid availability, 409, 410
Potatoes,
    mineral content, 253
    protein, high in S. American variety, 251
    protein source, 253-255
    source of Vitamin C, 250, 255
Poultry, 225-240
    chemical composition, 227, 233-239
    growth on hydrocarbon-produced protein, 320-323
    nutritive value, 226
    products, in world food supplies, 226
Precooking, in catering, 392
Preference, protein-free and protein-imbalanced dietaries, 432
Preheating, of milk, 221
Preservation,
    additives in, 66, 67, 109
    by antibiotics, 102, 109
    by dehydration, 115-118
    by fermentation, 102, 109, 118
    by heat, 109-111
    by irradiation, 102, 103, 109, 111-113
    by proteinaceous foods, 66, 67, 100-103, 107-122
    by reducing $a_w$, 100, 109
    by refrigeration, 101, 109, 113-115
Press-cake, proteinaceous microbial susceptibility, 96, 100
Pressure-cooking, of protein foods, 373
Processing,
    fish, effect of collagen, 209
    of milk, 220-222
    soya protein, 347-350, 353
        effect on nutrients, 348
Production,
    bulk, hot food, 394, 395

Production—*cont.*
of protein, comparison of methods, 331
Proline, 172
ProNutro, 43
Protein bodies, in cereals, 287
'Protein gap', 33, 39, 46
'Protein paradox', 42, 475
Protein-protein interactions, 131
Proteins,
abnormal metabolism, 458-472
aggregates,
distribution of particle size, 134
size and shape, 133-135
algal,
amino acid composition, 336, 337
nutritive value, 335-341
alterations in processing, 126-138, 203-210
animal, 18, 32, 33, 51, 55, 141-163
species effect on production, 144-147
animal sources under-utilized, xvii, 18, 56, 201, 246
body weight relationships, 161
in cereals, 246, 257, 258
cereal,
in bread manufacture, 306
classification, 283-289
distribution in grain, 281-284
fractionation, 285, 286, 288
nutritional properties, 289-297
quantity and type related, 294, 295
U.K. consumption, 300
cereal endosperm, synthesis, 286
changes in, during bread manufacture, 306
changes and meat flavour, 379
comparison of sources, 264
concentrates, 42, 116, 118
accumulation of toxins, 75
local adaptation, 42, 43
soya, 347-350
consumption,
*per caput*, xiii, 3, 6, 15, 47, 50, 51, 213
form of, xiv, 6, 15, 18, 23, 202, 246

Proteins—*cont.*
consumption—*cont.*
future increase, xiv, 9, 12, 46, 246
national and regional differences, 3, 9, 10, 34, 200, 213
content
in muscle, and slaughter weight, 158
in unicellular algae, 330, 339
in wheat, 281, 282
contractile, 167-172
cooking changes, 370, 371
cooking procedures, 371-373
deficiency diseases, xv, 38, 39, 50
deficiency, faulty development, 49
denaturation
in processing, 119-122
in stored fish, 392
in diet, response genetically determined, 162
differential content in muscle, 147
digestion and absorption, 458, 459
dissociation of, resistance of covalent links, 132
efficiency ratio, 449, 450
in eggs, nature of, 228-233
of eggs,
structure-forming ability, 228, 232
as thickening agents in cooking, 376, 377
energy relation, 8, 10, 32, 33, 37, 46
essential, synthesis, 422
evaluation
by amino acid composition, 451
indices, 450, 451
nitrogen balance, 450
procedures, 448-457
faulty utilization, 38
fish,
adverse properties in processing, 203-208
content variability with species, 210
and eating quality, 381, 382
extraction methods, 203, 207
fatty acid interaction, 206, 208
nutritive properties, 201, 202, 203

Proteins—*cont.*
  fish—*cont.*
      and suitability for processing, 188, 209
      texture in cooking, 382, 383
  gels,
      average pore size, 135
      in cooking, 370
      and fish quality, 209, 210
      gel strand thickness, 135, 136
      soya, 348, 353
      value of eggs, 228, 232
  globular, gel formation, 133
  groundnut,
      fibre structure by E.M., 135, 136
      gel structure by E.M., 135
  heat stability, 109, 110
  human requirements, 9, 33, 35, 36, 37, 47, 49
  hydration of, 121, 122
  from hydrocarbon fermentation, 317-326
  indices of requirement, 9, 14, 47, 48, 50
  intolerance to, 469-472
  from leafy vegetables, 260-264
  life-span curtailment, 48
  maximum production by meat animals, 157
  meat,
      differential changes in cooking, 380
      properties of, 167-182
  metabolism,
      microbial involvement, 467-469
      regulation, 403-415
  microbial spoilage, in catering, 389, 390
  milk,
      amino acid composition, 216-218
      amounts consumed, 213, 216
      different components, 214
      efficiency of utilization, 218
      level of, 215, 223
  molecules of,
      average degree of aggregation, 127
      collision frequency efficiency, 128
      interchain links, 127, 131

Proteins—*cont.*
  of muscle,
      denaturation in freezing, 177, 205-207
      denaturation in freeze-drying, 178, 204
  non-commodity nature, 20
  novel, 57, 58, 246, 260, 271, 317-326, 328-343, 346-360
  nuclear transportation of m-RNA, 404
  photosynthesis, 329, 330
  plant,
      enrichment, 266-279
      genetical influences, 245-264
  potato,
      increase by fertilizers, 255, 259
      nitrogen balance, 249-251
      prevention of pellagra, 249
  products of different sources, 331
  properties significant in cooking, 370, 371
  poultry, extractability in ageing, 236, 237
  quality of, 3, 15
  ratio to water, in carcass, 153
  reasons for cooking, 373
  reheating effects in catering, 395, 396
  requirements, xiii, 7, 9, 36, 47-49, 50
      physiological variability, 270
  returns from land use, xv, 146
  sarcoplasmic, 173, 175, 178, 179, 205
  soya,
      composition of isolate, 350, 351
      fibre-forming ability, 353, 354
      isolation procedure, 347-349
      processing, 347-350, 353
      properties, 351-354
      yield of isolate, 349, 350
  stabilization of conformation, 119, 120
  storage life limited, 422
  surplus production, 21, 24, 25, 30
  synthesis,
      amino acid imbalance, 436
      daily fluctuation, 413-415

Proteins—*cont.*
  synthesis—*cont.*
    inhibitors, 405, 406, 409, 410, 411
    mechanism saturated, 437
    organization in cell, 404, 405
    regulation of cytoplasmic mechanisms, 407-412
    regulation of nuclear mechanisms, 406, 407
  and taste sensation, 367
  texture, 126, 209, 246
  tolerance, human variability in, xvi, 37, 48
  transferability limited, 21, 25, 26, 31, 52
  vegetable, in cooking, 383-384
  vegetable origin, 14, 15, 41, 52
  wheat, role in dough development, 305-307
  world requirement, potential of algae, 332
  world supply, means of enhancing, xvii, 10, 14, 19, 27, 46-60
  yields from potato, 259
Proteolysis, 113, 115
  in cooking meat, 381
  and cheese flavour, 374
  excessive, in gastro-intestinal diseases, 466
  ferritin, inhibition by excess iron, 408
  post-mortem, and meat tenderness, 176, 177, 178
  in poultry, 236, 237
Proteoplasts, of cereals, 286, 287
*Pseudomonas,*
  egg spoilage, 232
  sensitive to irradiation, 113
'ptomaines', 96, 97
Pulses, as protein source, 15, 43, 52
Puromycin, inhibition of protein synthesis by, 406
Putrefaction, 91, 96

$Q_{10}^{\circ}C$,
  for destruction of bacteria, 110
  for protein denaturation, 110, 119
Quail, resistance to hemlock, 477

Quality,
  fish, control envisaged, 196, 197
  in meat, 141, 174

'Radappertization', 112
'Radicidation', 112
Rate, cooking, with microwaves, 397
Red meat, in poultry, 233, 234
Reducing agents, in bread manufacture, 304, 305, 306
Refrigeration, of proteinaceous foods, 101
Regulation,
  protein synthesis,
    cytoplasmic mechanisms, 407-412
    nuclear mechanisms, 406, 407, 412
Reheating,
  by microwaves, 398
  of precooked foods, 395, 396
Renal tubules, defective amino acid transport, 462
Rennin, and casein coagulation, 215, 216
Reticulum,
  endoplasmic, 287, 404-406
  sarcoplasmic, 172, 177, 179
Rheology,
  of wheat endosperm, 289
  soya protein, 353
Ribose, in browning, 111
Ribosenucleic acid (RNA)
  breakdown control by amino acid supply, 409
  protein synthesis, 404, 405, 409-411
  synthesis, inhibitors, 405, 406
Ribosomes,
  free, and amino acid deficiency, 410
  inhibition of transcription, 406
Rice,
  fortification, 277
  high yielding, 41
  intolerance to gluten, 470
  supplemented by algal protein, 340
Rice-milk, in Indian Dietaries, 219
Rigor mortis,
  in fish, 190, 191
  in meat animals, 172, 175, 176

Rigor mortis–*cont.*
  in poultry, 234, 237
  resolution, in fish, 191
Roasting, of protein foods, 372
Ruminants,
  urea as nitrogen source, 319
  as utilizers of non-protein nitrogen,
    146
Rye, amino acid content, 290


*Salmonellae,*
  in animal carcass, 92
  destroyed by irradiation, 112
  in dried foods, 100
  in egg, 109
Salmonellosis, 92, 93, 100
Salt, table, fortification by lysine, 278
Sampling, problems in fish plants, 197
Sarcomeres, 168, 172, 175, 176
  in poultry, 233
Sauerkraut, vitamin C supply, 262
Sausages,
  refrigerated storage of, 102
  soya protein in, 355
  water-holding capacity of, 181
Season, effect on fish texture, 187,
    188
Seasonality, protein foods, 391
Seaweed, as food, 341, 342
Serine, in methionine toxicity, 425,
    428-430, 445
Serotonin, in plantains, 76
Sex,
  and meat production, 149-153, 160
  and nutrition, interaction, 150, 151
Sewage, and algal culture, 335
Sheep,
  age and carcass composition, 161
  breed, and carcass composition,
    148
  as protein producers, 143-146
  sex effect on development, 150
Shellfish, toxicity, 73
Shortening, of muscle, and toughness,
    176
Shorthorn, as meat producer, 147
Shrinkage, ice-cream, in catering, 393
'Skins', formation in heat stored food,
    395

Smoluchowski, general theory of
  molecular aggregation, 137
Sole,
  lemon,
    browning of, 111
    free amino acids in, 189
    myosin relatively stable, 208
Solvents, organic, in food dehydration,
    116, 117
Sorghum, high lysine, 297
Sounds, and eating quality of food,
    366, 367
Soup, soya protein component, 355
South Africa, protein concentrates in,
    43
Southdown, 148, 150
Soya,
  concentrates, 42, 43
  as protein source, 54, 57, 346-360
  protein,
    amino acids in, 319
    in drying banana puree, 357
    food uses of, 354-357
    nutritional value, 247, 358-360
Species, and meat production, 143-146
Spoilage,
  associations, 89
  fish, 192-194
    and overfeeding, 189
  of harvested algae, 333
  microbial factors determining, 90,
    107, 108
  microbial, protein foods in catering,
    389, 390
  microflora, changes on storage, 91
  non-microbial, 107, 119-122
  of protein
    by infestation, 79
    by micro-organisms, 89-103
    by rotting, 52
Spray-drying,
  of milk, 221, 222
  soya protein, 353
Staling, bread, 311
*Staph. aureus,* food poisoning from,
    94, 97
Sterilization, in preservation, 110, 111
Staple foods, poor protein sources, 6,
    33
Starch,
  gluten-free, coeliac disease, 471

Starch—*cont.*
    granules, in endosperm, 283, 284, 289
    yield from potato, 259
Starvation, plasma amino acid level maintained, 420
Statistical forecasting, of nutrient requirements, 36
Stewing, of protein foods, 372
Stimuli,
    sensory, and food assessment, 366-369
Stomach, emptying, glycine and serine effect, 431
Storage,
    of dried milk, 221, 222
    of hot food, in catering, 394, 395
    problems in catering, 391-394
    protein, in cereals, 287
    protein foods, regulations, 389, 390
Streptococci, toxin production by, 98, 102
Sucrose, in protection of frozen yolk, 115
Sulphide, in fish canning, 111
Sulphur,
    of cereal endosperm, 286
    in egg proteins, 230
Sulphydryl-disulphide, exchange, 231
Supplementation,
    by algal protein, 340, 341, 343
    bread, by soya protein, 359, 360
    of deficient dietaries, 14
    dietary, value of milk, 218, 219
    mutual, of deficient proteins, 266, 267
    of protein, costs, 273
Supply,
    balance with demand, 3-19, 28, 34
    problems in catering, 391-394
Surplus, of amino acids, 418
Surpluses, destruction of, 25
Sweden, accumulation of mercury in eggs, 85


Taste,
    basic sensations, 368
    and eating quality of foods, 367, 368

Temperature,
    and amino acid imbalance, 438-441, 444
    and eating quality, 369
    of fish, importance for quality, 191, 194, 204
    on micro-organisms, 108, 113-115
    post-mortem, and meat quality, 176
    and protein aggregation, effect on chain/sphere ratio, 133
    protein food storage, 389, 390
    ranges, effect on meat proteins, 179, 180
Teratogenicity, of nitrosamines, 68
Texture,
    of algae, 343
    bread, 303, 309, 310
    cheese, 374, 375
    and eating quality of foods, 369
    of egg foods, 376, 377
    in fabricated foods, 126-138, 246
    of fish,
        altered in processing, 204, 206, 207, 210
        in cooking, 382
        defects by washing pre-rigor, 210
        and lipid content, 187, 193, 206
        and rigor mortis, 191, 192
        and starvation, 188
    of food,
        evaluation procedure, 369
        nomenclature, 368, 369
    in foods, value of egg proteins, 228, 232
    formation from soya protein, 353, 354
    of meat,
        in cooking, 380, 381
        on freezing, 113, 119, 120
        in freeze-drying, 118
        and hydrocarbon-produced feed, 326
    poultry, 239, 240
    spoilage, in warm stored food, 395
    in microwave cooking, 398
Thaw-rigor, in fish, 192
Thiol groups, in bread dough, 306, 307
Threonine, 291, 412, 419, 434-436, 439-441

Time, for quality retention, frozen foods, 392
Tissues, order of development, 158, 160
Tofu, 357
Toughness,
    in fish,
        and freezing, 194, 204-206
        and rigor onset, 191, 192
    of meat,
        and ageing, 176
        on cooking, 180
        and freeze-drying, 178
        and muscle proteins, 173, 176
        and rigor mortis, 175
    in poultry, 236, 238-240
Toxicity,
    of algae, 341
    amino acids, 423, 424, 431, 438, 444, 445, 477
    and hydrocarbon fermentation, 318, 319, 326
    and intestinal bacteria, 468
    of micro-elements to algae, 334
    phenylalanine, 465
    of soya bean, 347, 358
Toxins,
    of *Cl. botulinum,* 93
    marine, 72, 73, 93
    of moulds, 94-96, 100
    naturally occurring, 70-72
    in plant tissues, xv, 54, 70, 76
    protein association with, 54, 65-87, 91
    of *Staph. aureus,* 94
    summation of effects, 70
Trace elements, as toxins, 75
Tracers, radioactive, in cereal protein synthesis, 286
Trade, in protein foods, 26
Transport,
    amino acids, mechanisms, 461
    of ribosenucleic acid, and protein synthesis, 406
Trimethylamine oxide, in fish spoilage, 192-194
Tropomyosin, 168, 171
Troponin, 171
Trypsin Inhibitors, xv, 54, 232, 358
Trypsinogen, deficiency, disease, 460, 461

Tryptophan, 15, 65, 181, 246, 249-251, 256-258, 262, 293, 296, 409, 410, 412, 423, 451, 461, 462, 463
    malabsorption disease, 463
Tubers, potato, amino acid content, 255
Tuna,
    myosin stability of, 209
    post-mortem proteolysis, 193
Tunisia, field trial of enriched protein, 275, 276
Tyrosine, 97, 423
    treatment of phenylketonuria, 465

UHT, milk, 374
Ultimate pH, high, resistance to proteolysis, 113
United Kingdom,
    pre-war protein insufficiency, 38
    protein imports, 35
    wartime nutrition, 35, 36
United Nations, 3, 9, 38-40, 273, 274, 346
Urea,
    on biopolymers, effect of, 120, 121
    feed for ruminant, 319
    and protein production, 55

Vacuum-drying, 117, 118
Varieties,
    better-yielding, 15, 24, 40, 41, 51, 250, 251, 274
    selection of high-yielding maize, 296, 297
Vegetables, green leaf, protein source, 247-249, 260-264
Veterinary products, as toxic residues, 86
Vibrio, in fish, 92
Viscosity,
    of egg proteins, in cooking, 377
    intrinsic, of serum albumin, 130, 137
    protein, in cooking, 371
Vitamin B complex, xvi, 32, 43, 246
Vitamin B$_{12}$, xiv, xvi, 226, 469
Vitamin C, from potato, 250

Vitamins,
  deficit, 32, 37
  general, in potato, 255
Vitellins, 229, 230

Wastage, of protein, 52, 54, 474
Waste, protein foods, in catering, 389
Water,
  'bound' and 'free', 174
  vaporization, in microwave cooking, 397
Water Activity ($A_w$) and microbial spoilage, 90, 99, 100, 107, 108
Water-holding capacity,
  of fish, 205
  of meat, 173, 174, 178, 181
  enhancement, soya protein, 355
Wedge protein, 283, 284
Welfare Foods Scheme, 36
Wheat,
  amino acid content, 290, 293, 294
  fortification, 269, 272, 273, 275-278
  grain distribution of protein, 281
  hard and soft, 281, 285, 293, 294
  intolerance to gluten, 470
  protein/calorie source in Tunisia, 275
  proteins, 246, 309
  world resources, economic use by Chorleywood process, 312
Wheat flour, fortification, 41

Whey, in bread manufacture, 304
White of egg, 109, 110
  composition, 230, 231, 232
  in cooking, 376, 377
  freezing point, 229
  structure, 230-232
White meat, in poultry, 233, 234
Wholesomeness, microbial lowering of, 91,
Wiking Eiweiss, 118
World Health Organization, 39, 47, 67
World population, increase, 46
Wound-healing, and protein deficiency, 50
Wrapping, of food, in catering, 391, 392

Yeasts,
  hydrocarbon-grown, 317-326
  pig feeding, 323-325
  poultry feeding, 320-323
Yolk,
  in cooking, 376
  freezing point, 228, 229
  proteins, freezing damage, 114, 115
  solids, chemical composition, 229
  structure, 229

Zein, 287, 293, 296
Z-lines, of muscle, 168, 176